## What's New in this Edition?

This is the second edition of "Citrix MetaFrame XP: Advanced Technical Design Guide." In addition to completely rewriting the first edition of this book, several new topics were added. Here's a partial list:

- Feature Release 2
- Citrix Secure Gateway
- NFuse Classic 1.7
- Enterprise Services for NFuse

Additionally, three entirely new chapters were added:

- Server Sizing and Performance Optimization
- MetaFrame XP Server Deployment in the Enterprise
- Ensuring Availability and Server Redundancy

## Reader Comments about the First Edition of this Book

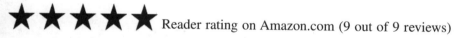

★ ★ ★ ★ ★ Reader rating on Amazon.com (9 out of 9 reviews)

If you really want to understand the MetaFrame XP products, you must read this book! As an engineer by trade, I've read more technical books than I care to remember. One thing I've noticed is that a product or technology needs to mature somewhat before adequate readings are available to explain it all. Citrix technology has certainly matured, and of the book authors currently writing about Citrix technologies, Brian Madden has emerged the undisputed master. His writings are easily understandable and utterly complete. How rare it is that a brilliant engineer can actually write.
*John Carver, Citrix Certified Instructor*

On top of the incredibly thorough technical content, this book has one thing that most other technical guides do not—personality. The writing style isn't the normal, monotonous style that is found in so many tech books, it is conversational and sometimes even entertaining. The technical merits of the book speak for themselves—Real world experiences plus the theory behind them. This isn't just a reiteration of the Metaframe XP Admin Guide, it SHOULD BE the Metaframe XP Admin Guide.
*Gabe Knuth, Principal Consultant*

If you are working with Citrix, you NEED this book!
*Matthew Unger*

# Citrix® MetaFrame XP™
## Advanced Technical Design Guide

Including Feature Release 2

**Brian S. Madden**

BrianMadden.com Publishing
Washington DC
www.brianmadden.com

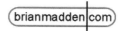

**Citrix MetaFrame XP: Advanced Technical Design Guide**
**Including Feature Release 2**
Copyright © 2002 by Brian Madden

International Standard Book Number (ISBN): 0-9711510-3-2

Library of Congress Catalog Card Number: 2002094060

Printed in the United States of America

First Printing: November 2002

BrianMadden.com Publishing offers discounts of this book when ordered in bulk quantities. For more information, contact brian@brianmadden.com.

**Trademarks**
All terms mentioned in this book that are known to be trademarks or service marks have been appropriately capitalized. BrianMadden.com Publishing cannot attest to the accuracy of this information. Use of a term in this book should not be regarded as affecting the validity of any trademark or service mark.

**Editor**
Leah Ogonek

**Technical Reviewers**
Shane Broomhall
Sean Casey

**Reviewer**
Gabe Knuth

**Cover Magic**
Natalie Black

**Cover Design**
Brian Madden
(so Natalie doesn't
get blamed for it)

**Publisher's Cataloging-in-Publication Data**

Madden, Brian S.
  Citrix MetaFrame XP: advanced technical design guide, including feature release 2 / Brian S. Madden -- 2nd ed.
  p. cm.
  Includes index.
  LCCN 2002094060
  ISBN 0-9711510-3-2

  1. Citrix MetaFrame. 2. Client/server computing.
I. Title.

QA76.9.C55M33 2002                    005.4'4769

# Contents at a Glance

**Part I. The MetaFrame XP Server Environment**     **21**

1. MetaFrame XP Overview     23
2. MetaFrame XP Server Architecture     37
3. MetaFrame XP Network Architecture     55

**Part II. The Application Environment**     **107**

4. Application Strategies and Installation     109
5. Creating the User Environment     153
6. Server Sizing and Performance Optimization     229
7. Printing     259
8. Integration with Novell NetWare     315

**Part III. Connecting Users to Servers**     **335**

9. User Access Methods and Devices     337
10. Deploying and Configuring ICA Clients     353
11. Building Web Portals with NFuse Classic 1.7     431

**Part IV. Deploying Your MetaFrame XP Servers**     **499**

12. MetaFrame XP Server Deployment in the Enterprise     501
13. MetaFrame 1.8 Migration and Integration     533
14. Licensing     577

**Part V. Running Your MetaFrame XP System**     **623**

15. Security     625
16. MetaFrame XP Server Management and Maintenance     719
17. Ensuring Availability and Server Redundancy     751

Appendixes     766
Index     778

## How This Book is Structured

This book is made up of seventeen chapters divided into five parts.

Technical books such as this are not always read straight through from cover to cover. Instead, many of readers immediately turn to the chapter that is most relevant to their current environment. To facilitate this, each chapter of this book has been structured and written like an independent white paper so that all of the information you need is in the chapter that you're reading. When outside information is needed, the chapter where it can be found is referenced.

If you have some experience with MetaFrame XP, Chapters 1 and 2 of this book are probably the most boring since they contain a lot of overview and introductory information. However, if you're new to MetaFrame XP, the chapters of this book have been structured logically so you can read them in the order that they are arranged.

Another important thing about this book is that the topics of each chapter are "solutions focused" instead of "tool focused." For example, you will not find a chapter that explains what every single option does in the Citrix Management Console. (If you want that, read the Citrix product documentation.) Instead, this book details where certain options can be configured only when you need to configure them as part of your design.

Lastly, this book is designed to provide a "real world" look at how MetaFrame XP is really used and how real environments are put together. You will not find any screen shots in this book. In highly technical books, they are a waste of space and they are often used to make the books appear to be thicker. (No one needs to read a passage about how to install MetaFrame XP with a screen shot of the "Click Next to Continue" screen.) If you need screen shots, read the Citrix product documentation.

# Contents

How This Book is Structured ................................................................. 6
Contents .............................................................................................. 7
A Note from the Author ..................................................................... 18
Acknowledgements ............................................................................ 19
Using this Book with Citrix Certification Practice Exams ................... 20

## Part I.  The MetaFrame XP Server Environment

### 1. MetaFrame XP Overview

The MetaFrame XP Solution ................................................................. 24
MetaFrame XP Server-Based Computing Components ....................... 25
Independent Computing Architecture (ICA) ...................................... 26
ICA Protocol ...................................................................................... 26
ICA File Type ..................................................................................... 26
MetaFrame XP Features ..................................................................... 27
MetaFrame XP Optional Features ....................................................... 30
Managing MetaFrame XP with the CMC ............................................ 31
Extending MetaFrame XP with Feature Releases ................................ 31
FR-1 Enhancements to MetaFrame XP ............................................... 31
FR-1 Enhancements to MetaFrame XPa and XPe .............................. 33
FR-1 Enhancements to MetaFrame XPe .............................................. 33
FR-2 Enhancements to MetaFrame XP ............................................... 34
FR-2 Enhancements for MetaFrame XPe ............................................ 35

### 2.  MetaFrame XP Server Architecture

How MetaFrame XP Works .................................................................. 38
How Microsoft Windows Terminal Server Works ............................... 38
MetaFrame XP Interaction with Terminal Server ............................... 41
MetaFrame XP Components ............................................................... 42
MetaFrame XP Server Requirements ................................................. 47
Software Requirements – Base Operating System ............................. 47
Server Hardware Requirements ......................................................... 49
The MetaFrame XP Installation Process ............................................ 49
Server Drive Letter Remapping ......................................................... 50
Feature Release 2 Installation ........................................................... 52

Should you use MetaFrame XP Feature Releases? ............................. 54

## 3. MetaFrame XP Network Architecture

Independent Management Architecture (IMA) ............................................ 56
Placement of MetaFrame XP Servers ...................................................... 58
    Why should you care about server placement? ................................. 60
    What are the server placement options? ............................................... 61
    Considerations when Choosing Server Locations ................................ 65
MetaFrame XP Server Farm Design ........................................................ 69
    Why should you care about server farm design? ................................. 70
    What are the server farm design options? .......................................... 71
    Considerations when Designing your Server Farm ............................ 73
Server Farm Zones ................................................................................ 74
    Why should you care about zone design? ........................................... 82
    What are the zone design options? ..................................................... 83
    Considerations when Designing your Zones ...................................... 85
The IMA Data Store ............................................................................... 87
    Why should you care about IMA data store design? ........................... 91
    What are the IMA data store options? ................................................. 92
    Considerations when Designing your Data Store ............................... 95
Future MetaFrame XP Server Relocation ............................................... 97
Real World Case Study .......................................................................... 98
    Option 1. One Company-Wide Farm with One Zone ....................... 100
    Option 2. One Company-Wide Farm with Multiple Zones ............... 102
    Option 3. Multiple Server Farms ..................................................... 104
    Analysis of the Proposed Worldwide Architectures ......................... 105

## Part II. The Application Environment

## 4. Application Strategies and Installation

Installing Applications .......................................................................... 110
    Problems with Applications in Multi-User Environments ................. 111
    Installing New or Untested Applications ........................................... 114
    Knowing Which Application Options to Use ..................................... 115
    Legacy Application Compatibility ..................................................... 115
Application Publishing Strategy ............................................................ 118
    Things to Consider when Creating your Strategy ............................. 118

What are the Published Application Strategy Options? ...... 120

Choosing What Types of Files are Opened Where ............... 122
   Publishing Content ................ 123
   Client to Server Content Redirection ................ 125

Multi-Server Application Load Management ........................ 131
   How does Citrix Load Manager Work? ............... 131
   The MetaFrame XP Load Management Process ............... 133
   How Load Evaluators are used in Load Management ...... 135
   How "Rules" Affect Load Management ............... 136
   The Zone Data Collector's Role in Load Management ...... 140
   Load Management Strategies ............... 142
   Load Evaluators—Which rules to compare? ............... 145
   Applying Load Evaluators to Published Applications ...... 146

Application / Server Installation Groups ............... 147
   What are the Application Location Options? ............... 148
   Considerations when Deciding where to Install Applications ...... 150

## 5. Creating the User Environment

User Profiles ............... 154
   How User Profiles Work ............... 155
   Why should you care about user profile design? ............... 162
   What are the User Profile Design Options? ............... 163
   How will you manage cached copies of roaming profiles? ...... 174
   Considerations when Designing User Profiles ............... 177

User Policies ............... 178
   Windows User Policies ............... 179
   Citrix User Policies ............... 181
   Why should you care about user policy design? ............... 186
   What are the user policy design options? ............... 186
   Things to Consider when Designing User Policies ............... 194

Home Drives ............... 195
   How Windows Home Drives Work ............... 195
   Why should you care about Home Drives? ............... 199
   What are the Home Drive Design Options? ............... 199
   Considerations when Designing Home Drives ............... 208

Logon and Logoff Scripts ............... 208
   How Logon and Logoff Scripts Work ............... 209
   Why should you care about logon script design? ............... 209
   What are the logon script options? ............... 210

Considerations when Designing Logon Scripts ................................. 216
Real World Case Study .................................................................. 217
    Parker HealthNet Implementation Summary ............................. 227

## 6. Server Sizing and Performance Optimization

MetaFrame XP Server Hardware .......................................... 230
    MetaFrame Server Memory Usage ................................ 231
    MetaFrame Server Processor Usage .................................. 233
    MetaFrame Server Hard Drive Usage .............................. 233
    MetaFrame XP Server Hardware Redundancy .................... 234
Real-World Sizing Strategies ................................................ 234
    Why Should You Care About Server Sizing? .................... 235
    Server Sizing Options ................................................ 235
Server Sizing Techniques .................................................... 238
    Server Capacity Planning ............................................ 239
Performance Tuning your Environment .................................. 252
    Tuning Servers .......................................................... 252
    Tuning Applications .................................................. 253
    Tuning the Network .................................................. 254

## 7. Printing

How Windows Printing Works ............................................ 260
    Phase 1. Windows Application .................................... 261
    Phase 2. Print Spooler .............................................. 261
    Phase 3. Printer ........................................................ 262
How MetaFrame XP Printing Works .................................... 262
    Client Printers .......................................................... 264
    Server Printers .......................................................... 283
Managing Printer Drivers .................................................... 285
    How Windows Printer Drivers Work ............................ 285
    How MetaFrame XP Manages Printer Drivers ................ 287
Configuring Printers for Users ............................................ 293
    Assigning Printers to Users ........................................ 293
    Letting Users Choose Their Own Printers .................... 297
Third Party Printing Solutions ............................................ 299
    Problem 1. Multiple Printer Drivers must be Managed .... 300
    Problem 2. Client Printer Performance is Poor .............. 301

Problem  3. Printing in WAN Environments ........................................ 303
Real World Case Study ............................................................. 305
   The Main Office ................................................................. 306
   The Regional Offices ......................................................... 308
   The Small Offices .............................................................. 312
   Home Users ...................................................................... 312
   Summary .......................................................................... 314
   Why should you care about the method of integration? ...................... 316
   What are the NetWare integration options? ......................................... 317

## 8. Integration with Novell NetWare

Microsoft's Gateway Services for NetWare ............................... 318
   Configuration of Gateway Services for NetWare ............................... 319
Microsoft's Client Services for NetWare ...................................... 319
   Configuration of Client Services for NetWare ..................................... 320
Novell's NDS Client ..................................................................... 321
   Configuration of Novell's NDS Client ................................................. 322
NDS Integration with Feature Release 1 or 2 ............................................. 328
   Requirements for Using MetaFrame XP's NDS Features ................... 328
   Configuration of NDS Integration with Feature Release 1 or 2 ......... 330
   Feature Release 2 Refinements to NDS Integration ........................... 331
Issues to Consider for the NetWare Options ............................................. 332

## Part III.  Connecting Users to Servers

## 9.  User Access Methods and Devices

Methods of End User Access ..................................................... 338
   Why is the method of access important? ........................................... 338
   What are the user access method options? ......................................... 339
Client Device Planning Considerations ...................................... 343
   Technology Management Issues ........................................................ 343
   Political Issues ..................................................................... 344
   Cost ..................................................................................... 345
   Environmental / Facilities ..................................................... 346
   Applications ........................................................................ 346
Types of Client Devices .............................................................. 348
   Option 1. Traditional Computer Workstations ..................................... 348

Option 2. Thin Client Devices and Appliances .................................... 349
Option 3. Traditional Workstations, Managed as Thin Devices ......... 351
Option 4. Mobile Wireless Devices ..................................................... 352

## 10. Deploying and Configuring ICA Clients

ICA Client Functional Overview ............................................................... 354
    ICA Client to MetaFrame XP Server Communication ....................... 354
ICA Client Features and Options ............................................................. 357
    ICA Session Features .......................................................................... 358
    Client Performance Enhancing Options ............................................. 365
    Administrative Features ...................................................................... 369
    Connection Launching Features .......................................................... 370
    Which options work on which platforms? .......................................... 374
Windows 32-bit ICA Clients ................................................................... 374
    Technical Overview ............................................................................ 374
    Differences Between Downloadable Win32 Client Packages.............. 375
    32-bit Windows Program Neighborhood Client ................................. 377
    32-bit Windows Web Client ................................................................ 392
    Program Neighborhood Agent ............................................................ 401
Java ICA Client ....................................................................................... 403
    Technical Overview ............................................................................ 404
    Launching ICA Sessions with the Java Client.................................... 408
    ICA Java Client Launch Parameters ................................................... 409
ICA Client Auto Update .......................................................................... 418
    How ICA Client Auto Update Works .................................................. 419
    Configuring ICA Client Auto Update ................................................. 420
Real World Case Study ............................................................................ 425
    ICA Client Platforms .......................................................................... 426
    The Windows ICA Client Package ...................................................... 427
    NFuse Versions .................................................................................. 432
    Why use NFuse? ................................................................................. 434

## 11. Building Web Portals with NFuse Classic 1.7

Understanding NFuse Classic .................................................................. 435
    NFuse Components .............................................................................. 435
    How NFuse Classic Works .................................................................. 437
NFuse Web Server Configuration ............................................................ 441
    The NFuse Configuration Process ...................................................... 441

Configuring the NFuse Java Objects ............................................. 445

Working with NFuse Web Pages .................................................... 448
    Configuring Default Web Page Options ................................... 449
    Where is the Citrix Web Site Wizard? .................................... 454
    Understanding the Default NFuse Web Site ............................. 454
    Modifying the Default NFuse Web Site ................................... 457
    Creating NFuse Web Sites from Scratch ................................. 466

NFuse Web Clients .................................................................... 466
    NFuse Client Requirements ................................................... 466
    ICA Client Source Files and Locations ................................... 467
    Using NFuse to Automatically Instal the ICA Client ................ 467

Using Enterprise Services for NFuse ............................................ 472
    How Enterprise Services for NFuse Works ............................. 473
    Understanding the ESN Components ....................................... 475
    Designing your ESN Solution ................................................ 478
    Configuring Enterprise Services for NFuse ............................. 481

NFuse 1.5x and 1.6x Considerations ............................................ 481
    New features available in NFuse 1.7 ...................................... 482

Leveraging NFuse with the PN Agent .......................................... 484
    Understanding Program Neighborhood Agent Files .................. 485
    Configuring PN Agent with the Config.xml File ...................... 485
    Designing your PN Agent Solution ........................................ 497

What happened to Project Columbia? ........................................... 497

# Part IV. Deploying Your MetaFrame XP Servers

# 12. MetaFrame XP Server Deployment in the Enterprise

Deploying MetaFrame XP ........................................................... 502
    Server Drive Imaging ......................................................... 502
    Unattended Installations ...................................................... 505

Deploying Applications ............................................................. 507
    An Overview of Automated Software Distribution ................... 508
    Automated Software Distribution Considerations ..................... 511
    Citrix Installation Manager Overview .................................... 513
    Understanding Installation Manager Components ..................... 516
    Using Installation Manager in the Real World ......................... 522

## 13. MetaFrame 1.8 Migration and Integration

Concepts for Mixing MetaFrame 1.8 and XP ........................................... 534
   MetaFrame 1.8 and XP Product Level Correlations ......................... 534
   MetaFrame XP Interaction with MetaFrame 1.8 .............................. 535
   MetaFrame 1.8 Technical Components ............................................... 536
   Mixed Mode Server Farms ................................................................. 538
   IMA Service ....................................................................................... 538
   Server Farm Design .......................................................................... 539
   Administration Tools ......................................................................... 540
   ICA Browser Service ......................................................................... 541
   ICA Client to MetaFrame Server Communication ........................... 542
   Network Ports and Protocols ............................................................. 543
   Published Applications ...................................................................... 543
   Load Balancing ................................................................................. 547
   Licenses ............................................................................................. 549
Native Mode Server Farms ....................................................................... 549
   Client Communication with Native XP and 1.8 Farms ...................... 550
Add-on Management Services from 1.8 to XP ......................................... 551
   NFuse Classic .................................................................................... 552
   Installation Manager ......................................................................... 553
   Resource Manager ............................................................................. 556
MetaFrame 1.8 to XP Server Farm Migrations ......................................... 557
   Prerequisites ...................................................................................... 557
   Farm Migration Strategies ................................................................. 559
   Target XP Farm Operating Mode ...................................................... 560
   User Access during the Migration ..................................................... 562
   Farm Consolidation .......................................................................... 564
   Other Product Upgrades / Migrations ............................................... 566
   Server Migration ............................................................................... 568
   Publishd Application Migration ......................................................... 569
Real World Case Study ............................................................................. 571
   Current Business Environment .......................................................... 571
   Current Technology Environment ...................................................... 571
   Future MetaFrame XP Environment .................................................. 572
   The Project Team's Thoughts about the Migration ........................... 572
   Migration Plan .................................................................................. 573

## 14. Licensing

Microsoft Licensing ................................................................................. 578

Microsoft Licensing Requirements ................................................... 578
How Microsoft Licenses Work .............................................................. 581

Citrix Licensing ................................................................................... 601
Citrix MetaFrame XP Licensing Requirements ............................. 601
How MetaFrame XP Licensing Works ............................................ 602
Configuring MetaFrame XP Server License Usage ....................... 611
Managing Licenses with the Citrix Management Console ............... 613
When Multiple Licenses are Applied to One User ........................... 614
License Differences Between MetaFrame XP and 1.8 ..................... 615

Application Licensing ....................................................................... 615

Real World Case Study ..................................................................... 618

# Part V.  Running Your MetaFrame XP System

## 15.  Security

Security Configuration Layers ........................................................... 627

Server Security ................................................................................... 629
MetaFrame XP Application Server Security .................................... 629
IMA Data Store Server Security ..................................................... 633
NFuse Server Security ..................................................................... 634

Application Security ........................................................................... 636
Published Application Security ........................................................ 636
Windows Desktop Application Security ............................................ 639

Connection Security ........................................................................... 643
Connection Properties ..................................................................... 643
Connection Permissions ................................................................... 649
Strategies for Using Multiple Server Connections ......................... 651
Connection Configuration in the Registry ..................................... 652

Network Security ............................................................................... 652
MetaFrame XP Network Data Security / Encryption ...................... 653
Network Perimeter Security / Firewall Configuration .................... 681

Client Device Security ....................................................................... 693
Saving User Credentials on ICA Client Devices ............................. 693
Using Local ICA Files to Connect to ICA Applications .................... 694
Pass-Through Authentication ......................................................... 695
Preventing Users from Changing Their Client Settings .................... 695
Client Web Browser Security ........................................................... 697
Navigating Client-Side Proxy Servers ............................................ 703

User Account Security .............................................................................. 704
    User Account Configuration .............................................................. 704
    Secure User Authentication .............................................................. 706
    Domain Configuration ...................................................................... 709

Secure System Administration Environments........................................... 712
    MetaFrame XP Administrators ........................................................... 712
    Session Shadowing ........................................................................... 715
    MetaFrame XP User Auditing ............................................................. 716

## 16. MetaFrame XP Server Management and Maintenance

Managing Servers with the CMC ........................................................... 720
    Choosing a CMC Connection Server ................................................. 720
    Run the CMC Locally on a MetaFrame XP Server ........................... 721
    Configuring Data Refresh in the CMC............................................... 721
    Number of Concurrent CMC Consoles ............................................. 722
    Configuring Server and Application Folders ...................................... 722
    Using the Citrix Web Console .......................................................... 723

Server Farm Maintenance ....................................................................... 724
    Changing Zones............................................................................... 724
    Changing Farm Membership ............................................................ 724
    Migrating to a New IMA Data Store ................................................. 726
    Replacing MetaFrame XP Servers .................................................... 727
    Renaming a MetaFrame XP Server .................................................... 728

Periodic Farm Maintenance Tasks ......................................................... 729
    Compact the Access Database .......................................................... 729
    Cycle Boot MetaFrame XP Servers .................................................. 730
    Stop and Start the IMA Service ........................................................ 730
    Keep the Operating System Warm and Clean ................................... 730
    Check Resource Manager or Load Manager Logs ............................. 730
    Check for New Hotfixes or Service Packs ........................................ 731

Citrix Resource Manager ....................................................................... 731
    Monitoring Servers and Applications ............................................... 734
    Working with Metrics...................................................................... 736
    How Resource Manager Works ........................................................ 741
    Using Resource Manager in the Real World ..................................... 744

Citrix Network Manager ........................................................................ 744
    Network Manager Installation .......................................................... 745
    Network Manager Configuration ...................................................... 745

Real World Case Study ........................................................................... 748

## 17. Ensuring Availability and Server Redundancy

MetaFrame XP High Availability Strategies .......................................... 752
    ICA Client Devices ............................................................ 753
    Network Connection ............................................................ 754
    NFuse Web Server ............................................................ 754
    MetaFrame Server Redundancy ....................................... 756
    User and Application Data ................................................ 759
    MetaFrame XP Support Components ............................... 760
MetaFrame XP Backup Strategies ......................................... 762
    Backing Up the License Database ................................... 763

# Appendixes & Index

## Appendixes

A. The Future of Citrix in a Microsoft .NET World .............................. 766
    Microsoft's .NET Strategy ................................................ 766
    The Future of .NET .......................................................... 769
    How does .NET Relate to MetaFrame? ........................... 770
    The Evolution of Citrix .................................................... 771

B. Acronyms Used in this Book .............................................. 772

C. MetaFrame Component Configuration ............................... 774

D. MetaFrame XP TCP Ports ................................................ 775

E. MetaFrame XP Scheduled Events ..................................... 775

F. Websites Referenced in this Book ..................................... 776

## Index

## A Note from the Author

I did my best to write this book with the reader in mind. As a writer, I'm always interested in hearing your thoughts about what worked, what didn't, what was good, and what was bad. I would love to hear any feedback or comments that you might have.

Any mistakes or clarifications that are found in this book will be posted to www.brianmadden.com. This site contains up-to-date information about this book and future books.

For those of you who are wondering, I work for Hewlett-Packard Consulting & Integration's US Federal practice in Washington DC. I do not work for Microsoft or Citrix. (I just happen to like their products a lot!) All the views and opinions expressed in this book are mine--not Citrix's, Microsoft's, or HP's.

Also, throughout this book, I make several references to online thin client communities, including The THIN List at http://thethin.net, run by Jim Kenzig, www.twaekcitrix.com run by Rick Dehlinger, and www.dabcc.com run by Doug Brown. I try to help out (and I receive help from) these group as much as I can. They are excellent resources for Meta-Frame XP information. Even though I mention these groups several times throughout the book, I am not "officially" affiliated with them, which means that I do not represent them and I do not have any financial interest in them. In fact, I do not have any financial interest in any of the companies that I mention in this book.

Thanks for reading. I look forward to hearing from you.

Brian S. Madden
brian@brianmadden.com

November 2002

## Acknowledgements

The response to the first edition of this book has been phenomenal. As excited as I was to write an expanded and updated follow-on edition, there are two people who really made this book possible: my boss and my wife (Yes there is a difference although sometimes it's hard to tell.)

At Hewlett-Packard, Jeff Goldstein gave me the flexibility needed to get this book done in a timely manner. At home, my wife Holli was (again) very supportive of my writing. While she remained in the same country as me through the entire process this time, she let me write even as we found a house, placed a bid, closed, fixed it up, and moved in.

In addition to their support, I decided that if this book was going to be mainstream I needed to get an editor. I was absolutely blown away by the work that Leah Ogonek did. She has an amazing ability to turn a techie rambling style into actual english.

I'd also like to point out that I thought the orange fruit on the cover was a hilarious play on words (Citrus = Citrix, get it?), and Natalie Black was very helpful in making my "citrus vision" a reality.

## Using this Book with Citrix Certification Practice Exams

After I wrote the first edition of this book, several people asked me if it would be a good resource for studying for the CCA or CCEA exams. I personally feel that it's important to have a solid understanding of the technology before taking an exam, and my book can provide that. However, this book is designed to be a technical field guide, not an exam study guide.

That being the case, I set out to find a way for readers of my book to have access to quality practice tests. I considered a CD-ROM that contained sample tests, but I feared that it would become outdated too quickly.

Instead, I have partnered with the Citrix training website www.learncitrix. com. LearnCitrix.com offers the best practice tests, available in online or offline modes. As a reader of this book, you can get a 25% discount on Citrix practice tests from www.learncitrix.com.

I have no financial interest in LearnCitrix.com and I do not receive any kind of compensation or kick-back if you choose to purchase practice tests from them. I just feel that they are the best on the market.

For more information or to sign up and receive your 25% discount, visit www.learncitrix.com/brianmadden.

# PART I

## The MetaFrame XP Server Environment

In this section

1. MetaFrame XP Overview     23

2. MetaFrame XP Server Architecture     37

3. MetaFrame XP Network Architecture     55

# CHAPTER 1

# MetaFrame XP Overview

**In this chapter**

The MetaFrame XP Solution                                24

Independent Computing Architecture (ICA)                 26

MetaFrame XP Features                                    27

Extending MetaFrame XP with Feature Releases             31

This book is designed to provide you with practical, real-world information about the use and design of Citrix MetaFrame XP systems. In order to study the advanced technical details, we need to ensure that you have a good baseline understanding of MetaFrame XP's features.

If you have already read and understand the MetaFrame XP instruction manual, or if you are very familiar with previous versions of MetaFrame, you'll probably just want to skim this chapter.

As you read through this book, keep in mind that each chapter was written separately and that it is okay for you to read them out of order. Of course if you're new to MetaFrame XP, the chapter sequence will guide you through a logical progression of the components, beginning in this chapter with an overview of Citrix's MetaFrame XP solution.

# The MetaFrame XP Solution

In case you don't know why you're reading this book, Citrix MetaFrame XP for Windows allows real Windows applications to be remotely accessed by many different types of client platforms, including Windows, Macintosh, UNIX, and Linux workstations, as well as wireless devices, laptops, set top boxes, mobile handheld devices, the X-Box, and network appliances. This access is provided via the Internet, LAN, WAN, dial-up or wireless connections, via TCP/IP, IPX, SPX, NetBIOS, or SLIP/PPP protocols.

When MetaFrame XP is used, Windows applications are executed on Meta-Frame XP servers, and users access the applications from their client devices via "remote Windows" sessions. Even though applications are running on the servers, the applications' screen images are transmitted to the users, so the users feel that the applications are running locally on their own client devices. One single MetaFrame XP server can support dozens or even hundreds of simultaneous users.

Applications running on MetaFrame XP servers can have complete access to users' local system devices, including disk drives, ports, printers, audio, and the Windows clipboard. Users can resize remote application Windows and "Alt-Tab" through the application list. A single user may have several Meta-Frame XP application sessions open in addition to their local applications. This means that from a user's standpoint, all applications look and feel the same. The users probably (and ideally) don't even realize that some applications are actually executing on centrally controlled and managed MetaFrame XP servers while others are local. Because MetaFrame XP allows users to use their regular Windows applications, their productivity remains high. This computing model is known as "Server-Based Computing."

## MetaFrame XP Server-Based Computing Components

In order to understand how Citrix server-based computing works, you need to understand its components. There are three main components that make up MetaFrame XP server-based computing environments:

- A multi-user operating system.
- Citrix MetaFrame XP application server software.
- Citrix client software and devices.

Let's examine each of these components.

### Component 1. A Multi-user Operating System

The foundation for the servers that run Windows server-based computing environments (and therefore MetaFrame XP) is a "special" version of the Microsoft Windows Server operating system that allows multiple simultaneous users to connect and run applications independently of each other. This is different from a standard Windows server. Standard Windows servers allow multiple users to simultaneously connect to *resources* (such as files, printers, and applications), but only one user can be interactively logged onto the console at a time. A multi-user operating system allows multiple users to connect and run *interactive* sessions (like remote control sessions) on the server, independently of what any other user is doing.

For MetaFrame XP server-based computing environments, valid multi-user operating systems include Microsoft Windows NT Server 4.0 Terminal Server Edition and Windows 2000 Server with the Terminal Services network service installed in "application mode." (Citrix also makes derivative versions of MetaFrame for UNIX-based servers, but they are not the topic of this book.)

### Component 2. MetaFrame XP Server Software

The Citrix MetaFrame XP server software installs as an application on top of the multi-user operating system. MetaFrame XP is the middleware that allows users to connect to the server to run applications. In addition to providing the client connection, MetaFrame XP increases the manageability and scalability of the default Microsoft Windows server-based computing environments.

### Component 3. Citrix ICA Clients

In order to use applications running on MetaFrame XP server-based computing servers, end users need to have client software loaded on their client devices. This client software is known as the "Citrix ICA client." The exact meaning of this will become apparent as you read more of this book. For now, it's important to know that in order for users to access applications on a MetaFrame XP server, they need to have the "Citrix ICA client" software installed on their client devices. Fortunately, there are versions of the Citrix ICA client software for almost every operating system and type of device, including Windows, Linux, UNIX, Macintosh, Windows CE / Pocket PC, JAVA, and Psion.

# Independent Computing Architecture (ICA)

When working with MetaFrame XP server-based computing environments, the term "ICA" will come up frequently. It is important to understand the context in which it is used, because ICA (Independent Computing Architecture) is both a *protocol* and *file type*.

## ICA Protocol

The ICA protocol is the network protocol used by Citrix ICA client devices and MetaFrame XP servers for client-to-server session communication. The ICA protocol actually transmits keystrokes and mouse movements from the client to the MetaFrame XP server, and screen images from the server to the client. This protocol is also responsible for the "advanced" features of MetaFrame XP, such as mapping a user's clipboard, local drives, and local ports, as well as printing and encryption.

The ICA protocol is a high-level protocol that can run on top of many standard network protocols, including TCP/IP, IPX/SPX, and NetBIOS.

## ICA File Type

"ICA" is also a type of file. ICA files (with the ".ica" file extension) are text-based files that contain instructions and parameters for connecting to MetaFrame XP servers. Users with Citrix ICA client software installed on their computers can double-click an ICA file to launch the Citrix ICA client software, establishing a session (via the ICA *protocol*) with the MetaFrame XP server. This session is established based on the parameters contained in the

ICA file. An ICA file has the "ini" file format, so it may be viewed and edited with any text editor.

It is important to note that while using ICA files allows users to connect to MetaFrame XP servers, there easier ways of accomplishing this. These other ways are covered throughout this book.

# MetaFrame XP Features

For the sake of those of you who are new to MetaFrame XP, let's take a brief look at the features available features. We'll look at each of these features in depth throughout this book, not just from a "features" standpoint, but also from a design and best practices standpoint. If you've used previous versions of MetaFrame but are new to MetaFrame XP, you will notice that several core features have been carried over from earlier products while others are completely new.

*Application Publishing.* MetaFrame XP's "application publishing" capability allows users to connect to applications by a friendly application name instead of a server name. For example, with application publishing enabled, a user can connect to an application called "Word 2002." The MetaFrame XP system would automatically connect the user to the proper server based on that application name. Without application publishing, a user would need to connect to a specific server, such as server01.yourcompany.com, and then run a specific application, such as winword.exe.

*Server Farms.* Multiple MetaFrame XP servers can be logically grouped together to form what's known as a "server farm." All servers in a server farm can then be managed together as one single unit. This is similar to the concept of a Microsoft Windows domain. Larger farms can even be partitioned into multiple "zones," allowing them to efficiently scale a wide variety of networks. We will spend a great deal of time in Chapter 3 drilling into the details of server farm and zone design.

*Program Neighborhood.* This feature allows your users to make one single connection to a group of MetaFrame XP servers. Based on that one connection and their network logon credentials, users are presented with a complete list of published applications that they have permissions to access. Program Neighborhood (coupled with application publishing) greatly simplifies your life as an administrator. By using Program Neighborhood, you do not have to worry about how to provide your users with access to a new application. All you have to do is grant them permissions to the application. The next time your user connects, the icon for the new application will automatically be available in their Program Neighborhood.

*Session Shadowing.* This feature is similar to "remote control" features in some helpdesk applications. Shadowing allows any user with appropriate permissions to remotely view the screens of other users' sessions. This is most often used for training and support purposes.

*NFuse Classic.* NFuse Classic is a free Citrix component that allows MetaFrame XP environments to be extended to web-based application portals. Users simply access a web portal and log on. Based on their credentials, users are presented with links to launch MetaFrame XP applications. NFuse greatly simplifies access to MetaFrame XP servers. All you have to do is give users the URL to the web server—the web pages will do everything else. (It's important to note that the NFuse feature included with MetaFrame XP is the "NFuse Classic" product. Citrix also has a product called "NFuse Elite." NFuse Classic and NFuse Elite are not the same product. For more information on NFuse, see chapter 11.)

*Web-Based Client Installation.* Users that will access your MetaFrame XP environment through the web (and NFuse Classic) do not need local ICA client software on their computers. Upon their first visit to the website, users will be prompted to automatically download and install the required client software.

*Encryption.* All MetaFrame XP-related network traffic can be encrypted. This includes traffic between the ICA clients and the MetaFrame XP servers, between the ICA clients and the NFuse web servers, between the NFuse web servers and the MetaFrame XP servers, and between various MetaFrame XP servers in the server farm.

*Universal Client Access.* The Citrix ICA client has been written for over twenty platforms, ensuring that users can connect into MetaFrame XP environments from almost any type of client device.

*Seamless Windows.* MetaFrame XP application sessions can totally integrate with users' existing Windows desktop environments. For example, old-fashioned remote application environments (like PCAnywhere) were confusing for users because they had a second desktop (complete with a second start menu) inside the remote application window. It was painfully obvious that the application was being run remotely. However, with MetaFrame XP's Seamless Windows feature, applications look and feel like they are local. They can be minimized, maximized, and dynamically re-sized. Users can even "Alt-Tab" between local and remote applications.

*High Color Depth and Resolution.* MetaFrame XP sessions can support 24-bit color at resolutions up to 64,000 x 64,000. This means that MetaFrame XP can support the graphics requirements of any application.

*Access to Local System Resources.* Applications running on MetaFrame XP servers can map back to a user's local disk drives, ports, printers, and clipboard. Even though applications running via MetaFrame XP ICA sessions are remote, the remote applications can totally integrate with a user's local applications.

*Client Time Zone Support.* Users do not need to have their client devices set to the same time zone as the MetaFrame XP server. In fact, MetaFrame XP servers can differentiate between local time and the user's time zone, enabling each user's session to operate in the proper time zone. One MetaFrame XP server can support multiple simultaneous users in different time zones.

*Citrix Management Console (CMC).* Most MetaFrame XP systems management tasks are done via a Java application called the Citrix Management Console (CMC). This is similar in concept to (although not compatible with) the Microsoft Management Console (MMC).

*Centralized Printer Management.* Printer drivers and configurations from one MetaFrame XP server can be automatically replicated to other MetaFrame XP servers in the server farm. This saves time in large environments because you don't have to manually configure the same printer connection over and over for every single server.

*Centralized License Management.* All MetaFrame XP licenses for multiple users and servers are managed at the server farm-level from one central location.

*Active Directory Support.* MetaFrame XP is fully Active Directory compliant, meaning that administrators, users, and permissions can be configured based on Active Directory groups. MetaFrame XP does not extend the schema of Active Directory.

*Pass-Through Authentication.* If you have users connected to MetaFrame XP sessions from Windows client devices that are already logged onto the network, the Citrix ICA client software can be configured to automatically pass the user's current credentials to the MetaFrame XP server, without the need for the user to re-enter their logon information.

*SpeedScreen*. This feature allows users to experience a quick, responsive ICA application environment, even over slow WAN connections, by providing instant mouse feedback and screen response.

*Panning and Scaling*. MetaFrame XP sessions can be dynamically scaled if the session resolution does not match the resolution of the ICA client. In addition to being able to scale a MetaFrame XP session, a high resolution session can have scroll bars and be panned on lower resolution clients. (Of course even with these features, it's still hard to use real applications on a palm–sized CE device.)

## MetaFrame XP Optional Features

MetaFrame XP comes in three versions: XPs, XPa, and XPe. MetaFrame XPs is the "base" version, and all the features previously described are available to MetaFrame XPs servers. The XPa and XPe versions have some advanced features and options not found in MetaFrame XPs. These options include:

*Application Load Management*. Users and applications can be load-balanced across multiple MetaFrame XPa and XPe servers, increasing scalability and redundancy. For example, a user can simply connect to "Word 2002," and MetaFrame XP will (behind the scenes and transparent to the user) figure out which actual server of all the MetaFrame XP servers is least busy and connect the user automatically.

*Application Packaging and Delivery*. In larger environments where many MetaFrame XPe servers run the same applications, Citrix Application Packaging and Delivery (known also as Citrix Installation Management) allows you to create application packages on one MetaFrame XPe server and automatically deploy them to multiple target MetaFrame XPe servers.

*System Monitoring and Analysis*. Also known as Citrix Resource Management, System Monitoring and Analysis allows you to proactively monitor Meta-Frame XPe servers. This is useful in larger environments.

*Network Management*. MetaFrame XPe can be plugged into your existing SNMP-based management tools, both for monitoring and management purposes.

## Managing MetaFrame XP with the CMC

The Citrix Management Console (CMC) is the main configuration utility used to view the status and change the settings of MetaFrame XP servers. This tool is similar in concept to the Microsoft Management Console (MMC), although unfortunately is in no way compatible with the MMC.

For some reason, Citrix decided to write the CMC in Java. This means that even through it's a Windows application, it doesn't perform like one. For example, the scroll-wheel on a mouse does not work in the CMC.

No one is really sure why Citrix reinvented the wheel and wrote their own Java-based management tool from scratch, instead of making a management plug-in for the MMC. Citrix claims that they chose Java for compatibility reasons. Because the MMC only runs on Windows NT/2000, they wanted to write their tool to work on any platform. (Apparently they couldn't think of any other way to provide a Windows application to non-Windows clients.) What's really funny is that the CMC requires fairly heavy communication between the machine that it runs on and the MetaFrame XP server that it communicates with. Because of this, Citrix's official recommendation is to run the CMC on a MetaFrame XP server and connect to it through an ICA session anyway.

The CMC will be covered in greater detail in chapter 16.

# Extending MetaFrame XP with Feature Releases

MetaFrame XP was released in February 2001. In October 2001, Citrix released a "Feature Release" for MetaFrame XP. This feature release, called "Feature Release 1" (FR-1) contained updated options and functionality for MetaFrame XP. This is *not* a free upgrade. It is similar in concept to a "minor release" of a software platform, for example, version 1.0 to version 1.1.

In May 2002, Citrix released Feature Release 2 (FR-2) for MetaFrame XP. In addition to its own new features, Feature Release 2 includes all new features that were introduced with Feature Release 1.

## FR-1 Enhancements to MetaFrame XP

Let's take a look at the increased functionality that you get with Feature Release 1. This section will detail the functionality that is added to all versions of MetaFrame XP (XPs, XPa, and XPe.)

*SSL Encryption Support for ICA Sessions.* Using FR-1, ICA client to Meta-Frame XP server session traffic can be 128-bit encrypted using standard encryption methods. This replaces MetaFrame XP's old proprietary encryption (SecureICA) with industry standard SSL encryption. The major advantage to this is that SSL traffic uses common TCP ports and is most likely able to traverse standard firewalls.

*NDS Support.* When FR-1 is applied to a MetaFrame XP server, applications and content may be published to NDS users and groups. Additionally, pass-through authentication has been updated to support NDS logins. Previously, in order to use NDS, you had to duplicate users in the NT domain and then associate their NT user accounts with their NDS accounts, since MetaFrame XP would not recognize native NDS accounts. With Feature Release 1, Citrix ICA clients and NFuse can pass NDS credentials in addition to a user's NT domain credentials when an ICA session is launched. See chapter 8 for complete information about integrating MetaFrame XP with Novell.

*Program Neighborhood Agent.* Remember that one of the features of Meta-Frame XP is Program Neighborhood, which allows you to easily push connection icons to end users. The major drawback to Program Neighborhood is that there are many configuration files that need to be configured on the client device in order to make it work and customize it the way you want it. With the Program Neighborhood Agent introduced as part of FR-1, you can automatically push connection icons to the Start Menu, desktop, or system tray of your users' workstations. Everything is controlled from the server, so you don't have to worry about users breaking or changing the configuration of their clients.

*Citrix Universal Print Driver.* Printing in MetaFrame XP environments can be challenging. The Citrix Universal Print Driver included in FR-1 is a print driver that theoretically works for all printers. Using it can reduce print job sizes by up to 50% (and therefore print times can by reduced by 50%). However, the downside of the Universal Print Driver is that it only supports 300 dpi monochrome printouts.

*Content Publishing.* This functionality takes the concept of "published applications" a step further, to "published anything." Without FR-1, the only things that you could publish to users were executable applications. However, the content publishing features of FR-1 can be used to publish video, audio, Word documents, web pages, or any other files. When a user clicks a content published icon, the content is opened on their client device. This ultimately allows users to seamlessly access both MetaFrame XP applications and local applications from one single location.

*Citrix Web Console.* This is a web version of the Citrix Management Console, which can be used for performing common administrative tasks via a standard web interface.

*Improved Performance.* Advances in the ICA protocol allow for improved bandwidth usage across the board, highlighted by a 50% bandwidth reduction when using 24-bit color over low bandwidth connections.

*Auto Client Reconnect.* ICA client devices that are unintentionally disconnected from a MetaFrame XP server when their session is interrupted by a bad network connection can now be configured to automatically attempt to reconnect without any user intervention.

*Citrix Management Console Improvements.* When FR-1 is used the CMC displays more detailed information about MetaFrame XP servers, including the Feature Release and Service Pack levels and the operating system platform.

# FR-1 Enhancements to MetaFrame XPa and XPe

Feature Release 1 also provides enhancements that are only available to Meta-Frame XPa and MetaFrame XPe servers.

*Connection Control.* This enhancement allows you to limit the number of concurrent user and/or application connections and is convenient for applications that are licensed on a "per concurrent user" connection basis.

*CPU Prioritization.* This enhancement allows you to assign CPU priority to applications running on Windows 2000 servers, ensuring that one user's "Solitaire" session is not taking away valuable CPU cycles from a payroll processing application.

# FR-1 Enhancements to MetaFrame XPe

The following enhancements are only available when Feature Release 1 is installed onto MetaFrame XPe servers.

*ICA Session Monitoring.* This enhancement allows you to monitor ICA network traffic, all the way down to the "virtual channel" level. With ICA session monitoring, you can see the exact amount of bandwidth that is being consumed by a single ICA session and tune your network accordingly.

*Installation Management Improvements.* With FR-1 installed, you can now filter Installation Management's target MetaFrame XPe servers according tooperating system type (Windows 2000 or NT 4) and whether or not Installation Management is installed. You can create and modify folders that can contain installation packages and also schedule target servers to reboot after a package has been successfully delivered. FR-1 also allows you to customize the message that is displayed to users when the system is pending a reboot after an Installation Management package has been installed.

*CA Unicenter TNG Plug-In.* Before FR-1, MetaFrame XPe's network management utilities only plugged-in to HP OpenView or Tivoli NetView. Feature Release 1 allows it to also plug-in to Unicenter TNG.

## FR-2 Enhancements to MetaFrame XP

Feature Release 2 adds many new features to MetaFrame XP.

*Windows 2000 Server is Now Required.* Okay, maybe this isn't exactly a "feature," but before you get excited about any of the new features of FR-2 you should know FR-2 does not work on Windows NT Terminal Server 4.0.

*User Policies.* The CMC can be used to set user and group policies that allow you to easily specify which MetaFrame XP features can be accessed by which users. Similar to Windows policies, you can specify multiple policies with multiple priorities. For example, you might create a policy that disabled sound support for all users, and another policy for executives with sound enabled.

*Delegated Administration.* Before FR-2, MetaFrame XP administration was "all or nothing." User accounts configured as administrators had full rights over all servers in the server farm, and there was no way to limit the administration or to give certain users administrative rights over smaller subsets of the server farm. However, by using FR-2, you can designate certain administrative roles for certain Windows groups or users. For example, you might allow one administrative group to manage MetaFrame XP printers without giving them the ability to change any published application properties.

*Transport Layer Security Encryption.* FR-2 supports Transport Layer Security (TLS) encryption. TLS encryption is even more secure than SSL, and is used more and more in the real world.

*Non-Administrator Shadowing.* This feature allows users to shadow other user sessions without needing to have administrative rights on the server of the user that they are shadowing. Many users can thus share a single session for online collaboration and training purposes.

*Smart Card Support.* The ICA protocol has been slightly modified with the release of FR-2. One of those modifications is the inclusion of support for Smart Cards (assuming you have the proper Smart Card reader hardware for your client devices).

*Content Redirection.* FR-2 provides an easy way for you to specify the location of applications that should open when users click on certain types of documents. For example, content redirection on the server allows users to double-click a Word document from within their ICA session while the document is opened locally on their client device instead of being opened with a copy of Word running on the MetaFrame XP server.

*More Enhancements to the CMC.* The Citrix Management Console has been further refined, with FR-2 introducing search capabilities, pass-through authentication, and better integration with Active Directory.

*Windows Installer Support.* Beginning with FR-2 (and Service Pack 2), all MetaFrame components are distributed as Windows Installer MSI files. This makes it easier to package MetaFrame XP for distribution to remote sites.

*IBM DB2 Support.* All MetaFrame XP server farms require a database to store configuration information. Prior to FR-2, that database had to be Microsoft Access, SQL Server, or Oracle. FR-2 adds support for IBM DB2.

*Printer Management Enhancements.* FR-2 further refines the management of printers for users. For example, with FR-2 you can set default printing preferences for autocreated printers and force users' printer settings to be refreshed every time they start an ICA session.

*Citrix Web Console Enhancements.* The Citrix Web Console has been modified to support more features, although it is still nowhere near as easy to use as the real Citrix Management Console.

## FR-2 Enhancements for MetaFrame XPe

The advanced features of MetaFrame XPe also receive new functionality when Feature Release 2 is used.

*Application Packaging and Delivery.* The big FR-2 enhancement here is that you can stagger package delivery across multiple groups of MetaFrame XPe servers. This is useful when you want to deploy a single package to many MetaFrame XPe servers but don't want them all to get it at the exact same time. Also, with FR-2 you can configure a single package to be installed from multiple network share points. This allows Installation Management to actually be useful in WAN environments.

*System Monitoring and Analysis.* With FR-2, a centralized database can now be used to store all collected information from multiple MetaFrame XPe servers. (Before FR-2 each server maintained its own information.) Also, pretty reports can now be generated based on data collected and predefined Crystal Reports templates. This is useful in situations where you want to send invoices to users based on their system usage or the fact that you don't like them.

# MetaFrame XP Server Architecture

In this chapter

How MetaFrame XP Works                    38

MetaFrame XP Server Requirements          47

The MetaFrame XP Installation Process     49

This chapter and the next can be logically grouped together because both focus on the architecture of MetaFrame XP environments. Chapter 2 covers the architectural components of specific MetaFrame XP servers. You can think of this as the architecture of MetaFrame XP itself. Chapter 3 covers the architecture of the MetaFrame XP network environment, including those factors that affect how the MetaFrame XP servers are placed on the network and hooked together.

In Chapter 2, we'll first look at how MetaFrame XP works. To do this, we'll take a quick tour of the various pieces and subsystems of a MetaFrame XP server. Then we'll look at some of the decisions that you will have to make when you install MetaFrame XP and any of the Feature Releases or Service Packs.

# How MetaFrame XP Works

In order to understand how MetaFrame XP really works, we need to look at the components that make up a MetaFrame XP server. Because MetaFrame XP is an add-on product to Microsoft's Terminal Services (the required multi-user operating system), we need to understand how Terminal Services works and interacts with MetaFrame XP before we can examine the actual MetaFrame XP components.

## How Microsoft Windows Terminal Server Works

We mentioned in Chapter 1 that MetaFrame XP is an add-on product to either Microsoft Windows NT Server 4.0 Terminal Server Edition or Windows 2000 Server with Terminal Services running in Application Mode. (Throughout this book, we will refer to these two operating systems as "Terminal Server." This term is used to generically describe either platform.) MetaFrame XP is really no different than any standard Windows application because it requires an operating system to be installed in order to function.

Terminal Server is basically the same as the regular Windows Server operating system except that in Terminal Server, key components have been added or modified to provide support for multiple simultaneous users.

In case you're wondering, Microsoft Windows has always been a "multi-user" operating system in the sense that multiple users could be connected to a single server at any given time. However, these users were connected to file services or printer services on the servers. They ran their local Windows interfaces on their local computers. The server only supported one single desktop interface via the local keyboard, mouse, and monitor. The main difference with Terminal Server is that multiple users can each run their own Windows desktop sessions on the server, so Terminal Server is "multi-user" in the sense that it supports multiple desktop interfaces. Some people like to think of this as a "remote control" environment, except that the Terminal Server can support many different users "remote controlling" it at the same time with each user doing something different. Conceptually, this is similar to UNIX X.11 servers.

In order for Terminal Server to support multiple user sessions, some changes had to be made to it from the regular Microsoft Windows server software. There are two fundamental differences between Terminal Server and regular Windows Server:

- Certain core components of the Windows operating system have been modified in Terminal Server to support multiple simultaneous user interfaces. For example, the virtual memory manager and the object manager have been modified so that they can support multiple simultaneous desktop interfaces without getting confused.

- New services and components have been added that allow Terminal Server to support the multiple user "sessions." The most important new component is the "Terminal Server" service. This service, which runs deep inside the server, is responsible for interfacing the multiple user sessions with the operating system. The Terminal Server service is responsible for functions such as creating sessions, receiving users, and ending sessions.

In order to understand how the various Terminal Server components work together in the real world, let's look at what happens as a Terminal Server is booted and a user connects.

1. The Terminal Server boots like a normal server, except that many of the core components are "multi-user aware."

2. The Terminal Server service (`termserv.exe`) is started. This service immediately begins waiting for user session connections. Every single user session that connects to a Terminal Server is given a "session ID" which is an integer appended to every process that the session runs. Each Terminal Server tracks its own Session IDs, and the session ID numbers start over at zero whenever the server is rebooted. The unique session IDs are what allow two different users to run the same application at the same time without the Terminal Server getting

confused. Session IDs also allow the server to keep all processes and memory separate for each user's session.

3. The server console (the local keyboard, mouse, and monitor) session starts and connects automatically. The console session is always the first one, so it always has the session ID "0." Once the console session connects, its display, mouse, and keyboard drivers are loaded.

4. Next, the Terminal Server service calls a component called the "Session Manager" (smss.exe). The Session Manager is responsible for managing user sessions (which are all the sessions other than the server console with session ID "0."

5. The Session Manager invokes the process csrss.exe to create two new user sessions (session ID "1" and session ID "2") that remain idle on the server. Whenever a user connects to the Terminal Server to establish a session, the Session Manager connects them to one of these "idle" sessions, and a new idle session is created. The idea behind this is that idle sessions have the memory space, session IDs, and interface drivers all set up and loaded so that when a user connects, all they have to do is grab one of these idle sessions. This shaves a bit of time off of the user session connection process.

6. After the Session Manager completes its startup tasks, the Terminal Server creates connection listeners that watch certain network cards and protocols for new user session connection requests. When a new session connection request is received, the session listener passes the request over to the Session Manager, and then the connection listener goes back to listening for more connections.

7. Once the Session Manager receives a new session request from the connection listener, the Session Manager negotiates with the requesting client for the security encryption for the session.

8. Next, the Microsoft licenses are verified. The server client access license is verified first, and then the Terminal Server client access license is verified. (Licensing is covered in detail in Chapter 14.)

9. At this point, the user session is ready to begin. If there is an existing disconnected session for that user, that session stack is loaded. Otherwise, the server maps one of the idle sessions to the user's account, and the user is ready to go.

In environments where MetaFrame XP is not used, Terminal Server provides its own thin client protocol, called RDP, which allows other Windows clients to connect to the server and run remote sessions. However, the server startup and session connection processes are the same regardless of whether MetaFrame XP is used.

# MetaFrame XP Interaction with Terminal Server

MetaFrame XP is an add-on product to Terminal Server. It uses the existing Terminal Server core components and services. In MetaFrame XP environments, Terminal Server is responsible for uncoupling the user interface from the application execution. All MetaFrame XP does is package that user interface in a protocol (the ICA protocol) and send it to the end users.

MetaFrame XP also plays a role in helping the end users find and connect to servers. However, after a user connects, they run a regular Terminal Services session with the Citrix ICA protocol.

Because MetaFrame XP is just an add-on product that provides the interface to end users, it is essentially nothing more than a set of services and management tools. MetaFrame XP does not break any of the existing Terminal Services components or interfaces. In fact, even though MetaFrame XP users connect via the Citrix ICA protocol, other Terminal Server users can still connect to the same server at the same time via the Microsoft RDP protocol.

Figure 2.1 shows how the MetaFrame XP software and Terminal Server operating system interact on a single server. As you can see, while the core multi-user operating system is based on Terminal Server, both user connection subsystems operate in a parallel fashion, allowing users to connect to MetaFrame XP or Terminal Server sessions.

*Figure 2.1  MetaFrame XP and Terminal Server Interaction*

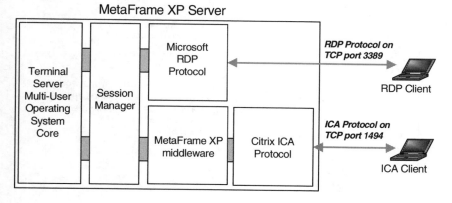

## MetaFrame XP Components

As we mentioned previously, MetaFrame XP is really nothing more than a middleware software application. Fundamentally, MetaFrame XP only does two things:

- It provides a method for users to locate and connect to servers.
- It provides a protocol (ICA) for users to run their remote sessions.

The diagram we looked at on the previous page (Figure 2.1) shows MetaFrame XP as a self-contained box. Of course in the real world, nothing is quite that simple. Even though it only does two things, MetaFrame XP is made up of several different components, subsystems, and interfaces. A more complete diagram of the MetaFrame XP components is shown in Figure 2.2. Refer to that diagram as you read through the next few sections describing each of the components that make up MetaFrame XP.

*Figure 2.2    The MetaFrame XP components, services, and interfaces*

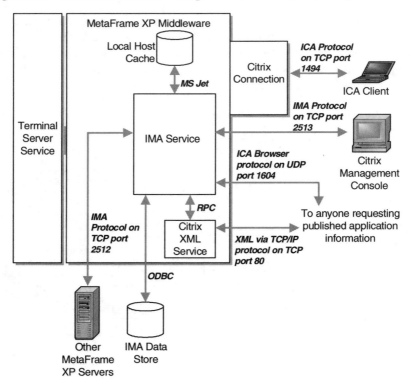

## Component 1. The IMA Service

As you can see by its placement in Figure 2.2, the IMA Service is the central nervous system of MetaFrame XP. This service is responsible for just about everything MetaFrame-related, including tracking users, sessions, applications, licenses, and server load. It also communicates with other MetaFrame XP servers and administrators, and knows which users have permissions to access which applications. The IMA service runs on every MetaFrame XP server in your environment. If that service stops then your server is out of commission. The IMA service itself is made up of many components and subsystems. As you read this book, you will become more familiar with these various components.

## Component 2. The Citrix XML Service

The Citrix XML Service is the primary interface between the MetaFrame XP server and anything else in the world that wants to get information about what services, applications, and content are available on it. The Citrix XML Service does not figure out anything on its own. Rather, it gets its information from the server's IMA Service and sends that information to whomever requested it.

As its name implies, the Citrix XML Service transmits this information via XML. Remember that XML is a language, not a protocol. The Citrix XML Service sends XML files to client devices that need information about the services offered. These XML files are generated by the XML Service dynamically and contain the information that the clients need. The XML service transmits XML files via standard protocols, usually HTTP running on TCP/IP.

## Component 3. The ICA Protocol

Chapter 1 mentionedthat the Citrix ICA protocol is the protocol used for the remote application sessions between users and MetaFrame XP servers. The ICA protocol is a high-level protocol, and it can run on top of TCP/IP, NetBIOS, or IPX/SPX. While Terminal Server is technically responsible for separating an application's execution logic from its user interface, the ICA protocol is responsible for transmitting the user interface elements (screen updates, mouse movements, and keystrokes) between ICA client devices and MetaFrame XP servers. Also, the Citrix ICA protocol is responsible for transmitting background information between the ICA clients and the MetaFrame XP servers, including the port mappings, drive mappings, print jobs, and sound.

### Component 4. Citrix Connection Listeners

Every MetaFrame XP server allows users to connect via explicitly defined ICA connection listeners. These listeners are similar to the Terminal Services listeners, except that MetaFrame XP listeners listen for connections based on the Citrix ICA protocol instead of the Microsoft RDP protocol. One connection listener is required for each network card / protocol combination. For example, an ICA connection listener waiting for connections on TCP/IP via NIC #1 would be a separate connection listener from one waiting for ICA connections over SPX via NIC #1, and so on. In the real world, these connection listeners and all of their related configuration properties are simply referred to as "connections."

If no connections were defined on a server, then no users would be able to connect, because there would be nothing to listen for and receive the user session connections. By default, the MetaFrame XP installation program automatically creates a connection for each protocol that is installed on the server when MetaFrame XP is installed.

Because each defined connection only supports one unique combination of a network protocol (TCP, IPX, async), a thin client protocol (ICA, RDP), and a network card, you can get very creative when you define connections. Imagine the following scenario:

*Figure 2.3   A MetaFrame XP server with multiple NICs*

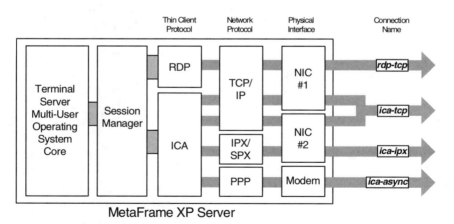

Figure 2.3 shows a MetaFrame XP server running TCP/IP and IPX/SPX with two network cards. When MetaFrame XP was installed, a connection called "ica-tcp" was automatically created and applied to both network cards. This connection is used by all users connecting via the ICA protocol running on

TCP/IP via either of the two network cards. This connection was created in addition to the "rdp-tcp" connection that was automatically created when Terminal Services was installed. The "rdp-tcp" connection allows users to connect via the Microsoft RDP protocol over TCP/IP, via either network card. On the server shown in Figure 2.3, the administrator previously removed NIC #2 from the configured list for the RDP protocol. This means that only users connecting via NIC #1 can use the "rdp-tcp" connection.

When users connect to MetaFrame XP servers, they do not choose which connection they use. In fact, just the opposite happens. The user connects via a certain network card and protocol combination, and the appropriate connection receives them. For example, in Figure 2.3, if a user tries to establish an ICA session via the IP address of NIC #1, they will be picked up by the "ica-tcp" connection. If a user tries to establish an ICA session via the IP address of NIC #2, they will also be picked up by that same "ica-tcp" connection. However, if they try to establish an RDP session via the IP address of NIC #2, their session will not connect, because no RDP connection is configured for NIC #2.

As you will see throughout this book, almost everything that you configure in MetaFrame XP environments is configured via the Citrix Management Console. However, the connections and their associated listeners are configured via a different utility called "Citrix Connection Configuration" (CCC). You can use CCC to configure options for Citrix ICA connections and Microsoft RDP connections, such as settings, permissions, and over what network card a connection is valid. Full connection details are available in Chapter 17.

In case you're wondering, the reason why connection settings are configured with their own utility instead of the Citrix Management Console is because each MetaFrame XP server maintains its own settings in its Windows registry. This is different from all other MetaFrame XP settings, which are maintained in a central database. This database (the "IMA Data Store") will be introduced in Chapter 3.

Anyway, you can only create one connection for each unique thin client protocol / network protocol / network card combination. This is because if you created multiple connections, each connection could have different properties, and the server wouldn't know which properties applied to user sessions that connected via the ambiguous connections.

The properties that you configure for a connection affect all of the users for that connection, regardless of whether the users have conflicting options configured somewhere else, such as in their user account properties. For example, if you set the properties of a connection that is ICA on TCP/IP, bound to all network adapters to "disable" client drive mappings, then every user that connects via that protocol / network card combination (i.e. that connection) will be bound by those settings, even if the user has different settings in his profile or is an administrator.

In the real world, you can use the power of multiple connections to customize parameters for different users that connect in various methods. For example, if you are using asynchronous ICA dial-in capabilities, then you can customize that specific connection to disable sound support in an effort to save precious dial-in bandwidth. In this situation, your LAN users would use a separate connection (maybe ICA on TCP/IP or ICA on SPX) that did not have the same restrictions. This is detailed in Figure 2.4.

*Figure 2.4 Multiple connections with different parameters*

|  | Thin Client Protocol | Network Protocol | Physical Interface | Connection Name | Unique Connection Options |
|---|---|---|---|---|---|
|  | RDP | TCP/ IP | NIC #1 | rdp-tcp | Administrators Only |
|  | ICA |  |  | ica-tcp | Medium Sound Quality No Compression Encryption |
|  |  | IPX/ SPX | NIC #2 | ica-ipx | Medium Sound Quality No Compression No Encryption |
|  |  | PPP | Modem | ica-async | No Sound Compression No Encryption |

MetaFrame XP Server

At this point, it's important to note that there are several different ways to restrict user access. One of the problems with setting access at the connection layer is that whatever restrictions you configure are in place for all users on the connection. This could present a problem if, for example, you have users that you want to restrict that are coming from one subnet and users without restrictions coming from another. From the connection standpoint all would be using the same connection because all would connect via ICA on TCP/IP.

Of course you could install two network cards in your MetaFrame XP server and set up two different connections—one for each network card—each with different settings and restrictions. This is not always practical because you would then need two network cards and two IP addresses for each server.

Fortunately, there are other ways to address needed security, as detailed in Chapter 15 of this book.

# MetaFrame XP Server Requirements

This section addresses the requirements of a Windows server that need to be in place before MetaFrame XP is installed. We'll begin by looking at the software requirements.

## Software Requirements – Base Operating System

MetaFrame XP can be installed onto a server running Windows NT Server 4.0, Terminal Server Edition (simply referred to as "Terminal Server 4.0" or "TSE" in the industry) or Windows 2000 Server with Terminal Services enabled in Application Mode (referred to as "WTS"). Minimum operating system requirements are as follows:

- Windows NT Server 4.0, Terminal Server Edition: Service Pack 5
- Windows 2000 Server or Advanced Server: Service Pack 1

These are just the minimum requirements needed for the MetaFrame XP installation to be successful. In the real world, you should use the latest service pack that you can support within your organization. As of this writing, those are Service Pack 6 for Terminal Server 4.0 and Service Pack 3 for Windows 2000.

### Should you use Terminal Server 4.0 or Windows 2000?

MetaFrame XP installs in exactly the same way on either platform. Furthermore, it acts the same on both platforms. At this point in time, Windows 2000 is stable enough that it should be the default platform for MetaFrame XP unless you have some specific reason to stay with Terminal Server 4.0. Besides, Citrix has officially decided to stop developing new products for Terminal Server 4.0, so you must use Windows 2000 if you want the "latest and greatest" from Citrix.

When designing a MetaFrame XP environment for your enterprise, the important thing is that the version of MetaFrame on all your servers is the same. The underlying operating system is less important. The lowest common denominator is key when deploying MetaFrame XP across platforms. You will not be able to use Group Policy across your entire environment if only half of your MetaFrame XP servers on running on Windows 2000 (obviously).

One thing you do need to be careful about when deploying MetaFrame XP across multiple operating systems is application publishing. If you publish one application across multiple platforms, your users will randomly get different platforms when they connect on different days. Depending on the application, this would be very confusing for your users. (More on application publishing in Chapter 4.)

### Using MetaFrame on Terminal Server 4.0

If you're using Terminal Server 4.0, be aware that Terminal Server service packs and Windows NT service packs are not the same and are not compatible. In order to download the proper service pack, make sure that you choose Service Pack 5 or 6 for Windows NT Server, Terminal Server Edition. Service Pack 6 for Terminal Server 4.0 is based on Service Pack 6a for Windows NT 4.0, so there is no such thing as Service Pack 6a for Terminal Server 4.0.

In addition to Windows Service Pack 5, MetaFrame XP running on Terminal Server 4.0 also requires MDAC 2.5 with Service Pack 2. (That's Service Pack 2 for MDAC, not Windows.) You will also need to manually install the JET components. It is recommended that you install JET 4.0 with Service Pack 3.

You can download the necessary JET and MDAC components from the Microsoft Universal Data Access Website, at www.microsoft.com/data. You should be very careful to test any new versions of MDAC that you download. For example, MDAC 2.6 caused major problems with MetaFrame XP when it was first released. For up-to-date information about MDAC versions and common problems with MetaFrame XP, you should consider joining a free online users group, such as the THIN list at http://thethin.net.

### Using MetaFrame XP on Windows 2000 Server

If you are using MetaFrame XP on Windows 2000 servers, Windows 2000's Service Pack 2 includes and automatically updates MDAC to Service Pack 2. However, it's recommended that you use Service Pack 3 for Windows 2000. If you can't do this, then be sure to read the rest of this book before deploying MetaFrame XP in your environment, because there are several post-Service Pack 2 hotfixes that you should apply prior to installing MetaFrame XP.

### Windows 2000 – Server or Advanced Server?

If you decide to use Windows 2000 Server as the platform for your MetaFrame XP environment, you will need to decide which version of Windows 2000 you will use—Server or Advanced Server. Fortunately, from the MetaFrame XP standpoint, it doesn't matter which platform you use. All MetaFrame XP functions and options are available on both Windows 2000 Server and Windows 2000 Advanced Server.

The real decision about which version of Windows 2000 you should use will be based on the underlying functionality of Windows 2000 that you require. In probably 99% of all cases, the only reason that people choose Advanced Server instead of Server is that Advanced Server supports more processors and more memory. While it's true that Advanced Server also supports additional functionality such as clustering, this functionality is rarely (if ever) used in MetaFrame XP environments. This is because MetaFrame offers its own, application-specific versions of this advanced functionality. (For details, read the next 700 pages.)

## Server Hardware Requirements

In addition to the underlying operating system, there are certain server hardware requirements that your MetaFrame XP servers must meet. From a "bare minimum" standpoint, any computer that can run Terminal Server can run MetaFrame XP. From a "practical" standpoint, however, there are many different factors that you need to consider when thinking about server hardware.

Truthfully, properly sizing a MetaFrame XP server is more of an exercise in the performance optimization of your overall MetaFrame XP environment than it is meeting a raw hardware requirements checklist. For this reason, the topic of MetaFrame XP optimization and server sizing deserves its own chapter, and the topic is covered in-depth in Chapter 6.

# The MetaFrame XP Installation Process

This book focuses on the advanced technical concepts of MetaFrame XP and what you need to know to design MetaFrame XP environments for the real world. Because of this, a walk-through of the MetaFrame XP installation that takes you from screenshot to screenshot is not included. If you need that then you should refer to the MetaFrame XP product documentation. However, this section does describe (from a technical standpoint) the process that takes place as MetaFrame XP is installed.

MetaFrame XP is installed onto a server just like any other application. Before you install MetaFrame XP, you will need to put your server into "install mode." Chapter 4 describes the details of this mode and how it works. However, if you just want to get MetaFrame XP installed and worry about "install mode" later, then open a command prompt and type change user /install.

Ideally, you'll be able to read through this entire book before you build your production MetaFrame XP servers. If you just want to install MetaFrame XP as fast as possible, then you should be safe by just selecting the default options. A lot of people do this to build a test server, and then they read through this book trying the different options as they go. When they are done, they complete their design and rebuild their server for "production" use.

Theoretically, you should install MetaFrame XP onto a clean system that doesn't have any applications installed. If this isn't possible, you can install MetaFrame XP onto an existing system. If your existing system is Windows 2000 and you do not have Terminal Services installed, there is a good chance that installing Terminal Services will break most of your installed applications.

During the MetaFrame XP setup routine, you will need to choose a data store. For details about the various data store options, see the "IMA Data Store" section of Chapter 3.

If you choose to install all of the ICA clients during MetaFrame XP installation, you will need about 200MB of disk space. For details and more information about installing ICA clients on your MetaFrame XP server, see Chapter 10.

During the installation, you'll need to enter a Citrix license number and a product code. Entering this from your product is pretty straightforward, although you'll want to read Chapter 14 before you create the strategy for licensing your enterprise.

The installation program will also ask if you want to install NFuse, which is the web portal used to access MetaFrame XP applications. If you have IIS installed on your server, then you can choose to install the NFuse components along with the installation of MetaFrame XP. Detailed NFuse information is available in Chapter 11.

## Server Drive Letter Remapping

One of the things that you will need to decide before you install MetaFrame XP is whether or not you want to remap your server drive letters. Essentially, this option gives you a one-shot chance to change the current server drive letter assignments. By default, this will change current server drive letters from C, D, E... to M, N, and O...

You are given this option during the MetaFrame XP installation unless you are installing MetaFrame XP from the SP-2/FR-2 .MSI file. In this case, drive letter remapping is *not* an option during the installation. You must remap your server drives *before* installing MetaFrame with the `DriveRemap.exe` utility contained in the MetaFrame XP installation folder. If you choose either one of these drive remapping options, the utility will make the necessary changes in disk administrator and scan the registry, looking for references to the old drive letters and changing them to the new drive letters.

Why does it matter in a MetaFrame XP environment what drive letters your servers use? It matters because MetaFrame XP has the ability to automatically map client devices' disk drives to their session within the MetaFrame XP server. Typically, client device's drives begin with C: and move up from there. A default MetaFrame XP server will also have a C: drive. When a user connects to sessions in this type of environment, the C: drive refers to the drive on the MetaFrame XP server. In order to map back to the client's C: drive, another drive letter must be used (default V:). While there is nothing technically wrong with this scenario, it can be confusing to users, because they see their local drive as C: when using local applications, and see it as V: when using MetaFrame XP applications.

### Advantages of Remapping Server Drive Letters

- Users will be able to see their own local disk drives as the correct drive letters.
- If you need to change the drive letter, the MetaFrame XP installation program provides an easy way to do this.

### Disadvantages of Remapping Server Drive Letters

- Any previously installed applications will most likely stop working.

By changing the MetaFrame XP server drive letter to something other then C: the sessions on the server have the C: letter available for client use. Users access their local files on the C: drive regardless of whether they are running local or MetaFrame XP applications.

This server drive letter remapping is only necessary when users will be accessing data on their local client devices through MetaFrame XP sessions.

There are some people who have chosen to remap server drives only to discover at a later time there is a reason that the server must access its own local drive as C:. If this is the case, you can use the `subst` command to add a mapping to the root drive as C:.

For example, if your system drive is M:, you can execute the command `subst c: m:\` from the command prompt. This will give you a C: drive that is identical to the M: drive. It is important to note that this is a temporary command. Any substituted drives will not be retained when the server is rebooted. If a drive substitution needs to be permanent, you can add the subst command to a login script.

## Feature Release 1 Installation

If you are planning on using Feature Release 1 (FR-1), then you should install it just after you finish installing MetaFrame XP. FR-1 requires MetaFrame XP Service Pack 1. If you do not have Service Pack 1 installed, the FR-1 installation program will install it for you. The same source installation files are used to install both FR-1 and Service Pack 1. Basically, you will install Service Pack 1 no matter what. Then, if you want to use FR-1, you add the FR-1 license, and the FR-1 components that came with Service Pack 1 are "unlocked."

One thing that's tricky about FR-1 is that in order to use it you need to install and activate a FR-1 license. Even though an unactivated FR-1 license will indicate that there is a grace period before you must activate the license, the reality is that the features of FR-1 are not available until the FR-1 license is activated. (See Chapter 14 for details about what this means.) At this point no one is really sure whether the product was designed this way on purpose or if this is a bug.

If you decide to use FR-1, then you should install it on all of your MetaFrame XP servers. (The same can be said for Service Pack 1.) You'll want to make sure that all of your MetaFrame XP servers are runnings the same version of the MetaFrame components. If you have servers with different versions of MetaFrame software installed then your system might not perform as expected. (More on this later in the book.)

In Chapter 1, you saw a list of the features that FR-1 offers. The features of FR-1 fall into the "cool, but not ground-breaking" category. As you read through this book, you'll notice that there is not a single entire section dedicated to FR-1. Rather, as MetaFrame XP design components are discussed, a note will be made if FR-1 is needed.

## Feature Release 2 Installation

The installation of Feature Release 2 is very cool. As with FR-1, Citrix released FR-2 and Service Pack 2 at the same time. Also as with FR-1, the FR-

2 and Service Pack 2 installation files are 100% identical. The same installation process is used for both FR-2 and Service Pack 2, and you "enable" the FR-2 functionality by installing Service Pack 2 and adding the FR-2 license.

Citrix did a couple of cool things when they released Feature Release 2 and Service Pack 2. Namely:

- SP-2/FR-2 now comes packaged in standard Windows Installer (.msi) files. This means that it is much easier for you to package FR-2 to deploy it to remote servers. The downside to this is that the SP-2/FR-2 installation program requires that the Windows Installer version 2.0 is installed on your server. This updated Windows Installer is part of Service Pack 3 for Windows 2000. If you're not using Service Pack 3 then it can be downloaded for free from www.microsoft.com.

- The SP-2/FR-2 installation program can also be used to install MetaFrame XP. If you are building a new MetaFrame XP from scratch, you can simply run the installation of SP-2/FR-2. The installation will install MetaFrame XP pre-patched to SP-2/FR-2. This is really nice because it saves you from having to immediately install SP-2/FR-2 after installing MetaFrame XP. Another nice thing about installing MetaFrame XP this way is that if you're installing MetaFrame XPe, the installation program will automatically install the Resource Management, Network Management, and Installation Management options. (This means no more "CD swapping" during the installation process of MetaFrame XPe.)

In addition to these two cool things that Citrix did when they released FR-2, they did one "uncool" thing. Namely:

- Windows 2000 is required for FR-2 and Service Pack 2. By making this requirement, Citrix essentially announced that they were stopping all new product development for Terminal Server 4.0. This offended and shocked a lot of people initially, although realistically, support for Terminal Server 4.0 was getting harder and harder anyway. Plus, when SP-2/FR-2 was released, Windows .NET Server was just around the corner, so Citrix had their hands full writing their product for both Windows 2000 and Windows .NET.

## Should you use MetaFrame XP Feature Releases?

The concept of the "feature release" is certainly not unique to Citrix, although those of you familiar with only Microsoft products might find it a bit strange. Some people argue that Feature Releases should be free, because they are released every year along with service packs. Others point out that by charging for Feature Releases, Citrix is actually able to get more new features released to the public sooner.

Either way, the bottom line is that if there are components of a Feature Release that are actually useful to you, then you should use the Feature Release. However, keep in mind that Feature Releases are released at the same time as service packs. This means that you can update your MetaFrame XP system code to the most recent service pack without having to pay for the feature release. After all, sometimes the new "features" of a Feature Release are actually properties of the free service pack or a new version of the ICA client software (which is also free).

# CHAPTER 3

# MetaFrame XP Network Architecture

In this chapter

| | |
|---|---|
| Independent Management Architecture | 56 |
| Placement of MetaFrame XP Servers | 58 |
| MetaFrame XP Server Farm Design | 69 |
| Server Farm Zones | 74 |
| The IMA Data Store | 87 |
| Future MetaFrame XP Server Relocation | 97 |
| Real World Case Study | 98 |

In this chapter, we're going to look at the considerations you need to take into account when designing your MetaFrame XP network architecture. By "network architecture," we mean the MetaFrame XP environment as it relates to the network, not the specifics of individual servers.

It is crucial that your MetaFrame XP architecture is able to support your users over your existing network. Regardless of whether you're planning on scaling your MetaFrame XP environment to support worldwide users, or you're building one server that may be the foundation for the future, you should address several things, including:

- MetaFrame XP server placement. (The location of your servers on the network.)
- MetaFrame XP server farm design.
- Server farm zones.
- IMA data store usage.

We'll close the chapter with a case study that details a real world design for a toy company. We'll look at several possible designs that this company considered and the advantages and disadvantages of each option.

Now, before we start looking at the details of the MetaFrame XP network architecture, it's important to fully understand Citrix's new Independent Management Architecture (IMA). Let's take a peek now.

# Independent Management Architecture (IMA)

MetaFrame XP is the first Citrix product that uses Citrix's Independent Management Architecture (IMA). The Citrix product literature describes IMA as if it's a magical solution that makes working with MetaFrame XP effortless. In the real world, MetaFrame XP's IMA consists of two components that we actually care about.

Independent Management Architecture is:

- **A data store**, which is a database for storing MetaFrame XP server configuration information, such as published applications, total licenses, load balancing configuration, MetaFrame XP security rights, and printer configuration.
- **A protocol** for transferring the ever-changing background information

between MetaFrame XP servers, including server load, current users and connections, and licenses in use.

In MetaFrame XP, IMA does *not* replace the ICA protocol. The ICA protocol is still used for client-to-server user sessions. The IMA protocol is used for server-to-server communication in performing functions such as licensing and server load updates, all of which occur "behind the scenes."

*Figure 3.1  MetaFrame XP network communication*

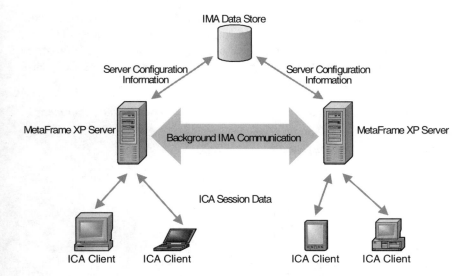

If you're familiar with previous versions of MetaFrame, MetaFrame XP's IMA *does* replace the ICA Browser Service. Not to be confused with the ICA protocol, the ICA Browser Service (in previous versions of MetaFrame) was used to replicate MetaFrame server configuration information between servers. This was needed because that information was stored in the local registries of each server. (They didn't use a central database, like IMA does). That ICA Browser Service was notoriously bug-ridden, extremely chatty, and didn't scale very well. Today, of course, all of that information is stored in the IMA data store. (For more information about integrating MetaFrame XP with the previous version of MetaFrame, see Chapter 13.)

Today, every MetaFrame XP server runs the "IMA Service." This service is the actual component that communicates with the IMA data store and other MetaFrame XP servers. Additionally, this IMA service communicates with the Citrix Management Console to allow administrators to manage and configure servers.

## Placement of MetaFrame XP Servers

The first major thing you need to consider when designing your MetaFrame XP network architecture is the physical placement of MetaFrame XP servers on the network.

The key here is to determine where MetaFrame XP servers should be located in relation to the data and the users. In simple cases, this determination is not very difficult. Consider the environment in Figure 3.2 consisting of two office locations. Let's assume that users from both offices need to access a database-driven application housed in the main office.

*Figure 3.2  Users in two offices need access to the same database application*

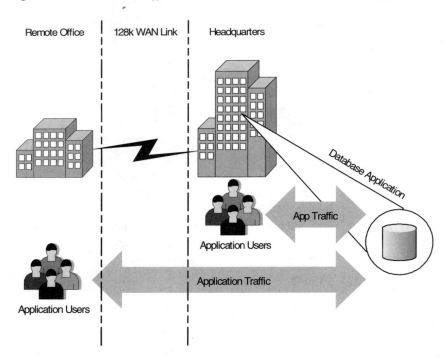

This company's IT department has decided to use MetaFrame XP to ease application deployment and to get the best possible performance for remote users. The company is faced with two choices when it comes to the location of the MetaFrame XP server for the remote users: they can put the Meta-Frame XP server at the remote office with the users, or at the main office with the database.

While both choices would allow the company to manage the users' applications, putting the server near the database will yield the best performance. (See Figure 3.3.) This is because the network traffic between the database and the client application running on the MetaFrame XP server is much heavier than the ICA user session traffic between the MetaFrame XP server and the end user. By placing the MetaFrame XP server at the main office, the database client software that is installed on the MetaFrame XP server is located near the database itself. Application performance is excellent due to this close proximity, and only MetaFrame XP ICA session traffic has to cross the expensive, slow WAN link.

*Figure 3.3  A MetaFrame XP server at the main office*

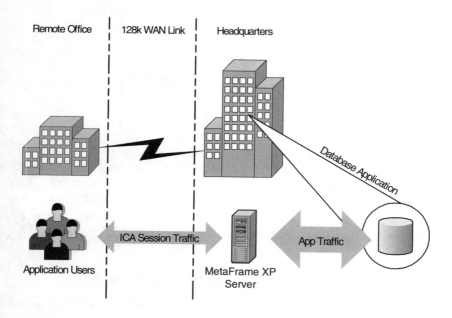

Now consider the other possible server placement option for this company. If the MetaFrame XP server were located at the remote office (as in Figure 3.4 on the next page), the heavy database traffic would still have to cross the WAN while the light, efficient ICA session traffic would be confined the remote office's local LAN, where bandwidth is plentiful. The server located at the remote office would not help application performance from an end user's point of view because the level of database traffic on the WAN is no different than if they weren't using MetaFrame XP.

*Figure 3.4  MetaFrame server placement at the remote office*

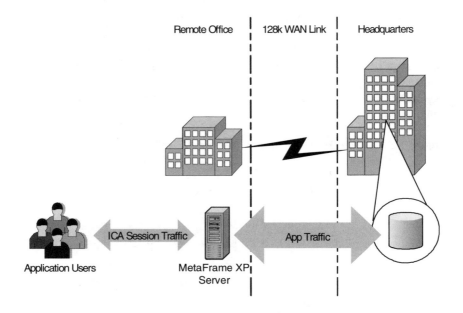

As this simple example shows, it's desirable to place the MetaFrame XP server close to the data source instead of close to the users. MetaFrame XP's ICA protocol is designed to work over great distances and slow WAN links. This allows heavy application data traffic, flowing between the MetaFrame XP server and the data server, to remain on a local LAN.

## Why should you care about server placement?

As shown in the previous example, the placement of your MetaFrame XP servers will directly impact several areas, including:

• Users' session performance.
• Network bandwidth usage.
• Server management.

## Users' Session Performance

The performance of the users' sessions depends not only on the network speed between the user and the MetaFrame server, but also between the MetaFrame server and the data the user needs to access. It does no good to put a Meta-Frame server on the same LAN link as a user if that server must access files that are located across a 56K connection.

However, this must be balanced with the network latency between the user and the MetaFrame XP server. Users won't want to use MetaFrame applications if there's a two second delay from the time they hit a key until the time the character appears on their screen.

## Network Bandwidth Usage

Network bandwidth usage is directly affected by the location of the Meta-Frame XP servers. Average MetaFrame XP ICA user sessions only require about 20KB per second. Many n-tier business applications (such as Baan, SAP, and PeopleSoft) require much more than that. If your MetaFrame XP server is on the wrong side of the network then you won't save any bandwidth by using MetaFrame.

## Server Management

Ultimately someone is going to need to maintain and manage the MetaFrame XP servers. It's usually much easier for administrators to maintain them if the application servers and the MetaFrame XP servers are both at the same physical location.

# What are the server placement options?

Even after looking at the complexities that arise when deciding where to put your MetaFrame XP servers, there are still really only two possible solutions.

- Distribute the servers throughout your environment, balancing some near each data source.
- Put all MetaFrame XP servers in the same place, in one big datacenter.

As with all decisions, each point has distinct advantages and disadvantages that must be considered when designing the final solution.

## Option 1. MetaFrame XP Servers Placed in many Locations

When users need to access data that is in multiple geographic areas, multiple MetaFrame servers can be used, with some servers in each location, physically close to each data source.

By placing MetaFrame XP servers in multiple locations throughout your environment (see Figure 3.5), a user can concurrently connect to multiple MetaFrame XP servers. This allows each server to have quick, local access to the data. An added benefit of this is that there is not one single point of failure. Losing access to one data center only affects some applications.

*Figure 3.5  Multiple MetaFrame XP servers provide fast access to data*

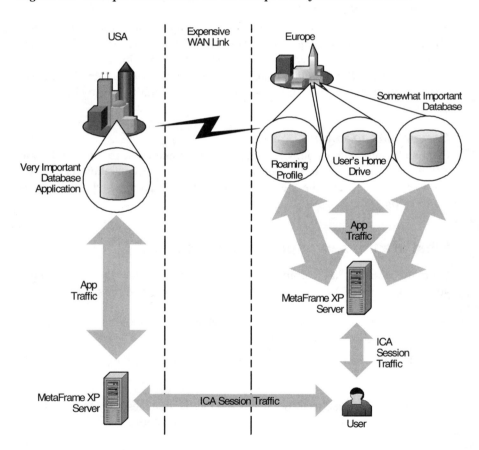

MetaFrame XP can even be configured to automatically route users to secondary servers in the event that a user's primary servers are inaccessible. (See Chapter 4 for details on how to do this.)

The downside to having MetaFrame servers in multiple locations is that your overall environment becomes more complex. Servers must be managed in several physical locations. User access must be designed so that they can seamlessly connect to multiple MetaFrame XP servers. On top of all this, it is inevitable that some data will only exist in one place, and that users will need to access it from every MetaFrame XP server, regardless of location. (Windows roaming profiles are a good example of this.) Lastly, a multi-server MetaFrame XP environment requires that each MetaFrame XP server communicates with other MetaFrame XP servers to transfer background information. When all MetaFrame XP servers are located on the same LAN, managing this communication is not an issue due to the high availability of bandwidth. However, when MetaFrame XP servers span multiple physical locations connected by WAN links, this communication must be managed. (Managing this communication is certainly possible; it just becomes another thing that must be planned for.)

As you can see in Figure 3.5, there are several advantages and disadvantages to placing MetaFrame XP servers in multiple locations throughout your environment.

### Advantages of Placing Servers in Multiple Locations

- Users' MetaFrame XP sessions are always close to their data.
- Efficient use of WAN bandwidth.
- Local departments can own, control, and manage their own servers.
- Increased redundancy.

### Disadvantages of Placing Servers in Multiple Locations

- More complex environment.
- Users may need to connect to multiple MetaFrame XP servers in order to use all their applications.
- Your servers might require additional local (onsite) administrators because they are not all in the same building.

## Option 2. All MetaFrame XP Servers in one Central Location

Instead of sprinkling MetaFrame XP servers throughout your environment, you can put all of your servers in one datacenter (see Figure 3.6 on the next page). After all, providing remote access to Windows applications is what MetaFrame XP is really designed to do.

*Figure 3.6  All MetaFrame XP servers in one datacenter*

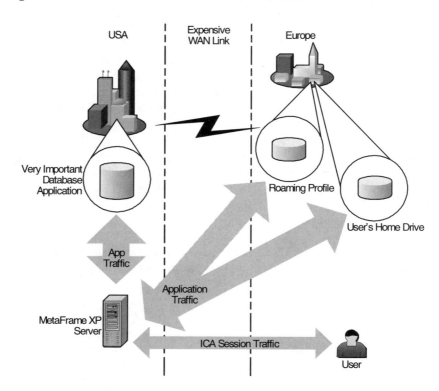

Having one central datacenter that contains all of your MetaFrame XP servers is easy to administer, but it causes other issues to arise.

For example, any users that need to access data outside of the data center where the MetaFrame XP servers are located must do it via a WAN link. While the performance of the ICA session between a user and MetaFrame XP server won't be a problem, significant performance problems could exist within the application sessions themselves due to potential great WAN distance between the MetaFrame XP server and the user's data.

Different applications handle data latency in different ways, but your users will become frustrated if they have to wait a long time to open or save files. Additionally, WAN bandwidth might be wasted because users would be forced to connect to all MetaFrame XP applications via the WAN.

### Advantages of Placing all MetaFrame XP Servers in one Location

- Simple environment to administer.

- Users can connect to one MetaFrame XP server to run all of their applications.
- MetaFrame XP servers are all in the same physical location.

### Disadvantages of Placing all MetaFrame XP Servers in one Location

- Access to data may be slow if the data is located across a WAN.
- WAN bandwidth may be wasted because users would be forced to connect to a remote server for any MetaFrame XP application.
- No option for local MetaFrame XP servers (local control, local speed, etc.)
- Single point of failure.

As you can see, the location and placement of your MetaFrame XP servers will directly impact many aspects of your MetaFrame XP environment. While part of the design will be easy, other aspects will take some time and thorough planning.

## Considerations when Choosing Server Locations

The previous example showed that the data location directly affects the placement of the MetaFrame XP server. However, in the real world, there are many more factors than were outlined in this simple example. The subsequent list includes all necessary considerations and is followed by descriptions of why each item is important.

- Where are the users?
- Where is the data?
- How much (and what type) of data is each user going to need?
- How many different applications are the users running?
- Where is the IT support for the applications?
- What does the WAN look like?

### User Location

The location of the users is a major factor to consider when deciding where to put the MetaFrame XP servers. Are all of the users in one central location, or are there multiple pockets of users? Is there a datacenter at every location where the users are, or are the users at remote offices?

## Data Sources

The data that users need to access from within their MetaFrame XP sessions is probably the most important consideration when deciding where to put your servers. When you look at the sources of data, it is important to consider all types of data that a user may need to access from a MetaFrame XP session. This includes back-end application data and databases, as well as files and file shares, home drives, and Microsoft Windows roaming profiles. (See Figure 3.7)

Are the users at the same physical location as all of their data sources? Is all application data at the same location on the network as users' home drives and Windows roaming profiles, or will users need to pull data from multiple network locations for a single session?

*Figure 3.7  Users often need to access multiple types of data from one session*

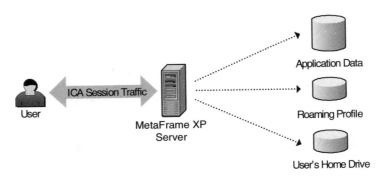

When considering the data that users need to access, consider how each data source will be used throughout their sessions. Will they need to access the data only during session startup or shutdown, or will they need constant access throughout the entire session? For each data source, will users only need to read the data, or will they need to write as well?

Lastly, consider the impact of each data source on the users' sessions. What happens if the path to each data source is congested? Will users be merely inconvenienced, or will they not be able to do their job?

To help understand the importance of these questions, refer to Figure 3.8 (facing page). This diagram details a situation that is becoming more and more common as organizations grow.

In this example, a user works for a company with a worldwide presence. Apparently this company followed the advice of consultants from the nineties, because all of their crucial business data has been consolidated into one single database in the US. Obviously, one of the main reasons that this company chose to use MetaFrame XP is so that their European users can have fast access to the database application. This company put a MetaFrame XP server in the US, right next to the database server, allowing the European user to access the database through a bandwidth-efficient ICA session. Sounds great! Very simple. Unfortunately, in the real world it is not always as simple.

In reality, the European user must access applications other than that one US database. Since the user is already running applications via ICA sessions to a MetaFrame XP server in the US, they might access other applications via that same MetaFrame XP server, right?

*Figure 3.8  A user in Europe needs to access data throughout the world*

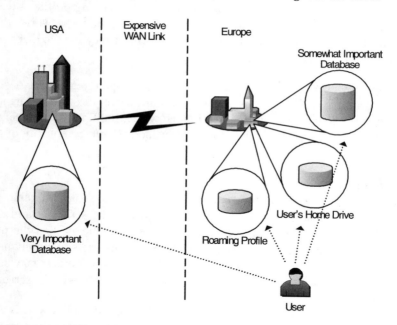

Let's think about this before we jump to an easy answer. Should a European user really be accessing all applications via servers in the US? Sure. If the user is already crossing the WAN to connect to the database, there is no real impact to adding more applications. But will the user always be utilizing the database? What if the user just wants to use other applications? Should the company pay for the transatlantic bandwidth so that the user can create a PowerPoint presentation? What about the user's home drive? Most likely, the user will want to save files and work with others. Should he use PowerPoint running on a US server while saving files to a file server in Europe? What about PowerPoint's auto-save feature? Will this user have the patience to wait while his file is auto-saved across the ocean WAN every ten minutes while he's trying to work?

The point here is that users need to connect to multiple data sources, and they frequently need to access data that resides in many different geographic regions. While this European example is a geographic extreme, the same ideas apply anywhere. A slow WAN is a slow WAN. The previous example also applies to users in Washington DC accessing databases 30 miles away in Baltimore over a 56k frame relay.

This example illustrates a situation in which a user only needed access to a database and a home drive. Other users may need to access files and data from many different groups in many different locations. Also, don't forget about Windows roaming user profiles. If one single roaming profile is to be used for all MetaFrame XP sessions on servers throughout the world, then that profile needs to be accessible to the user wherever they log on. (More on roaming profiles in Chapter 5.)

If a user only needed to access data from one geographic region, the design would be simple. You would just put a MetaFrame server next to the data and have the user connect via an ICA session. However, multiple geographic regions that all have important data for the user increase the complexity of the design.

### *Applications*
The number and types of applications that you want to make available via MetaFrame XP also affect the decision as to where the servers should be located. The application mix needed by one user may dictate that the user must connect to multiple MetaFrame XP servers. Some users may only need to access applications on single MetaFrame XP servers while others may need to access applications across departments via many MetaFrame XP servers.

The mix of local applications and remote MetaFrame XP applications is also a factor. Will any applications be loaded locally on the users' computers or will everything be done via MetaFrame XP? If everything is done via MetaFrame, and the MetaFrame servers are located across the WAN from the users and the WAN link goes down, all productivity stops. Is that an acceptable risk to the organization or should some servers and data be local—even though all data may not be local?

### IT Support of Applications

How does your organization's IT department support applications? If all application support is from one site then it makes sense for all MetaFrame XP servers to be located at that site. However, large organizations usually have many applications that are supported by different people from different locations, as shown in Figure 3.9 on the next page. In these cases you may have to place MetaFrame XP servers in multiple locations, with each server placed near the people that support its applications.

### WAN Architecture

The wide area network can also affect where MetaFrame XP servers should be located. If bandwidth is congested, MetaFrame XP servers should be located across WAN links because they are generally more efficient than the native applications over WAN links.

*Figure 3.9  Application support from multiple people in multiple locations*

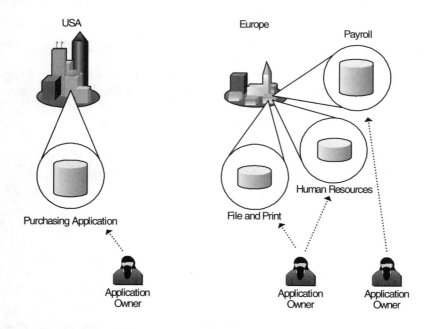

## MetaFrame XP Server Farm Design

Remember from Chapter 1 that a server farm is a logical group of MetaFrame XP servers that are managed together as one entity, similar in concept to a Microsoft Windows domain. With MetaFrame XP, one single farm can scale to hundreds of servers to support a very large enterprise. Of course, there are also reasons that organizations might choose to have multiple, smaller server farms.

When deciding on the boundaries that separate server farms, one geographic location does not always correlate to one server farm. There are many situations that call for a server farm to span multiple locations, even if those physical locations are connected via slow WAN links. Conversely, there are also reasons that one physical location would need to have multiple MetaFrame XP sever farms, or even multiple farms within one datacenter. The decision as to the number and locations of farms needs to balance technical and business requirements.

Even though we've used the analogy of Microsoft Windows domains to explain the concept of MetaFrame XP server farms, the server farm boundaries do not have to be aligned to Windows domain boundaries. One server farm can span multiple domains, or one server farm can be made up of MetaFrame XP servers that belong to different domains.

## Why should you care about server farm design?

You should design you server farm boundaries independently of your MetaFrame XP server locations. This means that you should first decide where you're going to put your servers. Only then should you start to think about their farm memberships and how many farms you will have.

The decision to create one all-encompassing server farm or several smaller server farms impacts several areas in your environment, specifically:

- Ease of management.
- Network bandwidth usage.
- End users' ability to logon.

### *Ease of Management*

All of the MetaFrame XP servers in one farm can be managed together. They are managed via the same tool, and many security and configuration settings are configured on a farm-wide basis. MetaFrame XP servers that belong to different farms must be managed separately. Applications cannot be load-balanced across servers in different server farms (although users can simultaneously run sessions on MetaFrame XP servers that are members of different farms).

## Network Bandwidth Usage

MetaFrame XP servers in a server farm must communicate with other servers in the same farm. (Remember the new IMA server-to-server communication protocol?) Therefore, having many servers in a farm increases network communication overhead.

## End Users' Logon Ability

One single server farm can span multiple domains. In these multi-domain farms, it is possible for one published application to be load-balanced across MetaFrame XP servers that are members of different domains. If this is the case, users may experience intermittent logon problems if they are routed to a load-balanced server from another domain that does not trust their domain.

# What are the server farm design options?

When thinking about your MetaFrame XP server farm layout, there are really two choices. You can build large farms that include MetaFrame XP servers from multiple geographic areas, or you can build multiple small farms, each including a single group of MetaFrame XP servers.

Note that the "geographic area" referred to here relates to geographic area of the MetaFrame XP servers only, which is why we design the server farm after we design the placement of the MetaFrame XP servers. If you have users all over the country, but you have decided that all the MetaFrame servers will be in one location, then that would be considered a single "geographic area," in regards to server farm design.

## Option 1. One Large Server Farm

There are many advantages of having one large server farm. Remember, one large server farm does *not* mean that all of your servers must be in the same physical location. Some companies have MetaFrame XP servers in several datacenters throughout the world, with all of those servers belonging to the same server farm.

By creating one server farm, all administration can be done by one group of people. Farm-wide changes affect all the MetaFrame XP servers in the company because all company servers are in the same farm. Additionally, each user only needs a single ICA connection license, even if they connect simultaneously to multiple MetaFrame XP servers in different parts of the world.

Unfortunately, there are also drawbacks to the single farm model. Because all farm servers need to keep in communication with each other, farms that span slow WAN links will need to use part of that link for farm communication. (A farm can be divided into logical "zones" that help manage that communication. These zones are covered in the next section.) Also, server farms are designed to be administered as a group, and this administration is "all or nothing." You can't give some people administrative rights to some farm servers while preventing them from administering others. This becomes a real issue if you have farms that span great distances and you want local administrators to be restricted to managing local servers only.

### Advantages of Creating One Large Server Farm

- Efficient license usage.
- Single point of administration.

### Disadvantages of Creating One Large Server Farm

- Cannot segment farm server administration.
- Intra-farm network communication.
- All farm-wide settings must apply to all servers.

## Option 2. Multiple Smaller Server Farms

Many companies choose to segment their MetaFrame XP servers into multiple farms. Again, this segmentation does not have to follow geographic boundaries. Some companies have several server farms for MetaFrame XP servers that are in the same datacenter because different departments have different needs, users, and servers.

Splitting your MetaFrame XP environment into multiple farms allows local groups or departments to manage their own servers and to purchase and manage their own licenses. Larger companies with several locations can save WAN bandwidth by keeping MetaFrame XP servers on both sides of the WAN in separate farms.

Of course, if separate farms are created then one user connecting into multiple farms will need a MetaFrame XP connection license for each farm that is used. (See Chapter 14 for full license usage details.) Also, any enterprise-wide changes made by MetaFrame XP administrators will need to be manually configured for each farm.

### Advantages of Creating Multiple, Small Farms

- Intra-farm network communication is not as broad.
- Departmental licensing.
- Local administration.

- Different farms can have completely unrelated configurations and settings.

### Disadvantages of Creating Multiple, Small Farms

- One user connection to multiple farms requires multiple licensees.

- Enterprise-wide configuration changes need to be separately applied at each farm.

# Considerations when Designing your Server Farm

There are several considerations that will help you make your decision as to whether you will have one large farm or several smaller farms. If you choose to have several smaller farms, these can also help you choose your farm boundaries and how you should segment your server farms.

- How will your MetaFrame XP servers be administered?
- How much network bandwidth is available?
- What are your licensing requirements?
- What is the Windows domain / Active Directory design?
- Where are the users located?

### Administration

The desired administration of your MetaFrame XP environment will drive the server farm design. A MetaFrame XP server farm is designed to be managed as one group. Because of this, any farm administrative rights that you grant to users in your farm apply to all servers in the farm. It is not possible to grant users administrative rights on some servers while preventing them from administering others in the farm. If you need to segment the administration of MetaFrame XP servers, then you need to create multiple server farms.

Feature Release 2 for MetaFrame XP does introduce the concept of segmented administration. However, this administration is segmented by role, not by server. What this means is that if you have a large farm, you can give some users administrative rights over certain roles, such as printer management or application management, while preventing them from having the ability to change the network configuration of servers or add new servers to the farm. The problem with this is that these rights also apply to all servers in the farm. Users who are only granted the right to manage printers have that right on all farm servers. There is still no way to let some users administer certain servers while preventing them from administering other servers in the same farm.

### Network Bandwidth

MetaFrame XP servers in server farms need to communicate with each other. For this communication, consistent network connectivity is needed. If you have any network connections that are extremely limited or unreliable, you may not want to span one farm across them, choosing instead to create two farms, one on each side.

### Licensing

MetaFrame XP licensing is connection-based, which means that one user can simultaneously run sessions on multiple MetaFrame XP servers in the same farm and only use one license. However, if one user connects to servers in two different server farms, one license is required for each server farm. If you want users to only use one license, you must put all of the MetaFrame XP servers they use in the same server farm.

### Windows Domain / Active Directory Design

The design of your underlying Windows NT domain or Active Directory can also impact your MetaFrame XP server farm design. There is no problem with having multiple MetaFrame XP server farms in one Windows domain. However, the opposite is not necessarily true. Ideally, a farm should not span multiple NT domains or Active Directory forests. While there is no technical reason that one server farm could not span multiple domains; management becomes much more complex. (Refer to Chapter 17 for more details.)

### User Location

When designing server farm boundaries, you need to think about the locations of your MetaFrame XP servers in addition to the locations of the users that will be accessing the servers. For example, if you have decided that you need to have multiple groups of MetaFrame XP servers in different geographic areas, but users from each area only connect to their local MetaFrame XP servers, then you can easily make the decision to create multiple server farms.

## Server Farm Zones

MetaFrame XP server farms can be partitioned into multiple logical segments called "zones." Every server farm has at least one zone (which is created by default when the server farm is established). As an administrator, you can add additional zones and reconfigure existing MetaFrame XP farm servers so that they belong to zones other than the default zone.

Server farm zones in MetaFrame XP serve two purposes:

- Zones allow for efficient collection and aggregation of MetaFrame XP server statistics.

- Zones allow for efficient distribution of server farm configuration changes.

As you have probably guessed, zones are intended to allow server farms to grow efficiently. Large server farms that have their zones properly designed will allow end users to have quick and efficient logons and server connections. A server farm that is partitioned into multiple zones can contain many more servers than a farm that has only one zone. Server farm zones only affect the technical communication aspects of server farms. Zone configuration does not affect any administration or security components.

All MetaFrame XP servers must belong to a server farm, and every server farm must have at least one zone. Therefore, every MetaFrame XP server must also belong to a zone. One zone can contain up to 100 MetaFrame XP servers before performance dictates that more zones should be created. However, this does not necessarily mean you must wait until you have 100 servers before you should create more zones. In the real world, your network architecture will drive the number of zones that you will create.

Each MetaFrame XP server monitors itself for many events, including user logons, logoffs, connections, disconnections, and its server load and performance-related statistics. This self-monitoring is necessary for load-balancing and license tracking to work. Each server actively tracks its own statistics and sends periodic reports to a central location. It is not practical for every single MetaFrame XP server to notify every other MetaFrame XP server in the farm each time one of these user or performance metrics changes. (This is how MetaFrame 1.8 worked and is the reason why it didn't scale very well.) However, it's important that all MetaFrame XP servers know the current status of all the other servers so that farm-wide load balancing and license tracking can function.

As shown in Figure 3.10 (on the next page), a lot of network communication occurs between MetaFrame XP servers in a zone. Considering the fact that the environment in the diagram is made up of only nine servers, you can imagine how much communication would take place if this environment was made up of twenty or thirty servers. This is where zones become necessary.

*Figure 3.10  The communication between multiple servers in one zone*

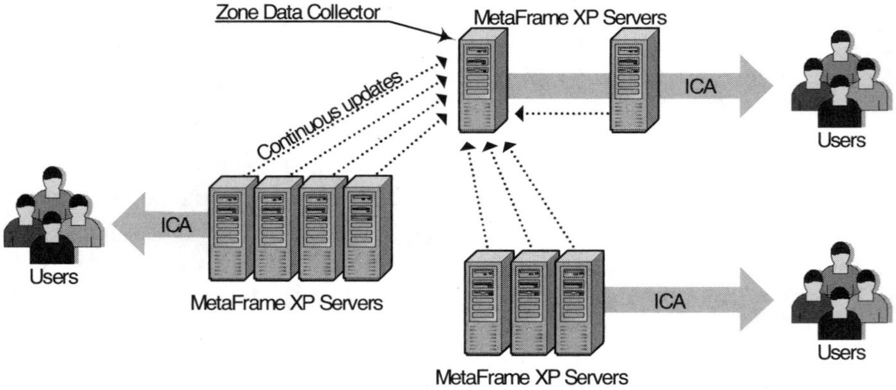

A server farm zone is a logical group of MetaFrame XP servers. These Meta-Frame XP servers exclusively communicate user load, performance, and licensing statistics with each other. One chosen server within each zone communicates with one chosen server from each of the other zones. Within this model, only one server from each zone sends server-to-server communications throughout the farm, instead of every single MetaFrame XP server trying to communicate with one single MetaFrame XP server.

The "chosen" MetaFrame XP server that communicates with other zones is known as the Zone Data Collector (ZDC). There is only one ZDC per zone, and every zone must have one. The ZDC is the server responsible for knowing all up-to-date statistics about every MetaFrame XP server in the zone, including user load, performance load, and license usage. Whenever any of these monitored parameters changes on any MetaFrame XP server, that server sends notification of the change to its local zone's ZDC. The ZDC then notifies all other ZDCs of the other zones in the farm.

All ZDCs from each zone within a server farm maintain an open connection with all other ZDCs in the farm, forming a hierarchical communication chain that ultimately touches every MetaFrame XP server in the farm.

Figure 3.11 (facing page) shows what the server from Figure 3.10 would look like if it was partitioned into multiple zones. As you can see, network communication is vastly reduced when compared to the diagram that only had one zone.

Because each ZDC must maintain an open link to all other ZDCs in the farm, you should try to keep the total number of zones in the farm as *low* as possible while still having enough zones to be efficient. There is a fine line between too many zones and not enough. We'll take a more in-depth look at this in a bit. For now, remember that any time a user logs on or off, connects or disconnects, or any server load changes, server updates are sent to all ZDCs in the entire farm.

*Figure 3.11  Multiple MetaFrame XP servers in multiple zones*

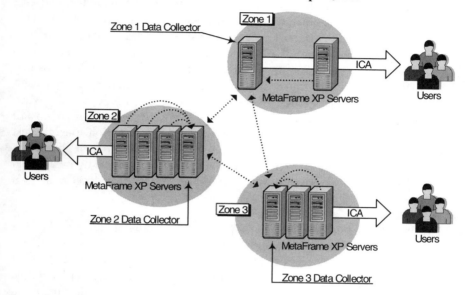

## Zone Data Collector (ZDC)

The Zone Data Collector is a role that one MetaFrame XP server performs for each zone within a server farm. You do not have to explicitly configure a server to be a ZDC, because anytime there is more than one MetaFrame XP server in a zone an election takes place to choose the one server that will act as the ZDC. You can, however, change the election preferences of individual servers to affect the outcome of an election, essentially allowing you to select which server you would like to become the ZDC. These preferences range from "most preferred" to "least preferred." Election preference settings are set via the Citrix Management Console (CMC) in the server farm's properties box. (CMC I Farm I Properties I Zone I Highlight Server I Preference)

## Zone Data Collector Elections

Zone elections take place automatically within each zone to designate the MetaFrame XP server that will act as the Zone Data Collector. The outcome of the election is decided by the following three criteria, listed in order of precedence:

1. Software version number. (The newest version will always win.)
2. Manually configured election preference. (As configured in the CMC.)
3. Host ID. (The highest host ID will win.)

As you can see by the election criteria, the software version number carries a higher precedence than the manually configured preference in the CMC. This is like an insurance policy, just in case Citrix ever decides to make any radical changes to the operation of the ZDC (in the form of a hotfix or service pack, for example). By designing the election criteria this way, Citrix ensures that the ZDC will always be the most up-to-date server in the zone. As an administrator, it is important to remember this version precedence, especially when you are testing new or beta versions of MetaFrame XP software. If you install a new test version of MetaFrame XP into an existing production zone, the test server will become the ZDC because it will be a newer build than your existing production MetaFrame XP servers. Of course, this can easily be avoided by installing test servers into their own server farms, or at least their own zones.

The final election criterion, the "host ID" parameter, is essentially a tie-breaker if the first two items are the same on more than one server. The host ID is a random number that is generated when MetaFrame XP is installed. The server with the highest host ID will win the ZDC election. You cannot change the host ID. If you would like to change the outcome of an election then you should simply change the "Election Preference" parameter of a server in the CMC.

Now that you understand how the outcome of a ZDC election is determined, let's look at what causes an election to take place.

There are several events that initiate a ZDC election, as outlined below. Any one of these "triggers" can cause an election and there is no order or precedence. Any MetaFrame XP server can call an election by sending out an "election request." Election requests are sent out when any of the following events occur:

- A MetaFrame XP server loses contact with the ZDC. (That MetaFrame XP server will send out an election request.)
- The ZDC goes off-line. (If the ZDC is shut down gracefully it will send out an election request before it shuts down its local IMA service. If the ZDC is unexpectedly shut down then the next MetaFrame XP

server that tries to send an update to it will notice that the ZDC is gone and will send out the election request.)

- A new server is brought online. (It sends out an election request as soon as the local IMA service is started.)

- An election is invoked manually by an administrator. This is done with the "querydc -e command." (The server where this command is executed sends out an election request.)

- The configuration of a zone changes (when a MetaFrame XP server is added or removed, or a new zone is created). The server that receives the update from the CMC sends out an election request. Depending on the servers affected by the change, election requests could be sent out to multiple zones.

After a ZDC election is complete, if a new server is elected as the ZDC then every other MetaFrame XP server sends the new ZDC its complete status information. If the newly-elected ZDC is the same server as before the election, the other MetaFrame XP servers are smart enough not to resend their information because they know that the ZDC has their up-to-date information from just before the election.

Remember that each ZDC maintains connections to all other ZDCs in the farm. If a ZDC loses an election, it notifies the ZDCs in other zones that it is no longer the ZDC for that zone. If a ZDC goes off-line, ZDCs from other zones figure out that there is a new ZDC when the new ZDC begins contacting them for information.

If you're familiar with MetaFrame 1.8, then you know about the ICA browser service and the ICA master browser elections. Zones and ZDCs perform similar functions (but are *much* faster and more reliable). Also, unlike MetaFrame 1.8, there are no backup zone data collectors in MetaFrame XP.

### Communication between MetaFrame XP servers and the ZDC

The ZDC maintains the dynamic information of all the MetaFrame XP servers in the zone. Each MetaFrame XP server in the zone notifies the ZDC immediately when any of the following events occurs:

- There is an ICA session logon, logoff, disconnect, or reconnect.
- The server or application load changes.
- Licenses change (used, released, added, or removed).
- A MetaFrame XP server comes online or goes off-line.
- Any published application's settings change.

• A MetaFrame XP server has an IP or MAC address change.

All of this information is collectively known as "session data." No session data is stored permanently on the ZDC. It is all kept in memory for use only by the IMA service. You can view any of this data at any time with the queryds command-line utility.

If a ZDC does not receive any communication from a MetaFrame XP server in its zone after 60 seconds, the ZDC will perform an "IMA Ping" to determine whether the server is still online. You can change this interval by adding the following registry value:

Key: HKLM\Software\Citrix\IMA\Runtime

Value: KeepAliveInterval

Type: REG_DWORD

Data: The interval in milliseconds, entered in hex notation. (The 60 second default would be 60,000 milliseconds, or 0xEA60 in hex.)

When entering the registry value, remember that you can use the Windows calculator to convert from decimal to hex. (View Menu | Scientific | Enter your decimal number | click the "hex" button.)

### Communication between Zone Data Collectors

As soon as a ZDC receives an update from a MetaFrame XP server, it forwards the information to all other ZDCs in the farm. If the ZDC fails to connect to one of the other ZDCs, it will wait five mintues and then try again. This five-minute interval is also controllable via the registry:

Key: HKLM\Software\Citrix\IMA\Runtime

Value: GatewayValidationInterval

Type: REG_DWORD

Data: The interval in milliseconds, entered in hex notation. (The 300 second default would be 300,000 milliseconds, or 0x493E0 in hex.)

Looking at the large amount of frequently-changing session data that a ZDC must deal with leads to one question:

## Should you build a dedicated Zone Data Collector?

Once your environment grows larger than a few MetaFrame XP servers you may begin to wonder whether you should build a "dedicated" MetaFrame XP server that acts only as a zone data collector without hosting any user sessions.

The ZDCs of larger zones can get very busy. Building a dedicated server is a good way to minimize the risk that a busy zone will impact live user sessions due to a MetaFrame application server that is too busy acting as ZDC.

There are no hard numbers to dictate the point at which you should build a dedicated ZDC. In the real world, if a zone has more than ten servers or so, people tend to build a dedicated ZDC. Of course hardware is always getting faster and faster, so this number may change.

If you are at the point where you don't know whether or not you need a dedicated ZDC, the best thing to do is to look at the performance of the server acting as the ZDC and compare it to servers that are not acting as the ZDC. Refer again to the previous section for a list of how much work the ZDC must do.

If you don't want to dedicate one server to be the ZDC, there is a trick that you can use to still get the best performance possible. All you have to do is pick the server that you want to be your ZDC and configure it for the "most preferred" election preference in the CMC. Then, configure the load balancing for that server so that it takes on fewer users than your other servers. (See Chapter 15 for details.) Doing this will ensure that your ZDC is not impacted by user sessions, allowing the ZDC to perform its tasks as needed.

On the other hand, if you decide to create a dedicated ZDC, the process for configuring it is simple: Install MetaFrame XP on the server; add it to your farm and zone; configure it for the "most preferred" ZDC preference in the CMC; and don't publish any applications to it.

If you build a dedicated ZDC, be sure to remember that you must install any Citrix hotfixes or Service Packs to your dedicated ZDC first, otherwise you run the risk that your dedicated ZDC could lose a ZDC election to a more up-to-date server somewhere else.

### Advantages of Building a Dedicated ZDC

- You won't have to worry about the ZDC overhead impacting one of your production MetaFrame XP servers that is hosting user sessions.

- Because MetaFrame XP licensing is connection-based, your dedicated ZDC will not require a Citrix license.

### Disadvantages of Building a Dedicated ZDC

- You will need to find, buy, steal, or otherwise acquire an extra server.
- You will need to buy a Microsoft Windows server license for that server.

# Why should you care about zone design?

Proper zone design is important. There are several areas that are directly affected by the number of zones and the location of the zone data collectors. These areas include:

- WAN performance.
- Application enumeration.
- Application connection speed.
- Farm change propagation speed.

### WAN Performance

In a large environment with multiple WAN locations, you need to consider the network bandwidth cost of placing separate zones at each WAN point. Because every ZDC establishes a connection with every other ZDC in the farm, and because all ZDCs update each other whenever anything happens, too many zones will adversely affect WAN bandwidth with all the ZDC traffic. This means that fewer zones are better.

### Application Enumeration

When users request a list of available MetaFrame XP applications, the zone data collector is contacted to return the list of applications that are available to that user. If the ZDC is far away or too busy (because the zone is too large), the user will have to wait a long time for the ZDC response that provides them with their application list. This means that more zones are better.

### Application Connection Speed

When users connect to published load-balanced applications, the ZDC is contacted to find out which MetaFrame XP servers run the application and which server has the lightest load. As with application enumeration, if the zone data collector is far away or busy, the user will have to wait a long time for the ZDC response that allows them to attach to the appropriate MetaFrame XP server to start their application session. This also means that more zones are better.

## Farm Change Propagation Speed

Any farm-wide configuration changes that are made in the Citrix Management Console must be propagated down to every MetaFrame XP server in the farm. Fortunately, the Zone Data Collectors are leveraged for this update. The ZDCs receive the updates from the server running the CMC and forward the changes to the MetaFrame XP servers in their respective zones. The more zones there are, the faster these updates reach every MetaFrame XP Server. This means that more zones are better, but this is not as important as the first three factors.

As you have seen, there are advantages and disadvantages that will apply no matter how many zones you have.

# What are the zone design options?

After the complete analysis of how zones work, everything that they affect, and everything that can affect them, it's finally appropriate to look at the options available when designing zones. There are really only two choices.

With a server farm that spans multiple, physical locations, you can:

- Configure one zone that spans physical locations.
- Configure each location to be its own zone.

Let's look at the details of each option.

## Option 1.  Create One Zone

Because a server farm zone does not have to be confined to a single geographic location, it's possible to limit WAN communications between locations by creating a large zone that includes MetaFrame XP servers from multiple locations. This is clearly evident back in Figures 3.10 and 3.11.

However, potentially severe consequences could result if only one zone is created for multiple locations. Since this one zone will have only one ZDC, user logons and application enumerations could be slow since each of these actions requires contact with the ZDC which could be on the other side of the WAN. Also, because the ZDC is responsible for distributing farm configuration changes to all MetaFrame XP servers in the zone, one giant zone will force the ZDC to communicate with every single MetaFrame XP server in the zone, potentially sending the same change across the WAN multiple times. (This fact can be seen in the case study at the end of the chapter.)

### Advantages of Creating One Zone that Spans Multiple Sites

- All session update information is only sent across the WAN once, to the zone data collector.

### Disadvantages of Creating One Zone that Spans Multiple Sites

- User logons, queries, and application enumerations could be slow if the zone data collector is far away from the users.

- More traffic could be generated by MetaFrame XP server-to-ZDC session information updates than is saved by having one zone.

- The MetaFrame XP server-to-ZDC session update information cannot be configured, timed, parsed, queued, or limited (unlike ICA Gateway traffic in MetaFrame 1.8). This is because by definition, it is assumed that all servers in one zone are well-connected, and that bandwidth is plentiful and cheap.

- Farm configuration changes must traverse the network once for every server, because having one zone removes the hierarchy.

Obviously, there can be substantial network performance degradation if only one zone is created when multiple zones are needed.

### Option 2. Create Multiple Zones

Splitting a farm into multiple zones is a logical option, especially for larger environments. However, you need to be careful that you do not create too many zones.

Because all ZDCs maintain open connections to all other ZDCs, updates are continually sent between zones. This can affect performance if the bandwidth between zones is limited. There is no way to cut down these updates (unless a third party Quality of Service device is used, like those from Packateer or Sitara. These devices are discussed in Chapter 6.)

### Advantages of Creating Multiple Zones

- Local zones allow for fast user logons, application queries, and available application enumerations.

### Disadvantages of Creating Multiple Zones

- All background information is replicated to all zone data collectors. (Such is the price for having continuous local, up-to-date information about all zone servers.)

- All zone data collectors need direct access to all other zone data collectors.

In general, you should be careful that you do not create too many zones. Don't create another zone just for the sake of having it, because too many zones can actually hurt your network performance more than not having enough zones.

## Considerations when Designing your Zones

Remember that the way you design your zones does not affect the management of the server farm. The number and locations of zones should be based purely on technical factors, which is why the factors listed here are technical. The answers to the following three questions will directly affect zone traffic, and therefore zone design:

- In what ways will users access the applications?
- How many servers are there?
- What is the bandwidth and connectivity between servers?

### User Access to Applications

The ways that users access their MetaFrame XP applications and the configuration of those applications will help you determine your zone design. The following four items need to be considered:

- **Number of users**. The more users there are, the more zones are needed, as more ZDCs will be needed to service user requests.

- **Length of the average session**. If users log on to their applications and stay on all day, no session information will change on the MetaFrame XP servers and the ZDC will not be contacted, allowing for larger zones. If users log on and off constantly, ZDC updates will be frequent, causing more ZDC load and requiring smaller zones (more ZDCs).

- **Number of simultaneous logons**. ZDCs are used most heavily as users enumerate and connect to MetaFrame XP servers. Thousands of users logging in simultaneously may overwhelm one ZDC. If all your users start working at the same time, you may need more zones.

- **Number of load-balanced published applications**. More applications require more zones because there is more application information that must be updated across the farm via the ZDCs.

When designing zones, you need to consider everything that communicates with the ZDC. In general, the more IMA communication going on inside the farm, the more ZDCs are needed, which means more zones.

### Number of MetaFrame XP Servers

One zone can support about 100 servers. This is not a hard limit, but rather a practical performance-based limit determined by internal Citrix research. If you have more than 100 servers in a single zone, you will most likely need to partition it into two zones. Of course, servers will continue to get faster, which means that by the time you are reading this, you can probably build a ZDC powerful enough to support more than 100 servers. At that point, however, you will probably have other reasons to create multiple smaller zones.

### Bandwidth and Connectivity Between MetaFrame XP Servers

The available bandwidth between MetaFrame XP servers needs to be assessed when looking at zone design. Keep in mind that every dynamic change to any MetaFrame XP server in the environment is sent first to a local ZDC, which in turn sends the change to the all other ZDCs in the farm. Consider the environment in Figure 3.12:

*Figure 3.12    A single server farm with servers separated by WAN links*

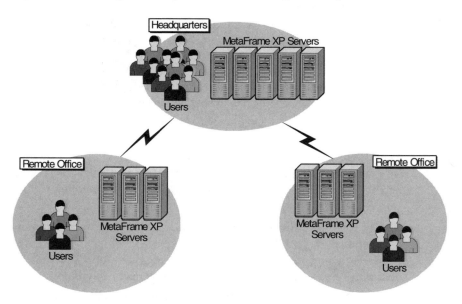

This WAN environment is configured with MetaFrame XP servers in three separate locations. If three zones are created, every time a dynamic event (such as a user logon) occurs, the local ZDC will send that event to ZDCs in the other two zones. This single event ends up crossing the WAN link two times, once to each other zone data collector. If, instead, the environment is configured as a single zone (with one ZDC), every time a dynamic event occurs, the event traverses the WAN link only once to the central ZDC. The downside to the single zone is that when any information is needed from the ZDC (such as for a user logon), the information may be across the WAN, instead of local (because the ZDC may be across the WAN). It is this balance that you must consider when designing zones.

Usually, you will end up creating a unique zone for each physical network location within a server farm. However, this does not always have to be the case. You can configure any server to be a member of any zone. Zone boundaries do not have to fall in line with IP subnets or network segments.

# The IMA Data Store

Now that we've seen how zone data collectors are responsible for tracking and maintaining server information that changes frequently, let's take a look at the components of a MetaFrame XP server farm that maintain information that does *not* change frequently. This information is stored in a database called the IMA data store.

The IMA data store is *not* the same as the zone or the Zone Data Collector. (In fact, the two aren't related at all.) The IMA data store is an ODBC-compliant database containing persistent configuration information, whereas the zone data collectors contain dynamic information that changes frequently. To view or change configurations stored in the IMA data store, you use the Citrix Management Console. Any information that it displays is pulled from the IMA data store, and when you click the "OK" button after making a change, that information is written to the IMA data store.

All server farm configuration information is saved in the IMA data store, as opposed to being saved on individual MetaFrame XP servers. Whenever a MetaFrame XP server starts up, it contacts the IMA data store and downloads its configuration information. (Actually, this contact occurs whenever the IMA Service is started, which usually coincides with the server starting up, but not always.)

MetaFrame XP servers always know where the data store is because they each have a local file-based DSN called mf20.dsn. This DSN contains the information for connecting to the IMA data store. (More on this file in Chapters 12 and 16.)

After a MetaFrame XP server initially contacts the IMA data store and downloads its configuration information, the server will check for changes every 10 minutes. This default interval can be changed via the following registry key:

Key: `HKLM\Software\Citrix\IMA`

Value: `DCNChangePollingInterval`

Type: `REG_DWORD`

Data: The interval in milliseconds, entered in hex notation. (The 600 second default would be 600,000 milliseconds, or `0x927C0` in hex.)

### Local Host Cache

As previously stated, every MetaFrame XP server downloads its configuration information from the server farm's IMA data store. Each server is smart enough to only download information from the IMA data store that is relevant to it. Information about other servers is ignored and not downloaded. Once the information is downloaded, it is saved locally in a Microsoft Access-style database known as the "Local Host Cache." This local host cache is maintained on every MetaFrame XP server. It serves two purposes:

- **Increased Redundancy**. If communication with the IMA data store is lost, the MetaFrame XP server continues to function for up to 48 hours (96 hours with Feature Release 2) because the vital configuration information it needs is available in its local host cache.

- **Increased Speed**. The local host cache contains information that the MetaFrame XP server needs to refer to often. By maintaining the information locally, the MetaFrame XP server does not have to access the IMA data store across the network every time any bit of information is needed.

Even though all application publishing information, domain trust rights, and application user rights are retained locally at each MetaFrame XP server in its local host cache, the Zone Data Collector is still contacted whenever a user launches an application. This contact is made so that the ZDC can keep an accurate count of each server's user load.

You can manually refresh a MetaFrame XP server's local host cache with the command `dsmaint refreshlc`. Real world experience shows that this manual refresh is something you'll do more often than you care to; particularly if you are testing new applications and do not want to wait for the changes to be propagated down to every MetaFrame XP server.

## IMA Data Store Database Type

The IMA data store can be in one of four database formats: Microsoft Access (MS Jet), Microsoft SQL Server, Oracle, or IBM DB2. (IBM DB2 requires Feature Release 2 for MetaFrame XP.) The IMA data store works like any standard database, which means that the best performance, reliability, and scalability will be found when SQL Server, Oracle, or DB2 is used. Of course in order to get these benefits you need to address the additional management, hardware, and licensing requirements of these databases.

## IMA Data Store Access Mode

Every MetaFrame XP server must belong to a server farm and have access to that farm's IMA data store. MetaFrame XP is designed to be able to access the data store in either "direct" or "indirect" mode.

When direct mode is used, a MetaFrame XP server connects directly to the database server that is running the IMA data store. A MetaFrame XP server that accesses the IMA data store via indirect mode accesses the database by connecting to another MetaFrame XP server. That other server then forwards the requests directly to the database, and then sends the information back to the original server.

If the IMA data store is a Microsoft Access database, it must be accessed via indirect mode. IMA data stores running on SQL, Oracle, or DB2 platforms can be accessed via direct or indirect mode.

## IMA Data Store Replication

MetaFrame XP servers need to have regular communication with the IMA data store to ensure that they always have the current configuration information for the server farm. (Even though we say "regular" communication to describe the communication between a MetaFrame XP server and the IMA data store, keep in mind that this communication is not nearly as frequent as the communication between a MetaFrame XP server and its zone data collector.)

Because of this regular communication, slow network links between Meta-Frame XP servers and the IMA data store can cause problems, such as extremely long IMA service start times and timeouts during sequential reads from the data store.

Obviously, this is a situation that should be avoided. One way to avoid this is to split the server farm into multiple, smaller farms. While this would technically solve the problem of MetaFrame XP servers having a slow connection to the data store, it would introduce the complexities and additional management requirements associated with multiple server farms.

Alternately, the IMA data store can be replicated throughout your network environment, so that multiple database copies exist in different locations for various MetaFrame XP servers to access. This data store replication is not a feature of MetaFrame XP; rather, database replication is a native feature of Microsoft SQL Server or Oracle.

Microsoft Access-based data stores do not support replication, because Microsoft Access itself does not support replication. This should not be a problem for you, because if your environment is big enough that you need data store replication, then you shouldn't be using Microsoft Access to run your data store anyway.

Also, IBM DB2 databases cannot be used for IMA data stores if you plan to replicate the database. This is because MetaFrame XP uses the binary large object data type to store information in DB2 databases, and DB2 does not support the use of that data type for replication.

One of the downsides of database replication in general is that the multiple replicas of the database must stay synchronized with the master copy. This can get to be a problem if many changes occur to the database simultaneously. Fortunately, MetaFrame XP servers only read data from the IMA data store. The only time that information is written to the data store is when a configuration change is made through the Citrix Management Console. Because these changes are manually performed by administrators, there is no risk that too many will occur simultaneously. In fact, in many cases, only one change will be made at a time.

### Advantages of Replicating the IMA Data Store

- Increased performance in large server farms.

### Disadvantages of Replicating the IMA Data Store

- You need multiple database servers.
- Adding MetaFrame servers to the farm is more complex.
- Only SQL and Oracle data stores can be replicated.

## How to Configure IMA Data Store Replication

Detailed step-by-step procedures for replicating an IMA data store can be found in the "MetaFrame XP Advanced Concepts Guide" available for free at www.citrix.com/support. Ultimately, you need to configure one database so that it is the "master" copy of the data store. Changes made to the master copy are replicated to read-only copies throughout your environment. All MetaFrame XP servers are then configured, via their local mf20.dsn files, to point to the nearest replica of the data store.

The only caveat to replicating the IMA data store is that in order to make any changes to the farm or publish new applications, you must use a CMC that is connected to the read/write master copy of the data store. The easiest way to do this is to configure the CMC as a published application on one of the servers that connects to the master copy.

More details about configuring the DSN that a MetaFrame XP server uses and publishing the CMC can be found in Chapter 16.

### How to Add a New Server to a Replicated Environment

When you add a new MetaFrame XP server to an environment with a replicated data store, you will need to point it to the read/write master copy of the data store during the installation process. Once MetaFrame is completely installed, you can configure the server (as described in Chapter 16) to use a closer read-only copy of the data store.

## *IMA Data Store Size*

Regardless of the mode of access or the database platform, the IMA data store will require approximately 200 KB for each MetaFrame XP server in the farm. This will vary slightly based on the number of applications published, how print drivers are used, and the exact configuration of the farm. The good news is that the database will always be relatively small. Even the largest environments only have data stores that are around 50 MB or so.

# Why should you care about IMA data store design?

As you have seen, there are many technical components that you need to understand when designing the IMA data store for your server farm. Based on these components, it's easy to see that the design of the IMA data store has the potential to impact several areas of your MetaFrame XP environment, including:

 • WAN bandwidth.

- IMA service startup times.
- Server farm reliability.
- Scalability.

### WAN Bandwidth

Because each MetaFrame XP server needs to read from the IMA data store, your WAN bandwidth can be adversely affected if you do not adequately plan for the location of the data store and its replicas. You want to make sure that you know how and when these database reads will occur.

### Speed for the IMA Service to Start

Every time the IMA service is started on a MetaFrame XP server, the IMA data store is queried and the necessary information is downloaded to the Meta-Frame XP server's local host cache. If the nearest copy of the IMA data store is across a slow network link, the IMA service could take a long time to start as it downloads its information. No users can log on until the IMA service is fully started, after the IMA data store read is complete.

### Reliability

If the IMA data store is not available, MetaFrame XP servers default to their local host cached copies. If this occurs, you will not be able to make any configuration changes to the farm or to any published applications. Also, after 48 hours (or 96 hours with MetaFrame XP Service Pack 2) without contact with the IMA data store, local MetaFrame XP servers' license service will fail and users will not be able to log on. This 48 or 96 hour limit is an artificial cut-off built into the product and cannot be changed.

### Scalability

All servers in a server farm need to contact the single IMA data store. If you want your farm to grow to several hundred servers, you'll need to scale your IMA data store to support the large number of data requests and consider the location of local data store replicas to service all of those requests.

## What are the IMA data store options?

When it comes down to actually designing your data store, there are really two different areas to look at that can be matrixed into three options. For your IMA data store, you can have:

- A Microsoft Access database in indirect mode, accessed through one server.

- SQL, Oracle, or DB2 database in indirect mode, accessed through one server.

- SQL, Oracle, or DB2 database in direct mode, accessed directly via the database server.

If you have existing SQL, Oracle, or DB2 servers in your environment then you can put the IMA data store on them. SQL Servers must be at least SQL Server 7.0 with Service Pack 2, and Oracle servers must be version 7.3.4. In order to use IBM's DB2 database for your data store, your MetaFrame XP servers must use Feature Release 2, and you must use at least DB2 version 7.2 with FixPak 5.

If you use a database other than Microsoft Access, you should know that the MetaFrame XP installation process cannot automatically create the database for you. You will need to manually create the empty database using the native database tools and specify that database during the MetaFrame XP installation. The installation program will automatically create and configure the tables it needs.

## Option 1. Access Database IMA Data Store

Using the Microsoft Access database platform for your IMA data store is cheap and can be run on one of your MetaFrame XP servers. Access-based data stores are designed for small or test environments. The database cannot scale too large, and even if it could, other MetaFrame XP servers must always access the data store through the server that hosts it (via "indirect" mode).

Realize that even though we call this solution a "Microsoft Access" solution, it doesn't actually mean that you have a copy of Access installed on your MetaFrame XP server. Technically, this solution uses a "Microsoft Jet" database. The drivers and support files needed to read and write Jet databases are included as part of the Windows operating system. Microsoft Access is an application that also just "happens" to use the Jet database format.

### Advantages of MS Access-based Data Stores

- Inexpensive.

- No dedicated database hardware. (It can be run on a MetaFrame XP server.)

### Disadvantages of MS Access-based Data Stores

- Single point of failure.

- Limited to 50 servers (for performance reasons).

- Slow.

- Data store cannot be replicated.
- The IMA data store often gets corrupted when Access is used.

## Option 2. SQL, Oracle, or DB2 via Indirect Mode

A data store hosted by a SQL, Oracle, or DB2 server will be fast and reliable. However, just because the data store is on one of these platforms doesn't automatically mean that all MetaFrame XP servers in the farm are accessing the database via "direct" mode.

For example, if you have five MetaFrame XP servers that all access a Microsoft Access-based IMA data store via indirect mode hosted on one server, at any time you could convert the database from Microsoft Access to SQL Server. The MetaFrame XP server that previously hosted the Access database would then connect directly to the SQL Server. However, the other four servers would continue to connect to the first server where the database was previously located. Technically, this configuration would work, but you would not realize the full benefits of the SQL Server and would still have a single point of failure.

In this case, you would still be accessing the IMA data store via "indirect mode," connecting through one MetaFrame XP server. You would lose most of your potential gains over keeping with an Access database. (In this scenario, it would be easy to configure the other MetaFrame XP servers to access the new data store directly. See Chapter 16 for details.)

### Advantages of SQL, Oracle, or DB2 via Indirect Mode

- Stable database.
- Scalable database.
- For Oracle and DB2, you wouldn't have to install any custom database drivers on all your MetaFrame XP servers. (They would only be needed on the server that is accessing the database via direct mode.)

### Disadvantages of SQL, Oracle, or DB2 via Indirect Mode

- Single point of failure.
- A database server is needed.
- Performance bottleneck.

## Option 3. SQL, Oracle, or DB2 via Direct Mode

An IMA data store running on a Microsoft SQL, Oracle, or DB2 server connected directly to all the MetaFrame XP servers in the farm is really the way to go for an enterprise-wide environment. It will be fast, reliable, and scalable. Also keep in mind that you can configure native database replication for SQL or Oracle so that there is a local copy of the IMA data store near each group of MetaFrame XP servers. The only downside to using SQL, Oracle, or DB2 via direct mode is the potential cost associated with the database software and servers. However, if you're using this type of data store and you have MetaFrame XP servers through your enterprise, a few thousand dollars spent to ensure that the IMA data store is done right is money well spent.

### Advantages of SQL or Oracle in Direct Mode

- Quick, reliable access.
- Stable database.
- Scalable database.
- No single point of failure.
- For SQL or Oracle, database replication keeps copies of the database near MetaFrame XP servers.

### Disadvantages of SQL or Oracle in Direct Mode

- A database server is needed.
- One more server to purchase.
- One more server to manage.

## Considerations when Designing your Data Store

Because there are very different designs and strategies for an IMA data store, it's important that you determine which is right for you. Answering the following questions about your environment will help to make your decision as to what IMA data store options you should use:

- What is the WAN distribution of your MetaFrame XP servers?
- How many MetaFrame XP servers will there be?
- How crucial are the applications running on the MetaFrame XP servers?
- What is the budget?
- Is there already a database server that you can use?
- What is your tolerance for pain?

### WAN Distribution of Servers

If your MetaFrame XP servers in a single server farm are located on opposite sides of a WAN, then you should consider database replication. This means that you would have to use SQL or Oracle for your data store. With servers in one location, database replication becomes less important (and your choice of database platform becomes less important).

### Number of MetaFrame XP Servers

A Microsoft Access-based data store can support up to about 50 servers before performance bottlenecks would dictate moving it to a real database (i.e. SQL, Oracle, or DB2). If your MetaFrame XP environment will just be a handful of servers, then you can get away with choosing Microsoft Access for your data store platform.

### Importance of your MetaFrame XP Environment

If MetaFrame XP is not mission critical in your environment, then it's probably not worth spending the extra money to build a dedicated SQL, Oracle, or DB2 server to host the IMA data store. On the other hand, if your applications are mission critical, you probably don't want to risk the single point of failure nature of a Microsoft Access-based data store.

### Budget

If you do not have the budget for an IMA data store then your design is simple: use MS Access. The Microsoft Access data store option is free. It requires no additional hardware or software. Then again, if you have the money, you should opt for the more reliable and efficient solution.

### Existing Database Server

If you are lucky enough to work in a large environment there may already be a SQL, Oracle, or DB2 database server that you can use for your IMA data store. If you are really lucky, someone else might be responsible for administering that server, which would be one less thing for you to worry about.

### Pain Tolerance

There have been numerous problems with IMA data stores based on Microsoft Access. Many administrators spend time repairing and restoring their data stores that are Microsoft Access-based. This is most likely due in part to bugs in the MetaFrame XP software and part to the fact that Microsoft Access is a desktop database. It is much more suited to track kitchen recipes than it is enterprise data stores. If you want the "real" solution then you need to use SQL Server, Oracle, or DB2.

# Future MetaFrame XP Server Relocation

Perhaps one of the most important properties of any technical design is knowing that it is not static and that changes will always need to be made. To that end, with MetaFrame XP it is possible (at any time) to move MetaFrame XP servers in and out of any farm, to move them to a different or new zone, or to point them to a new IMA data store location.

The movement and reconfiguration of MetaFrame XP servers is not tied to any particular MetaFrame XP network architecture. This means that you can design your MetaFrame XP network architecture for your environment as it stands today and then you can modify it in the future as your requirements and environment change and grow. We'll look at the specifics of how to move and reconfigure servers in Chapter 16.

Now that we've looked at the components that go into the creation of your MetaFrame XP network architecture design, let's take a look at a real world case study (beginning on the next page). In this case, we'll look at the many designs that an international toy company considered for their MetaFrame XP architecture, and the design that they finally chose.

# Real World Case Study

## Lilydink Toy Company

The Lilydink Toy Company has decided to create a unified MetaFrame XP strategy for their entire enterprise. They currently have multiple pockets of users that use applications in multiple locations. Figure 3.13 shows their current business environment.

*Figure 3.13  The Lilydink Toy Company's business environment*

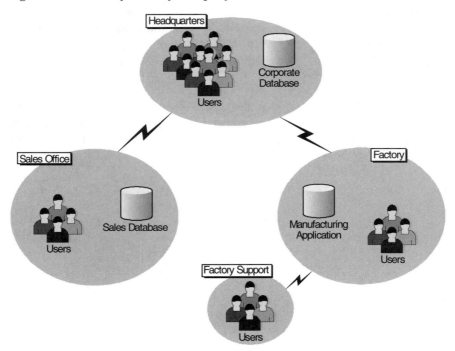

All users in the remote sites need to access the corporate database application at the headquarters. Additionally, remote users will need to access applications at their respective remote sites.

After studying their environment, there were some technical design decisions that the project team could easily make. Lilydink decided that they would place MetaFrame XP application servers throughout their environment instead of placing them all at the headquarters. They figured that by doing this the users' sessions would always execute in close proximity to their data. Also, they didn't like the idea of application data from the remote sites traveling across the network to central MetaFrame XP servers, just to be sent right back to the remote user via an ICA session.

They next decided that they would have a local IMA data store at each physical site. If each site was its own server farm, then this would be a given. However, if they have a single, large server farm, they will place local data store replicas at each remote site that has MetaFrame XP servers.

Even with these preliminary questions answered, The Lilydink Toy Company still wasn't sure what their server farm architecture should look like. After some lengthy discussions, they boiled it down to two questions:

- Should they create one large server farm or a separate server farm for each location?
- If they create a large server farm, should they partition it into separate zones or just have one large zone?

Lilydink decided to map out all possible solutions based on answers to these two questions. They came up with three different architectures worth considering:

- One company-wide server farm with one zone.
- One company-wide server farm with multiple zones.
- Multiple server farms.

The sections on the following pages compare three MetaFrame XP network architectures. While no architecture represents the "perfect" solution, each has very specific advantages and disadvantages. Most likely, a combination of architectures will work best for the Lilydink Toy Company.

## Option 1. One Company-Wide Farm with One Zone

The first company-wide MetaFrame XP architecture that Lilydink considered was the creation of one large server farm not split into separate server zones. In this scenario, there would only be one zone data collector for the entire company. All session update information would traverse the WAN to the single zone data collector.

Lilydink's IT staff created architectural diagrams to represent where the different MetaFrame XP components would be and to get a visual feel for the amount of network traffic between sites. Their first diagram is shown in Figure 3.14 on the next page.

*Figure 3.14 One large server farm with a single large zone*

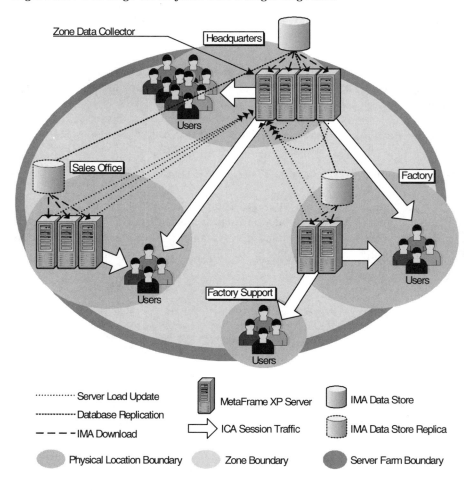

The first thing that you may notice when looking at this layout is that there is quite a bit of network traffic between remote sites. In addition to users' ICA traffic from their application sessions, every remote MetaFrame XP server creates a connection back to the zone data collector at the headquarters.

The design team was also concerned that having a zone data collector on the opposite side of a busy WAN link could frustrate remote users if they try to logon during busy periods.

The Lilydink project team created the follow list of advantages and disadvantages for this architecture:

### Advantages of One Large Farm

- Licenses are pooled across all sites. Each remote user will only need one license, even though they will access applications on local and remote MetaFrame XP servers.

- Simple maintenance and administration, because all servers will be in the same server farm.

- All session update information is sent across the WAN once, to the zone data collector at the headquarters.

### Disadvantages of One Large Farm

- Even though it happens only once, all session update information must be sent across the WAN to the zone data collector at the headquarters.

- Logons, queries, and enumerations could be slow for remote users, because the zone data collector is across the WAN.

- Firewall ports 2512 and 2513 must be opened to allow intra-farm communication if the WAN links connect through firewalls. (See Chapter 15 for more information on MetaFrame XP port usage.)

- Centralized administration only. Because all servers belong to the same server farm, remote sites cannot have their own administrators.

- Session information updates from each MetaFrame XP server to the zone data collector cannot be configured, timed, parsed, queued, or limited (unlike ICA Gateway traffic in MetaFrame 1.8).

## Option 2. One Company-Wide Farm with Multiple Zones

Instead of having one zone, the Lilydink project team decided that another architecture option was to create one company-wide server farm with separate zones for each geographic location. This would allow them to have a zone data collector at each local site.

*Figure 3.15  One farm, multiple zones*

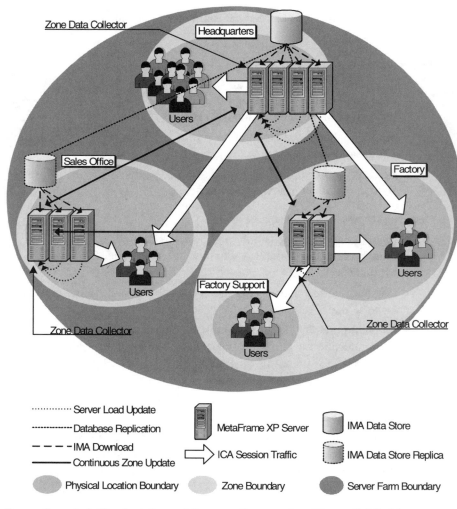

Even after a brief look at the architecture diagram (see Figure 3.15), it's easy to see that WAN network traffic could be less than the first design. The main difference here is that any and all session change information is passed from the first zone data collector to all of the others. For example, whenever a user logs on to a MetaFrame XP server, that server informs the zone data collector. If there is only one zone, no other communication takes place. Even if the zone data collector is on the other side of a WAN link, the update only crossed the link once. However, if there were many zones, the zone data collector that received the information from the MetaFrame XP server would immediately notify each and every one of the other zone data collectors. In a WAN environment, such as the illustrated environment of the Lilydink Toy Company, those immediate zone updates would travel across the WAN repeatedly—once for each zone data collector.

### Advantages of One Farm with Multiple Zones

- Licenses are pooled across all sites. Each remote user will only need one license even though they will access applications on local and remote MetaFrame XP servers.

- Simple maintenance and administration, because all servers will be in the same server farm.

- Local zone data collectors at each site allow for fast logons, queries, and application enumerations.

### Disadvantages of One Farm with Multiple Zones

- All background information is replicated to all zone data collectors. (Remember, this additional network load is the price you pay for having local, up-to-date information at each site.)

- Firewall ports 2512 and 2513 must be opened to allow intra-farm communication if the WAN links connect through firewalls.

- Centralized administration only. Because all servers belong to the same server farm, remote sites cannot have their own administrators.

- All zone data collectors need direct network access to all other zone data collectors.

## Option 3. Multiple Server Farms

Not sure if the WAN bandwidth could handle the traffic generated by a Meta-Frame XP server farm, Lilydink decided to consider the option of creating multiple server farms, one for each geographically separate location. With this design, each farm is essentially its own entity. While this design has virtually zero impact to the WAN, it also is the most difficult to work with on a daily basis.

*Figure 3.16 Multiple farms*

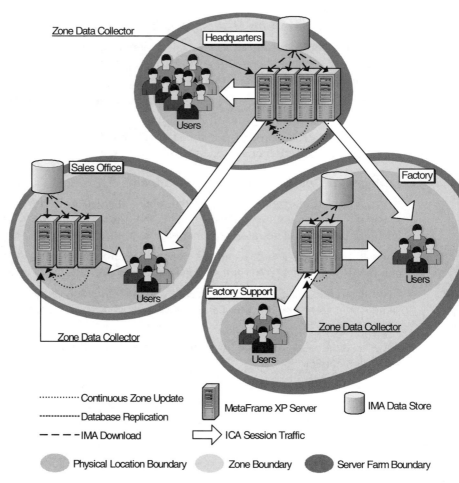

As you can see in the diagram (Figure 3.16), the only traffic that traverses the WAN in this situation is the actual ICA session traffic from the remote users accessing applications from the headquarters. Of course, this architecture is not without its problems, most notably the inability to share MetaFrame XP connection licenses between locations.

### Advantages of Multiple Server Farms

- No MetaFrame XP background IMA data replication.
- Departmental-based licensing.
- Each farm could have separate, local administrators.
- No IMA data store replication, since each farm has its own IMA data store.

### Disadvantages of Multiple Server Farms

- Licenses are not pooled across different geographic regions, causing each remote user that accesses corporate and local applications to consume two connection licenses.
- All security must be configured independently at each farm.
- All farms must be administered separately. While there are ways to configure the Citrix Management Console to simultaneously show both server farms (see Chapter 16), farm administrators must manually make changes to the configuration of each farm separately.

## Analysis of the Proposed Worldwide Architectures

After looking at the advantages and disadvantages of the three solutions outlined, the Lilydink IT staff decided that their MetaFrame XP company-wide architecture would be a combination of the three. In some places it would be logical to conserve bandwidth while in others it would be important to share licenses and management via common server farms.

The main advantage to having one giant worldwide farm is that one user will only need one license, regardless of the location or the number of servers that he accesses. With the abilities to replicate the IMA data store locally among sites and to segment the server farm into multiple zones, it is technically possible to build one large farm that spans multiple WAN locations.

However, if localized administration is important, having one giant farm can be a problem. Users are granted server farm administrative rights via the Citrix Management Console. These rights allow a user to access and change the IMA Data Store (which contains all configuration information about all farm servers). Server farm administration rights are "all or nothing." There is no way to segment a server farm into multiple administrative groups (unless you split the farm into multiple farms). Even if native Microsoft security was used to "lock-down" a server (with NTFS rights, policies, etc.), all server farm administrators would still be able to change that server's information in the IMA data store. This would be like revoking someone's local administrative rights from a server but then giving them full control of the registry (the IMA data store in this case). This lack of administrative delegation ability within one server farm is a disadvantage to the many advantages of having one unified, global farm. (Note that not even Feature Release 2's delegated administration helps in this case, since it delegates administration by role, not by server.)

In addition to the major farm design, another decision must be made as to the numbers and locations of server zones. Most likely, organizations will want to split any farm that traverses geographic locations into multiple zones. This is primarily due to the fact that all servers in one zone need constant access to the zone data collector. Additionally, having local zones will always ensure that a zone data collector resides on the same subnet as a MetaFrame XP server that a user would like to use.

Ultimately, the Lilydink Toy Company will create multiple zones, some spanning physical sites, others not. For example, several remote sites may have MetaFrame XP servers that all connect into Europe. It is possible that all of those remote sites would be one zone, while the US sites would be in another zone.

# PART II

## The Application Environment

In this section

4. Application Strategies and Installation     109

5. Creating the User Environment     153

6. Server Sizing and Performance Optimization   229

7. Printing     259

8. Integration with Novell NetWare     315

# CHAPTER 4

# Application Strategies and Installation

In this chapter

Installing Applications                                    110

Application Publishing Strategy                            118

Choosing What Types of Files are Opened Where  122

Multi-Server Application Load Management         131

Application / Server Installation Groups            147

The previous chapters detailed necessary considerations for designing your MetaFrame XP environment. This chapter discusses the core of your MetaFrame environment—your applications. MetaFrame XP exists for one reason—to allow users to run applications. In fact, the only reason that any IT department exists is to support applications for users. Clearly, it's important to build your MetaFrame XP design around the applications that your users require and the methods that by which they be accessed.

This chapter begins with a study of what it takes in install applications onto a MetaFrame server. After that we'll examine how applications are published in MetaFrame XP environments and some strategies that you can use in your environment. Next we'll discuss application load management. This chapter will close with a section about how you can apply your new application knowledge to the design of your server farm.

# Installing Applications

With MetaFrame XP, application installation is a bit more complex than on standard workstations. You must prepare your MetaFrame XP servers (or any Terminal Servers) for a new application before it can be installed. The reason for this is that when Microsoft Windows was designed, only one user could be interactively logged onto a computer at any given time. With Terminal Server, hundreds of users can be logged on "interactively" at the same time.

By the way, a user is said to be logged on "interactively" to a Windows computer if he is viewing that computer's screen and using its keyboard and mouse. In traditional network environments, users are "interactively" logged onto their local workstations, but they are not interactively logged onto the servers because they are only accessing server resources through the network rather than using the server's keyboard and mouse and viewing its screen. Logging onto a server "interactively" is Windows NT 4.0 terminology. In Windows 2000, the term logged on "locally" is used. These two terms can be used interchangeably. Technically, to say that a user is logged on "locally" in Windows 2000 is a bit deceptive, because Terminal Services or MetaFrame ICA users are said to be logged-on to a server "locally," even though they are connecting through the network.

Either way, installing applications in multi-user environments like MetaFrame is more complex than installing applications on regular computers. In this section, we're going to take a look at some of the decisions you'll have to make and the problems that you'll likely encounter when installing these applications.

# Problems with Applications in Multi-User Environments

Before you think about installing any applications onto your MetaFrame XP servers, you should examine how applications function in multi-user environments like Terminal Server and MetaFrame. There are a few problems that can arise that don't exist in traditional single-user workstation application installs. The two main problems are:

- Application configuration files are not correctly used.
- The Windows Registry is not correctly used.

Let's take a more detailed look at each of these problems and why you need to be concerned with them when you install applications onto your MetaFrame XP servers.

### Problem 1. Application Config Files are not Correctly Used

A lot of older applications store their configuration options in .INI files located in common folders, such as `c:\program files\old application name\appconfig.ini`. This is usually okay if only one user will ever use the application (like in standard workstation-based computing environments), but it doesn't work when multiple users need to use the application on the same computer (i.e. the MetaFrame XP server). In MetaFrame XP environments, any configuration options that one user changes would affect all of the users because they are all pointing back to the same .INI configuration files.

### Problem 2. The Windows Registry is not Correctly Used

Some applications that you might need to install will not properly use the Windows registry. Usually these are expensive industry-specific applications written by small companies (which coincidentally tend to be the types of applications most used in MetaFrame XP environments).

To understand how applications often incorrectly use the Windows registry, we should first look at how applications correctly use the registry. The Windows registry has several main sections, or "hives." Applications store their configuration information in two hives: the "machine" hive and the "user" hive:

- The machine hive (HKEY_LOCAL_MACHINE, or simply HKLM) contains settings and configurations for applications that apply machine-wide (for all users that log onto that particular computer).
- The user hive (HKEY_USERS, or HKU) contains application

settings and configurations that apply to each individual user, allowing different users to have different settings.

The HKU hive has a subtree (a registry folder) for each locally (or "interactively") logged on user, named by the user's Security Identifier, or SID. Remember from your basic Windows training that a SID is a unique serial number (like S-1-5-21-1993962763-920026266-854245398-1002) that is used internally by Windows to keep track of each user.

Every time users logon in a Terminal Services environment, their own subtree is added to the HKU hive. If you have two users logged onto a server then you will see two SIDs listed under the HKU hive with each user's unique settings stored in the registry structure under their SID name. Fifty users logged in at the same time will mean that there are fifty SIDs listed in the HKU hive.

Incidentally, if you look in the registry, you will notice a hive called HKEY_CURRENT_USER, or HKCU. This hive does not contain any real data, rather, it is simply a pointer to the current user's SID in the HKU hive. The only reason that this hive exists is to make it easier for you to know which HKU hive belongs to the active user. If you view the HKCU hive from an ICA session that is logged on as "Brian" you will see one set of data. Viewing the HKCU from another session logged on as "Holli" will reveal a different set of data. You can edit a user's registry settings in either place—the HKCU hive or the user's SID subtree in the HKU hive.

For an application to be properly installed onto a multi-user server, the application must store each user's personal configuration options in their personal registry keys in the HKU hive, not in the server-wide HKLM hive. Unfortunately, many of today's applications store configuration information in the HKLM hive, which means that the same settings will apply to all users. Fortunately, there are ways to avoid this scenario in Terminal Services environments.

### How Terminal Services Addresses These Two Problems

The main problem that these two application scenarios cause is that certain applications do not recognize user-specific application settings. Individual users cannot customize their own applications. Another way to describe this problem is that any changes one user makes to the application are suddenly applied to all users who use the application.

To prevent this from happening, you need to put your Terminal Server into an application "installation mode" before you attempt to install any applications. When you do this, your Terminal server captures all registry and .INI file changes during the software installation. These changes are all redirected to the HKLM\Software\Microsoft\WindowsNT\CurrentVersion\ TerminalServer\Install registry location, which acts as a caching area for the current application installation session. This registry location contains two subkeys: software and machine. Any changes or additions that the application's installation program makes to the current user's hive (HKCU) are copied to the software key. Changes or additions made to the machine hive (HKLM) are added to the machine subkey.

After application installation is complete, you need to take the server out of install mode. Then, whenever a user launches an application the server will check for the proper registry entries in the real HKLM and the user's HKCU and compare them to the entries that the system previously recorded from the software installation. If the entries to not exist in the proper HKLM and HKCU locations then the server will copy them from the install keys listed above to the proper locations in HKLM and HKCU.

Ordinarily, a Terminal Server operates in "execute mode." You can place a Terminal Server into "install mode" by installing new software via the "Add / Remove Programs" component of the Control Panel. When you add new software this way, you are given the choice as to whether you are installing the software for the current user only (causing the server to remain in execute mode) or for any user that logs on (temporarily setting the server into install mode). You can also manually set the server into install mode via the command change user /install. You can change it back to execute mode with the command change user /execute. If you forget which mode your server is in, you can check it with the command change user / query.

Install mode and execute mode work the same way for both Terminal Server 4.0 and Windows 2000 with Terminal Services enabled in application mode. The only small difference is that Windows 2000 includes additional logic to "force" you to remember to use install mode for installing applications. Basically, if you try to run a program like setup.exe, Windows 2000 will pop up a dialog box saying that the server must be in install mode before the application can be installed. When this happens, you can quickly jump to a command prompt, type change user /install, and then rerun your setup program. This is a nice feature, because there are many occasions with Terminal Server 4.0 where people install applications only to realize later that they forgot to place the server into "install mode." The only remedy was to uninstall the application, change the server to "install mode," and then reinstall the application.

If an application needs to wait for a reboot in order to complete certain installation tasks then the application installation programs can add scripts to the
"runonce" key (HKLM\Software\Microsoft\Windows\CurrentVersion\
RunOnce). Any program listed in this key is executed one time after the server
is rebooted. Terminal Server is smart enough to use install mode for all entries
that are listed in the runonce key, even if it's after a reboot.

## Installing New or Untested Applications

Now that you know about placing your servers in install mode you can begin
to install your applications. Even though installing an application on a Meta-
Frame XP server is like installing an application on any standard workstation,
there are some best practices that you should follow to ensure your application is installed properly.

- Install all of the application options that you think any user would
  ever need. Disk drive space is so cheap and plentiful these days that
  it really doesn't do any good to restrict certain application features
  by not installing them (unless you have business reasons to prevent
  users from using certain application features). For example, if you're
  installing Microsoft Office, perform a "custom" setup and select all
  the options.

- Check out the applications "readme" file. Because Terminal Server
  deals with applications a bit differently than regular computers, there
  are often little tweaks and tricks that you will need to apply to
  applications to get them to run right. Terminal Server has been around
  for awhile now, and most applications are written to support it. More
  often than not, Terminal Server-specific information is included in
  the application's readme file. The THIN list online community gets a
  few requests per week from novice administrators asking how to install
  Microsoft Office XP on a Terminal Server, even though the exact
  process is described step-by-step in the Office readme file.

- Refer to an online community, such as the THIN list at http://
  thethin.net. Regardless of the application that you're trying to
  install, there's a good chance that someone else has already installed
  it on a MetaFrame server. Visit http://thethin.net and search
  the THIN list archive for your application's name. (This archive grows
  by about 2000 messages every month.) If you don't find anything in
  the archive, try sending a message out to the group asking about your
  application.

# Knowing Which Application Options to Use

Many applications used in MetaFrame XP environments have "workstation" and "server" install modes. These types of applications have two components: the server component and the workstation component. Since your MetaFrame XP servers are basically nothing more than gigantic shared workstations, you need to perform a "standard" workstation install on your MetaFrame XP servers.

If there's ever a situation in which you don't know which installation options you should choose for an application when you're installing it on a Meta-Frame XP server, just choose the options that you would use if you were installing the application onto a standard user's workstation.

For example, some applications have a "thin client" mode of installation. At first this might seem like the perfect installation option to use on a MetaFrame server. However, for a lot of applications the "thin client" mode of installation means that the bulk of the application's client files have been preinstalled onto a file share somewhere, and that the local workstation install only needs to contain user configuration information. Lotus Notes, Baan, SAP, and PeopleSoft are all examples of these types of applications.

If your application offers it, there's nothing wrong with using this type of "thin client" installation option for an application on your MetaFrame server—but you shouldn't automatically use this option just because you're using Citrix. Again, the bottom line is that you should install your application with the same options as if you were performing a standard end user workstation install.

# Legacy Application Compatibility

Microsoft and Citrix had to do quite a bit of engineering and redeveloping of many Windows components to allow multiple users to be simultaneously logged on "locally" to servers in Terminal Server environments. However, the people who write the software applications often create applications that were only meant to be used in old-fashioned (i.e. 1998) single-user environments where only a single user is logged on "locally." This means that many applications installed onto a Terminal Server might not realize that multiple users will be accessing the application simultaneously.

"Application compatibility" is a dying term used to describe the process of making applications that were never intended for use in multi-user environments. This term is mainly used for applications that were released prior to

Terminal Server 4.0 (Summer 1998). Out of the box, Windows 2000 with Terminal Services and Terminal Server 4.0 have some default logon scripts that run and are very confusing. You've probably noticed that an empty DOS box titled "usrlogon.cmd" pops up each time a user logs onto the server (this pops up minimized in Windows 2000). This logon script (which is launched from the registry) is used for legacy application compatibility purposes.

"Application compatibility" is achieved through scripts that run in order to "fix" any problems that specific applications have in Terminal Server environments. Application compatibility scripts are located in the folder "%system root%\application compatibility scripts\." You will find that this folder comes populated with dozens of scripts, most of which are useless because they are for applications that are now so old nobody uses them anymore. Most applications released after 1998 are Terminal Services–savvy and do not require application compatibility scripts.

Most of these old application compatibility scripts contain two parts. The first, located in the install subdirectory, is a script that is meant to be executed just after the application has been installed. It "fixes" the application to work in a Terminal Server environment by changing locations and permissions of registry keys and ensuring that custom settings are saved per user instead of per machine.

The second part of an application compatibility script, located in the logon subdirectory, is executed at the time a user logs on. It creates the application's directory structure and .INI files in the user's home directory. For example, the Microsoft Word 97 application compatibility script creates several items, including the user's custom dictionary and a folder for storing clipart.

These application compatibility scripts create a system variable called %ROOTDRIVE%. The %ROOTDRIVE% variable is a drive letter that is created and used by legacy applications when local home drives are used. The drive letter specified by the %ROOTDRIVE% variable is mapped to a user's home drive. By doing so, an application can refer to the %ROOTDRIVE% drive letter in the registry, allowing each user to have a different drive location because the drive letter is mapped to a different location.

Figure 4.1 details the Terminal Services default logon scripts, how they're run, and when they are called. If all of the applications that you're using were written after 1998 then you can probably ignore this entire chart. However, it is worth being familiar with this application compatibility process because there are times when it comes in handy for use with tricky, newer applications.

*Figure 4.1  The application compatibility logon script process*

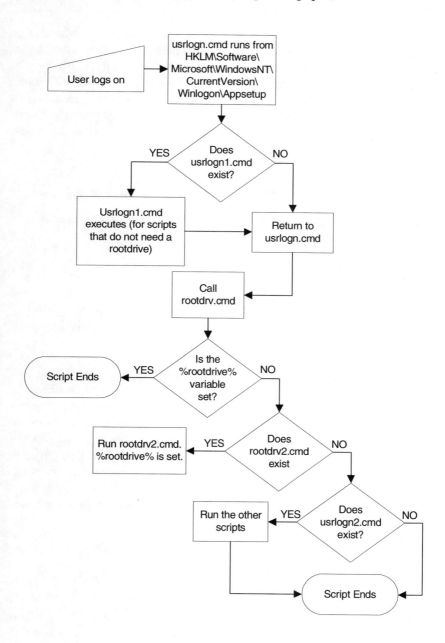

# Application Publishing Strategy

Now that you know how to get your applications installed (and where to go for help when you run into trouble), we can look at some different strategies that you can use when you publish applications for your users. You'll need to create an application publishing strategy that answers several questions, among them: Will you publish the full Windows desktop or multiple individual applications? If you decide to publish multiple applications, will you publish one copy of each application or multiple copies with different options for different users?

## Things to Consider when Creating your Strategy

In order to help you create your application publishing strategy, consider the answers to the following:

- What type of client hardware devices will be used?
- How many different applications will each user need?
- How many applications will be on each server?
- Will different types of users need to access the same application?

### Client Hardware Devices

If your users are connecting from client devices that have a local Windows desktop, such as Windows 95 or Windows NT clients, there is no need for them to run a remote desktop on your MetaFrame server. Running a remote desktop in addition to a local desktop could be confusing for your users because they would have two start menus, two recycle bins, etc. Most users probably would not understand the concept of having a "local" desktop and a "remote" desktop anyway. Besides, with local Windows desktops users can access published applications in "seamless" mode, allowing the applications to look and feel like local applications. (See Chapter 9 for details about seamless Windows.)

However, if your users are connecting from client devices that do not have local Windows desktops, such as Windows CE or UNIX, then running a remote MetaFrame XP desktop could make it easier for users to run their applications. Also, some non-Windows client devices only allow one ICA session at a time; if you want to allow users to multitask you will need to let them connect to a full Windows desktop on the MetaFrame XP server since they would not be able to connect to more than one individual published application at a time.

## Number of Applications per User

If your users open and close several applications throughout the day, a remote desktop shell will probably be faster and easier to use as opposed to connecting and disconnecting to several published applications. Of course if users only access a few applications and keep those applications open all day then the full remote desktop is not needed.

## Number of Applications per Server

If you have a lot applications installed on each of your MetaFrame XP servers then the chances are pretty high that all of a user's applications will be located on the same server. If this is the case, you have the option of publishing the desktop for the user to access their applications.

However, if a user's applications are spread across multiple MetaFrame XP servers then it doesn't make sense to force the user to connect to a published desktop on each server. If you did this your users would have to navigate the full desktop shell for each different server—very confusing for them.

## Different User Types for the Same Application

If all of the users for an application have the same configuration you can publish a single copy of that application. However, there are some situations where different groups of users need to access the same application with different parameters. If this is the case, you may need to publish multiple copies of the application.

Often times, the configuration of these applications can be set with a text file referenced via the command line when the application is launched. If you have applications like this you can create two different configuration files, one for each group, and then publish two copies of the application. You can specify a different configuration file in the command line of each published application

Consider for example a sales application called "Sales Tracker" that has a different database for each region. The first copy of this application you publish could be for the North region.

Published Application Name: `Sales Tracker - North`
Command Line: `"m:\SalesTrack\tracker.exe /d:north.dsn"`

You could then publish a second copy of the application for the south region.

Published Application Name: `Sales Tracker - South`
Command Line: `"m:\SalesTrack\tracker.exe /d:south.dsn"`

This would allow you to run the applications off of the same MetaFrame XP servers for different groups of users. You could even set the permissions of the published application so that only users from the proper region had access to their application. That way your users would not be confused by seeing multiple copies of the application. The application's permissions would cause users to only see their own copy.

# What are the Published Application Strategy Options?

Given everything that you need to consider when creating your published application strategy, there are really only two options available:

- Publish individual applications.
- Publish the Windows desktop.

### Option 1. Publish Individual Applications

Your first option is to publish individual applications for your users. When you do this, users will need to separately connect to each application. Once the application is launched it will smoothly integrate with their local desktops. In fact, many users will not even realize that they are running a remote ICA application (which is a good thing). Users are not running the Windows desktop from a MetaFrame XP server, published applications can be easier to secure because some of the local security policies that affect access to items such as the start menu and "My Computer" do not need to be used (the server's start menu and "My Computer" are not available to the user when an application is published).

A downside to having users connect directly to published applications is that it can give you a false sense of security. You might feel that the users' environment is secure because they don't have a desktop. However, if a user can get to a server's remote desktop there would be no security in place. One famous example is with old versions of Microsoft Word. Even as a published application, a user could click "Help | About" from within Word. From there, they could launch the System Information utility, from where they could choose "File | Run." This would allow them to run `explorer.exe`, thus opening up a remote desktop shell session.

Another downside to running only published applications is that non-Windows users would not receive the full Windows experience. They would be forced to switch between ICA applications with their local client device, instead of the clean Windows interface.

### Advantages of Publishing Individual Applications

- One user can use applications from multiple servers or multiple farms and geographic locations.
- Seamless windows.
- Can be easier to secure.
- Works well with NFuse web portals.

### Disadvantages of Published Applications

- No desktop for non-Windows users.
- False sense of security.
- Many published applications to manage.

## Option 2. Publish the Server Desktop.

In shear contrast to publishing individual applications only, you can choose to give users access to MetaFrame XP applications via a published desktop. This allows users connecting from non-Windows clients to get the full Windows experience (although only you can decide if this is actually a good thing). Users will be able to quickly switch between applications because they will all be running in the same window of one server session. A full desktop will also allow users to do those "little things" that they do with desktops, like adjusting printers, using calculator, and editing files with notepad.

In general, users with access to the full desktop have a fair amount of power and often spend their entire day in remote desktop sessions. There are, of course, some companies that use the full remote desktop and completely lock it down with policies. This protects the servers from users who would otherwise try to change important settings. Some of these locked down desktops have no icons, just a start menu with a few programs. (See chapter 5 for details.)

Remote desktops are not convenient if a user needs to connect to applications that are on multiple servers because the user would then need to run multiple remote desktops. Also, Windows-based clients already have a local start menu, so the duplicate start menu that is presented via the remote desktop ICA session can be confusing. With remote desktops, the ability for users to do those "little things" is a double-edged sword. End users could potentially have access to a lot more than you intended. When giving users access to full desktops, even with policies in place, it is crucial that security is adequately addressed. (See Chapter 15 for details.)

### Advantages of the Published Desktop

- Quick switching between applications.
- Non-Windows client devices get the full Windows experience.
- Users can more easily do "the little things."

### Disadvantages of the Published Desktop

- All applications must be on one server.
- Full Windows clients receive second start menu and a duplicate desktop environment.
- Users can more easily do "the little things."
- Security must be carefully applied.

### Applying Published Application Strategy in the Real World

In most environments, the manner in which end users access applications depends on many factors. Almost never is the configuration identical for all users across the board. For example, many companies have task-based workers that only use three or four applications per day, all day, every day. For these users, it makes sense to use Windows-based thin client terminals configured to run remote Windows desktops. Of course, these desktops only have a handful of icons and no access to configuration information. (See chapter 9 for more information about thin client devices and chapter 5 for more information about creating the locked down desktops.)

Often, these same companies will also have users with legitimate needs for full PCs. These users, however, can still access specific applications through ICA sessions. They often connect to the published applications directly (without first accessing a published desktop). These published applications fully integrate with their local desktop computers via Seamless Windows.

It's also possible to mix both of these scenarios in the same environment. In fact, many companies have these two environments mixed on the same servers with the same applications—some accessed directly as published applications and some accessed via published desktops.

# Choosing What Types of Files are Opened Where

What a weird section title, huh? Let's try to figure out what this means. In the early days of MetaFrame, people were happy with the fact that they could publish applications and that users could connect to "applications" instead of connecting to "servers."

However, the way that people use MetaFrame has evolved in the past few years, causing MetaFrame itself to evolve. A big piece of this evolution has to do with how users access files and content.

Now that MetaFrame has become a large part of many environments, there is a need to integrate it even more with users' everyday activities. In many organizations, users have grown accustomed to using NFuse or Program Neighborhood as their main "launching point" into their computing environment. Users use MetaFrame everyday to launch their applications. Wouldn't it be great if they could also use that same launching point to get access to network shares, important memos, or corporate training videos?

Additionally, there are situations in which you might want a user to be able to double-click a file on their local desktop computer and have that file open up via a remote MetaFrame session. Just imagine the possibility of allowing any user to be able to open any file of any type. Perhaps you could install applications like Microsoft Visio, MapPoint, and Project on MetaFrame servers. Then, a user receiving a Visio drawing via an email attachment (on their local computer) could just double-click that attachment and (without Visio being installed locally) have the drawing be opened by Visio via a remote Citrix ICA session. You would never have to worry about installing rarely-used applications for users ever again!

Maybe for you the opposite is also true. Perhaps you've chosen to deploy Microsoft Outlook via MetaFrame XP. What if a user receives an email that contains a hyperlink to a website? By default, when the user clicks on that hyperlink a copy of Internet Explorer will be launched on the MetaFrame server. Your user would then be using your expensive MetaFrame server to surf the web. Wouldn't it be great if there was a way to force the user to use their local web browser, even if the user clicks a hyperlink from within a MetaFrame session?

All of these "what if's?" are possible with MetaFrame XP today. As an administrator, you have the ability to decide *what* types of files are opened *where* by *which* users. How's that for flexibility? Let's look at what it takes to make this happen.

## Publishing Content

If you're using Feature Release 1 or 2, you can publish content in addition to publishing applications. Publishing content allows you to make computer files available to end users through the standard Citrix ICA client tools such as Program Neighborhood, NFuse, or the Program Neighborhood Agent. When users click on an application icon for published content, the content is opened with their local client device.

For example, in addition to several published applications, you could publish an FAQ document with information for your users about your Citrix server farm. That document would appear to users in the published application list along with any other published applications. If a user clicked on the published document, it would open on the user's computer just like a standard document.

In fact, if you publish content and your users access their applications via NFuse and a web server, the published content acts just like a hyperlink to any standard file, such as documents, videos, or MP3's. The advantage to providing the file via MetaFrame XP's "published content" function is that users can access the content through their standard ICA client methods of access, and you can set the permissions of the content just like you can on any published application. Users will never see the icon for content without the proper permissions.

You publish content just like you publish any other ICA application. To do this, select the "publish content" option in the application publishing wizard that is launched when you begin publishing anything via the Citrix Management Console. When you publish content you need to specify its location. You can specify a whole directory or a single file. Either way, you need to specify the content location in the HTTP address format, such as http://www.brianmadden.com, ftp://www.brianmadden.com/document.doc, or file://server1/share/document.doc.

### Advantages of Publishing Content

- Access to files (content) can be controlled like any published application.
- Users can access non-Citrix content through familiar ICA client interfaces.

### Disadvantages of Publishing Content

- The content viewers for each type of content must be installed locally on the client devices.
- If you are making published content available via a web server, then you must configure the MIME types for each type of content that you want users to be able to open automatically.
- Feature Release 1 or 2 is required.

- Published content only appears as part of an application set, either via Program Neighborhood or a web portal. This means that you cannot create a custom ICA connection to a published content item.

# Client to Server Content Redirection

Traditionally, one of the biggest problems users face when their applications are loaded on MetaFrame servers instead of their local computers has to do with content (or file) redirection. To understand this problem, let's look at how it happens. Imagine an environment where Microsoft Word is available to end users via a published application on a MetaFrame server. Users with Windows desktops will undoubtedly find Word documents that they want to open while they are browsing the network or their local computers. In traditional environments, the user can simply double-click the document and Word is automatically launched with that document open.

In the MetaFrame XP world, it's not quite that simple. If Word is not installed on a user's workstation then the ".doc" file type extension is not associated with Word on that workstation. Even if the user uses Word on a MetaFrame server, double-clicking a ".doc" file on the workstation will probably just open a local copy of WordPad with an error that says that the document type is not registered.

In order to combat this, you could manually register the ".doc" file type association so that it launches the Word published application when a ".doc" file is double-clicked. While this would work for launching Word, it still wouldn't be a full solution because Word would not automatically open the file that the user clicked. This means that the user would have to manually browse back to the location where the file was located and open it from Word within their ICA session.

The solution to this is for the user's workstation to be configured so that when they click on a ".doc" file it opens a remote session of Word *and* passes the path of the file to the server so that Word can open that file.

There are actually a few different ways that this can be addressed. The exact method that you use will depend on which Feature Release you are using and how your ICA clients are configured.

## Content Redirection Using Feature Release 1 or 2

If you're using Feature Release 1 or 2, then you'll be happy to know that the MetaFrame XP product has been extended to "officially" support a solution for this problem. To implement this content redirection, you need to configure both the MetaFrame XP published application and the Windows client device.

With Feature Release 1 or 2, MetaFrame XP supports client to server content redirection by adding the ability for an ICA client to pass the path of a file to a published application via a command line parameter. This is known as "parameter passing." The use of parameter passing to published applications is enabled by adding a ""`%*`"" to the command line of the published application. This is similar in concept to the way that Windows supports parameter passing by adding a "`%1`" to a command line. To enable parameter passing for a published application, all you have to do is add the ""`%*`"" to the end of the published application's command line via the Citrix Management Console. (Note that you need to add the quotes when you type this into the CMC, so you end up adding a space-quotes-percent-asterisk-quotes to the end of a published application's command line.)

For example, if you have a published application called "Microsoft Word" with the command line `m:\program files\microsoft office\office10\winword.exe`, you would enable the parameter passing by changing the command line to `m:\program files\microsoft office\ office10\winword.exe "%*"`.

You can add the ""`%*`"" parameter to the end of any published application. Then, if the ICA client passes parameters, the MetaFrame XP server dynamically replaces the ""`%*`"" with the actual parameters. If the client does not offer any parameters, the server ignores the ""`%*`"".

Once you configure your MetaFrame XP servers to support the extended parameter passing, you need to configure your client devices. To do this, you need to change the file associations of the three-character file extensions for each type of file that you want to pass to a MetaFrame XP server. Usually, file type associations are configured so that they open an application that can read the file. For example, when a user double-clicks on a ".doc" file, their local computer knows to launch Microsoft Word and open the file that they double-clicked. However, when you're using extended parameter passing to open MetaFrame XP applications, double-clicking a ".doc" file needs to do three things:

1. Launch the local ICA client software.

2. Instruct the ICA client software to connect to a published application (Microsoft Word in this case).

3. Tell the published application to automatically open the file that the user just double-clicked.

To do this, you need to add the file type association. (Windows Explorer | Tools Menu | Folder Options | File Types Tab | New) For example, you can configure the ".doc" file type to open a "Microsoft Word" published application by associating the ".doc" file extension with the command line `c:\Program Files\Citrix\ICA Client\pn.exe /pn:YourAppSetName /app:Microsoft Word /param:"\\client\%1"`. The "app" command line switch instructs `pn.exe` to launch the specified published application. The "param" switch instructs it to attach the enclosed parameter to the tail end of the command to launch the application. In this case, the "%1" is the standard Windows command-line parameter passing variable. If you wanted to, you could add any parameters you wanted after the "param" switch.

This example assumes that the user is using the full Program Neighborhood client, which is launched with "pn.exe." If you use this client then your users must connect into the server farm via their local Program Neighborhood at least once so that the ICA client can build a list of published applications that are available. If the user does not connect first then the published application will not be found. Alternately, you may need to use "wfica32.exe" or "wfcrun32.exe" depending on your ICA client options. (See Chapter 10 for details.) No matter which client executable you need to use, you can get the command-line syntax by typing the client executable followed by a "/?" at a command prompt.

### Content Redirection with Feature Release 2

In addition to the method of content redirection outlined in the previous section, there is one more option that you have if you're using Feature Release 2.

One of the problems with the type of content redirection mentioned previously is that you have to manually configure every ICA client device's file type association for each type of file that you want them to open via a MetaFrame application.

If you're using Feature Release 2, you can actually configure file type associations via the Citrix Management Console. These file type associations are then used by all ICA PN Agent clients.

Does this sound too good to be true? In a way, it is. The list of requirements you need to meet in order for Feature Release 2's "automatic" content redirection is pretty steep. These requirements include:

- You must use Feature Release 2.

- Users must use the "Program Neighborhood Agent" ICA client. (See Chapter 10 for details on the PN Agent.)
- Your users must access MetaFrame via NFuse Classic.
- You must enable client drive mapping.

There is really no way around these requirements. This is because the PN Agent client works by pulling all of its configuration information from a central location, so it's easy for a MetaFrame XP server to modify the properties of the ICA client to force them to pass the full path of the file that was clicked. Client drive mapping is how the published application finds the file.

You can enable this type of content redirection on an application-by-application basis. When FR-2 is used, you are presented with a "Content Redirection" screen during the initial application publishing process. (A "Content Redirection" tab has also been added to the published applications' properties page.) From here, you can select a checkbox next to each file extension that you would like redirected to this published application for your PN Agent users. Checking this box does two things:

1. If it's not there already, it appends the ""%*"" to the end of the published application's command line setting.
2. It modifies the PN Agent configuration file to have the ability to recognize that a type of file extension should now be used to open an application on a remote MetaFrame XP server.

For this to work, you need to import the file types from the registry (CMC | Right-click the server | Update File Types from Registry).

### Advantages of FR-2's Content Redirection

- It's easily applied to all users.
- It's easy to turn on or off.

### Disadvantages of FR-2's Content Redirection

- The requirements are pretty steep.

## Content Redirection without Feature Release 1 or 2

All of that ""*%"" stuff we just talked about is only available if you're using one of the Feature Releases for MetaFrame XP. If you're not using a Feature Release then you'll have to configure content redirection the old-fashioned way.

There are several steps that you must take in order to configure file type association content redirection without using a Feature Release. What's interesting here is that the fundamental process used is conceptually identical to that of a Feature Release. The only difference is that you need to configure everything manually when you're not using a Feature Release.

In order to understand how this configuration must be done, let's step through an example. This example is for Microsoft Word, but you can use these techniques for any application.

1. Create a batch file that is in a publicly accessible network location, such as \\server\share\LaunchWord.bat.

The batch file should look like this:

```
@echo off
```
*(the next three lines are one line that is wrapped)*
```
echo n:\Program Files\Microsoft Office\Office10\
winword.exe %1 %2 %3 %4 %5 %6 %7 %8 %9 >
p:\OpenFile.bat
pn.exe /app:"Microsoft Word"
```

As you can see, there are two drive letters used in this batch file, N: and P:. The N: drive and path is the application's installed directory on the Meta-Frame XP server. The P: drive is the user's personal home drive. This P: drive can be a network share or part of the user's local profile. The exact location of the P: drive is unimportant. What is important is that the P: drive is accessible *only* by the current user.

2. Create a published application on your MetaFrame XP server to run p:\OpenFile.bat.

3. Create an association on your user's local workstation for .doc files that runs the batch file from the network location in step 1.

Then, when the user double-clicks a ".doc" file on their local computer, it will run the batch file from step one (since you configured the file type association in step 3). The batch file will dump the command to start Word and the document path into a new batch file on the user's home drive and it starts the ICA connection to the published application. That published application runs the new batch file on the MetaFrame XP server (as configured in step 2).

The %1 %2 .. %9 in the command line allows this to work if there are spaces in the document path. If you only had a %1, then the code would stop dumping the path if it encountered a <space> character. For instance, if a user's file is in the folder "c:\My Documents," this code would input "c:\My" into the OpenFile.bat. Extending to %9 allows for nine spaces in the path and file name.

The pn.exe /app:"Microsoft Word" command instructs the local ICA client software to connect to the "Micrsoft Word" published application. If you go to the command prompt and type, pn.exe /? you will see that there are many options. You can specify custom .INI files, and create a custom appsrv.ini file that pointed to the right server farm. You could put this .INI file in the same public location as the batch file.

Lastly, you might need to change the batch file to run pn.exe from the proper path, or add the path of it to your client's "PATH" statement. By default, pn.exe is in the \Program Files\Citrix\ICA Client\ directory.

## Server to Client Content Redirection

Now that you understand how content redirection can help users to launch applications on remote MetaFrame servers, let's look at how users can click on content from within their MetaFrame XP sessions that is launched on their local client workstations.

If you're using Feature Release 2, you can configure your MetaFrame XP servers to allow users to click on certain kinds of links and have the content open on their local client workstations instead of on the MetaFrame server. In probably 99% of all cases this configuration has one purpose—to prevent users from surfing the web on MetaFrame servers.

In order to enable content redirection in FR-2, all you need to do is check a box in CMC. You can enable this on a farm-wide basis (CMC | Right-click on server farm | Properties | 'MetaFrame Settings' tab | check 'Enable Content Redirection from Server to Client') or on a server-by-server basis (CMC | Right-click on server | 'MetaFrame Settings' tab | 'Content Redirection from Server to Client' section | Uncheck 'Use farm settings' | Check 'Enable Content Redirection from Server to Client').

Once content redirection is enabled, whenever a user clicks an HTTP link the web page is opened on their client browser.

Server to client content redirection has several requirements:

- You must use Feature Release 2.
- Only Win32 and Linux clients are supported.

- Only HTTP, Real Media, QuickTime, and Windows Media types of content are supported.

- The application containing the hyperlink must "properly" use the Windows shell to launch a web browser. Interestingly, Microsoft Office does *not* properly use the Windows shell to launch a browser. Instead, it calls IE directly. (This is probably why Microsoft is experiencing a little legal problem with IE integration.) Server-to-client content redirection does not work from within Microsoft Office.

# Multi-Server Application Load Management

By this point, we've already covered everything related to applications when it comes to installing them on a single MetaFrame XP server. However, your MetaFrame environment will most likely consist of more than one server. You'll probably want to install certain applications onto multiple servers. This is often done for scalability (if you have 1,000 users then you'll need more than one server) and reliability (if you have ten servers then you can lose one without affecting all users).

When you outgrow a single server or want to load-balance applications across more than one MetaFrame XP server, you'll need to use Citrix Load Manager (LM). Load Manager is the component of MetaFrame XPa and XPe that allows you to specify the criteria that make applications available for end users. It also allows you to customize the load balancing schemes when an application is published across two or more servers. With Citrix Load Manager enabled, users will continue to connect to published applications as they always have. The difference is that when Load Manager is used, the system will check all MetaFrame servers running the same application and automatically connect the user to the least busy server.

Citrix Load Manager is not a separate product from MetaFrame XP. It is built-in to MetaFrame XPa and XPe, and is required when applications are published across multiple servers. (If you have MetaFrame XPs then you will not be able to use Load Manager until you upgrade to XPa or XPe.)

## How does Citrix Load Manager Work?

There are several components involved when users are load-balanced between multiple MetaFrame servers. Some components are specific to Citrix Load Manager and some are standard MetaFrame XP components that take on additional roles in load-balanced environments. The specific components that play a role in load-managed environments are:

- Load Evaluators.
- Rules.
- Zone Data Collectors.

### Load Manager Component 1. Load Evaluators

Load Evaluators are little programs that run on servers in the server farm that monitor the server's ever-changing utilization and usage. They calculate a "load index" for each server or application where they are applied. The load index always has an integer value somewhere between 0 and 10,000, its value changing depending on the actual load. A value of zero means that the load evaluator has calculated no load, and a value of 10,000 means that the load evaluator has calculated the maximum load. In the real world, the values of the load evaluators are constantly changing as server and application loads change.

Load evaluators are created via the Citrix Management Console and their properties are stored in the IMA data store. After they are created, Load Evaluators can be applied to farm servers or published applications.

### Load Manager Component 2. Rules

Rules are the specific sets of criteria that the load evaluators use to calculate their load index. Each load evaluator is made up of one or more rules. For example, a rule might be established that correlates to CPU utilization—returning a load index value of 0 for 0% CPU utilization, and 10,000 for 100% utilization (and 5,400 to 54% utilization, etc). Many parameters exist that can be used to establish rules, including CPU or memory usage or the number of users logged into the server.

The number and configuration of rules that make up a load evaluator are also stored in the IMA data store.

### Load Manager Component 3. The Zone Data Collector

Any time the load index of a MetaFrame server changes, that server sends the new load index to the zone data collector. (Remember from Chapter 3 that the zone data collector then sends that information to all other zone data collectors in the server farm.)

Because the zone data collector knows which of the servers has the least load at any given time, it is always ready to direct ICA clients to the least busy server when they request the address of a published application.

Figure 4.2 shows how the three components of Citrix Load Management work together.

*Figure 4.2 The Citrix Load Manager components*

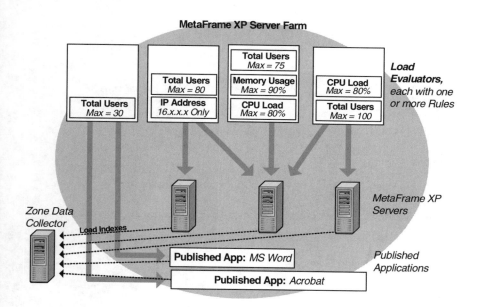

## The MetaFrame XP Load Management Process

The three Load Manager components work together to perform their tasks in a logical format. To illustrate this, let's look at the steps taken when a user connects to a published application that is load-balanced across multiple Meta-Frame XP servers:

1. Even before an ICA user connects, each MetaFrame XP server's Load Evaluator keeps the zone data collector up to date on their server load, based on the various configured rules. This is shown in figure 4.3 on the next page.

*Figure 4.3 Load Evaluator's on each server update the ZDC*

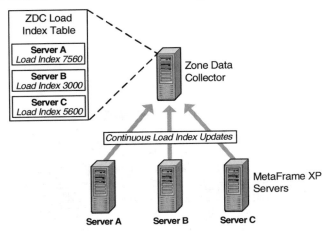

2. Figure 4.4 picks up with step 2, when the ICA client requests a connection to the "MS Word" published application.

*Figure 4.4 The client connecting process in a load-managed environment*

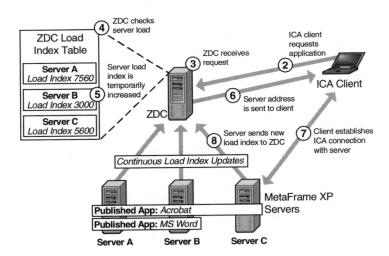

3. As with any published application request, this request is received by the zone data collector (ZDC).

4. The ZDC knows which servers have the published application and what those servers' last reported loads were. From among those servers, the ZDC selects the one with the lowest load index.

5. The ZDC temporarily increases that server's load index in its own table by 200 points. (More on what this number means later.)

6. The ZDC sends the address of the server with the least load to the ICA client.

7. The ICA client connects to a MetaFrame XP server, based on the address received from the ZDC.

8. The MetaFrame XP server updates the ZDC with the new load number changed since the user connected.

Now that we have an overview of how the components of load balancing work together, let's examine each of them in depth, beginning with the Load Evaluators.

## How Load Evaluators are used in Load Management

A Load Evaluator in a MetaFrame XP server farm is responsible for analyzing the various rules applied to it and returning a load index to the zone data collector. Remember that the load index can be any integer from 0 to 10,000. A value of 10,000 indicates that the server is full and is not accepting connections. Any value less than 10,000 indicates that the server is accepting connections. The zone data collector will ultimately send users to the server with the smallest load index. The load indexes get higher as they approach 10,000, starting all the way from a value of zero—meaning that a server has no detected load.

Each Load Evaluator has a name, description, and one or more assigned rules. When you assign a rule to an evaluator, you specify the parameters for that rule, such as when it reports a full load (10,000). These parameters vary depending on the rule you are working with. Each load evaluator must have at least one rule configured for it, although a single load evaluator could have all twelve different types of rules applied to it.

Load Evaluators are stored in the server farm. Depending on the rules they have configured, they are then applied to specific servers or published applications. You can create as many different Load Evaluators as you want in a single MetaFrame XP server farm. However, each server in the farm must have one (and only one) Load Evaluator applied to it. Published applications can also have one Load Evaluator applied to them.

Not all Load Evaluators will be used for every ICA client request. For example, different Load Evaluators will be applied to different published applications or different servers. When determining the load index for a server, the zone data collector will look at all the applicable Load Evaluators and use whichever one is greatest. That greatest number is compared to the greatest number of the other servers.

Having Load Evaluators is required in MetaFrame XP with Load Management enabled. There are two default evaluators that can be configured but not deleted. These evaluators always apply, even if you only have one server.

## How "Rules" Affect Load Management

Remember that in order to calculate its load index, a Load Evaluator must have one or more "rules" applied to it. The Load Evaluator will use the rules to process current server utilization and generate the load index.

There are four classes of rules (and twelve rules total) that are based on various MetaFrame XP performance components. Each rule is used to create a load index based on a different type of information. There are different types of rules each used differently, depending on the type of performance data to be evaluated. The four types of rules are as follows:

- Moving average, based on percentages.
- Moving average, based on manual parameters over time.
- Incremental.
- Boolean.

### Moving Average Rules, Based on Percentages

Percentage-based rules evaluate performance-based server metrics expressed in terms of percentages (such as the percentage of CPU utilization). To use percentage-based rules, you must specify two parameters: a high value and a low value. The Load Evaluator will then return a load index value based on your parameters. If the performance counter being evaluated is less than your configured minimum, the Load Evaluator will return a value of zero, indicating no server activity. If the counter is higher than the high parameter configured, the Load Evaluator will return a value of 10,000. If the performance counter falls between the high and low configured parameters, the server will return a value proportional to the configured parameters.

Even though the configured parameters are entered as percentages, this does not mean that the returned Load Evaluator will always match that percentage. (A 70% performance counter does *not* automatically mean that the load evaluator will return 7,000.) Let's consider an example to illustrate how this value is calculated.

Assume that you've configured the CPU utilization rule and have set the low value to 50% and the high value to 90%. Any time the CPU utilization is below 50% the Load Evaluator will return a load index of zero, effectively meaning that there is no load. Any actual CPU utilization over 90% will cause our Load Evaluator to return a load index of 10,000, indicating that the server is fully loaded and not taking on any more ICA sessions. With a high of 90% and a low of 50%, you are left with a 40% range that the Load Evaluator will use for its 0 to 10,000 load index. Simple arithmetic will show that each percentage point of CPU utilization is equal to 250 points in the load index (10,000 / 40 = 250). Therefore, an actual server load of 67% would cause the Load Evaluator to create a load index of 4250 (17 percentage points above 50% (because 50% = 0) multiplied by 250). This makes sense since 67 is 42.5 percent of the way between 50 to 90 (50 and 90 are the respective minimums and maximums that you configured for this rule).

These rules are called "moving average" rules because the actual load index is based on an average of the most recent ten samples. This method evens out unexpected spikes. Each MetaFrame XP server sends new load index samples to the ZDC each time a user event occurs or every 30 seconds. Because of this, the ten sample moving average window could be as long as five minutes or as short as a few seconds if ten people log on at once. There is no way to reset this average, other than by stopping and starting the IMA service.

Of the twelve rule types available, two operate in this percentage fashion:

- *CPU Utilization.* On multiprocessor systems this is the average of all the processors.
- *Memory Usage.* This is the percentage of the total memory used, including physical and virtual.

### Moving Average Rules, Based on Manual Parameters over Time

Similar to the percentage-based moving average rules, some rules are based on actual performance metrics from the server. Instead of specifying the high and low percentages, you specify the actual high and low values. The load evaluator returns a load index between 0 and 10,000 proportionally based on the values you've specified.

There are five types of these rules available. Since they are time-based, they all are based on "per-second" values. Valid values for the high and low inputs for each of these are 0 to 2,147,483,647.

- *Context Switches.* Occurs every time the server switches from one process to another.

- *Disk Data I/O*. Evaluated based on the actual disk I/O throughput in kilobytes.

- *Disk Operations*. The number of disk assesses per second, based on the percentage of high and low configured values.

- *Page Fault*. Occurs every time the system must access memory that has been paged to disk.

- *Page Swap*. Occurs when the system swaps data in physical memory to the pagefile on the disk.

As the previous type of rules, these rules are also "moving average" rules whose load index is based on an average of the ten most recent values.

In order to get starting points for these rules, you can use Performance Monitor to watch each appropriate counter. As your environment grows, you will most likely need to adjust these settings.

### Incremental Rules

Incremental rules are based on the total number of users or licenses in use. Unlike the previous types of rules, incremental rules are not based on performance monitor metrics. You can configure the values that correspond to a full load for these incremental rules.

When an incremental rule is used, the Load Evaluator will return a load index of zero if the item specified for the rule evaluates to zero. If the item meets or exceeds the limit you set, the load evaluator sets the value to 10,000.

For incremental rules, you configure only one parameter—the maximum (because the minimum is assumed zero). Any number between zero and your configured maximum generates a load index proportional from 0 to 10,000.

There are three types of incremental rules. Each has a maximum configurable value of 10,000 (in case there is anyone out there that can actually fit 10,000 users on one server).

- *Application User Load*. This is the total number of users accessing the published application that this rule is applied to. It can only be applied to one application. If you have multiple applications that you need to limit then you must create multiple Load Evaluators. This rule is useful if you only have a limited number of licenses for a published application. Be careful though; this rule only applies when running instances of the published application. It does not know about other users who might have connected directly to a server and started the application from there.

- *Server User Load.* This rule is similar to the Application User Load rule except that it applies to all users connected to one server. It is based on active ICA sessions. It will not prevent users from reconnecting to disconnected ICA sessions.

- *License Threshold.* This rule supports thresholds for two license types: assigned licenses and pooled licenses. You can enter two different limits for this rule, one for each license type. The license threshold will always evaluate to the higher of the two numbers. For example, consider the environment in Figure 4.5.

*Figure 4.5 License threshold sample configuration*

| License Type | Rule Threshold | Actual Licenses In Use |
|---|---|---|
| Assigned Licenses | 80 | 26 |
| Pooled Licenses | 120 | 32 |

In this case, assigned licenses are 32% in use (26 / 80) and pooled licenses are 27% in use (32 / 120). This means that the license threshold rule would evaluate based on the higher number—the assigned licenses. The load index calculated is 3250 (26 / 80 as a proportion from 0 to 10,000).

If you would like the license threshold rule to evaluate based on only one type of license, simply enter a value of 0 for the type that you would like to ignore.

## Boolean Rules

The final rule type that can be configured are Boolean rules. Boolean rules are based on whether the criterion evaluates to be true or false. Unlike other rules that return a sliding scale load index from 0 to 10,000, Boolean rules have no load values. As the name implies, they have two states: "yes" or "no." They can return a value of 0 or 10,000—nothing in between.

Boolean rules are based on an external parameter, such as the time of day or a user's IP address. They are not based on actual performance or load of a MetaFrame XP server. This means that all Boolean rules must be used in conjunction with other rules. (Remember that you can add as many rules as your want to a single Load Evaluator.) As an example, suppose you had only one Boolean rule applied with no other rules across five servers. When the Boolean rule was true it would evaluate to "0" for all five servers—causing them all to have equal load balance indexes. In this case, the client would be connected to the machine with the lowest host ID. Subsequent ICA clients would experience the same scenario. Because the load index would never change they too would connect to the server with the lowest host ID. All users would connect to the same server because the load index would never change with only the Boolean rule applied, and the host ID would never change since it's a permanent internal setting.

Boolean rules can only be used to determine whether an ICA client can connect to a published application. These rules do not prevent a user from connecting to a server directly and running the application from the remote desktop session.

There are two types of Boolean rules:

- *IP Range*. The Load Evaluator can enable or disable access based on an ICA client's IP address. You can configure multiple IP address ranges for this rule. The IP Range rule is evaluated through a two step process. First, the client's IP address is checked to see whether it's within any of the specified ranges for the rule. To be within range, the client's IP address must be greater than or equal to the first value and less than or equal to the second value. (Warning: When you configure this rule, there is no logic to ensure that the first value is less than the second value. If the first value is greater than the second, no IP addresses will ever evaluate within range.) If a client's IP address is determined to be in range, then access is granted or denied based on the setting of the rule, either granting access to all IP addresses within range or denying access to all IP addresses within range.

- *Scheduling*. This rule's evaluation is based on the day of week and time of day as specified by the server's clock. This is useful if you only want to allow access to servers during business hours. (Hint: when you're applying this rule, you don't need to click in each individual little square. You can click and drag to turn on or turn off complete ranges.) However, this rule will not force users off of the system if they're already connected. Of course, you can use the native Microsoft tools to enforce logon hours. See the Chapter 15 for more details.

## The Zone Data Collector's Role in Load Management

The zone data collector constantly keeps track of load indexes for every server in the farm. (Note: This is not a typo. Each zone data collector always knows the load information of every server in the entire server farm, not just its local zone.) When an ICA client makes a request to launch a published application, the zone data collector will return the address of the server with the least load. If all servers have a value of 10,000, the client connection is refused.

MetaFrame XP servers send their load index updates to the zone data collector anytime a user event occurs. Remember from Chapter 3 that "user events" include activities such as user logon, logoff, connection, or disconnection. If you perform a network analysis of that transaction, you'll see that a MetaFrame server sends both its load index and its current user count to the zone data collector.

Additionally, the MetaFrame XP server sends an updated load index value if no user events occur over a period of five minutes. You can change this interval via the Citrix Management Console. (CMC | Farm | Actions | Load Manager | Load Manager Settings) When Load Management is in use, MetaFrame XP servers will also update the zone data collector if their load index changes (up or down) by more than 500 points within a 30 second period.

When the zone data collector checks farm servers' load indexes (as when a client requests a connection to a published application), it does not take into consideration any user or protocol restrictions. If a user requests an application via the IPX protocol and the least loaded server only has TCP/IP, then the user will not be able to connect, because the zone data collector will provide the user with the address of a server that is not running the same protocol as the user. Realistically, this should not be an issue, because you should only publish applications where any user of the application could access it on one of the servers where it is configured. If you need to get more granular with user rights then you'll need to publish multiple applications. .

Citrix Load Manager is only used when an ICA client starts a new session via a published application. There are some situations where Citrix Load Manager is not used to route users to a server, even if Load Management is enabled. These situations are as follows:

- *Direct connection to a MetaFrame XP server.* If a user connects directly to a MetaFrame server (instead of a published application), their ICA client does not request server information from the zone data collector, so the zone data collector never has a chance to affect which server the user accesses.

- *Reconnecting to a disconnected session.* When a user reconnects to a disconnected session, his session already exists on one server, causing their client device to connect back to that server. In this case, the ICA client still requests connection routing from the zone data collector, but the fact that an existing disconnected session is running takes precedence over the load balancing numbers, even if the server load is 10,000.

- *Session sharing with Seamless Windows.* If a Windows client has one session established with a MetaFrame XP server via Seamless Windows, connecting to another published application will launch that application on the same server as the first session, unless that application is not published on the same server.

In all three cases, the MetaFrame XP server will notify the zone data collector of its new load index once the user connects.

## Load Management Strategies

Now that you understand how load management works, let's see how it can be used in the real world. Figure 4.6 shows three servers, their specifications, and the applications that will be published on each.

*Figure 4.6 A typical load-managed environment*

|  | Server A | Server B | Server C |
|---|---|---|---|
| Processors | 1 x 1.26 GHz | 2 x 1.26 GHz | 2 x 1.26 GHz |
| Memory | 1 GB | 2 GB | 4 GB |
| Published Applications | Word<br>Excel<br>Acrobat | Word<br>Excel<br>Visio | Word<br>Excel<br>Visio<br>Acrobat |

### Configuring Server Load

Remember that each MetaFrame XP server must have one Load Evaluator applied. A generic Load Evaluator called "Default" is applied to each server out of the box. This Load Evaluator consists of one rule—"Server User Load"—with the maximum number of users set at 10,000. Even without any additional configuration, this default Load Evaluator will successfully equalize the user load in the environment shown in Figure 4.6. However, because both Server B and Server C have twice the processing power as Server A, you wouldn't want your users distributed evenl between the servers. Ideally, you'd like twice as many users to go to Servers B and C. The easiest way to do this is to create a unique Load Evaluator for each of the two types of servers. Let's take a look at that process:

1. Create a Load Evaluator for Server A called "1x1.26GHz."

2. Create a Load Evaluator for Servers B and C called "2x1.26GHz."

3. Like the default Load Evaluator, you would only need to apply one rule to your custom Load Evaluators. Also like the default Load Evaluator, you could use the "Server User Load" rule.

4. Configure the maximum number of users for each Load Evaluator's rule so that the "2x1.26GHz" Load Evaluator's maximum is twice as large as the maximum for "1x1.26GHz."

Now that you've decided that the user load rule value for the "2x1.26GHz" rule should be twice as high as the "1x1.26GHz" rule, you need to decide what the rule's values should be. Should you enter realistic numbers that match your licenses, like "80" and "40," or should you enter false, high numbers, like "5,000" and "10,000?" To address this, think back to how load manager works.

In both cases, the load of the servers will be managed effectively. Consider this scenario:

*Figure 4.7 Light usage load indexes with various "Server User Load" values*

| Server | Current Users | Load Index with Max Users Set at 80/40 | Load Index with Max Users Set at 10000/5000 |
|--------|---------------|----------------------------------------|---------------------------------------------|
| Server A | 3 | 750 (3 out of 40) | 6 (3 out of 5000) |
| Server B | 5 | 625 (5 out of 80) | 5 (5 out of 10000) |
| Server C | 4 | 500 (4 out of 80) | 4 (4 out of 10000) |

Notice that the ratios of the load indexes between Servers A, B, and C are identical, regardless of whether the Load Evaluators have rules with maximum user limits that are sky-high (10000/5000) or more down to earth (80/40). In this case, the next user that connects will be routed to Server C. Now, let's re-examine this scenario taking into account servers more heavily used.

*Figure 4.8 Heavy usage load indexes with various "Server User Load" values*

| Server | Current Users | Load Index with Max Users Set at 80/40 | Load Index with Max Users Set at 10000/5000 |
|--------|---------------|----------------------------------------|---------------------------------------------|
| Server A | 40 | 10000 (40 out of 40) | 80 (40 out of 5000) |
| Server B | 80 | 10000 (80 out of 80) | 80 (80 out of 10000) |
| Server C | 80 | 10000 (80 out of 80) | 80 (80 out of 10000) |

As you can see in Figure 4.8, no additional users would be able to connect with the lower limits (80/40) because a load index of 10,000 will not allow any more users to connect to a server. With high limits (10000/5000), the servers can take on more users. Because the load indexes for all three servers is the same (80), the user requesting the connection will be given the address of the machine with the lowest host ID.

## *Fine Tuning Load Evaluators*

You'll probably want to fine-tune your farm's load evaluators after you build your initial environment. This fine tuning usually involves adding more rules to the existing Load Evaluators. (Remember that even though only one Load Evaluator can be applied to each server, that Load Evaluator can be built upon more than one rule.)

For example, you might be worried that some of your servers will run out of memory because the current Load Evaluators are based only on one rule— "Server User Load." This means that even if a server runs out of memory the zone data collector will still try to have users connect to it because the Load Evaluators are not configured with any rules that look at memory usage. Ideally, you should create a Load Evaluator that would prevent users from connecting if the memory utilization was full.

*Figure 4.9 The current Load Evaluator for Server A*

| Rule | Server User Load |
| --- | --- |
| Maximum Users | 40 |

Figure 4.9 shows the current Load Evaluator (named "1x1.26GHz") that is applied to Server A. This load evaluator has only one rule applied, the "Server User Load." Figure 4.10 shows the properties of the second rule—based on the memory usage—that could be added to the existing "1x1.26GHz" Load Evaluator.

*Figure 4.10 Properties for an additional rule for Server A's Load Evaluator*

| Rule | Memory Usage % |
| --- | --- |
| Minimum | 80 |
| Maximum | 90 |

Once the second rule is added, the Load Evaluator will calculate its load index based on both rules. By setting the second rule's memory usage minimum to 80%, the second rule will always evaluate to zero until memory utilization hits 80%. At 90%, that rule will evaluate to a load index of 10,000, causing the server to be unavailable. (That rule will evaluate to a number between 0 and 10,000 for memory utilization between 80 and 90%.)

By adding this second rule, no additional users will be able to connect if the memory usage gets really high—even if only 10 or 20 users are currently connected. In effect, the memory utilization rule becomes a type of "circuit breaker," protecting the server from memory over-utilization.

### Checking Server Load

As you're tuning your Load Evaluators, it's helpful to be able to view the various load indexes. This can be done with the "qfarm" command-line tool. There are two options that will return load management numbers:

- **qfarm /load**. This command displays information about the load balanced servers in your farm.

- **qfarm /app**. This command displays information about the load balanced published applications in your farm.

The "qfarm" command line utility will display the load indexes for servers or applications. Additionally, the qfarm utility can report other information about Load Manager (as detailed in Figure 4.11).

*Figure 4.11 Load Manager values as reported by the qfarm utility*

| Load Value | Description |
| --- | --- |
| 0-9999 | Load index value. |
| 10000 | The server or application is full. |
| 20000 | The server is not a Load Managed server. |
| 99990 | There is a problem with Load Management on the server. |
| 99999 | There is no Load Evaluator attached to the application |

## Load Evaluators—Which rules to compare?

You can essentially build a customized load management environment by creating load evaluators with multiple rules applied. You can also create unique Load Evaluators based on completely different rules and apply them to different servers. You don't have to configure each Load Evaluator to calculate its load index in the same way.

The million-dollar question then becomes, "How do the Load Evaluators calculate their load indexes when multiple rules are applied?"

The "common denominator" in these cases is the load index calculated by each Load Evaluator. Remember that all the zone data collector cares about when looking at load is the load index (that number between 0 and 10,000 that each server sends to the zone data collector). The zone data collector isn't concerned with how the load index was calculated. For example, it is perfectly acceptable for one server (with one Load Evaluator applied) to cal-culate its load index based on memory utilization and another server (with another Load Evaluator applied) to calculate its load index based on proces-sor utilization.

How does the zone data collector compare the processor utilization of one server to the memory utilization of another? It uses the load index numbers. Whichever server has the lowest load index gets the user. Consider the sce-nario in Figure 4.12. Each of the servers has a different Load Evaluator ap-plied to it. Each Load Evaluator has one rule applied based on different crite-ria: processor utilization, memory utilization, or current users.

*Figure 4.12 Load indexes with different Load Evaluators applied*

| Server | Load Evaluator Rule | LE Rule Max / Min | Actual Number | Load Index |
|--------|---------------------|-------------------|---------------|------------|
| Server A | % Proc Util | 60 / 0 | 50% Actual | 8333 (50 out of 60) |
| Server B | % Mem Usage | 90 / 0 | 70% Actual | 7777 (70 out of 90) |
| Server C | Current Users | 50 / na | 41 current users | 8200 (41 out of 50) |

If an ICA client requests the address of the least busy server, the zone data collector will have no problem returning the address of Server B, since its load index is the lowest (7777) out of the three servers. However, can we, as administrators, really say that memory utilization alone made that server less busy than the processor utilization or number of users on Server A or C? In the real world, load scenarios like this are rare, mainly because they're con-fusing.

## Applying Load Evaluators to Published Applications

So far, all analysis we've done regarding Load Evaluators relates to server load. If you think back to the introduction to this section, we also said that you can apply Load Evaluators to published applications (CMC | Published Ap-plications | Right-Click | Select Load Manage).

Load Evaluators are configured for each instance of the published application running on each server. As with server-based Load Evaluators, it's possible to apply a different Load Evaluator to each instance of the published application on each unique server. This allows you to create extremely complex load management environments.

When a MetaFrame XP server sends its load information to the zone data collector, it sends the load index for itself (calculated via the Load Evaluator applied to the server) and any load indexes applied to published applications (calculated via the Load Evaluator applied to a specific published application on that server).

The main reason that you would use application-based Load Evaluators is if you had different types of applications with different requirements. You might create one Load Evaluator with the "Total User Sessions" rule and apply it to a server, and create another Load Evaluator with the "Schedule" rule and apply it to a published application. That way you can still get server-based load management while having scheduled time to take applications offline.

Creating Load Evaluators based on published applications could get you into a situation where a user is making a connection to a server and two load indexes apply—one for the server and one for the published application the user requested on that server. In this case, the zone data collector uses the higher of the two indexes. The zone data collector then sends the client to the server with the lowest load index.

### Load Management Performance

Citrix Load Manager includes a Load Management logging tool (CMC | Load Evaluators | Logging). This logging tool can be used for troubleshooting the load manager. (Note that this tool should not be used for security auditing purposes because it is not always 100% reliable.)

When using the Citrix Management Console, you will notice that the performance is slow, especially when selecting servers for Load Management and when attaching Load Evaluators to servers. Interestingly, in large environments, the CMC will report that it is done enumerating servers and has found them all. Even after this message, the CMC may continue to find more servers.

# Application / Server Installation Groups

Now that you understand how application publishing and load management work, you need to think about your strategy for deciding which applications you'll put on which servers.

In smaller environments with only a few applications, you'll probably put all applications on all servers. However, if you have a larger environment you might be faced with a tougher decision; What should you do if you have twenty applications and twenty servers? Do you put one application on each server? Do you put all twenty applications on all twenty servers? Most likely your solution will be a mixed environment, grouping some applications to-gether on some servers and other applications on other servers.

## What are the Application Location Options?

When deciding which applications to put on which servers, there are two basic options:

1. Install a few related applications on each MetaFrame XP server, creating several different server configurations.
2. Install all applications on all MetaFrame XP servers, creating only one type of server configuration.

Similar to other design options that we've been reviewing in this book, each of these works well in different situations. Let's take a look at each one now.

### Option 1. Install A Few Related Applications on Each Server

If your MetaFrame environment has to support a large number of applica-tions, you might choose to install only a few of your applications on each server, even if all the servers are members of the same farm. This will essen-tially create a server farm made up of multiple groups of load-balanced serv-ers, each group containing a subset of the entire farm's applications. These small groups of servers are called "load-balancing groups" or "silos." (Au-thors Note: I used to call these "farmlets," but that term didn't catch on. The de facto industry term is "silo.")

All servers from all of the silos can still belong to the same server farm. In fact, the decision as to how you will design your server farms does not change. The application location decision only comes into play after you've decided how you will design your server farms and where your servers will be lo-cated. Consider the environment outlined in Figure 4.13 (facing page).

In this environment, one large server farm of 89 MetaFrame XP servers is broken down into four separate silos. Each silo contains servers that are load-balanced with similar applications. With this design, an update to a payroll application will not affect servers outside of the HR silo. Additionally, appli-cation integration and testing time is drastically reduced because there are fewer applications per server to potentially interfere with any new update.

If a user needs to access applications from multiple silos, they will need to establish ICA connections with multiple MetaFrame XP servers. Of course as long as the servers are members of the same server farm, the user will not consume multiple ICA connection licenses.

*Figure 4.13 Applications installed on various silos*

| Applications per Server | Number of Load-Balanced Servers in the Silo |
| --- | --- |
| Word<br>Excel<br>PowerPoint<br>Internet Explorer<br>Outlook | 60 |
| Data warehouse<br>Production Line Manager | 10 |
| Research Application | 15 |
| HR Application<br>Payroll | 4 |

By limiting each MetaFrame XP server to a few applications, the overall environment is generally easier to support and maintain. This is true for several reasons. First, because only a few (or even only one) application is installed on each server, the chance of applications not being compatible with each other is greatly diminished. Also, fewer applications mean fewer application updates with hotfixes and service packs. In general, the fewer number of applications per server, the more static—and stable—the server can be.

Of course this added stability comes at a price. Because applications are spread across many servers, servers (and applications) are not used as efficiently as they could be. Not only does this mean that more servers could be needed, it also means that servers will most likely be underutilized.

## Advantages of Installing a Few Related Applications on Each Server

- Ease of support. There are no conflicts between applications.
- Simpler application upgrades. Application version compatibility tests are easier when there are fewer applications that could potentially interfere.
- More static servers. If application hotfixes are released quarterly, six applications on one server result in new server code every other week.

## Disadvantages of Installing a Few Related Applications on Each Server

- Higher Cost. More servers are needed.
- Potentially under-utilized servers.

## Option 2. Install All Applications on All Servers

Alternatively, you could choose to configure your MetaFrame XP servers to be 100% identical. This would mean that you install all of your applications onto all of your servers. If there are a total of five applications in a server farm, then every server in the farm would run all five applications.

There are several benefits to doing this. Users who access multiple applications only need to connect to one server. Greater economies of scale can be realized since every user can be crammed onto a few servers. No user has any reason not to do everything on one server. Certain aspects of this environment could make it easier to manage, especially since all the servers are configured the same.

Unfortunately, deploying each application to every server is not always feasible. This can cause complex application upgrades because many applications on one server increases the chance that there will be some incompatibilities. Also, the MetaFrame XP servers will need to be taken out of service frequently due to the large number of applications on each server and the inevitability that there will always be something that will need to be updated. Finally, installing all applications on every server will not allow your environment to realistically grow any larger than a few dozen applications.

### Advantages of Putting All Applications on All Servers

- Better economies of scale.
- Fewer servers.
- All servers can be 100% identical.

### Disadvantages of Putting All Applications on All Servers

- Extremely complex application upgrades.
- Frequent server servicing.
- Constantly changing server environment.
- You need to install one application many times.
- Difficult to troubleshoot.
- Not realistic in large environments.

## Considerations when Deciding where to Install Applications

Unfortunately, the decision as to which MetaFrame servers you'll use for each application can be complex. The good aspect of this complexity is that while there are many issues to consider, each issue on its own is relatively simple solve.

To understand these issues, ask the following questions about each application:

- Who owns and maintains the application?
- How often is the application updated (including new versions, service packs, and hotfixes)? How long does this take?
- Can this application be grouped with others into a logical family (such as Microsoft Word and Excel)?
- How much server power does the application require?
- What is the total number of applications that you have?
- What type of server hardware do you have?

### Application Ownership

If certain groups of applications are owned or maintained by the same groups of administrators, then it makes sense to keep all of their applications together on the same servers. That way, each department only has to deal with their own applications. However, if all of the applications are supported by one large group of administrators (i.e. you), then this is not a factor.

### Application Complexity

Applications that are updated frequently should be kept away from applications that are almost never updated. For example, imagine that you have two applications each hosted by two servers. Application A is updated every other week, and application B is updated quarterly. If you publish both applications to all four servers then you will need to touch and update all four servers every other week. However, if you limit each application to two servers then you will only need to update the two servers for application A every other week.

### Application Groups

If you have certain groups of applications that are used by the same groups of users, it might make sense to confine them to selected servers. Many companies keep all applications specific to a department on MetaFrame XP servers separate from those that host company–wide applications.

### Server Resources Needed

If you have many applications that require significant server power, it may not be possible (or economical) to put them on the same server as other applications that also have high resource requirements.

## Number of Applications

The more applications you have, the more likely it is that you will need to put specific applications on specific servers. If you only have three applications, you can afford to put them all on each server. However, if you have one hundred applications, there is no way that you would put them all on every Meta-Frame server.

## Server Hardware

The type of server hardware you have (or plan to have) will also help you decide whether you should put all applications on all servers or whether you should divide your farm in silos. Obviously, if you have six quad-processor servers then your application installation options would be a bit different than if you had twenty single-processor servers. A full analysis of server hardware and server sizing as it relates to your application and farm design is covered in Chapter 6.

# CHAPTER 5

# Creating the User Environment

In this chapter

| | |
|---|---|
| User Profiles | 154 |
| User Policies | 178 |
| Home Drives | 195 |
| Logon and Logoff Scripts | 208 |
| Real World Case Study | 217 |

In this chapter, we'll look at the technical components that shape the environment of your users' MetaFrame XP sessions. These include the elements that work together to ensure each user gets customized access to their environment and information, including:

- User profiles
- Policies
- Home directories
- Logon scripts

We'll end this chapter with a real world case study detailing the solution that a hospital network came up with for their users.

The key to success when creating MetaFrame XP environments is to create a balance between giving users total freedom to configure their environment and locking down a system to provide no ability to customize anything. This chapter analyzes the many ways that you can manage your user's environment.

# User Profiles

Microsoft Windows user profiles allow customization and configuration of your users' environment. Profiles form a collection of settings, configurations, and personal files that are unique to each user. They permit multiple users to have different environments, even if they're all connected to the same server at the same time.

For example, correctly implementing user profiles allows one user to set his Windows background to a picture of his kids, his mouse pointer to a dinosaur, and his menu color to purple—while another user can log on with normal settings.

There are hundreds of components that can be configured via user profiles. Some of these components include:

- Windows desktop configuration and settings.
- Internet connection settings.
- Printers and mapped drive connections.
- Temporary Internet file locations.
- Application settings, such as file paths, options, and preferences.

In addition to the hundreds of Windows components that can be configured with a user profile, every application loaded on a server introduces more of its own settings. (Microsoft Word has hundreds of settings, including file save locations, custom dictionary locations, grammar checking preferences, etc.) In fact, you can use a profile to customize practically any setting stored in the registry.

Before discussing how user profiles are used, let's see how they work.

## How User Profiles Work

A user that logs on to any Windows NT or Windows 2000 computer uses some form of a Windows user profile. This user profile is made up of two parts:

- A collection of user-specific files and folders.
- Registry settings.

The files and folders that make up a Windows user profile allow each user to have his or her own unique environment. One user's "My Documents" folder can be different from another user's "My Documents" folder because even though each user sees the folder as "My Documents," they are two separate destinations accessed by two separate paths.

In addition to "My Documents," user profiles also include folders such as Desktop, Temporary Internet Files, Start Menu, and Favorites. (Basically, any folder containing files specific to a user is part of the user profile.) User profiles are important in MetaFrame environments since there can be hundreds of users on the same server at the same time, and each needs access to his own custom folders.

In addition to the collection of folders, a user profile also contains Windows Registry settings that are used to maintain the user's individual application preferences and settings. These include the file save locations in Microsoft Word, the proxy settings for Internet Explorer, the mouse cursor and scroll speed of Windows, and mapped printers and network drives.

Registry settings are stored in each user's profile in a file called ntuser.dat. Then, whenever a user logs on to Windows, his preferences are read from the ntuser.dat file in his user profile and merged into the system registry for the session. (Remember from Chapter 4 that the HKEY_CURRENT_USER registry hive maintains the user's settings during the session.)

Because each user has his own HKCU hive (even when multiple users are logged on at the same time), each can have his own settings on a MetaFrame server. This means that each user also has his own `ntuser.dat` file to permanently store his settings.

What about the few applications that use .INI configuration files instead of the registry for their configuration information? How do user profiles support different .INI files for different users? Fortunately, the architecture of Terminal Server allows multiple users to each have their own copies of centralized .INI files, even if these .INI files are stored in common locations. This architecture is set up automatically when a server is placed into "install mode" for application installation. (Refer to the previous chapter for more details on install mode.)

Whenever an application is installed while the server is set to "install mode," any .INI configuration files usually written to common folders are instead diverted to the user profile location. For example, if an application installation procedure tries to create a file called `application.ini` in the `c:\windows\` folder, Terminal Server will add a "Windows" folder to the user profile and put the `application.ini` file in that new folder. Then, whenever the application looks for its application.ini configuration file, it is redirected to the stored in the user profile, not the one in the common Windows folder. This allows each user to have his own unique settings for applications, even if the applications don't properly use the Windows registry.

In order to further understand user profiles, let's examine at a sample one. Figure 5.1 (facing page) lists the files and folders that together make up the "default" user profile. In the real world, all user profiles are different, but this table lists the basics.

It's important to note that every user who logs on to your MetaFrame XP server has some form of user profile, even if that user only runs published applications with no Windows desktop. This is because when you run a published application there is still a Windows desktop executing on the server. MetaFrame XP hides this desktop from the user so that the user can use his own local desktop.

Now that we've reviewed the basics of Windows user profiles, let's take a look at the three different types that there are:

- Local profiles.
- Roaming profiles.
- Mandatory roaming profiles.

Every Windows user profile must be one of these three types. Each is useful in different situations.

*Figure 5.1 Elements of a user profile.*

| File or Folder | Description |
| --- | --- |
| NTUSER.DAT | Registry file containing all HKCU registry settings for that user |
| ntuser.dat.LOG | Transaction log file for ntuser.dat |
| Application Data | User specific application configuration information |
| Cookies | Internet Explorer cookies |
| Desktop | Contents of the Windows Desktop |
| Favorites | Windows Favorites shortcuts |
| Local Settings for the user | Contains Temp, Temporary Internet Files, and History folders |
| My Documents | My Documents |
| SendTo | Shortcuts for the user's "Send To..." context menu |
| Start Menu | Custom shortcuts for the user's Start Menu |
| Windows | Any Windows folder components that are specific to that user, usually configuration and log files |

## User Profile Type 1. Local Profiles

A "local profile" is a user profile stored locally on one computer. Local profiles contain the files, folders, and registry settings for each user as previously discussed. However, local profiles are only applied to the user environment when the user logs on to the computer where the local profile is stored. By default, local profiles are stored in the `\%systemroot%\Profiles \%username%\` folder on Windows NT 4.0 computers. For Windows 2000 computers, local profiles are stored in the `\Documents and Settings \%username%\` folder.

Because local profiles only apply when the user logs on to the particular computer where the profile is stored, they work best when users are allowed to save their settings and configurations in single-server environments.

As outlined in Figure 5.2, whenever a user with a local profile logs on to a Windows NT or Windows 2000 computer, the system will search its local hard drive to see if the user has an existing local profile. If the user's profile is found, it is loaded into memory and its settings are applied. If the system cannot find an existing local profile for the user, then a new local profile is created by making a copy of a generic profile template. This creates a local profile for the user, and any changes made to the configurations or preferences are stored in the user's new local profile. When the user logs off, the system retains the user's local profile so that the next time the user logs on to that computer own customized environment is loaded (complete with pink background and dinosaur cursors).

*Figure 5.2  The user logon process with local profiles*

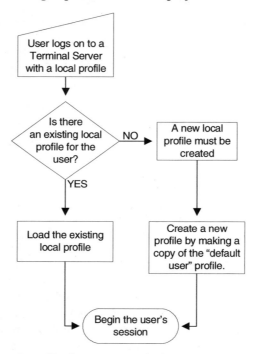

Local profiles work well when users only log on to one server. The main disadvantage of local profiles is that they are always "local" to the computer where they were created. If a user has a local profile on one computer and logs on to another computer, a different local profile will be used or created. There is no way for the second computer to access the profile that the user has created on the first computer.

Obviously, local profiles can cause problems in an environment with multiple MetaFrame XP servers since each server will contain a different local profile for each user. In an environment with five MetaFrame XP servers, each user has five different user profiles. Users would get a different profile depending on which server they logged on to. Confusion would be compounded when users connected to load-balanced applications where they are automatically connected to the least busy server. One day, a user might connect to Server A. The next day, they might get Server B. From the user's standpoint, each day could bring a different profile with a Windows background or different application settings.

In light of this scenario, wouldn't it be great if there was a way to store user profiles in a centralized location, allowing the user to get his own profile no matter what MetaFrame XP server he is logged on to? Roaming profiles accomplish just that.

## User Profile Type 2. Roaming Profiles

A roaming profile is a user profile stored on a network share instead of on a local computer. When the user logs on to a computer, the computer checks to see if that user is configured to use a roaming profile. If so, the computer copies the contents of the user's profile from the network share to the local drive, and the profile is loaded into its memory. In this way each user gets his own environment no matter where he logs on. Any changes that the user makes throughout the session are saved in the profile. When the user logs off, the profile is copied back to the network share. That way, the next time the user logs on, the environment is exactly as they left it, even if they log on to a different computer.

For a user to have a roaming profile, you simply specify the network path where the profile will be stored. (Do this by editing user's properties in User Manager for Domains or Active Directory Users and Computers.) When configuring a user's domain account, you will see two profile fields listed in the user's properties. One is labeled "User Profile" and the other is labeled "Terminal Services Profile." Both of these fields allow you to enter the network share path where the roaming profile will be stored. (In Windows NT 4.0 environments, you must use the version of "User Manager for Domains" from a Windows NT 4.0 Terminal Server Edition server. If you use a "User Manager for Domains" from a regular Windows NT Server, you will not see the extra Terminal Server-specific fields in a user's properties.)

By default these two fields are empty, indicating that the user is configured for a local profile. To configure a roaming profile, you must understand the differences between these fields and how they relate to each other. Let's consider what happens when a domain user logs onto a Terminal Server. You can visualize this process with Figure 5.3 (next page).

*Figure 5.3   The user logon process with roaming profiles*

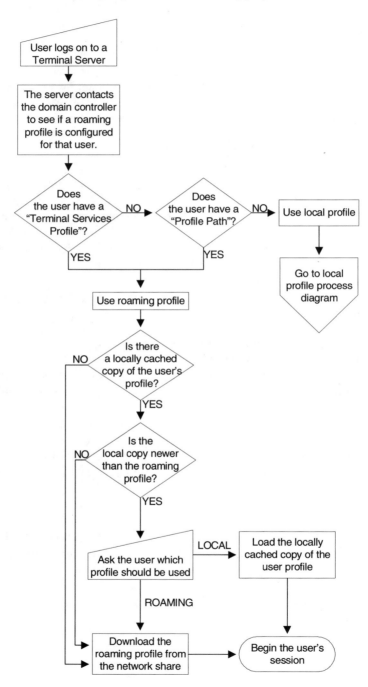

When a domain user logs on to a Terminal Server, the server contacts a domain controller and attempts to load that user's roaming profile from the network path specified in the "Terminal Services Profile" text field property of the user's account. If that field is blank, the server will attempt to load the roaming profile from the path specified in the "Profile Path" text field. If that field is also blank, the server knows that no roaming profile has been specified, and so it creates or uses a local profile.

If a user logs onto a non-Terminal Server, the system will immediately look for the roaming profile in the "Profile Path" location, bypassing the "Terminal Server Profile" text field. This allows you to specify different profiles for users, depending on whether they log on to a Terminal Server or a regular computer. This is very useful in the real world because profiles on Terminal Servers tend to be different from profiles on regular workstations.

When a user with a roaming profile logs off of a computer, the roaming profile is copied from the computer back up to the roaming profile master location. As a result, the user will access the most up-to-date profile the next time he logs on, including any changes made during his last session.

*Figure 5.4  The user logoff process with roaming profiles*

Roaming profiles contain the same components, files, and folders as local profiles. In fact, if you were to compare the two types of profiles, you would find them to be 100% identical. The only difference is a profile stored in the network location specified in the user's domain account properties is called a "roaming profile." If the profile is stored locally on a computer not specified in the user account, it's called a "local profile."

## User Profile Type 3. Mandatory Roaming Profiles

There's an additional type of user profile that offers stricter control over your users known as the "mandatory profile." Mandatory profiles are a form of roaming profiles. They operate in the same way, except that with mandatory profiles, the user's settings are not saved when they log off. This means that any configurations or settings that the user changes are not retained.

Mandatory profiles allow you to create standard profiles distributed to multiple users. They prevent users from "breaking" anything, since their changes do not get copied back up to the master profile location when they log off. The next time they log on, their mandatory profile is downloaded again, exactly the same as it was the first time.

## Why should you care about user profile design?

The options you choose when designing the profiles for your MetaFrame XP environment will impact several areas, including:

- The administrative effort needed to add a server or a user.
- The amount of manual configuration a user must make to begin using MetaFrame XP applications.
- A user's ability to customize his environment.
- The overall continuity of the user's environment.
- The time it takes to launch an application or server session.

Let's detail each of these items that can be affected by the way you design user profiles.

### Adding Users or Servers

If user profiles are designed properly, adding a server or user will be as simple as adding it to the domain. You won't have to worry about custom configurations or settings. However, if user profiles are not designed properly, you will need to perform manual customization before bringing new servers or users into your environment.

### Amount of User Configuration

The first time that a user logs on to a Windows NT or Windows 2000 system, a profile must be created. If this profile is created from scratch, then the user must manually configure everything himself. That could take a fair amount of time, and there's always the risk that the user won't configure things properly. On the other hand, if you pre-configure the user's profile then the user can begin working immediately. All of the options will be set up properly.

### Users' Ability to Customize Their Environment

If you give users mandatory profiles without telling them, then they may try to save their settings, only to find that their settings were not retained the next time they log on. Mandatory profiles will prevent users from saving any preferences or settings to their application environment. Roaming profiles will allow them to save those settings.

## *Continuity of the Users' Environment*

If you use local profiles in an environment where users will try to save the settings from their MetaFrame XP sessions, the users may become confused because their environment could change from day to day as they connect to different servers. This would decrease productivity and increase users' frustration.

If your users use the same roaming profile on their local computer as they do when running sessions on MetaFrame XP servers, configuration settings or data could be lost from one of the sessions, since whichever session is logged off last will overwrite the master profile.

## *Application Launch and Session Start Time*

When a user with a roaming profile logs onto an ICA session on a MetaFrame XP server, he must wait as his profile is copied from its network storage location to the local MetaFrame XP server. If the profile is large or if the network connection is slow, the user will be forced to wait a long time, causing more frustration.

Roaming and mandatory profiles are entirely copied down from the network when the user logs onto a MetaFrame XP server. Roaming profiles are copied back up to the network when the user logs off. Profiles can easily be several or even dozens of megabytes in size. If many users simultaneously log on and try to download their roaming profiles at the same time, it could negatively impact the network. You must consider the size of the profile, the speed of the network, and the number of users logging on or off together to determine if your network can support your users' profiles.

# What are the User Profile Design Options?

When creating your strategy for managing the profiles of your MetaFrame XP users, you'll need to provide answers to several design questions. There are many configuration options available:

- Will you pre-configure any user profiles?
- What types of profiles will be used?
- Will you limit the size of roaming profiles?
- Where will roaming profile master copies be stored?
- How will you manage cached copies of roaming profiles?

### *Will you pre-configure user profiles?*

All settings and configuration information contained in a user profile must be configured at some point. It can either be preconfigured by you before the user logs on or configured by the user after they log on.

If you're using local or roaming profiles, a copy is made of the local computer's "Default User" profile whenever a user who does not have a profile already created logs on. As an administrator, you can use this to your advantage because any changes that you make to the "Default User" profile will be included in every new copy of it.

There are two ways to configure the "Default User" profile. The first is manually:

1. Open the registry editor. In this case, you must use regedt32.exe not regedit.exe.
2. From the menu, choose Registry | Load Hive.
3. Browse to the local "Default User" profile folder.
4. Load "ntuser.dat" from the default user's profile.
5. When the dialog box appears asking for a name for the new hive, enter any name you want. This name is what the newly loaded hive will be called within the Registry Editor. This name is temporary.
6. Make any changes to the newly loaded registry hive.
7. When you have finished, choose Registry | Unload Hive.
8. From Windows Explorer, copy any files and folders that you want to be part of the profile into the "Default User" profile folder.

Rather than configuring the "Default User" profile manually, there is a neat shortcut that is much easier to use:

1. Create a dummy user on the MetaFrame XP server called "Profile Template."
2. Configure that user with the same rights and options as your new users.
3. Log onto the MetaFrame XP server as that "Profile Template" user.
4. Configure each option as you'd like the default to be for all of your new users. This could include file "save as" locations, the Internet Explorer home page, or any other desktop or application settings.
5. Log out and log back on as the administrator.

6. Copy the entire contents of the "Profile Template" user profile folder into the default user profile, overwriting everything.

Either of these methods will update the "Default User" profile, causing new users to receive their profiles based on this modified default user profile. You can make additional changes to the default user profile at any time, but be aware that any changes you make will not affect the current profiles that have already been created.

Also, if you have more than one MetaFrame XP server, then you should copy the "Default User" profile that you modified to all of your servers, since new user profiles are always generated from the local "Default User" path. If you don't copy the profile, you might get users with profiles based on the wrong template, depending on which server they logged on to.

### *Advantages of Preconfiguring User Profiles*

- All users are ensured to receive the proper settings.
- The MetaFrame XP environment will be ready for users as soon as they log on.

### *Disadvantages of Preconfiguring User Profiles*

- Preconfiguration is more work for you.
- All users are forced to get same the profile template.

Instead of preconfiguring user profiles, you can simply choose to have your user profiles generated from the generic "out of the box" profile.

### *Advantages of not Modifying the Default User Profile*

- Allows users to configure things just as they like them.
- Good for environments where nothing will be the same across users.
- Good for environments where policies will be used to enforce settings. (See the next section for information about policies.)
- Less administrative work.

### *Disadvantages of not Modifying the Default User Profile*

- Users must manually configure everything.
- Users might misconfigure a component.

## What type of profile will be used?

At some point you must decide whether you will use local, roaming, or mandatory profiles. As you are making this decision, keep in mind that you do not need to have an "all or nothing" solution. You may want to give some users roaming profiles, while still restricting another group's ability to change settings with mandatory profiles.

Local profiles can be used where the settings in the profile don't matter. This is usually the case when you're using policies to define desktop settings or when users are connecting to restricted published applications without connecting to a full desktop.

Also, if you're just starting out and you only have one MetaFrame XP server, you can begin with local profiles. As your environment grows, you can copy the existing local profiles to network share locations; allowing them to be used as roaming profiles.

### Advantages of Local Profiles

- They are the default option that works right out of the box.
- No administrative configuration is needed.
- Users can create a full, custom environment.
- Users can configure and change any settings.

### Disadvantages of Local Profiles

- Only applied to local servers.
- Users can configure and change (break) any settings.

The next option is roaming profiles. Roaming profiles are used most often in real world environments for the convenience that they provide over local profiles.

### Advantages of Roaming Profiles

- The same user profile can be applied across servers.
- Users can create a full, custom environment.
- Users can configure and change any settings.

### Disadvantages of Roaming Profiles

- The network share location where the master profile is stored must be close to the MetaFrame XP server where users log on.
- Users can configure and change (break) any settings.

- There is no way to disable a roaming profile for users on specific machines

Finally, mandatory profiles are mostly used in locked-down environments, although they are not necessary if policies are configured properly.

### Advantages of Mandatory Profiles

- Good for locked-down environments.
- Users cannot configure or change any settings.

### Disadvantages of Mandatory Profiles

- User cannot configure or change any settings.
- No user settings are saved between sessions.
- There is no way to disable a mandatory profile for users on specific machines

## Will you limit the size of roaming profiles?

By default, user profiles contain many files and folders. Because every user's roaming profile is copied to the MetaFrame XP server at logon and copied to the master network share location at logoff, it is important to keep the roaming profile as small as possible.

Left unchecked, a user's profile can easily grow to dozens or even hundreds of megabytes. When a user logs on, they must wait for the entire profile to be copied to the MetaFrame XP server from the master network share. If the profile is large, the logon process will be slow. It will seem to "hang" while the profile is copied. This is easily the most frequent cause of slow logons in MetaFrame XP environments.

There are a few strategies that you can use to limit the size of roaming profiles:

- Redirect certain folders to network locations outside the user's profile.
- Exclude certain default folders from the roaming profile.
- Apply an artificial size limit which will not allow the profile to exceed a certain MB size.

Let's take a look at what each of these strategies entails.

### Redirect Folders to Network Locations Outside of the User's Profile

By default, any folders that contain user-specific data are part of the user profile. These include folders containing configuration information and application settings and folders containing large amounts of user data, like the "My Documents" folder. If the "My Documents" folder is part of a user's roaming profile, then the profile can grow rather large as the user stores more and more documents in it.

To mitigate this size issue, you have the option of "redirecting" certain folders to locations outside of the user profile. For example, this redirection could allow the "My Documents" folder to point to a static network location that never changes, instead of a folder inside the user's roaming profile. Users with a redirected "My Documents" folder continue to open, save, and browse "My Documents" as usual. They would not be aware that any redirection is taking place.

The advantage to redirection is that the contents of the "My Documents" folder would be stored in one location. This content would not be copied to and from the MetaFrame XP server with the rest of the roaming profile. Users would access a single "My Documents" network location, no matter what Meta-Frame XP server they use. Often, these folders are redirected to the user's home drive. (More on home drives in the next section.)

As an administrator, you must choose which folders to redirect from user profiles. Choosing these folders creates a balance between keeping the user profile as small as possible while allowing users to have fast, local access to their data.

You can evaluate which folders to redirect on a folder-by-folder basis. If a folder contains configuration information or data that will be accessed in every session, then you should not redirect it. However, folders containing user data files are good candidates for redirection because not all user files are used during every session. A user's "My Documents" folder might be 50MB, containing 200 Word documents. However, throughout the course of a Meta-Frame XP session, a user will only actually use a fraction of those documents. There is no reason that all 200 documents should be copied to the MetaFrame XP server every time the user logs on.

The one exception to this rule is the "Desktop" folder. Users often store files on their Windows desktop, which corresponds to the "Desktop" folder in their user profile. Even though this folder may contain large amounts of user data, you should not redirect the desktop folder to a location outside of the user profile. The desktop folder was designed to be a local folder on each computer. If you redirect it to a remote network location, then the MetaFrame XP server will continually refresh it across the network, adversely affecting the performance of your network and your MetaFrame XP server.

### Advantages of Redirecting Folders

- Redirected folders are not part of the roaming profile that is frequently copied across the network.

- Profiles can be smaller, allowing quicker logon times.

### Disadvantages of Redirecting Folders

- Redirected folders must be accessed across the network from within MetaFrame XP sessions.

### Procedure for Redirecting Folders

Redirecting folders is a "user" registry setting of the MetaFrame XP servers. Folder redirection can be set manually with the registry editor or applied via a policy. There are many folders that can be redirected, including the following partial list:

| | |
|---|---|
| Application Data | Network Neighborhood |
| Cache | My Documents |
| Cookies | My Pictures |
| Favorites | Start Menu |
| History | Templates |
| Local Settings | |

When specifying a target for the redirected folder, you may enter a UNC name instead of a hard-coded path. If your target path ends with the `%username%` variable (example: `\\servername\sharename\%username%`) then the path will automatically be created, so long as the user has "modify" share and NTFS rights.

### Registry Location

A user's folders can be redirected in the registry with the following path: `HKCU\Microsoft\Windows\Current Version\Explorer\User Shell Folders\`

This registry folder contains several values. When you are editing the registry, you can change the data of any value to point to any path you wish. UNC paths are acceptable.

### System Policy Editor Location

The system policy editor for Windows 2000 or Windows NT 4 can also be used to redirect folders. When using the system policy editor, the following folders can be redirected:

| | |
|---|---|
| Programs | Desktop |
| Startup | Network Neighborhood |
| Start Menu | |

To configure folder redirection, navigate to the following path: User | Windows NT Shell | Custom Folders.

### Group Policy Location

Within the Windows 2000 Group Policy MMC snap-in, you can redirect the following folders:

| | |
|---|---|
| Application Data | Desktop |
| My Documents | My Pictures |
| Start Menu | |

Within the group policy snap-in, navigate to the following path: User Configuration | Windows Settings | Folder Redirection.

### Exclude Certain Folders from Being Copied to the Roaming Profile

You may determine that some folders in a user's profile contain data not worth saving. In order to further decrease the size of roaming profiles, you can choose to exclude those folders from the roaming profiles altogether. Excluding folders causes them not to be copied up to the master profile network share after a user logs off.

In Windows 2000, by default, the Local Settings, Temporary Internet Files, History, and Temp folders are excluded from a user's roaming profile. If you choose to exclude any additional folders or any folders in Windows NT 4, you should do this before you go live with your MetaFrame XP environment.

When a user with a roaming profile logs onto a MetaFrame XP server, the entire contents of the roaming profile are copied to the MetaFrame XP server from the user's master profile network share, regardless of whether you have excluded certain directories.

Directory exclusion only affects roaming profiles as they are copied from the MetaFrame XP server back to the master profile network share, after the user logs off. This only indirectly affects the size of the profile at the master location, because if you implement directory exclusion after a user has estab lished a roaming profile with a master copy stored on the network share, the directory exclusion will not make the profile any smaller.

The reason for this is that the excluded folders will already be part of the user's master roaming profile on the network share. They were put there when the user logged off with a roaming profile before you configured the directory exclusion. Even though the newly-excluded directories will never be copied from the MetaFrame XP server up to the master profile location when the user logs off, they will already exist in the master copy, and so they will be copied down every time a user logs on.

If you want to exclude directories from the roaming profiles of existing users with established roaming profiles, you need to manually delete the folders from their roaming profile master locations. Of course you won't need to do this for new users that have never logged on, because their master profile will be created on the network only after they log off of a MetaFrame XP server that has the exclusion applied.

If you choose to exclude directories from roaming profiles, be sure to set the same exclusions on each of your MetaFrame XP servers. Even one server without set exclusions would cause the unwanted folders to be copied to the master profile network share, becoming a permanent part of the user profile copied down every time a user logs on. You would then need to manually delete the folders from the master profile.

### Advantages of Excluding Certain Folders

- Reduces the size of the roaming profile.

### Disadvantages of Excluding Certain Folders

- Information in the excluded folders is not retained between sessions.

### Procedure for Excluding Certain Folders

User profile folder exclusion requires at least Windows NT 4.0 Service Pack 4, although this shouldn't be a problem since MetaFrame XP requires Windows NT 4.0 Service Pack 5. Folder exclusion is a registry setting that can be set manually or set via a user policy. (User policies are covered in detail in the next section.)

### Registry Location

In the registry, folders can be excluded via the following path:

Key: HKCU\Software\Microsoft\Windows NT\Current
Version\Winlogon

Value: ExcludeProfileDirs

Type: REG_SZ

Data: Directory names to be excluded, relative to the root path of the
profile. Multiple directories can be separated by semicolons.
(Example: temp;local settings\temporary internet files)

### System Policy Editor Location

Note: Many of the design options listed in this section can be implemented
via a system policy or a group policy (in addition to the manual registry setting). System and group policies are fully discussed in the next section of this
book, but the references are made here so that you'll know where to implement these profile settings once you read about policies.

User | Windows NT User Profiles | Exclude directories in roaming profile.

### Group Policy Location

User Configuration | Administrative Templates | System | Logon / Logoff |
Exclude Directories in Roaming Profile.

### Apply an Artificial Size Limit

In addition to the various methods by which roaming profile size is kept under
control, there is another method that can be used as a last resort if other methods fail. As an administrator, you can specify the maximum size, in kilobytes,
of roaming profiles on MetaFrame XP servers. This size limit acts as a sort of
"circuit breaker," kicking in when the profile gets too large.

In addition to the actual size limit specification, there are several other options you can configure:

- Should the user's registry file be included in the calculation of the
  profile size?
- Should users be notified when their profile exceeds the maximum?
- Do you want them to be notified with a custom message?
- How often should that message be displayed?

### *Advantages of Setting a Profile Size Limit*

- Guarantees that a profile won't get too big.
- Works in concert with other methods.

### Disadvantages of Setting a Profile Size Limit

- Should not be used as a surrogate for other methods.
- Can cause user confusion when the limit is reached.

### Procedure for Setting a Profile Size Limit

Limiting the size of a roaming profile can be accomplished by configuring a series of registry keys manually or through a policy. The artificial limit can be set up to 30MB. If you would like to set a limit larger than 30 MB, refer to the Microsoft Knowledge Base article Q290324.

**System Policy Editor Location**
User I Windows NT User Profiles I Limit Profile Size.

**Group Policy Location**
User Configuration I Administrative Templates I System I Logon / Logoff I Limit Profile Size.

### Choosing Not to Limit the Roaming Profile Size
Even after reviewing the options available for limiting the size of user profiles, you might make the decision not to limit the size. In small environments, it is not worth the extra effort that goes in to managing profiles.

### Advantages of Doing Nothing

- Least amount of work.

### Disadvantages of Doing Nothing

- Logons can be slow.
- MetaFrame XP servers can run out of disk space.
- If the environment grows, you will need to address profile size at some point.

## Where will roaming profile master copies be stored?
The convenience of using roaming profiles produces one side effect: the roaming profile must be copied over the network when the user logs on and logs off. In a perfect world, you would always be able to store the master copy of a user's roaming profile near the MetaFrame XP servers that they will be using. In the real world, this is not always possible, specifically with users that travel or connect to multiple MetaFrame XP servers in multiple locations. Consider the environment illustrated in Figure 5.5 (next page).

*Figure 5.5 Users often connect to multiple MetaFrame XP servers*

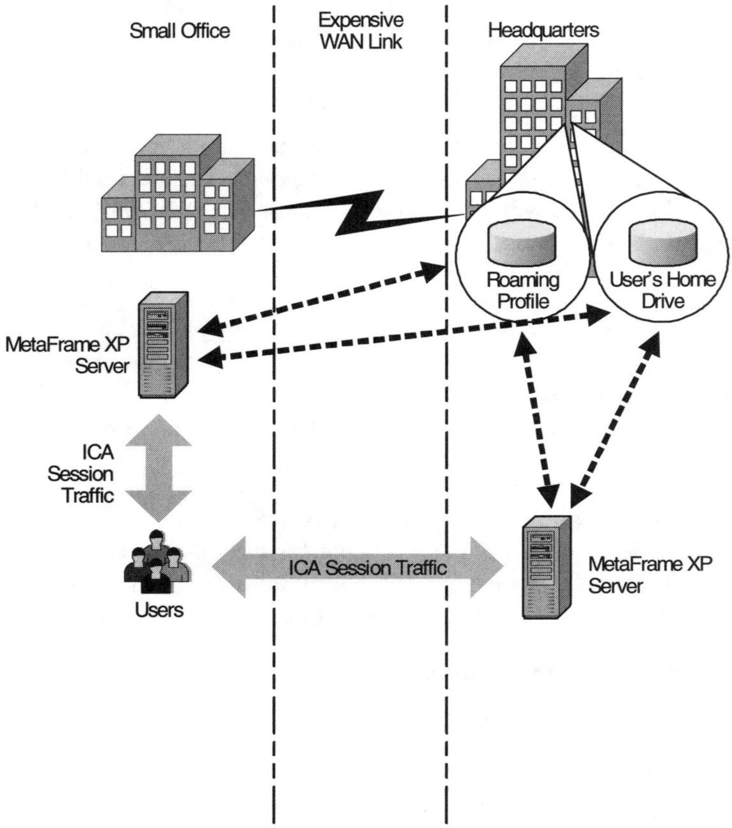

In environments such as this, where users log into multiple locations, the location of the master roaming profile becomes more difficult. You need to choose a location from which the user can copy the profile no matter where they log on.

## How will you manage cached copies of roaming profiles?

When a user with a roaming profile logs on to a MetaFrame XP server, the profile is copied from its network storage location to the local MetaFrame XP server. After the user logs off, the profile is copied from the local MetaFrame XP server back up to the network location. At this point, by default, the Meta-Frame XP server retains a local copy of the user's profile. This copy is saved locally so that if the user logs onto that server again before the roaming profile changes, the roaming profile does not need to be copied across the network, saving time and bandwidth.

However, in large environments, this profile "caching" could cause the MetaFrame XP servers to run out of disk space, sincethere could be hundreds of user profiles saved locally. After all, any user that logs on once will have a locally cached profile taking up space. Plus, the more servers you have, the less likely it is that a user will actually connect to the same physical server twice in a row.

To combat this, you can configure your MetaFrame XP servers not to retain the locally cached copy of roaming profiles. In doing so, whenever a user logs off of a MetaFrame XP server, his profile is copied back up to its master network share location and the local copy is deleted.

You can save server hard drive space by deleting locally cached profiles from MetaFrame XP servers. However, this hard drive space could come at the price of logon speed. By configuring MetaFrame XP servers to delete all locally cached copies of roaming profiles, every user's profile will be copied across the network when they log on, without exception. If the MetaFrame XP server had an up-to-date locally cached copy of the user profile, logon speed is faster because the profile would not have to be copied across the network.

Many people wonder if it is worth trading hard drive space for logon speed. Consider this situation:

> If a user with a session on Server A logs off, her profile will be copied to her master network profile location. Her locally cached profile on Server A will have the same timestamp as the roaming master copy.

> If the user then runs a session on Server B, when she logs off, her profile will be copied to her master profile location. Her locally cached profile on Server B will now have the same timestamp as the roaming master copy. At the next logon, if she logs on to Server B, no network copy will be needed because the local cached profile is the same as the network version. However, sif he logs on to Server A, the network copy will take place because the master profile has been updated since she last logged onto Server A. Even though Server A copied the profile to the network share, Server B overwrote it later. In this two server environment, the user only has a 50% chance that she will log on to the server that has the same

profile as the network, thus saving the network transfer time. If there were ten servers, she would only have a one in ten chance. Twenty servers would be one in twenty.

Saving locally cached copies of roaming profiles was designed for traditional (non-Terminal Server) environments, where users were logging on to the same workstation every day.

Having the locally cached copy of the profile only helps if the local profile is as new as the remote roaming profile. In MetaFrame XP environments, the hard disk space is usually more important than the chance of good network speed, causing most administrators to configure their servers to delete locally cached roaming user profiles.

### Advantages of Deleting Cached Copies of Roaming Profiles

- Saves drive space.

### Disadvantages of Deleting Cached Copies of Roaming Profiles

- Could cause slower logons.

### Procedure for Deleting Cached Copies of Roaming Profiles

This feature, like so many others, is simply a registry setting on your Meta-Frame XP servers. That means you can configure it manually with the registry editor or you can specify it in a policy.

**Registry Location**

Key: HKLM\Software\Microsoft\Windows NT\Current Version\Winlogon\

Value: DeletaRoamingCache

Type: REG_DWORD

Data: 1 (enable)

**System Policy Editor Location**

Computer | Windows NT User Profiles | Delete cached copies of roaming profiles.

**Group Policy Location**

Computer Configuration | Administrative Templates | System | Logon | Delete cached copies of roaming profiles.

Instead of deleting user profiles to save storage space, some people choose to store them in a location other than the default system drive. This allows the profiles to be stored on a large drive, since many of the MetaFrame XP servers' system drives are extremely small.

There is no real disadvantage to moving cached profiles to another drive, as long as that drive is local. If you try to put cached profiles on a remote drive or network share, you will get extremely poor performance. All session interaction between the MetaFrame XP server and the local profile assumes that the profile is local.

### Advantages of Changing Cached Copy Location

- Often MetaFrame XP servers have large drives other than the system drive.

- Get the performance of cached profiles without the risk of running out of disk space.

### Disadvantages of Changing Cached Copy Location

- Cached drive must be local to each server.

### Procedure for Changing Cache Copy Location

When you change the profile path, you can only change the profile root directory, which means that the "Default User" and "All Users" profiles are also moved to the new location.

**Registry Location**

Key: HKLM\SOFTWARE\Microsoft\Windows NT\Current Version\ProfileList

Value: ProfilesDirectory

Type: REG_EXPAND_SZ

Data: The new folder (Windows 2000 default is %SystemDrive%\ Documents and Settings.)

## Considerations when Designing User Profiles

Now that we've reviewed all of the options available when choosing how to apply user profiles, let's consider the questions that you need to answer. Answering these questions should make your design pretty simple:

- Are users authenticating individually?

- Does each user need his own customized environment?

- How much network bandwidth is available?

- What are the locations of servers that users will log on to?

### User Connections and User Authentication

If users are connecting anonymously, then they're not logging in with a unique domain account that will need to support individualized profiles. You can, however, configure a user profile that will be used by the anonymous accounts so that all anonymous users have any needed custom settings. On the other hand, if users are connecting explicitly, then you can support them with whatever type of user profile meets your needs. (See Chapter 15 for more information about explicit and anonymous applications.)

### Custom User Environments

If all of your users will share the same environment, then your profile design job is straightforward—you won't need to worry about custom profiles for each user. If users do need custom environments, then you will need to spend time thinking about how user profiles will be used.

### Network Bandwidth Availability

If bandwidth is plentiful, then you won't need to worry about the location of the master roaming profile network share or the size of roaming profiles. If bandwidth is scarce, you may spend significant time designing these components.

### Server Location

If all of your MetaFrame servers are in the same location then it's relatively simple to decide on the location of the server that will contain master roaming profiles. Of course in the real world, it's usually not that easy. If you have users that log onto MetaFrame XP servers in different physical locations or across WAN links, the decision of the master profile server location becomes difficult. You need to balance profile size and functionality with loading speed and network bandwidth availability.

# User Policies

While user profiles allow users to customize the settings of their own environments, policies allow you (the administrator) to force settings in your users' environments. Policies (and their mandatory configuration settings) can be applied to servers globally, affecting all users that logon, or conditionally, affecting only specific users that logon. This conditional application can be based on user accounts or group memberships.

There are two types of user policies: Microsoft Windows user policies and Citrix MetaFrame user policies. Conceptually, these two types of policies work in the same way. Windows user policies allow you to control Windows-related settings, and Citrix user policies allow you to control Citrix-related settings.

# Windows User Policies

Before we look at the details of how Microsoft Windows policies work, it's important to understand the differences between policies and user profiles.

## Differences between Windows User Policies and Profiles

Both policies and user profiles affect registry settings. A user profile contains registry settings (in the ntuser.dat file) that are used to create the user's unique HKEY_CURRENT_USER registry hive when they log on. Policies also contain registry settings. They dictate which values are allowed or not allowed in the HKEY_CURRENT_USER registry hive as its being created from the user profile. Policies can also affect computer-wide HKEY_LOCAL_MACHINE settings, which are applied as the computer is booted before any users log on.

Application settings and configurations that are maintained in the registry can be set with either a user profile or a policy. If there is a conflict, the policy setting will take precedence over the user profile setting.

For example, a user might configure their desktop background to be bright red. Doing this would set the bright red color value in a desktop settings registry key in the user's HKEY_CURRENT_USER registry hive. This updated value would become part of the user's profile, taking effect at every logon. At any time, the user could decide to change the desktop background color.

However, if you wanted to force the user's desktop to be a specific color, then you would apply a policy. The policy would affect the exact same value in the same registry location as when the user set it (in their profile), except that the policy could not be changed by the user. That's all policies really are—an administrator's way to force settings onto users.

Of course, you don't generally use policies to set the desktop color in Windows. You would use policies to set elements that affect how the users use the system such as Start menu items, file save locations, search options, and local drive access.

*Figure 5.6  Differences between profiles and policies*

| User Profile | Policy |
| --- | --- |
| Applied to a user | Applied to a computer, group, or user |
| Only one per user | Many can be layered per user |
| Settings are the user's choice | Settings are the administrator's choice |
| Affects the user's registry hive | Affects the user's or server's registry hive |
| Registry settings, folders, files | Registry settings only |

People often wonder whether they should use profiles or policies to manage the user environment. In the real world, the two are meant to complement each other and are used together. Situations are rare where one is used to the exclusion of the other.

## Creating and Editing Windows Policies

Policies are created and edited in different ways, depending on what type of policy you are working with.

Windows NT 4.0-compatible policies, which can be applied to Windows NT 4.0 and Windows 2000 servers as well as Windows NT 4.0 domains, are created and edited with the System Policy Editor (poledit.exe). Windows 2000 policies, configured as part of the Active Directory, are edited with the Group Policy snap-in for the Microsoft Management Console (gpedit.msc).

Since policies are no more than a collection of registry keys and values, these policy editing tools are merely graphical interfaces that allow you to set registry values. These registry values can then be directly applied to the local server or saved as policy files.

Whether you're using Windows NT or Windows 2000, you'll need at least one ADM policy template file in order to create a policy. ADM files contain all of the policy settings and options, as well as the corresponding registry keys and values needed to create a policy. ADM template files are added as plug-ins to the policy editing utilities. Without any ADM template files plugged-in, the policy editing tools are useless, kind of like the MMC without any snap-ins. Once the ADM files are plugged-in to the policy editing utility, you can point-and-click your way through the configuration of policies.

ADM policy templates are simply text files with the ".adm" extension, such as winnt.adm or common.adm. The policy editors for both Windows NT and Windows 2000 come with several ADM files plugged-in out of the box. These default ADM files let you configure policies for several Windows options. However, if you have other applications installed, such as Microsoft Word, you'll probably want to extend your policy editor to include Microsoft Word options. This is because the default ADM templates only cover Windows options. You can't use them to configure any Microsoft Word options.

In order to create policies that include Microsoft Word options, you would need to obtain a Microsoft Word ADM policy template file. There are hundreds of Microsoft Word templates available. You can download the "official" ones from Microsoft's web site. (They are included as part of the Office Resource Kit.) As soon as you add the Microsoft Word ADM template to your policy editing utility, you will instantly see options for configuring Microsoft Word settings. For example with Microsoft Word, these policy settings include paths to office assistants, the ability to disable certain features, and menu options.

You will need to find (or create) ADM policy templates for all the applications that you want to regulate with policies. Check out the THIN list at http://thethin.net for a great collection of ADM policy templates.

Really, ADM policy template files are nothing more than cool interfaces that give you a graphical way to set and force desktop and application settings onto users.

## Citrix User Policies

One of the new features included with Feature Release 2 for MetaFrame XP is "Citrix User Policies." Citrix User Policies are similar to Windows user policies, except that Citrix user policies only contain Citrix-specific information. You configure Citrix user policies via the CMC, and you can apply them to groups or users. You can create multiple policies and set relative priorities, allowing you to create an extremely granular environment. Citrix user policies are the "killer app" of Feature Release 2. They make the Feature Release 2 upgrade worth paying for.

There are dozens of different configuration options that you can specify within Citrix policies, including client device settings, drives, printers, ports, limiting concurrent logon sessions (with XPa or XPe), shadowing, and encryption. Basically, Citrix user policies allow you to turn on or off any Citrix setting on a per-user or a per-group basis. The policies are then stored in the IMA data store.

The nice thing about Citrix user policies is that they apply to the user session itself, and so are enforced no matter what type of client or connection each user is using. In fact, Citrix user policies override all settings that are configured in other places, including the CMC-configured properties of a server or farm.

Refer to the chart in Appendix C of this book for a listing of all the Meta-Frame XP configuration options (including policies) and where they can be set.

## Creating Citrix User Policies

Creating a Citrix user policy is a two-step procedure. First, you need to create the policy itself. This is where you specify its name and configure the policy rules for it, such as enabling client drive mappings, disabling LPT port mapping, etc.

Every Citrix user policy contains dozens of policy rules, and you can set each individual policy rule to be "Enabled," "Disabled," or "Not Configured." Let's look at an example to understand what each setting means. If you create a Citrix user policy and set the client drive mapping policy rule to be enabled (by highlighting "Client Drive Mapping" in the left pane and selecting the "Rule Enabled" radio button in the right pane), then all users or groups who have that policy applied will have client drive mapping enabled. Similarly, if you set the policy rule to "Rule Disabled," then all users or groups who have that particular policy applied will find that client drive mappings are disabled.

The "Rule Not Configured" option is the default setting for all policy rules in new policies. This option indicates that this rule is not set to "Enabled" or "Disabled," allowing it to be configured by another policy. In our example, configuring the client drive mapping rule for "Rule Not Configured" would mean that the policy would not affect client drive mappings, allowing us to set the options for client drive mappings as part of the server's connection properties, or as part of another policy applied to different people. In the real world, you use the "Not Configured" policy option whenever a Citrix policy option is going to be configured somewhere outside of the policy.

## Applying Citrix User Policies

Once you create and configure a Citrix user policy, it doesn't affect anything until you apply it to users or groups. You can literally have hundreds of Citrix policies listed in the CMC that don't affect anything if you don't apply them to anyone.

You can create as many Citrix user policies as you want. In fact, large server farms might have dozens of policies. Applying Citrix policies to users or groups is pretty straightforward (CMC | Policies | Right-click on the Policy | Assign Users).

Citrix user policies get interesting when you have users that are affected by multiple policies. For example, you might decide to create one policy called "Farm Users" and apply it to your "Domain Users" group so that it affects everyone who logs on to your servers. You would use this "Farm Users" policy to configure all your MetaFrame configuration options.

Then, you might decide to create a second policy called "Remote Users" and apply it to users who dial-in to your MetaFrame environment. You could use this policy to turn off bandwidth-intensive features, such as client drive mapping.

However, if you do this a user logging on to your MetaFrame XP server from home would have two Citrix policies applied—the "Farm Users" policy applied to their domain group, and the "Remote Users" policy applied to their user account. On the surface, this may seem fine, but what happens if there is a conflict between settings from policy to policy? What happens, for example, if the "Farm Users" policy is configured to enable sound, but the "Remote Users" policy applied to the user is configured to disable sound?

You might think that "standard" Windows rules apply here and that the most restrictive policy settings would win out. However, policies don't work like that. When you configure multiple policies in a server farm, you need to "rank" the policies in order of precedence.

Every Citrix user policy in your server farm has a rank. A policy's rank (or "priority") is a unique integer that directly affects the order in which it is applied. The first policy that you create has a priority of "1." The next policy you create has a priority of "2," and so on.

Whenever a user logs on that has more than one policy applied (via their user account and any groups that they belong to), the system resolves any conflicting policy settings by using the setting from the policy with the higher priority. (Remember that with Citrix user policies, a smaller priority number equates to a higher priority. The policy whose priority is set to "1" has the highest preference, and so on.)

You can change the priority of any policy at any time via the CMC (CMC | Right click on the policy name | Priority). One interesting quirk about the

CMC is that by default, the CMC displays the list of the farm's Citrix user policies in "list" mode. As with anything in the CMC, "list" mode shows the policy names only. It does not indicate their priorities. Even worse, the CMC lists the policies in alphabetical order, not priority order. This means that the policy order you see may not be the order in which they are applied.

To effectively work with Citrix user policies in the CMC, you need to change the CMC's view to "details" mode (CMC | View Menu | Details). This mode will show the policy's name, priority, status, and description. Once you switch the view to details mode, you can click the "priority" column header in the CMC to sort the list of the policies in the order that they will be applied.

As you start to apply multiple policies, you will begin to appreciate the "Rule Not Configured" policy option, since this option does not affect the policy rule one way or the other. While the "Enabled" setting will force that option to be enabled and the "Disabled" setting will force that option to be disabled, the "Not Configured" setting causes the policy processor to ignore that option—allowing it to be applied with a different policy (or with a different method altogether, such as a Citrix connection option).

### Managing Citrix User Policies

Once you create more than a few Citrix user policies, they will become hard to manage. The main challenge is that when you have several policies applied to different users and groups, it can be hard to figure out the "effective" policies that are applied to single users. This comes from the fact that a single user account could have multiple policies in effect for it, depending on the groups that the user belongs to and the policies that affect those groups.

The easiest way to find all the policies that affect a single user is to use the CMC's "search" capabilities (New with SP-2). Right-click on the "Policies" item in the left-hand pane, and then click "Search" from the little menu that pops up. You can then search for policies that apply to a specific user or group.

Whenever you perform a search, your search results will include all policies that apply to the user or group you searched for. The results will also contain an additional policy called "Resultant Policy" with a priority of "0." You can double-click this "Resultant Policy" to see the effective policy rules that will be applied to the user or group that you searched.  Basically, this Resultant Policy is like a query result that sorts through the policy rules and priorities of all policies that apply to the user or group you searched for, and then displays the specific policy rules and configurations that will actually apply. Since the Resultant Policy is not a "real" policy, you cannot change any policy options when you view it.

If you ever run into problems when using Citrix user policies, the Resultant Policy is an excellent troubleshooting tool. It can help you figure out what's really happening, especially if you have many policies.

Another technique that's useful when troubleshooting policies is to disable certain policies. At any time, you can disable a policy via the CMC (CMC | Right-click on the Policy | Disable). Disabling a policy causes it not to be applied as users log on, although the policy is still listed in the CMC.

If you're doing a lot of troubleshooting with policies in the CMC, remember that each MetaFrame XP server in the farm needs to receive the updated policy information from the IMA data store before you can successfully test new policy settings. Some people make a policy change and then instantly log on to a server to test that change. Then they curse when their change did not work, when in fact they just didn't wait long enough for the server that they tested on to receive that change. (Remember that any time you change anything in the CMC, the CMC writes the change to the IMA data store, and each server's local host cache must receive the new information from the data store.)

An easy way to ensure that a MetaFrame XP server has received the change from the IMA data store is to use Windows Explorer to view the timestamp of the local host cache. (The local host cache was discussed in Chapter 3.) By default, the local host cache is `%systemroot%\Program Files\Citrix \Independent Management Architecture\imalhc.mdb`. Most people keep one session logged on to the MetaFrame server with an Explorer window open to the path. Then they make their policy change within the CMC. As soon as the timestamp of the local host cache file changes to the current time, they log in via another session to test the policy.

### Advantages of Citrix User Policies

- Because they are applied at the server level, they apply no matter what type of client is connecting.
- Multiple policies and be layered and ranked to create customized environments.
- They provide an easy way to configure and control MetaFrame options.

### Disadvantages of Citrix User Policies

- Feature Release 2 is required.

## Why should you care about user policy design?

Now that you understand the basics or how user policies work, you can see that there are two reasons that you need to think about user policy design on your system:

- Policies affect your users' ability to customize their own environment.
- Policies affect the security of your system.

### *Users' Ability to Customize Their Environment*

If policies are too restrictive, then users will not be able to do their jobs or to fully use the system. If policies are not restrictive enough, security and integrity of the MetaFrame XP system will be affected. Users may be able to use unauthorized programs or even worse, they may be able to access configuration and system administration areas of the server that affect everyone.

### *Security*

User profiles and policies will directly affect the options and settings users see in their MetaFrame XP sessions. Properly designed policies will allow them to use the servers without risk of the users changing inappropriate settings or accessing unwanted areas.

Shane Broomhall, a Citrix instructor, says it best:

> Most likely, you have a certain user in your environment with a copy of "MCSE for Complete Brain-Dead Idiots in 24 Hours" on his desk. This person is the really dangerous one. The one with a little knowledge and even less common sense. The one who (just by reading one thing) can completely break his desktop computer. From your perspective, if this person has broken his desktop by playing around with it (because it was not locked down) it's no big deal, because he has only really affected himself. However, now that you're using Meta-Frame XP, when this user does the same thing with a MetaFrame XP desktop that has not been locked down properly, he's affecting potentially hundreds of other users. It is this user that forces us to spend time designing policies and profiles.

## What are the user policy design options?

When it comes down to actually designing your policies, you have a few options depending on your platform.

## What type of NT 4.0 policies will you use?

If your MetaFrame servers are running Terminal Server 4.0, you can create and apply policies in three different ways:

- Local computer policy.
- Domain-wide policy.
- Manual, computer-based policy.

Windows NT 4.0 policies are configured with System Policy Editor, available in the administrative tools or from the command line (poledit.exe). Policy Editor has the ability to open two types of policies:

- The local registry.
- Policies saved as files with the ".pol" extension.

### NT 4.0 Local Computer Policies

You can edit the policy of the local server by opening its registry from within the System Policy Editor (File | Open Registry). Editing the policy in this way produces the same result as if you manually edited the registry. Most people choose to use the System Policy Editor because it is easier than editing the registry. With Policy Editor, you don't have to know where anything is or what the options are. Just find what you want to change and check the box.

While editing the local registry of a server will work, most people choose not to because it must be manually done on each server.

### Advantages of Local Computer Policies

- Simple to apply.
- Easy to change.
- Works well for single-server environments.
- Allows each server to have unique policy settings.

### Disadvantages of Local Computer Policies

- Must be manually configured at every server.
- Do not scale very well.

There are two ways that NT 4.0 policies can be applied to more than one computer. The first allows you to create a policy that is applied to all computers in the entire domain.

## NT 4.0 Domain-Wide Policies

Instead of manually editing the registry of every MetaFrame XP server in your environment with System Policy Editor, you can create a single policy applied to an entire domain. To do this:

1. Use System Policy Editor to create the settings and configurations you want. This can include entries for multiple computers, groups, or users.

2. Save the policy as a file called "ntconfig.pol."

3. Copy ntconfig.pol to the domain controller with the master Netlogon$ share (repl$ share).

4. Directory replication between the domain controllers' Netlogon$ share will ensure that this policy file is updated on all domain controllers. There is no additional configuration that must be done.

You'll have many users, groups, and computers that will all require unique policy settings within your domain. Users and groups may have unique HKEY_CURRENT_USER settings, and Terminal Servers may have unique HKEY_LOCAL_MACHINE settings. Fortunately, you can add different policy settings that apply to different users, groups, and computers—all within a single ntconfig.pol file. From within the System Policy Editor (as in step one above), click the Add User, Add Group, or Add Computer button to add a specific user, group, or server that does not get the Default User or Default Computer policy settings. (There are more details in the System Policy Editor's help menu.) If you decide to create custom policies for users, you should first create a policy for the "administrator" that is excluded from other policies that you create. This is important because it is very easy to "accidentally" create a policy that locks everyone out of important system functions, including the administrator.

By specifying unique policy settings for your MetaFrame XP servers in a domain policy file, you can create restrictive computer policies that only apply to the MetaFrame XP servers in your domain.

One of the downsides to creating policies that affect the entire domain is the fact the users log onto MetaFrame XP servers with the same accounts they use at their local workstations. Because of this, it's not possible to create user-level policies that apply on some computers and not others. All computers on the domain will get the same ntconfig.pol policy file from the domain controllers.

Additionally, because only one policy file can exist for the entire domain, that policy will become quite large as it fills with dozens of computer, user, and group settings. Anytime the policy is applied, the target computer will need to sort through the entire policy, looking for entries that apply to it. If users or groups are specified in the policy, the computer must sort through the policy when they log on, increasing logon time and network utilization.

### Advantages of Creating NT 4 Domain-Wide Policies

- Simple to create and implement.
- Easy to maintain, since only one file needs to be updated for the entire domain.
- Multiple computer, user, and group entries can exist in the single policy file.

### Disadvantages of Creating NT 4 Domain-Wide Policies

- Complex policies can take a long time to be applied.
- Large policies could increase logon time for users.
- "All or nothing" approach. There is no way to allow the policy to apply to users when they log into some computers but not others.

### NT 4.0 Manual Computer-Based Policies

Instead of applying a single policy to an entire domain, it is possible to create a policy that is only applied to selected computers. This will allow you to have different policies for different computers.

In order to do this:

1. Use System Policy Editor to create the settings and configurations you want.
2. Save the policy as a file with any name.
3. Copy the policy file to a location where it can be accessed by the computers you want to apply it to.
4. Each computer that you want to use the policy file must be configured for it. To do this, you must edit the registry of each computer. (See the procedure below.)

Even though you must manually configure each computer to access the policy file, you can change the policy for all the configured computers simply by updating the policy file. (Open it in Policy Editor, make the changes, save the policy file.)

### *Advantages of Creating Manual Computer-Based Policies*

• Different policies can be applied to different computers.

• These "localized" policy files are usually smaller than domain-wide policy files.

• Local files allow fast policy application.

### *Disadvantages of Creating Manual Computer-Based Policies*

• Increased management effort.

### *Procedure for Creating Manual Computer-Based Policies*

After you create your policy file with the System Policy Editor, you need to edit the registry of the MetaFrame XP server to tell it to use the new policy file. You can do this manually via the registry or by using the System Policy Editor to edit the local registry.

When you specify the location of the policy file, you can use the %LogonServer% variable in your UNC path. Using this will prevent you from having a single point of failure as long as you copy the policy file to the same location on all of your domain controllers. You can use the Netlogon$ share's directory replication for this. Just name your policy something other than ntconfig.pol, so that your policy is not accidentally applied to all computers.

**Registry Location**

Key: HKLM\System\CurrentControlSet\Control\ Update

Value: UpdateMode

Type: REG_DWORD

Data: 0 = no policy. 1 = automatic policy from domain controller. 2 = manually specify the location of the policy file (via the data in the "NetworkPath" value.)

Value: NetworkPath

Type: REG_SZ

Data: UNC or local network path to the policy file.

**System Policy Editor Location**

Policy Editor | Open Registry | Local Computer | Network | System Policies Update. Check the "Remote Update" box. Set the update mode to "Manual." Enter the UNC path to the policy file.

## What type of Windows 2000 Policies will you use?

The manner in which policies are applied in Windows 2000 environments is different from Windows NT 4.0 environments. Policy techniques outlined in the Windows NT 4 section are still applicable for Windows 2000 servers, allowing for backwards-compatibility in mixed environments. However, if you have Windows 2000 MetaFrame XP servers, you'll probably find the Windows 2000-specific policies more flexible and easier to apply.

As with Windows NT 4 policies, Windows 2000 policy application varies, depending on what you want the policies to affect. There are two different types of Windows 2000 policies:

- Local computer policies.
- Group Policy Objects.

### Windows 2000 Local Computer Policies

Local computer policies are a fancy way of saying "the local registry settings" of a Windows 2000 computer. They are applied with the Group Policy MMC snap-in (gpedit.msc). By default, there is no shortcut for this procedure. You can launch the Group Policy snap-in manually (Start | Run | gpedit.msc). Just as in Windows NT 4.0, changing settings in the local computer policy sets registry values on the local server. After you are done changing policy settings, you can simply close the Group Policy editor. Nothing needs saved because the Group Policy editor, in this case, is in direct connection with the local computer's registry. The downside to editing the registry directly with Group Policy editor is that any policy settings you change will only apply to the local computer.

### Advantages of Local Computer Policies

- Simple to apply.
- Easy to change.
- Works well for single-server environments.
- Allows each server to have unique policy settings.

### Disadvantages of Local Computer Policies

- Must be manually configured at every server.
- Does not scale very well.

### Windows 2000 Group Policies

If your MetaFrame XP servers belong to an Active Directory domain, policy application becomes very flexible (and very cool). In Active Directory environments, policies are stored in the directory as "Group Policy Objects." A Group Policy Object (GPO) is a single policy file containing policy settings for users and computers. GPOs are stored in the directory itself, and there is no limit to the number that can be stored. Once they are created and stored in the directory, GPOs are applied to Active Directory Sites, Domains, or Organizational Units. The policies defined within the GPO apply to whatever objects (such as users and computers) are in the container where they are applied.

Such policy architecture allows you to create extremely flexible policies. For example, you can put all of your MetaFrame XP servers into one Organizational Unit (OU). You can then create a locked-down Group Policy Object and apply it to the OU, effectively securing your MetaFrame XP servers while not restricting user access to other systems not part of that OU.

Because Group Policy Objects can be applied at multiple levels, (sites, domains, and organizational units), designs can become complex very quickly when you apply different GPOs at different levels to the same objects.

The details of Active Directory GPO design will not be covered in this book. If you plan to make heavy use of them, there are several excellent white papers on Microsoft's website that explain how they are applied and how settings are inherited between levels. The important thing to realize is that GPOs are often used with great success in MetaFrame environments.

### Advantages of Group Policy

- Extremely flexible.
- Granular application.
- Easy to apply.
- The best policy solution in existence (so far).

### Disadvantages of Group Policy

- Requires Active Directory.
- Multiple policies can be difficult to maintain and troubleshoot.

## How will you apply policies? (All platforms)

When applying policies, there are several design decisions that you will have to make regardless of whether your MetaFrame XP servers are running Windows NT 4.0 or Windows 2000. To make these decisions, you must answer the following questions:

- Where will the policy files be stored for manual computer-based policies?

- What settings will you configure in the policy?

Typically, you would only use manual policy files if you do not have Active Directory and do not want to create one large domain–wide policy. Manual policies are technically NT 4.0-specific, but they can be used on Windows 2000 servers as well.

If you decide to use manual computer-based policies, you must decide where the policy files will be located. (This is the file that the computer will access when it is booted.) You have two choices for the location of this policy file:

- One file locally on every server.

- A central policy file, accessible to every server via a network connection.

By storing a policy file locally on every MetaFrame XP server where it is to be applied, you can rest assured that the policy will always be applied quickly and efficiently. The only downside is that if you make a change to the policy, you will need to copy that new policy file to every server where it is used. (Of course, this copying can be scripted with little effort.)

### Advantages of Storing Policy Files on Individual Terminal Servers

- Fast access to policy files.

- Fast logons.

- Policy will always be applied.

### Disadvantages of Storing Policy Files on Individual Terminal Servers

- Policies can be difficult to update.

- There is a chance that the policy files could get out of sync, with different versions on different servers.

Alternately, some administrators choose to keep the policy files in a centralized location. Often there may be a dozen or more policy files in one location, with each file unique for different groups of servers. Every server that has the policy applied connects to the central location and downloads the policy when it is booted. This method allows you to easily update policy files, with MetaFrame XP servers automatically receiving the new policy when they are rebooted.

### Advantages of Storing Policy Files in Central Locations

• Only one file has to be updated each time the policy changes.

### Disadvantages of Storing Policy Files in Central Locations

• Policy files must be acquired via the network every time the server is booted.

• If the master policy location is not available, the server will not receive a policy.

## What settings will you configure in the policy?

There are literally hundreds of options that can be configured with policies. (The options are almost endless with the availability of plug-in ADM policy template files.) It is important to consider the various choices before starting to actually build your policies. You don't want to have to make decisions about policy options on the fly. Many policy options affect more than one component, so an uninformed policy setting can have adverse consequences.

When deciding what aspects should be locked down with a policy, remember that roaming profiles will retain user settings from one session to the next. In general, you should only use policies to specify settings that you want to force upon the users. Settings that the users should be able to customize are better left to user profiles.

# Things to Consider when Designing User Policies

Now that you know what your user policy options are, you can begin to design your policies. As you design them, consider the following:

• Will users run full desktops or just published applications?

• How important is security?

• Which MetaFrame XP Feature Release are you using?

### User Applications

If users are running full desktops on your MetaFrame servers then it's important that you lock down those desktops with policies. On the other hand, if users only run published applications then you don't need to worry as much about policies.

### Security

The tighter you lock down your policies, the more secure your environment will be. Of course, this will also lead to more restrictive, less flexible environments. See Chapter 15 for the full details about securing your MetaFrame XP environment.

### Feature Release Level

Citrix user policies are extremely useful and convenient, except that they require Feature Release 2.

# Home Drives

As in any computing environment, home drives in MetaFrame XP environments provide a private location where users can store their personal files and data. In MetaFrame XP, home drives can be used in addition to user profiles for storage of application configuration information.

The golden rule for home drives in a MetaFrame XP environment is this: the more users store in their home drives, the less they are forced to store in their user profile. This is crucial, because a user's entire roaming profile must be copied on to the MetaFrame server when they log on, and off of the server when they log off.

Traditionally, users' home drives are network shares mapped to drive letters when the users log on.

In some MetaFrame environments, users won't need to save their own files, so you won't need to make use of explicit home drives for each user. However, users in these environments will still technically have a home drive location, even though they wouldn't have an explicit drive letter mapped to it. To understand this, let's take a look at how Windows home drives work.

## How Windows Home Drives Work

Whenever a user logs on to a Terminal Server, the server designates one folder to be the user's home folder (home drive). You can specify the exact location of the folder that becomes a user's home drive via User Manager for Domains (for Terminal Server 4.0 environments) or via the Users and Computers MMC snap-in (for Windows 2000 environments).

Similar to a user's profile path, you can specify two home drive locations per user—one that is used when users log on to regular computers and one that is used when users log on to Terminal Servers. In either case, the home drive can be a local path on the computer where the user logs on or a drive letter that is mapped to a UNC share.

Configuring a user's home drive as a property of his user account is an easy way to give each user his own private storage space while ensuring that drive letters will be mapped properly and permissions will be set correctly. Other than that, there's really nothing special about home drives configured as part of the user's account—they simply provide a location for users to store personal files and data.

When a user logs on to a MetaFrame XP server, the server contacts a domain controller to retrieve the user's home drive location. It first checks for a Terminal Services home drive. If no home drive is specified, the server will then check for a regular home drive location. If no home drive is specified in either place, the server will create a home drive in the user's local profile. This process is outlined in Figure 5.7.

Whenever a user logs on, the server sets two system variables to indicate the path of the home drive: %homedrive% and %homepath%. These variables allow Windows applications to locate a user's home drive no matter where it's located. For example, let's assume that a user's home drive can be found in the following location: h:\home\.

In Terminal Server 4.0 environments, the %homedrive% variable would be set to "h:" and the %homepath% variable would be set to "\home\." In Windows 2000 environments, the %homedrive% variable would be set to "h:\home" and the %homepath% variable would be set to "\." The change in usage of these two variables between platforms has to do with the fact that Windows 2000 environments support "deep shares." A deep share allows you to map a drive to a path like \\server\share\subdir1\subdir2\subdir3\. The root of the share would be anchored at "subdir3." In Windows NT 4.0 environments, drive mappings could only be anchored at the share level, meaning that the root of the above share would be anchored at "share."

In the real world, it's confusing to the user when he accesses his home drive letter and sees several subfolders, one for each user. This would cause the user to have to browse through the file structure to find his own home folder. More often, users' home drives are located at the root level of a drive mapping, such as "h:". In these environments, %homedrive% is set to "h:" and %homepath% is set to "\."

*Figure 5.7 Home Drive Mapping Process*

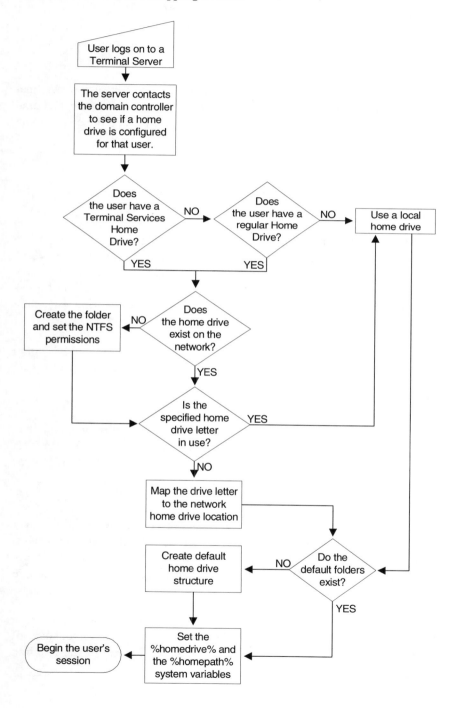

If you're not sure what the %homedrive% and %homepath% variables are in your environment, you can always check them from the command prompt by typing echo %homedrive% or echo %homepath%. Of course, you can also view all of the environment variables that are set by typing "set."

## How are Home Drives Used?

Most people think that home drives are only used to store users' personal files. While this is a primary use for them in MetaFrame environments, home drives also serve a few other important purposes. In MetaFrame XP, home drives are used for:

- Windows system configuration information.
- Application data and configuration information.
- Personal files.

### Windows and System Configuration Information

By default, the system creates two folders in each user's home drive: windows and windows\system. Any application looking for the server's windows or system directories to read or write .INI or configuration files is routed to the appropriate directory in the user's home drive. That way, each user can have his own configuration for applications.

These two folders are the only items automatically created in a user's home drive, and you should not remove them. Of course, most users will create many more folders on their own.

### Application Data and Configuration Information

Many applications require configuration folders to store user settings and data. Often these folders are created in addition to the windows and system folders. By putting this data in the user's home drive, an application can ensure that its settings will be unique for each user.

### Personal Files

Perhaps the most important use for home drives is to store users' personal files. In addition to the data files that users store directly in their home drives, many administrators configure a policy that redirects the user's "My Documents" and "Application Data" folders into their home drives. This procedure was discussed in the User Profiles section of this chapter.

By utilizing a user's home drive for personal data storage, you can leverage the advantages of roaming profiles without them growing too large, since all personal files would be located in the home drive, instead of the roaming profile.

# Why should you care about Home Drives?

There are several factors impacted by the way the home drive system is designed in MetaFrame XP. Because home drives are used throughout users' sessions, it's important that they're designed to support the needs of the users. Areas that are specifically impacted include:

- Logon speed.
- File open/save speed.
- User data integrity.

### Logon Speed

If the home drive is part of the user's profile that must be copied down to the MetaFrame server every time the user logs on, logons will be slow. On the other hand, if the home drive is located on a separate network share, allowing the profile to be small, user logons will be fast.

### File Access Speed

Many files will be read from and written to the user's home drive. If that home drive is located across a slow WAN link from the server running the user's MetaFrame XP server session, opening and saving files will be slow.

### User Data Integrity

A well-designed home drive environment will protect the data and the files that users store on their home drives. If the home drive design is sloppy, or worse yet, if home drives are kept on MetaFrame XP servers, user data could be lost if problems occur.

# What are the Home Drive Design Options?

Using home drives is fairly straightforward. There are a few options that you need to think about when deciding how home drives will be used in your MetaFrame environment. These options include:

- Home drive size.
- Home drive location.
- Number of home drives.
- Methods of specifying home drives.

## Home Drive Size

Remember the golden rule to roaming profiles? (Hint: Keep them as small as possible.) Home drives make it possible to keep profiles small. After all, in order to shrink the size of a profile you need to have somewhere to put the data that you take out of the profiles. That "somewhere" is in users' home drives.

While roaming profiles should always be kept as small as possible, there is nothing wrong with a home drive that is several gigabytes or more. They're only limited by the amount of hard drive space you have on the server that stores the home drives. From the network bandwidth standpoint, large home drives do not pose a problem, because data is only copied across the network as it is needed.

So far, everything we've mentioned about home drives reduces to the idea that it's okay if they are large. However, there may be situations in which you actually need to limit the size of users' home drives. In Windows 2000 environments, it's possible to limit the size of home drives with disk quotas.

Disk quotas allow you to specify the maximum drive space that a user can use on an NTFS volume. Users are only charged for files and folders that they own. You can set two limits per user per disk volume. A "soft" limit produces an event log and a warning for the user that they are nearing their disk limit. A "hard" limit is the actual disk limit. When this limit is reached, the user receives an "out of disk space" error if they try to copy anything else to their home drive.

In many environments, politics prevents disk quotas from "officially" being used. Even so, you might want to set quotas anyway. Set really high, just in case a slick user decides to store his entire MP3 collection in his MetaFrame XP home drive.

### Advantages of Disk Quotas

- Helps prevent servers from running out of space.
- Different users can have different quota sizes.

### Disadvantages of Disk Quotas

- Users are charged per volume, not per directory.
- Requires Windows 2000.
- Hastily-configured quotas could prevent users from doing their jobs.

- Disk space is cheap, and quotas might be more trouble then they're worth.

## Procedure for Implementing Disk Quotas

Disk quotas only work on NTFS volumes on Windows 2000 servers. They're managed through the "Computer Management" MMC plug-in (Administrative Tools | Computer Management | Storage | Disk Management | Right-click on Disk Volume | Properties | Quota Tab).

Configuring disk quotas is fairly easy. You can set both the limit and warning levels for new users. You can also click the "Quota Entries" button to configure a custom list for existing users. Interestingly, the drop down box for the quota limit starts at "KB" and goes all the way up to "EB," which is one billion Gigabytes, in case you have users that you want to "limit" to a certain number of EB's.

## Location of Home Drives

In addition to home drive size, you also need to decide where your home drives will be located. Be careful when choosing the locations of home drives in relation to your network. While home drives must be located on a server that has the storage and processing capacity to support them, they should also be located in close proximity to the MetaFrame XP servers so users have quick access to their data from MetaFrame XP sessions.

When you specify the location of your users' home drives, it is important that you *not* put them inside your users' profiles. This does not mean home drive can't be on the same server as the profiles, it just means that home drives should not be part of the directory structure that is copied to and from the MetaFrame XP servers as part of a user's profile. If you put the home drives in the user profile, then all the work you do to minimize the size of the roaming profile is wasted.

When it comes down to the actual physical location of home drives, there are two choices:

- UNC share.
- Local drive on MetaFrame XP server.

### Home Drives Accessed via UNC Shares

In most environments, the appropriate home drive location will be on a server that is available to all MetaFrame XP servers. The home drive is accessed through a UNC share name, and a drive letter is automatically mapped when the user begins his MetaFrame XP session.

### Advantages of UNC Share-Based Home Drives

- The home drive server can be built with redundancy, including with RAID storage volumes.
- Individual MetaFrame XP servers can be taken offline without affecting the availability of user data.

### Disadvantages of UNC Share-Based Home Drives

- An additional file server is required.

### Procedure for Creating UNC Share-Based Home Drives

To create a home drive for a user, you simply specify the home drive in the user's profile configuration (via User Manager for Domains or the MMC). Choose the "connect to" drive letter and type the full UNC path to the home drive location. You may use the %username% variable. If you specify the home drive as "\\server\share\%username%," then the system will automatically create the home drive and set the appropriate permissions. (Be sure to double-check that the selected drive letter is not in use for that user. If it is, you will not receive any error messages, but the home drive will map to a local drive (see below), not the UNC path.)

### Home Drives Stored on MetaFrame XP Servers

In some situations, you may choose to locate users' home drives on the MetaFrame XP server. This is usually done in small environments where the MetaFrame XP server is only one server.

### Advantages of Storing Home Drives on MetaFrame XP Servers

- Cheap and easy.

### Disadvantages of Storing Home Drives on MetaFrame XP Servers

- The contents of the user's home drive are not available when they log on to another server.
- A new home drive will be created on each server where the user logs on.

### Procedure for Creating Home Drives on MetaFrame XP Servers

A local home drive is also configured in the user account properties in the "Local Path" section. The entry takes the form of "c:\path1\path2\%username%." Again, using the %username% variable will cause the drive to be set up automatically the first time a user logs on.

## Number of Home Drives

In most environments, each user will only have one home drive. However, there is no reason that each user needs to be restricted to only one home drive, or that multiple home drives for one user have to exist in the same physical location. Consider the following environment:

*Figure 5.8  Some users need data in multiple locations*

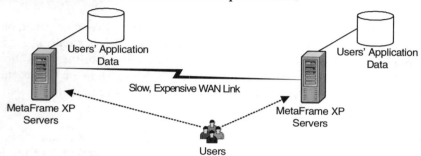

There are specific reasons that the user in Figure 5.8 must run his applications from MetaFrame XP servers in two different locations. This company will never have both applications installed on the same MetaFrame XP server because the databases are in two different locations. Because of this, there is no reason that the user's personal data for the application should be in one single location. The user can have one home drive at each location—each containing the user's files that are needed for that location.

Multiple home drives would make sense from a network standpoint, allowing the user to always have fast, local access to personal files from sessions on both MetaFrame XP servers. However, if you use multiple home drives you need to be careful. Don't try to make both home drives look the same to the user. You should probably not have both home drives mapped to the same drive letter (each in their own respective ICA sessions). While there is nothing technically wrong with doing so, it is confusing for the user to have a P: drive in two different ICA sessions that maps back to two different network locations. Users may switch back-and-forth between applications on different MetaFrame XP servers.  They won't understand, for example, drive P: from Microsoft Word has one set of files and drive P: from the data warehouse application has another.  Using multiple drive letters gives the user a clue that there are multiple network locations.

### Advantages of Multiple Home Drives

- Local data access from sessions on remote MetaFrame XP servers.

### Disadvantages of Multiple Home Drives

- Can be confusing if both drives have the same letter.

Instead of having multiple local home drives for each user throughout your enterprise, it's possible to configure directory replication so that the contents of one home drive are replicated to multiple servers throughout the environment.

Home drive replication is one of those things that sounds good on paper, but turns out to be a nightmare in real life. The data in home drives usually changes frequently, making it a bad candidate for replication. Also, the replication process takes time, so a user simultaneously using sessions on two MetaFrame XP servers that are far apart might have different versions of the same data, if the replication process has not completed.

Home drive data replication is mentioned here for the sake of thoroughness, because it has been used with limited success in some cases. In general, it is more trouble than it's worth.

### Advantages of Replicating Home Drives

- The same user data is locally available to a user's MetaFrame XP session throughout the enterprise.

### Disadvantages of Replication Home Drives

- User data can get out of sync.
- Replication times can be long.
- Bandwidth is wasted during the replication process.
- Additional management is required.

## Methods of Specifying Home Drives

So far, we've focused on how home drives are configured as part of a user's domain account properties. While this is the main method of specifying home drives, there are other methods that have limited uses. In this section, we'll take a look at all the methods you can use to specify a home drive for a user, including:

- User account properties configured in the domain or Active Directory.
- Logon script.
- Folder redirection via an Active Directory group policy.
- Do nothing (let the system create a home drive automatically).

## Method 1. User Account Home Directory Configuration

Before we look at some of the "alternative" methods of configuring home drives, let's look at the "official" way of doing it. In Active Directory or Windows NT 4.0 domains, domain users can be configured with a home drive that will be automatically mapped upon logon as part of their user account. Then, whenever that user logs on to a Terminal Server (any MetaFrame XP server), their home drive is mapped and set to the specified location without any extra configuration or scripting.

### *Advantages of Specifying Home Drives via User Account Properties*

- Easy to do.
- The "homedrive" and "homepath" variables are automatically set.
- This is the "official" method of creating home drives.
- The home drive is created and permissions are set automatically.
- Easy way to specify different home directories for Terminal Servers and non-Terminal Servers.

### *Disadvantages of Specifying Home Drives via User Account Properties*

- No flexibility.

### *Procedure for Specifying Home Drives via User Account Properties*

In Windows NT 4.0 environments, you can only configure the Terminal Services home drive path with the version of User Manager for Domains that comes with a Terminal Server (User Manager for Domains from a Terminal Server | User Properties | Profile Tab | Terminal Server Home Directory | Connect X: to UNC or local path).

In Windows 2000 environments, you configure home drives with the MMC (MMC | User Properties | Profile Tab | Home Folder | Connect X: to UNC or local path).

You can use the following procedure to create home drives in Windows 2000 or Windows NT 4.0:

1. Create a root folder to use for your home drives in the location of your choice.
2. Give the "Everyone" group "Change" permissions on this folder.
3. For each user, specify the home drives as "\\your folder\%username%."

In this case, you should literally type "%username%" in the box. This is a percent sign, the word "username," and another percent sign. Do not substitute the user's real user name for the %username% variable. If the username is "holli," then you would type %username% in the box, *not* %holli%.

When the user logs on for the first time, the system will automatically create the subdirectory for the username and give it the appropriate permissions. (Administrators get special access at the directory level only, the user maintains full control.) The windows and windows\system directories will also be automatically created, with administrators having full control.

### Method 2. Logon Script Home Directory Configuration

Another way to specify a home drive is to use a logon script to map a drive to a network share and then to execute a command setting the home directory environment variable to point to that drive. (See the next section of this chapter for more information about logon scripts.)

#### *Advantages of Specifying Home Drives via Logon Scripts*

- Extremely flexible implementation of home drives.

#### *Disadvantages of Specifying Home Drives via Logon Scripts*

- Scripts must be manually configured.
- "Homedrive" and "homepath" variables must be manually set.

#### *Procedure for Configuring Home Drives via Logon Scripts*

Specifics of this method are addressed in the logon script portion of this chapter.

### Method 3. Group Policy Folder Redirection

Active Directory group policies can be used to redirect local folders to network locations on computers running Windows 2000 and participating in Active Directory domains. For example, a user's "My Documents" folder can be redirected to a network share location that is centralized, so that no matter what computer the user logs on to, he would have access to the same data in his "My Documents" folder. Because this is a function of group policy, it can be applied only to the specific organizational units containing MetaFrame XP servers.

It should be pointed out that while redirecting the "My Documents" folder to a static network point can eliminate the storage of too much data in a user's profile, this is not technically a "real" home drive. In addition to a location for storing personal files, a home drive also contains certain system information, and a home drive is the target of the `%homedrive%` and `%homepath%` variables. That being said, if your users will only be using their "My Documents" folder for storage of personal files, you can probably get away with redirecting that folder and not worrying about the "official" home drive location.

### Advantages of Specifying Home Drives via Group Policy

- Folder redirection can be used in addition to "official" home drives.
- Easy way to keep data out of profiles. (After all, isn't that the only reason we really care about home drives anyway?)

### Disadvantages of Specifying Home Drives via Group Policy

- Not a "real" home drive.
- "Homedrive" and "homepath" variables will point to other locations.
- Applications that automatically write to the home drive will not write to a redirected "My Documents" folder (unless the home drive variables have been modified).

### Procedure for Specifying Home Drives via Group Policy

Detailed information about folder redirection can be found in the previous User Profiles segment of this chapter.

### Method 4. Do Nothing. Let the System Create a Home Drive

Finally, the "do nothing" approach is also a valid option with home drives. If no home drives are specified anywhere, the system will create a user's home drive in their local user profile (by creating a `windows` directory).

This solution can work for small environments where users will not store their personal files in the home drive. However, there can also be several problems with this method. If a MetaFrame XP server is configured to delete cached copies of roaming profiles at logoff, or if the local profile is overwritten by a roaming profile at logon, then the data in the home drive will be lost.

### Advantages of Doing Nothing.

- Least amount of work.
- Might be sufficient in small, single-server environments.

### Disadvantages of Doing Nothing.

- If local profiles are not cached, home drive data will be lost.
- If local profiles are overwritten by roaming profiles at logon, home drive data will be lost.

- The "doing nothing" approach will not work in multi-server environments.

## Considerations when Designing Home Drives

Now that you know all of the options, answering the following two questions should get your home drive design started in the right direction:

- Does each user need to store personal files?
- Will users be logging on to multiple MetaFrame XP servers at different physical locations?

### User File Storage

If your MetaFrame XP environment is used for specific applications only, it's possible your users will never need home drives during their MetaFrame sessions. Of course, if your users are running applications where they need to open and save files, or applications that rely heavily on personalized configuration (such as email), then it will be important to ensure that users have fast, reliable access to their home drives.

### Single Users with Multiple Server Locations

If users will be connecting to MetaFrame XP servers in multiple physical locations requiring access to home directories, your design will need to reflect this. The result will be a much more complex design than if each of your users only connects to one MetaFrame XP server.

When placing home directories, you also need to consider whether users will be using them just from MetaFrame XP sessions or if users will need to access them from anywhere on the network.

# Logon and Logoff Scripts

Logon scripts in MetaFrame XP environments are no different than in any other type of environment—they are just than batch files that run whenever a user logs on to the server. As with other components of MetaFrame environments, there are several different ways to use logon scripts, and some are more effective than others. Before we study the way logon scripts are used, let's take a look at how they work.

# How Logon and Logoff Scripts Work

Both logon and logoff scripts are batch files that execute when a user logs on or logs off of a MetaFrame XP server. These scripts can use system environment variables and can call other scripts.

## Logon Scripts

With logon scripts, you can assign a batch file to run when certain users log on or when a certain MetaFrame XP computer is used. They allow you to influence certain aspects of a user's environment without taking full control of it (as when policies or profiles are used). MetaFrame XP logon scripts are used to:

- Define and map a user's home drive (if this is not done automatically).
- Set up an application's environment in the user's home directory, by creating subdirectories and copying the necessary configuration files from a template directory.
- Verify or set permissions in a home directory.
- Start background processes.
- Configure and prepare any Windows components for use.
- Map network drives.
- Create icons and shortcuts for the user.
- Map printers.

## Logoff Scripts

In addition to logon scripts, you can configure logoff scripts to run whenever a user logs off of the MetaFrame XP server. These scripts serve several purposes, including:

- Delete unwanted temporary folders.
- Backup important files.
- Copy files to network locations.

# Why should you care about logon script design?

In most MetaFrame XP environments, logon scripts are used in addition to profiles and policies to create the user environment. If your system requires logon scripts, then you will need to use them. When designing logon scripts, the decisions you must make relate more to *how* the logon scripts are implemented, not *what* they do when they run.

If you don't carefully consider all logon script options available, you could limit the flexibility within your environment. For example, some logon script languages are more flexible than others, allowing more powerful scripts to be created.

## What are the logon script options?

When designing logon scripts, you'll most likely spend most of your time writing the script itself. However, there are a few decisions that you can make to help implement your scripts. Make these decisions by answering the following questions:

- What script language will be used?
- How will the scripts be launched?
- Will you use the same script on all of your servers?

### Script Language

There are hundreds of languages available for creating logon scripts. Realistically, there are few differences between the languages. In this section, we'll take a look at two of the most popular scripting languages. If you have a preferred language that you are comfortable with, use it with MetaFrame XP.

Two scripting languages that we will focus on here are Windows batch scripts and Kixtart scripts.

#### Windows Batch Scripts

Windows batch scripts are regular BAT or CMD scripts. Batch scripts are the most popular and easiest to use of all the available scripting languages, mainly because this is the script language that most of us have been using for fifteen years.

With Windows batch scripts, you can use system environment variables and create conditional logic. In fact, there are several advanced features built into this powerful scripting language. In many environments, you'll be able to do everything that you need to with Windows batch scripts. After all, if there is anything that you can't do with the native scripting language, you can always call another command-line utility from your script.

### Advantages of Windows Batch Scripts

- No third-party interpreter is needed.
- Scripts run in their own native language without needing to be compiled.
- Everyone knows how to write batch files.

### Disadvantages of Windows Batch Scripts

- Limited native advanced features.

### Kixtart scripts

The Kixtart scripting language and interpreter is a free script environment originally included in Windows NT Resource Kits. (You can download the Kixtart utilities for free from www.kixtart.org.) Kixtart scripts are more powerful and flexible than batch scripts, but they are written in their own proprietary scripting language. Many administrators use Kixtart scripts for their advanced features, like the ability to conditionally branch based on a logged-on user's group membership.

### Advantages of Kixtart Scripts

- More advanced than batch scripts.

### Disadvantages of Kixtart Scripts

- Written in a proprietary language.
- Requires the kix.exe script player.

## Launching Scripts

After you write your logon scripts, you must decide how the scripts will be launched. In the old days, this was easy (because there was only one option). Today, there are five different methods that can be used to launch a logon script for a given user. Some of these methods apply to all users that log on to a particular computer. Other methods apply to a particular user and follow that user to all computers. The five methods are:

- User's domain account properties.
- Group policy.
- Startup folder.
- Launch scripts via the registry.
- Launch scripts when certain applications are executed.

## Method 1. User's Domain Account Properties

Most people configure logon scripts on a "per user" basis as part of the user's domain account configuration. This is the "standard" way of configuring logon scripts. Logon scripts configured in this manner will run whenever the user logs on to any computer in the domain. It's really easy to apply different scripts to different users using this method.

### *Advantages of Scripts via Users' Domain Account Properties*

- Easy to set up.
- Scripts are automatically replicated between domain controllers (via the Netlogon$ shares).
- "Standard" way of configuring scripts.
- Different scripts can be applied to different users.

### *Disadvantages of Scripts via Users' Domain Account Properties*

- No way to prevent a script from running when a user logs on.

### *Procedure for Scripts via Users' Domain Account Properties*

In Windows NT 4.0 environments, logon scripts are configured with User Manager for Domains (User properties I Profile Button I Logon Script). In Windows 2000 environments, logon scripts are configured through the MMC (User properties I Profile Tab I Logon Script).

## Method 2. Group Policy

Group policy objects can contain logon and logoff scripts (in addition to computer startup / shutdown scripts) that are executed wherever the policy is applied. By using group policy, it is possible for you to "layer" scripts on the user, with different scripts applying at the site, domain, and OU levels. If a user is part of an OU structure several containers deep, it's possible to apply different logon and logoff scripts to each OU in the layer. All of the scripts will run for each user.

### *Advantages of Launching Scripts via Group Policy*

- Each group policy can have its own script, allowing for layering of scripts.
- Scripts (via policies) can be applied to specific OUs.

### *Disadvantages of Launching Scripts via Group Policy*

- Requires Active Directory.

### Procedure for Launching Scripts via Group Policy

Add the script names to the appropriate group policy via the group policy MMC snap-in (User Configuration I Windows Settings I Scripts).

## Method 3. Startup Folder

The "Startup" folder in a server's Start Menu contains programs that are run automatically when a user logs on. There are two startup folders that can be used. The first is in the "all users" profile. Logon scripts or application short-cuts placed in this folder are executed by every user when they log on. The second startup folder location is unique for each user. Any scripts stored in the "Startup" folder in the user's profile will execute every time the user logs on. If the user has a roaming profile and the scripts are stored in the "Startup" folder of that profile, the scripts will execute for the user on any server where that profile is applied.

### Advantages of Launching Scripts via the Startup Folder

- Different scripts can be configured for different users.
- If Terminal Server roaming profiles are used, you can easily create a logon script that only runs in Terminal Server environments.
- Each user can have multiple logon scripts.
- User-specific and server-specific logon scripts can be easily combined.

### Disadvantages of Launching Scripts via the Startup Folder

- If the profile doesn't load, the script won't run.

### Procedure for Launching Scripts via the Startup Folder

To launch logon scripts via a startup folder, all you need to do is copy the script into the appropriate startup folder. For "all users," the folder is unique on each server (*Local Profile Root*\All Users\Start Menu\Programs\Startup). For specific users, the logon script must be copied to their master profile location (*User Profile Root*\Start Menu\Programs\Startup).

When you put a logon script in the startup folder, you might wonder whether you should copy in the actual script or shortcuts to the script. Even though "best practices" dictate that you should only place shortcuts in the Start Menu, in this case you should put the entire script in the startup folder. Even the longest logon scripts are relatively small in size, and it's much easier to manage if the actual scripts are in the startup folder.

## Method 4. Launch Scripts via the Registry

The last method that you can use to launch logon and logoff scripts is to add entries to your MetaFrame XP server's registry. Every server has a registry key that specifies programs that are executed when the server is booted or when users log on. Adding your logon scripts to the list of programs executed when a user logs on is an easy and effective way to establish a logon script for all users on a particular server.

### Advantages of Launching Scripts via the Registry

- Script always runs, without exception.
- No dependency on profiles or network drives.

### Disadvantages of Launching Scripts via the Registry

- Must be configured manually on every server.

### Procedure for Launching Scripts via the Registry

The logon and logoff programs that are run when users log on or off are specified in the following locations:

**Logon Script**

> Key: HKLM\Software\Microsoft\Windows\Current Version\Run

> Value: Free-form name of your script.

> Type: REG_SZ

> Data: Full path and executable of script. Each script requires its own "value" entry.

**Logoff Script**

> Key: HKLM\Software\Microsoft\WindowsNT\CurrentVersion \Winlogon

> Value: LogoffApp

> Type: REG_SZ

> Data: List of applications that are to be run, separated by commas.

## Method 5. Launch Scripts when Certain Applications are Executed

You can write application-specific scripts that create the proper environment for applications (such as setting variables, mapping drives, etc.) when the application is run.

At first, you might want to simply add the logon script components to users' standard network logon scripts. After all, you could add logic into the logon script that would detect if a user was a member of a certain group or logging onto a certain machine and then customize the environment as needed. While this is a fairly complex process, it is possible to do.

You could also create a batch file that performs all of the necessary script functions and exits with a call to the application executable. You can publish the batch file instead of the application executable.

If you have users that need to access the applications from server desktops via the Start menu, you can modify the shortcuts in the Start menu so that they point to the batch files instead of the executables. You could even change the icons back to the original ones so that the applications seem identical to the users.

### Advantages of Launching Scripts when Certain Applications are Executed

- The scripts would work regardless of how the application was launched.
- The scripts will only run if the specific application is needed. Users will not need to wait while complex logon scripts are parsed every time they want to connect to a single application.
- There is no chance that an application could run without the script running first.
- Application-specific batch files could be easily managed by application owners. If a single, large logon script was needed, application owners would need to work with the logon script owner, resulting in increased complexity, the chance that something would go wrong, and the time needed to perform updates.

### Disadvantages of Launching Scripts when Certain Applications are Executed

- Increased Management. Scripts have to be configured manually on all servers (although you could store the scripts in a common location and then have all the shortcuts and published applications point to the central batch file via a UNC or mapped drive).

### Launching Different Scripts on Different Servers

Some methods of launching logon scripts allow you to configure different scripts on a server-by-server basis. While this allows you to have ultimate flexibility, it is difficult to manage multiple scripts across multiple servers, especially in large environments. The alternative is to launch a logon script via a method allowing you to specify one script that is executed no matter what server is used. The problem that arises is that the same script is run on every single server, even if there are particular servers where you don't want it to run. There are instances in which you might need custom scripts or custom components to run only on certain servers.

Fortunately, there's a simple solution. Add a line to your logon script that checks to see if a certain condition is true. If it is, the script will run. If not, part of the script can be skipped. This allows you to conveniently configure a logon script to run on all servers while being smart enough to know where it's running and what parts should run.

An easy way to accomplish this is to create a logon script that checks for the presence of a flag file on the server. If the flag file is present, the script is executed. If not, the script is aborted. Simply copy the empty flag file to the servers where you want your script to run. For example, you might add the following line of code to your logon script:

```
if exist %systemroot%\yourflagfile.txt goto exit
```

This would cause the script to exit if `yourflagfile.txt` was found on the server.

## Considerations when Designing Logon Scripts

When you begin to design your logon scripts and decide how they will be invoked, there are two questions to consider:

- Do you need scripts to run on a "per-user," "per-server," or "per-application" basis?
- Do you need different scripts to run on different MetaFrame XP servers, depending on which server the script is running?

The answer to the first question will help you determine how to launch the logon scripts. Figure 5.9 provides a snapshot of which script launching methods can be used in which situations.

The answer to the second question will help you determine what type of logic you will need to include in your logon scripts. With that, you should have all the information you need to design effective and efficient logon scripts, in turn making your MetaFrame XP environment easy to manage.

*Figure 5.9 The various methods that can be used to launch scripts*

| Method | Per-User | Per-Server | Per-Application |
|---|---|---|---|
| Domain Account | X | | |
| GPO | | X | X |
| Startup Folder | | X | X |
| Registry | | | X |
| Application | | | X |

# Real World Case Study

## Parker HealthNet, A Regional Healthcare Network

Parker HealthNet has decided to use MetaFrame XP to provide applications for 5000 users at nine hospitals and thirty remote healthcare facilities. Many of their users will need to access applications from multiple touch points. For example, doctors often travel between hospitals and remote medical offices, and nurses will use terminals spread throughout many locations in hospital complexes.

A project team was assembled to create a design for the MetaFrame XP application servers. Their design was based on the current environment, as outlined in Figure 5.10 (next page).

The project team first outlined their objectives. For the Parker HealthNet environment, several objectives were identified, including:

- **Security**. A secure environment was needed, since most of their applications are integral to patient care and they must be HIPAA compliant.
- **Availability**. If applications were not available, patient care would suffer.
- **Mobility**. Many users would need to simultaneously access applications running on multiple MetaFrame XP servers in multiple locations.

Based on their current environment and future needs, the project team was able to make several design decisions. First, they decided to place MetaFrame XP servers (with Feature Release 2) at each of the nine hospitals. They wanted to create one single server farm users to easily access applications from any location. They decided that users would primarily access applications running on MetaFrame XP servers installed locally in each of their own hospitals, but that there would also be some central medical applications for all users running on MetaFrame XP servers in the central datacenter. Figure 5.11 shows a typical hospital and how its users will access applications.

*Figure 5.10  Parker HealthNet's WAN Architecture*

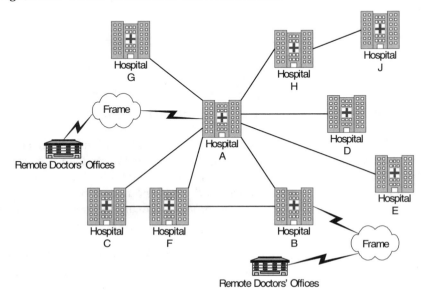

*Figure 5.11  Typical Hospital with MetaFrame XP Application Access*

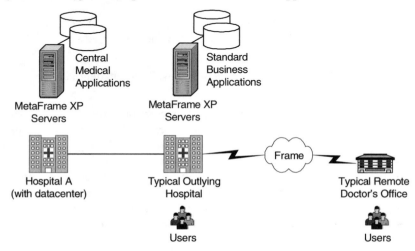

Parker HealthNet just migrated to Active Directory last year, so all of the MetaFrame XP servers will run on Windows 2000 and be part of the Active Directory. They have one active directory domain, with separate Active Directory sites configured for each hospital.

After these basic design decisions were made, the project team deliberated at length on more complex questions. They were able to consolidate all questions into five core issues:

- Should they use mandatory profiles or group policies to lock down the desktop?

- If they use group policies, at what level should the policies be applied?

- Should they use Citrix user policies? If so, how should they be configured?

- Considering that many users travel between locations, where should the master roaming profiles be located? What about the home drives?

- Some of the team members are very nervous about using roaming profiles.

## Issue 1. Desktop Lockdown

The major discussion around desktop lockdown was not "if" they should lock them down, but "how" they should lock them down. Should they use mandatory profiles or group policies? Initially, the project team thought that they had to use group policies, but some members pointed out that mandatory profiles also contained the same registry data as policies. By using mandatory roaming profiles, they could create locked-down template users and use them to manually create the mandatory roaming profiles.

The problem with such an approach is that while it would *technically* work, it would be difficult to update any parameter in a mandatory profile. Administrators would have to manually connect to the ntuser.dat file from every different profile and update the appropriate registry key. This created an inverse balance. If many profiles were created, there would be the ability to highly customize the environment for different users. However, that would also mean it would be more difficult to update all of the profiles when something changed. This inability to easily update profiles disqualified this method as a viable solution. Some users would need to change or modify certain parameters, and team members didn't feel comfortable with using mandatory roaming profiles across the board.

Leveraging Active Directory's group policies was %username%the real solution for Parker HealthNet. After some investigation, the project team found that there were only a few members on the team opposed to using group policy. Their reason for not wanting to use it was because they had "read that it was a nightmare," and had bad experiences with Windows NT 4.0 system policies.

To alleviate these concerns, the project team did extensive Group Policy testing in their lab. Also, because Active Directory was already in use in the environment, there were some real-world policies in place that could be studied to see how they really worked. Ultimately, Parker HealthNet decided to use group policies to lock down and protect their MetaFrame XP servers.

### Issue 2. Group Policy Level

After deciding to use group policies to lock down parts of the user environment, the Parker HealthNet MetaFrame XP project team still needed to decide how the group policies would be applied. The main issue they discussed was whether to create policies that apply to individual users or that apply to the MetaFrame XP servers themselves. Of course, all group policies in Active Directory must apply to a site, domain, or organizational unit. For Parker HealthNet, the policies would apply to an organizational unit. The discussion focused on whether the organizational unit should be populated with computers or users.

Team members that wanted the policies to apply to the actual computers argued that computer-based policies would be the easiest to administer. Other team members agreed, but noted that the ease of administration would come at a price—flexibility. They pointed out that if policies were created at the computer level, then any user that logged on would have those policies applied, including administrators. The first group then suggested that policy filtering could be used on the permissions of the policies so that they would not apply to members of the administrative group. (If you're lost at this point, pick up a book on Windows 2000 group policy design.)

Based on this information and some detailed lab testing, Parker HealthNet decided to create one OU in Active Directory called "Citrix Servers" to contain the computer accounts of all Terminal Servers. Then, they created a group policy which locked-down user settings and applied it to the "Citrix Servers" organizational unit.

## Issue 3. Citrix User Policies

After the project team designed their Windows group policy environment, they decided to think about how to implement Citrix user policies. (After all, Citrix user policies are the main reason that they paid for Feature Release 2.)

The project team was really excited about the fact that they could layer multiple Citrix user policies in their environment. They decided to first create a "baseline" policy that would be applied to all users who will ever use the MetaFrame system. They named this policy "Default Users" and applied it to the "Domain Users" group. Within the Default Users policy, the project team configured all standard options.  Figure 5.12 shows the options used.

*Figure 5.12  Parker HealthNet's "Default Users" Citrix User Policy*

| Policy Rule | Parker HealthNet's Setting |
| --- | --- |
| Client Drive Mapping | Enabled |
| Connect Client Devices | Enabled: Connect Client Drives at Logon |
| Client Printer Mapping | Disabled (This is like a double-negative. Enabling this policy rule turns off printer mapping, which means that disabling it forces printer mapping to be turned on.) |
| Connect Client Printers | Enabled: Connect Printers at Logon: All client Printers |
| Default to Client's Main Printer | Enabled: Default to Client's Main Printer at Logon |
| Client LPT Port Mapping | Not Configured |
| Client COM Port Mapping | Not Configured |
| Client Clipboard Mapping | Not Configured |
| Client Audio Mapping | Enabled: Turn Off Client Audio Mapping |
| OEM Virtual Channels | Not Configured |
| Limit Concurrent Logon Sessions | Enabled: 1 |
| Limit the Client Printer Bandwidth | Not Configured |
| Estimate Client Local Time | Not Configured |
| Use Local Time of ICA Clients | Not Configured |
| Configure User Shadowing | Enabled: Allow Shadowing |
| Assign Shadowing Permissions | Enabled: Administrators |
| Set Required Encryption Level | Enabled: 128-bit |
| Auto Client Update | Enabled: Turn Off Auto Client Update |
| Server Content Redirection | Enabled: Use Server Content Redirection |

Next, the project team determined how to deal with users that dial-in. Since those users only connect at modem speeds, the project team decided to create a policy called "Remote Users" that disabled certain bandwidth-intensive settings. This policy is detailed in Figure 5.13.

*Figure 5.13 Parker HealthNet's "Remote Users" Citrix User Policy*

| Policy Rule | Parker HealthNet's Setting |
|---|---|
| Client LPT Port Mapping | Enabled: Turn Off Client LPT Port Mapping |
| Client COM Port Mapping | Enabled: Turn Off Client COM Port Mapping |
| Set Required Encryption Level | Enabled: Basic |
| Server Content Redirection | Enabled: Do Not Use Server Content Redirection |
| All other rules | Not Configured |

The project team only configured specific policy rules for remote users that would directly affect bandwidth for them. The other rules were left at the "Rule Not Configured" setting, giving the project team the flexibility to set those options elsewhere if needed.

Next, the project team had to consider their "Super Users," an eclectic group who needed to use the MetaFrame solution to its full potential. Essentially, this group of users would need to *not* have any MetaFrame options disabled. To do this, the project team created a policy as outlined in Figure 5.14.

*Figure 5.14 Parker HealthNet's "Super Users" Citrix User Policy*

| Policy Rule | Parker HealthNet's Setting |
|---|---|
| Client Audio Mapping | Disabled (This is like a double-negative. Enabling this policy rule turns off audio mapping, which means that disabling it forces audio mapping to be turned on.) |
| Client LPT Port Mapping | Disabled |
| Client COM Port Mapping | Disabled |
| Client Clipboard Mapping | Disabled |

Since there was no domain group called "Super Users," the project team applied the "Super Users" policy on a user-by-user basis (as opposed to simply applying it to a group). This was relatively easy to do, and the project team used the CMC's "Add List of Names" **** functionality to import a list of users received via email.

Once this "Super Users" group was created, the project team felt that satisfied their Citrix user policy design. As a side note, the CIO's secretary complained bitterly when she found out that she could not play the audio emails that she received from her niece. To alleviate this, the project team created a special policy called "CIO's Secretary." They only configured one policy rule—Client Audio Mapping. The others they left as "Rule Not Configured." Then, they set the priority on that policy to be higher than the "Default User" policy. That way, the secretary received all the policy rules of the "Default User" policy, with her special audio rule applied in place of the standard "Default User" audio rule.

Parker HealthNet had four different Citrix user policies in place by the time they were done with all the configuring. These four policies are outlined in Figure 5.15.

*Figure 5.15  Parker HealthNet's Final Citrix User Policies*

| Policy Name | Priority |
|---|---|
| Super Users | 1 |
| CIO's Secretary | 2 |
| Remote Users | 3 |
| Default Users | 4 |

As you look at this table, remember that in the event of conflicting rules in policies applied to the same user, the rule explicitly configured in the higher priority policy will take affect.

## Issue 4. User Profile and Home Drive Locations

After figuring out how to use group policies, the project team needed to decide where on the network they would store users' roaming profiles and home drives. The easiest way to determine this was to look at how users would access their MetaFrame servers. From there, it would be easy to determine where to put user data.

The project team planned for all users across the entire health system to run the "standard" applications from MetaFrame XP servers at their respective local hospitals. Additionally, many users would need to access medical records applications that would reside on MetaFrame XP servers in the central datacenter in Hospital A. These users would therefore need to access two MetaFrame XP servers—one at their local site and one in the central datacenter. Generally, users would not need access to multiple MetaFrame XP servers at different local sites.

Now that the project team knew where the MetaFrame XP servers would be located and how they would be accessed, they needed to decide where on the network they would store roaming profiles and user data. They realized that they should try to keep the data as close as possible to the MetaFrame XP servers. They decided that there would be several storage locations throughout the health system, with one storage location at each of the nine hospitals. The exact data location for a specific user would depend on where the user was based. The project team appreciated the fact that just having data stored in multiple locations on the network does not mean each user's data will be located in multiple locations. It just means users' home drives and roaming profiles would be sprinkled throughout the WAN.

For example, for users in the remote medical offices, their roaming profiles and home drives would be stored at the nearest hospital where the MetaFrame XP servers are. (See Figure 5.16.) This is due to the fact that there will not be any MetaFrame XP servers at the remote office facilities, and remote office users will access MetaFrame XP servers located at the nearest hospital.

*Figure 5.16  Roaming Profile and Home Drive Locations*

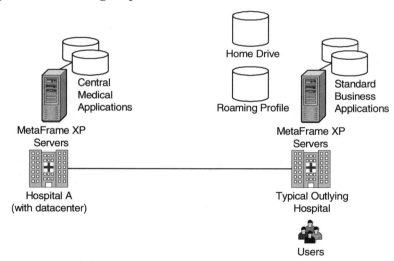

Because some users need to simultaneously access applications from MetaFrame servers in the central hospital and their local hospitals, the project team needed to decide where their roaming profiles and home drives would be located. Right off the bat, they discarded any notions of using data replication to copy user profiles or home drives to multiple locations throughout the WAN. They knew that by introducing data replication, they would needlessly complicate their environment and waste money on additional storage devices and replication software.

Ultimately, the project team decided to keep the user data at the local hospital site because the medical applications that ran on the central MetaFrame XP servers didn't really need access to the users' home drives. It wasn't that big of a deal for users with sessions on those servers to load their roaming profiles from their local hospital servers.

Once they figured out that issue, all the project team had to do was decide how to deal with users that travel between hospitals. Should those users access applications from local MetaFrame XP servers in the hospital that they are visiting, or should they access MetaFrame servers from their home sites?

After a brief discussion, the project team decided that traveling users would run applications off of MetaFrame XP servers at their home site, not the site to which they traveled. This decision was made for several reasons:

### Why Parker HealthNet Decided that Traveling Users Should Access their MetaFrame XP Applications from their Home Servers

- Easier to manage, there would be no need for any script logic to determine where the user is connecting from.
- Easier to size the MetaFrame XP servers, the user base for each site would be constant.
- Roaming profiles and home drives would be stored at the same local site as the MetaFrame XP server.
- Users could easily reconnect to disconnected sessions from any location, the sessions would always be running in the "proper" location.
- The ICA protocol is efficient and is the preferred protocol for WAN communication. (If local MetaFrame ICA servers were used, then the ICA protocol would only be used on the local LAN, and inefficient file transfer traffic would traverse the WAN. See Chapter 3 for details.)

Once this issue was finalized, the project team felt they had a solid profile and user storage strategy. It's interesting to note that Parker HealthNet is not currently using roaming profiles on their desktop workstations. Some members of the project team were not at all comfortable with them. In fact, some team members argued that roaming profiles should not be used at all, especially because the central medical applications at Hospital A did not really leverage profiles. These applications maintained user settings that were applied after the user logged into the application rather than Windows.

However, since it's not possible to have a domain user that uses roaming profiles on some servers but not on others, the project team decided just to keep the roaming profiles as small as possible. They redirected all static folders in the profile to users' home drives. They also made sure that no unneeded temporary directories were part of the profile. After some testing, they figured that most profiles would be less than 500k in size and that they would be able to use roaming profiles without any major problems.

### Issue 5. Concerns about Roaming Profiles

The last major issue that the Parker HealthNet project team addressed was roaming profiles. Remember that in the Parker HealthNet environment the master copies of roaming profiles are stored at local hospitals where the users logon most often. While testing roaming profiles, the project team found that the network was sometimes very slow. As outlined in the previous section, they knew that they would have to do as much as possible to keep the roaming profiles as small as possible, in case users ever needed to log onto servers from locations other than their home locations. In testing, they found that sometimes a roaming profile would timeout as it was being downloaded to the MetaFrame XP server from the master server storage location.

By default, the MetaFrame XP servers were configured to detect slow network connections to the master profile server locations. If a slow connection was detected (because the network was congested), the server would ask users if they wanted to wait to download their remote profile or if (instead) they would like to use their locally cached profile. Parker HealthNet's users were not trained for this, and the project team guessed that many of them would call the helpdesk if this message appeared. Even worse, users might choose to use the local profile. (After all, using the local profile was the default selection in this dialog box.) This would be a problem for Parker HealthNet because then users would not get their own customized environments.

Fortunately, there are several registry values that can be configured on the servers to change the behavior of the roaming profile slow network detection process. These values are all located under the following registry key:

Key: HKLM\Software\Microsoft\WindowsNT\CurrentVersion\Winlogon

There are several values under this registry key that work together to control the behavior of the slow network detection process.

Value: SlowLinkDetectEnabled

Type: REG_DWORD

Data: 0 = disabled

Value: `SlowLinkTimeOut`

Type: `REG_DWORD`

Data: Slow network connection detection timeout, in ms.

Value: `Show`

Type: `REG_DWORD`

Data: Dialog box timeout in seconds.

The project team ended up disabling slow network timeout detection altogether. Initially, they configured this manually on each server. (Actually, they created a .reg file that they used to apply these values to each of their servers.) Later on, the project team realized that because these slow network detection settings were just regular registry values, they could control them with a policy. Eventually they made these values part of their group policy.

## Parker HealthNet Implementation Summary

Ultimately, Parker HealthNet was able to successfully implement the MetaFrame XP environment as outlined. Even though it has only been six months since they completed the implementation, patient care has been positively affected. In fact, Parker HealthNet is planning on acquiring two or three hospitals in the next 12 to 18 months, and they view their MetaFrame XP environment as one of the key components that will allow them to quickly integrate the new hospitals into their existing business environment.

# CHAPTER 6

# Server Sizing and Performance Optimization

In this chapter

MetaFrame XP Server Hardware      230

Real-World Sizing Strategies      234

Server Sizing Techniques      238

Performance Tuning your Environment      252

Now that you've designed your application strategy, you need to think about how to size the servers that run your applications. MetaFrame XP server sizing involves three basic steps:

1. Understand how server sizing works in MetaFrame XP environments.

2. Create your server sizing strategy.

3. Test your server sizing strategy.

In this chapter, we'll look at the various elements affecting the performance of MetaFrame XP servers. Then we'll examine various real-world server sizing strategies so that you can create your own strategy. Lastly we'll explore the different methods that can be used to test your strategy.

# MetaFrame XP Server Hardware

Server sizing in MetaFrame XP environments is quite a bit different than server sizing in traditional server environments. Since multiple users simultaneously access MetaFrame XP servers, the hardware tends to be much more robust than that of standard servers. Additionally, because the Windows operating system has been "tweaked" in Terminal Server environments to support multiple users, Terminal Servers deal with hardware differently than standard Windows servers.

In order to be able to adequately create your server sizing strategy, it's worth inspecting how server sizing works in MetaFrame XP environments. To do this, we'll focus on each of the major server hardware components and how they affect multi-user (Terminal Server) environments.

Before addressing hardware, however, there are a few things that you should keep in mind.

First of all, when you design your MetaFrame XP servers, you need to make sure that you have "real" server hardware. Desktop computers turned on their side do not constitute "real" hardware. Even though many of your users might have faster computers than your servers, they will not perform well. A 1.8GHz Walmart PC with 512MB of memory will not perform nearly as well as an HP Proliant 1.8GHz with 512MB server.

This is especially true in MetaFrame environments. MetaFrame servers are usually pushed to their limits due to the aggregate user processing taking place on them. Low-end PCs typically do not have the internal bus speed or internal bandwidth to support many users, even if they have fast processors and a great deal of memory. For testing purposes, low-end PCs are adequate "just to see if it works," but you will not be able to extrapolate any performance numbers from low-end test PCs to real servers.

The bottom line is that you should use common sense and build your Meta-Frame XP server like a server. You're going to have a lot of users on this server, so it's not worth cutting corners to save a few dollars.

Now, let's get started with our exploration of server hardware in MetaFrame XP environments. We'll begin with memory utilization.

## MetaFrame Server Memory Usage

Every user that runs an application on a MetaFrame XP server will use the memory for that application just as if they were running it on a normal workstation. For example, a quick check of the task manager shows that Microsoft Word requires about 10MB of memory to run. Each user of Word will need 10MB, meaning that 20 simultaneous users will require 200MB of memory. Of course, this is on top of the overhead required for each user to run a session, which is about 4MB, so that 20 users running Word require a collective 280MB of memory on the MetaFrame XP server.

To this you must add the memory required by the base operating system. Microsoft laughingly recommends 128MB. Also, you need to add the 64MB that Citrix recommends for the base installation of MetaFrame XP.

If you add all of these together, you'll find that 20 users will theoretically require that a MetaFrame XP server has 672MB of memory.

Before you run out and start checking the memory usage of your applications, you should know the two reasons that any calculations you make based on these parameters will be totally useless:

1. Applications require varying amounts of memory. Even though task manager showed Microsoft Word to only consume 10MB of memory, you must remember that memory consumption will vary greatly depending on the documents that are open. Download and open a 300 page graphics-laden Windows 2000 white paper, and you'll see that Word can consume much more than 10MB. Another thing to watch out for is that the supporting files, such as DLLs, sometime consume the largest amount of memory.

2. Terminal Services treats multiple instances of the same executable in a special way. If 20 users are all using Word at 10MB each, then you would assume that 200MB of memory is being consumed, right? In actuality, Terminal Services is a bit smarter than that. Because all 20 users are using the same copy of winword.exe, the system figures that it doesn't need to physically load the same binary executable image into memory 20 times. Instead, it loads the executable only once and "points" the other sessions to that first instance. This is done discreetly. In fact, the components controlling each user's session think that they have a full copy of the executable loaded locally in their own memory space, when in fact all they have is a pointer to another memory space. If one session should need to modify the copy of the executable in memory, the server seamlessly (and quickly) makes a unique copy of the executable for that session.

What is particularly tricky here is the fact that if you look at the task manager, each user's session will report the full amount of memory being used. Only in the total memory usage statistics will you see that the numbers don't add up.

When you're thinking about the amount of memory to put in your MetaFrame XP servers, you should also think about how the pagefile will be used. The official pagefile recommendation for Terminal Server environments is 1.5 times the amount of physical memory. However, this does not need to be strictly followed. When determining your pagefile size, look at the types and numbers of applications that users will be using. Also consider the amount of total system memory. If you have a server with 512MB, then 1.5x pagefile is adequate. However, if you have 8GB of memory, you can probably get away with a smaller pagefile. Try a 4GB pagefile first and then increase from there if necessary.

Some people point out that if your pagefile is smaller than the amount of physical memory, you won't be able to collect any memory dumps when the server crashes. However, very few people actually analyze data from dumps. If you need to take the time to research and analyze dump data, then it is because you have a recurring problem. In this case, you can always bump up the pagefile as needed on the specific servers exhibiting the problems.

### Real-World Memory Recommendation

It is typically appropriate to estimate about 256MB for the base system. Then, for each user allow 13MB for the basic environment, plus the amount of memory each application requires. Realistically, there is almost never a reason to build a MetaFrame server with less then 512MB, and most servers now have at least 1GB.

# MetaFrame Server Processor Usage

When it comes to sizing MetaFrame server processors, don't take the time to calculate how many megahertz or gigahertz you need to support your users. Processor speeds are dictated by Intel and the hardware vendors, and you're pretty much forced to take what they offer. The real decision when sizing processors is the number of processors. In most cases, you need to figure out whether your MetaFrame servers will be single, dual, or quad-processor boxes.

In deciding how many processors you want in your servers, keep in mind that in Terminal Services environments, the multi-user kernel is based on a *cooperative* multitasking algorithm. Each user's session sends requests to the processor only as needed. If one user does not need much processor time, then more processing power is available for other users. Terminal Services does not work the same as old timesharing servers, where each user was allocated his particular time whether he used it or not.

Due to cooperative multitasking and the fact that each user's session operates several threads, MetaFrame servers tend to scale very well when two or four processors are used. (Just remember that the more processors you have, the greater your risk of running into a bottleneck in another part of the server.)

In a perfect world, your processor utilization would constantly be 99%. This would indicate that you didn't waste money buying too many processors, but also that no users have to wait for processing bottlenecks.

## Real-World Processor Recommendation

Processors are very fast and very cheap. When sizing servers, many people buy single processor servers that are dual processor capable. This allows them to test with a single processor and then add a second if the single processor does not give the results that they want.

Xeon processors will yield better performance in MetaFrame XP, as will those with more cache. The trick will be to determine whether they are worth the added cost. (See the sizing techniques section later in this chapter.)

# MetaFrame Server Hard Drive Usage

In most environments, your MetaFrame servers need only to contain the Windows operating system, the pagefile, the MetaFrame XP software, and your software application files. User and application data is usually stored on non-MetaFrame servers or a storage area network (SAN).

Ideally, all your servers will be identical to each other, so that users can successfully load balance across them and you can easily replace individual servers without affecting the entire system. (See Chapter 17 for more details.)

Because of the way that hard drives are typically used in MetaFrame environments, you don't need very much storage space on individual servers. Most people buy two drives and mirror them for redundancy. It's hard to find drives smaller than 18GB anymore, and 18GB should be more than enough storage space for each server, especially if you follow the guidelines from the previous chapter to prevent users' roaming profiles from being permanently cached on your servers.

The large hardware vendors are pushing 15k RPM drives. You'll have to test to determine whether you can actually fit more users on a server with 15k RPM drives over 10k drives. The price difference is currently so steep that if you're building more than a few servers, you can go with 10k drives and use the money saved to buy an entire extra server or two.

### Real-World Hard Drive Recommendation

Since MetaFrame XP servers don't store much data locally, you should be able to build your servers with two drives configured to mirror each other for redundancy. Today, most MetaFrame servers are the thin, 1U servers or blades with only two drives.

## MetaFrame XP Server Hardware Redundancy

Most name-brand servers now have options for redundant and hot-swappable components, including power supplies, fans, network cards, and PCI slots. Many people think these types of redundant devices are needed because the MetaFrame environment is so important to the business. While this is true, these devices are not always needed in MetaFrame environments.

Quite often, redundancy in MetaFrame environments is built-in at the server level. Instead of spending extra money on fancy servers, many administrators spend money on an extra server that can be added into the load-balance group to support users if a server is lost.

# Real-World Sizing Strategies

Now that you know how server hardware components work in MetaFrame environments, you need to think about your strategy for sizing your servers.

The objective is simple: you want to build your servers to be big enough to support your users, yet small enough so that you don't spend too much money on them.

At first, this statement may seem extremely obvious. Nevertheless, there's plenty to think about when you get ready to size your servers.

## Why Should You Care About Server Sizing?

Server sizing is not about buying the fastest processors and the most memory. When it comes to server sizing, the maximum number of users a server can support is less important than the maximum number of users you *know* it can support. If you build a server planning for fifty but only get ten users you will run into problems.

A proper server sizing strategy involves creating a balance between too many small servers and too few large servers. For example, it's possible to build a sixteen processor server with 48 gigabytes of memory. But just because you can build one gigantic server for all of your MetaFrame XP users—should you? There are plenty of servers out there that have terrible session performance with only 50% of their processors and 30% of their memory utilized.

## Server Sizing Options

By building several smaller MetaFrame XP servers, you're able to increase the redundancy of your MetaFrame XP environment. If you build one gigantic $60,000 server and something happens to it, all of your users are down. However, if you build three $20,000 servers and you lose one, only one-third of your users are not able to access their applications.

Your server environment will ideally balance between the two extreme options:

- Build a few gigantic servers.
- Build many small servers.

A similar topic was discussed in Chapter 4 with regard to the number of applications installed on a server. (Remember? All applications on all servers verses just a few applications on each server.) The difference here is that now we're thinking about the actual number of servers. For example, in Chapter 4 you might have decided to only put one application on each server. However, if you have 1,000 users accessing that application, you have a choice when it comes to server sizing. You can build a few gigantic servers (two servers supporting 500 users each) or many small servers (ten servers supporting 100 users each).

## Option 1. Build a Few Gigantic Servers

Drive space, processors, and memory are so incredibly inexpensive these days that many people are transfixed by the idea of creating a few massive servers that can each support hundreds of MetaFrame XP users. (See Figure 6.1) They like the concept of only having a few servers to manage and the fact that they can spend money on mission–critical redundant drives, processors, NICs, and power supplies.

*Figure 6.1  A few gigantic servers*

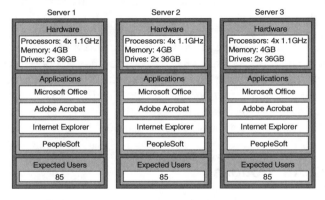

However, every server is going to have limits, and quite often, user load does not scale linearly. For example, there are situations in which one server with quad 1GHz processors and 4GB of memory will show 75 users only utilizing about one half of the system. Task manager shows that aggregate processor utilization is about 60% and memory utilization is 1.7GB. Unfortunately, environments like these often generate problems when adding additional users. Adding two additional users to such a scenario might cause the system to slow to a crawl, even though the task manager still shows that the system is only about one-half utilized. Further investigation reveals that the system has run out of page table entries (a known problem with 32-bit Windows servers running 6 or 8 processors), and that adding just two additional users caused the system to begin to get backed up.

In this case, two dual-processor servers with 2GB of memory each might have scaled better than the one large server.

### Advantages of Building a Few Gigantic Servers

- More economies of scale.
- Fewer licenses required.

### Disadvantages of Building a Few Gigantic Servers

- Single point (or fewer points) of failure.
- If you support multiple applications, many of them will need to installed (and therefore tested) together on the same server.
- The page table entry limit may prevent you from ever hosting more than 200-230 users on a single server, no matter how large that server is.

## Option 2. Build Many Small Servers

Instead of building a few gigantic servers, you might choose to build several smaller servers (as shown in Figure 6.2). This option lessens the risk that one system's failure could take out a significant user population.

*Figure 6.2  Many smaller servers*

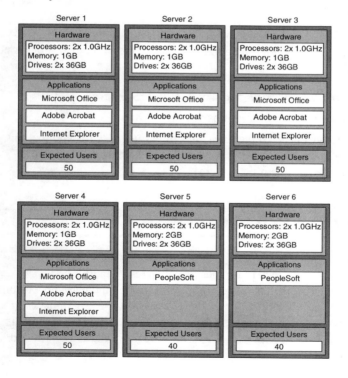

When thinking about building multiple smaller servers, two advantages become apparent, most notably redundancy and scalability. Because you have multiple servers, you could lose one without the entire user population going down. (This may mean that you might not get paged if this happens, allowing for a full night's sleep.) Also, you can schedule servers to be taken down for maintenance or to be rebooted without affecting everything.

Furthermore, you might be able to support more users with the same amount of money. (Or, you could look at this as being able to save money.) Many MetaFrame administrators also like the fact that building multiple smaller servers gives them more flexibility to dynamically deploy and re-deploy applications as users' needs change.

Another in favor of multiple, smaller servers is the ease with which servers are managed and provisioned today. Many companies are leveraging 1U "pizza box" servers or blade servers to build large farms of redundant servers. (Think of it as "RAIS"—Redundant Array of Inexpensive Servers.)

### Advantages of Building Many Small Servers

- Redundancy.
- Easier scalability.
- Flexibility. Redeploy applications and move them around as needs shift.

### Disadvantages of Building Many Small Servers

- Some utilization might be wasted.
- You will need to purchase additional licenses for applications that are licensed on a "per server" basis (such as the Microsoft Windows operating system).

# Server Sizing Techniques

Once you finalize your strategy (or perhaps in order to help you solidify your strategy), you will need to run performance tests on your servers to determine the number of users that they can support. Though there are dozens of Internet sites and research studies that provide server-sizing benchmarks, it's impossible to get exact results given the variations between environments, including network speed, protocols, Windows profiles, and hardware and software revisions.

One mistake that many people make after performing benchmark tests is to assume that the system will scale linearly based on high-level information available in task manager. Suppose that a server with no users has 4% processor utilization and 150 MB memory utilization. With five active users, the processor utilization rises to 14% and the memory to 200 MB. A quick estimate reveals that the processor would max out at 48 users, with 630 MB memory utilization.

However, real world tests might indicate that 25 users can connect, but any more cause the system to run extremely slow, even though plenty of memory and processing power is available. In these situations, the server bottleneck is not visible on the surface with task manager. The disks may be overused or the server's system bus may be full.

It is imperative that a detailed analysis be performed to determine the true system utilization. It should be no surprise that Citrix and Microsoft recommend purchasing the fastest server possible. In most situations, however, this is not feasible, so you will have to test your server hardware to determine your maximum load.

## Server Capacity Planning

There are several tools and techniques that you can use to determine the capacity and performance of your MetaFrame XP servers. To do this, you'll need to simulate user load on your servers and record the performance of the system. From there, you'll be able to determine the system's bottlenecks and capacity limits.

Regardless of the exact tool or technique that you use, all capacity planning and testing follows the same basic methodology:

1. Choose the application or applications that you would like to use for the load testing.
2. Determine what tasks a user will do within that application.
3. Determine what performance speed or response time is required.
4. Determine how users use the application.
5. Create a script or automated process that can simulate a user using the application.
6. Prepare to monitor the server's performance during the test.
7. Perform the test by executing the scripts.
8. Analyze the results.

9. Ask your boss for more money to buy a bigger server.

Results from this method of server testing should tell you two things:

1. How many users the server can support.

2. How the server performs when it is highly loaded. (For example, does performance lag for current sessions, or does it stop accepting new sessions?)

Let's detail each of the testing steps.

### Step 1. Choose your Test Application

When testing the performance of a server, the first thing you need to do is identify an application or applications to test. Ideally, you'll be able to test the applications that are most important to your business.

### Step 2. Determine Test Tasks

Once you've determined an application that you want to use for your testing, you need to think about what users will be doing with that application. Is it a line-of-business application where users will be entering data into forms and running reports on that data, or is it a spreadsheet application where users will be performing calculations? Maybe it's a word processing application where users write documents?

### Step 3. Determine Appropriate Response Times

Once you figure out how you will test the application, you need to determine what the appropriate application response time is. This will help you determine whether a server is too busy. For example, if your test application is Microsoft Word, you might determine that a letter must appear on the screen within 0.2 seconds of the user pressing the key. This would be your threshold for acceptable performance. Later on in your testing process, you may find that your server can support 130 simultaneous users before crashing, although each user has to wait 0.5 seconds for the key response delay. In this case, you may find that you can only support 80 users with the 0.2 second response time. Even though your consultant says 130, you would know that your server can really only support 80 users.

As another example, your users might need to pull up reports in a line of business application. You need to determine what the appropriate wait time is for them. If you decide that a user should not have to wait more than 15 seconds for a report, then it is unacceptable to put 60 users on a server if they must each wait 20 seconds for their reports.

## Step 4. Determine how Users Use the Application

Once you determine the appropriate responsiveness of your applications, you need to determine how active your users are. For example, some users enter data into a screen, then rummage around through papers at their desk, then enter more data. For these users, you might discover that they can enter the data in 10 seconds, but that they only do this once per minute. On the other hand, more active users might perform the same 10-second transaction six times per minute.

Knowing your mix of users is important, because a server that can support 75 "slow" users might only be able to support 40 active users.

## Step 5. Create the Application Simulation Script

Now that you've thought about the application that you would like to test and the way that users will use the application, you can begin thinking about the testing process itself. The main technique that you'll use in your capacity planning is to have multiple users access your application at the same time. By watching the performance of the system during this time, you can determine how the system will scale.

Instead of finding a bunch of users and asking them to "use the system" while you watch the performance, most people create user simulation scripts. These scripts simulate users using the system. The nice thing about creating a script is that you (as one single person) can test hundreds of users accessing the system at the same time. The other advantage of using a script instead of test users is that you can get consistent, repeatable loads and thus you'll know if any changes you make to the server actually affect performance.

An application simulation script is essentially a batch file that automates the process of a user launching and using an application. There are dozens of tools on the market that can be used to script your user sessions. The most popular ones detailed in Figure 6.3.

*Figure 6.3 Popular Windows application usage scripting tools*

| Product | URL | Cost |
| --- | --- | --- |
| AutoIt | www.hiddensoft.com/AutoIt) | Free |
| WinBatch | www.winbatch.com | US $100 |
| WinTask | www.wintask.com | US $100 |

These tools offer a "recording" mode that allows you to perform some functions (such as typing a document, browsing the web, using PeopleSoft, etc).

Once a script is recorded, you can play it back to simulate a user using the system.

When your application simulation script is complete, you should end up with a file or files that you can launch from the command line. (For example, "autoit.exe /word" or "myappscript.cmd.") The script should launch the application and then begin "playing back" the simulated user interaction.

### Step 6. Prepare to Monitor the Performance

Before you start your testing, you need to configure your system so that it records the performance of your server during the testing. It's very important that your testing data is logged and saved. While you're conducting the test, you will be focused on creating a good test. You don't want to worry about trying to view the results of the test as you're conducting it. It's much better to to record the results so that you can view them in detail at a later time.

There are two ways to measure performance in MetaFrame XP environments:

- Use the Resource Manager component of MetaFrame XPe.
- Use Windows Performance Monitor.

Resource Manager is fully discussed in Chapter 16, so we won't spend time on it here. Besides, Performance Monitor is much more appropriate for recording the results of user capacity testing.

Think back to your Windows 2000 training. Do you remember how to use Performance Monitor to record performance counters to a log file so that you can view them later?

1. In Windows 2000, launch the Performance MMC (Start | Programs | Administrative Tools | Performance).

2. Expand the tree under "Performance Logs and Alerts" in the left pane. Right-click on "Counter Logs" and choose "New Log Settings…"

3. Type a name for your new log file. (This should be a "friendly" name, such as "50 user test with MS Word.")

4. Click the "Add…" button on the screen that pops up. This is where you choose the specific counters to record. (Keep reading for a list of counters that actually matter when testing MetaFrame servers.)

5. Highlight each counter and instance that you would like to record and click the "Add" button to add them to the log file. After you've

selected all the counters you'd like, click the "Close" button to go back to the log file settings screen.

6.  By default, the system is configured to record a sample of the data every 15 seconds. Depending on your test size and hard drive space, you might want to increase the frequency to every 5 seconds or so.

7.  If you would like to change the path of the log file, you may do so by clicking the "Log Files" tab.

8.  You can also click on the "Schedule" tab to configure your log file so that it automatically starts and stops at specific times, although most people don't do this when they're running specific tests.

9.  Once your counter log is fully configured, it will appear in list in the Performance MMC. When it's time for your testing to begin, you can start the log by right-clicking it and selecting "Start" from the context menu. The icon next to the log will change from red to green.

Now that you know how to configure and save performance logs, there's one question that needs to be answered: What performance counters should you monitor? While there are many books that list "standard" performance counters and what they do, in the real world, there are only a few counters that matter when sizing MetaFrame servers.

## Performance Counters that Actually Matter

At a minimum, you should capture the following performance counters when conducting your tests:

### Memory: Pages/sec

This counter shows the number of times per second that the server looked for something in physical memory, but instead was forced to go to the paging file on the hard drive. (Technically, this is known as a "hard page fault.") Ideally this number stays around zero. Any sustained value up around 20 or 30 indicates that you need might need more memory (or fewer users).

It's important not to confuse the "Pages/sec" counter with "Page Faults/sec." The Page Faults/sec performance counter shows the total of hard *and* soft page faults. Soft page faults occur when the system is ultimately able to find what it needs in memory without going to disk. Soft page faults are not as bad as hard page faults. (It's like "good" cholesterol and "bad" cholesterol.) The important thing to remember here is that you track the "Pages/sec" counter, not the "Page Faults/sec" counter.

### Processor: % Processor Time: _Total

This counter shows how busy the processors are. If it pegs at 100% then you definitely need more of something. If the processor is too busy, don't automatically think that you need more processing power. For example, the processor might be busy because you're running out of memory, and the processor is spending a lot of unneeded time writing to and reading from the paging file.

If you notice that the processor utilization is fairly high, you might want to track the System: Processor Queue Length counter as well. This counter shows how many requests are backed up while they wait for the processor to get freed up to service them. By tracking this, you can see if the processor is very busy or too busy. (Yes, there is a difference.) A processor that is very busy might show 100% utilization, but it will back down as soon as another request comes through. You could see this because the Processor Queue Length would be almost zero. A processor that is too busy might also show 100% utilization, except that because it's too busy it cannot service additional requests, meaning that the Processor Queue Length would begin to fill up.

### Physical Disk: % Disk Time

This counter essentially shows you how busy your server's hard drives are. A value of 100% would indicate that the disks are 100% busy, meaning that you might need faster disks, more memory, or fewer users. Like with the processor counters, if your % Disk Time counter is at or near 100, you might also want to monitor the Physical Disk: Current Disk Queue Length counter. This counter will tell you how many disk requests are waiting because the disk is too busy.

If you have multiple physical disks in your server (that are not mirrored), you should record a separate instance of this counter for each disk instead of one counter for the total disks. That way, you can determine whether your disks are being used evenly, or if one disk is overworked while the other sits idle..

### Network Interface: Bytes Total/sec

If you're worried about the utilization of the server's network card, you might want to record the Bytes Total/sec of the card. If you do this, keep in mind that a 10 Mb/second network interface is 10 mega*bits*, and the performance counter tracks bytes. Since there are 8 bits in a byte, the performance counter would max out at 1.25M bytes. If you factor in physical network overhead, the actual maximum of a 10Mb network is about one megabyte per second.

In the real world, most MetaFrame servers are connected to the network at 100Mb speeds or faster, and other server hardware components max out long before the network interface.

**Terminal Services: Active Sessions**
This performance counter simply provides a count of the total number of ICA sessions (or RDP sessions) that are active on your server. This counter is extremely valuable when you're analyzing your performance logs after you've captured them. It lets you see exactly how many users were active at any given time during the log period.

In addition to these specific performance counters, there are six performance objects that are MetaFrame-specific and Terminal Services-specific. Most people forget that they exist. These object classes include:

- **Citrix IMA Networking** counters monitor IMA background communication traffic.

- **Citrix MetaFrame XP** counters monitor MetaFrame XP traffic such as zone elections, local host cache, IMA data store communications, and application enumerations.

- **Citrix Secure Ticket Authority** counters monitor Citrix Secure Gateway. (See Chapter 15 for more information about Citrix Secure Gateway.)

- **ICA Session** counters (available when using Feature Release 1 or 2) monitor the details of specific (or the aggregate totals of) ICA session bandwidth, including printing, compression, and the various virtual channels. (If you don't have MetaFrame XPe then you will only be able to see the latency-related ICA session counters.)

- **Terminal Services** counters monitor the total, active, and inactive Terminal Services (and MetaFrame) sessions.

- **Terminal Services Session** counters monitor the details of specific sessions from the perspective of Terminal Services. These counters are similar to the ICA Session counters, except that they monitor the Terminal Server-specific elements of each session. These elements include the percentage of processor time that a session uses, the number of handles and threads a session has open, session input and output bytes, frames, errors, and cache performance of a session.

### *Step 7. Conduct the Test*

Now that you have your application simulation scripts created and are ready to monitor the performance of the server during the test, you can begin the actual testing process. At first, you might think that you need to connect dozens of client workstations and manually invoke your scripts on each one, but fortunately there is a cool utility from Citrix called the Citrix Server Test Kit (CSTK) that can automate this process.

The CSTK is a utility used to run application simulation scripts from multiple ICA clients. It can even launch several sessions from a single client. Basically, it allows you (as a single person) to run tests that simulate dozens or even hundreds of users on one server. From there, you can watch your server's performance with different user loads. The CSTK is free, although you have to download it from the Citrix Developer Network (www.citrix.com/cdn). It does not come on the MetaFrame XP CD.

To use the CSTK, you will need several ICA clients in addition to the server that you want to test. These can be any platform and any type of ICA client, although there are advantages (that will become apparent later) to using 32-bit Windows clients.

The CSTK can run multiple ICA sessions from one client as long as the client device can support multiple ICA sessions and it has the resources to run as many sessions as you plan to test on it. Realistically, memory is usually the limiting factor. A good rule of thumb is that you need about 12MB of memory for each session that you want to run on a client device. For example, a Windows workstation with 128MB of memory should be able to support about 10 simultaneous ICA sessions. If you want to test your server with 100 user sessions, you would need 10 workstations, each with 128MB of memory.

Several components make up a complete CSTK environment:

- **The CSTK Console**. This is the main interface to the CSTK. It allows you to start and stop your tests, apply simulation scripts, and configure test user accounts.
- **The user simulation scripts**. These are the scripts that you created back in Step 5. The CSTK comes with some generic scripts for basic tasks (such as using Internet Explorer, calculator, notepad, etc). It also comes with more robust scripts for Office 97 and Office 2000.
- **The CSTK Client**. This is a small program that runs in every ICA test session. It is responsible for running the user simulation scripts.

It's added to the "All Users\Startup" folder when you install the CSTK.

- **The Client Launcher Utility**. This program can be used on 32-bit Windows clients to automatically launch multiple ICA sessions that are used to run the test scripts. In small test environments, this tool is not necessary. However, if you plan to test 20 sessions from a single workstation, this tool will save you from having to manually start and logon to 20 different sessions.

In order to understand how the CSTK works, let's review step-by-step how it's used:

1. The first thing you need to do is to prepare your environment. Ideally, you'll be able to run your tests on an isolated test network. Gather your MetaFrame server and the necessary ICA client devices. (You'll probably want to activate the Citrix licenses on your test server so that an annoying popup window does not break your scripts every 10 minutes. Just remember that "officially" Citrix advises against activating your server until it is finalized. It's your call. See Chapter 14 for the gory details of licensing.)

2. If you haven't done so already, install the CSTK on your server. (Remember to put your server into install mode first.) After the CSTK is installed, you'll notice that the "CSTK Client" is automatically launched whenever a user logs on. For now, you can just ignore that.

3. Launch the CSTK administrative console. (Start | Programs | Citrix Server Test Kit 2.1 | CSTK Console) You will use this console to configure your testing environment and run your tests.

4. Next, import the application simulation scripts you created in Step 5 into the CSTK environment. This process will make these scripts available to the CSTK. To do this, choose Tools | Add Application Scripts. You can specify anything you want for the Script Name. Use the "Browse" button to browse to the path of the executable of your script. You can specify any necessary command-line parameters in the "Parameters" box. For example, if you used AutoIt to create your script, you might need to specify `AutoIt.exe` in the "Program Name" box, and `yoursrcriptname.txt` in the "Parameters" box. Specify whether your application applies to "Normal Users" or "Power Users." Normal users will only run one script at a time, and power users will run multiple scripts simultaneously.

5. After you've added the application scripts, you need to configure groups of test users that will use your scripts (User Group | Add, or

click the "+" button on the toolbar). When you specify users, you're essentially indicating which application scripts run for which users when they log on. When adding a user group, the first question you're asked is whether you want to add a group of Normal Users or Power Users. Make your selection and click "OK."

6. Next, you need to specify a range of usernames that will run an application script (or scripts) when they log on. Specify the usernames by entering the basename and the number of users. For example, to apply a script to users "brian1" through "brian5," you would enter "brian" as the basename and "5" as the number of users. If this is the first time that you're using the CSTK and you don't have any test user accounts created, you can click the "Create Users" button. This will create the test user accounts based on the baseline name and number of users. These user accounts are created with blank passwords.

7. Before you click "OK," highlight the script or scripts that you want this user group to run and click the "Add" button. If you elected to create normal users, selecting multiple scripts will cause the users to run them one by one and the list of available scripts will only show those that you've designated for normal users. If you elected to create power users, selecting multiple scripts will cause the users to execute them all at the same time, and the list of available scripts will only show those that you've designated for power users. In a sense, normal users execute their application scripts in a "serial" fashion, and power users execute them in a "parallel" fashion.

8. Once you add a group of users and click "OK," you'll see them listed on the main CSTK console screen. You can add as many groups of users as you want (as long as the basenames are not the same in two different groups).

9. At this point, the CSTK is fully configured and you should save your testing environment configuration. You can save the entire configuration, including user groups and applications, by choosing File | Save Configuration File. Your settings are then saved as an INI file with a .CST file extension. You can load your settings into the CSTK so that you don't have to manually set up everything from scratch in the future. When you save a configuration file, it does not include the application script information. When adding application scripts to the CSTK, they are available until they are deleted. If you delete one, loading a configuration file where it was used will not bring it back.

10. In order to begin the testing process, choose Test | Start Test or click

the lightning bolt button on the toolbar. You'll notice that starting the test doesn't actually do anything. You have to log users on in order for the scripts to execute. This is also a good time to start your performance monitor logging process as described back in Step 6.

11. From one of your ICA client devices, log on as one of your test users. This should be a user that is configured in one of the user groups in the CSTK console. Since a shortcut to the CSTK Client was added to the "All Users\Startup" folder when the CSTK was installed, it will launch after logon and the appropriate application script or scripts will start to run.

12. In order to easily launch multiple ICA sessions from a single 32-bit Windows client device, you can use the CSTK Client Launcher. Log onto a client workstation and run `CSTKlaun.exe` from the "ClntLaun" folder of the CSTK directory. When you run it, it will detect the path of the ICA client executable (`wfcrun.exe`). Verify that this path is correct and enter the usernames that you want the sessions to be run from. The username entries follow the same baseline syntax as the groups within the CSTK. For example, if you have 10 test workstations that you plan to use for 10 sessions each, you would configure your CSTK for usernames "test1" through "test100." Then, you would configure the CSTK Client Launcher to use "test1" through "test10" on the first workstation, "test11" through "test20" on the second workstation, and so on.

13. After you specify the users that will run on a workstation, you need to click the "Create Entries" button in the CSTK Client Launcher to create custom ICA connections for each user in the workstation's Program Neighborhood. Clicking this button brings up a screen that allows you to specify the default options used for each connection (such as the name of the server to connect to, protocols, etc.) Configure your options as needed and click "OK."

14. Before you run your test, click the "Advanced Delay" button to specify the delay between sessions. This allows you to specify how much time passes between launching sessions. One of the nice features is that it allows you to specify progressively more time as more sessions are launched, allowing you to anticipate slower responses as the server gets more loaded.

15. After you've configured the delay, you can click the "Run" button on the Launcher's main screen. ICA user sessions will begin to be launched, and they will run the scripts that you specified for the user groups in the CSTK console.

As you add users to your testing environment, you should add them in small groups. For example, if you're testing 100 users, you might want to add 10 users every five minutes for the first hour or so, and then add users one-by-one. By doing this, you'll be able to figure out how each user affects the overall system.

Don't forget to stop your performance monitor recording log once your testing is complete. Once it's stopped, you can examine it to determine the results of your test.

## Step 8. Analyze the Results

Once you've stopped your performance monitor log, you can view the results within the Performance MMC console. With the "System Monitor" object highlighted in the left-hand pane, click the button with the picture of the cylinder on it and browse to your log file. This will configure the graph to pull its data from the log file instead of from the current system activity.

Even after you configure the graph to get its data from the log file, you'll notice that the graph is still blank. You need to manually add the performance counters that you want to view. Use the "+" button on the toolbar, just like you would with live data. The only difference is that when you're displaying data from a log file, the only performance counters listed will be the ones that you recorded in the log file.

As you analyze your results, keep in mind to look for the bottlenecks in your system. Every system will max out at some point. If your system seems to be running out of memory (due to high page faults) then you can probably add more. Once you do that and run the tests again, you might find out that you can support 10 additional users but then your processors start to max out (due to a consistent Processor Queue Length).

Another fact to keep in mind is that when you use the CSTK, the CSTK client utility takes about 2.8MB of server memory for each session that is tested. Also, capturing performance logs takes up system resources.

Based on the data from the log file of your test, you can probably figure out the point in which your server performance starts to fall drastically. Looking at the Active Sessions counter will tell you how many sessions there were when that performance drop occurred. Once you determine how many users your system can hold, you may want to run your tests again. For this second round of tests, you might ask live users to log on in addition to your test users. The live users will be able to tell you whether the system is usable or not.

## Third Party Server Sizing Tools

If your MetaFrame environment is really important to your business, or if you work for a consulting company, there are some third-party server sizing and stress test tools that are much easier to use than the CSTK, and they produce much more accurate results. (Of course the downside is that they are expensive.)

The two most popular tools are StressTest by Scapa Technologies (www.scapatech.com) and LoadRunner by Mercury Interactive (www.mercuryinteractive.com). These two tools are similar. In addition to being easy to use, they have the ability to test the performance of a MetaFrame server from end-to-end, instead of only testing the impact of multiple user sessions and application execution as with the CSTK. They can test the aggregate affects of server load, network bandwidth, compression, encryption, and ICA virtual channel use.

Also, because they work by using dedicated testing workstations to monitor session performance, the testing itself doesn't impact the results (unlike the CSTK which itself consumes server resources).

The process by which these third party tools are used is the same as when the CSTK is used. You still have to write application simulation scripts. However, the third party tools make it easier to run the tests and interpret the data.

Both the Scapa tools and the Mercury tools are widely used, and it's up to you to determine which is more appropriate for your environment. Mercury Interactive has always positioned themselves at the top tier of testing products, and their pricing for their MetaFrame tools reflects that. (Their product is more than twice the cost of Scapa's product.) However, if you work for a consulting company, Scapa offers a "roving" license that allows you to take their testing tools from customer to customer.

### Advantages of Third-Party Testing Tools

- They test the performance of the entire system, not just the server.
- They employ outside "control" testing stations, so the act of testing does not skew the testing results.
- They provide the most accurate, end-to-end MetaFrame sizing and stress testing.

### Disdvantages of Third-Party Testing Tools

- They are expensive (approximately US $25,000 for Scapa and US $50,000 for Mercury)

# Performance Tuning your Environment

In the previous section, we discussed server sizing. Server sizing and performance tuning are closely related. The main difference is that server sizing is about choosing the proper hardware, and performance tuning is about making software configuration changes that affect how efficiently the hardware is used. In this section, we'll look at several techniques and resources that you can use to tune your servers, their applications, and the network.

## Tuning Servers

If your server sizing tests showed that you can get 40 users on a MetaFrame server, there might be some configuration tricks that you can use to bump that up to 42, 44 or even 50 users.

It seems like almost every day another performance tweak or registry hack is discovered that can help MetaFrame XP servers run faster. In this book, we've focused on the techniques that you can use to get the best performance out of your MetaFrame XP environment from a design standpoint. If you want to tune your servers even further, there is one place that lists all the registry keys and the settings that can help you. That place is the website www.TweakCitrix.com. This site is run as a "side project" by Rick Dehlinger, a Senior Systems Engineer for Citrix. TweakCitrix.com is home to the famous "MetaFrame Installation and Tuning Tips" document. This document, compiled by Rick, contains hundreds of tuning tips and tricks sent in by Citrix administrators worldwide. TweakCitrix.com also features several message boards containing up-to-the-minute postings about performance tuning MetaFrame XP systems.

Rather than waste the paper required to list those tuning tips (which are constantly being updated anyway), you should go straight to the source at www.TweakCitrix.com.

Another phenomenal way to tune your MetaFrame XP servers is to purchase a utility called "TScale" from Kevsoft. (www.kevsoft.com) TScale is a small program that runs in the background on a MetaFrame XP server. It constantly monitors how the server uses its virtual memory. Then, in the middle of the night (every night), a batch process runs that applies optimizations based on what it saw that day.

It only takes a few minutes to install and configure TScale, and after a few days you will notice a performance increase of 30% to 40%, which means that you can support 30% to 40% more users. A 30-day evaluation copy of TScale is available, and you should definitely try it out. (Author's Note: I have no vested interest in TScale or KevSoft. I just really like their products, and I think that they work well.)

Lastly, as was mentioned elsewhere in this book, remember that you can always visit http://thethin.net for a lively source (about 100 new messages per day) of thin client topics, including performance tuning techniques.

## Tuning Applications

In addition to the techniques that you can use to tune your server, you also can specify the CPU priority of published applications if you're using Feature Release 1 or 2 and you have MetaFrame XPa or XPe (CMC | Published Application Properties | Application Limits Tab). There are five levels of priority settings that you can set: high, above normal, normal, below normal, and low. Configuring these settings directly affects the application's processes, similar to changing a process's priority with the Task Manager (Task Manager | Processes tab | Right-click on process | Set Priority)

When you configure the CPU priority of a published application, every instance of that application is launched with the configured priority, even if the application is load-balanced across more than one MetaFrame XP server.

Be careful when setting the CPU priority of a published application. Just about all of the processes on a MetaFrame XP server are, by default, set to "normal." If you configure an application to be above that, then you may run into trouble because that application may take processing time away from other critical operating system components.

Realistically, configuring application CPU priority should be done as a sort of "last resort," when other server planning and sizing methods fail to produce adequate performance results.

### Advantages to Setting Application CPU Priority
- Allows more important applications to preempt less important ones.

### Disadvantages of Setting Application CPU Priority
- Don't expect too much.
- Not a substitute for real server sizing planning.
- Can be very dangerous if hastily planned.

- Requires Feature Release 1 or 2.
- Does not work with MetaFrame XPs.
- Does not work with Terminal Server 4.0.

## Tuning the Network

The last MetaFrame XP performance tuning element to look at is the network. Before we explore the details of how you can tune your network, it's important to review some basics of network performance.

### *Factors Affecting Network Performance*

When thinking about network performance, you need to understand the difference between "latency" and "bandwidth." Both are used to describe the speed of a network. Bandwidth describes how much data can pass through the network in a given period of time, such as 10 megabits per second, or 256 kilobits per second. Latency describes the length of time, usually expressed in milliseconds (there are 1000 milliseconds in one second), that it takes for data to get from point A to point B. Bandwidth and latency are independent of each other.

The fact that bandwidth and latency are different from each other is an important concept to understand in MetaFrame environments. (This is so important that we're going to resurrect the "highway" analogy.)

Imagine that each bit of data is an automobile, and the network is a highway. In order for the data to get from point A to point B, an automobile would have to travel from one end of the highway to the other. In high-bandwidth environments, the highway has many lanes, and hundreds of automobiles can be on it at the same time. In low bandwidth environments, the highway is a narrow country road, and only a few automobiles can fit in it at the same time. The width of the highway is like the bandwidth of the network.

Since latency affects how long it takes data to traverse the network, the speed of the automobiles on the highway represents the latency. Even on narrow highways (low bandwidth), there might be people who drive really fast and travel the road quickly (low latency). Conversely, even if you have a large number of automobiles on a wide highway (high bandwidth), the drivers may choose to drive slowly (high latency).

We said that bandwidth and latency are not really related, because the width of the highway does not directly affect how fast you drive on it. However, as you've probably guessed by now, it's possible that bandwidth *can* affect latency.

Thinking again to our highway example, imagine a low-bandwidth environment that also has low latency (a narrow highway where the people drive really fast). If there are only a few automobiles on the road, they can go fast without problems. However, imagine that the hallway begins to fill up with more and more autos. Even though the people want to drive fast, they can't because the highway is too crowded. The effect is that it will take the longer for automobiles to get from one end of the highway to the other. In a sense, the latency has increased from low latency to high latency simply because there are too many vehicles on the highway.

There are several solutions to the overcrowded highway problem. You could:

- Widen the highway.
- Remove some of the vehicles.
- Force people to drive smaller vehicles.
- Install traffic signals and lane control devices to manage the traffic.

As you'll see, the four potential solutions to the overcrowded highway problem are also the four potential solutions to overcrowded networks in Meta-Frame XP environments.

Back in the real world, a network connection's bandwidth and latency each affect Citrix ICA session traffic in different ways:

- Bandwidth affects how much data the session can contain. Higher resolution sessions require more bandwidth than lower resolution sessions. Sessions with sound, printing, and client drive mapping all require more bandwidth than sessions without. If a particular session only has 15Kbps of bandwidth available, that session can still have decent performance so long as the resolution, color depth, and other virtual channel options are tuned appropriately.

- Latency is usually more critical in thin client environments. Since latency affects the amount of time it takes for communication to pass between the client and the server, environments with high latency can seem like they have a "delay" from the user's perception.

For example, imagine an environment where a user was using Microsoft Word via an ICA session. When they press a key on their ICA client device, the key code is sent across the network to the MetaFrame server. The server processes the keystroke and prepares to display the proper character on the screen. Because this is a Terminal Server, the screen information is redirected back across the network where it is displayed on the local ICA client device. In order for a character to appear on the screen, data must travel from the client to the server and then from the server back to the client again.

In this situation, if the latency of the network is 10ms, the network delay will only add 20ms (because the data crosses the network twice) to the time between the key press and the character appearing on the user's screen. Since 20ms is only 0.02 seconds, the delay will not be noticeable. However, if the latency was 200ms, the total delay to the user would be 400ms, or almost one-half of a second. This length of delay would be noticeable to the user, and would probably be unacceptable.

An easy way to get an approximation of the latency in your environment is to perform a TCP/IP ping. You can ping the server from the client or the client from the server, it doesn't matter which way. For example, if your server is called "server01" would you execute the following command from an ICA client workstation:

```
ping server01
```

(Be sure that you execute the ping command locally on the workstation, not via an ICA session on the server.) The results will look something like this:

```
Pinging server01 [10.1.1.42] with 32 bytes of data:

Reply from 10.1.1.42: bytes=32 time=378ms TTL=118
Reply from 10.1.1.42: bytes=32 time=370ms TTL=118
Reply from 10.1.1.42: bytes=32 time=360ms TTL=118
Reply from 10.1.1.42: bytes=32 time=351ms TTL=118

Ping statistics for 10.1.1.42:
    Packets: Sent = 4, Received = 4, Lost = 0
Approximate round trip times in milli-seconds:
    Minimum = 351ms, Maximum = 378ms, Average = 364ms
```

Notice that the time= section of each line shows you the approximate latency. This time is the time that the "pinger" waited for a response from the "pingee," meaning that the time shown represents the entire round-trip.

The above scenario with the 364ms latency could have occurred in a dial-up environment with a bandwidth of 28kbps or a frame-relay environment with

512kbps. In either situation, the performance would not be as good as an environment with less latency.

### Resolving Network Performance Issues

Once you've determined whether your network performance issues are bandwidth-related or latency-related, you can begin to address them.

If your network suffers from a lack of bandwidth:

- See what type of traffic you can remove from the network. This is like removing extra automobiles in our highway example.

- Make the ICA sessions as "small" as possible. For example, your current ICA sessions might be 24-bit color, with audio and port mapping enabled. Monitoring the network might show that your ICA sessions were consuming 40k bps. By switching to 16-bit color and disabling audio and port mapping, you might be able to get your ICA sessions down to 20k bps. This is like convincing everyone to drive smaller cars in our highway example.

- Install a hardware device to monitor and control application and ICA bandwidth. This is like adding a traffic cop and traffic signals in our highway example.

The two most popular types of bandwidth management devices are Packeteer's PacketShaper (www.packeteer.com) and Sitara's QoSWorks (www.sitaranetworks.com). Both are physical hardware devices that sit between your network and the WAN router, as shown in Figure 6.4.

*Figure 6.4  Third party bandwidth-management device usage*

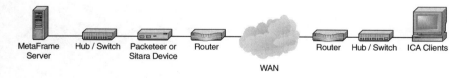

These devices allow you to analyze and capture current traffic usage (which is when you'll discover that 75% of your WAN traffic is web surfing).

You can then give Citrix ICA traffic priority over other types of traffic. You can even configure these devices to give different priorities to different IP addresses. You can also guarantee certain amounts of bandwidth to ICA (or any protocol).

These third-party devices are similar to Cisco Quality of Service (QoS) devices, except that the Sitara and Packeteer devices are "Layer 7" routers and can differentiate ICA traffic from other types of traffic.

If you determine that your network performance issues are due to high latency, there are also some steps that you can take to help improve performance:

- Enable Citrix "SpeedScreen" technology. This technology uses different kinds of caching and character generation methods to make user sessions appear faster in highly-latent environments. Full details on SpeedScreen are covered in Chapter 10.

If you have high latency, don't forget (as shown in our highway example) that freeing up some bandwidth might also have the positive effect of lowering your overall latency.

# CHAPTER 7

# Printing

In this chapter

| | |
|---|---|
| How Windows Printing Works | 260 |
| How MetaFrame XP Printing Works | 262 |
| Managing Printer Drivers | 285 |
| Configuring Printers for Users | 293 |
| Third Party Printing Solutions | 299 |
| Real World Case Study | 305 |

At some point during your MetaFrame XP system design you'll remember that your users will probably want to print something sooner or later. Printing is an important function to users within their MetaFrame XP sessions, yet it has traditionally been the biggest nightmare for MetaFrame administrators. Ideally, printing from applications via ICA sessions should be no different than printing from any other application. It should be seamless to the user, allowing them to click the print button within their application, easily select a printer, and quickly receive their printout.

All server-based computing environments pose unique challenges to printing. This is not due to any Citrix or Microsoft design flaw, but rather with the way processing occurs in server-based architectures. Because all application processing occurs on the server, users' print jobs are also created on the server. However, users' printers are usually located or configured at their client devices. The process of getting server-generated print jobs to a client-specified printer can be complicated.

In this chapter, we'll look at how Windows printing works and the printing options that are available when using MetaFrame XP. We'll also look at what it takes to assign printers to users when you have dozens or even hundreds of users connecting from the same server. We'll close this chapter with an in-depth case study that examines the challenges faced by one company's multi-faceted printing environment.

## How Windows Printing Works

Before we explore the challenges of MetaFrame XP printing and the many solutions, you need to understand how Windows printing works. After all, the process by which a MetaFrame XP server prints is no different than any other Windows computer.

There are a surprising number of steps that take place whenever a document is printed, even in a traditional computing environment. However, whether you're printing a document to a local printer, a network printer, or through a Citrix ICA session, the process is basically the same.

Behind the scenes, there are three phases that take place from the moment you hit the "print" button in your application to the moment the finished print job appears on the printer:

- Phase 1. Windows Application.
- Phase 2. Print Spooler.

• Phase 3. Printer.

*Figure 7.1 The Windows printing process*

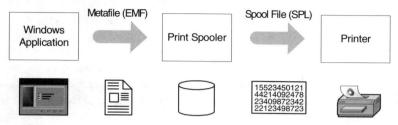

## Phase 1. Windows Application

When a user requests a printout from a Windows application, the application is responsible for generating its own output in preparation for printing. This output includes items such as formatting the pages properly and adding page numbers. The application processes its printer output via a Windows subsystem called the Graphics Device Interface (GDI). This GDI generates the application's output in the form of an enhanced metafile (EMF).

EMF files are not printer-specific. An application would generate the same EMF file for one printout no matter what kind of printer it was printing to. This is why any Windows application can print to any printer. The EMF file is the common middleman between the application and the printer. In order to understand this, let's consider how the following line of text would be printed:

All people seem to need data processing.

The EMF file for this line of text would contain instructions for the printout, including things like the color, font, characters, and the spacing. The EMF document is a vectorized document that is very small in size. As soon as the EMF file is generated, the application is no longer involved in the printing process. This is why you can close an application before it's done printing and the print job will still finish. The application is only involved in the beginning of the print process to generate the EMF print file. After that, it hands everything over to Windows. Windows then passes the EMF file to the print spooler.

## Phase 2. Print Spooler

The print spooler itself performs many printing-related functions. The easiest way to understand what the print spooler does is to break it up into logical steps. The print spooler is responsible for the following three tasks:

- Receiving the EMF print file from the application via the GDI.
- Translating the EMF file to another file in the printer's native language.
- Ensuring that the native file is successfully transferred to the printer.

After receiving the EMF file from the GDI, the print spooler uses the printer drivers to translate the EMF file into a printer spool file (.SPL). The printer spool file contains detailed instructions for the print device. Take another look at our example:

All people seem to need data processing.

In this case, the printer spool file would contain the printer-specific detailed instructions and formatting needed for printing in the printer's native language. This would include resolution, paper tray information, form feed data, and the rasterized image of the page. Printer spool files vary in size depending on the type of printer and how well the drivers are written. In all cases, however, the printer spool files are much larger than the EMF files.

Once the spool file is created, the print spooler ensures that the file is transferred to the printer.

### Phase 3. Printer

In the final printing phase, the printer receives the spool file from the print spooler. The printer prints this file no matter what. This is why printers will print garbage if the wrong drivers are used. Using the wrong drivers creates spool files that are not compatible with the printer. However, the printer doesn't know this and it tries to print whatever it receives.

# How MetaFrame XP Printing Works

Now that you understand how printing works in standard Windows environments, let's see how printing can be configured in MetaFrame XP environments. Before we get too far into the details of MetaFrame XP printing, we need to "redefine" some standard printing terms for the MetaFrame XP environment.

Even with the infinite number of printing scenarios available in the real world, there are only two major types of printing scenarios available in MetaFrame

XP. All MetaFrame XP printing is a variation on one of the following two themes:

- *Client Printers*. These are printers that are connected to the ICA client device when a MetaFrame XP session is launched. Depending on the client platform, this can include printers that are physically attached to the client or printers that are logically mapped to the client through the network.

- *Server Printers*. Server printers in MetaFrame XP environments are printers where the MetaFrame XP server has direct access to the print queue. This can include standard network printers that are accessible via a \\servername\printername share. It can also include printers where the print queue is located locally on a MetaFrame XP server, even including printers that are directly connected to MetaFrame XP servers.

*Figure 7.2 The various types of MetaFrame XP printers*

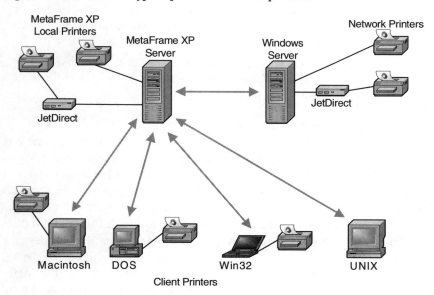

It's important that you understand the differences between client and server printers in MetaFrame XP environments. Each type has advantages and disadvantages is used or configured differently. For these reasons, we'll look at client printers and server printers separately in this chapter, beginning now with client printers.

# Client Printers

Different ICA client platforms support different types of client printers in MetaFrame XP. For that reason, we need to outline the differences of the various client platforms so that we know what client printer options are available:

- *On 32-bit Windows ICA client devices*, all printers configured in Windows before the user connects to the MetaFrame XP server are considered client printers. This is basically any printer that appears in the "Printers" folder on the client computer, including printers that are physically connected to the client computer, as well as network printers that are mapped by a logon script or user profile.

- *On Windows CE, DOS, and Mac OS client devices*, a client printer is a printer that is physically connected to a local port on the client device. This usually includes printers that are connected to the local LPT1 port. This is different from 32-bit Windows clients, because any network printers that are mapped by local users cannot be automatically used as client printers within MetaFrame XP sessions from these platforms.

- *On other Citrix ICA client platforms*, client printers cannot be directly used from MetaFrame XP sessions. Printing from these environments must be configured via server printers.

## How Client Printers are used by MetaFrame XP

Before we can look at how client printers are configured in MetaFrame XP, we need to understand how client printers are used by MetaFrame XP. When a user with client printers connects to the MetaFrame XP server, the user's local ICA client software automatically shares the printers that the user has installed locally. When the user needs to print a document from within a MetaFrame XP application, they invoke the print job as usual. From within their MetaFrame XP session, they will see the shares of their local client device's printers. These printers will have the name `\\clientname#\printername`. These printers are not fully installed locally on the MetaFrame XP server, they are just automatically shared on the client device by the ICA client software. When the user prints to one of his client printers, the process outlined in Figure 7.3 (facing page) takes place.

1. The user prints from his application running on the MetaFrame XP server.

2. The application creates the EMF file on the MetaFrame XP server.

3. The EMF file is sent to the print spooler on the MetaFrame XP server.

4. The print spooler creates the spooled print job, using the proper drivers for the client's printer. This is possible because the MetaFrame XP server has the appropriate printer drivers loaded on it for the client's printer.

5. The spooled print job is sent from the MetaFrame XP server to the ICA client device. This spool file is sent as part of the ICA protocol, although at a lower priority than things like screen updates and the user interface.

6. The client device receives the spool file. Because the MetaFrame XP server had the drivers loaded for the client's printer, the print job is spooled specifically for the client's printer, and the client device can send the print job right to the printer.

*Figure 7.3 Printing to a MetaFrame XP client printer*

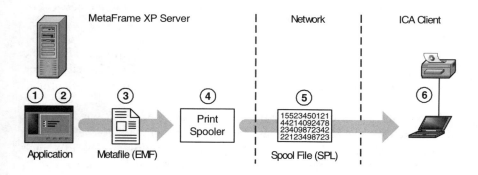

One thing that is immediately obvious when looking at the client printer process is the potential for a severe performance problem. Spooled print jobs are usually quite large, and they can take a long time to transmit to the client's printer, especially if the user is connected via a dial-up line. Additionally, the performance of the ICA session can be degraded because bandwidth is being consumed by the spooled print job that is being sent to the client.

One potential solution involves printing to clients' network printers. If your users connect from 32-bit Windows clients, any network printers that they have mapped are also shared and mapped in their ICA session when they connect to a MetaFrame XP server. If you think about it, printing to a client's network printer actually makes the problem worse, not better. Let's look at what happens in this case.

*Figure 7.4 MetaFrame XP printing to client network printers*

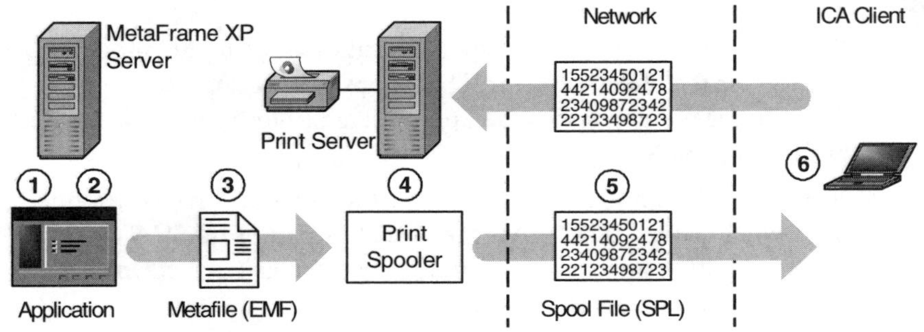

Steps one through five are identical to steps one through five in Figure 7.3, when a client's local printer is used. The only difference when a client's network printer is used is shown in step six.

6. The client device receives the spool file. Because the MetaFrame XP server had the drivers loaded for the client's mapped network printer, the client device can send the print job right to the network printer.

As you can see, if the client's printer is a mapped network printer, the spooled print job is sent across the network to the ICA client. The ICA client then immediately sends the print job across the same network to the network printer.

Of course the solution is to route the print job from the MetaFrame XP server directly to the print server, without channeling it through the ICA client. This is a commonly used alternative to the previously outlined scenario, which will be studied later in the "Server Printers" section of this chapter.

There are a few more downsides to client printer mapping, in addition to the performance impact. The first involves the printer driver requirement on the MetaFrame XP server. As you saw in Figures 7.3 and 7.4, a user's print job is created, rendered, and spooled on the MetaFrame XP server when client printer mappings are used. Because of this, the server must have the necessary drivers for the client's printer installed, so that the server knows how to create the print job. Remember, all of the work for printing is being done on the server, which means that the server needs the proper print drivers installed, not the ICA client.

If you have an environment in which your users have only a few different types of printers, then this might not be a problem. However, if you have hundreds of users with hundreds of different printers, installing and configuring printer drivers on your MetaFrame XP servers can be a nightmare. We'll study the use and management of printer drivers a bit later in this chapter.

Another downside to client printer mapping is that in order for a user to be able to use a printer, it must be installed and configured locally on the client device. This could be the exact opposite of what you're trying to do by using MetaFrame XP. Most likely, you want to move away from having to configure things on individual users' workstations. If a user installs, deletes, or otherwise modifies their local workstation printers (not your problem), it will affect how they print from their MetaFrame XP session (definitely your problem).

### Advantages of Printing with Mapped Client Printers

- Seamless connection of printers.
- Users see printers that they are familiar with.
- All supported local printers are available.
- Quick setup for existing client printers.

### Disadvantages of Printing with Mapped Client Printers

- Poor print performance.
- Bandwidth intensive.
- Printers must be installed and configured on local clients.
- Users can update, modify, or delete their local printers, directly impacting the MetaFrame XP client printer mappings.

### Configuring Client Printers

By definition, client printers are already set up and configured on the client devices, so there is nothing else that you need to do there. All client printer mapping configuration is done centrally at your MetaFrame XP servers. From a high level, allowing users to print to their client printers involves two steps:

1. Install the printer drivers on your MetaFrame XP Servers.
2. Configure your servers to use client printers.

### Step 1. Install Printer Drivers

The first thing that must be done is to install the necessary print drivers on servers in the server farm. Because the applications are running on the servers and the print jobs are spooled on the servers, you need to have the drivers installed on every MetaFrame XP server for every different client printer. There are many issues associated with the installation and management of printer drivers on MetaFrame XP servers. We will look at the specific details in the "Managing Printer Drivers" section of this chapter.

If a MetaFrame XP server cannot find an appropriate driver for a client printer when a user connects, then that client printer will not be available from within that ICA session.

### Step 2. Configure the MetaFrame Server to Connect Client Printers

After the printer drivers are installed, you need to configure MetaFrame XP to connect clients' printers when their ICA sessions are started. You will have to configure: MetaFrame XP server permissions, the MetaFrame XP server connection, and the user's domain account properties.

**Verify MetaFrame XP Server Permissions for Printing**

In order for users to be able to print on a MetaFrame XP server, they will need Read, Write, Execute, and List Folder Contents access to the print spooler's directory, %SystemRoot%\System32\Spool.

**Verify MetaFrame Server Connection Configuration for Client Printer Use**

With the Citrix Connection Configuration tool, you can configure the client printer options for all users that use a particular connection. In the "client settings" area of the connection properties, make sure that the "disable windows client printer mapping" or "disable client LPT mapping" boxes are *not* checked. Obviously, checking either one of these boxes will prevent client printers from being mapped.

If the "Inherit User Configuration" option is checked, then you will need to verify that the user's account is properly configured for client printer mapping.

**Verify Citrix User Policies**

If you're leveraging the Citrix user policy feature of Feature Release 2, then you need to make sure that the effective policies for your users allow for the auto-creation of client printers. See Chapter 5 for more information about Citrix user policies.

**Configure User Account Settings**

You can configure client printer connection settings on a user-by-user basis. In Windows NT 4.0 domains, this is done by editing the user's account properties with a copy of user manager for domains that came with Terminal Server (User Manager for Domains | User Configuration Button). In Active Directory environments, the client printer mapping properties are part of the user's

AD object (Active Directory Users and Computers | User Object | Environment Tab).

In either environment, selecting "Connect Client Printers at Logon" will cause the user's client printer to automatically be created when they log onto a MetaFrame XP server. When the user logs off and all his print jobs have printed, the printer is automatically deleted. If you do not set the "Connect Client Printers at Logon" option, a user will still be able to manually map to his client printer, it just will not be created for him automatically.

### Enable Auto-created Printers

Once you have everything set up, you will need to ensure that auto-created client printers are enabled in your server farm. (CMC | Right-click on Printer Management | Properties | Printers tab). If you're using Feature Release 2, you can also use this screen to configure the properties of auto-created printers, including how you want the properties to be updated, whether users can specify their own settings, and whether unfinished print jobs should be deleted when a user logs off.

### Auto-created Client Printer Names

When a printer is auto-created from an ICA client device, the printer will have the name `\\clientname#\printername`. The comment field will read "Auto Created Client Printer." If you modify or delete the text of the comment, MetaFrame XP will not realize that the printer was auto-created, and will not delete it when the user logs off. Upon subsequent logons by the same user, MetaFrame XP will use the existing printer information without modifying it. If a user changes his printer settings, those changes are not maintained. While this can be useful for preserving custom print settings, it will also cause all of the printers to remain installed on the server.

### *Printer Driver Problems when Using Mapped Client Printers*

Remember that your MetaFrame XP server must have the printer drivers installed locally for users to be able to print to their client printers, because the print jobs are rendered and spooled on the server.

When a user with client printer mapping enabled starts a MetaFrame XP session, the server checks the driver names of the user's client printers. It then looks at all the driver names of its own installed printers. If there's a match, the server knows that it has the appropriate drivers installed to support that printer and the printer is automatically mapped for that user's session. If there is no match, then that printer is skipped and the MetaFrame XP server moves on to the next client printer. For example, if the MetaFrame XP server has a driver installed called "HP OfficeJet 40xi" and the ICA client has a printer called "HP OfficeJet 40xi," the server will know that there's a match. However, if the client has a printer installed called "Canon BJC-620," then obviously the server knows that there is not a match.

This works fine if your ICA clients and your MetaFrame XP server are running on the same platform, since the exact same printer drivers will be installed on both ends. However, this leads to an interesting problem if your client platform is not the same as your MetaFrame XP server platform. For example, some printers have driver names in Windows 95 are not the same as in their Windows 2000 counterparts. If one of your users has a LaserJet 5P printer, the Windows 95 driver name of the printer on that user's workstation might be called "Hewlett Packard LaserJet 5P." However, the MetaFrame XP server will have the Windows 2000 version of that printer's driver installed. Instead of being called a "Hewlett Packard LaserJet 5P," the Windows 2000 driver might be called "HP LaserJet 5P." To human readers, the driver names seem the same, but to MetaFrame XP, the fact that one starts with "HP" and the other starts with "Hewlett Packard" causes the two driver names to be different. Because MetaFrame XP interprets these names as being different, ICA clients using Windows 95 will not be able to print to their own local printer, because MetaFrame XP thinks that it doesn't have a driver that can support it.

### Solution: Printer Driver Mapping

To address this, it's possible for you to correlate the driver names of client printers with the driver names of server printers. In this case, you would tell MetaFrame XP that the client printer "Hewlett Packard LaserJet 5P" is the same as the server printer "HP LaserJet 5P."

In order to do this, you can place a file on your MetaFrame XP server called wtsuprn.inf. This file, which you should put in the `%systemroot%\system32\` folder, contains server-name to client-name printer driver mappings. By default, this file does not exist. However, there is a template called wtsuprn.txt that you can modify. After you modify the template, you need to change its extension from .txt to .inf. Let's take a look at that template now.

*Figure 7.5 The wtsuprn.txt template file*

```
===========================================================
; WTSUPRN.TXT
;
[Identification]
        OptionType = PRINTER
[ClientPrinters]
```

```
;
;       Client Name                      Server Name
;            |                                |
;            |                                |
;            |                                |
;           \|/                              \|/
;"HP LaserJet 4/4M"              = "HP LaserJet 4"
;"HP LaserJet 4P/4MP"            = "HP LaserJet 4P"
;"HP LaserJet 4 Plus/4M Plus"    = "HP LaserJet 4 Plus"
;"HP LaserJet 4Si/4Si MX"        = "HP LaserJet 4Si"
;"HP LaserJet 4V/4MV"            = "HP LaserJet 4V"
;"HP LaserJet 5/5M - Enhanced"   = "HP LaserJet 5"
;"HP LaserJet 5/5M - Standard"   = "HP LaserJet 5"
;"HP LaserJet 5/5M PostScript"   = "HP LaserJet 5"
;"HP LaserJet 5L (PCL)"          = "HP LaserJet 5L"
;"HP LaserJet 5P/5MP (HP)"       = "HP LaserJet 5P"
========================================================
```

The printer driver names in this file are case sensitive and space sensitive. Basically, everything between the quotation marks must match the printer name *exactly*. As with many .inf files, the leading semicolon (;) indicates that the line is a comment and should be ignored. If you make any changes or additions or if you want to activate any of the mappings already in the file, you need to make sure that line does not start with a semicolon. When you use this file, be aware that you can have more than one client printer mapped to a single server print driver.

This wtsuprn.inf file must exist on every MetaFrame XP server where you want these print driver mappings to be applied. Keep in mind that you do still need to install printer drivers on your MetaFrame XP server when you use this file. This file merely tells the server which of its already installed drivers correlate to ICA client printer drivers.

### Finding the Exact Printer Driver Names

In order to be able to map printer drivers between the MetaFrame XP server and clients, you need to know the exact printer driver name for both the server and the ICA client. You can get this information from the printer properties dialog box (Start | Settings | Printers | Right-click Printer | Properties | Details). On Windows 9x computers, the driver is listed in the "Print using the following driver" box. On Windows NT and Windows 2000 computers, the driver box is on the "General" tab. Because the name of the printer driver can vary on the workstation depending on the platform, make sure you have the right driver name for the each client platform that is being used. For example, if you see "HP LaserJet 4000 Series PCL 5/5e," be sure to note all the punctuation, spaces, and case sensitivity.

If you already have the driver installed on your MetaFrame XP server, but you do not have a printer installed where you can check the properties, you can always begin the printer installation process. Just add the printer as a local printer on any port. When you get to the list of printers, browse to the manufacturer in the left pane. From there, you can view the full driver name in the right pane.

Once the driver names are added to your mapping file, your users will be able to print to their client printers from MetaFrame XP sessions. You do not have to reboot your server after you change the mapping file. Simply log the user off and then back on.

### Sequencing of Client Printer Driver Mapping

When a user with client printers logs on to a MetaFrame XP server, the server goes through several steps to try to find an appropriate printer driver to use.

1. The server looks for the printer name in one of the text mapping files. First, the `wtsuprn.inf` file is checked for a `clientname#\ printername` entry, and then just a *printername* entry. If nothing is found there, the server looks for the same two entries in the wtsprnt.inf file.

2. The server looks for the client printer driver name in one of the text mapping files. Similar to the search for the printer name, the `wtsuprn.inf` is first checked for a `clientname#\print drivername` entry, and then for a *printerdrivername* entry. If this fails, the server looks for the same two entries in the wtsprnt.inf file.

3. If the server cannot find any mapping information in either of the two text mapping files, it checks to see if the driver is already loaded locally on the server. To do this, it looks at `HKLM\System\Current ControlSet\Control\Print\Environments\Windows NT x86\Drivers\` in the registry.

4. If it can't find the printer driver information in the registry, that means that the printer driver is not installed. As a last resort, the server will check to see if the client's printer is one of the hundreds of standard printers that are available with Windows. To do this, it looks at the `ntprint.inf` file. If the printer is found and if the source files are available (usually via a CD or network share), then the print drivers are automatically and silently installed.

5. If the server is does not find the client's printer in the ntprint.inf file, the client's printer is not mapped for the ICA session. The MetaFrame

XP server will start this entire process over again for the next printer on the client's list.

## Using MetaFrame XP to Map Printer Drivers

Now that we've seen how printer driver mapping works under the hood, you'll be happy to know that there is an easier way to do it with MetaFrame XP.

During the MetaFrame XP installation, or whenever the IMA service is started on a MetaFrame XP server, the print driver mappings from the wtsuprn.inf or wtsprnt.inf files on the server are imported into the IMA data store. Any duplicate mappings are not written to the data store. Then, the server's local wtsprnt.inf file is populated from the mapping information stored in the IMA data store. If the wtsprnt.inf file does not exist, the IMA service creates it. If it does exist, it is overwritten with the mapping information contained in the IMA data store. This allows the print driver mappings from all MetaFrame XP servers in the farm to be automatically populated to all other servers.

But wait, it gets better. In the MetaFrame XP environment, you can configure printer driver mappings via the Citrix Management Console, instead of having to manually edit any .inf files (CMC | Printers | Right-click on driver name | Mapping). When you configure printer driver mappings via the CMC, you must choose a platform for the mapping. In this way you can have different mappings for Terminal Server 4.0 and Windows 2000 MetaFrame XP servers. Add the driver name of the client printer driver that correlates to the server printer driver name.

In addition to these methods, you can also manually import existing wtsuprn.inf or wtsprnt.inf files using MetaFrame XP's qprinter command line utility, available on the MetaFrame XP CD.

## Printer Driver Compatibility Problems

There's also another issue that can arise when you use client mapped printers. Think back to process that MetaFrame XP uses to create client printers. The very last thing the server tries before giving up is to locate a default driver for the printer. If a default driver is found and the Windows source files are available, the driver is automatically installed onto the MetaFrame XP server, allowing the user to access their client printer. While this may seem like a convenient way to install printer drivers, it actually tends to cause two major problems:

- *Users connect with untested client printers.* Most user communities are uncontrolled. It's likely that a user could connect to your MetaFrame XP server with almost any printer drivers installed locally.

By default, this will cause the printer driver to automatically be installed on the server, even if you have never tested (or even heard of) that printer. In some cases, users printing to unsupported drivers may crash the server. This is more of a problem if your MetaFrame XP servers are running on Terminal Server 4.0, because regular Windows NT 4.0 printer drivers are not automatically compatible with Terminal Server. In Windows 2000, this is less of a problem, but you still don't want untested printer drivers on your server.

- *Automatically installed printer drivers are not automatically removed.* One of the big concerns that many MetaFrame XP administrators have the number of printer drivers that are installed on their servers. If users with all types of printers are causing drivers to be installed on the MetaFrame XP servers, the servers will need to manage a lot of drivers. Additionally, if driver auto-replication is used (discussed later in this chapter), the printer driver replication process will take even longer.

In order to prevent these two situations from occurring, there are three options that you can implement:

- Use the CMC to mark certain printer drivers as "incompatible."
- Configure your MetaFrame XP servers to only use trusted drivers.
- Manually map known bad drivers to known good drivers.

**Solution 1. Use the CMC to Set Printer Driver Compatibility**
You can use the Citrix Management Console to prevent certain printer drivers from being used with client printers. This is done by configuring printer driver compatibility. In the printer driver compatibility box, (CMC | Printers | Right click on driver | Compatibility), you can add printer drivers that you will explicitly allow or explicitly prevent on your servers. In order to add a driver that is allowed, it must already be installed on one of your MetaFrame XP servers in the farm.

If client printer mapping is enabled, the MetaFrame XP server checks the client print driver compatibility list before it sets up any printers every time a user logs on. If a printer uses drivers that are on the prohibited list, the server does not set up that printer. It sends a message to the user and writes a message in the server's event log.

These compatibility settings only affect client mapped printers, not network printers. This is because the drivers for network printers must be manually installed by an administrator—there is no way for them to be automatically installed by the server. The idea here is that if you are manually installing printer drivers, then you know which are compatible and which aren't.

### Advantages of Setting Printer Driver Compatibility

- Settings are automatically applied to all servers in the farm.
- Easily configured, changed and updated.
- Choosing to "explicitly allow" printer drivers is an easy way to limit the total number of drivers installed.

### Disadvantages of Setting Printer Driver Compatibility

- In order to prevent certain drivers from being used, you need to know which ones are bad.
- You cannot have different driver compatibility settings for different servers in the farm.
- Only applies to client mapped printers.

### Solution 2. Use Only Trusted Drivers

Another interesting solution to the automatic printer driver installation problem is to configure your MetaFrame XP servers so that they only load drivers from a trusted source. Basically, you configure a network path in the registry of each of your MetaFrame XP servers, and your servers will only be able to load printer drivers from that path. Many people leverage a trusted driver path by creating a network share and then dumping the approved printer drivers into that share. If a driver is not in that share, it cannot be installed. This applies to drivers that would be automatically installed as part of the client printer mapping process, or drivers that you manually install as an administrator.

To configure your MetaFrame XP server to use trusted drivers, you need to configure two registry keys. This process is the same for Terminal Server 4.0 and Windows 2000. (Technically, Terminal Server 4.0 requires Service Pack 5 in order for this to work, but MetaFrame XP also requires Service Pack 5, so that shouldn't be an issue in your environment.)

Key: HKLM\System\CurrentControlSet\Control\
   Print\ Providers\LanMan Print Services\Servers

Value: LoadTrustedDrivers

Type: REG_DWORD

Data: 1

A value of "1" enables the trusted driver usage, indicating that printer drivers can only be installed from the share specified in the following registry value:

Value: `TrustedDriverPath`

Type: `REG_SZ`

Data: `\\servername\sharename`

After making this configuration, you must reboot in order for it to take effect.

The easiest way to produce the trusted printer driver files is to copy them from a server that already has the printer drivers installed. For complete details about the paths of driver files, see the "Managing Printer Drivers" section of this chapter. When you copy the drivers into your trusted source share, they must be under the version number folder. For example, if you copy the drivers from the "3" folder, then your drivers must be copied to a "3" folder in the sharename folder.

### Advantages of Configuring a Trusted Driver Path

- Allows you to control which printer drivers are installed.
- Applies to all printer drivers, no matter how they are installed.

### Disadvantages of Configuring a Trusted Driver Path

- Must be configured manually on every server.
- You still have to install the drivers before they can be used.

### Solution 3. Manually Choose Alternate Printer Driver Mappings

Sometimes you will know that certain printer drivers are not compatible with Terminal Servers, but users will need to be able to print to their printers anyway. In these cases, you might be able to find "alternate" printer drivers that would work for the user.

For example, if you have clients with Hewlett Packard 8000N drivers that cause your MetaFrame XP servers to crash, you can configure your servers to use HP LaserJet 4 drivers to print to the 8000N printer. For this configuration, all you have to do is map the client driver "Hewlett Packard 8000N" to the server driver "HP LaserJet 4." Nowhere does it say that the printer mappings must be for the exact same printers. In fact, there are some generic printer drivers, such as "HP LaserJet" or "HP DeskJet" that will work with hundreds of printer models.

An added benefit to mapping alternate drivers is that you can control the physical number of printer drivers that are installed on your MetaFrame XP servers, because you can map one server printer driver to multiple client printer models. Imagine how nice it would be if you could map 42 different laser printers to work with one generic "HP LaserJet" driver.

In some cases, mapping alternate printer drivers can also increase performance. This can happen because the spooled print file, which is transmitted via the ICA protocol to the ICA client, is created with the printer driver. All printer drivers are not created equal. Some printer drivers are very efficient, and create very efficient spool files. This is usually the case with name-brand printers. However, the whole reason that we need to use client printer mapping in the first place is because we, as administrators, do not have control over the printers that our users have connected locally to their ICA clients. They didn't buy the name brand printer that we recommended. They bought the cheapest $25 printer that they could find at the Price Club. These printers tend to have very inefficient drivers, which means that they can easily create spooled print files that are several megabytes per page. (To be fair, the people who created these drivers probably never imagined that anyone would actually want to transmit the spooled print files across a slow network.) To combat this, you can usually find "alternate" drivers that work for some printers that are much more efficient than the printer's native drivers. You can also use alternate black and white drivers for color printers. By definition, black and white drivers will produce smaller spool files because they will be monochrome instead of full color. Of course, your users will not be able to print in color, but monochrome is better than nothing.

When looking for alternate print drivers, whether for compatibility or for performance reasons, you can try to find these drivers through trial and error on your own. However, most administrators have better things to do and there are many resources on the Internet that maintain lists of alternate printer drivers and the printers that they seem to work with (try http://thethin.net).

The only drawback to using alternate printer driver mapping is that some of the functionality of the original printer driver on the MetaFrame XP server may not work on the printer. These functions are usually minor, like multiple paper tray settings, stapling, or duplexing options.

### Advantages of Alternate Printer Driver Mapping

- Allows users to print to printers whose native drivers are not supported.
- Controls the total number of printer drivers in your server farm.
- Allows you to substitute efficient printer drivers for inefficient ones.

### Disadvantages of Alternate Printer Driver Mapping

- Some printer functionality could be lost by using alternate drivers.

- You need to figure out which alternate drivers work for each printer.

- You must manually map the generic driver to the exact name of every driver it is to replace.

- If you make this change on one server, it needs to propagate to the other servers.

## Configuring Printer Auto-creation for DOS or WinCE Clients

The DOS and Windows CE ICA clients only support the auto-creation of printers that are physically connected to the client device. In the real world, this is most often seen with Windows-based terminals or thin client devices at remote offices that connect to corporate MetaFrame XP servers. Auto-created client printers on these platforms will have the name *clientname*#LPT*x*, where *clientname* is the user's ICA client device name and *"x"* is the LPT port that has the printer attached.

You can configure printer auto-creation settings on a client-by-client basis, using the Citrix Management Console (CMC | Right-click on printers | Client Printers). Use the Client Printers dialog box to add, remove, reset, edit, and delete the configuration for DOS and Windows CE client printers. These client printers are only available to the users of each individual client device.

After you configure a client printer, the ICA client software on that device downloads its printer configuration the next time an ICA session is started. This configuration is maintained in the IMA data store and can be downloaded by the client when it connects to any MetaFrame XP server in the farm. You can view the status of DOS and Windows CE client printers in the "Client Printers" dialog box in the CMC. Here, the word <downloaded> appears in the list when information for the client printer setup has been successfully sent from the MetaFrame XP server to the client device.

The fact that you can manage client printers centrally for DOS and Windows CE clients is a new feature of MetaFrame XP. Previous versions of MetaFrame required that users manage their client printers themselves, by running a Client Printer Configuration Utility from a MetaFrame server via an ICA session.

## *Improving the Performance of Client Printing*

As discussed previously, the architecture behind the use of client printers is fundamentally inefficient, because large spooled print jobs must be sent via the ICA protocol to the ICA client to be printed. Even though some of the other printing methods that we'll discuss later (such as server-based printers) are much more efficient than using client printers, the convenience of client printers is a compelling reason to use them. Because of this, there are some aspects of their performance that can be addressed, including:

- Limiting the bandwidth used by client printing.
- Configuring the Universal Print Driver.

### Limiting Client Printing Bandwidth

Because the entire spooled print job must be sent to the ICA client when Client Printer Mapping is enabled, users with slow connections may see degraded ICA session performance. This occurs because the available bandwidth is consumed by the print job, leaving no room for the remaining ICA traffic. In order to combat this, set a limit on the amount of bandwidth that an ICA print job can take, effectively increasing the bandwidth available to the more crucial ICA functions. The bandwidth settings can be configured through the CMC, on a farm-wide basis (CMC I Printer Management I Bandwidth) or on an individual server basis (CMC I Server name I Properties I Printer Bandwidth).

Limiting bandwidth will not help print jobs finish any faster. In fact, it might cause them to be slower. However, it can lessen the impact that printing has on a user, allowing them to do other work while they wait for the print job to be spooled to their local printer.

### *Advantages of Limiting Client Printing Bandwidth*

- Increases overall ICA session performance while printing, especially over slow connections.
- Can be configured on a farm–wide or server–wide basis.

### *Disadvantages of Limiting Client Printing Bandwidth*

- Client print jobs could take longer.

### Configuring the Universal Print Driver for Client Printer Mapping

If you're using Feature Release 1 or 2 and your ICA clients are running on 32-bit Windows platforms, you can use the universal print driver to increase client printing speed and decrease your management of printer drivers. The universal print driver is made up of two components: the print driver that is loaded on your MetaFrame XP servers and the ICA client component that renders print jobs on the client device.

*Server Component.* The universal print driver is automatically installed when Feature Release 1 or 2 is installed. It is a "generic" printer driver, capable of generating 300dpi monochrome print jobs that can be sent to any printer. This driver receives print jobs that are printed to it, and sends them to the ICA client to be spooled and printed.

*Client Component.* Support for the universal print driver is built in to the Windows 32-bit ICA client version 6.20 and newer. The ICA client receives unspooled print jobs from the MetaFrame XP server, spools them, and sends them directly to the user's printer.

### How the Universal Print Driver Works

With regular client printing in MetaFrame XP environments, the print job is created and rendered for the printer on the MetaFrame XP server. As you recall, this involves creating the enhanced metafile, which is then translated to a printer–specific spool file. This large spool file is then transmitted to the ICA client device. When the universal print driver is used, this process changes a bit, as shown in Figure 7.6.

*Figure 7.6 The universal print driver in action*

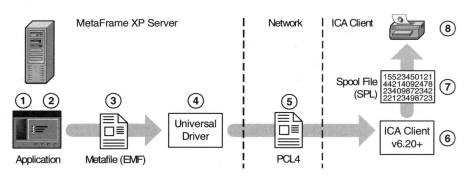

1.  The user prints from their application running on the MetaFrame XP server with Feature Release 1 or 2.

2.  The application creates the EMF file on the MetaFrame XP server.

3.  The EMF file is sent to the print spooler on the MetaFrame XP server.

4.  The print spooler uses the appropriate printer driver to create the spool file in preparation for printing on the client's printer. In this case, the driver used is the Citrix "universal print driver." This

driver creates a very efficient PCL4 file, instead of a standard print spool file.

5. The universal print driver sends the PCL4 file to the ICA client via the background printing channel in the ICA protocol. The PCL4 file is not printer-specific. It is very small and efficient.

6. The Windows 32-bit ICA client, version 6.20 or newer, receives the PCL4 file. It transfers the file to the ICA client's universal print driver component.

7. The client's universal print driver component produces the print job's spool file, based on the client's local print driver.

8. The print job is sent to the appropriate printer.

As you can clearly see, with the universal print driver, client printers can be used with much more efficiency than when regular print drivers are used. Because the universal print driver is not printer-specific, it can be used to print to virtually any printer. This means that you do not have to worry about managing too many printer drivers on your MetaFrame XP servers. The more printers that can use the universal print driver, the fewer drivers you will need to install.

Of course there is a down side to this added convenience and performance. In this case, the universal print driver can only generate print jobs in black and white, and they are limited to 300 dpi. This does not mean that users can't print to 1200 dpi color printers. It just means that those printers will only produce 300 dpi monochrome output when used with the universal print driver.

In the real world, 300 dpi monochrome should be sufficient for most business documents. If your users have needs to print in color or at higher resolution, you'll need to either use the printer's regular driver or connect to the printer as a server printer (covered in the next section).

### Advantages of the Universal Print Driver

- Significantly increases print speeds, especially over slow connections.
- Prevents you from having to install and manage individual print drivers on all of your MetaFrame XP servers.

### Disadvantages of the Universal Print Driver

- Requires Feature Release 1 or 2.
- Requires Citrix ICA clients version 6.20 or greater.
- Only works with the 32-bit Windows clients.

- Limited to 300 dpi, monochrome.

- Does not use advanced features of printers.

### Configuring the Universal Print Driver

All universal print driver configuration is done via the Citrix Management Console (CMC | Right-click Printer Management | Properties). In addition to specifying whether or not you want to auto–create client printers at logon and what type of printers you want to create (default only, non–network, all, or inherit user configuration), you can control how you want the universal print driver to be used. There are four options:

- *Native Drivers Only.* This setting will disable the universal print driver. If the server cannot find the native printer driver for a user's client printer, then that printer will not be available during the user's session.

- *Universal Driver Only.* This setting will cause the MetaFrame XP servers to ignore any print drivers that are installed when connecting to users' local client printers. If you use this, then you do not need to have any printer drivers installed on your servers to support client printers, other than the universal print driver.

- *Both Universal and Native Drivers.* Selecting this option will create a printer object for each client printer using the universal print driver. In addition, for any printers that also have regular printer drivers installed, another printer object will be created. This means that some printers will show up on the user's list twice. The only difference is that the printer using the universal print driver will have the text [MF:PCL4] at the end of the printer name. The idea behind this is that it gives users flexibility by letting them choose the driver to use. However, it can be confusing to users because they see the same printer on the list twice. Most likely they will end up printing to the printer using the regular driver, because that will show up first in the list (alphabetical order). In case you're wondering, you might have read some of the Citrix ad copy advertising that users were able to switch between the universal driver and the regular driver at any time. This is not some sort of fancy feature of the ICA client software, rather, it's possible when using this option, because the user can choose which printer driver to use at the time of printing.

- *Universal Driver Only If Native Driver Unavailable.* This option is the default, and probably works best for most real world situations. Many people use this as a sort of "catch all," allowing users to print with the universal driver if they connect to the server with an unsupported printer.

## Server Printers

Instead of dealing with the many complexities of client mapped printers, you can instead choose to use server-based printers for printing in your Meta-Frame XP environment. A server printer in a MetaFrame environment, just like in any environment, is any printer that is directly available via a server's print queue. This print queue can be Windows or NetWare, client or server based. Basically, any printer that can be accessed via a \\computername\ printername sharename is a server printer.

From within ICA sessions running on MetaFrame XP servers, users can set up their own server printers if they have permissions to connect to them. As an administrator, you can configure server printers for your users with logon scripts or roaming profiles. Actually, server printers are used and accessed in MetaFrame XP sessions just as they are in any Windows environment.

A server printer can also be a printer that has a print queue directly on a MetaFrame XP server. This could be a printer that is physically connected to the local LPT port of a MetaFrame XP server or an IP printer that has a print queue locally on a MetaFrame XP server.

Remember, if a user has a server printer mapped on his own computer before he launches an ICA session on a MetaFrame XP server, that server printer can be available during his session. However, that printer would be a client mapped printer (as covered in the previous section in Figure 7.4), not a true server printer. A true server printer is mapped directly to the print queue from the user's session on the MetaFrame XP server, as shown in Figure 7.7 (next page).

You'll notice when using server printers that if the print servers are on the same network as the MetaFrame XP servers, then printing performance is excellent. In fact, printing in this type of environment is no different than printing in any network environment. This is most often seen when the users, MetaFrame XP servers, and printers are all located in the same building.

*Figure 7.7 Server Printers in a MetaFrame XP environment*

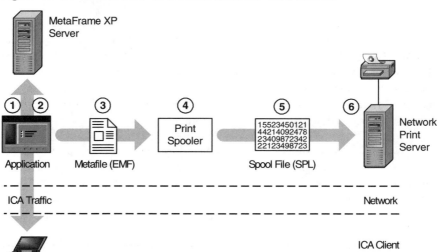

1. The user prints from his application running on the MetaFrame XP server.

2. The application creates the EMF file on the MetaFrame XP server.

3. The EMF file is sent to the print spooler on the MetaFrame XP server.

4. The print spooler creates the spooled print job, in preparation for printing on the network printer. The MetaFrame XP server has the proper drivers loaded for the network printer.

5. The spooled print job is sent to the network print server.

6. The network print server queues the print job to the printer.

Unfortunately, server printer performance is not as good in remote environments, where the users and printer are located in one building and the Meta-Frame XP servers are located in another.

### Advantages of Using Server Printers

- Good performance.
- Reliable.
- Users receive the same printers no matter where they log in.

### Disadvantages of Using Server Printers

- No local printer support.

- Users must browse the network for printers that are not configured.
- Printers must be configured for each user.
- To get good performance, the print server must be located in the same building as the user.

# Managing Printer Drivers

Whether you use client-mapped printers or server printers, you'll need to have printer drivers installed on each of your MetaFrame XP servers. Consequently, you will need to spend some time thinking about how to manage those printer drivers. Before we address this issue, however, let's look at what printer drivers really are, how they work, and how they're stored on Windows servers.

## How Windows Printer Drivers Work

Fundamentally, Windows printer drivers translate print jobs from an enhanced metafile format, which is printer-independent, into the native language that can be understood by a printer. This is the reason why a printer prints garbage when you use the wrong driver. Printer drivers need to be installed and registered on a computer before they can be used.

Two things happen when you install a printer driver onto a Terminal Server or Windows 2000 server. First, the necessary printer driver files are copied from the source location to the server. The server stores printer driver files in the `%systemroot%\system32\spool\drivers\w32x86\3\` folder. In this path, the w32x86 signifies an Intel Windows NT or Windows 2000 platform, and the "3" signifies the version of the printer driver (3 = Windows 2000, 2 = Windows NT 4.0).

Second, the driver's details are written to the registry in this path: `HKLM\System\CurrentControlSet\Control\Print\Environments\Windows NT x86\Drivers\Version-3\`*printerdrivername*. Similar to the file path, a Version-3 key means that the driver is a Windows 2000 driver and a Version-2 key means that the driver is a Windows NT 4.0 driver.

User's individual printer settings, such as print, duplexing, and paper tray options, are stored in the HKCU\Printers registry key. These settings are user-specific, just like any other customized Windows settings.

## Installing Printer Drivers

Installing print drivers onto a MetaFrame XP server is no different than installing print drivers onto any Windows computer. While it would be nice if you could point a wizard to an .inf file in the CMC, the easiest way is to use the standard Windows "Add Printer" wizard. Have the wizard copy the drivers from your source location to the server. Select a local port that is not in use for the printer, keeping in mind that there is no limit to the amount of printers you can add to one port. As soon as you install the printer, you may delete it. The print drivers will remain installed on the server. You may verify that the drivers are installed through the CMC (CMC | Printers | Drivers).

If you're running MetaFrame XP on Terminal Server 4.0, then you need to ensure that any print drivers you install are compatible with the Terminal Serer Edition of Windows NT 4.0, instead of just Windows NT 4.0. This is not an issue in Windows 2000 environments, because by definition, all Windows 2000 printer drivers must work in regular and Terminal Services modes.

## Removing Printer Drivers

When you delete a printer from the "Printers" folder on one of your MetaFrame XP servers, the drivers are not uninstalled from the server. This can be a problem, because if you've identified that a certain printer driver causes problems, you need to be able to remove that driver from the server to prevent clients from using it. Also, if a driver is no longer needed, removing it will mean that there is less for the IMA data store to manage.

Fortunately, you can manually remove a printer driver and all traces of its existence by following this simple procedure:

1. If you haven't done so already, remove the printer by deleting it form the "Printers" folder.
2. Stop the spooler service.
3. Browse to the following registry location: `HKLM\System\CurrentControlSet\Control\Print\Environments\Windows NT x86\Drivers\Version-x\`*`printerdrivername`*, where x is the version of the driver (2 = NT 4.0, 3 = Windows 2000).
4. Note the names of the files listed.
5. Remove the registry key *`yourprinterdriver`*.
6. Delete the referenced driver files from the `%systemroot%\system32\spool\drivers\w32x86\x` folder. If you have multiple printers installed, you may want to copy the driver files to

a temporary location before you delete them outright, because many similar types of printers use the same driver files.

7. If you're not able to delete the files, you will need to disable the spooler, reboot, and delete the files again. After you do this, remember to reset the spooler to "automatic" startup.

8. After the print drivers have been removed, you should reboot the server.

### What driver does a Printer Use?

Occasionally, you will need to figure out which drivers a printer uses that you haven't installed yet. This is especially handy if you allow your MetaFrame XP server to automatically install any needed printer drivers.

Every Windows NT and Windows 2000 server has a "master list" of default printers that it supports and the drivers that each printer needs. That master list is stored in the %systemroot%\inf\ntprint.inf file. You can open this file in a text editor to see which drivers each printer will request. Ntprint.inf is organized by manufacturer, with individual printers and their drivers listed under the manufacturer's section, as shown below.

```
[HP]
"HP 2000C" = HPV2000C.GPD.ICM
```

## How MetaFrame XP Manages Printer Drivers

The IMA data store maintains records of the configured printers and installed print drivers on every MetaFrame XP server in the server farm. The data store obtains this information via the following methods:

- *During MetaFrame XP installation*, the IMA Data Store records a list of printer drivers that have been previously installed on the server.

- *Whenever a print driver is installed on a MetaFrame XP server*, that server's IMA service updates the printer driver list in the IMA data store. If the IMA service is not running when a printer driver is installed, it synchronizes its local information with the data store the next time it starts. During synchronization, all appropriate drivers are added to the data store for any new printer drivers found on the MetaFrame XP server. Additionally, any printer driver entries that exist in the data store for print drivers that no longer exist on farm servers are removed from the data store.

If you ever feel that the printer drivers in the data store are not in sync with the printer drivers on a server, you can manually update the driver list in the IMA data store (CMC I Printer Management I Update Printer and Driver Information).

### Replicating Printer Drivers Between MetaFrame XP Servers

The reason that printer driver information is stored in the IMA data store is so that printer drivers can be replicated between MetaFrame XP servers in the farm. MetaFrame XP offers a few different methods for replicating printer drivers. This is useful because printer drivers need to be installed on MetaFrame XP servers regardless of which printing method (client printer mapping or server printers) that you choose. You can choose from four different methods for replicating printer drivers between MetaFrame XP servers. The first two are features of MetaFrame XP, and the last two are not:

- MetaFrame XP replication.
- Automatic MetaFrame XP replication.
- Manual Resource Kit replication.
- Manual replication.

### Method 1. MetaFrame XP Printer Driver Replication

MetaFrame XP printer driver replication is designed to copy printer driver files and registry settings to MetaFrame XP servers across the server farm, allowing you to install all required printer drivers on one MetaFrame XP server and then replicate the files and registry settings to all other servers in the farm. MetaFrame XP printer driver replication does not replicate printer properties such as default paper tray selection or paper orientation.

Using MetaFrame XP's print driver replication feature, you can manage all MetaFrame XP printers across the entire server farm via the Citrix Management Console (CMC I Printers I Right-click Print Driver I Replicate Drivers). Make sure that when you replicate drivers, you are not in the <any> server view by choosing a specific server name from the dropdown list or by selecting the server from the left pane. If you try to replicate drivers in the <any> view, MetaFrame XP will randomly choose the server that is to be used as the master to be replicated. This is not a good thing.

Choosing to replicate a driver will lead to a dialog box in which you can indicate whether to replicate the driver to all MetaFrame XP servers in the farm or to just the servers that you specify. Additionally, you can check a box that forces the source driver to overwrite the target driver, which is helpful when updating driver versions. Keep in mind that Windows 2000 and Windows NT use different printer drivers. Do not replicate between the two platforms.

When you're setting up printer driver replication, do not choose destination servers that are not operating and will not be within 24 hours. After 24 hours, the replication queue marks the job as incomplete. Even if the server comes back online, drivers will not be replicated.

If driver replication fails due to communication errors, the console displays an error message and records the error in the server Event Log for each server where the operation failed.

### Advantages of MetaFrame XP Replication

- Prevents you from having to install the same printer driver on multiple servers.
- Replicates printer drivers even if no printers are installed.
- Once the replication process begins, no user intervention is required.

### Disadvantages of MetaFrame XP Replication

- You must manually invoke the replication process.
- Source and target server platforms must be the same.
- Replicating too many drivers can degrade performance.
- Target servers that are not available for more than 24 hours will not receive new drivers.
- If bad drivers are replicated, all MetaFrame XP servers can be broken very quickly.
- Printer settings are not replicated.

## Method 2. MetaFrame XP Automatic Replication

A disadvantage to the MetaFrame XP printer driver migration is that you must manually invoke the replication process. If there are many print drivers that frequently change in your environment, you can configure your server farm for automatic printer driver replication. This automatic replication will occur whenever servers are added to the farm or whenever the IMA service is started. The IMA data store maintains two lists of drivers to be replicated, one for Terminal Server 4.0 servers and one for Windows 2000 servers.

You can add or remove drivers from the auto-replication lists with the CMC (CMC | Printers | Drivers Tab | Auto Replication). When auto replication is enabled for a driver, an entry is added to the appropriate data store list. When you edit the auto replication list, you can specify one server to use as the master source server or you can let MetaFrame XP pick any server where the driver is installed. If you specify <any> as your source server, MetaFrame XP will copy the driver from any server that is available in the farm at the time of auto replication to a new or restarted server. This will enable the replication to take place without a dependency on one specific server.

It's easiest to track printer driver versions within the server farm if you choose one server as your master printer driver server. This is not a technical requirement, but rather a practical decision. Additionally, if you have both Windows NT and Windows 2000 servers, you should select one printer driver master server for each operating system. Choosing one master printer driver server will make it easier to manage the automatic replication of printer drivers.

Unfortunately, when you configure auto replication, your source server must be a MetaFrame XP server. You cannot choose to replicate printer drivers from network print servers or other network sources. Citrix claims that this is because MetaFrame XP does not have guaranteed access to those servers or sources. Critics claim that this is because Citrix didn't spend the time to implement this feature. Either way, you'll need to install the drivers on at least one MetaFrame XP server before you can use MetaFrame XP's replication features to copy the drivers to the remaining servers.

### Advantages of MetaFrame XP Manual Replication

- "Hands off" print driver replication and management.
- Printer drivers can be configured for replication on a driver-by-driver basis.
- Can be configured with multiple source servers, preventing an unwanted single point of failure.

### Disadvantages of MetaFrame XP Manual Replication

- IMA service start times greatly increase.
- Driver replication can take a long time, especially with many drivers.
- Increased network traffic.
- Increased CPU load.
- Sometimes it doesn't work (for no apparent reason).
- The auto replication engine continuously checks for driver changes.
- Printer settings are not replicated.

If you choose to use auto replication for your print drivers, be careful. It should only be used in situations where you need to replicate a few drivers. In reality, the print drivers on your servers will probably not need to be changed that often, so you should be able to use manual replication when driver updates are needed.

Auto printer driver replication is known for being CPU-intensive. Make sure to monitor the CPU utilization of the source server when it is used, especially if you reboot more than one MetaFrame XP server at the same time.

### Method 3. Using Print Migrator 2000 to Replicate Drivers

The Windows 2000 Server Resource Kit Supplement 1 includes Printer Migrator 2000, a utility that can be used to replicate printer drivers between servers. This utility can be used with Windows NT 4.0 and Windows 2000 servers. For pure Terminal Server 4.0 environments, you can also use Printer Migrator 1.0, included in the Windows NT 4.0 Server Resource Kit.

Printer Migrator 2000 allows you to back up printers, print queues, ports, printer drivers, and printer shares to a .cab file. You can then restore the settings of that .cab file to another server. This utility can only restore Terminal Server 4.0 backups to Terminal Server 4.0 servers and Windows 2000 backups to Windows 2000 servers.

#### Advantages of Print Migrator 2000 Replication

- No overhead when it's not being used.
- Drivers and settings can be replicated to remote servers.
- Drivers can be replicated from network print servers to MetaFrame XP servers.

#### Disadvantages of Print Migrator 2000 Replication

- Must be manually invoked.
- The spooler service is stopped while this tool is used.

### Method 4. Manual Print Driver Replication

The last option that you have for replicating printer drivers is to do it manually. You must manually install or copy all of the needed printer drivers onto each of your MetaFrame XP servers.

#### Advantages of Manual Print Driver Replication

- No performance overhead of any replication services.
- No learning curve.

- Allows you to install different printer drivers to different servers.
- Works well in small environments with only a few drivers.

### Disadvantages of Manual Print Driver Replication

- Drivers must be manually installed onto each MetaFrame XP server.

## Printer Driver Replication Performance

When the IMA service starts, it must synchronize all installed printers and drivers with the IMA data store. This causes each MetaFrame XP server to read the new printers and drivers from the data store. Any time printers or printer drivers are installed or deleted, this information is updated in the IMA data store. The data store contains one record for each print driver, one for each server, and a complete list of the printer drivers installed on each server. The more print drivers installed on farm servers, the larger the printer records in the IMA data store become and the longer it takes the service to start. Something as "insignificant" as printer driver auto-replication can affect overall performance in three ways:

- MetaFrame XP server performance.
- Amount of IMA traffic.
- IMA service startup time.

Many factors, including network traffic and server load, affect how quickly printer drivers replicate. The IMA service handles MetaFrame XP printer driver replication and it contains information for printer drivers, auto-replication, and replication source and destination servers. The replication itself is performed by the IMA service's "printer driver replication queue." This replication queue operates at a low priority, allowing other critical services to access the bandwidth they need. Each printer driver/server combination creates an item in the printer replication queue. In your environment, you should take steps to ensure that this queue does not exceed 1,500 entries. To determine the queue size, multiply the number of installed drivers by the number of Meta-Frame servers. (10 drivers to 5 servers = 50 items, 5 drivers to 100 servers = 500 items)

In lightly used environments, this replication queue might be able to handle 50 entries per minute. In more heavily utilized environments, it might fall to 10 per minute. Remember that printer driver replication can be very CPU intensive on the source server, so you should avoid replicating drivers while the source server has a heavy load. You can monitor the replication queue items with the qprinter command. You can also find replication history and status messages from each target server's application event log.

If you decide to use printer driver replication or auto-replication, you should follow these best practices:

- Install as few printer drivers on MetaFrame XP servers as possible. This includes limiting the number of drivers, as well as not installing drivers on servers where they will never be used.
- Install "common" drivers where possible. For example, many HP laser printers can use the same basic driver.
- Remove unused drivers.
- Separate the server farm into multiple zones.

Following these basic steps will allow you to use MetaFrame XP printer driver replication without severely impacting the performance of your MetaFrame XP environment.

# Configuring Printers for Users

Now that you've completed the work needed to ensure that various printers will be available to the users on your MetaFrame XP servers, you need to provide a method for users to access their printers. In some cases, as when client mapped printers are used, configuration is easy because the printers are automatically created for the users.

However, client printers don't always work in the real world, so server printers must be used. When using server printers, you need to think about how your users will these printers. Will you assign certain users to certain printers? If so, how will you do this? Maybe you want to allow all users to be able to use all printers? If this is the case, how will users know which printers they should use? We'll look at two strategies to answer these questions:

- Assigning printers to users.
- Methods of letting users choose their own printers.

## Assigning Printers to Users

Once you decide that you would like to control which printers your users are able to print to, you need to determine how to provide that access. Setting permissions on printers is important, but permissions alone won't configure a printer for a user. For example, if you want the user "brian" to print to the `\\printerserver\fastlaser` printer, you can edit the properties of that print queue and grant "brian" print permissions. However, how will Brian know how to access that printer? Is he smart enough to be able to browse the network to the `\\printserver` computer, and then select the fastlaser printer? Most likely, if you decide that Brian should use the \\printserver\fastlaser printer, you need a way to assign that printer to him, so that when he selects "print" from a MetaFrame XP application, the \\printserver\fastlaser printer shows up in his printer list:

There are three methods that you can use to assign server-based printers to users.

- Use MetaFrame XP's printer configuration features.
- Map printers in users' logon scripts.
- Map printers as part of a user's profile and policy settings.

### Method 1. Using MetaFrame XP to Configure Printers

You can use the Citrix Management Console to manage two types of printers in MetaFrame XP server farms: network printers and local printers.

- *Network Printers.* MetaFrame XP gives you the ability to "import" network print servers into your server farm (CMC | Printer Management | Network Print Servers Tab | Actions Menu | Import Network Print Server). Nothing physically changes on the print servers, and there is no risk to your print servers when they are imported into the farm. (You can import print servers without their owner's permission!) Importing the print servers simply means that MetaFrame XP will take an inventory of which printers are available on the print servers that you import. This information is written to the IMA Data Store. If the printers available from an imported print server change, you can manually update the server farm's inventory (CMC | Printer Management | Network Print Servers Tab | Right-click Print Server | Update Network Print Server).

- *Local Printers.* Local printers are shared printers that have print queues locally on a MetaFrame XP server. This could be a printer that is physically connected into the parallel port of a MetaFrame XP server or it could be a network printer that is installed as a local printer (usually to a "local" TCP/IP port). Records of the local printers installed on all MetaFrame XP servers in the server farm are written to the IMA data store. You can view the properties of local printers farm-wide (CMC I Printers I Printers Tab) or on an individual MetaFrame XP server (CMC I Server Properties I Printers Tab).

Both network printers and local printers require that the proper printer drivers are installed on the MetaFrame XP servers. Ideally, these drivers should be installed on all servers in the farm, because the printers are available to users on all the servers.

You can configure auto-creation settings for a local and imported network printers (Right-click on printer I Auto-creation). This allows you to choose the Windows users or groups that will automatically have the printers mapped when they log on, ensuring that only the appropriate groups or users see the appropriate printers.

### Advantages of Assigning Printers with MetaFrame XP

- Works without user profiles or logon scripts.
- The ICA client does not need a preconfigured connection to the printer.

### Disadvantages of Assigning Printers with MetaFrame XP

- Can be time consuming to configure.

## Method 2. Configuring Printers via Logon Scripts

Instead of managing server printers with MetaFrame XP, you may choose to take a more traditional route. Logon scripts have always been (and will continue to be) a simple yet effective way to map printers for specific users. (Logon scripts were covered in detail back in Chapter 5.) When it comes to printing, there are a few different ways that you can use logon scripts to map users' printers.

One of the cool things about using logon scripts to map printers is that you can incorporate conditional branching into the scripts based on a user's group membership. That way, you can give a user access to a printer simply by adding them to the appropriate Windows group. You can even set the permissions of a printer based on the same user group.

### Mapping Printers with Standard Batch Files

If you want to use a regular batch file to map network printers for users, you can use the con2prt.exe command-line utility to add a printer connection for a user in a logon script. In order to use this utility, copy con2prt.exe to the %systemroot% folder on each of your MetaFrame servers. Then, call it from the logon script using the following format:

```
con2prt /c \\printserver\fastlaser
```

There are a few command-line options that you may need to use with the con2prt.exe utility.

/f - Deletes all printer connections.

/c - Connects the specified printer.

/cd - Connects the specified printer and makes it the default.

### Mapping Printers with Kixtart

If you have chosen to use Kixtart as the language for your logon scripts, you can use its own native capabilities to connect to network printers. For example, the following Kixtart code checks to see whether the user is in the "PrinterGroupName" Windows group. If he is, it adds the \\printserver \fastlaser printer connection and sets it to be the default printer for the user. Many Citrix administrators use code like this, adding this code segment for each printer in the environment. Their final logon scripts may have dozens of printers.

```
if ingroup("PrinterGroupName")
    addprinterconnection ("\\printserver\fastlaser")
    setdefaultprinter ("\\printserver\fastlaser")
endif
```

### *Advantages of Assigning Printers with Logon Scripts*

- You can assign printers on a per-user basis, or per-group basis.
- You can assign different printers for different servers.
- Logon scripts can be used in many different ways.

### *Disadvantages of Assigning Printers with Logon Scripts*

- Requires knowledge of the logon script language.

## *Method 3. Configuring Printers via User Profiles*

The third option for assigning printers to users is to use their user profiles. Full details of profile usage are available in Chapter 5. Srofile allow users to map printers and set defaults which can then become a permanent part of their profile.

# Letting Users Choose Their Own Printers

Instead of assigning printers to your users, you may have an environment in which users need to be able to choose their own printers. This makes your job much easier. If security is important, you can still set the printing permissions on the printers that you don't want everyone to be able to print to.

If you simply give a user permissions to print to a network printer, that printer will not be automatically set up for the user. However, the user will be able to browse the network and connect to the printer if he needs to print to it.

### Advantages of Letting Users Choose Their Own Printers

- You can still set security for printers that need limited access.
- There is less for you to configure.

### Disadvantages of Letting Users Choose Their Own Printers

- Users need to know how to connect to printers.
- Users need to know which printer they are looking for.

Users are able to configure their own printers via Windows Explorer, or the "Printers" folder in the Start Menu. However, in the real world, many people choose not to allow users to connect to the Windows desktop or Windows Explorer, and thus users are not able connect to network printers. To prevent this, make the "Printers" folder a published application, allowing users to connect and configure the printers saved in their user profiles. If your profiles are configured properly, any changes that a user makes in the "Printers" published application are available from within any published application that they run.

### Publishing the Printers Folder as Published Application

Publishing the Printers folder is not intuitive at all, although it is very easy to do. The Printers folder does not have its own executable; it's actually built into the Windows shell (explorer.exe). These types of Explorer shell components are called "shell extensions." Each shell extension has its own GUID, which is like a serial number that differentiates it from all other shell extensions. Information about different shell extensions are contained in the following registry location: HKEY_CLASSES_ROOT\CLSID\<unique guid>.

In this case, the Printer folder's unique GUID is {2227A280-3AEA-1069-A2DE-08002B30309D}.

Any Windows program can access a shell extension by calling explorer.exe and requesting the GUID of the extension it wants. You can create a Meta-Frame XP published application that points to the Printers shell extension.

Here's a neat trick to show how that shell extension will work: create a new folder on your Windows desktop; name the folder "`Printers.{2227A280-3AEA-1069-A2DE-08002B30309D}`" with no spaces anywhere in the name; press Enter, the icon for the folder will change into the Printers folder icon; and when you open that folder it will look just like the Printers folder from the start menu. To make the Printers folder available as a published application, you need to publish a folder like this. Here are the steps to take:

1. Create a folder called "`Printers.{2227A280-3AEA-1069-A2DE-08002B30309D}`." Make sure that there are no spaces in the name anywhere.

2. Put that folder somewhere it can be published. For example, use the `m:\print\` directory, so that the full path of our folder is `m:\print\Printers.{2227A280-3AEA-1069-A2DE-08002B30309D}\`.

3. Now, all you need to do is publish that folder. To publish a folder in MetaFrame XP, you need publish explorer.exe with command line switches that will open that folder. However, you need to first make a copy of explorer.exe. Your copy can be called anything *except* explorer.exe. This will force your published application to open a new instance of explorer.exe, since yours will have a different name than the background copy that is already running.

4. Put the new copy of explorer.exe (Let's call it printexplorer.exe) into the `m:\print\` folder.

5. Publish this application. The command line to publish will be the following: `m:\print\printexplorer.exe /n,/root, m:\print\Printers.{2227A280-3AEA-1069-A2DE-08002B30309D}`.

Let's take a closer look at the command line that you are publishing. It begins by launching `printexplorer.exe` with several command line options. The `/n` option tells explorer to open a single-paned window. The `/root` option tells explorer to open this window as the root, preventing users from being able to click the "Up" folder to browse back up through the directory structure. The command ends with the full path to your custom folder, telling explorer which folder should be used as the root.

# Third Party Printing Solutions

At this point we have examined all of the aspects of printing in MetaFrame XP environments. We have looked the various tools and techniques available from Citrix and Microsoft. Even considering everything we've seen so far, there are printing scenarios that can still cause trouble. Among these are the following:

1. Printer drivers must be installed and managed for each client printer on every MetaFrame XP server.

2. Client printing performance is poor. The universal print driver helps in some situations, but it has major drawbacks, including the fact that it only works for 32-bit Windows clients, it requires Feature Release 1 or 2, and it is limited to 300 dpi monochrome.

3. There are no good solutions for situations where ICA clients and printer servers are on one side of the WAN, while MetaFrame XP servers are on the other.

Fortunately, there are several third party printing solutions that are available to address these issues. Let's look at the four most popular companies now, in alphabetical order:

- *Emergent Online* is a fairly large consulting and training company that also creates various software packages to help administrators with many thin-client situations. They have several printing products that can help with many different aspects of printing. Their website is www.go-eol.com.

- *FutureLink Canada* should not be confused with the US FutureLink that went bankrupt in 2001. FutureLink Canada is a completely separate company. They own the UniPrint family of MetaFrame XP printing solutions. More information is available at www.uniprint.net.

- *ThinPrint* is a German company with a large US presence. As their name implies, they focus entirely on printing in thin client environments, and they have several good products. You can find them at www.thinprint.com.

- *triCerat Software* has several products that can help you manage server-based computing environments more effectively. These include several printing products. More information is available at www.tricerat.com.

These four vendors are extremely competitive. Because of this, they are constantly coming out with new and updated products. Also, these four vendors are not very large, which means that they will go out of their way to support you and to give you their products at an attractive price.

Because there are some very real drawbacks with MetaFrame XP's out-of-the-box printing solutions and because these third party tools are so popular, it's definitely worth looking at them. As for recommendations, we're going to study the printing challenges and how third party tools are used to address them from a technical standpoint. We are *not* going to study each of the vendors' different products and provide reviews.

After you read this section, you'll have a true understanding of why these products are needed and how they can help. This will enable you to be able to go to the different printing vendors and accurately assess their products and offerings. All four of these vendors offer 30-day trial versions of their products, and there is a wealth of unbiased, up-to-the-minute reviews of all of these vendors and their products at `http://thethin.net`.

The technical design information provided in this book, coupled with the online information about these four vendors should provide you with enough information to be able to make an informed decision that allows you to support the MetaFrame XP printing challenges that arise in these problem scenarios.

Now, let's take a look at how these third-party tools address each of the MetaFrame XP printing problems outlined previously.

## Problem 1. Multiple Printer Drivers must be Managed

Whether you use client mapped printers or server printers, you need to have the appropriate printer drivers installed on every MetaFrame XP server. While there are steps you can take to help alleviate this, each has its problems. MetaFrame XP printer driver replication has serious performance issues. Manual replication is a problem if you have a lot of servers or a lot of users. The alternatives to using many drivers, such as the universal print driver or alternate driver substitution often come at the expense of printer functionality.

Since the early days of MetaFrame, there has been a call for an easy way to manage printer drivers on multiple servers. This is where the third party tools come in. These vendors offer products that allow you to package and distribute any number of printer drivers to multiple MetaFrame XP servers. This Your servers will then have the necessary drivers installed to support the needed number of network and client mapped printers. By having these printer drivers preinstalled on MetaFrame XP servers, you can dramatically reduce the administrative effort of supporting auto-created client mapped printers.

These third party tools also offer better performance than the standard MetaFrame XP printer driver replication as well as an easy way to remove drivers.

### Advantages of Third Party Printer Driver Management Tools

- Printer drivers can easily be installed and removed from MetaFrame XP servers.
- No performance degradation.
- Multiple drivers can be installed simultaneously.

### Disadvantages of Third Party Printer Driver Management Tools

- These tools represent an additional cost.
- These tools do not address the fundamental driver requirement problems associated with client printer mapping.

## Problem 2. Client Printer Performance is Poor

Ideally, printing in a MetaFrame XP environment should not be something that you should have to worry about. Most users already have their printers configured locally on their workstations before they ever connect to your MetaFrame XP servers. The users are familiar with their printers. They know where they are located and how fast they print.

Remember how the standard MetaFrame XP client printer mapping works? It gives the users the ability to print to their own printers, except the performance is poor. The large spooled print job is sent across the network to the user, which could take some time.

As an alternative to this, all four printing software vendors have products that allow users to quickly, easily, and seamlessly print to their own local printers. These products install as printer drivers on the server and a small client component on the ICA clients. To understand how this works, think back to how standard Windows printing works. The application generates an EMF file that is small and efficient. The print spooler uses the EMF to generate the spooled print file which is large and printer-specific. The spooled print file is transmitted to the ICA client.

These third party printing tools operate by intercepting the print job after the EMF is created but before it is sent to the print spooler.

*Figure 7.8 Third party printing software installed on ICA clients*

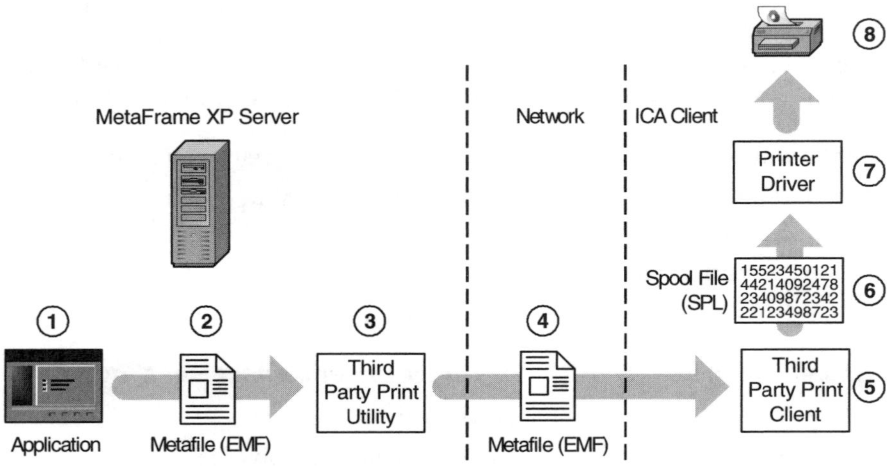

1. The user prints from an application on the MetaFrame XP server.

2. The application, via the GDI, generates an EMF file.

3. The third party software component running on the MetaFrame XP server receives that EMF file.

4. The third party software transmits the EMF file to the ICA client.

5. A third party software component on the ICA client receives the EMF file.

6. The third party software transfers the EMF file to the local print spooler on the client device.

7. The client device's local print spooler spools the print job.

8. The print job is transmitted to the client's printer, just like any print job in a non-MetaFrame XP environment.

Another thing that you may have noticed in this diagram is that if you use this type of third party tool, you do not need to have printer drivers installed on your MetaFrame XP servers. The printer drivers are not invoked until after the print job is sent to the client device. At that point, the client's printer drivers are used.

### Advantages of Using Third Party Client Printing Products

- Any client printer can be used.

- As an administrator, you do not need to worry about printing.

- Individual printer drivers do not need to be installed on the MetaFrame XP servers.

- The third party client software can be scripted to automatically install from an NFuse web page, just like the ICA client software.

- These tools can be used with all client platforms.

- These tools do not require Feature Release 1 or 2 (or MetaFrame for that matter).

### Disadvantages of Using Third Party Client Printing Products

- These third party tools represent an additional cost.

As you may have noticed, these third party tools are similar to the universal print driver functionality of Feature Release 1 or 2. (Actually, the universal print driver is similar to these tools, because they have been around a lot longer than Feature Release 1.) Even though they represent an additional cost, these tools have several benefits over the universal print driver of Feature Release 1, including the fact that they work on any client platform (instead of only 32-bit Windows) and can produce full color print jobs at any resolution (instead of being limited to 300 dpi monochrome).

## Problem 3. Printing in WAN Environments

Often, MetaFrame XP environments are designed so that the users are at one location, and the MetaFrame XP servers are at another location. This is the preferred design in many cases because it's desirable to place the MetaFrame XP servers close to the data sources which are usually located at corporate offices. One of the problems with this architecture is printing. Typically, the location that houses the users has its own print server. This is often the case with remote offices or factory floors, as shown in Figure 7.9.

*Figure 7.9 MetaFrame XP in a WAN environment*

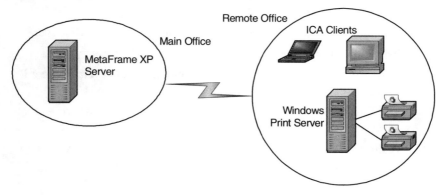

The problem with this environment is that the WAN is not used efficiently. If client printers are used, the MetaFrame XP servers will spool the entire print job before it's sent to the client devices. The clients then transfer the print job to the local print server. Alternately, the printer could be configured in Meta-Frame XP as a network printer. This would still mean that the print job would be spooled on the MetaFrame XP server, but in this case the spooled print job would then be sent directly to the print server instead of routed through the client device. Either way, inefficient print traffic is sent across the WAN.

The third party tools offer a solution where efficient print jobs are sent from the MetaFrame XP server directly to the print server. This is similar to the solution posed for Problem 2, except that the third party client software runs on the print server instead of the ICA client device.

*Figure 9.10 Third party software used with remote print servers*

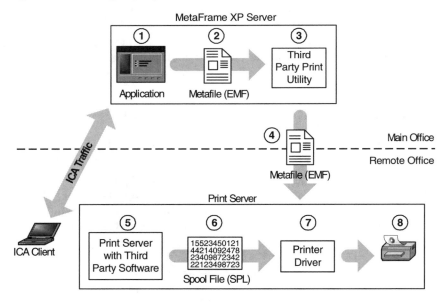

1. The user prints from an application on the MetaFrame XP server.
2. The application, via the GDI, generates an EMF file.
3. The third party software component running on the MetaFrame XP server receives that EMF file.
4. The third party software transmits the EMF file to the network print server.
5. A third party software component running on the print server receives the EMF file.

6. The third party software transfers the EMF file to the local print spooler on the print server.

7. The print server's local print spooler spools the print job.

8. The print job is printed without the large spool file ever traversing the network.

### Advantages of Third Party Print Server Software

- Perfect solution for ICA thin client devices that cannot have third party software installed locally.

- Keeps large print jobs from traversing the WAN.

- No software needs to be installed on the users' client devices.

- Process is completely transparent to the users.

### Disadvantages of Third Party Print Server Software

- These third party tools represent an additional cost.

# Real World Case Study

## Moxie Enterprises

Moxie Enterprises has decided to implement MetaFrame XP to provide several core applications for their users. They have 13 office locations and about 950 users. At this point, the project team has taken an inventory of their locations and users. Based on inventory findings, they were able to put together the basic design of their MetaFrame XP environment. Now, all they need to do is figure out how printing will work. In order to do this, the project team decided that it would be easiest to create a solution based on the type of printing scenario. In looking at their MetaFrame XP system design, they realized that there were basically four different printing scenarios:

- *Main Office*. There is 1 main office with 550 users and 14 MetaFrame XP servers. All printing is handled by local print servers.

- *Regional Offices*. There are 2 regional offices, each with 150 users and 5 MetaFrame XP servers. All printing is handled by local print servers. However, these users will also need to print from sessions running on MetaFrame XP servers at the main office.

- *Small Offices*. There are 10 small offices, each with 5 to 15 users. These offices do not have local MetaFrame XP servers—all their users run applications off of MetaFrame XP servers at the main office. Each of these small offices has a local file server that doubles as a print server, with a laser printer and a color ink jet printer.

- *Home Users.* There are fifty users that work from their homes. They each have a local printer connected to their laptop computers. A while back, the IT department issued a "Home Office Supported Equipment" list to the departments that listed four different printer models that would be supported.

In addition to identifying the different printing scenarios, the project team also created a list of business goals for their MetaFrame XP printing environment. These goals included the following:

- Users should be able to log in anywhere and be able to print.
- The printing process cannot be too confusing for the users.
- The printing process must work at a reasonable speed.

Keeping these three printing goals in mind, the project team decided to address each printing scenario separately, beginning with the main office.

## The Main Office

All of the printers at the main office are standard network printers. Most of the print servers are running Windows NT 4.0, although there are still a few Novell print servers. These printers are fairly standard with the print servers in the data center. The printers themselves have HP JetDirect cards.

*Figure 7.11 Network printers at the MetaFrame XP server location*

At the main office, users' printers are automatically mapped via their logon scripts. Because the project team wanted the users to have the same environment when they logged onto a MetaFrame XP server as when they logged onto their local workstation, the users will run their standard logon scripts (except for the virus update section which does not run if it detects that the user is logging on from a Terminal Server). Because the printers are configured via logon scripts, there will be no issues configuring printers for different users.

Some of the project team members commented that their printing performance would actually be faster when printing from MetaFrame XP than when printing from their workstations. This is because the MetaFrame XP servers are in the data center two racks down from the print servers. The print jobs that are generated by users on MetaFrame XP servers don't even have to leave the data center.

There was only one issue with the network printers at the main office that the project team had to address. That issue dealt with printer drivers and the drivers that need to be installed onto the MetaFrame XP servers. Some project team members wanted to install all of the drivers for all of the printers; other team members thought that only basic, generic drivers should be installed. To fully understand the differences of opinion, let's take a deeper look at the issue.

Moxie Enterprises has eight different types of network printers in their main office. Three-quarters of these are HP LaserJets. The rest are more specialized, such as color printers and a couple of dot-matrix printers for multipart forms. Some project team members felt that all of the LaserJet printers should use the same driver, most likely a LaserJet 4 driver. While they might lose some functionality of the more advanced printers, they would not have to support very many drivers.

Other team members felt that this was ridiculous and that they could easily support eight different printer drivers. They pointed out that because these were all network printers, there was no chance that non-supported printers would be ever be used. There was no risk that they would ultimately have to support hundreds of printer drivers.

In the end, this driver issue was escalated all the way up to the CTO. His vision was pretty compelling. He said, "We have already spent a lot of money on fancy printers that can duplex, collate, staple and bind. With our vision of moving everything to a server-based computing model, it seems that MetaFrame will be a key part of our infrastructure for the next few years. For that reason, we should do everything we can to ensure that we are able to realize the full benefits of our printers in the MetaFrame XP environment."

With that, the project team decided to install all of the native printer drivers on their MetaFrame XP servers.

## The Regional Offices

Moxie Enterprises has two regional offices, each with about 150 users. Most of the applications that users need to access will be served from local Meta-Frame XP servers. However, there will be a few users that will need to access some database applications from MetaFrame XP servers located at the main office. In either case, all printers at these regional offices are network printers. The print servers, which are all Windows NT 4.0, are located locally at the regional offices.

*Figure 7.12 Network printers at the regional offices*

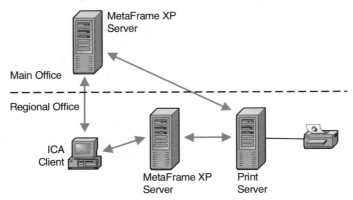

For the most part, printing in these offices will be done in the same way as the main office, with the users receiving their printer mappings via logon scripts. The users running ICA sessions on local MetaFrame XP servers will have extremely fast and reliable access to the printers.

The only issue here relates to the users that will need to print from applications running on the MetaFrame XP servers that are located back in the main office. In order to figure out how printing should be configured for those users, the project team decided to interview them to create a "printer user's profile." This document contains all of the vital printing information that the project team would need to figure out what type of printer support was needed.

The following questions were directed to the users to create the printer user's profile:

- How many different printers do you print to? Why?
- Do you use any advanced printer features, such as duplexing, collating, copying, or hole-punching?
- Do you print in color? How often?

- Do you ever use different paper types or sizes?
- Do you have any other special printing needs?
- Do you print forms, Word documents, images, or presentations?
- Who views your printouts?
- How many times per day do you print?
- What type of client device do you have? What operating system does it run?
- How many pages are usually printed at once?

In addition to the questions that where directed to the individual users, the project team also chose to look at the printers that they used. When looking at the printers, they tried to collect the following information:

- What is the printer's rated speed, in pages per minute?
- How often is the printer used throughout the day?
- How is the printer connected to the network? Can it be accessed via an IP address, or must it be accessed via a print server.
- What special features does the printer support that might be lost by using alternate generic drivers? How many people use these special features?

Remember, as far as the Moxie Enterprises MetaFrame XP implementation project team was concerned, they were only collecting this printer information to evaluate their printer options for the users at the two regional offices (with local print servers) that had to print from applications running on MetaFrame XP servers located at the main office.

The project team concluded from their evaluations that only about twenty people from each regional office needed to print from MetaFrame XP servers at the main office. Most of them were using Windows 2000 workstations, although a few people in the Customer Service Department were using HP Evo thin client terminals. These users didn't need to print in color, but they did print quite often from their central applications. The printers they used were HP LaserJet 8000N's, and they often printed on both sides of the page.

Based on this analysis, and the information that the project team received from their interviews, they built this list of requirements:

- Client platforms of Windows 2000 and Windows CE.
- Monochrome printing only.

- High speed.
- The printer must support duplexing.

Based on these requirements, the project team was able to outline four potential solutions. They decided that they would rank the advantages and disadvantages of each one and formally present them to the project steering committee along with their recommendations. The four potential solutions were as follows:

1. Use the Citrix Universal Print driver.
2. Install print queues locally on the MetaFrame XP servers.
3. Import the print servers into the MetaFrame XP server farm.
4. Use third party tools to send efficient print jobs to the print servers.

What follows is the information about each potential solution as presented to the steering committee.

### Potential Solution 1. Citrix Universal Print Driver
The first potential solution that the project team considered was to use the Citrix universal print driver available with Feature Release 1 or 2. Unfortunately, this did not meet the four basic requirements outlined previously since it only supports single-sided, monochrome print jobs and ICA clients running on 32-bit Windows platforms.

### Advantages of the Citrix Universal Print Driver
- No additional capital cost (The project team is planning on implementing Feature Release 2 for other reasons.)

### Disadvantages of the Citrix Universal Print Driver
- Does not meet the client device platform requirement. (Only works with 32 bit Windows clients)
- Does not meet the color printing requirement.
- Does not meet the duplexing requirement

### Potential Solution 2. Install Local Print Queues
The second solution was to install print queues locally on each of the MetaFrame XP servers. This is possible because the printers under consideration have HP JetDirect cards, so each printer's IP address can be added as a local port to each MetaFrame XP server. This can be done at no additional cost.

The disadvantage is the fact that these ports would need to be configured on every MetaFrame XP server, requiring significant time. Also, the performance over the WAN might be slow, especially during heavy printer usage. In this case, the entire spooled print job would be sent across the WAN.

### Advantages of Installing Local Print Queues

- No additional capital cost.

### Disadvantages of Installing Local Print Queues

- Might not meet the high speed requirement.
- Print queues must be installed on every MetaFrame XP server.

## Potential Solution 3. Import the Print Servers

Alternately, the project team considered importing the print servers into the MetaFrame XP server farm. While this wouldn't be quite as time-consuming as the local print queues, the performance wouldn't be any better.

### Advantages of Importing the Print Servers

- No additional capital cost.

### Disadvantages of Importing the Print Servers

- Might not meet the high speed requirement.

## Potential Solution 4. Use a Third Party Print Server Utility

The last solution that the project team considered was to use a third party utility like the one outlined in Figure 7.10. This utility would be installed on the MetaFrame XP servers and on the print servers, but nothing would need to be installed on the ICA client devices (which means the solution would work with both the Windows 2000 and Windows CE clients). Because this tool would be installed on both ends of the WAN, it would ensure that efficient metafile print traffic is transmitted across the WAN instead of large spool files.

### Advantages of Using a Third Party Print Server Utility

- Meets all technical requirements.
- Easy configuration.

### Disadvantages of Using a Third Party Print Server Utility

- Third party tool represents an additional cost.

The project team thought that the third party utility would provide the best overall solution for the regional office users that needed to print from applications running on the main office MetaFrame XP servers. The only real disadvantage that they could think of was the fact that the third party tool had to be purchased in addition to their Citrix and Microsoft software. However, they figured that the increased performance and decreased configuration effort would mean that this software would pay for itself very quickly.

## The Small Offices

All of Moxie's ten small offices have local print servers, but all MetaFrame XP application execution takes place at the main office. Again, because the print server is not located near the MetaFrame XP server, the spooled printer files must be sent from the MetaFrame XP server across the WAN to the print server, which can be time consuming.

*Figure 7.13 Network printers at remote office locations*

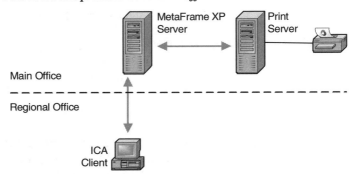

In this case, the project team was able to quickly make a decision without any arguments. They immediately decided to use the same third party printing utility that they will use for the regional offices. This will allow the users at those facilities to make full use of their color and laser printers without the need to install any client software on the users' workstations.

## Home Users

The final group of users that the project team addressed was the home users. The home users all run MetaFrame XP sessions off the servers at the main office. Almost all of the fifty home users have local printers installed. These printers are connected to their laptop computers via USB or the parallel port. As the project team discussed earlier, the big challenge with these users was that no one can be sure of what kind of printers they have. Some team members are estimating that there may be as many as thirty different types of printers out there.

*Figure 7.14 Local printers attached to client devices*

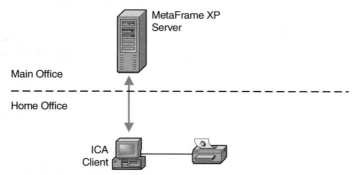

Fortunately, the printing technology decision for the home users was also easy to make. The project team knew that they were working with these requirements:

- Any client computer make and model.
- Any operating system.
- Any printer make and model.
- Extremely slow network connections (dial-up).
- No user intervention.

Some project team members wanted to use the Citrix universal print driver even though it only allowed printing in black and white. However, some home users connected from Macintosh platforms with the Macintosh ICA client software. The Citrix universal print driver only supports 32-bit Windows platforms.

All of these requirements naturally lead the team to one solution: third party printer management software. The server component of this software would be installed on each of the MetaFrame XP servers. A client component would be installed on every ICA client device. In this case, that was easy because users were connecting via an NFuse web portal. The project team simply modified the web page to check the user's IP address. If it is outside of the firewall, then the third party client printing software is automatically downloaded and installed to the user's computer.

Once this client software is installed, the MetaFrame XP servers send small, unrendered metafile print jobs to the client. The third party software installed on the client computer renders the print jobs locally, allowing any printer to be used, as shown back in Figure 7.8.

## Summary

By carefully analyzing all of the unique requirements of each printing scenario, the Moxie Enterprises project team was able to successfully design a MetaFrame XP printing solution that allows users to print documents with the speed and flexibility they need to run their business.

# CHAPTER 8

# Integration with Novell NetWare

In this chapter

Microsoft's Gateway Services for NetWare          318

Microsoft's Client Services for NetWare          319

Novell's NDS Client          321

NDS Integration with Feature Release 1 or 2          328

Issues to Consider for NetWare Options          332

Many businesses choose MetaFrame XP to provide anytime, anywhere access to existing applications. Many of today's applications and data still reside on Novell NetWare servers. The integration challenges of heterogeneous NetWare / Windows environments with MetaFrame XP environments are not new. These challenges have existed for a long time and will most likely continue to exist well into the future.

Fortunately, NetWare and Windows have been around much longer than MetaFrame XP, and so there are tried and true methods of integrating the two. Each method has its own advantages and disadvantages.

## Why should you care about the method of integration?

Because there are several different ways to integrate your MetaFrame XP servers with your existing NetWare environment, it's important that you evaluate the available options and the advantages and disadvantages of each. This will allow you to make the design decision that is most appropriate for your environment.

If you don't think carefully about your method of NetWare integration, you could choose an option that doesn't fit your environment. Even worse, you might choose an option that costs you more money and doesn't fit your environment. As you're reading through the different options, keep in mind that your choice affects several areas of your environment, including:

- Security.
- Additional components and software requirements.
- Flexibility of future servers.
- Users' ability to logon.

### Security
Some of the NetWare integration methods will "break" NetWare safeguards and user auditing that you have put in place. Others will cause NetWare user credentials to be cached in different areas. If having tight security is high on your priorities list, then you should be mindful of that as you evaluate different options.

### Additional Software Requirements
Some of the NetWare integration methods require that you configure various third party software components, such as ZENworks, in order to use them. While these methods work well in environments where ZENworks is already

deployed, it might not be practical to deploy ZENworks for the sole purpose of integrating MetaFrame XP users with NetWare.

Other integration methods require that you have Feature Release 1 or 2 installed on your MetaFrame XP servers. Similar to the ZENworks requirement, this is a nice perk of a Feature Release if you already have one deployed, but it may be cost-prohibitive to purchase a Feature Release for the sole purpose of integrating users with NetWare.

### *Future Server Flexibility*

You need to think about not only your present options, but your future options as well. Some of the NetWare integration methods are "all of nothing," meaning that your servers can either access a NetWare environment or a Windows domain environment, but not both. This may meet your current requirements if you have a 100% NetWare infrastructure, but it could prevent you from expanding your MetaFrame XP server farm into Windows domain or Active Directory environments.

### *Ease of User Logon*

In many cases, your users will need two user accounts—one for NetWare and one for Windows. Depending on the type of integration solution you choose, keeping these passwords synchronized can be easy or difficult, directly affecting the ease of the user logon process.

## What are the NetWare integration options?

Given everything that the NetWare integration strategy can affect and everything that you need to consider, there are four options that you can use to allow users on your MetaFrame XP servers to access resources from Novell NetWare environments. These options include:

- Microsoft Gateway Services for NetWare
- Microsoft Client Services for NetWare
- Install Novell's NDS Client.
- MetaFrame XP Feature Release 1 or 2

Throughout the remainder of this chapter, we'll take a detailed look at each one of these options, including the advantages, disadvantages, and how each is configured.

# Microsoft's Gateway Services for NetWare

Gateway Services for NetWare (GSNW) is a Microsoft tool that allows you to permanently map drives to NetWare volumes that are available to all users on a server. These drives appear to the users as local server drives. In most cases, the users do not even realize that the drives are *not* local to the MetaFrame XP server.

Gateway Services for NetWare works in a similar way to standard network drive mapping. When you create a regular mapping to a network drive on a MetaFrame XP server, the drive mapping is only available for the session (and the user profile) where it is mapped. For example, if you log on to a MetaFrame XP server and map the F: drive to the \\nov1\applications \data share, that F: drive will only be available in your user session. Other users won't see it at all. In fact, they could map their own F: drives to a totally different network location.

However, if you use Gateway Services for NetWare, you can configure a "gateway" to a network share, such as \\nov1\applications\data. This gateway is accessible locally on the MetaFrame XP server via a drive letter for all of your users in every session. To your users, the mapped drive will appear as a local drive.

Network drive gateways work well when you have some critical data on a NetWare server that you need to provide access to in cases where your users do not have NetWare accounts.

### Advantages of Gateway Services for NetWare

- Seamless access to NetWare data for your users.
- Users do not need NetWare accounts.
- No account password synchronization issues.
- You can configure different permissions on the gateway, so that only some users are permitted to access it. This is similar to setting NTFS permissions on a local drive.

### Disadvantages of Gateway Services for NetWare

- The performance of GSNW is less than stellar.
- From the NetWare standpoint, all users access the gateway share via the same account.
- A server list is only obtained from the first NetWare server that

GSNW attaches to, requiring proper SAP routing in your NetWare environment to access all NetWare servers.

## Configuration of Gateway Services for NetWare

You install GSNW the same way that you do any networking client. Once you install Gateway Services for NetWare, a new icon called "GSNW" will appear in the control panel. You can use this icon to configure the NetWare gateway and the client services settings. (Client settings are covered in the next section.)

To configure the gateway, you can follow this simple procedure:

1. Install the NWLink IPX/SPX/NetBIOS compatible protocol on each MetaFrame XP server that you want to use to access NetWare shares.

2. Install GSNW (Control Panel | Network | Install | Client | Add | Gateway (and Client) Services for NetWare).

3. Create a group on the NetWare server or in NDS called "NTGATEWAY."

4. Create a user account and grant it access to the resources that you would like to be available through the gateway.

5. Add the user account to the NTGATEWAY group.

6. Configure GSNW via the GSNW icon in the control panel. Click "Gateway" and check the "Enable Gateway" box. Add the name and password of the NDS or bindery account that you just created.

7. Specify a share name and drive letter that the MetaFrame XP users will use to access the NetWare drive.

8. Configure the maximum number of users, if you want. This number has nothing to do with licensing.

# Microsoft's Client Services for NetWare

When you install Gateway Services for NetWare, Client Services for NetWare (CSNW) is also installed. CSNW is client software created by Microsoft for connecting to NDS or Bindery NetWare volumes. This software allows users to uniquely connect to any NetWare resource.

### Advantages of Client Services for NetWare

- It uses the native Microsoft authentication and security components.
- Each user can log into the NetWare environment with their own unique credentials.
- Different users can access different NDS trees.
- CSNW is good for when only a few users need access to NetWare volumes.

### Disadvantages of Client Services for NetWare

- Much slower then Novell's NDS Client.
- Does not support NetWare IP.
- Does not support many "native" NetWare features, such as contextless login, ZENworks desktop, NetWare Application Launcher, or NDS Printing.

## Configuration of Client Services for NetWare

After you install CSNW/GSNW, the first time that a user logs on he will be presented with a NetWare login box immediately after he successfully authenticates with his Microsoft credentials. This NetWare login box is part of Microsoft's Client Services for NetWare, so this box is standard Windows gray and blue. (This is not the red and white "Novell" login box. To get that box, see the next section about Novell's NDS Client.) In this Microsoft Client Services for NetWare login box, the user can enter credentials for NDS or Bindery NetWare volumes. He can also select "none" as his NetWare server if he prefers not to connect to any NetWare resources. Whatever option he chooses is stored in his user profile.

With each subsequent logon, the user's Windows domain username and password are automatically and seamlessly passed to the bindery or NDS context that he logged into last. If his Windows username and password match his NetWare username and password (for the context or bindery saved in his profile), he is automatically logged on to that NetWare resource. If his Windows username and password are not valid in the NetWare environment, then the same NetWare login screen is presented to him, and he can: (1) enter new credentials; (2) choose a different context or server; (3) choose "none" to not log onto any NetWare resource,;or (4) choose "cancel" to cancel this request and keep his old credentials in his user profile..

At any time, if the user wants to change the NetWare settings that are saved in his user profile, he can access the "GSNW" icon in the control panel from within his user session.

# Novell's NDS Client

Instead of using Microsoft's Client Services for NetWare, you can choose to use Novell's version of the NetWare client software. When you install Novell's NDS Client software, available as a free download from www.novell.com, the Microsoft GINA will be replaced with Novell's Client GINA.

In Windows, a "GINA" is the Graphical Identification and Authentication component. This is the part of the operating system responsible for logging users on. In Windows NT and Windows 2000, you use the GINA every day when you press CTRL+ALT+DEL and type in your username and password. With Novell's NDS Client installed, the Microsoft GINA is replaced by the Novell GINA, which is why the "Press CTRL+ALT+DEL" screen changes from the gray and blue Microsoft box to the red and white Novell box.

The fact that Novell's Client replaces the Microsoft GINA is really not that big of a deal. In fact, in environments where NetWare and NDS are heavily used, it is actually a good thing, because Novell's GINA is much more compatible with Novell's features then the Microsoft GINA. However, in order for the Novell GINA to work in a Terminal Server environment, it must know that multiple users will be simultaneously logged on to a server, each with his own credentials. Novell made their client software "Terminal Server aware" several years ago with Service Pack 2 for the Novell NDS Client version 4.6.

Even though the Novell NDS client software is smart enough to know how Terminal Server works, there is still a fundamental challenge in MetaFrame XP environments. In MetaFrame XP environments that use NDS, users need several parameters to log on, including their Windows username, password, and domain, as well as their NDS tree and context, and possibly a separate NDS username and password. However, the ICA client software only has the capability to pass three parameters on to the MetaFrame XP server: the username, password, and domain.

Because of this, the Novell NDS client must work with only these three parameters and make assumptions about the rest. A majority of your configuration planning for Novell's NDS client involves choosing which user logon parameters are statically assumed and which parameters are passed by the user.

### Advantages of using Novell's NDS Client

- Fast access to NetWare resources.

- Many of the "advanced" Novell features can be supported, such as NDS printing, ZEN works, and Novell Application Launcher.

### Disadvantages of Novell's NDS Client

- Because the ICA software is not NDS-aware, you must make some trade-offs between user flexibility and NDS access.

- In order for users to have unique desktop environments, they must have domain accounts and NDS accounts (unless ZENworks is used).

- All Novell NDS Client configuration options apply globally for all users on a server.

## Configuration of Novell's NDS Client

As was mentioned previously, to use Novell's NDS client with MetaFrame XP, you need to install a minimum version of Novell Client 4.6 with Service Pack 2. In the real world, version 4.8 or newer is recommended. Remember that these are the only versions of the Novell NDS Client that are Terminal Services-aware. With these versions, you can control how the Novell Client software deals with the limited logon parameters available via ICA and what assumptions are made. All of these parameters and features are enabled and configured via the registry. They mostly control the behavior of the logon components that the users see and the behind-the-scenes authentication behavior. All of the options that we will look at for Novell NDS Client apply globally to all users at the server.

In order for these options and configurations to work, you obviously need to have the Novell-branded client software installed. Also, it needs to be configured to use the NetWare GINA, not the Microsoft GINA. Let's take a look at each of these steps.

First, in a perfect world, you would install the Novell NDS Client software before you install MetaFrame XP. This has to do with our new friend GINA. When the Novell NDS Client software is installed, it replaces the Microsoft GINA with the Novell GINA. However, when MetaFrame XP is installed, it replaces the Microsoft GINA with a Citrix GINA. Ultimately, everything will work together—it's just that you need to make sure everything is configured in the proper order.

If you have a brand-new server, install the Novell NDS Client software before you install MetaFrame XP. If you already have MetaFrame XP installed you can still install the Novell Client—you just have to add steps to change some GINA settings in the registry. In order to install Novell's NDS Client after MetaFrame XP is installed, follow these steps:

1. Change the GINA from the Citrix GINA to the Microsoft GINA. You need to do this because the Novell NDS Client software will not install properly unless it finds the Microsoft GINA in the registry. This GINA change is done through the registry.

   Key: `HKLM\Software\Microsoft\Windows NT\Current Version\Winlogon`

   Value: `GinaDLL`

   Type: `REG_SZ`

   Old Data you Should Change: `Ctxgina.dll`

   New Data you Type over the Old Data: `Msgina.dll`

2. Do not reboot the server. Instead, install the Novell NDS Client software as normal.

3. After the Novell NDS Client software is installed, change the GinaDLL value outlined in Step 1 from Msgina.dll back to Ctxgina.dll.

4. Again under the same registry key, add a new REG_SZ value called `ctxGinaDLL`. Set its value to "`nwgina.dll`." This new value will be the GINA that is used by the user sessions connecting via MetaFrame XP. In this case, the `nwgina.dll` is Novell's GINA.

5. Reboot the MetaFrame XP server.

Once these steps are complete, you will have the Novell NDS Client software installed. At this point, there are four different ways that it can be used:

- Use a generic "common" Windows login.
- Use a generic "common" NetWare login.
- Prompt the user for their NetWare credentials.
- Logon to Windows only without logging into NetWare.

Before we look at the specifics of each of these methods of configuring the Novell NDS Client software, we should look at some basic concepts for what you will be configuring.

Since the ICA client can only pass Windows credentials to the server, you need to make the decision as to whether you would like to automatically log in all users with the same generic NDS credentials, or whether you want to present a Novell login box to the user and let them enter their own NDS credentials. However, before you make this decision, you should decide if your users are going to have unique Microsoft credentials, or if they will logon generically with common user credentials.

### *Option 1. Use Common Windows Credentials*

There are many advantages and disadvantages to deciding to have your users all connect to the MetaFrame XP servers using a common Windows account. These details are discussed in Chapter 15. If you do decide to use this option, there are several different areas in which it can be configured, including the server registry, the ICA connection, the published application, or an ICA file. For the purposes of NetWare integration, configuring the common Windows credentials via the MetaFrame XP server's registry works the best. In this case, this is called "auto-logon," because the users will not be presented with a logon box since they are all connecting with the same user account.

You can enable the Windows auto-logon account with the following registry value:

Key: `HKLM\Software\Microsoft\Windows NT\Current Version\Winlogon`

Value: `AutoAdminLogon`

Type: `REG_SZ`

Data: 1 = enable

Even though the registry value is called "AutoAdminLogon," it does apply to all users and all user sessions, not just to people who connect from the server console. Once you enable auto-logon, you need to specify the user, password, and domain that will be used for the auto-logon. All three of these values are found in the same registry location as the AutoAdminLogon value, and they all are type REG_SZ. The three registry values are as follows:

- `DefaultUserName`
- `DefaultPassword`
- `DefaultDomainName`

Once these values are configured, any user that connects to the server will be automatically logged onto Windows as this user. Remember that these values affect the Microsoft Windows logon only (either workgroup or domain), and that they have nothing to do with NetWare logon that you will configure later.

### Option 2. Use Common NetWare Credentials

Novell's NDS client also allows you to specify an "AutoAdminLogon" value to enable users to logon to the NetWare environment with automatic credentials in the registry. However, in the Terminal Server environment, that NetWare "AutoAdminLogon" value only affects users that logon to the server console. Users that connect from client ICA sessions are affected by a different registry value, as show below:

> Key: HKLM\Software\Novell\Login
>
> Value: TSClientAutoAdminLogon
>
> Type: REG_SZ
>
> Data: 1 = enable

Once you enable this value, you will need to tell the software what settings you want to use to log in. With the Novell Client software, these settings are called "Location Profiles." A location profile is similar to a user profile for Windows, except that a location profile only exists within the Novell Client software. Each location profile includes things like the username, context, and NDS tree. The most commonly used Location Profile is called "default." However, you can specify the name of any Location Profile to be used for the auto-login. If you are not sure of the names of your Location Profiles, you can view a list in the registry at HKLM\Software\Novell\Location Profiles\Services\{1E6CEEA1-FB73-11CF-BD76-00001B2 7DA23}.

Once you decide which Location Profile you want to use for auto-login, specify it in the following location:

> Key: HKLM\Software\Novell\Login\
>
> Value: DefaultLocationProfile
>
> Type: REG_SZ
>
> Data: The name of the Location Profile to use for the automatic login.

For security reasons, a user's password is not stored in the Location Profile. In order for auto-login to work, it must be specified separately in the following registry key:

> Key: HKLM\Software\Novell\Login\DefaultPassword

Value: DefaultPassword

Type: REG_SZ

Data: Password for the autologin NDS user.

There are some situations in which you might want to provide users with the default auto-login settings for NDS while also giving them the option of over-riding them and selecting their own credentials. If this is the case, you can set a registry value that enables the Novell Login box to appear. When this is used with the NDS auto-login settings, the Novell Client login box appears pre-populated with the auto-login parameters. Users can click "Login" to login with those credentials, or they can enter their own unique credentials. This is enabled with this registry key.

Key: HKLM\Software\Novell\Login\

Value: AutoAdminQueryNDS

Type: REG_DWORD (Be careful here. Some of the Novell documentation incorrectly states that this should be a REG_SZ value, instead of a REG_DWORD.)

Data: 1 = enabled 0 = disabled

### Option 3. Prompt for NDS Credentials

As you saw in Option 2, when the TSClientAutoAdminLogon registry value is enabled (with a value or "1"), users connecting via remote sessions are automatically logged into the NDS tree. If you want to prompt users for their NDS credentials, then all you have to do is set that value to "0."

Previously, we also mentioned the AutoAdminQueryNDS value. In case you're wondering what the name "AutoAdminQueryNDS" stands for, it means when the Windows *Auto Admin* logon is used, *Query* the user for his *NDS* credentials. If you enable the AutoAdminQueryNDS value (by setting it to "1"), the NDS login box will appear for every user at logon time. Because you do not have any Location Profiles specified, no information will be pre-populated in the box, forcing users to type in their own credentials.

If you use this option in combination with the Windows AutoAdminLogon settings, then the Novell NDS Client login box will still appear, but the Windows logon settings will be grayed out, preventing users from changing them.

### Option 4. Do Not Logon to NDS (Workstation Only)

If you have the Novell NDS Client 4.8 or newer installed and you decide that you do not want your users to log into the NDS tree when their session begins, you can configure the following registry value:

Key: HKLM\Software\Novell\Login

Value: Default WS Only

Type: REG_DWORD

Data: "1" causes the "Workstation Only" checkbox to default to "On." "0" causes the "Workstation Only" checkbox to default to "Off."

If you choose this option, your users will be able to login to the NDS tree manually from within their user session. This method is used a lot when only some users need access to NDS resources and they only have access to the full Windows desktop instead of specific published applications.

### Summary of Novell NDS Client Registry Keys and Values

Because multiple registry keys, values, and data were mentioned in this section of the chapter, it's worth listing them all together, along with their different uses.

The following settings apply only to the Novell NDS Client software. Each listed item is a value in the HKLM\Software\Novell\Login registry key. In order for these settings to be valid, the MetaFrame XP server must use the NetWare GINA:

- *AutoAdminLogon*. Enabling this causes users to be automatically logged into the NDS tree when using the server console.
- *DefaultLocationProfile*. Specifies the Location Profile to be used for auto-login.
- *DefaultPassword*. Specifies the password to be used for auto-login.
- *TSClientAutoAdminLogon*. Enabling this causes users to be automatically logged into the NDS tree when connecting via user sessions.
- *AutoAdminQueryNDS*. Enabling this forces the Novell Login box to be displayed, even if Windows auto-logon or NDS auto-login is enabled.
- *Default WS Only*. When enabled, the "Workstation Only" login option is selected by default.

The next group of registry settings apply only to the Windows logon. They are set in the HKLM\Software\Microsoft\Windows NT\CurrentVersion\Winlogon registry key. These settings are valid for MetaFrame XP servers using the NetWare, Microsoft, or Citrix GINA:

- *AutoAdminLogon.* Enabling this causes users to be automatically logged onto the server, both from the console and from remote sessions.

- *DefaultUserName.* Specifies the user name when auto-logon is used.

- *DefaultPassword.* Specifies the password when auto-logon is used.

- *DefaultDomainName.* Specifies the domain when auto-logon is used. If the MetaFrame XP server is not part of a domain environment, then this value should be set to the local server name.

# NDS Integration with Feature Release 1 or 2

As you learned earlier in this chapter, one of the traditional challenges of integrating MetaFrame XP environments with NetWare environments has been that the ICA clients were only capable of passing the three Windows authentication parameters (username, password, and domain) to launch an ICA session. Citrix began to address this problem with the version 6.20 release of their ICA client software. This software is able to pass full NDS credentials to a MetaFrame XP server in place of Windows credentials.

The ability to do this makes it a lot easier for NDS users to use your servers. From the user standpoint, they can enter their credentials directly into the ICA client software or the NFuse web page. Once their ICA sessions are launched, they do not have to worry about retyping their credentials. The logon and authentication process is as seamless as it is in any full-Microsoft environment.

## Requirements for Using MetaFrame XP's NDS Features

In order to use NDS integration with ICA clients, there are several requirements that must be met, as outlined in the following list. This list represents the minimum requirements. For each of these items, newer versions are also acceptable:

- *Feature Release Level.* You need to have at least Feature Release 1 installed on each MetaFrame XP server that you want to make available to NDS users.

- *NDS 8.73 or eDirectory 8.5.* NDS 8.73 is only supported on NetWare 5. eDirectory can run on multiple platforms, including Windows 2000 Server.

- *ZENworks for Desktops 3*. MetaFrame XP's NDS integration leverages ZENwork's "Dynamic Local User" technology. (More on this later.)

- *Novell NDS Client version 4.8*. This software must be installed on each MetaFrame XP server that you want to make available to NDS users.

- *ICA Client Software 6.20*. This is needed on each ICA client device that you want to integrate with MetaFrame XP's NDS features.

- *A Single NDS tree*. The NDS tree that MetaFrame XP server users log in to is configured at the server farm level. If you have more than one tree that you need to log in to, then you will need to connect to each tree from separate server farms.

- *Dedicated MetaFrame XP Servers*. If you configure MetaFrame XP servers to authenticate users via NDS, then they cannot authenticate users via Microsoft domains. You will have to choose which servers use Windows authentication, and which use NetWare authentication.

If you've met all of these requirements, then you can use MetaFrame XP's NDS integration features. If you don't meet them, then you'll need to use one of the other methods of integrating your NetWare users with your MetaFrame XP servers.

### Advantages of FR-1 or FR-2 NDS Integration

- Users can log on with their existing NDS credentials.

- No need to duplicate user accounts between your Windows and NDS environments.

- Tight integration with MetaFrame XP features, including application publishing, NFuse 1.6 and 1.7 Classic, pass-through authentication, connection control, printer management, and Program Neighborhood.

### Disadvantages of FR-1 or FR-2 NDS Integration

- Only one NDS tree can be supported per server farm.

- ZENworks is required.

- A single MetaFrame XP server can only be configured to support Windows users or NDS users—not both.

- You must manage the NDS components or your MetaFrame XP environment while logged onto the CMC as an NDS user.

- NDPS print queues are not directly supported, although this can be configured via ZENworks.

- Feature Release 1 or newer is required.

## Configuration of NDS Integration with Feature Release 1 or 2

If you decide that you would like to use the NDS integration features of Meta-Frame XP, you can use the following process to configure everything. This process assumes that Feature Release 1 or 2 is enabled on the MetaFrame XP servers that you're using:

1. Enable the Dynamic Local User policy in ZENworks for Desktops. This allows your users to logon to your MetaFrame XP servers without explicitly-configured local Windows accounts. To do this, ZENworks uses a "Dynamic Local User" account (DLU). Basically, when a user needs to log onto a MetaFrame XP server, ZENworks uses its own domain administrator rights to create a new local user account on the MetaFrame XP server. ZENworks builds the user's custom desktop as needed from their NDS profile. When the user logs off, the account is deleted. This entire process is transparent to the end user. From their standpoint, they logged onto the server by only using their NDS account.

2. Install the Novell NDS Client software, version 4.8 or newer. Refer to the process outlined in the "Configuration of Novell NDS Client" section earlier in this chapter.

3. Enable NDS support in the server farm. Connect to a MetaFrame XP server that has Feature Release 1 or 2 enabled and the Novell client installed. Enable NDS support by adding the NDS tree name in the CMC (CMC | Right-click on Farm | Properties | MetaFrame Settings Tab | NDS Preferred Tree). When you do this, the "TSClientAutoAdminLogon" registry key will automatically be configured on all farm servers.

4. Give at least one NDS account farm administrator rights (CMC | Right-click Citrix Administrators | Add a Citrix Administrator | Double-click NDS tree | Show Users | Select User | Add button). As with standard administrators, NDS administrators can be Read-Only or Read-Write. If you select an NDS object that has objects below it, then the child objects will have the same permissions.

5. Open a CMC session as an NDS administrator. You do this by launching the CMC as normal, except that you enter NDS user credentials into the authentication box instead of Windows

credentials. (If you're using Feature Release 2's pass-through authentication to launch the CMC, you'll need to logon to the server as the NDS user.) Because there are no extra fields for the NDS tree or context, you must log on with the full distinguished name. This is simply the full path to your user account in the NDS tree, with a leading period and periods between each object (.username.your-ou.organization). Of course you might have more than one OU in your distinguished name. Also, when logging into the CMC, you need to enter the NDS tree name in the domain field.

6. Publish applications for NDS users that only NDS users will use. To do this, you publish the application or content as usual (CMC | Right-click Applications | New Application), except that you specify users from the NDS tree instead of a Windows domain. Again, any permissions that you set also apply to the child objects below the object for which you grant the permissions.

Once you complete these steps, your server farm will be fully integrated with NDS. For ICA client-specific configuration issues, see the ICA Clients chapter (Chapter 10). For NFuse-specific NDS configuration, see the NFuse chapter (Chapter 11).

## Feature Release 2 Refinements to NDS Integration

For the most part, Feature Release 2 does not affect how Novell NDS integration works with MetaFrame XP servers. However, there is one slight change in FR-2 that can allow you to use Novell NDS integration without using the ZenWorks Dynamic Local User (DLU) policy. With Feature Release 1, the ZenWorks DLU is required because the when farm-wide NDS integration is enabled, the Windows username and domain fields are actually used to pass the NDS credentials from the ICA client. Since NDS credentials show up in the fields normally used for Windows credentials, the logon would fail if these credentials were simply passed to Windows.

However, since FR-1 uses ZenWorks DLUs, any information on the "Windows" tab of the Novell NDS Client login box is ignored since the Windows logon information is pulled from the ZenWorks DLU policy. This means that NDS users can successfully logon even with invalid credentials on the Windows tab.

With FR-1, if an NDS user tries to logon with NDS credentials from an ICA session when ZenWorks DLU is not used, the logon will fail because the credentials from the "Windows" tab are applied (since ZenWorks was not used to replace them). The system is trying to use the Windows username and domain information as-is, but those credentials fail because the domain field actually contains the name of the NDS tree (because the farm is in NDS mode).

With Feature Release 2, a new "`SyncedDomainName`" registry key is available to prevent this problem from occurring:

> Registry Location: `HKLM\SOFTWARE\Citrix`
>
> Key: `NDS`  (You will need to create this key.)
>
> Value: `SyncedDomainName`
>
> Type: `REG_SZ`
>
> Data: The name of your Windows domain

You can use this parameter to specify the name of a Windows domain that will be used to log the user on. This is needed because your farm is operating in NDS mode, meaning that the domain parameter from the user's ICA logon is interpreted as the NDS tree. By adding the "SyncedDomainName" value, a valid Windows domain will be available that the TSClientAutoAdminLogon can process to log the user on. The only disadvantage of this is that your usernames and passwords will need to be the same in NDS and Windows.

### Advantages of the SyncedDomainName key

- You can use MetaFrame XP's "official" NDS integration without using ZenWorks' Dynamic Local User policies.

### Disadvantages of the SyncedDomainName key

- Feature Release 2 is required.
- Users' Windows usernames and passwords must match their NDS usernames and passwords.
- This only works if your NDS tree name is less than 15 characters long (the limit for Windows domain names).

# Issues to Consider for the NetWare Options

Now that you understand the technical details and intricacies of the various MetaFrame XP and NDS integration options, you need to figure out which ones will work best in your environment. To do this, you will need to answer the following questions:

- Do all of your users need to access the same data on NetWare servers, or do they each need to access their own data?

- Do users need to use applications where they are authenticated as NDS users, or do they just need access to their data?

- Do users need their own unique desktop environment, or can they use a common MetaFrame XP environment?

- Do you have Feature Release 1 or newer?

- Is NDS going to be in your environment long-term, or are you migrating to Active Directory?

- Do your NetWare users also have Windows domain or Active Directory accounts?

- Do your users need to access NetWare resources from all MetaFrame XP servers in the farm, or just certain servers?

## Data Access

If all of your users need to access the same data, then you can use one of the options where all users login to NetWare with the same credentials, such as a NetWare auto-login or a NetWare gateway. If users each need to access different components in the NetWare environment, then they will need to login to NetWare with their own unique accounts.

## User Access to NDS

If users need to access an NDS application, then they will need to authenticate to the tree. If they just need to access data that is stored on NDS volumes, then the NetWare gateway should work.

## User Environment

If your users do not need their own unique Windows desktop environment, they can share a Windows account which can be configured to auto-logon. This means that each user would only need a NetWare account, saving you from having to create or migrate too many Windows accounts. However, if users need their own unique desktops, they will need their own Windows accounts or you will need to use the ZENworks for Desktops to create Dynamic Local User accounts.

## Feature Release Level

Obviously, if you don't have or are not planning on using Feature Release 1 or 2 then you cannot use any of MetaFrame's native NDS integration options.

## Future User Account Platforms

If you have users with NDS accounts that you're planning on migrating to Windows or Active Directory accounts, it might be worth migrating them now for use with MetaFrame XP. However, if you're planning on NDS as your primary directory, then creating Windows accounts for your users would be counterproductive. In this case, your best solution would be to use the NDS integration features of Feature Release 1 or 2, or use the Dynamic Local User functionality of ZENworks.

## User Account Types

If your NetWare users already have Microsoft accounts that they use on a daily basis, they are familiar with the account integration and synchronization issues. In this case, you can probably just install Novell's NDS Client software or Microsoft's Client Services for NetWare, and your users will already know what to do when they see the NetWare login screen. If your users do not currently have both types of accounts, then you will need to plan on educating them when you roll out MetaFrame XP.

## MetaFrame XP Servers that will Access NetWare Resources

If you have MetaFrame XP servers that you dedicate to NDS users, you will be able to use the Feature Release 1 or 2 NDS integration features of MetaFrame XP. However, if you will need to have some servers that support users authenticating via NDS and Microsoft methods, you will need to choose an alternative method of integration.

# PART III

## Connecting Users to Servers

In this section

9.  User Access Methods and Client Devices       335

10. Deploying and Configuring ICA Clients        353

11. Building Web Portals with NFuse Classic 1.7  431

# CHAPTER 9

# User Access Methods and Client Devices

**In this chapter**

Methods of End User Access 338

Client Device Planning Considerations 343

Types of Client Devices 348

This chapter focuses on connecting your users to their applications running on your MetaFrame XP servers. Clearly, you've already made the decision that you will use MetaFrame to make this access easy.

Now you just have to figure out how you will do this with MetaFrame. There are two basic questions that you'll need to answer:

- What process and methods will your users use to access their applications?
- What types of hardware devices will be used to access the applications?

To answer these two questions, we'll present the myriad of available options and the advantages and disadvantages of each. Additionally, we'll outline the issues that you should think about when planning your own environment. When looking at client device options, we'll explore everything from full-blown Windows PCs to Linux workstations to Windows-based thin client devices. We'll also consider the time and effort it takes to configure, manage, and troubleshoot these devices, as well as the situations in which different types of devices are appropriate.

Let's begin with the different methods by which your users can access Meta-Frame XP ICA applications.

# Methods of End User Access

Probably the primary reason that anyone uses MetaFrame XP is to provide simple end-user access to Windows applications. By "methods of end user access," we're talking about how your users actually launch their applications on your MetaFrame XP servers. Do they have icons for MetaFrame XP applications in their Windows Start Menu or on their Windows desktop? Do they launch applications through a web portal? Are they running complete remote desktops or only specific applications?

## Why is the method of access important?

By spending some time up front to consider how your users will access their applications, you can build their environment to be easy to use. (This will make your life easier as a MetaFrame administrator.

The way that you configure your user access will directly affect several aspects of your users' experience, including:

- What users can do with their applications.
- How easily users can use and get access to their applications.
- How easy everything is to administer.
- How quickly the users can access the system and switch between applications.
- How secure the system is.
- Total cost of ownership.

## What are the user access method options?

Ultimately, all users will access the MetaFrame servers via some form of ICA client software from a hardware device that supports that software. Once a user is connected, their experience is controlled by the server—it doesn't really matter how they connected or what kind of client device they have. All of the user access method options really affect what steps the users will need to take to establish their connections.

From the management standpoint, the various user connection options fall into two general categories:

1. Options that require configuration on client devices, such as the traditional Program Neighborhood client.
2. Options that do not require configuration on client devices, such as deploying applications via web portals.

Regardless of the access methods you choose, your users will need some form of ICA client software loaded on their client device. However, some access methods require that you manually configure or update the client configuration on every single client, while other methods allow you to make configuration changes one time at the server, with ICA clients receiving the new settings automatically.

Let's take a detailed look at each of the following methods of end user access:

- Placing icons on your users' desktops and in their Start Menus.
- Creating websites or web portals with links that launch MetaFrame applications.
- Installing and configuring the full Program Neighborhood ICA

client software on each client workstation.

- Using the Program Neighborhood Agent, which allows users to launch MetaFrame applications via links on their desktop or in their Start Menu, while allowing you to administer those links centrally. (This option requires Feature Release 1 or 2.)

### Option 1. Traditional Icons on the Desktop and Start Menu

You can choose to put icons and shortcuts to your MetaFrame applications in your users' Start Menu or on their desktop. To your users, these icons look just like "regular" Windows applications. Your users would be comfortable with accessing applications this way, since it's really no different than the way they launch applications currently.

However, simply placing a shortcut on a computer does not mean that the computer will know what to do when that icon is clicked. You still have to install some form of ICA client software. In addition, if you ever want to change the parameters of an application that a user is accessing, you will have to do it manually.

### Advantages of Connecting via Traditional Icons

- MetaFrame XP application access is identical to locally-launched applications.
- Icons placed in this fashion can contain detailed connection configuration information.
- Each icon could point to applications from different server farms.

### Disadvantages of Connecting via Traditional Icons

- The ICA client software must be manually installed on each client workstation that users will use to access their applications.
- Any application shortcut configuration changes must be done manually.

### Option 2. Web Page / Web Portal

Many MetaFrame administrators provide their users with web access to applications, either through static web pages or dynamic web portals. These web pages are usually configured so that they will automatically install the ICA client software onto the user's client device if it's not installed when they visit the site.

Additionally, most application web portals are configured so that the user is provided with a login screen when they first access the site. After successful authentication, the list of MetaFrame applications is custom-built for each user based on his credentials. This application list consists of hyperlinks and icons for each application. Clicking one of these application hyperlinks launches an ICA session which is fully integrated into the user's desktop experience.

See Chapter 11 for full details on creating web application portals for your MetaFrame XP users,.

### Advantages of Connecting via a Web Page

- Access to MetaFrame XP applications can be from any machine, without preconfiguring client software.
- Since many organizations already use web pages and intranets for important information and announcements, MetaFrame XP applications can be configured as part of a user's home page or corporate portal.
- Because application configuration is done at the web server, you can easily change parameters or options. Every client device recognizes the changes the next time they access the web site. There is no need to manually configure every client.
- One web page can contain links to applications from multiple MetaFrame servers or server farms.

### Disadvantages of Connecting via a Web Page

- Visiting a web page for their applications may be an added step for your users.
- This could be a single point of failure. If the web server goes down, the users lose access to their applications.
- You'll have to maintain the web server in addition to all of your MetaFrame XP servers.

## Option 3. Full Program Neighborhood from a Local ICA Client

If you choose to install the full Program Neighborhood ICA client on your users' workstations, they can launch their MetaFrame XP applications via the Program Neighborhood software. The Program Neighborhood software can even push application icons to the users' desk or Start menu. More information on the Program Neighborhood client is available in Chapter 10.

### Advantages of Connecting via a Full Client

- Users will only see the icons for applications that they are configured to use.

### Disadvantages of Connecting via a Full Client

- You will need to manually update any configuration changes to the client software on your users' workstations.

- It can be difficult for your users to connect to applications from more than one server farm.

- It's easy for your users to "break" things, since the client software will be installed on their workstations just like any application.

## Option 4. Program Neighborhood Agent

If you're using Feature Release 1 or 2, you can use the Program Neighborhood Agent to push MetaFrame XP application icons to 32-bit Windows clients. With the PN Agent client, icons can automatically appear in a user's Start Menu, on the desktop, or in their system tray. All configuration of the PN Agent client software is done via a URL, so you can change client configuration parameters automatically without having to visit every single client. More information about how to use this client is available in Chapter 11.

### Advantages of Connecting via the Program Neighborhood Agent

- As an administrator, you can easily update and change the configuration of the users' client software.

- The Program Neighborhood Agent software can seamlessly connect to multiple server farms.

### Disadvantages of Connecting via the Program Neighborhood Agent

- This only works with 32-bit Windows clients.

- The Program Neighborhood Agent client software must be manually installed.

- You must use NFuse 1.6 or newer.

- You must use Feature Release 1 or 2.

## Focus on Applications

It is important to remember when figuring out how your users will launch their MetaFrame XP applications that your users only care about their applications. The ideal environment will allow your users to access their applications in an easy and intuitive manner, helping them to remain productive.

# Client Device Planning Considerations

A major advantage of server-based computing technology is that the type of client platform and device that determines which applications you can use is removed from the equation . While this is a good thing from a business perspective, it can have the negative effect of making your technology decisions difficult. It was easy when applications only worked in Windows environments. If a user needed to use the application, they needed a computer running Windows—period.

Now that MetaFrame has come along, users can access Windows applications from virtually any platform and virtually any device. Since each platform and device combination offers slightly different options for you (the administrator) and your users, you now need to spend time thinking about which client devices will be used.

In order to evaluate which types of client devices are best suited to your environment, you need to answer a series of questions. These questions can be broken into five broad categories:

- Technology management issues.
- Political issues.
- Cost.
- Environment and facilities aspects.
- Applications.

Let's take a look at these questions now.

## Technology Management Issues

### How will the client devices be configured?
Do you need client devices that do not require local configuration, as all parameters are pulled from a central area? If you have devices that require local configuration, do you have the skills or ability to automatically script and push out this configuration, or will you need to visit each client device manually?

### How much time should be spent troubleshooting the clients?
If each client device contains custom data and configuration information for its user, then IT support personnel could potentially spend significant amounts of time troubleshooting and hunting down problems within each client de-

vice. Traditionally this has been the case with Windows-based PC workstations.

In the MetaFrame XP world troubleshooting doesn't require that kind of time. Many companies deploy generic client devices to end users with all of the users' applications executing on MetaFrame XP servers and their data stored on network drives. Then, if a client device stops working properly, the IT staff doesn't have to waste valuable time troubleshooting it. They can pull it out and replace it with a new device.

These devices can be thin client devices or full PC workstations that are managed as generic devices. When a PC workstation that is managed like a thin client device breaks, the IT staff simply replaces it with a generic, newly-imaged PC.

### What kind of local IT support is available?

If your user environment is located at a main corporate campus or if there are local IT department staff, it's possible to have client devices that require some manual configuration or expertise to install. However, if there are no IT staff at the users' site, then you need to choose client devices that a non-technical person can troubleshoot. Usually, this means using thin client devices. If one stops working, a non-technical person can go to the closet, get a new one, and plug it in where the broken one is. The cables are color-coded, and all configuration information and application information is either preset or downloaded from a server.

## Political Issues

### How is the relationship between the IT department and the users?

Do your users respect the IT department or are they hostile? If there is mutual respect and the relationship is strong, it will be possible to introduce new technologies and devices to the end users. However, if the relationship is strained, every detail of the IT department's technology decisions will be scrutinized. Any aspect of the new technology that the users feel is lacking will cause a user revolt.

### Have users become attached to their ability to "personalize" their computers?

In traditional environments where full PC workstations sit on each user's desk, many users have gotten used to being able to "personalize" their computers. You probably see this every day in the custom desktop themes, screen savers, wallpapers with pictures of users' kids, and animated dinosaur mouse pointers.

You might choose to replace your users' customizable PCs with thin client devices that are managed as generic company assets and that are replaced if they break, much like the telephone.

Even though these thin client devices provide a 100% identical look and feel of business applications, users can be put off if they were to lose some "freedoms," such as the ability to customize settings and use floppy disks.

### How smart are your users?

Will your users be able to adapt well to new solutions or technologies, or will they call the helpdesk every day for a month? Even worse, are they too smart (or crafty)? Will they try to break or get around whatever procedures are put in place? You should spend time trying to understand what your users' true needs are. Keep in mind that some users are never happy. No matter what you do, they will always want more.

### How easy is it for users to break the client devices?

Most users tend to meddle with whatever configuration settings and options they can find on their client computers. When looking at client devices, it's important to assess how easily they can be "locked-down," preventing users from breaking them.

### What is the security level needed in the end user environment?

Will end users need secure access over the network, or will they need secure authentication, such as smart cards or biometric authentication? How about the client devices themselves? If they're located somewhere in which theft is a problem, thin client devices are more attractive than PC workstations, because thin client devices are worthless to thieves outside of the office environment (unless the thieves set up a MetaFrame XP server in their hideout). Even if they are stolen, thin client devices are cheaper to replace.

## Cost

### Is there a significant investment in the current client devices or licenses?

Sometimes MetaFrame XP is deployed in environments that haven't had new desktop technology for many years, so it's easy to justify the cost of new client devices that are purchased as the MetaFrame XP applications are rolled out.

Much more common, though, are the environments that lease or refresh their desktop technology every few years. Even if the IT department decides that thin client devices are the cheapest, easiest, and coolest client devices they could use, it may not be a possibility because the end user departments "just got new PCs last year, we're not pulling them out now."

If politics force you to use the existing client devices, then your client device selection process shouldn't take long.

### Who pays for new end user hardware?

Often end user departments pay for their own client devices. In these cases, you need to know whether they typically purchase what the IT department recommends or if they purchase whatever they want (usually based on cheapest price). If they go by IT recommendations, are there particular vendors that must be used or price caps that must be observed?

Of course, even if the IT department pays for the end user devices, these same political and pricing issues may still apply.

## Environmental / Facilities

### Are there any special environment site needs?

If the end user environment is harsh or dirty, client machines may break more often, requiring ones that are inexpensive and easy to replace. If the client environment has sanitary requirements, as in hospitals, the client devices might need to be hermetically sealed or have the ability to be easily disinfected.

### What are the power consumption requirements?

Many traditional computers require 200 to 300 Watts to operate, while many thin client devices operate on 25 Watts or less. When you consider that these devices are used for at least 2000 hours per year, and with energy prices always increasing, the power cost savings can be tremendous even with a few hundred users.

## Applications

### What types of applications will be used?

If only MetaFrame ICA applications will be used, then client devices can be almost anything (thin client, Windows CE, full PC, etc.). But, if users will ever need to access an application that is not delivered via MetaFrame XP, then they will need client devices that support other applications. Interestingly, this issue drives the balance between the number of applications in the

MetaFrame XP environment and the complexities and expenses associated with different client devices.

### How many different applications will be used?

In addition to the types of applications that are used, you must evaluate how many applications a user will need.

If the user is using less than five applications every day (word processor, email, web, and a line of business application), then it makes it easy for you to recommend thin client devices. However, the more applications a user requires, the tougher it becomes to use thin client devices. You might also need to consider other factors, such as the length of application usage. How many times is the user switching between applications per day?

### What kinds of graphics and sound support will clients need?

Do the users have applications with high graphics requirements? Some thin client devices have much better graphics performance than others. This is especially evident with high resolutions and color depth.

Do the users need audio support on their client devices? Remember that even though audio support might not be perceived as necessary by the IT department, the users may be very upset if they "lose" sound when moving to a MetaFrame XP-based solution.

### Do the end users require wireless mobile access?

If users need to be able to move around while using their ICA applications, is this movement confined to one area or one building, or will they need to access their applications from anywhere in the country?

How will mobile devices be used? Users that need access primarily from one location with the ability to roam are very different from users that primarily need to roam. Battery life is also a big factor.

### What types of peripherals are used?

Some environments may require specific peripherals, such as bar code readers or scanners. If this is the case in your environment then you will need to evaluate whether applications will support the barcode readers through thin client devices and ICA sessions or if the applications will need to be installed locally on traditional PCs.

### Will the users travel with their client devices?

If users will be traveling with their client devices, such as laptops, then you must make provisions for the users to have access to applications when they are offline.

# Types of Client Devices

There are literally hundreds of different types of client devices that can be used to access MetaFrame XP environments via ICA sessions. While that list is always changing and it's not practical to discuss all of them here, these client devices can be broadly broken down into four groups:

- Traditional computer workstations, including standard Windows PCs, Macintosh computers, and UNIX workstations.
- Traditional computers, managed as generic dumb terminals. These are usually standard computers, complete with local operating systems and hard drives, that are created with disk "images." If one stops working properly, it's replaced with a new computer, or it is "re-imaged." Significant troubleshooting time is not wasted.
- Thin client devices and "dumb" appliances. This includes devices that are usually based on Windows CE, Windows XP Embedded, or Linux on-a-chip. These devices have no local hard drives and typically boot off of servers or have chip-based operating systems. While some of these devices may have local web browsers or terminal emulators, they usually run most applications from backend servers.
- Mobile wireless devices, including dedicated wireless ICA devices and palm-sized computers.

Let's take a look at each of the four families of client devices in greater detail.

## Option 1. Traditional Computer Workstations

Traditional computer workstations are currently deployed in almost every organization throughout the world. From a MetaFrame XP standpoint, if traditional computers are out there and they're paid for, then why not use them? MetaFrame XP works very well when accessed from standard computers, whether users access their MetaFrame XP applications through the locally installed Program Neighborhood or through a web portal.

Additionally, because traditional computers have local processors and hard drives, the Citrix ICA protocol can cache certain information and graphics locally, increasing performance, especially over high latency connections.

However, as more applications become server-based and as more companies use MetaFrame XP, traditional computers quickly become overkill for many users. They are expensive to maintain and users often break them through "trial and error" misconfiguration.

### Advantages of Traditional Computer Workstations

- Already deployed in most locations.
- Users are comfortable with them.
- Local processor and storage allows for better ICA session performance.
- No perception of "IT is taking this away from us."
- Local, non-MetaFrame XP applications can also be used.
- Many peripherals are available and compatible.

### Disadvantages of Traditional Computer Workstations

- Expensive to purchase and maintain.
- Proprietary for each user.
- Difficult to troubleshoot.
- Must be manually configured or complex scripts and policies must be created.
- Require local IT staff for support.
- Prone to being broken by "curious" users.
- Increased risk of "accidental" local data storage, which is not secure and not backed up.
- Target for thieves in unsecured environment.
- Many more options and models make it harder to enforce standards.
- High power consumption.
- Many moving parts that can break or get dirty.

## Option 2. Thin Client Devices and Appliances

Thin client devices and appliances are purpose-built machines used primarily for accessing server based computing environments, including web browsing, terminal emulation, and Citrix ICA sessions. These devices usually have no local hard drives or moving parts.

There are several flavors of thin client devices, most easily categorized by their local operating system. Most of these devices run some form of chip-based Windows (Windows CE.NET or XP embedded), Linux, or Java. In order to connect into the MetaFrame XP environment, they therefore need to have the appropriate local ICA client software installed.

There are several advantages to using thin client devices. Because they don't have any in-depth local configuration, users are not able to break them as easily. They have few (if any) moving parts, which means that there is less to break. If something does break, it's usually cheaper and easier to replace the entire terminal.

For example, one company headquartered in Euclid, Ohio has manufacturing facilities in Ontario, Canada. Their entire shop floor is run off of applications on MetaFrame XP servers located in Euclid. All application access in Canada is done via thin client devices. Due to the harshness of the manufacturing environment, traditional PCs were always breaking. The thin client devices they chose had no moving parts—not even cooling fans—so they don't break nearly as often. This is especially nice because there is no IT staff in Canada. When a thin client device does break, the shop foreman goes to the closet and grabs a replacement terminal. The user connects back into his session right where he left off with only a few minutes of total downtime.

However, be careful that you're not fooled by the seemingly endless advantages of thin client devices, because there are several major drawbacks.

First and foremost is the fact that with thin client devices, all major processing must be done somewhere else. With full-blown PCs, you have the *option* of running applications centrally. With thin clients, all applications *must* be run centrally. Do you, as an administrator, really want your clients surfing the web or writing email to their kids with valuable server processing time? Of course, many thin clients now have local browsers and local email programs, but you get the idea.

### Advantages of Thin Client Devices

- Low maintenance costs. If one breaks, throw it away, plug in a replacement, connect back into MetaFrame XP, done.
- No local user troubleshooting.
- No local IT staff is needed.

- Little-to-no local user configuration, so users can't break them (as easily).
- Low power consumption.
- No black market value, so they're less likely to be stolen.

### Disadvantages of Thin Client Devices

- Less flexibility than PCs.
- Essentially, all applications must run through host server.
- If they are purchased to replace PCs, people will be upset. ("We just spent $2500 on new PCs, and now they're replacing them?")
- In politically charged environments, users perceive that their full PC's are being "taken" from them.

Thin client devices are great, but unless you have a compelling reason *not* to use PCs, be careful of the "nothing" approach (as in "all or nothing") that you get with thin clients.

# Option 3. Traditional Workstations, Managed as Thin Devices

It is possible to combine the traditional computer workstation hardware with the management style of thin client devices to create a solution that has some of the advantages of each.

This entails keeping full computer workstations for every user, but building a standard workstation image that is deployed to all users. All of the applications (except maybe a web browser) are server-based. The idea is that if a computer workstation breaks, a new hard drive or new workstation can be brought in to replace it.

One company that did this created a "five minute rule." Basically, the desktop computer technicians would visit an end user whenever they had a problem and called the helpdesk. If it was something simple, they fixed it. However, if the desktop technician could not fix the problem within five minutes, the user's computer was wiped clean and a new image was put on.

This worked well because all of their applications were delivered via Meta-Frame XP and NFuse, and all of the users' data was stored on the network. All of the users' computers in the entire company had the same image, which was just a base operating system, a web browser, and the ICA client software.

A very popular trend right now for accessing MetaFrame XP applications is to use your current user workstations with a Linux image and the "five minute rule."

### Advantages of Traditional Workstations Managed Like Thin Clients

- Current hardware can be utilized.
- Efficient use of time for IT staff.

### Disadvantages of Traditional Workstations Managed Like Thin Clients

- The hardware still breaks.

## Option 4. Mobile Wireless Devices

"Mobile wireless devices" are actually a legitimate option when deciding how your users will access MetaFrame XP applications. As with all mobile wireless devices, the primary drawback is still battery life. There are really two classes of wireless devices, LAN devices and public WAN devices.

LAN devices are usually laptop computers or Windows CE / Pocket PC devices with 802.11 wireless network cards. Although there are some companies with wireless devices purpose-built for Citrix ICA sessions, (similar to wireless thin client devices), they are not widely used because they are expensive and generally geared towards specific vertical markets. (Hermetically sealed for healthcare, built in barcode readers for warehouses, etc.) Most people just buy full-blown laptops with wireless LAN cards.

The public wireless WAN is where the real fun begins (for true geeks). The wireless public WAN is the system that you pay a monthly access fee to use. There are many networks throughout the world, and most are based on CDPD, CDMA, PCS, GPRS, or similar networks. There are millions of palm-sized computers out there today, and most of them can run the Citrix ICA client. They can be used for wireless, go-anywhere access to the Internet.

### Advantages of Mobile Wireless Devices

- Access to critical applications from anywhere.
- Very, very cool.

### Disadvantages of Mobile Wireless Devices

- Expensive service (US $30-$100 per user per month).
- Tiny screens on devices.
- Do we really need to access our applications on the golf course?
- Battery life.

# CHAPTER 10

# Deploying and Configuring ICA Clients

In this chapter

ICA Client Functional Overview                 354

ICA Client Features and Options                357

Windows 32-bit ICA Clients                     374

Java ICA Client                                403

ICA Client Auto Update                         418

Real World Case Study                          425

Citrix has created ICA client software for dozens of different platforms. While the basic functionality of the different clients is the same, each platform has specific features, options, and methods of configuration and deployment.

In this chapter, we'll review the two most popular clients—the 32-bit Windows and Java ICA clients. We'll look at how the different configuration options work and how they impact client use.

For each client platform, we'll study:

- Technical overview.
- Configuration.
- Deployment.

Before we begin examining the details of each client, let's see how ICA client software works and what the different configuration options are.

# ICA Client Functional Overview

The ICA client software is the fundamental element allowing a computing device to attach to and run sessions off of a MetaFrame XP server. Without ICA client software installed, a device cannot run ICA sessions. From the MetaFrame XP server's perspective, it doesn't matter which ICA client platform is used or how a client connects to the server. This is actually the true beauty of MetaFrame XP. All users get the exact same application experience—regardless of their client platform.

## ICA Client to MetaFrame XP Server Communication

Fundamentally, the ICA client software needs to do two things to allow users to access MetaFrame XP applications:

- It locates the MetaFrame XP server and the application that the user wants to use.
- It establishes the remote sessions, via the ICA protocol, with the MetaFrame XP server.

Just about any type of client software in the world needs to take these two steps to connect to a server resource. For example, if we were talking about web browsers instead of ICA software, then our client software would be the web browser. The first step (the location of the server) is done by the user typing in the name of a website, such as www.citrix.com. The second step (establishing the session) is accomplished as the server sends web pages to the client via the HTTP protocol.

Let's observe these two steps from and ICA client perspective.

### Step 1. ICA Client Locates Servers and Applications
In order for any ICA client software to connect to a MetaFrame XP server, the client software needs to be able to find the MetaFrame XP server. There are six different ways that this can occur, although not all versions of the ICA client software support all methods.

Throughout this chapter, we'll look at different ICA client platforms and how they can be configured to automatically connect to specific servers via specific protocols. However, any configuration that you set up will always use one of these six protocol combinations to find a server:

- *TCP/IP.* Using the TCP/IP method, the ICA client software will send out a broadcast to UDP port 1604. Any MetaFrame XP servers listening on this port will respond.
- *IPX.* Using the IPX method, the ICA client software will send out a broadcast via the IPX protocol.
- *SPX.* Using the SPX method, the ICA client software will send out a broadcast via the SPX protocol.
- *NetBIOS.* Using the NetBIOS method, the ICA client software will send out a NetBIOS broadcast.
- *TCP/IP + HTTP.* When the TCP/IP + HTTP method is used, the ICA client software will try to connect via the HTTP protocol to a host called "ica" in order to automatically download configuration information for servers and applications.
- *SSL + HTTPS.* When the SSL + HTTPS method is used, the ICA client software will try to connect via an HTTP request encrypted with SSL, to a host called "ica."

In many instances, users establish their ICA sessions with MetaFrame XP servers by specifying the name of a published application rather than the name of a specific server. This was discussed back in Chapter 4.

The ICA client software is responsible for displaying a list of the available published applications (and published content if the servers are running Feature Release 1 or 2) for the user. Any time a user uses the ICA client software to view the available applications in a server farm or to refresh the list of applications in a server farm, the following process takes place:

*Figure 10.1 How the ICA client software obtains a list of available applications.*

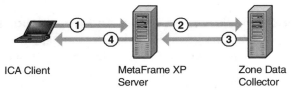

ICA Client          MetaFrame XP          Zone Data
                    Server                Collector

1. The ICA client software contacts a MetaFrame XP server to obtain the list of applications that are available.

2. The MetaFrame XP server sends the user's credentials to the zone data collector.

3. The zone data collector compiles the list of applications for that user and sends it back to the MetaFrame XP server.

4. The MetaFrame XP server sends the list to the ICA client.

### Step 2. ICA Client Software Establishes Session

Once a MetaFrame XP server is located, the ICA client software is able to connect to it for the user session. This user session can take place over one of several protocols:

- TCP/IP.
- IPX.
- SPX.
- NetBIOS.
- Async (modem).

Figure 10.2 illustrates the process that occurs when a user chooses to launch an ICA session via a published application.

1. The user selects a published application to run from the list of applications presented in their ICA client software (from the list the software previously obtained from a MetaFrame XP server and the zone data collector). In the example in Figure 10.2, the application selected is "Word 2002."

2. The name of the application that the user selected is passed to the MetaFrame XP server.

*Figure 10.2 A user launches a published application*

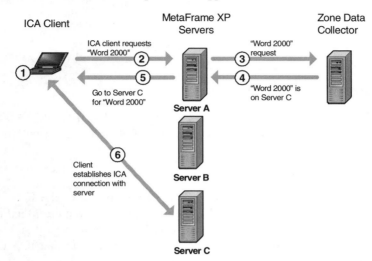

3. The MetaFrame XP server passes the name of the application to the zone data collector.

4. The zone data collector sends the address of the MetaFrame XP server running Word 2002 back to the first MetaFrame XP server. (This might also involve a load balancing calculation as outlined in Chapter 4.)

5. The MetaFrame XP server that the user initially contacted sends the address of the server running Word 2000 to the ICA client.

6. The ICA client software on the user's client device establishes an ICA connection with the application.

# ICA Client Features and Options

In addition to providing the core functionality of ICA sessions, the ICA client software has several features that can enhance the quality and performance of ICA sessions making them easier for users and administrators to use.

These ICA client features and options can be broken down into the following four categories.

- ICA session features.
- Performance-enhancing options.

- Administrative features.
- Connection establishment features.

Let's take a look at each of these features now.

## ICA Session Features

There are several options that ICA clients have that affect users' ICA sessions and how their client devices work with the MetaFrame XP server within their ICA sessions.

### Client Device Mapping

Client device mapping allows certain hardware elements of the ICA client device to be accessed through ICA sessions running on remote MetaFrame XP servers. This process is called "mapping" because it is very similar to mapping a network drive or printer port on a server, except that ICA client device mapping occurs in the opposite direction. For example, consider the following diagram.

*Figure 10.3 ICA client drive mapping from a MetaFrame XP server session*

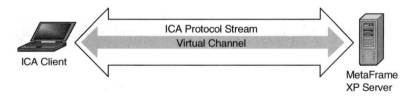

ICA Protocol Stream
Virtual Channel

ICA Client

MetaFrame
XP Server

1.  When the ICA session is established with the MetaFrame XP server, the ICA client software on the client device sends the server a list of local components that are available to be mapped.

2.  If the appropriate mappings have been enabled on the MetaFrame XP server, the mapping process continues and a dynamic mapping is made to the client device.

3.  Part of the ICA protocol, called a "virtual channel" is used for the mapping. One channel is used for each of the different types of device mapping. This channel allows the mapping data to flow back and forth between the ICA client and the MetaFrame XP server.

These mappings are dynamic. They only exist for the current user and the current session. As soon as the user logs off, the mappings are deleted.

There are several types of devices that can be mapped to client devices in ICA sessions.

## Client Drives

MetaFrame XP servers have the ability to connect to and map client drives from the local client device to the sessions running on the MetaFrame XP server.

When client drives are mapped, users have the ability to access data stored on their local hard drives or floppy drives from within their MetaFrame XP server sessions. By default, client drives are mapped using the same drive letter that is configured for the drives on the local client. This allows users to access their local drives via drive letters that are familiar to them.

Obviously, the server can't map a drive to the client device if the drive letter is already in use. In this case (whether because the server has a local drive with the same letter or a network drive is mapped with the same letter), the client drive is mapped with a new drive letter, starting with "V" and moving backwards through the alphabet.

This drive letter conflict is why you have the option of remapping the server drives when MetaFrame XP is installed (as discussed in Chapter 2). The idea is that most client devices will have drive letters that are "C", "D", and "E." If your MetaFrame XP server also uses these drive letters, then the client drives will be available via drive letters "V", "U" and "T" during their server sessions.

In some situations, you might want to configure your MetaFrame XP server so that it does not automatically assign a drive letter to mapped client drives. If you do this, you can still configure it so that users can browse to their client drives through network neighborhood. To do this, you need to make a change to the properties of the connection, which means that you need to use the Citrix Connection Configuration utility to configure it. Use this utility to edit the properties of the connection, and ensure that the "Connect client drives at logon" box is not checked (CCC | Edit Connection | Client Settings). If you're using Feature Release 2, you can also configure this via a Citrix user policy (Client Devices | Client Drives | Connect Client Drives).

Whenever any client devices are mapped from within ICA sessions, your users will see a "Client Network" item in their Network Neighborhood (Network Neighborhood | Entire Network | Client Network). Underneath the Client Network item will be a computer called "client." Browsing this computer will reveal a drive share for each local drive on the client device. These drive share names are made up of the drive letter plus a dollar sign, which means that you will see the shares as \\Client\C$ or \\Client\D$.

If you would like to disable all access to ICA client devices' local drives, then you can check the "Disable Client Drive Mapping" box in the connection's properties (CCC | Edit Connection | Client Settings) or enable the "Connect Client Drives" Citrix user policy with a value of "Do Not Connect Client Drives at Logon". If you do this, the client drive shares will not appear in the client network.

### Printer Mapping
Similar to the drive mappings, printers can be mapped with the ICA client software. There are many different parameters that will affect your printing solution in your MetaFrame XP environment. For that reason, you can find everything that you need to know about printing in back in Chapter 7.

### Port Mapping
You can map LPT and COM ports from the local ICA client devices so that they are available to users via their server sessions. This is also configured as a property of the connection (Citrix Connection Configuration | Edit Connection | Client Settings | Ensure that "Disable Client LPT Port Mapping" or "Disable Client COM Port Mapping" is not checked) or as part of a Citrix user profile. When you enable port mapping, the ports are not mapped in MetaFrame XP server sessions automatically. Instead, they are available via the client device in Network Neighborhood (From a MetaFrame XP server session | Network Neighborhood | Entire Network | Client Network | Client). You will see that one port is shared for each local port on the client device, such as \\Client\COM2, or \\Client\LPT1.

LPT ports are mapped automatically when your session begins, but COM ports are not. In order to use a mapped COM port, you need to manually map it from within your MetaFrame XP server session. This is most easily done with the "change client" command. The "change client" utility is included with MetaFrame XP and it is meant to be run by users (or logon scripts) from within their ICA sessions. This utility allows you to change the current mapping settings for a particular client device.

When you first use this command, try typing "change client" at the command prompt of a MetaFrame XP server session. This will show you a list of the current devices that are mapped to the local client device.

The "change client" command has the following syntax:

```
change client hostport clientport
```

For example, in order to map COM1 so that the ICA client's COM1 port is available via COM1 from a server session, you would type "`change client com1 \\client\com1:`" Notice that the trailing colon (:) is part of the device's share name. When you use this command, you do not have to map it to the same port on the server as it is on your client device.

In order to view the list of devices that are available on your client device, type "`change client /view`".

Once your ports are mapped, you can do just about anything with them that you can with a local port on a regular Windows computer, including synchronizing Palm Pilots and Windows CE devices.

## Audio Support

If your users' client devices have speakers, they will be able to hear audio from their sessions on the MetaFrame XP server. This is known as "client audio mapping," and it works in a similar way to the other client mapping features.

If you decide to enable client audio mapping, you should know that only certain kinds of sounds are redirected to the ICA client devices. Only audio from applications in which the programmers "properly" used the Microsoft sound APIs fall into this category. Because of this, certain types of sound that are played from server sessions do not make it to the ICA client.

In the real world, you will have to test any applications that require sound. Citrix designed the audio mapping capabilities of the ICA client so that the general "beeps" and "bings" that users receive throughout the day can be sent to the client. It's not really meant for users to use to watch multimedia presentations from the server.

On your MetaFrame XP servers, you enable client audio mapping as a property of a connection (Citrix Connection Configuration | Edit Connection | Client Settings | Disable Client Audio Mapping box unchecked) or as part of a Citrix user policy (Client Devices | Client Audio Mapping) in Feature Release 2 environments.

In addition to enabling or disabling audio mapping, you can also configure the quality of the sound that is sent to ICA client devices. This quality can also be configured as a property of a connection (Citrix Connection Configuration | Edit Connection | ICA Settings | Client Audio Quality). There are three quality options: high, medium, and low:

- *High*. You should only use the "High" quality when you have more bandwidth than you know what to do with and when you need really accurate sound. The high quality setting plays audio at the native data rate, which equates to about 1.3Mbps. If you choose to use the high setting, remember that your MetaFrame XP server will need to spend more time processing audio, because it will need to send 1.3 MB across the network every second.

- *Medium*. With the "Medium" setting, the sound quality is lower, but it only uses 64Kbps.

- *Low*. Most people who use client audio mapping use it with the "Low" setting. This quality setting allows users to hear system sound while only consuming about 16Kbps.

The bandwidth requirements for each of the three quality levels only apply when sound is actually being played. However, when sound is enabled, a small amount of bandwidth is always used even when no sound is playing. This happens because the "Audio" virtual channel of the ICA protocol is enabled anytime audio mapping is enabled. Even though this additional bandwidth usage is small (less than 1Kbps), a lot of people choose to disable audio mapping altogether.

However, it is better to think twice before choosing to disable sound altogether. Disabling sound usually upsets users. When they get upset, your job becomes more difficult. If you use the "low" quality setting, your users will get to hear their audio without overtaxing the network. Besides, your users won't be able to tell the difference between the low, medium, and high settings anyway.

### Hotkey Mapping

Within MetaFrame XP environments, there are several keystroke combinations that users might need from within their ICA sessions that are not possible. For example, imagine that an application running on a MetaFrame XP server requires the user to press CTRL + ALT + DEL. How would the user do that from their MetaFrame XP session? If they press CTRL + ALT + DEL on their local client device, the local CTRL + ALT + DEL screen will pop up, not the one on the server.

In order to send CTRL + ALT + DEL to the server, a user can press a special key combination on the ICA client device. There are several hotkey combinations, including the task list, closing remote applications, CTRL + ESC, ALT + TAB, and CTRL + ALT + DEL. The exact configuration of these hotkey combinations is done on the ICA client, and the exact method changes depending on the client platform.

## Clipboard Integration

When users run a combination of locally and remote ICA applications, they will often need to cut and paste data from their local applications to their remote applications. Since both sets of applications are running on two different computers, this clipboard integration is not inherently possible. Fortunately, the Citrix ICA client software allows local and remote applications to share clipboard data.

When this feature is enabled, any data that is written to the clipboard of either the client or the server is instantly replicated to the clipboard of the other.

As with other configurations, clipboard integration is enabled or disabled as a property of a connection (Citrix Connection Configuration | Edit Connection | Client Settings | Disable Client Clipboard Mapping check box) or a Citrix user policy (Client Devices | Client Audio Mapping).

## Color Depths

MetaFrame XP servers support 4-, 8-, 16-, and 24-bit color depths. This works out to 16, 256, 64K, or 16M colors. Ordinarily you would think that the fewer colors you use, the lower the bandwidth requirements would be. As with almost everything in MetaFrame XP, this is not necessarily the case. The 16 and 256 color modes use just about the same amount of bandwidth, so there is really no reason to limit yourself to 16 colors unless you have older client devices or you are mad at your users.

When you step up to the 16 or 24 bit color depths, things get even more interesting. Ordinarily, you would expect that these color depths would require more bandwidth, because more colors are used. In fact, the opposite tends to be true. This is because Citrix has continuously upgraded the compression algorithms that the ICA client uses, but for legacy compatibility reasons, these new algorithms cannot be applied to the older clients that only support 16 or 256 colors. This "feature" has been corrected with Feature Release 2.

In the real world, it's probably best to keep your servers set to 24-bit color. If bandwidth is a problem, then you can use the monitoring tools of MetaFrame XPe to determine the exact ICA virtual channels in use and the amounts of bandwidth that different options require. Just remember that a lower color depth does not automatically equate to lower bandwidth requirements.

### Screen Resolution

ICA clients can theoretically support ICA session resolutions up to 32,000 by 32,000 pixels (although limitations in Windows reduce this to more like 2,700 x 2,700 pixels). Either way, since there are no display devices that can actually show this resolution, you can set the screen resolution of your remote MetaFrame XP session so that it's higher than the physical resolution of your ICA client device. If you do this, you will be able to pan the remote session window with scroll bars.

In the real world, not too many people use this on a daily basis, mainly because the scroll bars are annoying to use. Panning the screen is most often used when you are connecting to an ICA session from a device with a tiny screen, such as a HP iPAQ handheld running Windows CE.NET.

### Seamless Windows

If the ICA client device is running a local operating system with a windows interface (for example, Microsoft Windows or Linux x-Windows), the user can run applications in "Seamless Windows" mode. This means that remote applications appear in resizable windows that look and feel just like local applications. Seamless Windows are one of the "killer app" features of Meta-Frame.

Seamless windows applications do not run in their own desktop windows. For Microsoft Windows users, the remote application will not have its own Start Menu, and users can maximize, minimize, resize, and "ALT + TAB" to their application, just as if it were local. In fact, most users that access MetaFrame XP applications in Seamless Windows mode do not even realize that their applications are running on the remote server.

Refer back to Chapter 4 for more details about seamless windows,

### Multiple Monitor Support

ICA client devices running Windows across multiple monitors can run single ICA sessions that can span multiple monitors. This support happens automatically for systems that have multiple monitors when users connect to applications with fixed resolutions (not seamless window mode).

### Local Time Zone Support

Citrix ICA clients support per-user time zones when connecting to MetaFrame XP servers. This allows each user's session to run in the time zone (and local time) of the local ICA client software.

When local time zone support is enabled (CMC | Farm Properties | Meta-Frame Settings Tab | Client Time Zones | Use local time of ICA clients) the ICA client sends the name of its local time zone to the MetaFrame XP server. The MetaFrame XP server compares the client's time zone to its own time zone and adjusts the clock for that user's session appropriately. It is possible for a single MetaFrame XP server to simultaneously support users from any number of time zones throughout the world.

### Multi Button Mouse Support
The ICA client can support mice with multiple buttons, even if the local client operating system does not. (Attention Macintosh users!)

### Wheel Mouse Support
As part of the mouse movements and clicks that are passed to the MetaFrame XP server via an ICA session, the scroll wheel on newer mice is also supported. This means that users who are accustomed to using the wheel on their mouse can use it for both local and remote applications.

### Encryption
The newest ICA clients support three types of ICA session encryption: SSL, TLS and SecureICA. The details of these encryption features are covered in the security chapter of this book, Chapter 15.

## Client Performance Enhancing Options

The ICA client software also several features that you can use to enhance the performance of your users' sessions.

### Bitmap Caching
ICA clients with local storage capabilities can use that space to cache bitmap images from the MetaFrame XP servers. This increases the performance of a session because popular objects can be retrieved from the local cache instead of needing be retrieved from the MetaFrame server.

Bitmap caching is generally a good thing, especially with applications that have a few main screens that most users flip through. It also works very well in WAN environments.

When you configure bitmap caching, you need to specify the amount of disk space that is used for the cache, the location of the cache, and the minimum bitmap size that will be cached. In general, you can't have too much cache, so if your clients have big hard drives, go ahead and use them. Typically, the performance increases of the bitmap cache will level off after your cache exceeds about 10MB.

You can also choose the location of the cache files on the client device. When you do this, be sure to choose a local drive. If you choose a network mapped location, then your ICA client performance will probably be worse than having no cache.

Lastly, you can configure the minimum size of the bitmap to be cached. This defaults to 8K and works well for most environments. If you change the minimum size, be sure to test your changes to determine if they actually make a difference and to ensure that they do not negatively affect performance.

The bitmap cache settings, like all client settings, can be configured on a client-by-client basis, meaning that you can have different options configured on each of your ICA client devices.

### Session Compression
Most ICA client platforms support data compression. This option can only be configured at the ICA client itself (as opposed to enabling on the server- or farm-basis). Citrix's ICA protocol data compression works pretty well and there's no real reason not to use it.

### SpeedScreen Latency Reduction
Remember from the last chapter that "latency" in MetaFrame environments is the time it takes from when a user performs an action until he receives feedback of that action. For many users, the inherent latency of MetaFrame environments causes problems with typing and clicking, as when the user enters several keystrokes before seeing output of them on the screen.

MetaFrame XP can make the user think that there is less latency through the use of SpeedScreen Latency Reduction (SLR). SLR decreases the users' perception of latency in two ways:

- SLR can provide instant feedback whenever a mouse button is clicked.
- SLR can be used to echo text to the screen locally.

#### Mouse Click Feedback
When mouse click feedback is enabled, the Citrix ICA client will change the cursor from the "normal select" pointer (usually an arrow) to the "working in background" pointer (usually an arrow next to an hourglass). Since mouse click feedback is a property of the ICA client, it can provide instant "click

feedback" to the user, even in environments with high latency where the server does not respond quickly.

Enabling mouse click feedback will prevent users from clicking on items too many times and getting multiple copies launched. This usually happens when impatient users click on something, and then they think that nothing has happened, so they click on it again. Ultimately, they get multiple instances of their item being opened.

### Local Text Echo

Local text echo allows the ICA client software to render fonts locally on the client device rather than waiting for them to be sent down by the MetaFrame XP server. Ordinarily, MetaFrame XP works in a "screen-scrape" mode, in that the MetaFrame server sends information about the pixels that change color to the ICA client. For example, if a user is using Microsoft Word, the keystroke is sent to the MetaFrame XP server each time they type a letter. The server processes the keystroke and the application responds by displaying the letter that was typed on the screen. The MetaFrame XP software sends the screen update information to the ICA client, which would probably be a list of pixels that were white that should now be changed to black, representing the new letter.

This method can be inefficient, especially over slow network links. In order to address it, SLR can be used to generate the characters locally on the ICA client device. When local text echo is enabled, the ICA client sends the server a list of fonts that it has installed as soon as the session begins. Then, as a user types from within their application, the ICA client device displays the text on the local device the instant the key is pressed, before receiving confirmation from the server to change the color of the appropriate pixels. Local text echo works well with applications in which users type very quickly, and it's annoying to have even the slightest delay from the time that a key is pressed until the time the character appears on the screen.

### Configuring SpeedScreen Latency Reduction

In order to use either or both of the components of SLR, you must configure them on your MetaFrame XP server. This is done with the SpeedScreen Latency Reduction Manager (Start | Programs | Citrix | MetaFrame XP | SpeedScreen Latency Reduction Manager).

When you launch the SLR manager on a MetaFrame XP server, you are presented with a list of servers in your farm. If you double-click on a server, you can view the default SLR configuration options for that server.

The mouse click feedback configuration is simple—either it is "on" or "off." There are no additional options to configure.

The local text echo is a bit more complex. This stems from the fact that not all applications are ideal candidates for using SLR's local text echo. In fact, some applications have some screens that would work well and others that would not. For example, if you wanted to enable local text echo with Microsoft Word, it would work well while you're using the main document screen. However, it might not work so well with some of the property pages.

For this reason, you need to configure the local text echo components of SLR so that it knows which applications (and which windows of those applications) it should be enabled for, and which ones it should avoid.

To configure local text echo properties for applications, open the SLR Manager. By clicking the "new" button, you can define a new policy for an application. When you do this, a wizard will be launched that will walk you through the SLR configuration of the application. Basically, you are given the opportunity to use the application while the SLR manager is running in the background. You can select different windows or fields and give them each different SLR properties, including whether you want to enable local text echo, the font size, and how text is displayed.

You can use local text echo with any application so long as it was written using the standard Microsoft APIs. (You cannot use local text echo with the Citrix Management Console, since it was not written with Microsoft APIs.)

Once you get your SLR settings configured the way you want them, they are saved into the `%systemroot%\system32\ss3config\` folder. This folder will not exist until you save some SLR settings. Within this folder, subfolders will be created for each application for which you created an SLR policy. You can copy application SLR policies from one server to the next simply by copying the application's folder in the `\ss3config` folder.

### Queue Mouse Movements and Key Strokes

On an ICA client, you can configure the rate that mouse movements and keystrokes are sent to the server. This is not the same as SpeedScreen. Adjusting these settings helps to reduce network traffic by reducing the frequency of mouse and key data sent, while SpeedScreen's purpose is to improve the user's perception of performance.

## Administrative Features

To make your life easier as an administrator, there are a few features that are common to many ICA clients.

### Auto Client Update

Auto client update allows you to automatically deploy new versions of the ICA client software to your users. To do this, you maintain a database that contains the new versions of the clients for the platforms that you support on your MetaFrame XP servers.

For details about the auto client update, refer to the "Auto Client Update" section of this chapter.

### Logging

Many of the ICA client platforms support logging that you can enable to record the following types of information:

- *Connections and Disconnections.* When enabled, a record is written to the log file anytime an ICA connection is enabled or disabled. That record indicates the time, date, and the name of the server farm or application. This option is enabled by default.

- *Errors.* Error logging causes an error event to be written to the log file anytime an ICA error occurs. This option is also enabled by default.

- *Data Transmitted.* If you choose to enable logging of the data that is transmitted, the contents of every single ICA packet sent from the client to the MetaFrame XP server are written to the log file. This causes the log file to grow very, very quickly (about 1MB per minute). This logging is meant only for advanced troubleshooting purposes. If you are a geek, then you might also want to enable this logging for a minute or two, because studying the outputs of this log will teach you how the ICA client really works.

- *Data Received.* This is similar to the data transmitted, except that it logs the contents of the ICA stream sent from the MetaFrame XP server to the ICA client.

- *Keyboard and Mouse Data.* If you enable this, the log file will contain a record of the mouse movements and keystrokes. Be aware that this represents a huge security hole if you're not careful. When enabled, someone viewing the log file can see everything that a user typed, including passwords. (See Chapter 15 for more security information.) As with data logging, having the keyboard and mouse data logging enabled will cause your log file to grow quickly.

If you enable logging, all five types of logging information are written to the same log file. You have the option of specifying whether you want to append the data to the current log file or start a new log file every time a new connection is made. In the real world, most people disable logging for the day-to-day operations of their environment. Logging is usually only used for troubleshooting purposes.

## Connection Launching Features

There are quite a few features of ICA clients that help users find and connect to their applications on your MetaFrame XP servers.

### Program Neighborhood

Program Neighborhood allows your users to log into a MetaFrame XP server farms once, after which they are presented with icons for each application that they can access. This prevents users from having to log in separately to each application. It also simplifies your administration, since icons for newly-configured applications are automatically made available to users as soon as they log into Program Neighborhood.

Your users can use Program Neighborhood to configure multiple Application Sets. An Application Set is a listing of applications from a single server farm. By accessing multiple application sets, your users can access multiple server farms from a single ICA client.

For example, a user may log into Program Neighborhood and be presented with multiple icons, each icon representing a different server farm. Clicking on a specific server farm will expose the icons for published applications in that server farm configured for that user.

### Program Neighborhood Agent

The Program Neighborhood Agent client is similar to the Program Neighborhood client, except that MetaFrame XP application and content icons are placed in the system tray, Start menu, or desktop folder. When the Program Neighborhood Agent is used, no configuration information is stored locally on the client device.

Details about configuring the servers needed to support the Program Neighborhood Agent ICA client can be found in Chapter 11. Details about the use and installation of the Program Neighborhood client can be found later in this chapter.

## Web Browser Launching

Most Citrix ICA clients support web browser launching, which means that the ICA client software can be automatically launched by a user clicking a hyperlink on a web page. Full details about the integration of Citrix ICA clients and the web can be found in Chapter 11.

## Pass-Through Authentication

Users connecting from Windows 32-bit clients can choose to have the credentials they used to log onto their workstation transparently passed through to MetaFrame XP servers when they establish an ICA session. This pass-through authentication works with both NDS and Windows authentication methods. For details about configuring pass-through authentication on your servers, refer to Chapter 15.

## Business Recovery

Many ICA clients have redundancy built into them in the form of "business recovery." Essentially, this redundancy allows you to create multiple lists of servers that the client software will contact when looking for an application list or trying to connect to a published application.

This feature is implemented in the form of a "Server Group List." ICA clients divide the MetaFrame XP servers that are to be contacted into three groups: primary, backup 1, and backup 2. Each group can contain up to five servers, listed by their DNS name, NetBIOS name, IP address, or MAC address. When the user clicks an icon to launch a session, the ICA client simultaneously sends out the request to all servers in the primary group. If no server responds, it tries again. After the third try, the ICA client software automatically moves on to the servers in the backup 1 group. After the third try to the backup 1 list, the client tries the backup 2 list.

If you have chosen an HTTP protocol as your method for locating servers, then the ICA client software treats all three lists as one, methodically stepping through each server.

As an administrator, you can put the servers in specific lists to control the order that they should respond. However, you need to keep the server list within reason. Even though you could have fifteen servers spread out across your three lists, you wouldn't really want a situation in which a user had to wait for fourteen servers to timeout before finding one that works.

## Multiple Sessions

Some ICA client platforms can support multiple simultaneous ICA sessions. This allows users to be connected to two different MetaFrame XP servers at the same time.

## NDS Authentication

All of the ICA clients version 6.20 and newer can authenticate users to an NDS tree instead of a Windows domain (if Feature Release 1 or 2 is enabled on your MetaFrame XP servers). For details, refer to Chapter 8.

## Auto Session Reconnect

ICA clients version 6.20 and newer can be configured for auto client reconnect. This option will prompt the client software to automatically attempt to reestablish a connection with the MetaFrame XP server if an ICA session is unexpectedly disconnected. This usually occurs over slower network connections when the sessions occasionally timeout, or when your cat walks across your desk and pulls out your modem cable.

## Dialing Prefixes

The ICA clients that support dial-in modems can support dialing prefixes, allowing users to save settings for the phone dialer that can be applied across multiple ICA connections.

## Local File Type Support

The ICA clients version 6.20 and newer support launching published application by opening a local document on a client device that is associated with the remotely published application. Detailed information about configuring this on the MetaFrame XP server was outlined back in Chapter 4. Information about configuring this for different ICA client platforms is contained in the appropriate section of this chapter.

## Desktop Integration

Windows-based ICA clients allow you to automatically place icons for Meta-Frame XP applications and content directly on your users' desktops or start menus, without the need to visit their client devices. This can make it easy to make new applications available to your users.

## Save User Credentials

Many ICA clients allow users to save their credentials associated with ICA connections so that they do not have to manually type them in whenever they launch an ICA session. See Chapter 15 for more information.

*Figure 10.4  (facing page) Available options for popular ICA client platforms*

| Feature | Win32 | Java | UNIX | Win CE | DOS | MAC |
|---|---|---|---|---|---|---|
| **Session Features** | | | | | | |
| Client Drive Mapping | X | X | X | X | X | X |
| Client Printer Mapping | X | X | X | X | X | X |
| Client COM Port | X | X | X | X | X | X |
| Audio Support | X | X | X | X | X | X |
| Hotkey Mapping | X | X | X | X | | X |
| Clipboard Integration | X | X | X | | | X |
| 16 and 24 bit color | X | X | 6 | X | | |
| Huge Resolution | X | X | X | X | | |
| Multi Monitor Support | X | | | | | |
| Seamless Windows | X | | 6 | | | |
| Local Time Zone Suport | X | | 6.2 | X | | 6.2 |
| Multi Button Mouse Support | X | X | X | X | X | 6.2 |
| Wheel Mouse Support | X | | | | | |
| Citrix Universal Print Driver | 6.2 | | | | | |
| SecureICA Encryption | X | X | 6 | X | X | X |
| SSL Encryption | 6.2 | 6.2 | 6.2 | 6.2 | | 6.2 |
| | | | | | | |
| **Performance** | | | | | | |
| Bitmap Caching | X | X | X | | X | X |
| Session Compression | X | X | X | X | X | X |
| SpeedScreen Enhancements | X | X | X | X | | |
| Queue Mouse and Keys | X | | | | | |
| | | | | | | |
| **Administrative** | | | | | | |
| Auto Client Update | X | | X | X | X | X |
| Logging | X | | | | | |
| | | | | | | |
| **Connection** | | | | | | |
| Program Neighborhood | X | X | | X | | |
| PN Agent | 6.2 | | | | | |
| Web Browser Launching | X | X | X | X | | 6.2 |
| Application Publishing | X | | X | X | X | X |
| Pass Through Authentication | X | | | | | |
| DNS Name Resolution | 6.2 | | | | | |
| Business Recovery | X | X | X | | | X |
| Multiple Sessions | X | | | | | X |
| Per Connection Browsing | | | | | | 6.2 |
| NDS Authentication | 6.2 | | | | | 6.2 |
| Auto Session Reconnect | 6.2 | X | | X | | |
| Dialing Prefixes | X | | | | X | |
| Local File Type Support | 6.2 | 6.2 | 6.2 | | | 6.2 |
| IPX / SPX Sessions | X | | | | | |
| TCP/IP Sessions | X | X | X | X | X | X |
| NetBIOS Sessions | X | | | | | |
| TCP/IP HTTP Location | X | X | X | X | | |
| Desktop Integration | X | | | | | |
| Save User Credentials | X | X | X | X | X | X |

## Which options work on which platforms?

The previous section outlined the generic options that are available with ICA clients. It's important to note that not all of these options are available on all client platforms. The chart in Figure 10.4 shows several popular ICA client platforms and the specific options that are supported on them.

As you look at this chart, keep in mind that it only shows the options that *could* be used on different client platforms. As an administrator, you have the ability to restrict certain options from users, and many of these restrictions can be configured in many places. The appendix of this book contains a chart detailing every configuration option (all of those shown below and then some), and the location at which each option can be configured.

Now that you've seen all of the options that are available to various client platforms, let's take a detailed look at some of the more popular ICA clients. To do this, we'll first study the family of numerous and popular 32-bit Windows clients. After that, we'll look at the Java clients, since they can be used on any platform.

# Windows 32-bit ICA Clients

In the real world, about 80 percent of all users that access MetaFrame XP do so from client devices with a 32-bit Windows operating system running locally. For this reason, Citrix has spent considerable effort creating and maintaining the 32-bit Windows ICA clients, which also have several features that others do not. In order to study the 32-bit Windows ICA clients, we'll look at the following areas:

- Technical overview of the 32-bit Windows family of ICA clients.
- Configuration.
- Differences between the many downloadable 32-bit Windows ICA client packages.

## Technical Overview

All 32-bit Windows ICA clients created after the year 2000 are known as "Universal Win32 Clients." This is because the same core client files are used universally on any Win32 platform, including Windows 9x, ME, NT, 2000, XP, XP Embedded, and all web browsers on these platforms, such as Internet Explorer and Netscape Navigator. If you still remember the dedicated ActiveX control and Netscape Navigator plug-in ICA clients from a few years ago, forget them—they no longer exist. They've both been replaced by this new universal Win32 client (which still can be configured to automatically download when a user visits a web page).

Fundamentally, the core of the Citrix ICA Universal Win32 client is made up of a single executable: `wfica32.exe`. Of course, there are many configuration files and DLLs that support additional functionality, but all core functionality on any Win32 device is accomplished by this one executable. This is the file that is executed by any user on any Win32 device, whether they connect through Program Neighborhood, Internet Explorer, or Netscape Navigator.

In addition to the `wfica32.exe` executable, there are two other major types of components to the Win32 Universal Citrix ICA client:

- INI Configuration files.
- Feature-specific DLLs and executables.

### INI Configuration Files

Each client device stores its own configuration information in INI files. Some of these files are user-specific and stored in the user's Windows profile. Others are machine-specific and stored in common folders. Later in this chapter, we'll examine these files in detail and discuss how they are used.

### Feature-Specific DLLs and Executables

The other major component of the Win32 Universal ICA client software is the collective DLLs and executables that provide additional functionality over the basic connection to a MetaFrame XP server. Even though `wfica32.exe` is the core client component, it provides only the basic ICA session support. Almost all of the client features that make ICA attractive (and that we discussed earlier in this chapter) are performed by separate DLLs or executables. Among these features are compression, encryption, client device mapping, Program Neighborhood, and the ICA connection center. We will look at these files in depth later in this chapter when we explore client installation methods.

## Differences Between Downloadable Win32 Client Packages

Once you decide to use the Win32 ICA client, a quick check to the Citrix download website (`www.citrix.com/download`) reveals that there are six different downloadable packages for the Win32 clients. Some of these packages are current, and others have been officially retired (although for some reason they are still available for download). The Citrix website does not make a clear distinction between the different versions. Because all are readily available, it's important to know which are current and which are old, and how each package is used today. The following six different ICA 32-bit Windows client installation packages are available today:

### Current Win32 ICA clients

- Full Program Neighborhood Client – CAB file.
- Full Program Neighborhood Client – EXE file.
- Full Program Neighborhood Client – MSI file.
- Web Client – CAB file.
- Web Client – EXE file.
- Program Neighborhood Agent Client – EXE file.
- Program Neighborhood Agent Client – MSI file.

Let's look at what each of these packages represent.

## *Current Win32 ICA Clients*

The current universal Win32 ICA client is available in three versions—one with Program Neighborhood, one without Program Neighborhood (known as the Web version), and one with the Program Neighborhood Agent.

### Full Program Neighborhood Client

The universal Win32 ICA client with Program Neighborhood is the traditional "full client." This package includes the Program Neighborhood executables and is fully installed on a Win32 PC, complete with icons and Start menu integration. This Win32 client contains all of the standard client installation files, including all DLLs and all INI files.

This version comes packaged in three different formats: an executable (`ica32.exe`), a cab file (`wfica.cab`), and a Microsoft Installer package (`ica32.msi`). The contents of these three packages are 100% identical, allowing you to choose which package is best for your particular deployment situation.

### Web Client

The universal Win32 web client is identical to the Program Neighborhood Win32 client, except that the web client does not contain any of the Program Neighborhood files (Program Neighborhood being the actual Windows user interface). When installed, this version of the client does not show up on the user's desktop. There are no help files, and no Start menu item. (It also does not support pass through authentication.) This ICA client must be launched through an external source, such as a website (like NFuse) or an ICA file.

There are two reasons that the Program Neighborhood files have been left out of the ICA web client:

- The client installation is smaller.
- There are no components that end users will discover and alter.

This Win32 web client comes packaged in two different formats: an executable (ica32t.exe) and a cab file (wficat.cab). Notice that these files are named like the full Program Neighborhood versions, except that the letter "t" has been added to the end of their names. Also like the Program Neighborhood clients, the files contained in these two packages are 100% identical.

### Program Neighborhood Agent Client

The Program Neighborhood Agent client also contains the same core files as the other two types of universal Win32 clients. Like the web client, the Program Neighborhood Agent client does not include the full Program Neighborhood software. However, in its place it includes the components needed to use the Program Neighborhood Agent.

There are also two different packages for the Program Neighborhood agent: an executable (ica32a.exe) and a Microsoft Installer package (ica32a.msi). Again, these two packages contain identical contents, so you can choose whichever is easier for you to deploy. Also, notice the naming convention. The Program Neighborhood Agent client packages end with the letter "a."

## 32-bit Windows Program Neighborhood Client

The Program Neighborhood client is the "standard" 32-bit desktop ICA client. This client includes the full Windows ICA user interface. This main feature that the Program Neighborhood client offers over the other clients is the "Program Neighborhood," a desktop interface that allows users to establish connections with server farms or to create custom connections to individual published applications or servers.

### *Program Neighborhood Client Configuration*

In the appendix you'll find a chart listing all of the MetaFrame XP configuration options and where those options can be configured (farm, server, client, connection, etc.). In the 32-bit Windows desktop world, those options that can be configured at the ICA client are configured from within Program Neighborhood.

In order to understand how configurations are made to the Program Neighborhood ICA client software, it's important to understand how the Windows 32-bit Program Neighborhood software works.

Program Neighborhood supports two different types of ICA connections:

- *Application Sets.* From within Program Neighborhood, connections to server farms are referred to as Application Sets. A single user can have many application sets, and so will be able to access many different server farms. Program Neighborhood only shows one icon for each application set. When a user double-clicks that icon, he will be logged into that server farm. The icons that are then displayed are based on the published applications and content that are configured for that user.

- *Custom ICA Connections.* Through Program Neighborhood, users can also manually create shortcuts for individual published applications or specific servers. These are known as custom ICA connections. Most likely, your users will not have any custom ICA connections because they will be connecting through an Application Set. As an administrator, however, you'll probably have many custom ICA connections configured in your Program Neighborhood on your personal workstation. At minimum, you'll want to create one custom ICA connection for each MetaFrame XP server, so that you can connect to a specific server for troubleshooting purposes.

When you first open the Program Neighborhood client software (Start | Programs | Citrix ICA Client | Citrix Program Neighborhood), you are taken immediately to the "Custom ICA Connections" page. This page contains a single icon called "Add ICA Connection." Obviously, this is where you can manually create icons and specify connections for custom ICA connections.

If you click the "up" button on the toolbar, you will be taken to the Program Neighborhood home screen. This screen contains two icons, "Find new application set" and "Custom ICA Connections." Double-clicking the "Find new application set" icon launches a wizard that allows you to connect to a server farm. When this wizard has completed, an icon for the new application set will be placed on the Program Neighborhood home screen, along with the existing "Find new application set" and "Custom ICA Connections" icons.

There are several different areas in which to configure properties of components of the Program Neighborhood. The two main areas are the Custom ICA Connection Properties and the Application Set Settings. Configuring the properties of an application set allows you to change the settings for that single application set only, (Program Neighborhood | Right-click Application Set | Application Set Settings) or (Program Neighborhood | Highlight the Application Set | click the Settings button on the toolbar).

Additionally, you can configure the properties of a Custom ICA connection. To configure the default properties for all new custom ICA connections, highlight the "Custom ICA Connections" icon in the Program Neighborhood home screen and click the "Settings" button on the toolbar (or right-click the "Custom ICA Connections" icon and choose "Custom Connections Settings). You can also configure the settings for one single custom ICA connection by applying this procedure to the connection's icon instead of the generic "Custom ICA Connections" icon.

Figure 10.5 (next page) shows which settings can be configured for custom ICA connections or for application set settings. A value of "CD" in the connection settings means you have the option of specifying that an individual setting will inherit the "Custom ICA Connection Default." A value of "SD" in the application set settings column indicates that you have the option of configuring that setting to user the default from the server. In both cases, you can override the default if you need to. For option columns that simply contain an "X," the options must be specified explicitly for that connection or application set.

In addition to options that are configured on a per-connection or per-application set basis, there are also some options that are only configured on a client-wide basis. For the most part, these options apply to specific hardware components of the ICA client that will be used for all ICA connections.

With the Program Neighborhood client, you can access these client-wide options via the tools menu (Program Neighborhood | Tools | ICA Settings). Because the tools menu contains all of the options that apply client-wide, you can access the "Tools" menu from any screen of the Program Neighborhood, regardless of whether your current view is a custom connection or an application set.

*Figure 10.5 Where options can be set with Program Neighborhood*

| | Custom ICA Connection Properties | Application Set Settings |
|---|---|---|
| Connection Type | X | X |
| Connection (Server or Published App) | X | n/a |
| Protocol | CD | X |
| Server Group | CD | X |
| Compression | X | X |
| Disk Bitmap Cache | X | X |
| Queue Mouse and Keystrokes | X | X |
| Desktop Integration | | X |
| Sound | CD | SD |
| Encryption | CD | SD |
| SpeedScreen Options | X | X |
| Color Depth | CD | SD |
| Resolution | CD | SD |
| Credentials or Smart Card Use | X | X |
| App to Run | X | n/a |

The following options are configured on a client-wide basis:

- Client Name. This is the name of the client device that will show up on the server through the Citrix Management Console.
- Serial Number. This is for legacy licensing situations. You can leave it blank.
- Keyboard Layout & Type. By default, this will pull the layout from the user profile, and the type from the current keyboard that is installed.
- Dial-In settings (Connect to Screen and Terminal Window).
- Enable or disable auto client updates.
- Whether pass-through authentication is enabled.
- Bitmap cache disk usage amount and cache directory.
- Minimum size bitmap that will be cached.
- Hotkeys shortcut configuration.

• Log file Settings.

## Program Neighborhood INI Configuration Files

Now that you understand how the different options can be configured via the Program Neighborhood interface, we need to look at how these options are saved under the hood.

For some reason, the 32-bit Windows ICA client software configuration information is still saved within INI configuration files, instead of being written to the registry. All of the configuration changes that users or administrators make via the menus and options of the Program Neighborhood are written to configuration files.

In some ways, this is helpful. For example, saving configuration information makes it easy to copy the configuration of one ICA client to another, because all you have to do is copy some INI files. You don't have to worry about the registry at all.

The Program Neighborhood Windows 32 ICA Client software uses the following configuration files:

- appsrv.ini
- module.ini
- pn.ini
- wfclient.ini
- uistate.ini
- wfcname.ini
- wfcwin32.log
- webica.ini

Let's take a look at each of these files and what they do.

### Appsrv.ini
*Location*: `%UserProfile%\application data\ICAclient\`

*Purpose*: `Appsrv.ini` contains settings that define preferences related to custom ICA connections. These settings are configured through the Program Neighborhood GUI when you click the "settings" button (Or through File | Custom Connection Settings).

### Module.ini

*Location*: ICA client installation directory. (Default `%ProgramFiles%\Citrix\ICA Client\`)

*Purpose*: This file contains information about which ICA modules are installed, including their versions and options. Essentially, this is just a list of ICA client DLLs. You will generally not have to worry about editing the contents of this file.

### Pn.ini

*Location*: `%UserProfile%\application data\ICAclient\`

*Purpose*: This file contains settings that define server farm application sets for the Program Neighborhood. Obviously, this `pn.ini` file does not exist in the web only or Program Neighborhood Agent Win32 clients, since these clients do not use Program Neighborhood.

The `pn.ini` file has two sections: a "Program Neighborhood" section and an "Application Set" section. The Program Neighborhood section contains information that applies to the Program Neighborhood in general. Additionally, each application set (or server farm) that you connect to has a corresponding section that contains settings for that server farm.

Let's take a look at a sample `pn.ini` file:

```
[Program Neighborhood]
Corporate=4839r93j

[Corporate]
ICASOCKSProtocolVersion=0
ICASOCKSProxyPortNumber=0
ICASOCKSTimeout=0
SSLEnable=Off
SSLProxyHost=*:443
SSLNoCACerts=0
SSLCiphers=COM
PNName=CorporateSet
UseDefaultSound=Off
ClientAudio=On
UseDefaultWinColor=Off
DesiredColor=2
```

The first section is the same for every `pn.ini` file in the world. That section begins with `[Program Neighborhood]`. The Program Neighborhood section simply contains a list of all the server farms that the user has previously set up in their Program Neighborhood software. Next to each server farm is an eight-character random identifier. This random identifier is created by the ICA client software when a user first connects to the server farm. It is simply used as a way for the ICA client software to internally keep track of multiple farms. This identifier has nothing to do with the MetaFrame XP servers. In fact, it will be different on every single ICA client.

In this sample `pn.ini` file, the user has only connected to one server farm. That farm's name is "corporate," and the random identifier is "4839r93j."

The random identifier also corresponds to two files saved in the same directory as the INI files. These two files have the extensions `.idx` and `.vl`. For this example, these files would be called `4839r93j.idx` and `4839r93j.vl`. The `.vl` file contains a cached list of all the applications that are available for the server farm, and the `.idx` is an index for the `.vl` file.

If the user has chosen to save his password locally (Program Neighborhood | Application Set Settings | Login Information tab), the `.vl` file also contains an encrypted version of that password.

After the `[Program Neighborhood]` section of `pn.ini`, there is one section for each server farm. In the previous sample file, the only server farm is "corporate," so the only other section is `[Corporate]`. As you can see in the example, the `[Corporate]` section of the `pn.ini` file contains the connection options for that server farm.

### Wfclient.ini
*Location*: `%UserProfile%\application data\ICAclient\`

*Purpose*: This file contains hardware settings for the ICA client software, including the keyboard layout, color depths, resolutions, and COM port mapping names. All of these settings can be configured via the tools menu in the Program Neighborhood GUI (Program Neighborhood | Tools | ICA Settings | General tab).

### Uistate.ini
*Location*: `%UserProfile%\application data\ICAclient\`

*Purpose*: The `uistate.ini` file contains information about the ICA session window. ("Uistate" stands for User Interface State.) This file is modified whenever an ICA session ends. It specifies the size and location of the windows, so that the software can place the session window on the local desktop right where the user left it. A sample `uistate.ini` file is shown below:

```
[Desktop]
WindowXPos=40
WindowYPos=28
DeskTopWidth=640
DeskTopHeight=300
ScaledWidth=0
ScaledHeight=0
```

### Wfcname.ini

*Location*: Root of the system drive.

*Purpose*: For ICA clients prior to version 6.30, this file specifies the name of the ICA client device. It only contains two lines, as shown below:

```
[WFClient]
ClientName=brian
```

You can change the name of the client in the Program Neighborhood (Program Neighborhood | Tools | ICA Settings | General tab | Client Name). When you make this change, the `wfcname.ini` file is updated, which means that you can change the name simply by bypassing the Program Neighborhood GUI and changing the value in the file directly. Many people configure logon scripts to automatically update the `wfcname.ini` file when a user logs on, so that the ICA client name will always match the username.

ICA clietns version 6.30 and newer store the name of the ICA client device in the registry instead of the `wfcname.ini` file. The following registry location is used:

Location: `HKLM\Software\Citrix\ICA Client`

Key: `ClientName`

Type: `REG_SZ`

Data: The name of your client device.

### Wfcwin32.log

*Location*: The name and location of this file are configurable. By default, this file is located in the ICA client installation folder.

*Purpose*: This file is the log file that is used for logging the various ICA client options (Program Neighborhood | Tools | ICA Settings | Event Logging tab).

### Webica.ini

*Location*: `%systemroot%`

*Purpose*: This file is contains security settings for ICA applications that you access through web browsers. It allows you to specify the amount of local access that different ICA applications have to your computer when they are launched from the web browser. A detailed discussion of the use of this file is covered in Chapter 15.

## Program Neighborhood Client Deployment Configuration

Once you decide which features and options of the ICA client software to use, you need to figure out how to deploy the software to your users. If you have many users, you'll also want to configure the ICA client software before it is installed on all of their workstations. That way, you won't have as much work to do and the chance that users will not configure things properly themselves is diminished.

### Advantages of Preconfiguring ICA Client Software

• Saves time if you have many users.

• Decreases the chance that an individual user might not install something properly.

### Disadvantages of Preconfiguring ICA Client Software

• Additional time must be spent configuring the client software before it's deployed.

• All users will receive the same options.

In order to prepare the ICA client software for your users, there are several steps that you must take:

1. Extract the installation source files from the ICA client installation package downloaded from the Citrix website.

2. Preconfigure specific ICA client options and settings.

3. Configure a silent install routine.

4. Repackage the installation files.

Let's focus on these steps.

### Step 1. Extract the Files from the Single-File Source Package

Usually it's fairly easy to edit the installation source files for an application that you need to install. Most of today's applications come on CD-ROM, and you simply copy the contents of the CD to your hard drive and make whatever changes are needed. From there, you can usually burn a new CD or copy the installation files to a network share where users can access them.

Editing the source files of Citrix's ICA client software is not so easy. None of the 32-bit Windows ICA clients are in a form that allows you to directly access the files. Instead, they come consolidated and compressed into one single file. Depending on the package, that one file is a CAB, MSI, or EXE.

Because of this, you'll need to extract the real source files from the compressed installation package before you can edit the source files and change certain client options.

The exact method that you must use to extract the files depends on whether you have chosen to download the CAB, MSI, or EXE package. Citrix provides the three different packages as a matter of convenience. They all contain the exact same files. For that reason, you should pick whichever file type is easiest for you to work with. In fact, you can even choose to download one type and then repackage it into another.

### Extracting Files from the CAB Package

If you're using Windows 2000 or Windows XP, you can open CAB files simply by double-clicking them in Windows Explorer, causing you to "explore" the contents of the CAB. From there, you can drag and drop the entire contents of the CAB file into a temporary directory where you can work with them. If you're using Terminal Server 4.0, you will not be able to open the CAB file by clicking it in Explorer. Instead, you'll have to use a command-line tool called `expand.exe`, which is located in the `\system32\` folder.

### Extracting Files from the MSI Package

MSI files are created with the "Windows Installer." The Windows Installer is a program from Microsoft that developers use to create installation routines for their software. Anyone can install an MSI file, but in order to edit the contents of one, you need to have a copy of the Windows Installer. (You can get this with many of the Microsoft Development tools.) For more information about the Windows Installer, check out the Microsoft Developer Network, at `msdn.microsoft.com`. (From the MSDN homepage, navigate to the MSDN Library link. Follow the table of contents to Setup and System Administration | Setup | Windows Installer.)

If you are familiar with the Windows Installer, you might want to use it to edit the files in the in MSI package. Otherwise, choose the CAB or EXE package.

### Extracting Files from the EXE Package

The EXE version of the ICA client installation package is a self-unzipping executable. Running the executable will not unzip the files, it will just install the ICA client. However, you can use the following command line options to extract the files from the EXE package without installing the ICA file:

```
ica32.exe /a /extract /path c:\yourextractpath
```

Alternately, you can use a third party tool such as WinZip to extract the files.

## Step 2. Preconfigure ICA Client Options and Settings

Once you've extracted the ICA client installation source files from the down-loaded package, you can modify certain configuration files. Preconfiguring the client settings and options relieves users from needing to manually con-figure their client software. In order to preconfigure the Citrix ICA client software, you can configure the options that are saved into the INI files. Then, when users install the ICA client software, they get the INI files configured exactly as you want them.

Even though the Windows 32-bit ICA client software uses several different .INI files to hold configuration data, most of the important information is stored in three main files: `appsrv.ini`, `module.ini`, and `pn.ini`. You can build custom versions of these three files to be included in your ICA client installation package. That way, your users will get certain options con-figured for them as soon as they install the client software. Most people use this to preconfigure connection options for the server farm.

In order to configure options that will be installed into these three INI con-figuration files, you need to configure the "source" versions of the files, which are included in the installation package and named `appsrv.src`, `module.src`, and `pn.src`. When the ICA client software is installed, the installation routine uses the appropriate .SRC file as a template to generate the .INI files.

You can open the .SRC files with a standard text editor. When you do this, you'll see that they look exactly like their .INI counterparts. This means that you have two choices when it comes to preconfiguring these files. You can edit them directly, or you can configure a Program Neighborhood client ex-actly as you like it, copy the three .INI files to a temporary folder, rename them with the .SRC extensions, and copy them into your ICA source file pack-age.

## Step 3. Configure the ICA Client for a Silent Install

A "silent install" is an installation routine that does not require any input whatsoever during the installation process. Silent installs are used when you want to automatically deploy the ICA client software to the users without any chance that they could choose the wrong option.

In order to create a silent install, you need to install the Citrix ICA client software on a test workstation. When performing that installation, configure it so that all of your inputs and answers for the dialog boxes are recorded into an "answer file." Then, when you install the software on your users' workstations, the setup program uses the answer file to provide the answers to the dialog boxes, instead of presenting the user with the choices.

With the 32-bit Windows ICA client software, this silent installation option is automatically available because Citrix chose to package their client installation with tools from InstallShield. This ability to create silent installations is one of the great things about InstallShield. Citrix did not have to do any extra work to enable this silent install functionality. It's automatically available anytime InstallShield is used to package application installation routines. In fact, the silent install methods discussed here can be used with any application whose installation routine was created with InstallShield, which is probably 90% of all applications in the world (except for those written by Microsoft, because they use the Windows Installer instead).

To create a silent install for the 32-bit Windows Citrix ICA client, follow these simple steps:

1. Start with a test workstation that closely resembles your target workstations. If all of your users already have an old version of the ICA client that they will be upgrading, then make sure that your test workstation has that same ICA client installed. If they do not have any clients installed, then make sure that your test workstation does not have any clients installed.

2. Start the installation routine from the command line by typing `setup -r`. (This assumes that you have extracted the files as outlined previously.) In this case, the "`-r`" option tells the installation program (InstallShield) that you want to "record" this installation.

3. Install the ICA client as usual, choosing whatever options you want for the ICA client software on your target workstations.

4. When the installation is finished, a text file called `setup.iss` will be created in the `%systemroot%` folder. (ISS stands for "InstallShield Script.") This file contains all the answers to the dialog boxes from your installation and allows you to perform future installations using those same answers. Copy the `setup.iss` file into the same directory as your unpacked ICA client installation files.

5. In order to use the silent install script that you just created, you must

run "setup -s" to kick off the installation. For this to work, the
setup.iss file must be in the same directory as setup.exe.

Every option and action that can be set during an application's graphical installation process is saved in the setup.iss file. Let's take a look at a sample setup.iss file now. Comments as to how the different parts of the file are used have been inserted throughout the file.

The setup.iss file begins with the [InstallShield Silent] tag, indicating that this is a recorded file for an InstallShield silent install routine.

```
[InstallShield Silent]
Version=v5.00.000
File=Response File
```

The Version= line refers to the InstallShield version, not the ICA Client version. The File item tells InstallShield that this is a response file that contains answers for installation.

```
[DlgOrder]
Dlg0=SdWelcome-0
Count=7
Dlg1=SdLicense-0
Dlg2=SdAskDestPath-0
Dlg3=SdSelectFolder-0
Dlg4=SdShowDlgEdit1-0
Dlg5=AskOptions-0
Dlg6=MessageBox-0
```

The DlgOrder section contains an overview of the dialog boxes that will be encountered during the installation. The next part of the file contains a section for each dialog box. Each of these sections contains the button that was pressed (Result=1) and any options that were selected on the screen (as indicated in the lines beginning with "sz").

```
[SdWelcome-0]
Result=1
[SdLicense-0]
Result=1
```

As you can see by these two entries, the first two dialog boxes that a user sees when installing the ICA client software are the welcome screen and the licenses agreement. Neither of these screens have any options, and the Result=1 line indicates that the confirmation button was pressed when the recording was made.

```
[SdAskDestPath-0]
szDir=C:\Program Files\Citrix\ICA Client
Result=1
```

This dialog box asks the user for the destination path for the installation of the ICA client software. You can edit this section of the setup.iss file directly, if you want to have different silent install package options.

```
[SdSelectFolder-0]
szFolder=Citrix ICA Client
Result=1
```

This "SdSelectFolder" section indicates the name of the program group that will be added to the user's start menu that will contain the shortcuts to Program Neighborhood.

```
[SdShowDlgEdit1-0]
szEdit1=YOURICACLIENTNAME
Result=1
```

This "SdShowDigEdit" section contains the name of the ICA client device. This name is written to the wfcname.ini file. If you are automating the client install for your users, but you want each of them to have their own unique client name, it's probably easiest to leave this section of the setup.iss file with a generic name, and then to change the name in the wfcname.ini file later.

```
[AskOptions-0]
Result=1
Sel-0=0
Sel-1=1
```

This "AskOptions" dialog box is the final confirmation that comes up before the installation begins. This simply provides the user with a confirmation of their choices. Like the other dialog boxes, the Result=1 indicates that the user has pressed "OK."

```
[Application]
Name=ICA Client
Version=4.0
Company=Citrix
[MessageBox-0]
```

```
Result=1
```

This last section represents the dialog box that appears after the installation has successfully completed.

After you examine this `setup.iss` file, you can clearly see that this file is created simply by recording the answers, inputs, and buttons pressed as you installed the ICA client software. This is why it's important that your test workstation has the same configuration as your production workstations. If the configuration of your test workstation is different from the configuration of your users' production workstations, then the dialog boxes presented during the installation of the ICA client software could be different.

For example, if the ICA client software is installed onto a fresh workstation that does not have any previous versions of the ICA client installed, the third dialog box of the installation procedure asks the user to specify the path they want to use to install the new software.

In contrast, if the ICA client is installed onto a workstation that already has a previous version of the ICA client installed, then the third dialog box is different. Instead of asking about the install location, it asks the user if he wants to upgrade the current ICA client or install a fresh copy.

Clearly, you cannot use the same `setup.iss` script for both of these environments, because the script will fail if the installation dialog boxes are not 100% identical to when the script was recorded.

## Step 4. Repackage the Installation Files

After the source files are configured for your environment, you need to prepare them to be distributed to your users. If you will be installing the ICA client software from a network share, floppy disk, or burned CD, then you can simply copy the files as they are and instruct your users to run `setup.exe -s` to kick off the installation. You can even use a utility such as WinZip to create a self-extracting executable.

However, if you will be deploying the ICA client installation files to users via a web browser, then you will not be able create a normal self-extracting EXE. You will need to create a digitally "signed" package. If you don't do this, then the security settings of many users' web browsers will not allow them to run your EXE or install your CAB.

The easiest way for you to package and sign your ICA client installation source file is to use InstallShield's PackageForTheWeb product. This product is available for free from the InstallShield website (`www.installshield.com`).

Basically, PackageForTheWeb allows you to combine a directory full of source files into a single CAB file or self extracting EXE. It also allows you to apply the proper digital signatures to your packages so that they can be downloaded by your users.

If you will only be deploying this package internally, then you can run your own certificate server and generate certificates that you can use to sign your installation packages. However, if you will need to deploy this package externally, you will probably find it easier to purchase a digital certificate from a real certificate authority. VeriSign offers a Commercial Internet Software Distribution License for only $400 per year (www.verisign.com/installshield). For more information about how digital certificates work, see Chapter 15 of this book.

## 32-bit Windows Web Client

If you have users that will only access MetaFrame XP applications via links from websites, they can use the 32-bit Windows ICA web client. The web client is the full Program Neighborhood client without Program Neighborhood. This version of the client requires that users launch ICA sessions via an external source, since there is no Program Neighborhood. The ICA web client is most often used in situations where users access ICA applications through the web from Citrix NFuse servers. (NFuse is discussed in detail in the next chapter.)

### Web Client Configuration

Even though the ICA web client does not have a local Program Neighborhood interface, it is identical to the full Program Neighborhood client in every other way. All of the "web" functionality of the ICA web client is also included as part of the Program Neighborhood and Program Neighborhood Agent clients.

In years past, Citrix has always created a dedicated version of the ICA client for use with the web. This was an ActiveX control or Netscape plug-in. Users who wanted to access ICA applications launched from web browsers could install these dedicated web ICA clients instead of the standard ICA clients. However, with today's new ICA clients this is no longer done, because the functionality needed to integrate with Internet Explorer or Netscape Navigator is included in all ICA client packages.

Because the web integration functionality is built into all new ICA client packages, the current ICA "web client" integrates with the web in the exact same way as the "Program Neighborhood" client or the "Program Neighborhood Agent" client.

## How the ICA Client Integrates with Web Browsers

In order to access an ICA application via a web browser, a user surfs to a web page that contains hyperlinks to ICA application sessions (in the form of ICA files). When the user clicks on a hyperlink, the web browser receives the information about the ICA session and passes that information over to the ICA client. The ICA client receives the connection information from the web browser, and establishes a connection with the MetaFrame XP server.

This web browser to ICA client software integration is possible because the ICA client is registered as a COM component. A COM (Component Object Model) component is a piece of executable code that has registered its interfaces with the operating system allowing different applications to interact with each other.

In order for the operating system to be able to keep track of all the different COM components, each has its own serial number, called a "class ID." When application vendors create COM components to be part of their applications, they register the class IDs of their components so that they are guaranteed to be unique from the class IDs of all other COM components in the world.

For example, the class ID of the Citrix ICA client is 238F6F83-B8B4-8771-00A024541EE3. This is the class ID number that Citrix reserved several years ago. Even though it is the same for every ICA client on every computer in the world, this class ID uniquely defines the ICA client and will never be used by any component other than the ICA client.

The ICA web client uses the class ID of the COM component to make its services available to the web browser. This is what allows the ICA client software to automatically launch ICA applications using information received from the web browser. An ActiveX control (wfica.ocx) contains the specific code needed to link the two. When the ICA client is properly set up on a user's machine and configured to launch ICA sessions from web page information, the following registry key will exist:

Key: HKLM\SOFTWARE\Classes\CLSID\{238F6F83-B8B4-8771-00A024541EE3}

Value: InprocServer32

Type: REG_SZ

Data: C:\PROGRA~1\Citrix\ICACLI~1\WFICA.OCX

The data is the path to the ActiveX control, which is the `wfica.ocx` file located in the ICA client installation directory.

## Web Client Installation and Deployment

Even though the ICA web client is made up of the same core files as the full Program Neighborhood client, the installation routines of the two are not the same. Since the ICA web client is primarily designed to be downloaded and installed from websites, Citrix has chosen to streamline its installation routine, so that little user intervention is required.

For example, instead of asking a lot questions and displaying several dialog boxes, the ICA web client installation only has two dialog boxes. The first tells the user that the web client is about to be installed, and the second tells the user that the installation is complete.

The ICA web client installation is invoked with "`ctxsetup.exe`" instead of "`setup.exe`." The "`ctxsetup.exe`" program is written as a silent install that doesn't ask the user many questions. You can configure the installation options by editing an .INI file instead of having to go through the trouble of recording a silent install.

In order to understand how the ICA web client can be used in the real world, let's take a look at the process that is used to configure and deploy it:

1. Configure the ICA web client options.
2. Reduce the size of the web client installation package.
3. Configure the ICA web client installation process.
4. Repackage the modified installation files.
5. Use the web to deploy the client.

### Step 1. Configuring the ICA Web Client Options

Because the 32-bit Windows ICA web client contains the same core components as the full Program Neighborhood client, you can configure many of the options in the same way. The ICA web client comes from Citrix in two different packages: a CAB file and an EXE file. In order to work with these files, you will need to extract their contents to a temporary folder, just as you did with the full Program Neighborhood client. See the full Program Neighborhood client section (previous section) of this chapter for information about the ICA client packages and how they can be extracted.

After you extract the ICA web client source files, you can modify the parameters that will be contained in the .INI files by editing the appropriate .SRC files, just like when you preconfigured the full Program Neighborhood client. Again, see the previous section of this chapter for details. In general, the .INI and .SRC files are the same for the web client as they are for the full Program Neighborhood client except that the ICA web client does not contain a pn.ini or pn.src file, since it does not have a Program Neighborhood.

Once you get the ICA web client installation source files extracted and configured, you can continue preparing the ICA client for distribution. The next thing that you should do is take a look at the files contained within your installation procedure and figure out if you need all of them or if there are some that can be removed.

### Step 2. Reducing the Size of the Web Client Installation Package

Usually, the ICA web client is installed onto users' computers automatically when they visit a website that establishes an ICA connection to a MetaFrame XP server. When this happens, the ICA web client source package is automatically downloaded from the website and executed on the user's computer.

Even though the ICA web client is only about half the size of the full Program Neighborhood ICA client (1.8MB for the web client compared to 3.4MB for the Program Neighborhood client), there are situations in which bandwidth is tight and you might want to further decrease the size of the downloaded ICA client software. This is most often done when users will be downloading the ICA web client over a slower Internet connection.

In order to further reduce the size of the ICA web client installation package, you can decide which features your users will need to use and then delete the source files that support those features that will not be used. This creates a smaller CAB or EXE file for your users.

### *Advantages of Reducing the Size of the Client Installation*
- Download time is decreased.

### *Disadvantages of Reducing the Size of the Client Installation*
- Some functionality will be lost.
- Extra administrative time is required to remove the files and reconfigure the client.

The first step to reducing the size of the ICA web client is to select the files that you want to remove from the source installation package. After you have unpacked the installation files from the CAB or EXE file, refer to Figure 10.6 to determine which files you can remove for features that you will not use.

Take note of any files that you delete, because you will need to refer to them in the next step.

For example, if you want to disable audio from remote ICA sessions, then you can remove the files needed to support audio. Referring to Figure 10.6 shows that you can remove the `adpcm.dll`, `audcvtN.dll`, and `vdcamN.dll`.

*Figure 10.6 Specific roles of the files in the Win32 ICA client*

| File | Function |
|---|---|
| acrdlg.dll | Auto Client Reconnect |
| adpcm.dll | Audio |
| appsrv.ini | INI configuration file |
| APPSRV.SRC | Source file for INI |
| audcvtN.dll | Audio |
| clientn.ico | Icon |
| concentr.cnt | Seamless Windows |
| concentr.dll | Seamless Windows |
| CONCENTR.hlp | Seamless Windows Help |
| ctxsetup.exe | Setup Executable |
| ctxsetup.ini | Setup Options |
| cudhlpt.dll | CUD Helper |
| ICACIObj.class | Netscape Plug-in |
| license.txt | License Agreement |
| migrateN.exe | WinFrame File Migration Tool |
| module.ini | INI configuration file |
| MODULE.SRC | Source file for INI |
| npicaN.dll | Netscape Plug-in |
| pcl4rast.dll | Client Printing |
| pdc128N.dll | SecureICA and Logon Encryption |
| pdcompN.dll | Compression |
| sslasock.dll | SSL Encryption |
| sslsdk_b.dll | SSL Encryption |
| update.ini | Auto Client Update |
| vdcamN.dll | Audio |

*Figure 10.6 Continued...*

| File | Function |
| --- | --- |
| vdcmN.dll | Auto Client Update |
| vdcom30N.dll | COM Port Mapping |
| vdcpm30N.dll | LPT Port Mapping |
| vdfon30n.dll | SpeedScreen |
| vdtw30n.dll | Display Driver |
| vdzlcn.dll | SpeedScreen |
| version.dat | Text File w/ ICA version info |
| wfclient.ini | INI configuration file |
| WFCLIENT.SRC | Source file for INI |
| wfcmoveN.exe | Auto Client Update |
| wfcrun32.exe | Seamless Windows |
| WFCSETUP.INI | Setup INI options |
| wfcwinn.dll | Client DDE |
| Wfica.ocx | ActiveX Control |
| wfica32.exe | Core Client Executable |
| wficat.inf | CAB file list |

If you choose to remove any source files, it is important to remember that the functionality of the files that you removed will be permanently disabled on the client devices that receive the installations with files removed. If you were to decide that you would like to support audio through ICA sessions after you deployed the ICA client without audio support, then you would have to figure out how to get the missing audio files to your users.

After you delete the files for the features that you do not need, you will need to tell the ICA client software that you removed some files. If you don not, the installation will fail because it thinks that the files are missing and the installation package has been corrupted.

To do this, open the configuration file ctxsetup.ini. This file contains the file information for the ICA client setup. Within ctxsetup.ini, locate the section for each file that you have deleted. The section will have the file name in brackets, like this: [FILENAME]. Delete the file name in brackets and the TargetDir, SourceFileName, and TargetFileName sections for each file that you have removed. For example, if you decide that you will

never use audio, then you would remove the following lines from
ctxsetup.ini:

```
[adpcm.dll]
TargetDir=%TARGETDIR%
SourceFilename=adpcm.dll
TargetFilename=adpcm.dll
RequiredCopy=1

[audcvtn.dll]
TargetDir=%TARGETDIR%
SourceFilename=audcvtn.dll
TargetFilename=audcvtn.dll

[vdcamN.dll]
TargetDir=%TARGETDIR%
SourceFilename=vdcamN.dll
TargetFilename=vdcamN.dll
```

You will also need to remove the references to the names of the files you are
removing from the [AddFiles.Win32] section of the ctxsetup.ini
file, which would be the following three lines:

```
adpcm.dll
audcvtn.dll
vdcamN.dll
```

### Step 3. Configuring the ICA Web Client Installation Process

As mentioned in the introduction of this section, the installation options of the
ICA web client are configured with an .INI file instead of recording options
for a silent install. These options are saved in a file called ctxsetup.ini,
located in the web client CAB or EXE source file. The ctxsetup.ini file
contains many different sections. The section that is used to specify the behavior of the installation is the [Setup] section at the beginning of the file.
Figure 10.7 shows a sample [Setup] section from this file.

*Figure 10.7 The default [Setup] section from the ctxsetup.ini file.*
```
[Setup]
Product=Citrix ICA Web Client
InitialPrompt=1
TARGETDIR=%PROGRAMFILES%Citrix\icaweb32
UninstFile=%TARGETDIR%uninst.inf
DisplayLicenseDlg=1
AddUninstallLink=1
PromptForCopyingPlugins=0
```

Let's define what each option entails:

- *InitialPrompt*. If you disable this (by changing the "1" to a "0"), the initial dialog box that tells the user that the ICA web client is about to be installed will not be displayed. Most people set this to "0."

- *TARGETDIR*. This represents the directory on the client device where the ICA web client files will be installed to.

- *UninstFile*. This specifies the path to the .INF file that will contain the uninstall information.

- *DisplayLicneseDlg*. If this is enabled (value is set to "1") then the License agreement dialog box is displayed to the user when the installation takes place. A value of "0" causes this box to not appear, and it is assumed that the user accepts the terms of the license agreement. In the real world, most people set this to "0."

- *AddUninstallLink*. When this is set to "1," a link to remove the ICA web client is added to the Windows Add / Remove Programs list in the control panel. A value of "0" means that this link will not be added.

- *PromptForCopyingPlugins*. When this is enabled (value is set to "1") the user will be prompted when the ICA client plug-in is copied to the Netscape plug-ins directory.

As long as this `ctxsetup.ini` file is located in the same directory as the other installation files, the settings that you configure will be used for the installation.

## Step 4. Repacking the Modified ICA Web Client Installation Files

In order to deploy the ICA web client to your users, you need to repackage your modified group of files into a package that can easily be distributed via the web. This is most easily done by grouping them into a CAB file. For details about how this is done, see the repackaging information in the previous section when packaging was discussed for the full Program Neighborhood client.

## Step 5. Deploying CAB Files via Web Sites

The easiest way to deploy the ICA web client to end users is to configure a web page to automatically install the client if the current version is not already installed. If you are using NFuse, the NFuse web pages will automatically be configured to allow users to automatically download the ICA web client. See the next chapter for information on how this works with NFuse.

If you are not using NFuse, the easiest way to allow the ICA client to be automatically downloaded and installed is to add this line to your web page:

```
<object
classid="clsid:238f6f83-b8b4-11cf-8771-00a024541ee3"
codebase="/clients/wficat.cab#Version=6,30,1050,0"
width=0 height=0>
</object>
```

The `classid` attribute is the class ID of the ICA client COM object. This value should never change.

The `codebase` attribute specifies the location and version of the ICA web client CAB source files. In the above example, the ICA client is in the form of the file "wficat.cab" which is located in the "\clients" folder in your web server's root web directory. In other words, this CAB file is accessible via the path http://yourwebserver/clients/wficat.cab.

The "version" value after the CAB file location indicates the version of the ICA web client that is contained in that CAB file. If you do not know the version, you can find it by locating the wfica.ocx file contained in the ICA client installation source files. Right-click on this file, and view the version information contained in the "version" tab. When you specify the version number in the web page, it is important to separate the groups of numbers with commas instead of periods.

When a user accesses a web page with this code added to it, his web browser will check to see if he has the COM object installed with the class ID in the tag specified in the web page. If he does, the browser will then check the version of the COM object to see if the version in the web page is newer than its version. If the user does not have the COM object installed, or if he has an older version installed, then the web browser will automatically download and install the CAB file specified in the web page.

As an administrator, if you ever get a new version of the ICA web client, you will need to copy the new CAB file to your web server. Then you will need to update the web page with the new version number. That will cause your users to automatically download the new version. If you want to create a web page that causes the CAB file to be downloaded and installed every time a user visits the page, then you can change the version number in your HTML code so that it read Version=-1,-1,-1,-1.

# Program Neighborhood Agent

The Program Neighborhood Agent version of the 32-bit Windows ICA client is something that was introduced with Feature Release 1 for MetaFrame XP. It's also including with Feature Release 2.

The Program Neighborhood Agent is "officially" covered in the next chapter. For that reason, we won't delve into the workings of the Program Neighborhood Agent here. We will cover how to install the PN Agent client in this chapter and then you can see in the next chapter how it is configured.

## Program Neighborhood Agent Client Configuration

Most of the settings for the Program Neighborhood Agent client are configured via an XML file on a web server. That's really the whole point of the PN Agent and its major advantage over the full Program Neighborhood client. As an administrator, if you need to change something, you simply change the settings in the XML file on your web server. Unlike the full Program Neighborhood client, there are no `appsrv.ini` or `pn.ini` files that must be individually updated on every single client device.

## Program Neighborhood Agent Client Deployment

The PN Agent client comes in two formats, an EXE and an MSI. Even though most options are configured via the XML file on the web server, there are some options that you can configure as part of the PN Agent client installation. These include installation options, such as which directory you want to install to and the path to your web server and the XML configuration file.

As you know by now (from reading about the full Program Neighborhood and web clients), if you want to edit the source files for the PN Agent installation package, you will need to extract them to a temporary directory, make your changes, and then repackage the files.

### Modifying Source Files

The PN Agent does not come from Citrix in the form of a CAB file—your only choices are the self-extracting EXE or the Windows Installer MSI file. In this case, it's probably easiest to work with the EXE package. As with the Program Neighborhood client, you can use the following command to extract the source files from the Program Neighborhood Agent installation file:

```
ica32a.exe /a /extract /path c:\yourextractpath
```

You can also use a third party utility such as WinZip.

Once you extract the source files from the PN Agent installation package, there are two files that you might want to modify:

- module.src
- install.ini

### Module.src

The module.src file is the only SRC installation INI file that is available with the PN Agent. This module.src file works in the same way with the PN Agent client as it does with the other 32-bit Windows clients. For the most part, there shouldn't be anything that you need to modify with this file.

### Install.ini

The install.ini contains the default settings that apply to the installation of the PN Agent client. The default install.ini file is shown here.

```
[install]
;ServerURL=
;InstallorUpdate=
;SetMachineNameClientName=
;Location=
;StartMenu=
;InstallSingleSignOn=
;AcceptClientSideEULA=
```

You can change the values for any of these lines. As with many text configuration files that you may have worked with, the leading semicolon on each line indicates that the line is a comment and the contents should be ignored. Therefore, if you configure any of the lines in this install.ini file, be sure to remove the semicolon from those lines. Let's interpret what each line means:

- *ServerURL.* This allows you to specify the URL of the XML configuration file that the Program Neighborhood Agent client will use. If you specify a URL to a server, the PN Agent client will append a path. For example, if you set this value to www.yourserver.com, the Program Neighborhood Agent will append /Citrix/PNAgent/config.xml, making the full path www.yourserver.com/Citrix/PNAgent/config.xml. If you specify the path directly to an XML file, such as www.yourserver.com/yourfiles/yourconfig.xml, then the PN Agent will not append anything.
- *InstallorUpdate.* This stands for "Install or Update." (It is not the

word "Installer" spelled incorrectly.) It allows you to specify whether to perform a maintenance update or a fresh install of the PN Agent client.

- *SetMachineNameClientName*. This allows you to specify the name of the ICA client.

- *Location*. This specifies the directory that the PN Agent will be installed into, for example `c:\PNAgent`.

- *StartMenu*. This specifies the location of the folder that the Program Neighborhood icon will be installed to in the start menu. For example, if you set this value to "PNA," then the Program Neighborhood Agent start menu icon will be in the Start I Programs I PNA folder.

- *InstallSingleSignOn*. This line allows you to specify whether single sign on support (pass-through authentication) is enabled or disabled. If it is disabled, you can only enable it by reinstalling the PN Agent client software.

- *AcceptClientSideEULA*. If you set this to "true" then the introduction screen and the license agreement screens will not be displayed.

For each line that you configure via this `install.ini` file, the corresponding dialog box will not be presented to the user during the installation. Therefore, if you want to create a totally "silent" install, you need to specify answers for every line, remove all of the leading semicolons, and set the "`AcceptClientSideEULA`" to "`true`."

Refer to the next chapter for more information on how the Program Neighborhood Agent client is used in the real world.

# Java ICA Client

The ICA Java client is the second most popular client platform (second to the Win32 clients). The ICA Java client will run on any operating system that has a Java Virtual Machine (JVM) installed. There are dozens of different client platforms that can run a JVM, including Win32, UNIX, Macintosh, OS/2, and BeOS. Many people choose to use the Java client because it supports features that might not be supported by the platform's native ICA client, such as Program Neighborhood. Also, if you have a diverse range of client devices, using the ICA Java client means that you only need to support one client platform instead of many.

### Advantages of the Java ICA Client

- Can be used on many different client operating systems.

- Can be embedded directly into web pages.

- Supports many advanced client features, such as Program Neighborhood.

### Disadvantages of the Java ICA Client

- Only supports TCP/IP sessions.

- Requires that a Java Virtual Machine be configured.

- The security context in which Java applications run sometimes prevents the ICA Java client from behaving properly.

## Technical Overview

The Java client comes packaged in a single installation file, `setup.class`. You can install the ICA client from this file onto web servers to allow users to run ICA sessions directly through web pages. You can also install this file onto each client device, so that the Java ICA client is installed locally, allowing users to access MetaFrame XP servers without having to go to a web page.

The ICA Java client is fully JDK 1.1 compliant. It will run in any environment that is also JDK 1.1 compliant.

### Differences between ICA Java Client Modes

The ICA Java client has two modes of operation, depending on how it is installed and used. The same `setup.class` file is used to install the ICA client for both modes. The two modes are:

- Applet mode.
- Application mode.

### Applet Mode

In applet mode, the ICA Java client is installed on your web server. Users launch ICA sessions and the ICA client by clicking on hyperlinks in web pages. All ICA client configuration is accomplished through parameters embedded in the web page that are passed to the ICA client when it's launched.

In applet mode, the ICA Java client never gets installed to the users' client devices and users do not have to have a JVM loaded locally. The ICA Java client is executed inside users' web browsers, and the ICA session appears inside their web browsers. When they close their browser, the ICA session is disconnected.

### Advantages of Applet Mode

- You can control what features are used.
- Easy for users to use.
- Nothing is installed locally on the client devices for the users to break.

### Disadvantages of Applet Mode

- ICA sessions run in the browser window.
- The Java runtime files must be downloaded every time a session is launched.

## Application Mode

In application mode, the ICA Java client is installed directly on the user's client device. This means that the client device must have a JVM installed locally as well. Once the ICA client is installed, however, users can launch ICA sessions from their local device anytime they want. They do not have to go through a web browser and their ICA session Windows are not embedded into a browser.

### Advantages of Application Mode

- Users can specify parameters when sessions are launched.
- User settings can be saved in .INI files, just like the 32-bit Windows clients.
- ICA sessions run in their own Window.

### Disadvantages of Application Mode

- You do not have tight control over what options the users choose.
- You need to figure out how to deploy the Java client software to all of your users.

## ICA Java Client Installation

The installation procedure for the ICA Java client is basically the same for both applet mode and application mode. The only difference is that with applet mode, the ICA Java client is installed onto your web servers, and with application mode, it is installed onto your client devices. To install the ICA Java client, follow these simple steps:

1. Install a Java Virtual Machine. The ICA Java client requires a JVM

that supports JDK 1.1, or JDK 1.3 or newer. For some reason, Citrix does not recommend that you use JDK 1.2, so you need to use 1.1, or 1.3 or newer. A JVM from any vendor can be used. Most people use the JVM that is built into older versions of Windows (jview), or they use the free JVM directly from Sun. Some newer versions of Windows do not have a JVM (due to a little legal problem with Sun) which means that you'll have to download one. If you go to Sun's website (www.sun.com), the JVM download will be listed as a JRE, which stands for Java Runtime Environment. Once you download and install the JRE, you won't notice much difference to your operating system, except that you'll have a directory with some new Java executables.

2. After you install your JVM, install the ICA Java client. This is done by running the downloaded setup.class file within the JVM environment. (A "class" file is a Java executable file.) The exact command that you use will vary, depending on the JVM you have chosen. With Microsoft's JVM, the command would be jview setup.class. If you have decided to use Sun's JVM, the command would be jre setup.class. On both platforms, you might also need to use the "cp" command line switch to specify the "classpath," which is the path to the setup.class file. Once you use the JVM to run the setup.class file, a GUI setup utility will be launched that graphically steps you through all of the ICA Java client setup options.

3a. Once the ICA Java client is installed, you need to configure it so that it can be used. If you installed the client on your web servers, you configure the client by building a web page that launches the client with certain options. Users launch ICA sessions by accessing the URL to your web page.

3b. If you installed the client directly onto your users' client devices, they can immediately access the Java client to launch ICA sessions. However, because the Java client's command-line environment is complex, you'll need to create batch files that contain the options and parameters your users need to access their ICA sessions. By default, two batch files are created for you, one called jicasession.bat that launches a command-line interface allowing you to specify ICA parameters, and a second batch file called pnsession.bat that launches the Java version of Program Neighborhood. These batch files are covered in detail later in this chapter.

4. As part of the ICA Java client installation procedure, a file called

`uninstall.class` is created in the client directory. This file can be used to remove the ICA Java client from a computer.

## ICA Java Client Files

When you install the ICA Java client, the installation directory will contain dozens of files. In addition to the batch files mentioned previously and some readme text files, most of the remaining files are either JAR or CAB files. A "JAR" file is an archive containing multiple files, just like a CAB file, except that JAR files are used with non-Microsoft platforms.

When you look at the files, you will notice that there are many groups of three files with very similar names. One has a "J" in the name, another has an "M," and the third has an "N." These are just three different types of archives for three different platforms. The "M" files are for use with Internet Explorer on Microsoft platforms, the "N" types are for Netscape browsers, and the "J" types are pure Java archives for use with other browsers or non-Windows environments.

For example, the security Java components are in a file called "cryptoj." If you look in the installation directory on your client device, you will see three files with the "cryptoj" name: `cryptojJ.jar`, `cryptojM.cab`, and `cryptojN.jar`. The contents of all three J, M, and N type files with the same name are identical, although the "M" type files tend to be about 25% smaller in size. In this case, the contents include Java executable files (class files), properties files, and GIF images for dialog boxes and menus. Also, all of these archives are "signed," which means that a digital signature has been applied by Citrix. This signature allows client devices to open the archives because they trust the creator.

In addition to the J, M, and N type archives, there are three different levels of the ICA client. Each level is a different size and represents different trade-offs. The more functionality an archive provides, the larger the file size and the longer the download time. When bandwidth is crucial, you can choose to use smaller archives that are faster to download but that do not support as many features. Let's look at the three different levels of the Java archives:

- *Full* (~800k). This contains all of the Java ICA client functionality.
- *Lite* (~400k). This includes most of the functionality. It is similar to the full package, except that it does not include Program Neighborhood, client drive mapping, or SpeedScreen latency reduction components.
- *Core* (~360k). The core package contains only the core ICA client

functionality with no options. However, you can combine this with individual options for an a la carte customized package.

If you actually look in the ICA Java client installation directory, you will see thirteen different sets of archives, each with three files, the J, M, and N types. Each of these archives contains files that perform a different function. Figure 10.8 describes each archive's role.

*Figure 10.8 The thirteen Java archives*

| Java Archive | Description |
| --- | --- |
| JICAEng | Complete "full" archive. |
| JICA | Complete "lite" archive. |
| JICA-core | Complete "core" archive. |

The following "a la carte" components can be added to the above archives.

| | |
| --- | --- |
| JICA-audio | Client audio mapping. |
| JICA-cdm | Client device mapping. |
| JICA-clipboard | Client clipboard mapping. |
| JICA-comm | Client COM device mapping. |
| JICA-pn | Program Neighborhood. |
| JICA-printer | Client printing component. |
| JICA-zlc | Zero Latency Windows component. |

The following three components are optional, and are NOT included in any of the main archives, including the "full" archive.

| | |
| --- | --- |
| cryptoj | Encryption component. This is required for SecureICA or SSL. |
| JICA-sica | SecureICA encryption component. |
| ssl | SSL encryption component. |

# Launching ICA Sessions with the Java Client

When you launch the ICA Java client, it doesn't do anything unless it receives parameters that contain information for the launch. For example, one of the many possible parameters is called "address." When you launch the ICA Java client, you can pass a value for this "address" parameter to the ICA client, which contains the address of the MetaFrame XP server that you want to connect to.

In this section, we'll name some of the most popular parameters. Then, we'll see how these parameters are incorporated into a web page to launch the ICA Java client in applet mode. After that, we'll look at how these parameters can be used with ICA Java clients installed on user workstations operating in application mode.

## ICA Java Client Launch Parameters

There are dozens of parameters that you can use when you launch the ICA Java client. We will take a look at the ones that you will most frequently use in the real world. For a complete list of parameters that are available, refer to the ICA Java Client Administrator's Guide, available on the Citrix ICA client download website.

The most popular parameters are as follows:

- *Address*. This is the address of the MetaFrame XP server that you will connect to. It can be an IP address, a NetBIOS name, or a DNS name. It can also be the name of a published application.

- *BrowserProtocol*. This specifies the protocol that will be used to locate the MetaFrame XP server. Valid values are "UDP" or "HTTPonTCP." The UDP protocol requires that a MetaFrame XP server is listening for ICA browser traffic and that UDP 1604 be open from the ICA client to the server. In the MetaFrame XP world, HTTPonTCP should be used.

- *HTTPBrowserAddress*. This is the address of a MetaFrame XP server used when TCP/IP+HTTP or SSL+HTTPS browsing is used. This parameter is only needed when you are connecting to a published application. If you do not specify a parameter for this value, the ICA client will try to connect to the hostname called "ica." If you want to specify more than one address, you can add a number after HTTPBrowserAddress. This number can range from 2 to 15. For example, the second address would be specified as HTTPBrowserAddress2. These 15 addresses are logically broken into three groups of five (primary, first backup, and second backup). These groups of servers behave as outlined in the "Business Recovery" section of this chapter.

- *Username*. This allows you to specify the username that will be used to launch the ICA session.

- *Domain*. This allows you to specify the domain that will be used to launch the ICA session.

- *Password*. This allows you to specify the password that will be used to launch the ICA session. This password will be sent in an unencrypted format and anyone will be able to view this password. If you need to automatically connect users to ICA sessions with a secure password, you will have to use an ICA file or specify an .INI file that contains an encrypted password.

- *InitialProgram*. This is the executable of the initial program that will be launched if you are connecting to a MetaFrame XP server. If you are connecting to a published application, then this value needs to be set to the name of the published application, preceded by a pound sign (#).

- *WorkDirectory*. This is the working directory for the executable specified in the InitialProgram section. If you are connecting to a published application, this value is ignored.

- *ICAPortNumber*. This is the TCP port number that the ICA client will use to connect to the MetaFrame XP server. If no value is specified, then the default port 1494 will be used.

- *UseAlternateAddress*. If this is enabled (value set to "1") then the ICA client will request the alternate (external) address from the MetaFrame XP server. Details of alternate address use and configuration are covered in Chapter 15.

- *SSLEnable*. When this is enabled (value set to "on") the ICA client will use SSL to encrypt the ICA data stream. This requires that the "crypto" and "ssl" Java archives are loaded, and that the MetaFrame XP server is running Feature Release 1 or newer. See Chapter 15 for details about using SSL.

- *EndSessionTimeout*. This specifies the disconnect time in seconds. After no activity, the session will be disconnected. The default value is 300 seconds.

- *Cabinets*. This allows you to specify additional Java cabinets. For example, if you decide to use SecureICA encryption, you would use this parameter to add the "cryptoj" and "JICA-sica" Java cabinets to the client execution.

- *IcaFile*. This parameter allows you to specify an ICA file that is used to establish the connection to your application. This is specified in the form of a URL.

- *Param*. The "param" parameter allows you to pass command-line parameters to the application as it is launched. This often includes options such as a file to open, in the form of `p:\personal\report.doc`.

In addition to these parameters that have been created specifically for use with the Java ICA client, you can create custom parameters based on the values of any standard `appsrv.ini`, `module.ini`, or `wfclient.ini` configuration files. This allows you to pass any possible parameter to the Java ICA client. To pass parameters based on the standard INI files, you need to create parameter names in the following format: `file.section.line`. Let's take a look at the three parts of this parameter format.

- *File*. This first part of the custom parameter specifies the type of .INI file that usually contains the setting that you are specifying in the parameter. For the `appsrv.ini` file, set this section to "user," for the `module.ini` file, set this section to "system," and for the `wfclient.ini`, set this section to "global."

- *Section*. This second part of the parameter specifies the section of the .INI file that you are referencing. The .INI file sections are always enclosed in brackets, for example, `[wfclient]` is a section of the `appsrv.ini` file.

- *Line*. The last third of the parameter represents the line item that you want to specify in the parameter. For example, "`DesiredColor`" is one of the many lines in the `[wfclient]` section of the `appsrv.ini` file.

For example, the `[wfclient]` section of the `appsrv.ini` file has a line called "`DisableCtrlAltDel`." You can set this value to "`on`" to prevent users from being able to send CTRL+ALT+DEL to the server. By default, this line does not have a preconfigured parameter that you can pass to the Java ICA client. However, because this line is part of the three main .INI configuration files, you can build a custom parameter to pass to the Java ICA client. In this case, the custom parameter would be called `user.wfclient.DisableCtrlAtlDel`, and you could set its value to "`on`."

You don't actually need an `appsrv.ini` file on your client device or webserver to build custom parameters from one. In fact, specifying the parameters when the Java ICA client is launched gives you the ability to configure any option that you would have otherwise needed an .INI file for.

### Creating a Web Page to Launch the Java Client
If you decide to use the ICA Java client in applet mode, you will need to create a web page that contains the information needed to launch it. Figure 10.9 shows at a very basic web page that could meet your needs.

*Figure 10.9 A very basic web page for launching the ICA Java client*

```
<html>
<body>
<applet code=com.citrix.JICA.class
codebase=http://yourwebserver/somedirectory
archive=JICA-coreM.cab
width=640 height=480>
<param name=address value=Word>
<param name=BrowserProtocol value=HTTPonTCP>
<param name=HTTPBrowserAddress
value=metaframexpserver.yourcompany.com>
<param name=HTTPBrowserAddress2
value=backupxpserver.yourcompany.com>
<param name=InitialProgram value=#Word>
<param name=EndSessionTimeout value=1800>
<param name=user.wfclient.DisableCtrlAltDel value=On>
</applet>
</body>
</html>
```

Let's take a look at how all of this works. As you can see, this is standard HTML. There are only two tags that we need to focus on, the "applet" tag that launches the Java applet and the "param" tags that pass parameters to the Java applet.

### The <applet> Tag

The applet tag allows you to imbed a chunk of Java code directly into a web page. In this case, that chunk of Java code is the ICA Java client. The applet tag begins with `<applet>` and ends with `</applet>`. The applet tag has several attributes that are included in the initial `<applet>` tag:

- *Code*. This is the name of the class file (Java executable) that starts and runs the applet. On most web servers this name is case sensitive. Figure 10.9 shows this as `com.citrix.JICA.class`. This will launch the ICA client. Alternately, if you want to launch Program Neighborhood, you can specify `com.citrix.pn.class`.

- *Codebase*. This is the path to the directory on the web server for the class file specified in the "code" attribute. The codebase attribute does not name the actual class file, just the path to it. This is usually a URL, and it must be in the same directory or a child directory of the web page.

- *Archive*. This is the name of the Java archive file that contains the

Java executables (class files), including the one specified in the "code" attribute. Notice that in the example web page in Figure 10.9, the "M" version of the archive is specified, meaning that this web page is intended for Internet Explorer users on Microsoft platforms. If visitors to this page will be using Netscape, then you would want the archive attribute to specify the Netscape version of the archive (`archive=JICA-coreN.jar`). This is where you specify the full, lite, or core archives. If you decide to specify `com.citrix.pn.class` in the `code` attribute, be sure that you specify the full client in this `archive` attribute.

- *Width and Height.* This is pretty self-explanatory. Remember that this is the size of the applet window inside the web browser. If you make this value too large, then your users will have scroll bars.

## The <param> Tag

The "param" tag allows you to specify the parameters and values that are passed to the ICA client. Any of the parameters listed in the previous section are valid. Each parameter consists of a "name" and "value" pair. The name indicates which parameter is being specified, and the value indicates the value that will be passed for that parameter. As you can see, each <param> tag can only hold one parameter name/value pair, but there is no limit to the total number of parameter tags that you can have.

In the example in Figure 10.9, the web page is configured to connect to a published application called "Word." Two server names are listed, one as the primary and one as the secondary. When a user establishes a session, the primary server is contacted (via the Citrix XML service). That server will communicate with the zone data collector to send the address of the least busy MetaFrame XP server to the user. See Chapter 4 for more on how load balancing works.

Notice that the "param" item is a separate tag, meaning that it contains its own "<" and ">" wrapper. The param tag is a subtag of the applet tag, and it is located between the opening <applet> and closing </applet> tags.

## Creating Web Pages in the Real World

If you decide to use the ICA Java client in applet mode, and you are not planning on using NFuse, then you will probably have to do some fancy programming. The reason for this is that one unique web page will have to be created for each different option that you would like to use.

For example, if you have users that use both Netscape and Internet Explorer, you would need to create two different web pages, one that specified the "N" version of the Java archive (`archive=JICAEngN.jar`), and one that specified the "M" version of the Java archive (`archive=JICAEngM.cab`).

Additionally, if you wanted different options, multiple web pages would need to be created, one for each set of options; for example, a page that launched sessions at 640x480 resolution with a `width=640 height=480` attribute, and a page that launched sessions at 800x600 resolution with a `width=800 height=600` attribute.

Obviously, this would get very complicated very quickly. An easy way around it is to use server side scripting, such as ASP pages with VB Script. For example, you could create a simple web page that detects the client browser platform, and then inserts the appropriate Java archive, so that Netscape users got the "N" archive, and IE users got the "M" archive.

If you are unfamiliar with server side web scripting, a high-level introduction is provided in the next chapter as NFuse is discussed. Additionally, a fantastic online resource for ASP scripting, help, and sample code is located at www.4guysfromrolla.com.

### Launching the Java Client in Application Mode

If you install the ICA Java client locally onto a client device, you can use the ICA client in "application" mode, which means that the ICA Java client is installed locally on your client device as an application.

Usually, when the ICA Java client is installed locally on a client device, the "full" Java archive is used because you don't need to worry about download times.

After you install the ICA Java client, two launch files are created. The exact names of these files vary depending on the platform, but they are something like "`jicasession.bat`" and "`pnsession.bat`."

`Jicasession.bat` is used to launch ICA sessions, and `pnsession.bat` is used to launch the Java version of Program Neighborhood. In actuality, these files are simple batch files that call the JRE and load certain classes. Let's look at a sample `jicasession.bat`:

```
"C:\Program Files\JavaSoft\JRE\1.1\bin\jre.exe" -cp
"c:\icajava\.;c:\icajava\JICAEngJ.jar;c:\icajava\cryptojJ.
jar;c:\icajava\sslJ.jar" com.citrix.JICA -
CDMPromptAlways:false %1 %2 %3 %4 %5 %6 %7 %8 %9
```

This sample `jicasession.bat` is from a Sun JVM environment, installed onto a 32-bit Windows client device. In your environment, the exact executables and path locations might be different, which is why these launch files are not generated until after the Java ICA client is installed.

All of the code in the launch file is actually one single command line. All it does is to launch the JRE (`jre.exe` in this case), give the location of all the class files (the JARs after the "cp" switch), and specify the Java command to be run (`com.citrix.JICA`).

The `pnsession.bat` file is used to launch the Java Program Neighborhood. It is identical to the `jicasession.bat` file, except that the `pnsession.bat` file calls the PN class file instead of the ICA client class file. This is done by replacing the `com.citrix.JICA` section seen in the `jicasession.bat` file with `com.citrix.pn`.

Both of the launching files accept parameters as command line options. You can specify these options by adding `-parameter:value` to the command line after the batch file. You can add multiple parameters. For example, to launch a Java ICA client connection to a MetaFrame XP server called "server1" with a disconnect timeout of 1800 seconds, use the following command:

```
jicasession.bat -address:server1 -EndSessionTimeout:
1800
```

It's the "`%`" values at the end of these command lines in these batch files that allow you to pass the command line parameters to the ICA client. Unfortunately, due to Windows limitations, you will only be able to pass 9 parameters. Any more will not be picked up. Of course you can get around this by modifying the batch files and adding the parameters there, right after the word "`false`" and before the "`%1`."

## Graphical Command Line

Occasionally, there may be situations in which you want to provide an opportunity for users to manually specify additional parameters. To do this, you can run the `jicasession` launch script with no parameters, or add the `-guicmdline` parameter to the list. This will cause a small graphical box to appear that will allow users to manually type in as many parameters as they want, using the familiar `-parameter:value` syntax. When the user has added all the parameters they need, they can click the "run" button. This graphical command line is especially helpful for troubleshooting purposes and for use with client platforms that do not have command line interfaces (such as Macintosh 9.x and OSX).

## Using Existing INI Configuration Files

One advantage that you have when using the ICA Java client in application mode that you do not have when you use it in applet mode is that with application mode you can configure it to use `appsrv.ini, module.ini,` and `wfclient.ini` files.

This is very convenient if you have other, non-Java ICA clients that are already configured properly and using these .INI files. This way, instead of having to manually build cumbersome command line launching scripts, you can just point your local Java client to the existing .INI files.

You can specify these .INI files for the ICA Java client just like any other parameter for the Java client running in application mode, as a *-parmeter:value* command line option.

*Figure 10.10 INI configuration file parameters for use with the Java client*

| Parameter | Description |
| --- | --- |
| Iniappsrv | Specifies the name and location of the appsrv.ini file. |
| Inimodule | Specifies the name and location of the module.ini file. |
| Iniwfclient | Specifies the name and location of the wfclient.ini file. |
| IniDir | Specifies the directory that contains any INI files not explicitly defined as parameters. |

Let's look at how these .INI parameters are used. Consider this command:

```
pnsession -iniappsrv:c:\somedirectory\appsrv.ini -
inimodule:c:\somedirectory\module.ini
```

This command will specify `appsrv.ini` and `module.ini` files to be used with the Java Program Neighborhood. A Program Neighborhood launched like this will contain all of the connections and information specified in these files.

Additionally, since an `appsrv.ini` can contain many connections, you can launch a single connection from an `appsrv.ini` file that contains many connections. Remember from the 32-bit Windows section of this chapter that a single `appsrv.ini` file can contain multiple connections, each headed with a `[connectionname]` section. To specify a single connection from an existing `appsrv.ini` file, add the connection name before the file, like this:

```
jicasession yourconnection -iniappsrv:
c\somedirectory\appsrv.ini
```

Remember that the only parameter that you must specify is the "address" parameter. However, that address doesn't have to be specified as a command-line option. As in the previous example, the address can be part of an `appsrv.ini` file, or part of an ICA file that is itself passed as a parameter, such as `jicasession -IcaFile:c:\somedirectory\yourapp.ica`.

As you can see, there are several different ways to specify many of the options and parameters that the ICA Java client will use. Let's summarize these options and how they relate to each other in terms of precedence:

1. Any parameter explicitly specified on the command line takes precedence over conflicting parameters set anywhere else. This includes all parameters specified in the `-parameter:value` format, or the `file.section.line:value` format.

2. Next, the options in an ICA file explicitly specified on the command line are applied. These options take precedence over anything below, and includes ICA files specified in the `-IcaFile:c:\directory \yourapp.ica` format.

3. Once all of the command line options have been parsed, the Java client looks to see if any .INI files have been explicitly specified on the command line. If they are, the client uses them. This includes files specified in the `-iniwfclient:c:\directory\wfclient.ini` format.

4. If the Java client still cannot find one or more of the three .INI configuration files, it will look to the `IniDir` parameter of the command line. If the `IniDir` parameter is specified (in the `-IniDir:c:\inifilelocation\` format), the client will search the specified directory for the needed .INI files.

5. If the Java client still cannot find one or more of the three .INI configuration files, it will look for an "`\ini`" directory off of the current working directory. It will look there for the missing .INI files.

6. If the Java client still cannot find one or more of the three .INI configuration files, it will give up and use the server defaults.

## Saving User Settings

One of the nice things about using the ICA Java client in application mode is that it allows you to store user settings in the three .INI files (`appsrv.ini`, `module.ini`, and `wfclient.ini`), just like the regular 32-bit Windows ICA clients.

The exact location where these files will be stored depends on your platform and the parameters that were passed to the Java ICA client when it was launched. Basically, the .INI files will be updated and stored in the location from which they were pulled when the client was launched. The only exception is if the Java client does not have write-access to that directory. In this case, the Java client will attempt to store the modified .INI files in a `\Citrix\` directory in the location specified by the "`user.home`" JVM environment variable. Depending on your JVM vendor and platform, this `user.home` path sometimes maps to a logical home drive. Other times, it maps to the system root or the location where the JRE is located.

In the real world, if you want to save user settings to .INI files, you should manually copy the .INI files to the user's home drive. Then, specify that path when the Java ICA client is launched. Since your users have write-access to their home drives, they will be able to save whatever settings they need.

# ICA Client Auto Update

One of the drawbacks to using MetaFrame XP in large environments is that the Citrix ICA client software must be installed and configured on every single client device that accesses your applications. This can cause problems whenever Citrix releases new versions of their client software, because you will need to find a way to update the software on all of your client devices.

Fortunately, MetaFrame XP supports ICA client auto update, which allows you to keep the ICA client software on your workstations up-to-date automatically. To use this, copy the new ICA clients to a MetaFrame XP server. Then, as users launch ICA sessions, their local ICA client software is updated automatically with the new client software from the server.

### Advantages of Using Client Auto Update

- Easy way to keep client devices up to date.
- Works with many ICA platforms.
- Automatically restores the old client version if update problems occur.
- Automatically detects old clients.
- Clients are updated with no end user intervention.

### Disadvantages of Using Client Auto Update

- "All or nothing" approach.
- Client auto update only updates clients. It cannot be used to install new clients.

## How ICA Client Auto Update Works

In order to use ICA client auto update, configure a database containing all of the ICA client installation files and their associated update settings. Then, whenever a user launches an ICA session on a MetaFrame XP server that has client auto update enabled, the server queries the user's ICA client software to determine its version number and operating system platform.

The MetaFrame XP server then checks the user's ICA client version information against the database of available ICA clients and platforms. If the client version is the same as an entry in the database, the user's logon. However, if the server finds that it has a newer version of the ICA client software, the ICA client auto update process begins.

The exact steps that take place to update the user's ICA client software depend on how you configure the client auto update options in the database. These options include whether the user is notified, whether the update is mandatory, and whether the user is able to continue with their ICA session while the new client software is downloaded in the background.

Once it is determined that new ICA client software should be deployed to the user, the request is forwarded to the client update database. Each MetaFrame XP server can have its own copy of this database, or, multiple servers can share the same database located on a network share, depending on your configuration.

The new ICA client software is downloaded from the client update database over the existing ICA protocol connection. This means that ICA client auto update works over any protocol and any connection type.

Once the download is completed, an updater program is launched that updates the user's old ICA client software to the new client software. Just in case there are any problems with the update, the old ICA client files are retained on the client device in a folder called "\backup" under the root of the ICA client folder.

## Configuring ICA Client Auto Update

Configuring ICA client auto update in your MetaFrame XP environment is fairly straightforward. As we discussed in the previous section, the client update options are configured as part of the client update database itself. There are only a few steps that you need to take to begin using ICA client auto update:

1. Configure the MetaFrame XP server to use a client auto update database.

2. Unpack and prepare your ICA client source installation files for the database.

3. Add the ICA client source installation files to the database.

4. Configure the database options for your ICA client installation.

Let's take a look at each of these steps in depth.

### Step 1. Configure your MetaFrame XP Servers

In order to use ICA client auto update features, you need to have at least one ICA client auto update database in your server farm. All ICA client auto update functionality is configured with the "ICA Client Update Configuration" utility on your MetaFrame XP server (Start | Programs | Citrix | MetaFrame XP | ICA Client Update Configuration). This utility allows you to configure the ICA client database, add new clients to the database, and configure the various client auto update options.

When you installed MetaFrame XP, you were given the option of installing an ICA client auto update database. If you chose to install this option, the client database was installed locally on the server in the %systemroot%\ica \clientdb\ folder.

If you chose not to install the client update database when you installed Meta-Frame XP, or if you want to create a new client update database that is located in a central network location, then you can do that with the ICA Client Update Configuration utility.

If you create a new client update database (Database | New) that you want to use as the default for the current MetaFrame XP server, you need to set the new database as the "default" client update database (Database | Set Default... | Set as Default Database on Local Machine checkbox).

If you have already created a new client update database and you just want to configure the current MetaFrame XP server to use this database instead of its local default client update database, then you can use the ICA Client Update Configuration utility on that server to open the database (Database | Open | Browse to existing client update database) and then set it as the server's default. Using this method, you can configure multiple servers to point to one update database. This is nice in larger environments because you only need to maintain and configure one copy of the database.

If you have a lot of MetaFrame XP servers that you want to point to the same client update database, you can easily configure them by double clicking the domain name and selecting the servers that you want to set, holding down the CTRL key to select multiple servers (Database | Set Default...).

Once you configure your MetaFrame XP servers to point to their respective client update databases (whether they share databases or each use their own), you can begin updating the properties and contents or the databases themselves.

### Step 2. Unpack and Prepare the ICA Client Installation Files
To begin using the ICA client auto update database you need to add ICA client software to that database. Unfortunately, the client update database requires that the ICA client installation files be in their native format. As you recall from previous sections, all of the ICA client installation programs from Citrix come packaged into single file installs. You must first unpack all of the source files from the ICA client package. The exact procedure for doing this was outlined in the previous sections of this chapter.

### Step 3. Add the ICA Client Files to the Database
Once your ICA client source installation files have been unpacked, add them to the client update database. To do this, use the ICA Client Update Configuration utility (Client | New) to browse to the update.ini file in the ICA client's installation files. This .INI file contains the settings and information for that ICA client that is needed for the client update database.

By using this update.ini file, you save time when you add new ICA clients to the client update database, because many of the "New ICA Client" wizard's questions are prepopulated with answers based on information contained in the update.ini file.

Let's look at a sample update.ini file. This sample is from the 32-bit Windows ICA client, version 6.30.1050.

*Figure 10.11 A sample update.ini file*

```
[ICAClient]
ProductID=1
Model=3
Version=6.30.1050
Enabled=yes
ClientDescription=Citrix ICA Win32 Client
UpdateDescription=Citrix ICA Client Version 6.30
IconPath=clientn.ico

[Intel]
UpdateHelper=cudhlpn.dll

[Update.ini]
DoNotUpdate=yes

[appsrv.ini]
DoNotUpdate=yes

[wfcmoven.exe]
UpdateImmediate=yes

[wfica32.exe]
FileExistenceRequired=yes

[migraten.exe]
ExecuteFile=yes
```

As you can see, all of the information and instructions for adding new ICA clients to the client update database are contained in this sample update.ini file. You can add as many different ICA clients to the database as you want. In fact, you can even add multiple copies of the same ICA client for the same platform to a single database. If you do this, you can only have one ICA client for each platform "enabled" at a time (see the next section for a description of this). However, by having multiple instances of the same ICA client in a single client update database, you have the flexibility to quickly enable and disable different ICA clients with different options.

If you ever want to remove an old ICA client from the client update database, you can also do this with the ICA Client Update Configuration utility. (Client | Delete)

## Step 4. Configure the Database Options

Once you have the ICA client installation source files added to the client update database, you need to configure the options that will be used when users' ICA clients are updated. There are two places that you can configure client update options, depending on what you want the options to affect. If you want to configure global options that apply to all clients in the client update database, then you need to configure the options via the Database I Properties menu in the ICA Client Update Configuration utility. If you want to configure options that only apply to one specific ICA client within the database, then you need to highlight that client and choose Client I Properties. In case of conflict, options configured at the individual client level will always take precedence over those default options specified at the global database level.

Let's take a look at the client update options that are available.

### Enabling and Disabling Clients

When editing the properties of the client update database, you can specify whether that database is enabled or disabled. Disabling a database is a simple way to disable ICA client auto update functionality. In the real world, many people disable the entire database after all the users' ICA clients have been updated.

You can also disable individual ICA clients within the database by editing the properties of the client itself. If you have multiple copies of the same client in a single database, you will only be able to have a single copy enabled at a time.

### Client Download Mode

The client download mode options allow you to specify the level of input that a user has when a new ICA client needs to be downloaded.

- *Ask user.* This setting informs the user that a newer ICA client is available and asks them if they would like to download it or if they would like to do it at a later time. This setting is not recommended because many users will always choose the "later" option, causing them to never receive the new ICA client software.

- *Notify User.* The notify user setting informs the user that a newer version of the ICA client software is available and it immediately begins downloading the software from the client update database to the user's client device, whether the user likes it or not.

- *Transparent.* This setting causes the new ICA client software to be downloaded to the user's client device without their knowledge. No indication whatsoever is provided to the user.

### Version Checking

The version checking option allows you to specify the conditions when the new ICA client software will be installed onto the client device.

- *Update older client versions only.* As its name implies, with this setting, the auto update process will only be invoked if the user's ICA client software is older than the version of the software in the client update database. This is the setting that most people use in the real world.

- *Update any client version.* This setting will cause the ICA client software to update any version. This will essentially cause the software to be updated every time the user connects. Normally, this option is used only if you have deployed a new version of the ICA client software that caused trouble and need to force the update client update to install an older version of the ICA software on top of the newer version.

### Update Mode

The update mode options allow you to specify how the ICA client software interacts with the user's current ICA session.

- *Force Disconnection.* When this is enabled, users are required to disconnect and complete the update as soon as the new ICA client download is complete. Otherwise, users have the option of disconnecting, but they are not forced to.

- *Allow background download.* As long as this is enabled, users will be able to use their ICA applications while the new ICA client is downloading. If you uncheck this box, your users will have to sit and do nothing while they wait for the ICA client to download.

In the real world, the "force disconnection option" is only enabled and the allow "background download" is only disabled if there is some kind of problem with the users' current ICA client that requires a new client before the users can continue. These cases are rare, and the default settings can usually be used.

### Log Download Clients

If you choose to log the downloaded ICA clients, an event log item will be created for every client that is updated. This can be annoying, but is a nice feature to have for troubleshooting purposes.

## Logs Errors during Download

This option only logs the errors that occur during ICA client downloads. This log item is enabled by default, and it is a good idea to keep it enabled. It will only fill the event log if you have problems, and if you have enough problems to fill the event log, then you definitely want to know what's going on.

## Maximum Number of Simultaneous Updates

You can specify a maximum number of concurrent client updates that can occur per MetaFrame XP server. Technically, this setting defines the number of concurrent downloads. If this number is reached, new users can log on but they will not receive an updated version of the ICA client.

This is useful in large environments where many users log on at the same time. It prevents your ICA client database network shares from becoming overloaded with users downloading the client.

# Real World Case Study

## Ruppert Scientific

The Ruppert Scientific Company plans to use MetaFrame XP to provide about 1500 users access to a few core scientific applications. They have just completed the design of their server farm, and they are now planning the deployment of the ICA client software to their users.

Of their 1500 users, 1200 run some form of 32-bit Windows operating system. However, as a scientific company, they also have about 200 UNIX workstations (various flavors) and 100 Macintosh users.

Additionally, about 275 of their Windows users are currently accessing one application on a MetaFrame 1.8 server, which means that these users have an older version of the ICA client installed.

About a year ago, an intern attempted to use the Auto Client Update features of MetaFrame 1.8 to update the Citrix ICA client for those users, but was not entirely successful—only 75 users ended up receiving the update.

Figure 10.12 (next page) details Ruppert Scientific's initial user scenario. As you can see by their client environment, the Ruppert Scientific project team had some work to do in determining their ICA client strategy.

*Figure 10.12 The initial client environment at Ruppert Scientific*

| Number of Users | Platform | Current ICA Client |
|---|---|---|
| 625 | Windows NT 4.0 | none |
| 300 | Windows 98 | none |
| 120 | Windows 98 | 4.21 |
| 80 | Windows 2000 | 4.21 |
| 25 | Windows 2000 | 6.0 |
| 50 | Windows NT 4.0 | 6.0 |
| 100 | Mac OS | none |
| 120 | Solaris | none |
| 60 | Irix | none |
| 20 | Linux | none |

There were two important decisions to be made:

- Which version of the ICA client would be used for their new deployment?
- How will the users with current ICA clients be dealt with?

Let's take a look at how the Ruppert Scientific project team addressed each question.

## ICA Client Platforms

The project team first decided to address the ICA client version. Specifically, they wanted to decide whether they should use the native ICA clients for their non-Windows users or the Java client. Ultimately, they decided that the Java client was the way to go. There were two reasons for this:

- The Java client would be used in the same way for all platforms, which means that instead of supporting a Mac client and four different Unix clients, they only had to support a single Java client.
- The Java client had a lot more features than the native Mac and UNIX clients, such as Program Neighborhood.

For the Windows clients, the Ruppert Scientific project team decided that they would use the standard 32-bit Windows Program Neighborhood ICA client.

By choosing these clients, Ruppert Scientific's ICA client environment was very simple, as shown in Figure 10.13.

*Figure 10.13 The new Ruppert Scientific ICA client environment*

| Number of Users | Platform | New ICA Client |
|---|---|---|
| 1200 | 32-bit Windows | Full PN v6.30 |
| 300 | All non-Windows | Java, v6.30 |

## The Windows ICA Client Package

The Ruppert Scientific project team decided to create a silent install for the 32-bit Windows ICA clients. This way, they could deploy the client to the users via their logon scripts.

Creating the silent installation was easy. The project team modified the .SRC files so that each user's ICA client and Program Neighborhood would be preconfigured for the Ruppert Scientific server farm. They also created a "setup.iss" installation script so that the ICA client install would happen without the user's knowledge.

After testing the ICA client installation, the project team felt that it was stable enough to be added to the production logon script. However, in final testing they discovered that it only worked for users that did not have any previous version of the ICA client installed. For users that had previous ICA clients installed, a few problems arose, including:

- The setup.iss script that the project team created only contained answers for the ICA client installation on a "fresh" workstation. The script failed when a previous version of the ICA client was detected, because the installation routine is different.
- Many of the user's with old ICA clients already have .INI configuration files that point to the old MetaFrame 1.8 servers. When the new ICA client was installed, the settings from the old .INI files were automatically migrated to the new ICA client, causing the clients to point to the old servers.

The project team discussed several possible solutions for each problem.

### Problem 1. Install Failed with Previous ICA Clients Loaded

The project team was divided over how to solve this issue. Half of the team wanted to create a second "setup.iss" script, so that there would be one containing settings for new ICA client installs and one containing settings for computers that already had the ICA client installed in which the new silent install was only performing an upgrade.

The other half of the project team wanted to create an uninstall program that ran first to remove the old ICA client. Then, the new ICA client could be installed as if every machine was a fresh one with no previous versions of the ICA client.

As with many computing issues, each method had its advantages and disadvantages. Either way, some kind of detection mechanism would have to run first that determined whether or not an old version of the ICA client was installed. The easiest way to do this was to query the registry for the uninstall registry keys. If these keys exist, then the ICA client was installed. The exact location in the registry varies depending on the version of the ICA client installed, so the project team had to look for several keys.

The 32-bit Windows ICA client InstallShield uninstall registry keys can be found in the following location:

```
HKLM\Software\Microsoft\Windows\CurrentVersion\Uninstall\
Citrix ICA Client
```

The older version of the ICA client InstallShield uninstall registry keys are in this location:

```
HKLM\Software\Microsoft\Windows\CurrentVersion\Uninstall\
WinFrame ClientV1.6
```

If this registry key was found, the project team decided that they would go ahead and execute the uninstall program located in that key, so that the old ICA client would be removed. They decided to do this so that all of the users in their environment would get the exact same version of the new ICA client and so that they didn't have to worry about weird settings in old clients that would be updated to become weird settings in new clients.

Each of the above registry keys contains a value called "UninstallString" which is the full path to an executable that can be used to remove the ICA client. (For example, `C:\WINDOWS\ISUNINST.EXE -fC:\PROGRA~1\Citrix\ICACLI~1\Uninst.isu -cC:\PROGRA~1\Citrix\ICACLI~1\ uninstpn.dll`)

Because Citrix has used InstallShield for years, the command line specified in the data of the UninstallString value can be modified to created a "silent" uninstall be adding a "-y  -a" to the end of the uninstall command line.

Any ICA clients that were installed via the MSI file from Citrix use the registry a bit differently than the InstallShield versions, so the project team decided to query for those keys as well.

MSI files are uninstalled using the Windows Installer executable (msiexec.exe) which is automatically loaded onto any computer that uses the Windows Installer. You need to know the GUID of an MSI package in order to uninstall it via the command line. These GUIDs are stored in the registry in the same location as the InstallShield uninstall information. (HKLM\SOFTWARE\Microsoft\Windows\CurrentVersion\Uninstall\). The GUID for the full ICA client is {DAA13EB6-C53F-4038-9880-C310500B49E9}. You can perform a silent uninstall of the MSI version of the client with the following command:

```
MsiExec.exe /x {DAA13EB6-C53F-4038-9880-C310500B49E9}
/qn
```

Most often, software vendors produce software installation routines with either InstallShield or the Windows Installer. The fact that Citrix offers both is rare. However, it is nice because it gives you several options when installing software. However, it also means that you need to look for both types of clients when performing uninstalls.

### Problem 2. How to Address Old User Settings

Because the new ICA client install does not replace or add new settings to existing settings, the project team had to get rid of the old settings. The easiest way to do this was to search for and delete the old .INI configuration files. They decided to search the user's profile for appsrv.ini and pn.ini, and delete any occurrences that they found.

### Final Client Installation Steps

Once these two problems were addressed, the project team could create the last part of the logon script, which simply launched the silent install of the ICA client.

Figure 10.14 (next page) shows the complete process that Ruppert Scientific's logon script followed. They used this script to successfully deploy the ICA client to their 1500 users.

*Figure 10.14 The final process for the ICA client installation logon script*

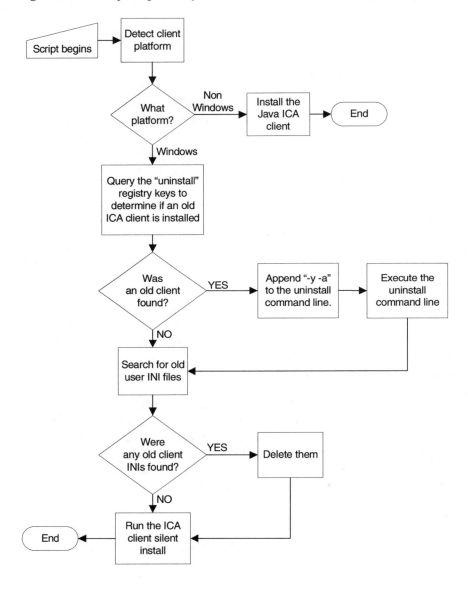

# CHAPTER 11

# Building Web Portals with NFuse Classic 1.7

In this chapter

| | |
|---|---|
| Understanding NFuse Classic | 435 |
| NFuse Web Clients | 466 |
| Using Enterprise Services for NFuse | 472 |
| NFuse 1.5x and 1.6x Considerations | 481 |
| Leveraging NFuse with the PN Agent | 484 |
| What happened to Project Columbia? | 497 |

NFuse Classic is a Citrix server product that allows you to create web application portals for your users to access MetaFrame XP published applications and content. With NFuse Classic, users connect to a website where, after authentication, they are presented with links to their MetaFrame XP applications. In a sense, the user's web browser becomes their "Program Neighborhood," because it contains a custom application list dynamically built for each of them based on their credentials.

When users visit an NFuse Classic web portal, the ICA client software is downloaded to their client device if they do not already have it installed. This allows you to provide true "URL Access" to Windows applications, because the URL of your NFuse Classic portal is all that users need in order to be able to access their MetaFrame applications. NFuse Classic can provide users with seamless access to multiple server farms, including mixtures of MetaFrame 1.8 and MetaFrame XP farms.

Citrix's NFuse Classic software, which is included free with MetaFrame XP (and the newest version is available as a free download), needs to be loaded on to your web server. NFuse Classic works with almost any web server, including Microsoft IIS, iPlanet, and Apache. This software uses your existing MetaFrame XP server farm to provide the application links to your users. In fact, ICA sessions launched from NFuse Classic web portals are identical to sessions launched from regular ICA clients. There is no difference to the look and feel of the applications, and your users do *not* need to run ICA sessions from within their web browsers.

Due to its versatility and ease of use, NFuse Classic has become the de facto standard in MetaFrame XP application deployment. In this chapter, we will look at how NFuse Classic works and how you can use it in your own MetaFrame XP environment.

## NFuse Versions

Within the Citrix product line, "NFuse" is the name of the family of web portal products. Currently, there are two different NFuse products: NFuse Classic and NFuse Elite.

- NFuse Classic is the product available for free that's used exclusively with MetaFrame XP.

- NFuse Elite is a standalone web portal product. (Think of it more like Microsoft SharePoint Portal Server or Plumtree Corporate Portal.)

NFuse Classic is an extension of MetaFrame XP, while NFuse Elite has nothing to do with MetaFrame XP. Technically, you can integrate MetaFrame XP applications into NFuse Elite portals, but this integration process is no different from MetaFrame XP applications being integrated into SharePoint or Plumtree portals.

This book does not cover NFuse Elite (just as it doesn't cover SharePoint or Plumtree). The objective here is to provide you with the knowledge you need to design your MetaFrame XP server farms. Since NFuse Classic is used to extend MetaFrame XP to the web, this chapter covers NFuse Classic.

There are several different versions of NFuse Classic that can be used with MetaFrame XP, ranging from NFuse 1.51 to NFuse Classic 1.7. NFuse 1.51 is the version included with the MetaFrame XP CD set. NFuse Classic 1.7 is a newer version with many updated features. It's available for download from www.citrix.com at no cost.

NFuse Classic 1.7 is required if you want to use the advanced features of MetaFrame XP servers introduced in Feature Release 2. However, NFuse Classic 1.7 works fine with MetaFrame XP servers that are running any Feature Release and any Service Pack (including the base product out of the box).

In reality, all versions of NFuse Classic from 1.51 through 1.7 are similar and work in basically the same manner. This chapter focuses solely on the newer version of NFuse, NFuse Classic 1.7. Because NFuse Classic 1.7 is available for free and it works with all versions of MetaFrame XP (and MetaFrame 1.8 with Service Pack 2), there is really no reason that any new NFuse deployments shouldn't be done with NFuse Classic 1.7.

### Advantages of Focusing on NFuse Classic 1.7 Instead of NFuse 1.51

- It's a free upgrade from NFuse 1.51.
- It works with all versions of MetaFrame XP.
- It's easier to configure than NFuse 1.51.
- It has more native features than NFuse 1.51.
- If you want your NFuse portal to use the new features of Feature Release 2, you must use NFuse Classic 1.7.

Of course, by choosing to focus on NFuse 1.7, we may leave those that have existing NFuse 1.51 deployments in the dark.

### Disadvantages of Focusing on NFuse 1.7 Instead of NFuse 1.51.

* You can only load one instance of NFuse 1.7 per web server.

If you currently have an NFuse 1.5x or NFuse 1.6x environment, there is a section towards the end of the chapter that covers what you need to know about NFuse 1.7 when you upgrade from older versions of NFuse. The good news is that if you are just using the basic features of NFuse 1.5x or 1.6x, you can upgrade to NFuse 1.7 without any problems. However, if you have a highly-customized NFuse 1.5x environment, you will probably need to rewrite some code to use NFuse 1.7. If you fall into this category, read this chapter to learn about the new features of NFuse 1.7 and decide for yourself if it's worth your time to upgrade (remembering that once you go to Feature Release 1 or 2, you will be forced to upgrade). Either way, many of the concepts covered here will apply to NFuse no matter if you are using NFuse 1.5x, 1.6x, 1.7.

Throughout the rest of this chapter, the term "NFuse" will refer to "NFuse Classic 1.7."

## Why use NFuse?

Before we get too far into this chapter, it's probably worth our time to take a look at the advantages and disadvantages of using NFuse. These advantages and disadvantages will become clear after you finish reading this chapter, but let's glance at them now.

### Advantages of Using NFuse

* All users can access all of their MetaFrame XP applications via one URL.

* You do not need to visit users to make configuration changes because application lists are dynamic and they reflect changes to users' configured applications the next time the user visits the NFuse web page.

* There is no need to manually install ICA client software or worry about client auto update.

### Disadvantages of Using NFuse

* There are some client devices (particularly older thin clients) that do not work with NFuse.

* You need a web server (although this could be one of your MetaFrame XP servers).

# Understanding NFuse Classic

In order to illustrate how NFuse works, lets deal separately with two crucial topics: the components that make up NFuse; and a descriptions of how these components work together, providing the NFuse experience.

## NFuse Components

There are three primary components that exist in a MetaFrame XP NFuse-enabled environment:

- NFuse web server.
- MetaFrame XP server farm.
- Client devices.

### NFuse Component 1.  Web Server

The web server is the primary interface for users in NFuse environments. After all, the whole purpose of NFuse is to allow users to access their applications through the web, and this is done with the web server. NFuse works with just about any web server. Throughout this chapter, we'll refer to an "NFuse web server." An NFuse web server is a regular web server with the following three NFuse web server pieces installed:

- *NFuse Java Objects*. These are the actual web server executable files that interact with the MetaFrame XP servers. These Java Objects are what enable the web server to provide lists of applications and authenticate users. You can think of the NFuse Java Objects as the "NFuse executable code."

- *NFuse Web Pages*. NFuse installs web pages that the users access to connect to MetaFrame XP applications. These web pages serve many purposes, including accepting user credentials, showing lists of ICA applications, logging users out, detecting whether ICA clients are installed, and providing help to users. These web pages are just like any other web pages on any other web server. The content of these pages allows them to interact with the NFuse Java Objects.

- *ICA Client Installation Source Files*. NFuse 1.7 can detect whether a user's client device has the Citrix ICA client software installed. If no ICA client is installed, the web pages will detect which platform the client device is and direct the user to a page from which the ICA client software can be downloaded and installed. In order for users to be able to download and install ICA client software from the NFuse web server, all of the source files for the different ICA client platforms must be copied to the web server to be available for download.

### NFuse Component 2. MetaFrame XP Server Farm

The NFuse web server obtains the list of published applications and content for users via a connection to a MetaFrame XP server farm. A MetaFrame XP server farm connected to an NFuse web server is identical to any other MetaFrame XP server farm. NFuse does not require that you make any customizations or modifications to the farm. In fact, MetaFrame XP server farms can be simultaneously accessed by users through NFuse and through traditional clients.

The NFuse web server communicates with a MetaFrame XP server farm in the same way that any client device communicates with a server farm—it uses the Citrix XML service. After a user connects to the NFuse web server, the NFuse web server contacts a MetaFrame XP server in order to authenticate the user and get the list of published applications for the user. The MetaFrame XP server uses its own Citrix XML service to send the application list back to the NFuse server.

If you're familiar with MetaFrame 1.8, you can think of the Citrix XML Service as nothing more than the ICA browser that uses the HTTP protocol to transfer information instead of UDP broadcasts. The Citrix XML service is installed by default with MetaFrame XP (or with Service Pack 2 for MetaFrame 1.8).

The MetaFrame XP servers play another role in NFuse environments. They host the users' ICA sessions after a user launches one via an NFuse web page. When a user clicks a link to launch an application via an NFuse web page, the user's session starts on a MetaFrame XP server, just like any other session. In fact, there is no difference in a user's session whether they launch it from NFuse or from a regular Citrix ICA client.

### NFuse Component 3. Client Devices

The last major NFuse component is the client device. An NFuse client is composed of two parts: a web browser and the Citrix ICA client software. The web browser allows users to view the NFuse web pages, and the Citrix ICA client software allows users to run MetaFrame XP sessions. Just about any client device that can run a browser and ICA client software can access applications via an NFuse web portal.

## *Where to go for More Information on These NFuse Components*

As you've just learned, there are three important components that make up an NFuse environment: the NFuse web server, the MetaFrame XP server farm, and client devices. Further, the NFuse web server has three of its own components: the NFuse Java Objects, NFuse web pages, and ICA client source files. These components are addressed in other places in this book, as follows:

- NFuse Web Server (covered in this chapter)

  - *NFuse Java Objects* ("NFuse Web Server Configuration" section of this chapter)
  - *Web Pages* ("Working with NFuse Web Pages" section of this chapter)
  - *ICA Client Source Files* ("NFuse Web Clients" section of this chapter)

- MetaFrame XP Server Farm (Chapters 2 and 3 of this book)

- Client Devices, web browser and ICA client (Chapters 9 and 10 of this book)

## How NFuse Classic Works

Let's look now to how all of the components of an NFuse environment work together.

Figure 11.1 (next page) shows the NFuse components and the processes that take place in NFuse environments. Each circled number corresponds to a step in the description following the diagram. Read through the steps while referring to the diagram. Then, we'll analyze each of the fourteen steps.

*Figure 11.1  How NFuse works*

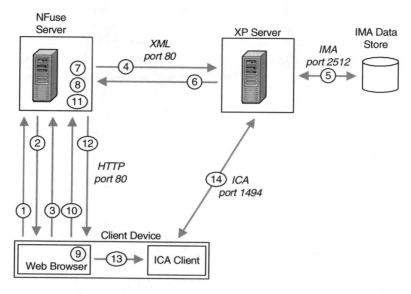

1. A user with a web browser and an ICA client requests the NFuse portal web page by typing in a URL.

2. The web server sends down the HTML login page via the HTTP protocol.

3. The web user enters credentials and sends them back to the web server.

4. The web server forwards the user's information to a MetaFrame XP server running the Citrix XML service.

5. The MetaFrame XP server validates the credentials and retrieves the user's list of applications for the server farm.

6. The MetaFrame XP server sends the application list to the NFuse web server.

7. The NFuse web server builds a web page containing all of the user's application icons.

8. Each icon is hyperlinked with its application properties.

9. The user selects an application to run by clicking on an icon in the web browser.

10. The web browser sends a request to the web server for the link that the user selected.

11. The NFuse Java Objects on the web server retrieve an ICA file

template. That template is modified with the application's and user's specific information. This creates a custom ICA file for the user.

12. The custom-built ICA file is sent to web browser on the client device.

13. The web browser receives the ICA file and passes it to the ICA client software loaded on the ICA client device.

14. The user's local ICA client starts the MetaFrame XP session with the information contained in the custom ICA file.

Now that you've seen the overview of the steps, let's examine each step more closely. For each, we'll look at what happens and why.

1. A user with a web browser and an ICA client requests the NFuse portal web page by typing in a URL.

2. The web server receives the user's request and sends down the web page that allows the user to login to NFuse. This web page contains text fields that allow the user to enter her credentials. It is sent to the user via the HTTP protocol, just like any standard web page.

3. The user enters her credentials and clicks the "submit" button. This action sends the credentials back to the web server. When this happens, scripting code in the web page creates a cookie that holds the user's credentials. This cookie is stored on the client device and it allows other web pages to request information about the current user. The password field is encrypted. Details of this encryption can be found in the "Security" chapter of this book, Chapter 15.

4. The NFuse web server forwards the user's credentials to a MetaFrame XP server running the Citrix XML service. The web server can be on the same physical server as the MetaFrame XP server. In this case, the NFuse web server would forward the users credentials to itself. The actual server and port that the NFuse web server contacts is specified in the NFuse.conf file (detailed later in this chapter).

5. The MetaFrame XP server validates the credentials and retrieves the user's list of applications for the server farm. The user's credentials are validated via the IMA service. A list of published applications and content is then provided based on the user's credentials. This list is created in the exact same way that it would be created if the user didn't use NFuse, as if they were getting a list of applications through Program Neighborhood with their regular ICA client software. If the user's credentials are not valid, the

MetaFrame XP server notifies the NFuse server which delivers the "logon failed" message to the user.

6. The MetaFrame XP server sends the application list to the NFuse web server. The NFuse Java Objects on the NFuse web server receive this list of applications.

7. The NFuse web server builds a web page containing all of the user's application icons. That web page is sent down to the user's web browser.

8. Each application icon is hyperlinked with its application properties. Each hyperlink points to a `launch.asp` file (or `launch.jsp`, depending on the web server platform).

9. The user selects an application to run by clicking on an icon in the web browser.

10. The web browser sends a request to the web server for the link that the user selected. The link contains information about which application the user clicked on.

11. The link is to the `launch.asp` file which performs several actions. It contains code that causes the NFuse Java Objects on the web server to retrieve a generic ICA file template. This ICA file template is like a regular ICA file, except that not all of the information it in is complete. Some important information (like the username or application name) contains dummy "placeholder" information. The NFuse Java Objects scan through the ICA file and replace any of the dummy information with the real information of the current user and application. This has the effect of creating a custom ICA file just for that user.

12. The custom-built ICA file is sent to web browser on the client device.

13. The web browser receives the ICA file and passes it to the ICA client software loaded on the ICA client device. This transfer of the ICA file (from the web browser to the ICA client software) is completely transparent to the end user. It's similar to when you click on a file with a .DOC extension from your web browser, and your computer automatically opens it with Word.

14. The user's local ICA client starts the MetaFrame XP session with the information contained in the custom ICA file. From this point on, the user has a regular ICA session established with the MetaFrame XP server. The web browser and the NFuse web server are totally out of the picture at this point. In fact, the NFuse web server could burst into flames and the user would never know it.

# NFuse Web Server Configuration

Now that you understand how NFuse works, we can start looking at how we make it do want you want.

## The NFuse Configuration Process

Since the NFuse Java Objects are the main executable components of an NFuse web server, you actually change the properties of an NFuse web server by changing the properties of the NFuse Java Objects themselves. There are two different methods that can be used to configure those Java Objects:

- Modify a text configuration (NFuse.conf) that contains NFuse settings.
- Use a set of administrative web pages to graphically and interactively make certain changes.

Let's take a detailed look at these two configuration options.

### Understanding the NFuse.conf File

When you install NFuse onto an IIS web server, all of the Java Objects and their related configuration and properties files are installed into the %programfiles%\Citrix\NFuse\ folder. When you install NFuse on an iPlanet or Apache web server, you must specify the location where you want the various components to be installed.

The NFuse Java Objects store all of their configuration information in a file called NFuse.conf, (located by default in the %programfiles%\Citrix \NFuse\conf\ folder on IIS web servers). You can directly edit this file with any text editor in order to make changes to NFuse. After you make changes to this file, you need to stop and start the web server service for the changes to take effect. (Using the iisreset command is an easy way to do this on IIS platforms.)

The NFuse.conf file controls all of the settings and behaviors of an NFuse web server, but the way the settings are used differs depending on the type of setting:

- Some of the settings affect the NFuse Java Objects directly (and therefore the NFuse server behavior). The NFuse Java Objects read the values of these settings from the NFuse.conf file when the web server is started. These settings are detailed in the "Configuring the NFuse Java Objects" section of this chapter.

- Some of the settings affect the NFuse web pages. Many NFuse web pages are built dynamically at run time by referring to settings in the NFuse.conf file. This allows the NFuse.conf file to control those web page options or behaviors. These settings are detailed in the "Configuring Default Web Page Options" of this chapter.

By having both types of settings controllable via the same NFuse.conf file, Citrix ensured that NFuse web sites could be language independent, since web pages written in any language can access the same settings in the NFuse.conf file.

The easiest way to understand an NFuse.conf file is to see an example of one from the real world. We'll take a look at an entire file right now. Then we'll focus on the specific configuration items that you'll actually be concerned with as a MetaFrame XP administrator.

*Figure 11.2  A sample NFuse.conf file*

```
UnrestrictedSessionFields=NFuse_CurrentFolder,NFuse_App...
SessionField.NFuse_ContentType=text/html
SessionFieldLocations=PNAgent,Script,Template,Url,Post...
Timeout=60
Version=1.7
SessionField.NFuse_CitrixServer=citrixserver1
SessionField.NFuse_CitrixServerPort=80
AlternateAddress=Off
SessionField.NFuse_IconCache=/NFuseIcons/
#SessionField.NFuse_RelayServerPort=[TCP port pf SSL
Relay]
SessionField.NFuse_IconCache=/Citrix/NFuse17/
NFuseIcons/
SessionField.NFuse_TemplatesDir=C:\\Program
Files\\Citrix\\NFuse
URLMapping./=C:\\Inetpub\\wwwroot
HttpOutputEncoding=8859_1
TemplateFileEncoding=8859_1
CacheExpireTime=3600
SessionField.NFuse_TicketTimeToLive=200
#SessionField.NFuse_Transport=HTTP
SslKeystore=C:\\Program Files\\Common
Files\\Citrix\\keystore\\cacerts\\
DTDDirectory=C:\\Program Files\\Citrix\\NFuse\\
```

```
AllowCustomizeWinSize=On
AllowCustomizeWinColor=Off
AllowCustomizeAudio=Off
AllowCustomizeSettings=On
AddressResolutionType=IPv4-port
OtherClient=default
#OverrideClientInstallCaption=[Place your text here]
Win32Client=default
Win16Client=default
SolarisUnixClient=default
MacClient=default
SgiUnixClient=default
HpUxUnixClient=default
IbmAixClient=default
ScoUnixClient=default
Tru64Client=default
LinuxClient=default
LoginType=default
#ForceLoginDomain=[Place your domain here]
#NDSTreeName=[For NDS logins place NDS Tree name here,
and also change LoginType to NDS]
#SearchContextList=[NDS context1, NDS context2, ...]
StaticStringTextFile=C:\\Program
Files\\Citrix\\NFuse\\nfuse.txt
StaticStringTextFileEncoding=8859_1
AuthenticationMethods=Explicit
#ClientAddressMap=[clientAddress,AddressType...]
#ServerAddressMap=[normalAddress,translatedAddress...]
#SOCKSProxy=[clientAddress,proxyAddress...]
BypassFailedServerDuration=60
EnableServerLoadBalancing=On
EnableSTALoadBalancing=On
AllowUserPasswordChange=Never
AutoDeployWebClient=Off
#WebClientVersion=6,30,1000
ShowClientInstallCaption=Auto
RequestPassThru=Auto
RequestICAClientSecureChannel=Detect-AnyCiphers
SmartCardToMF=Auto
EmbedApplications=Off
#EmbedMethod=Auto
AllowCustomizeEmbedApplications=Off
#JavaClientPackages=COMPortMapping,Thinwire1,PrinterMapping,SSL
#AllowCustomizeJavaClientPackages=Off
IgnoreClientProvidedClientAddress=Off
```

Let's state some more facts about this NFuse.conf file. First of all, remember that in order for any changes to take affect, you will need to stop and start the web server service. Secondly, recall that this single file affects all of the NFuse web sites that you have on one web server. However, as we'll see later, it's possible to override the settings in this file on a page-by-page basis.

You will notice that some lines in the NFuse.conf file begin with a pound sign (#). This sign is the "comment" sign and lines that begin with it are ignored. If you change the contents of a line that starts with #, you need to remove the # for the changes to take affect.

Also, in the NFuse.conf file, the double backslash (\\) is the escape character that represents the "\" in a file path. So, for the path c:\winnt\brian, you would need to specify it as c:\\winnt\\brian.

As you can see, there are many configuration parameters included in this file. The "NFuse Classic Administrator's Guide" (NFuse_Guide.pdf included with the NFuse 1.7 download) provides a fantastic reference for details of all the options. However, as a real world NFuse administrator, only a subset of these fields will actually matter to you. Those are the fields that we will discuss here.

### Using the NFuse Administrative Web Pages

If your NFuse web server is running on Internet Information Services on Windows 2000, there are graphical administration web pages that you can use to view and change the behavior of many of the basic NFuse options. These administrative web pages are essentially a graphical "front end" to the NFuse.conf configuration file. However, if your web server is not IIS 5.0 or newer, or if you want to make any advanced configuration changes, you'll need to edit the NFuse.conf file directly.

When you connect to the NFuse Administration web pages (at http://yourNFuseserver/Citrix/NFuseAdmin), you are presented with a pretty cool diagram that illustrates the different components of NFuse. You can click on different parts of the diagram to bring up a web page containing NFuse settings that affect that part. Each configuration page pulls its information from the NFuse.conf file.

There is a "Save" and a "Discard Changes" button on every configuration web page. After you enter the settings that you want, clicking the "Save" button writes those changes to the NFuse.conf file. However, it's important to remember that the NFuse Java Objects only read the settings from the NFuse.conf file when they are initially loaded. Therefore, in order to apply any changes that you make with the administrative web pages, you need to go into the "Apply changes" section of the administrative web site and click the "Apply changes" button after saving the changes. This button resets the NFuse Java Objects, causing them to reload the NFuse.conf file.

You don't really need to know much more about the NFuse administrative web pages. Throughout this chapter, as we describe specific options of the NFuse.conf file, we'll make a note if that particular option can be configured via the administrative web pages. This note will be in the form of (NFuse Admin Web Pages | ...)

## Configuring the NFuse Java Objects

The NFuse.conf file controls the properties of the NFuse Java Objects. These properties can be broken down into three broad categories:

- Properties that affect how the NFuse web server communicates with MetaFrame XP servers (via the Citrix XML service).
- Properties that affect how the NFuse web server formats the address of the MetaFrame XP server that it sends to the clients.
- Properties that affect the security of the NFuse web server.

We'll take a look at the first two types of properties next. We won't cover the NFuse security properties until we get to the security chapter, Chapter 15. After all, it does no good to secure NFuse until the rest of your system is secure.

### The NFuse Communication with the XML Service

Remember from the explanation of how NFuse works that NFuse is able to function because it communicates with MetaFrame XP servers. This communication is conducted via the Citrix XML service running on one or more MetaFrame servers.

The following lines of the NFuse.conf file affect the NFuse server's communication with the Citrix XML service:

```
SessionField.NFuse_CitrixServer=citrixserver1
EnableServerLoadBalancing=on
Timeout=60
RetryCount=5
BypassFailedServerDuration=60
SessionField.NFuse_CitrixServerPort=80
```

Notice that these lines are not in the same order as in the production NFuse.conf file listed in Figure 11.2. They are listed here together as a matter of convenience. However, you can generally put options in the NFuse.conf file in any order you like. In case of conflict, the last line wins.

### SessionField.NFuse_CitrixServer

(NFuse Admin Web Pages | MetaFrame Servers | Server list | Server addresses)

This line specifies the MetaFrame XP server (running the Citrix XML service) that NFuse will contact for all application information. This can be an IP address, a NetBIOS computer name, or fully qualified domain name. By default, the NFuse server will be configured to attempt to contact one server (the server that you specified during the initial NFuse setup):

```
SessionField.NFuse_CitrixServer=server1
```

An NFuse web server gets all of its information from the Citrix XML service running on a MetaFrame XP server in a server farm. If the one server that NFuse contacts goes down, then NFuse will not be able retrieve any user application information, even if all of the other MetaFrame XP servers in the farm are operational. For redundancy purposes, you can specify more than one server on this line with each server separated by commas:

```
SessionField.NFuse_CitrixServer=server1,server2,server3
```

The exact method of redundancy used depends on the setting in the EnableServerLoadBalancing line.

### EnableServerLoadBalancing

(NFuse Admin Web Pages | MetaFrame Servers | Server list | Use the server list for load balancing)

When this line is set to "On," the NFuse web server will use a "round robin" load balancing scheme to contact each server, selecting a different server from the SessionField.NFuse_CitrixServer line each time information is needed from a MetaFrame XP server.

If you set this line to "off," then NFuse will always contact the first server listed on the SessionField.NFuse_CitrixServer line. If this server ever fails, it will move on to the next one and so on.

## Timeout

After the NFuse web server opens a connection to a MetaFrame XP server via the Citrix XML service, this line specifies how long it will wait for a response before the server is deemed "unresponsive."

## RetryCount

This line specifies how many times the NFuse server must contact an unresponsive MetaFrame XP server from the `SessionField.NFuse_CitrixServer` list before the NFuse server decides that the MetaFrame XP server has failed.

## BypassFailedServerDuration

(NFuse Admin Web Pages | MetaFrame Servers | Server list | Bypass any failed server for __ minutes)

This item specifies the length of time (in minutes) that NFuse will not try to communicate with a MetaFrame XP server that has failed the number of times specified in the `RetryCount`. After this duration has passed, the server is added back to the list. This property applies whether `EnableServerLoadBalancing` is "on" or "off."

## SessionField.NFuse_CitrixServerPort

(NFuse Admin Web Pages | MetaFrame Servers | Settings for all servers | XML service port)

This is the TCP port that the Citrix XML service is running on the MetaFrame XP server specified on the previous item. If you have more than one MetaFrame XP server listed on the `SessionField.NFuse_CitrixServer` line, the XML service must be running on the same port on all the servers. By default, the Citrix XML service runs on port 80.

## *The NFuse Java Objects' Communication with the ICA Client*

The `NFuse.conf` file also specifies the format of the MetaFrame XP server address that NFuse sends to the ICA client. This address format is controlled by the following line:

```
AddressResolutionType=IPv4-port
```
This allows you to specify the type of address that will be returned for the MetaFrame XP server in the ICA file that is sent to the client device. Valid options for the address include `ipv4`, `ipv4-port`, `dns`, and `dns-port`. Rather than explaining the different options, let's take a look at examples of each of the different types:

```
ipv4: 128.242.82.212
```

```
ipv4-port: 128.242.82.212:1494
dns: citrix.brianmadden.com
dns-port: citrix.brianmadden.com:1494
```

If you change the port that ICA uses (1494 by default), then you will need to use one of the two options that specifies the port in addition to the address. It is recommended that you use one of the port options regardless, just in case any of your users fouled up the configuration of their ICA clients by setting it to a different port. If you specify the port here, it will override a user's client setting.

If you plan to use one of the DNS-based options (which is required for SSL), you will need to have Feature Release 1 or 2 installed on the MetaFrame XP server running the Citrix XML service that the NFuse server communicates with.

# Working with NFuse Web Pages

Now that you understand how NFuse works and how it can be configured, we can take a look at the web pages that NFuse uses. When you install NFuse 1.7 on your web server, the default NFuse web site is installed in the \Citrix\NFuse17 folder under the web root. The installation program asks if you want to change the default page to the NFuse page. If you choose to do this, then you can access NFuse directly via your web server's address. If not, then you can access NFuse via http://yourwebserver/Citrix/NFuse17. Similar to most web pages, the default NFuse web pages work no matter how you access the web server, whether by NetBIOS name, DNS name, or IP address.

In order to learn how to work with these NFuse web pages, we'll look at the following items:

- Setting web page options
- Where is the Citrix Web Site Wizard?
- Understanding the default NFuse web site.
- Modifying the default NFuse web site.
- Creating NFuse web sites from scratch.

# Configuring Default Web Page Options

The same `NFuse.conf` file and administrative web pages that you used earlier to configure the settings of the NFuse Java Objects are also used to configure the behavior of the NFuse web pages. You can probably customize the pages as much as you need without ever having to edit any web page source code.

Let's take a look at the specific lines in the `NFuse.conf` file that can be used to customize the look and feel of the web pages. These lines can be split into two categories:

- Fields that specify the login and authentication options.
- Fields that specify which application options the users see.

Again, remember that if you make any changes to any of these fields, you will have to stop and start your web server service.

## Specifying Login and Authentication Options

There are five fields in particular that affect the login options presented to users via NFuse 1.7 web pages. To prevent yourself from having to flip backwards through this book, let's list those specific lines again here:

```
AuthenticationMethods=Explicit
#ForceLoginDomain=[Place your domain here]
LoginType=default
#NDSTreeName=[For NDS logins place NDS Tree name here,
and also change LoginType to NDS]
#SearchContextList=[NDS context1, NDS context2, ...]
```

**AuthenticationMethods**
(NFuse Admin Web Pages | Authentication | Methods)

This specifies the manner of user authentication that your NFuse web server will support. There are several options, and you can support multiple options by adding multiple entries to the line, separated by commas.

A value of "Explicit" means that users must log in to the NFuse portal with their own usernames and passwords.

A value of "Guest" will cause a radio button to appear on the login page allowing users to choose "guest" access (or the standard "explicit" access). If guest access is chosen, web visitors do not have to enter any user credentials. When they click the "login" button, they are presented with a page containing links to all anonymous applications in the server farm. If "Guest" is listed without the "Explicit" option on this line, no login fields are displayed. Users that connect to the website are forwarded directly to the application list page which shows anonymous applications. In this case the logout feature is also disabled.

A value of "Integrated" enables pass-through authentication. When users access NFuse, the credentials that they used to logon to their local workstations are used, and the user is forward directly to their list of applications. This only works if users' client devices are Windows 2000 or Windows XP.

Usually, this option is used in combination with the "Explicit" option. Then, if pass-through authentication works, users have direct access to their applications. If pass-through authentication does not work, they are still given a chance to login manually.

You can also specify a value of "Certificate" on this line. This is the setting that you need to use if your users authenticate with smart cards. See Chapter 15 for the details of smart card authentication.

### ForceLoginDomain
(NFuse Admin Web Pages | Authentication | Explicitly login | Use NT authentication | with force login domain)

If all of your users will be logging in from the same Windows domain, you can add the domain name to this field after removing the leading "#." When you do this, the domain box won't appear on the login page.

If you are using NDS authentication, you can force users to type in their full user principal name by leaving this item blank, after removing the leading "#."

### LoginType
(NFuse Admin Web Pages | Authentication | Explicitly login)

A "default" setting means that users will be authenticating to a Microsoft domain or server. You can change this field to "NDS" if your users will be authenticating to an NDS tree. If you use this setting, you need to specify an NDS tree (see the next item). NDS authentication requires Feature Release 1 or 2 on the MetaFrame XP servers that the users will log in to. (See Chapter 8 for details about NDS integration.)

**NDSTreeName**
(NFuse Admin Web Pages | Authentication | Explicitly login | Use NDS authentication | with tree name)

Use this line to specify the NDS tree that your users will be using to log in. Remember to remove the leading #, and to set the "LoginType" to "NDS."

**SearchContextList**
(NFuse Admin Web Pages | Authentication | Explicitly login | Use NDS authentication | with search context list)

If you're using NDS authentication, you can add a comma-separated list of contexts to be searched by NDS users when they login. This can speed up your login time if all users are coming from just a few contexts, because the entire NDS tree will not have to be searched. If you specify this option, then only the specified contexts are searched, and if the user is not found there then his login will fail. If you leave this field blank or if you leave it commented out (#), then all of the contexts in the tree will be searched until the user's object is found.

### Specifying what Options the Users can Change

You can use the NFuse.conf file to configure which options your users will see when they login to NFuse. Specifically, you can prevent them from being able to override certain default settings that you specify. Any settings that users make are saved locally to their client devices as cookies, unless a user has connected as a guest.

There are seven fields that affect the options that users can change via the web pages. All seven of these fields can be set to "On" or "Off." A value of "On" means that users can change the default application settings via a special NFuse web page, accessible via the little toolbox icon on the main application list page. A value of "Off" means that the setting is not displayed and the published application's default setting as configured in the CMC is used. The seven options fields are as follows:

```
AllowCustomizeWinSize=On
AllowCustomizeWinColor=Off
AllowCustomizeAudio=Off
AllowCustomizeSettings=On
AllowCustomizeEmbedApplications=off
EmbedApplications=Off
AllowUserPasswordChange=never
```

### AllowCustomizeWinSize
(NFuse Admin Web Pages I ICA Customization I Window size)

This allows the users to change the default resolution of published applications.

### AllowCustomizeWinColor
(NFuse Admin Web Pages I ICA Customization I Window color)

This allows the users to change the default color depth of published applications.

### AllowCustomizeAudio
(NFuse Admin Web Pages I ICA Customization I Audio quality)

This allows the users to change the default audio quality of published applications.

### AllowCustomizeSettings
If this is set to "On," users are able to set the "Remember folder location," "Show current folder location," and "Application detail display options" settings.

### AllowCustomizeEmbedApplications
If this is set to "Off," users cannot change the options for how their applications are launched. Whatever options you configure via the `EmbedApplications` and `EmbedMethod` lines are used.

If you set this line to "On," your users will be able to override your default `EmbedApplications` and `EmbedMethod` settings.

### EmbedApplications
This line allows you to specify how users' applications are launched. A value of "off" (which is what most people choose in the real world) means that applications are launched in separate windows. A value of "On" causes applications to be launched within the confines of a browser window.

The `EmbedMethod` line controls how the ICA client is used with embedded applications. There are many considerations to think about with the ICA client, so this line is discussed again in the "NFuse Web Clients" section of this chapter.

**AllowUserPasswordChange**
(NFuse Admin Web Pages | Authentication | Methods | Allow user to change password)

When set to "always," a little keychain icon is displayed on the main NFuse applications page. Clicking this pops up a web page where users can change their Windows domain password. In order to use this feature, the Citrix XML service that NFuse communicates with must be running on a MetaFrame XP server with at least Feature Release 2.

A value of "never" disables this functionality via NFuse.

You can also set this to "expired-only." Then, when a user logs into NFuse with an expired password, they are automatically forwarded to the password change webpage.

Code running on the Citrix XML service server performs the actual password change. Therefore, you can still use this functionality if your NFuse server is in a different domain than your Citrix XML server. In fact, it even works if your NFuse server is not in any domain.

## How the NFuse.conf File Affects Web Pages

Many people wonder how the NFuse.conf file has the ability to affect the options that are available in NFuse web pages, because the NFuse web pages stay the same regardless of the settings of the NFuse.conf file. When the web server service is started, the NFuse Java Objects read the values of all the fields from the NFuse.conf file into memory. This is why you must stop and start the web server service after you make a change to the NFuse.conf file, because that file is only read once when the service is started.

When a web user requests a web page from the web server, the scripts in the web page check the NFuse Java Objects to find the values of the parameters they need to use. For example, the script code contained in the login page might look something like this (from a logical perspective):

```
If the LoginType in the NFuse.conf is "default," then
I will draw username, password, and domain boxes.
If the LoginType in the NFuse.conf is "NDS," then I
will draw username, password, context, and tree boxes.
```

As you can see, the people that wrote the NFuse web pages put in the necessary logic to check the values of the NFuse Java Objects (read from the NFuse.conf file) to see what custom options it should use as each web page is being constructed. In actuality, the fact that the NFuse.conf file can be used to affect web pages is a feature of the web pages themselves, not NFuse. This causes the NFuse web pages to be more complex (and to be harder to write), but it makes it easier for you to configure them.

## Where is the Citrix Web Site Wizard?

If you have used any versions of NFuse prior to NFuse 1.6, you probably used the Citrix Web Site Wizard to create your web pages. The Citrix Web Site Wizard was a stand-alone tool to build NFuse web sites for NFuse versions prior to 1.6. It was a GUI program that stepped through the different options available for NFuse web pages and then generated the pages. From there, you could copy the pages into your web server directory.

With NFuse 1.6x and 1.7, there is no need for the Citrix Web Site Wizard because all of the options that you could change with the Web Site Wizard can now be set with the NFuse.conf configuration file or via the NFuse administration web pages.

Some people like to point out that the Citrix Web Site Wizard also allowed you to apply different "themes" to the websites it created. These themes changed the look and colors of the website, similar to the website themes available in Microsoft FrontPage. The Web Site Wizard only came with three themes (all pretty lame), and Citrix never released any more. The fact that these themes do not exist in NFuse 1.7 is not a big loss. If you want to, you can change the themes of the default NFuse 1.7 websites with any web editing tool, including FrontPage. Just be careful that you don't delete any of the web scripting code.

## Understanding the Default NFuse Web Site

Before going much farther in our exploration of the NFuse web pages, we need to understand NFuse's default web pages, what they are, and how they work. We'll do that in the next section. Now, let's take a high-level look at web page scripting in general. This will help you understand how the NFuse web pages work. If you're already an expert on website scripting, skip directly to the "NFuse Default Website Flowchart."

### *An Overview Web Page Scripting*

It seems that most MetaFrame XP administrators grew up as network engineers, as opposed to application developers. Because of this, it can be difficult to understand how the NFuse web pages really work. Fortunately, with NFuse 1.7, we can configure most options via the NFuse.conf file or the administrative web pages without needing to worry exactly how the web pages fit together. Still, it's worth taking a look at the basics of web page scripting.

First, let's consider standard HTML. HTML is a "tag-based," document language. This means that HTML documents are viewed as written, except that there are some special sequences of characters or "tags," that the viewing program knows indicate special formatting. For example, consider the following HTML code:

```
Hello. The current temperature is 14 degrees.
```

If you viewed this HTML code in an HTML viewer (i.e. web browser), it would look like this:

```
Hello. The current temperature is 14 degrees.
```

It looks exactly as it was typed because there are no "tags," or special formatting instructions. However, the next sample HTML code is a bit different:

```
<p><b>Hello</b>. The current temperature is <i>14
degrees</i>.</p>
```

This code contains some special instruction tags between the < > symbols (or "tags.") This code will display text with the following formatting applied:

**Hello**. The current temperature is *14 degrees*.

The HTML viewer (web browser) knows that the letters enclosed in the < > brackets are special characters that represent instructions for the browser. In this case, the browser follows the instructions by applying special formatting to the words. <p> means paragraph, <b> means bold, and <i> means italics. The web browser knows what these special tags mean because they are defined in the international HTML standard. Pure HTML works well for static content, but fails if the web page must display information that may change. How do you include information that changes in HTML pages?

The answer is with web page server-side scripting. Web server-side scripting takes HTML a step further. With server-side scripting, regular HTML code is used as the foundation, with special executable instructions (in the form of a scripting language) included, sprinkled throughout the HTML. When a web browser requests a page, the web server knows that special scripts are included within the HTML. The web server scans the page for the scripts, executes the scripts, and replaces the script code with the result of the script execution.

Imagine that you wanted to create a web page containing information that might change often, such as the current temperature. The final web page as viewed in a web browser might look like this:

**Hello**. The current temperature is *42 degrees.*

The HTML source code of the web page has an executable script in it that inserts the current temperature. The source code for this example might look like this:

```
<p><b>Hello.</b> The current temperature is <i> <%
Here is the script code that goes out and finds the
current temperature %> degrees </i></p>
```

In this example, the script section `<% Here is the script code that goes out and finds the current temperature %>` is executed before the page is sent to the client. The results of the script are put in place of the script code, in this case, "42". The final web code that the client browser sees then looks like this:

```
<p><b>Hello.</b> The current temperature is <i> 42
degrees </i></p>
```

The web browser's doesn't know that any server side scripting took place—even though the web administrator was able to give each web browser client a custom page.

In the real world, static HTML pages usually have the file extension .HTM or .HTML. Pages that are dynamically generated from scripts usually have an extension that indicates the language of the scripts, such as .ASP (Active Server Pages), .JSP (JavaServer Pages), or .CFM (Cold Fusion Pages).

Undoubtedly, as you surf the web, you probably notice that many of the web pages you view have a script extension, like .ASP, instead of a static extension, like .HTM. However, if you view the source code of these pages (view | source), you will notice that they are standard HTML pages and you won't see any special scripts. The reason for this is that when you view the source code on your web browser, the scripts have already executed on the web server. The scripts generated their content (like the "42" in our temperature example) and produced a standard HTML web page that you view in your browser.

This is how the default NFuse web pages work. Some of the pages are .HTM pages and others are .ASP (or .JSP for iPlanet and Apache servers). With the dynamic server script-enabled web pages, NFuse is able to create standard web pages that are viewable by any web browser—even though each user will see different applications listed.

### NFuse Default Website Flowchart

After you install NFuse 1.7, you will notice that several web page files are placed in the web directory. As you begin to use NFuse, you can start to notice the different files used by the address in your web browser's address bar. In order to understand how the default web site is really set up, it's easiest to view it as a flowchart. Figure 11.3 (next page) on follows the process as a user logs into an NFuse Classic 1.7 web portal.

## Modifying the Default NFuse Web Site

In order to begin modifying the default NFuse web pages beyond what can be done with the `NFuse.conf` file and the administrative web pages, you need to understand how the pages work. The flowchart from the previous section detailed how the pages interact. However, even to a seasoned web programmer, the source code of the NFuse web pages looks a bit foreign at first. This is because the NFuse web pages have special methods of interacting with the NFuse Java Objects.

If you haven't figured it out already, the default web pages that are included with NFuse 1.7 are very powerful. If there is any additional functionality that you need, you can usually just modify the existing pages. Modifying the default NFuse pages is legal and encouraged by Citrix.

In this section, we're not going to talk about all of the modifications that could be made—your imagination will take care of that. What we will do is show you enough about the default NFuse website and how it interfaces with the NFuse Java Object that you are able to what to modify and how to modify it.

### How Web Pages Interact with the Java Objects

There are three ways in which the NFuse web pages can interface with the NFuse Java Objects

- Session Fields.
- Substitution Tags.
- Via Java functions defined in the Java Objects.

*Figure 11.3 The NFuse web portal process*

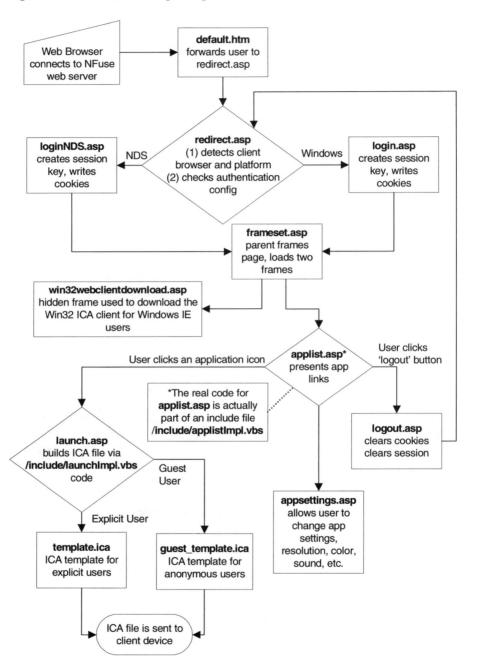

The details of the NFuse Java functions are beyond the scope of this book. Fortunately, you can change all sorts of things without knowing anything about Java. If you would like to explore the functions available for interfacing with the NFuse Java Objects, a full Java Objects reference is available in the Citrix NFuse document titled "Customizing NFuse 1.7," available as part of the NFuse download.

By skipping the Java functions, we now have only two items to look at: session fields and substitution tags. Let's start with session fields.

### Session Fields

A session field is a bit of NFuse-specific data as it relates to a user's NFuse session. Session fields hold all types of information, such as the current user name, the MetaFrame XP server name and address, and application settings. The values of session fields are stored in the NFuse Java Objects on the web server, causing a session field to behave like an "NFuse-specific" variable.

For example, when you login to a default NFuse web portal, the default login web page asks for three items: username, password, and domain. After you type each of these in and press "Submit," the value of each is written to an NFuse session field object.

Session field object names always begin with "NFuse_." In the login example mentioned above, the code in the login.asp web page might look something like this:

```
Username box = SessionField.NFuse_User
Password box = SessionField.NFuse_Password
Domain box = SessionField.NFuse_Domain
```

After the user "brian" logged in, the three session fields would hold the three following values:

```
NFuse_User = Brian
NFuse_Password = montypython
NFuse_Domain = bigdomain
```

Session fields exist so that multiple web pages can all have the same information. For example, after the user logs in to the login.asp page, he is forwarded to the applist.asp page which is responsible for drawing his list of MetaFrame XP applications. One of the first things that the applist.asp page will do is read the values from these three session fields so that it knows who the user is.

Each user that logs into an NFuse web portal has his own set of session fields so that the session field values between multiple users do not get mixed up. For those of you familiar with web programming, NFuse session fields are similar to web server session variables.

There are many ways that session field values can be set. In addition to a web page setting a value like we saw in the previous example, session field values can be set via URL parameters, web browser cookies, ICA files, or the NFuse.conf file. Because session fields can be set in multiple places, it's possible that a single session field might get set in two places with conflicting values. Whenever there is a conflict, the NFuse Java Objects look to the NFuse.conf file to see what precedence the different methods should take. This is done via the following line:

```
SessionFieldLocations=PNAgent,Script,Template,Url,Post,
Cookie,Properties
```

In addition to specifying the precedence of session field values (values listed from highest to lowest precedence), this line also specifies where session fields can be set. If an entry is not in the line, the Java Objects will ignore session fields set in this manner. For example, if you remove the "Url" entry from the SessionFieldLocations in the NFuse.conf file, you will not be able to set session fields via URL parameters. Let's take a look at what each of these locations means:

*PNAgent.* Session field values can be set from values in the Program Neighborhood Agent, via the config.xml file. (See the PN Agent section towards the end of this chapter for more details.)

*Script.* Session field values can be set from a web page server side script, such as an ASP or JSP page. For example, the web page script could have a line that says:

```
NFuse Session Field Name = Brian
```

*Template.* Session field values can be set from an HTML or ICA template file. Such a template file would contain substitution tags (covered in the next section) that are replaced with real data by the NFuse Java Objects when the file is requested by a client. Some of these substitution tags can request that the Java Objects update the value of a session field.

*URL.* Session field values can be set from parameters passed via an HTTP URL. For example the URL /myfile.asp?name=Brian&state=Ohio

would set the session field values "name" equal to "Brian" and "state" equal to "Ohio."

*Post.* Session field values can be set from the HTTP post method. This method is usually used with HTML forms. For example, a login HTML page might have a text field called "name" where users enter their name. Upon clicking the "submit" button, the web page would forward (post) the inputted text as a "name" value, write the value to the "name" session field, and then open the next web page.

*Cookie.* Session field values can be set from an HTTP cookie stored on the client web browser's machine.

*Properties.* Session field values can be set from settings in the NFuse.conf file.

### Substitution Tags

NFuse substitution tags are used to access the information stored in session fields. Substitution tags can be used in standard HTML web pages or in template ICA files. When a client web browser requests a file containing NFuse substitution tags, the NFuse Java Objects template parser scans the file and replaces any substitution tags with the real value stored in the session fields.

Every bit of user-specific NFuse data has an NFuse_*xxxxx* session field name and substitution tag. The session field is a way for data to be written to and read from the session field, and the substitution tag is a simple way to display the data stored in a session field.

NFuse substitution tags are enclosed in [  ] brackets. Let's look at some simple HTML code that uses substitution tags to access the session fields of the NFuse Java Objects to show the name of the currently logged on user. The HTML source code might look like this:

```
The current user is [NFuse_Domain]\[NFuse_User].
```

When this HTML page was sent to a web client, the NFuse Java Objects template parser would replace the substitution tags ([NFuse_Domain] and [NFuse_User]) with the actual session field data, in this case "briansdomain" and "Brian." This would cause the actual HTML code sent to the client to look like this:

```
The current user is briansdomain\Brian.
```

Substitution tags can also be used to provide information about applications. For example, consider the following HTML code:

```
The current application is [NFuse_AppName]. The
resolution is [NFuse_WindowWidth] x
[NFuse_WindowHeight].
```

The substitution tags could be replaced in this HTML code to form the following:

```
The current application is Word 2000. The resolution
is 800 x 600.
```

There are two ways to use NFuse substitution tags:

- Put them in HTML pages.
- Put them in the template ICA files.

Adding substitution tags to HTML files is very straightforward. All you need to do is to add the tags to your HTML code. We're going to focus on the template ICA files and how they use substitution tags, because understanding how those work is very important in the real world.

### ICA Template Files

Remember that whenever a web user clicks a hyperlink to launch an NFuse application, the web server sends an ICA file for that application down to the user. However, there is not a folder full of ICA files that are ready to go. Rather, the ICA file is dynamically built for that particular user as soon as the icon is clicked. In order to build that ICA file, NFuse starts with a preconfigured ICA template. This template is a file stored on the web server as template.ica. This is similar to a regular ICA file, except that the information that would be specific to one user or application is in the form of NFuse substitution tags. When a web user requests an application, the NFuse Java Objects retrieve the template.ica file and replace the NFuse substitution tags with the actual data relevant to that user or application.

Remember that the default NFuse website has two template ICA files: template.ica and guest_template.ica. The default web pages have logic to detect if a user is logged on anonymously or not. If they are, the guest_template.ica file is used. If not, then they are given an ICA file based on the template.ica file. Let's look at the template.ica file now. As you examine it, scan for the following three types of data:

- Substitution Tags, enclosed in the [   ] brackets, that begin with NFuse_.
- Session Fields, enclosed in the < [   ] > brackets.
- Actual, legitimate ICA information.

The two ICA files are compared side-by-side on the following two pages.

As you can see in this sample ICA file, most of the application information from the real ICA file has been replaced by substitution tags in the template ICA file. If for some reason there is any ICA setting that you want to be the same for all of your NFuse users, you can just overwrite the substitution tag with the real data in the template.ica file.

In case you're wondering, the guest_template.ica file only has a few lines that are different from the regular template ICA file. There are two session field declarations at the beginning of the guest template that are not in the regular template:

```
<[NFuse_setSessionField
NFuse_ClientName=AnonymousClient]>
<[NFuse_setSessionField
NFuse_UseCredentialType=UseAnonCredentials]>
```

Additionally, the two lines that contain user credential information in the regular template are not present in the guest template:

```
AutologonAllowed=ON
[NFuse_Ticket]
```

*Figure 11.4  The template.ica file from the default web site.*

```
<[NFuse_setSessionField NFuse_ContentType=application/
x-ica]>

[WFClient]
Version=2
ClientName=[NFuse_ClientName]

[ApplicationServers]
[NFuse_AppName]=

[[NFuse_AppName]]
Address=[NFuse_AppServerAddress]
InitialProgram=#[NFuse_AppName]
DesiredColor=[NFuse_WindowColors]
TransportDriver=TCP/IP
WinStationDriver=ICA 3.0

AutologonAllowed=ON
[NFuse_Ticket]

[NFuse_IcaAudio]
[NFuse_IcaWindow]

[NFuse_IcaEncryption]

SessionsharingKey=[NFuse_SessionSharingKey]

[EncRC5-0]
DriverNameWin16=pdc0w.dll
DriverNameWin32=pdc0n.dll

[EncRC5-40]
DriverNameWin16=pdc40w.dll
DriverNameWin32=pdc40n.dll

[EncRC5-56]
DriverNameWin16=pdc56w.dll
DriverNameWin32=pdc56n.dll

[EncRC5-128]
DriverNameWin16=pdc128w.dll
DriverNameWin32=pdc128n.dll
```

*Figure 11.5  A real ICA file*
```
[WFClient]
Version=2
ClientName=valhalla-bmadden

[ApplicationServers]
Word 2000=

[Word 2000]
Address=10.1.1.1:1494
InitialProgram=#Word 2000
DesiredColor=4
TransportDriver=TCP/IP
WinStationDriver=ICA 3.0

AutologonAllowed=ON
Username=brian
Domain=\FE2F7F5D1F55D72D
ClearPassword=2BBF9C702CE551

ClientAudio=On

DesiredHRES=640
DesiredVRES=480
TWIMode=On

SessionsharingKey=4-basic-none-server1-brian-bigfarm

[EncRC5-0]
DriverNameWin16=pdc0w.dll
DriverNameWin32=pdc0n.dll

[EncRC5-40]
DriverNameWin16=pdc40w.dll
DriverNameWin32=pdc40n.dll

[EncRC5-56]
DriverNameWin16=pdc56w.dll
DriverNameWin32=pdc56n.dll

[EncRC5-128]
DriverNameWin16=pdc128w.dll
DriverNameWin32=pdc128n.dll
```

## Creating NFuse Web Sites from Scratch

Some people choose to build NFuse web sites from scratch. There is nothing technical to prevent this, and all of the NFuse Java Objects and substitution tags can be used. While this method may give the most flexibility, it can be time consuming to build a website from the ground up. Most people end up customizing the default pages.

### Advantages of Building NFuse Web Pages from Scratch

- Most flexibility.
- NFuse "nuggets" can be created to integrate with existing pages or portals.
- When you're done, you will really know what you are talking about.

### Disadvantages of Building NFuse Web Pages from Scratch

- Time consuming.
- You must know exactly what you are doing.
- You will probably reinvent the wheel a few times along the way.

# NFuse Web Clients

Of course, NFuse-enabled MetaFrame XP environments require client devices to access the ICA applications. When working with NFuse clients, there are several things to consider.

First, we'll look at what the requirements are for client devices to be able to use NFuse web application portals. Then, we'll see where on the web server we need to copy the ICA client installation files. Lastly, we'll review the different methods of automating the deployment of that software to client devices.

## NFuse Client Requirements

In order to access a MetaFrame XP environment via an NFuse web portal, a client device must meet three requirements:

- The client device must have a web browser.
- The client device must be capable of running ICA client software.

- The client must be capable of launching the ICA client software by following an "ICA" file type hyperlink from the browser.

Basically, almost any web browser can view NFuse web server default web pages, and ICA clients exist for almost every type of device. That means that the first two requirements are almost always met. The show stopper for most devices that cannot access NFuse environments is the third point. The NFuse client device must be capable of launching the ICA client software based on a user clicking a hyperlink to an ICA file on a web page. Some old Windows CE and Java devices do not have this capability. On Macintosh and Java clients, there are some manual steps that must be taken to ensure NFuse applications are launched properly.

## ICA Client Source Files and Locations

In order for the default NFuse web pages to be able to provide links for users to install the ICA clients, the ICA client installation files must be located on the NFuse web server. The default web site assumes that the client installation files are located in the following path:

```
<WebServerRoot>\ICAWEB\<two letter language code>\<ica
client version>
```

For example, the English 32-bit Windows ICA client on an IIS server is located in the `\wwwroot\ICAWEB\en\ica32\` folder.

During the installation of NFuse, you are asked if you want to copy the client installation files to the web server. If you choose not to, the default web pages will still point to the default client installation locations. You can then manually copy the ICA client source files to the web server at any time.

## Using NFuse to Automatically Instal the ICA Client

Once you ensure that the ICA files are placed on your NFuse web server, you can configure NFuse to automatically install the ICA client software onto a user's client device if they visit the web site from a computer without the client software installed.

As an administrator, you have the ability to customize this process. Similar to the other NFuse configuration options, you can customize the ICA client installation options simply by modifying the `NFuse.conf` file or via the NFuse administrative web pags.

There are several items that control the action of the ICA client installation from the NFuse web pages:

```
AutoDeployWebClient=Off
#WebClientVersion=6,30,1000
ShowClientInstallCaption=Auto
Win32Client=default
OtherClient=default
#OverrideClientInstallCaption=[Place your text here]
#EmbedMethod=Auto
AllowCustomizeEmbedApplications=Off
#JavaClientPackages=COMPortMapping,Thinwire1,PrinterMapping,SSL
#AllowCustomizeJavaClientPackages=Off
```

### AutoDeployWebClient
(NFuse Administration Web Pages | ICA Client deployment | Enable automatic download of ICA Win32 Web Client)

When this is set to "On," the web client (icat.exe) is automatically deployed to users that connect to NFuse from 32-bit Windows clients if they do not already have the ICA client installed. In order for this to work, you need to have the ICA client source files in the proper location as described in the previous section.

A setting of "Off" will disable this Win32 automatic client deployment.

### WebClientVersion
(NFuse Administration Web Pages | ICA Client deployment | with version)

This line is used in conjunction with the AutoDeployWebClient setting. It allows you to specify the version of the 32-bit Windows web ICA client that is loaded on your web server for deployment. NFuse will compare the value of the WebClientVersion line with the actual version of the ICA client on the user's Win32 machine. If the version in the WebClientVersion line is newer, NFuse will invoke the Win32 ICA client installation process using the ICA client files loaded on the web server.

When you specify a WebClientVersion value on this line, you must enter it with commas instead of periods. Remember from Chapter 10 that you can find out the version of the web client by viewing the properties of the ActiveX control (Right-click wfica.ocx | Properties | Version tab | File Version). For example, if you would like to deploy version 6.30.1050.0 of the ICA web client, you would enter "6,30,1050" on this line. Then, whenever a user connects with a version of the Win32 ICA web client that's older than 6.30.1050 (or whenever a Win32 user connects with no client at all), NFuse will install the new client.

### ShowClientInstallCaption

(NFuse Administration Web Pages | ICA Client deployment | Display ICA Client installation caption)

NFuse has the ability to detect the client platform of visiting users. However, it can only detect whether users have the ICA client installed if they are using a Win32 platform. Since NFuse can also only automatically install the ICA client on 32-bit Windows platforms, this ShowClientInstallCaption line allows you to specify how the client installation process works for other platforms.

A value of "on" means that NFuse will display a link for the user to download and install the ICA client in the "NFuse Message Center" section of the main NFuse page. Since NFuse can detect the client platform, this link will be customized for the user for their specific platform.

Setting this value to "off" means that the client installation links will not be displayed, and you will need to figure out some other way to get the client software to your users.

You can also set this line to "auto," which is similar to the "on" setting, except that Win32 users will only see the ICA client installation link if they do not have the client installed. Users connecting from all other platforms will always see the link.

### Win32Client or similar

For each ICA client platform, there is an entry in the NFuse.conf file in the format platformClient (for example Win16Client, JavaClient, or Tru64Client). By default, these all have values set to "default." Changing any of these values allows you to specify the text and URL location for the ICA links shown in the NFuse Message Center, which is the area to the right of the application icons on the main NFuse page. To change this, enter the new caption text, followed by an ampersand (&), followed by the URL for that caption. You can string multiple caption/URL pairs together by separating each entry with a comma.

For example, by default, the NFuse web pages offer 32-bit Windows users the "web" version of the ICA client (ica32t.exe, no Program Neighborhood, see Chapter 10 for details). In some cases, you might decide that you would like to offer the full version (ica32.exe) or the Program Neighborhood

Agent (ica32a.exe) client in place of the web client. To do this, simply copy the new versions of the ICA clients that you want to use into the \ica32\ clients folder on your web server. Then, update the Win32Client field in the NFuse.conf file so that it points to your new files. In this case, you would change the line Win32Client = default to:

```
Win32Client=Click here for the full client&/ICAWEB/
ica32/en/ica32.exe,Click here for the PN Agent
client&/ICAWEB/en/ica32/ica32a.exe,Click here for the
web client&/ICAWEB/ica32/en/ica32t.exe
```

The root URL location is specified by the URLMapping field in the NFuse.conf file. Usually, this is the root of the website.

If you want to give you 32-bit Windows users the full client without giving them a choice of the other clients, then set your Win32Client value appropriately. For example:

```
Win32Client=Click here to download the client&/ICAWEB/
en/ica32/ica32.exe
```

You could also use these settings to use one client in place of another. For example, since NFuse can detect the platform from which a user connects, it will always display the "platform-specific" client installation link. However, what happens if you want to use the Java client for your Mac users, but you want everyone else to use their platform-specific clients? Configuring this via the NFuse.conf file is simple. Out of the box, Mac platforms are configured to use their default Mac clients (in the /icaweb/en/icamac/ macica_sea.hqx location on the web server). This is seen in the following line:

```
MacClient=default
```

To change the setting so that Mac users receive the Java client, you would need to change that line to read:

```
MacClient=Click here to download the client&/ICAWEB/
en/icajava/JICAEngJ.jar
```

### OtherClient
This line allows you to specify the caption and links for ICA clients where the client platform cannot be detected. The "default" setting uses the ICA Java client's links, but you can change this just like any of the other client links. Remember that the NFuse web page can usually detect the platform that a

user is connecting from, it just can't detect whether or not that user's client device has the ICA client software installed.

### OverrideClientInstallCaption
This line allows you to customize the message that is displayed in the client download box when a client needs to be installed. The exact message varies depending on the client platform, but says something to the effect of, "You need to download the ICA client software. To do so, click on the proper link below."

### EmbedMethod
(NFuse Administration Web Pages | ICA Client deployment | Embedded applications | Launch applications as embedded applications)

This line is used to specify the version of the ICA client that will be used if you've specified that ICA applications should be embedded in web pages via the EmbedApplications setting described earlier in the chapter.

A setting of "auto" will cause NFuse to detect the user's platform and automatically deploy the platform-specific client. A setting of "JavaClient" will cause NFuse to use the Java ICA client.

### JavaClientPackages
(NFuse Administration Web Pages | ICA Client deployment | Embedded applications | Select Java Client packages)

This line allows you to specify which Java packages are sent to the client when the Java ICA client is deployed. (Refer to Chapter 10 for details of how these packages work.) You can specify as many options as you want, placing them all on the same line separated by commas (with no spaces between entries). You can choose Audio, ClientDriveMapping, Clipboard, COMPortMapping, ConfigUI, PrinterMapping, SecureICA, SSL, Thinwire1, and ZeroLatency.

### AllowCustomizeJavaClientPackages
(NFuse Administration Web Pages | ICA Client deployment | Embedded applications | Select Java Client packages | Allow user to choose packages)

By setting this line to "on," you can let your users choose which Java modules are downloaded to their clients. They are presented with a list of checkboxes, and can pick and choose whatever they want. The default options are preselected based on the modules listed in the JavaClientPackages line.

Of you set this option to "off," then users are not given this option and the values from the `JavaClientPackages` line are used.

# Using Enterprise Services for NFuse

Out of the box, NFuse Classic 1.7 only has the ability to provide applications to users from a single server farm (because it only communicates with the Citrix XML service from a single server). This is unfortunate since (as we learned in Chapter 3) there are plenty of real world situations in which your MetaFrame XP environment might need to consist of multiple server farms.

Luckily, there is a solution that allows you to use a single NFuse web site to seamlessly and securely access published applications from multiple server farms. This is possible with a Citrix product called "Enterprise Services for NFuse 1.7" (abbreviated as ESN).

ESN is a standalone product from Citrix that sits between an NFuse web server and multiple server farms, as shown in Figure 11.6. When ESN is used, the NFuse web server communicates with ESN, and ESN communicates with the Citrix XML service running on multiple MetaFrame XP servers in multiple server farms. ESN stores all of its configuration in a SQL database. That database can be shared between multiple ESN servers for scalability and redundancy.

*Figure 11.6  How ESN fits into the NFuse architecture*

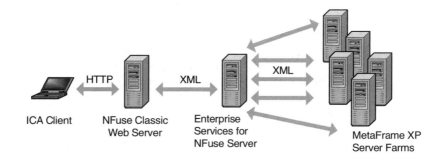

### *Advantages of using Enterprise Services for NFuse*

- Easy way to provide a single interface into multiple server farms.
- Can be used to "load-balance" multiple server farms.
- Leverages existing NFuse 1.7 technology and components.

- Fully supported by Citrix.

### Disadvantages of using Enterprise Services for NFuse

- Must be run on a Windows 2000 IIS web server.
- A SQL database is required.
- Requires MetaFrame XPe with Subscription Advantage.
- Other requirements are pretty steep.

Even though ESN is a separate product, it cannot be purchased. It is only available (via download) if you own MetaFrame XPe with a current Subscription Advantage license. See Chapter 14 for detailed information about licensing and Subscription Advantage.

The remainder of this section will focus on how ESN works and the design considerations that you need to think about for your environment. In Chapter 17 we'll describe how ESN can be used to load-balance multiple server farms for the ultimate in redundancy and high availability.

## How Enterprise Services for NFuse Works

In the beginning of this chapter, we outlined the step-by-step process of how NFuse Classic works. Figure 11.7 (next page) details that same process when ESN is also used.

*Figure 11.7 How ESN works*

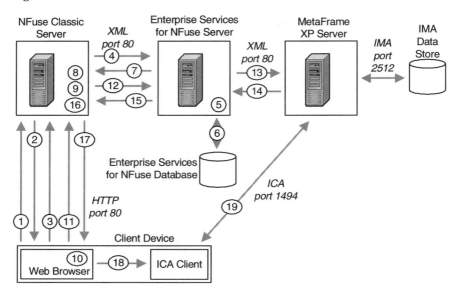

1. A user with a web browser and an ICA client requests the NFuse portal web page by typing in a URL.

2. The web server sends down the HTML login page via the HTTP protocol.

3. The web user enters credentials and sends them back to the web server.

4. The web server forwards the user's information to an ESN server.

5. The ESN server validates the credentials.

6. The ESN server retrieves the user's list of applications from its database. (ESN caches this information from the server farm, updating it every 24 hours.)

7. The ESN server sends the application list to the NFuse web server.

8. The NFuse web server builds a web page containing all of the user's application icons.

9. Each icon is hyperlinked with its application properties.

10. The user selects an application to run by clicking on an icon in thie web browser.

11. The web browser sends a request to the web server for the link that the user selected.

12. The web server sends the request to the ESN server.

13. The ESN server sends the request to the appropriate server farm via the Citrix XML service.

14. The MetaFrame XP server sends a response back to the ESN server.

15. The ESN server sends the information to the NFuse web server.

16. The NFuse Java Objects on the web server retrieve an ICA file template. That template is modified with the application's and user's specific information. This creates a custom ICA file for the user.

17. The custom-built ICA file is sent to web browser on the client device.

18. The web browser receives the ICA file and passes it to ICA client software that is also loaded on the ICA client device.

19. The user's local ICA client starts the MetaFrame XP session with the information contained in the custom ICA file.

## Understanding the ESN Components

There are five components that make up Enterprise Services for NFuse environments:

- NFuse Classic Web Server
- ESN Server
- ESN Database
- MetaFrame XP Servers
- ICA Clients

### Component 1. NFuse Classic Web Server

As you saw in Figure 11.7, the NFuse web server performs essentially the same role whether ESN is used or not. The main difference is that when ESN is used, the NFuse web server contacts the Citrix XML service on the ESN server rather than on a MetaFrame XP server. NFuse 1.61 or newer is required for ESN. Also, the default NFuse web pages are replaced with ESN web pages.

In order for this to happen, you need to put your NFuse web server into "Enterprise Mode." This will tell NFuse that it is communicating with an ESN server. You can put an NFuse web server into enterprise mode by viewing the

NFuse administrative web pages (NFuse Admin Web Site | Mode Link | Mode Setting) or by adding the following two lines to the `NFuse.conf` file:

```
NFuseEnterpriseMode=On
NFuseEnterprisePassword=yourESNpassword
```

Since NFuse Classic is still in place when ESN is used, you can still access and modify NFuse Classic settings. However, several NFuse Classic settings are also specified at the ESN level. For these particular settings, the system ignores the NFuse Classic settings when ESN is used. NFuse Classic pulls the configurations from the ESN server. These settings include:

- Load balancing of Citrix XML servers.
- Password change settings.
- Firewall configuration. (See Chapter 15)
- Alternate addressing. (See in Chapter 15)
- Citrix Secure Gateway. (See in Chapter 15)
- Authentication options, including pass-through authentication and smart card support. (See in Chapter 15)

### Component 2. ESN Server

The Enterprise Services for NFuse server is the main ESN component. It uses the Citrix XML service to poll all of the configured server farms (every 24 hours by default) and creates and maintains its own aggregated list of applications that are available across the farm.

Additionally, the ESN server maintains a list of user account mappings for NFuse user accounts that can be used to access MetaFrame XP servers in multiple farms.

The ESN server itself must be running Windows 2000 with Service Pack 2 and Internet Information Services. When you install ESN, a new web server component called "Tomcat Jakarta" is installed. (This is essentially an interpreter for the ESN web code, since that code is written as Java Server Pages which are not natively supported by IIS. More information is available at `http://jakarta.apache.org/tomcat/`.)

When you install ESN, you must choose whether it validates users against a Windows domain, an Active Directory, or an NDS tree. This is known as the "account authority." If you plan to use Windows NT 4.0 domain or NDS authentication, your ESN server must belong to a Windows domain. If you plan to use Active Directory authentication, your ESN server can operate in workgroup or domain mode.

All of these requirements apply to the ESN server only. Your NFuse Classic web server can be on a non-Microsoft platform.

### Component 3. ESN Database

ESN stores all of its information in a database. In addition to the cached lists of server farm applications and the user account mappings mentioned previously, the ESN database also stores all of the ESN configuration settings and any log files that you enable. (Unlike NFuse Classic, ESN does not store any information is text-based configuration files.)

The ESN database must be a Microsoft SQL 7.0 or SQL 2000 server. In large environments, a single ESN database can be used with multiple ESN servers. In a sense, the ESN database is kind of like the "data store" for ESN servers.

The exact size of the database will vary depending on the number of farms, applications, user mappings, and log files that you have. However, even the largest ESN databases are not especially large.

### Component 4. MetaFrame XP Servers

The last ESN server component is the MetaFrame XP servers. In ESN environments, MetaFrame XP servers perform the exact same role that they do in NFuse classic environments. The only difference is that they provide information about farm applications via the Citrix XML service to ESN servers instead of NFuse Classic servers.

In order for a MetaFrame XP server to work with ESN, it must have Feature Release 1 or 2 installed.

### Component 5. ICA Clients

ICA clients access the ESN environment in the same way that they access NFuse Classic environments. Similar to when NFuse Classic is used, once a MetaFrame XP ICA session is launched, both the ESN and the NFuse servers are no longer involved. At that point the user has a direct connection to the MetaFrame XP server.

At minimum, end users must have Internet Explorer 5.01 with Service Pack 2, 5.5 with Service Pack 2, or Netscape 4.7 to access ESN web portals. All ICA client platforms are supported except for the Java client version 6.30. (You can use the Java client version 6.20.)

## Designing your ESN Solution

Now that you know how ESN works, you can start to think about the design of your ESN environment. There are several issues to consider:

- What will be your strategy for aggregating published applications from multiple server farms?
- How will you configure user account mappings to ensure that all users can access MetaFrame XP servers from all farms?
- Where will you put your ESN servers?

### Published Applications from Multiple Farms

As long as published applications from multiple server farms have the same display names and application names, and as long as they are in the same Program Neighborhood folder, ESN will aggregate them into a single icon for on the ESN web site. This can be used to load-balance server farms.

You can use the ESN administrative web pages to specify default server farms for groups of users. Then, when users click on icons for applications published in multiple farms, they are sent to their preferred farm unless that farm is not available, in which case they are sent to the next least-busy farm.

### User Account Mapping Methods

The whole point of using ESN is to provide your users with access to multiple server farms. Unfortunately, there are many situations in which your users will not have rights to the MetaFrame XP servers in all the farms, since different servers from different farms are usually in different domains.

To address this, configure a user account mapping policy for each server farm to which ESN connects. This mapping correlates user accounts that are valid on the ESN web site with user accounts that are valid in each target server farm. The exact policy that you use for a farm depends on two items:

- Are your users' accounts valid in the target server farm?
- Is the target server farm in the same domain as the ESN server? (This does not have anything to do with the users' account domains.)

Based on your answers to these two questions, there are three possbile mapping modes:

- Manual account mapping.
- Automatic account mapping.

- No account mapping.

You must make this account mapping decision for every server farm that is part of your ESN environment. Let's take a look at each of the three options.

## Option 1. Manual Account Mapping

If your users already have valid accounts on the MetaFrame XP servers in the target farm, you can configure "manual account mapping." This setting causes the ESN web pages to ask the user to enter his account information for each farm the first time that he logs in to ESN. However, this information is then stored in the ESN database and users are not asked for their information again.

### Advantages of Manual Account Mapping

- No work for you.

### Disadvantages of Manual Account Mapping

- It only works when users have accounts that are valid on the target MetaFrame XP servers.
- The users must perform their own mappings. Even though this is explained in detail the first time the users login to the ESN web site, there is still a chance that the user could do something wrong.

## Option 2. Automatic Account Mapping

If your users do not have valid accounts on the MetaFrame XP servers in the target farm, and if you do not want to manually configure accounts for them, you can configure the farm for "automatic account mapping." To use this, you need to manually create a pool of user accounts in the target farm. (These accounts all need to be configured with the same password.) Then, when a user logs into the ESN web site, ESN automatically picks an unused account from the pool and creates a permanent mapping in the ESN database that locks the two accounts together. This allows users to log into the ESN website with their official account and be able to sign into the target server farm without re-entering their credentials.

### Advantages of Automatic Account Mapping

- The mapping process is transparent to the user.
- The auto-mapped accounts can be configured so that they never expire.

### Disadvantages of Automatic Account Mapping

- The account that the user is mapped to for use with the target

MetaFrame servers is picked randomly, and therefore it doesn't correspond to the user other than via the ESN mapping.

- You must manually set up a pool of user accounts for use with the target MetaFrame servers.

### Option 3. No Mapping

Lastly, if the MetaFrame XP servers in the target farm are in the same domain as (or a domain that trusts) the ESN server, you do not need to configure any account mapping (since you users will have authenticated to the ESN server already).

### Advantages of No Mapping

- No work for you.
- No work for the user.

### Disadvantages of No Mapping

- Only works when the account by which the user accesses the ESN web server also works on the target MetaFrame servers.

## *Placing ESN servers in your environment*

Now that you've designed all the other aspects of ESN, you need to think about where you're going to put your ESN servers. As you decide this, keep the following points in mind:

- The ESN server requires regular and consistent access to the ESN database since it queries it whenever a user logs into the ESN website.

- By default, ESN servers only contact MetaFrame XP farm servers once every 24 hours. The ESN servers do not necessarily have to be close to every server farm.

- You can have multiple ESN servers that share the same SQL database. You can even configure SQL replication to ensure that ESN servers in different parts of your environment have local SQL access.

- You can configure multiple ESN servers and multiple ESN databases to access the same MetaFrame XP servers.

- A MetaFrame XP server can communicate to NFuse Classic servers as well as ESN servers.

- As with NFuse Classic, a user's session on an ESN web server ends once he launches his ICA application.

## Configuring Enterprise Services for NFuse

Configuring ESN is relatively simple. While there are dozens of potential options (all outlined in the "Enterprise Services for NFuse Guide" that comes with the product), you can configure your ESN environment by following a few basic steps:

1. Configure your current NFuse server for ESN support.
2. Install ESN and SQL Server.
3. Configure the "one time only" settings of ESN by accessing ESN's administrative web pages at `http://yourESNserver/ NFuseEnterprise/admin/login`. (All ESN options are configured via web pages. The first time you access the web pages you are presented with the special "one time only" options.
4. Configure the SQL Server database connection.
5. Configure your user mapping and authentication method.
6. Configure the Windows group that you want to have administrative rights over ESN.

At this point, you have completed the "first time only" options.

7. Access the ESN administrative web pages again. You will be sent directly to the administration home page.
8. Add a MetaFrame XP server farm or farms (ESN Admin Web Pages | Farms | Add Farm). You add a farm by specifying the URL of a server running the Citrix XML service. (This URL is in the `servername:port` format.) You can add primary and backup servers for redundancy.
9. Configure account mapping for each farm

Once you do this, you will be able to begin using ESN.

# NFuse 1.5x and 1.6x Considerations

Because MetaFrame XP includes NFuse 1.51, Feature Release 1 includes NFuse 1.6, and Citrix Secure Gateway includes NFuse 1.61, there is a good chance that you might have an older version of NFuse running in your Meta-Frame XP server farm before you decide to install NFuse 1.7.

Because of this, we'll take a look at two things. First, we'll look at the features of NFuse 1.7 that are not available in previous versions to help you determine if you really want to upgrade. Then, we'll look at what happens when you install NFuse 1.7 onto a web server that already has NFuse 1.51 or 1.6x installed, and what you need to prepare for.

## New features available in NFuse 1.7

If you read Citrix's marketing literature about NFuse 1.7, you will see that it includes several new features. However, the structure of NFuse 1.7 is fundamentally no different from any previous version. The NFuse Java Objects perform the same role that they always have.

The "advanced" features of NFuse 1.7 stem from two areas:

- NFuse 1.7 supports Feature Release 2 for MetaFrame XP
- The default NFuse web pages are much more advanced than with previous versions of NFuse.

### New Features Based on Feature Release 2

We said earlier that NFuse doesn't really do anything, other than provide a web / Java interface into the MetaFrame XP environment. That same logic applies with NFuse 1.7 as well. The only reason that NFuse 1.7 supports most of its advanced features is because MetaFrame XP with Feature Release 2 supports those features. In order for these features to work, you must have Feature Release 2 installed and enabled in your MetaFrame XP server farm.

With Feature Release 2 installed, NFuse 1.7 supports the following features that are not supported in NFuse 1.6x:

- Smart Card Support. Users can seamlessly log onto MetaFrame XP servers with smart cards.
- TLS encryption. ICA sessions can be encrypted with transport layer security.

### New Features Based on Advanced Default Web Pages

The default web pages that come with NFuse 1.7 have been completely overhauled from previous versions. These web pages support many new features. Again, these features do not exist because the NFuse Java Objects have been radically overhauled (because they haven't). These features exist only because someone at Citrix spent a lot of time writing the default web pages.

- NFuse administrative web pages. The administrative web pages that were referenced so often throughout this chapter are a new feature of NFuse 1.7.

- Enhanced network address translation and SOCKS proxy support. NFuse 1.7 supports more firewall options than ever. These topics are discussed in detail in Chapter 15.

- Pass-through authentication. Pass-through authentication that was previously available only on Win32 clients is now available via NFuse. See Chapter 15 for more details.

- Users can change their passwords. Previously, this required third party add-ons.

- Load balanced XML requests. The NFuse Java Objects can now step through the server list in a round robin manner.

- Embedded application control. The embedded application options are new features of NFuse 1.7.

- Automatic delivery of the ICA Win32 web client. Instead of merely providing a download link, NFuse 1.7 can fully install the ICA client.

### *Upgrading from NFuse 1.51 or Newer to NFuse 1.7*

There are two ways that you can upgrade from NFuse 1.51 or NFuse 1.6 to NFuse 1.7. You can upgrade NFuse along with other MetaFrame XP components as you install Service Pack 2 or Feature Release 2, or you can upgrade NFuse all by itself by choosing to install just the new web server extensions.

If you install NFuse 1.7 by using the Feature Release 2 or Service Pack 2 installation program, your old NFuse configuration files (`NFuse.conf` or `NFuse.properties`) will be automatically backed up in the `%ProgramFiles%\Citrix\NFuse\BackedUpBy17\` folder. Any existing settings are then migrated from the old configuration files into the new NFuse 1.7 `NFuse.conf` file. On the other hand, if you upgrade to NFuse 1.7 by only installing NFuse, you are prompted for a directory to back up your existing files.

In either case, if you spent a lot of time customizing your old NFuse web pages, you will need to decide whether to customize the new NFuse 1.7 web pages. Any web pages that you created from NFuse 1.51 environments will not know how to take advantage of the new NFuse 1.7 features, such as the use of the NFuse.conf file. You will need to create new pages from the default NFuse 1.7 pages. Any pages that you created for NFuse 1.6 environments, however, should continue to function in NFuse 1.7.

# Leveraging NFuse with the PN Agent

As you are now aware, the real advantage of NFuse is not the fact that it "uses the web," but the fact that all client configuration is done centrally. What this means is that if you need to make any changes to your users' configuration, you can make the changes to your NFuse web server. Your client devices instantly begin using those changes the next time they connect to your NFuse website.

Unfortunately, NFuse has some drawbacks. One of these is the simple fact that users must access a web page to get their applications. This can be strange for users who are used to accessing all of their applications via their Start Menu or Windows desktop.

Start Menu and Windows desktop integration is one of the nice features of the full 32-bit ICA client. As an administrator, you can use this client to place application icons directly in the Start Menus or on the desktops of your users' workstations. While this is very easy to use, it has one major drawback. Because the full ICA client is used, any changes that you make to your backend cause you to have to update the pn.ini and appserv.ini files on every single client workstation. Plus, it's easy for users to foul things up because Program Neighborhood gives them so many configuration options that are easy to access.

To get the best of both worlds, Citrix introduced the Program Neighborhood Agent as part of Feature Release 1 for MetaFrame XP. (It remains unchanged in Feature Release 2, other than the ability to support the inherent changes introduced directly by FR-2.) The Program Neighborhood Agent allows you to place application and content icons on directly your users' desktops, Start Menus, and system trays.

### Advantages of the Program Neighborhood Agent

- All client configuration is done centrally, allowing you to easily change settings.
- No local client interface is installed. Users access MetaFrame XP applications simply by clicking on shortcuts.

### Disadvantages of the Program Neighborhood Agent

- It only works on 32-bit Windows clients.

NFuse 1.6 or newer is used as the logical backend for the PN Agent. The PN Agent is like NFuse without the web.

# Understanding Program Neighborhood Agent Files

In order to support Program Neighborhood Agent (PNA) functionality, the NFuse 1.7 setup program copies the needed files into the /Citrix/PNAgent web directory on your NFuse web server. The entire Program Neighborhood Agent server system is comprised of only eight files:

- *Enum.asp* This file is accessed by Program Neighborhood Agent clients to provide them with a list of published applications and content that they can access. This file works in the same way as the applist.asp file in a regular NFuse Classic website, except that instead of creating an HTML web page, it sends the results to the client agent. A similar file called smartcard_enum.asp is used for smart card application enumeration.

- *Launch.asp* This file is invoked by PNA clients when they launch an application or content. This file works in the same way as launch.asp in regular NFuse Classic websites. A similar file called smartcard_launch.asp is used for smart card application launching.

- *Template.ica* This template ICA file works just like the template ICA files in any NFuse website. If there are settings that you need to apply at the ICA file level for your PNA users, then you can make them here. Similar to NFuse Classic environments, there is also a guest_template.ica file for anonymous users.

- *Esninclude.asp* This file contains logic that is invoked when the PN Agent is used to login to Enterprise Services for NFuse environments.

- *Config.xml* This file contains all of the configuration for PNA clients. This file works in a similar fashion to the NFuse.conf file in a regular NFuse website, although the layout of the config.xml file is different because it is written in pure XML. Because this file controls everything, it's important that you understand it if you want to be able to use NFuse's Program Neighborhood Agent. Let's take a look at this file now.

## Configuring PN Agent with the Config.xml File

The settings that the Program Neighborhood Agent uses are centrally controlled by the config.xml located in the /Citrix/PNAgent web directory.

## Understanding XML Files

Since all PN Agent configuration is done via the `config.xml` file, and since the `config.xml` file is a standard XML file, it's probably worth spending a minute or two looking at what an XML file is.

An XML file is a type of document. It is based on a "markup language." While HTML documents are based on the "hypertext" markup language, XML documents are based on an "extensible" markup language (XML = eXtensible Markup Language). From a structural standpoint, XML documents are like HTML documents. The only difference is that there aren't any predefined tags in XML. That's why it's called "extensible." Since no tags are predefined, it can be extended in any way.

Think about how the HTML source code would look for this document:

**Hello.** My name is *Brian.*

The HTML code would look like this:

```
<p><b>Hello.</b> My name is <i>Brian.</i></p>
```

Within the international HTML standard, the "p" tag is reserved for a paragraph, the "b" tag is reserved for bold, and the "i" tag is reserved for italics.

Within an XML document, no tags are reserved. XML tags can be anything, and it's up to the application to determine how they're used. For example, an XML document might look like this:

```
<mylistofpeople>
        <firstname>Brian</firstname>
        <lastname>Madden</lastname>
        <title>author</title>
        <website>www.brianmadden.com</website>
</mylistofpeople>
```

Notice that each XML tag consists of an opening tag and a closing tag. Similar to HTML, the closing tag must start with a slash ("/"). In this document, the "mylistofpeople" tag is called the "root" tag, since it surrounds the entire document.

Some of the lines in this file have been indented purely for ease of viewing by human readers. That XML document could have just as easily looked like this:

```
<mylistofpeople><firstname>Brian</firstname><lastname>
Madden</lastname><title>author</title><website>www.bri
anmadden.com</website></mylistofpeople>
```

Since XML is extensible, you can use it however you want. For example, you can modify the previous example so that it contains two people:

```
<mylistofpeople>
      <person>
            <firstname>Brian</firstname>
            <lastname>Madden</lastname>
            <title>author</title>
            <website>www.brianmadden.com</website>
      </person>
      <person>
            <firstname>Doug</firstname>
            <lastname>Brown</lastname>
            <title>guru</title>
            <website>www.dabcc.com</website>
      </person>
</mylistofpeople>
```

Notice that we've added a tag called "person" that surrounds each set of tags for each person. By doing this, we've "extended" the XML document. This document now infers that there is a tag called "person," and that tag consists of "firstname," "lastname," "title," and "website" tags.

You can edit any XML file with a standard text editor. (If you double-click an XML file in Windows, it will open in a cool, interactive way with Internet Explorer.) There are also dozens of freeware and shareware XML file editors on www.download.com.

Now that you understand the basics of XML, let's examine PN Agent's config.xml file. Rather than display the entire file at once, we're going to break it down into several sections and review each section separately.

### Config.xml Header Information

The config.xml file opens with some standard XML header lines:

```
<?xml version="1.0" encoding="UTF-8"?>
<PNAgent_Configuration xmlns:xsi="http://www.w3.org/
2000/10/XMLSchema-instance">
```

The first line specifies the XML standard that this file follows (XML 1.0 in this case), and the second line is the "root" tag ("PNAgent_Configuration").

## Folder Options

The first tag after the header information is "FolderDisplay." The settings in this tag allow you to specify whether you want to display icons for Meta-Frame XP applications and content in the users' Start menu, system tray, or on their Windows desktop.

```
<FolderDisplay>
      <StartMenuDisplay>
            <Enabled modifiable="true"
forcedefault="false">true</Enabled>
            <RootFolder root="programs"
modifiable="true" forcedefault="false"/>
      </StartMenuDisplay>
```

Since this is the first config.xml tag that we're looking at, let's take a detailed looked at how it is structured.

The first section in the "FolderDisplay" tag is "StartMenuDisplay." (We call this the "StartMenuDisplay" section since it opens with a <StartMenuDisplay> tag and ends with a </StartMenuDisplay> tag.

Within the "StartMenuDisplay" section, there are two tags: <Enabled> and <RootFolder>. The opening and closing "Enabled" tags surround its value: "true," in this case. However, you'll notice that there is some extra data shoved in the "Enabled" opening tag. A standard opening tag would look like this:

```
<Enabled>
```
But in this case, the "Enabled" opening tag actually looks like this:

```
<Enabled modifiable="true" forcedefault="false">
```

In this case, the "Enabled" tag has extra attributes that have been applied to it. An attribute called "modifiable" has been added with a value of "true" and a "forcedefault" attribute has been added with a value of "false."

Take another look at the next tag:

```
<RootFolder root="programs" modifiable="true"
forcedefault="false"/>
```

At first glance, it appears that this tag doesn't have a closing tag to go with it. (You would expect to see a </RootFolder> closing tag. In this case, the "RootFolder" tag doesn't need to surround any data, so the people who wrote the XML file simply stuck the "/" in the end of tag right before the closing ">.">

With XML, you instead of specifying <tagname> and </tagname> opening and closing pairs, you can use the single tag (i.e. <tagname/>) shortcut if you don't need a pair of tags to surround some data.

Now that you understand the structure of the tags in the "StartMenuDisplay" section of the config.xml file, let's decipher what the values actually mean.

The "Enabled" tag in the "StartMenuDisplay" section is set to "true," which causes published applications to be automatically added to your users' Start menus. If you do not want any MetaFrame XP application icons to show up in your users' Start menus, you would change the value between the opening and closing "Enabled" tags to "false." A setting of "false" would look like this:

```
<Enabled modifiable="true"
forcedefault="false">false</Enabled>
```

Remember the "modifiable" and "forcedefault" attributes that have been shoved inside the opening <Enabled> tag? These two attributes refer to some of the PN Agent options that your users can edit via the properties screen of their local PN Agent software.

As you look through the config.xml file, you'll notice that many tags have "modifiable" and "forcedefault" attribute options. Each of these can be set to either "true" or "false." If "modifiable" is set to "true," users will be able to change the particular setting specified by that tag. If "forcedefault" is set to true, then the settings will be changed back to the default settings each time the Program Neighborhood Agent is started on the client. Usually, you set one of these to true and the other to false. In the "StartMenuDisplay" tag, we are allowing our users to be able to change this setting if they want to (modifiable="true") and we are not forcing our users to take our default settings when their systems are reset (forcedefault="false").

Now we can take a look at the next tag: "RootFolder." This tag allows you to specify which folder (in the user's Start menu) your Program Neighborhood Agent published application icons will appear in. As you can see, in this example, the folder is set to "programs." You can change this folder to anything that you want. Notice again that the "modifiable" and "forcedefault" attributes are present, allowing you to specify whether you want users to be able to change this option and whether the system should force it to be the setting you specify.

Before we move on to the next section, notice that the "StartMenuDisplay" section is closed out with the `</StartMenuDisplay>` closing tag. There is no "FolderDisplay" closing tag yet because the next section ("DesktopDisplay") is also part of the "FolderDisplay" section. Let's take a look at that "DesktopDisplay" section now:

```
<DesktopDisplay>
      <Enabled modifiable="true"
forcedefault="false">false</Enabled>
      <Icon>
            <Name modifiable="true"
forcedefault="false">My Program Neighborhood
Applications</Name>
            <Location modifiable="true"
forcedefault="false">http://yourNFuseserver/Citrix/
PNAgent/displayicon.ico</Location>
      </Icon>
</DesktopDisplay>
```

The "DesktopDisplay" section allows you to place a folder on the user's desktop that contains icons to their published applications. Like the other settings, the "enabled" tag can be set to "true" or "false" to turn that folder on or off.

The "Name" tag under the "Icon" section allows you to change the name of that folder. As you can see, the default setting of "My Program Neighborhood Applications" is pretty lame, and probably something that you'll want to change.

You should set the "Name" tag's "modifiable" attribute to "false." If you don't, your users will change the name of the folder and then forget that they changed it. Then they'll call you and you'll have to go to their desk to change it back.

The Location element allows you to specify a URL location to the icon that is used for the folder on the desktop. By default, this element does not exist in the `config.xml` file, and the default Program Neighborhood icon is used.

```
      <SystemTrayMenuDisplay>
            <Enabled modifiable="true"
forcedefault="false">true</Enabled>
```

```
      </SystemTrayMenuDisplay>
</FolderDisplay>
```

The next section, "SystemTrayMenuDisplay," allows you to place a little Program Neighborhood Agent icon in your users' system trays that they can use to access their published applications and content.

Notice that because this is the end of the Folder Display section, there is a final </FolderDisplay> tag that closes out the section.

### Desktop Integration

The Desktop Integration section of the config.xml file is shown below:

```
<DesktopIntegration>
      <StartMenu>add</StartMenu>
      <Desktop>add</Desktop>
</DesktopIntegration>
```

You shouldn't have to change any of the settings in this section. In fact, Citrix specifically insists that you don't. Supposedly, this section is for features that haven't yet been added to PN Agent.

### Configuration File

The configuration file section allows you to specify the URL of the config.xml file your clients will use for all their settings. By changing this, you can migrate users to different NFuse servers.

```
<ConfigurationFile>
      <Location modifiable="true" forcedefault="false"
replaceServerLocation="true">http://yourNFuseserver/
Citrix/PNAgent/config.xml</Location>
      <Refresh>
            <Poll>
                  <Enabled>false</Enabled>
                  <Period>8</Period>
            </Poll>
      </Refresh>
</ConfigurationFile>
```

With the "Location" section, you can specify the URL location of the XML file that clients will use to access their PNA settings. This is something that you should definitely NOT let users change, by setting the modifiable attribute to "false." One thing that's interesting about this is that if you change the location, but you have "forcedefault" set to "true," it's possible that your users will never get the default again. This is because if you change the location and the users connect to the new location, they will use the settings from the XML file in the new location instead of this XML file.

The "Refresh" tag allows you to specify whether you want this configuration data to refresh periodically. It's important to note that this refresh does not control the available applications or content refresh, it controls the refresh of client agent settings from this config.xml file. You can control the time between refreshes with the "Period" tag, specified in hours.

### *Request*

The Request section of config.xml allows you to specify where clients should look for published application data and how often they should refresh their information.

```
<Request>
      <Enumeration>
      <Location replaceServerLocation="true">http://
yourNFuseserver/Citrix/PNAgent/enum.asp</Location>
      <Smartcard_Location
replaceServerLocation="true">https://yourNFuseserver/
Citrix/PNAgent/smartcard_enum.asp</Smartcard_Location>
            <Refresh>
                  <OnApplicationStart
modifiable="true" forcedefault="false" >true</
OnApplicationStart>
                  <OnResourceRequest modifiable="true"
forcedefault="false">false</OnResourceRequest>
                  <Poll modifiable="true"
forcedefault="false">
                        <Enabled>true</Enabled>
                        <Period>6</Period>
                  </Poll>
            </Refresh>
      </Enumeration>
```

This "Enumeration" tag lets you specify where and how the application list is refreshed. By default, the application enumeration is performed by the enum.asp file which is located in the same directory is the config.xml file. Smartcard_enum.asp is used when your users authenticate with smart cards. You can change the URL for that file with the "Location" tags.

The "OnApplicationStart" tag refreshes the list only when the Program Neighborhood Agent is started. "OnResourceRequest" refreshes the application list whenever an ICA session is started or published content is accessed. If you enable the "poll" tag, the application list will be refreshed after the number of hours in the "Period" tag elapses.

```
<Resource>
<Location replaceServerLocation="true">http://
yourNFuseserver/Citrix/PNAgent/launch.asp</Location>
<Location replaceServerLocation="true">https://
yourNFuseserver/Citrix/PNAgent/Smartcard_launch.asp</
Location>
</Resource>
</Request>
```

The "Resource" tag points the PNA client to the file that is used to launch ICA sessions or content. By default, this tag points to launch.asp, located in the same folder as the other PNA NFuse files.

### Logon

The Logon section of the `config.xml` file contains settings that affect how users log on.

```
<Logon>
<LogonMethod>sson</LogonMethod>
<LogonMethod>prompt</LogonMethod>
<LogonMethod>smartcard_sson</LogonMethod>
<LogonMethod>smartcard_prompt</LogonMethod>
<EnableSavePassword>false</EnableSavePassword>
<SupportNDS>false</SupportNDS>
<NDS_Settings>
     <DefaultTree/>
</NDS_Settings>
</Logon>
```

There are several values that you can place into the "LogonMethod" tags, depending on how you want users to authenticate to their PNA clients. As you can see in the example, you can have multiple "LogonMethod" tags to support different logon options.

A value of "sson" will use the user's single sign-on credentials. A value of "prompt" will prompt the user for their credentials. Adding "smartcard_" to the front of these to logon types enables them for use with smartcards.

You can also set the "LogonMethod" tag to "anonymous" for use when you want to allow users to log onto anonymous applications.

If your users need to authenticate to an NDS tree, you can set the "SupportNDS" element to "true." When you do this, specify the default NDS tree in the "DefaultTree" tag. (Remember that since this tag is written as a single tag with the trailing "/," you'll need to write out the full tag set to specify the tree. Your tag will then look like this: <DefaultTree>yourtree</DefaultTree>.

### User Interface

The User Interface section of config.xml allows you to specify what components of the PN Agent client are available for users to view or edit.

```
<UserInterface>
     <ServerSettings>true</ServerSettings>
     <FolderDisplaySettings>true
     </FolderDisplaySettings>
     <RefreshSettings>false</RefreshSettings>
</UserInterface>
```

For each of these settings, a value of "false" means that the properties dialog box will not show up for PN Agent clients. The "ServerSettings" tag is associated with the "Server" tab in the PN Agent Properties box. The "FolderDisplaySettings" tag is associated with the "Application Display Tab," and the "RefreshSettings" tag is associated with the "Application Refresh Tab."

Throughout the XML file, if have you set your "modifiable" attributes to "false," then it really doesn't matter whether these "UserInterface" tags are set to "true" or "false," because the users won't be able to change anything anyway.

### File Cleanup

The file cleanup settings in the config.xml file allow you to specify whether the icons that have been placed on your users' desktops and Start menus should be removed.

```
<FileCleanup>
     <Logoff>false</Logoff>
     <Exit>false</Exit>
</FileCleanup>
```

A value of "true" in the "Logoff" tag causes the icons to be deleted when the user logs off. A value of "true" in the "Exit" tag causes them to be removed when the user exits the application. These file cleanup values aren't used very often, unless you have users that share workstations.

## ICA Options

The ICA options section of the `config.xml` file allows you to specify session options that are available to your PN Agent users.

```
<ICA_Options>
      <DisplaySize>
           <Options>
                <Dimension>
                     <Width>640</Width>
                     <Height>480</Height>
                </Dimension>
                <Dimension>
                     <Width>800</Width>
                     <Height>600</Height>
                </Dimension>
                <Dimension>
                     <Width>1024</Width>
                     <Height>768</Height>
                </Dimension>
                <Dimension>
                     <Width>1280</Width>
                     <Height>1024</Height>
                </Dimension>
                <Dimension>
                     <Width>1600</Width>
                     <Height>1200</Height>
                </Dimension>
                <Percent>75</Percent>
                <Mode>seamless</Mode>
                <Mode>fullscreen</Mode>
           </Options>
      </DisplaySize>
```

All of the "DisplaySize" tags dictate what display options are available to the users. The "Width" and "Height" tags of each "Dimension" tag specify the different resolutions that are available. For example, if you don't want users connecting at 640 x 480, then remove those tags, including the <Dimension> tag preceding it and the closing </Dimension> tag.

Notice that in addition to the "Dimension" tags, there is a "Percent" tag that allows you to specify session sizes as a percentage of screen size. You may add additional "Percent" tags as needed. Finally, there are two values available for the "Mode" tag. If you do not want seamless or full screen modes available, then remove the associated "Mode" tags.

```
<ColorDepth>
        <Options>1</Options>
        <Options>2</Options>
        <Options>4</Options>
        <Options>8</Options>
</ColorDepth>
```

The "ColorDepth" tags available here to PN Agent users are the same options that are available elsewhere. Within the config.xml file, the following color depth code is in place: 1=16 colors, 2=256 colors, 3=16-bit color, and 4=24-bit color. As with the other parameters, you may remove options that you do not want to present to users.

```
<Audio>
        <Options>high</Options>
        <Options>low</Options>
        <Options>medium</Options>
        <Options>off</Options>
</Audio>
</ICA_Options>
```

Similar to the other options, you can configure audio quality via the config.xml file. For example, if you want to disable sound for your PN Agent users, you would remove the excess tags so that your "Audio" section looked like this:

```
<Audio>
        <Options>off</Options>
</Audio>
```

The last tag in the ICA options section specifies the ICA template file that is to be used when users launch applications.

```
<ICA_TemplateFile>template.ica</ICATemplateFile>
```

Since PN Agent is based on NFuse technology, the ICA template file is used in the exact same way as it is in NFuse.

### Config.xml Closing Tag

In order to signify the end of the config.xml file, you need to close the very first tag (the root tag) that was opened at the beginning of the file.

```
</PNAgent_Configuration>
```

## Designing your PN Agent Solution

The PN Agent can read it's settings from a `config.xml` file from any URL. (This doesn't have to be an NFuse web server.) However, it does need to access an NFuse Classic server in order to receive the user's published application icons (via `enum.asp`) and to launch published applications (via `launch.asp`).

### Number of PN Agent Servers

Since the PN Agent ICA client only accesses the NFuse web server when applications are enumerated or launched, one NFuse server can support thousands of users. (Redundancy of these servers is discussed in Chapter 17.)

### Number of Config.xml files

You can have multiple config.xml files on a single NFuse server. This allows you to have different sets of users with different PN Agent configurations if you point them to unique `config.xml` files.

# What happened to Project Columbia?

If you worked with NFuse prior to version 1.7, you're probably familiar with Citrix's Project Columbia. Project Columbia was a set of web pages that replaced the default NFuse web pages. Columbia supported many advanced features, such as Citrix XML service load balancing and connecting NFuse web servers to multiple server farms.

Most of the core functionality of Project Columbia has been incorporated into NFuse Classic 1.7 or Enterprise Services for NFuse. Therefore, no versions of Project Columbia are compatible with NFuse 1.7, and no new versions are being developed.

# PART IV

## Deploying Your MetaFrame XP Servers

In this section

12. Server Deployment in the Enterprise     501

13. MetaFrame 1.8 Migration and Integration     533

14. Licensing     577

# MetaFrame XP Server Deployment in the Enterprise

**In this chapter**

Deploying MetaFrame XP        502

Deploying Applications        507

You've designed your MetaFrame XP environment. You know how you will publish your applications and how your users will connect. Now it's time to deploy your MetaFrame servers. This chapter does not focus on IT deployment methodologies or how to run a Citrix pilot project. Instead, this chapter focuses on the pure technical decisions you must make and steps you must take to move your MetaFrame XP environment from the design stage to the production stage.

Fundamentally, there are only two steps to this process:

1. Deploy the MetaFrame XP software to all your servers.

2. Deploy your applications to all your servers.

This chapter focuses on each step. Let's begin with your planning for the deployment of MetaFrame XP.

# Deploying MetaFrame XP

If your MetaFrame XP environment will consist of more than a few servers, then you will probably want to consider some method of automating their deployment so that you don't have to manually install and configure each one.

There are two different methods that you can use to deploy MetaFrame servers:

- Server Drive Imaging
- Unattended Installations

## Server Drive Imaging

As the name implies, server imaging involves creating a server image (or "clone") that will be used as the base image for target servers, then copying that image to other servers. To do this, you need to use third party drive imaging software, such as Norton Ghost (www.symantec.com) or StorageSoft ImageCast (www.storagesoft.com).

You can also create hardware-based images. These drive images can be created with an imaging machine that copies a source hard disk to one or more target disks. Alternately, you can configure your source server with two hard drives configured for RAID 1, and then break the mirror and use one of the drives in your target server.

Server imaging works well if all of your servers are going to be identical—both in terms or hardware and software. In order to use imaging to deploy your MetaFrame XP servers, create a source server with a generic configuration. Then, after that server's image has been deployed to your target servers, perform some minor configuration tasks on those servers to get them ready for production use. (These minor tasks include changing the server name and IP address.)

Even though imaging requires that you spend some time configuring the clone and then finalizing each server that has been imaged, you can usually save quite a bit of time overall, even with only a handful of servers. The more servers that you have to deploy, the more time you can save.

### Advantages of Server Imaging

- No need to install the base operating system on target servers before you image them.
- Applications can be imaged in addition to Windows and MetaFrame XP.

### Disadvantages of Server Imaging

- Target servers must be "cleaned up" after they are imaged.
- All server hardware must be identical.
- You need to take the time to create a source server that is good enough to image.

Imaging a MetaFrame XP server involves three steps:

1. Create the source server that will be imaged.
2. Create the image and deploy it to your target servers.
3. Finalize the target servers by making any post-image modifications.

## Step 1. Preparing the Source Server

There are a few considerations that you need to take into account when choosing the server that will have its drives imaged for your server deployment.

Your source server should not be one that hosts the data store. Also, if you chose to use MetaFrame XP's automatic drive letter remapping, be sure to test your imaging software. Sometimes the remapped drive letters confuse the software and the images that result are no good.

Once you choose your target server, following these steps to image it:

1. Install the base operating system, but do not add the server to a domain.

2. Install MetaFrame XP. Configure it to access the IMA data store that you want for your environment.

3. If your IMA data store is on an Oracle, SQL, or DB2 server, edit the file `\Program Files\Citrix\Independent Management Architecture\mf20.dsn`. In the `[ODBC]` section, remove the line that reads `WSID=YOURSERVERNAME`.

4. Delete the `wfname.ini` file from the root drive.

5. Stop the IMA service.

6. Set the IMA service startup method to "manual."

7. If you're running Resource Manager (see Chapter 16), delete both the files in the `%Program Files%\Citrix\Citrix Resource Manager\LocalDB\` folder.

8. Install all of your applications, but do not publish any of them.

### Step 2. Copy and Deploy the Image

Once you've prepared your server, perform the imaging process and deploy the image to your new target server or servers.

### Step 3. Clean up the Newly-Imaged Target Server

The following steps will need to be performed on each newly-cloned MetaFrame XP server before it can be used:

1. Turn on the server, but ensure that it is not connected to the network.

2. Give the server a new Windows Security Identifier (SID) because it has the same one as the source server (kind of like how two cloned humans would have the same DNA). Technically, when you add the server to the domain, it will receive a new domain SID, but you should also use a tool to create a new local SID for the server. If your cloning software doesn't come with a tool to change the SID, there are many SID changing tools available on the Internet.

3. Configure the server with its permanent IP address.

4. Configure the server with its new computer name.

5. Turn off the server.

6. Plug in the network cable.

7. Turn on the server.

8. Add the server to the domain and reboot.

9. Start IMA service.

10. Change the startup of the IMA service to "automatic."

11. Run the qfarm utility to verify that everything looks okay. This new server should show up in the list.

12. Configure the server's zone membership. After you image a MetaFrame XP server, the zone membership settings are not retained, and the server joins the default zone when IMA service starts.

Once you've completed these steps, your new server is ready to go. You can configure it just like any server.

## Unattended Installations

Instead of imaging your MetaFrame XP servers, you can perform unattended installations. When you perform an unattended installation of MetaFrame XP, the standard `setup.exe` installation file is executed on a server. However, an installation script is used to automatically specify MetaFrame XP installation options so that you don't have to manually install the MetaFrame XP software on each server.

### Advantages of Unattended Installations

- MetaFrame XP unattended installations can be sent to many different types of hardware.

### Disadvantages of Unattended Installations

- You must manually install the base operating system
- You must manually install the applications.
- You must create the unattended installation script.

There are two methods that you can use to perform unattended installations of MetaFrame XP. The one you choose to use depends on the version of MetaFrame XP you are planning to install.

If you're going to use MetaFrame XP without any Feature Releases or with Service Pack 1 or Feature Release 1, you need to install MetaFrame XP by itself and then install SP-1 or FR-1. This is done by creating an unattended answer file.

If you're planning on using Service Pack 2 or Feature Release 2, the SP-2/FR-2 installation program can be used to install the base MetaFrame XP product that is automatically at the SP-2/FR-2 level. SP-2 and FR-2 have been "slipstreamed" into the standard product installation. This installation program is available as an .MSI package, which means that there are several advanced options available to you. Of course you could choose to install MetaFrame XP without any Service Packs and then install SP-2 later, but installing the slipstreamed version of MetaFrame XP with SP-2 saves you a step.

### Creating an Unattended Answer File

The procedure for performing an unattended installation of MetaFrame XP without any Service Packs is very straightforward:

1. Install the first server of your server farm. This is necessary so that the server farm will be in place for future MetaFrame XP servers to connect to.

2. Copy the contents of the MetaFrame XP CD to the network.

3. If your IMA data store is based on a SQL, Oracle, or DB-2 database, copy the IMA data store DSN to a network share. This DSN is \Program Files\Citrix\Independent Management Architecture\mf20.dsn.

4. Edit the copied mf20.dsn file with a text editor. Remove the line WSID=YOURSERVERNAME.

5. Edit the unattend.txt file included with the MetaFrame XP installation files that you copied to the network in Step 2. Follow the instructions in the file to customize all the sections for your environment except for [Farm Settings], [Direct Connection Settings], and [Indirect Connection Settings].

6. From the new server that will have MetaFrame XP installed, map a drive to the network location.

7. Execute the installation program, specifying the "unattended" option, such as setup.exe /u:e:\unattend.txt. (The "e:" in this example represents the drive letter that you mapped in Step 6.)

When you use the unattended method for installing MetaFrame XP servers, be careful that you do not install too many servers at once. Each server locks certain tables in the IMA data store when it needs to add its own new information. The MetaFrame XP servers are smart enough to try again if they find that the data store is locked when they attempt to update it. However, if you try to install a huge amount of servers at once, the data store lockouts may cause the installation to fail on some servers.

### Creating Unattended Installs from the SP-2/FR-2 .MSI File

If you plan to install MetaFrame XP from the SP-2/FR-2 installation file, all of the source installation files are available in a single .MSI file instead of a standard `setup.exe` file. Because .MSI files are easy to work with and because most people use Service Pack 2, this method of installation is the one used most often.

In order to perform an unattended installation of an .MSI file, you need to apply "transforms." Transforms are files containing configuration options that are used to modify the installation of an .MSI file. Transforms are in the form of "transform files" with the `.mst` file extension.

The SP-2/FR-2 MSI file that is shipped from Citrix includes several sample transform files in the `\support\install` folder. These transform files contain generic settings, so they cannot be used directly. However, you can edit them to apply the properties that are appropriate in your environment.

To edit a transform file, you need a transform file editor. You can download a transform file editor from Microsoft for no charge. (To find this editor, go to `msdn.microsoft.com` and search for `orca.exe`.)

Once you have specified your installation options in your transform file, initiate the MetaFrame XP installation with the following command line:

```
msiexec.exe /i:mfxp001.msi /t:yourtransformfile.mst
```

After this command is executed on your all of your servers, you can start to think about your applications.

# Deploying Applications

It's kind of ironic, really. One of the primary advantages of MetaFrame is the fact that you can significantly decrease your software deployment timeframe since you only need to install applications once on a server instead of dozens of times on client devices. However, as your MetaFrame environment grows, it quickly becomes apparent that you need a solution for your servers, because with a large environment you need to install applications onto dozens of servers. Even though installing applications on dozens of servers is less work then installing them on hundreds of workstations, it is still a significant task that can be automated.

Fortunately, MetaFrame XP servers are the perfect candidates for using automated software distribution tools to install and update your applications on multiple servers. Before examing the details and design components of these tools, let's look at how automated software distribution works in general.

## An Overview of Automated Software Distribution

Automated software distribution is conceptually the same anywhere it is used, regardless of platform or tools. ZENWorks, SMS, Tivoli, Unicenter, IntelliMirror, and Citrix Installation Manager all work in exactly the same way.

Fundamentally, no software distribution tool has the ability to "push" software applications to target computers. These distribution tools simply evaluate a set of conditions on a target computer. If these conditions indicate that software should be deployed, the distribution tool causes the target computer to execute a command that launches the automatic software installation.

Software distribution environments are made up of three components. These components do not apply just to Citrix Installation Manager, but to all software distribution programs listed above.

- *Software Package*. This is a collection of the files (the source installation files) that are to be installed on the target computer.
- *Installation Command*. This is the command that is used to launch the installation of the software.
- *Software Distribution Agent*. This term describes the program that decides whether the software should be deployed. If it should, it executes the installation command on the target computer.

For example, imagine that you wanted to install Notepad onto some computers. You would create a software package that contained your source files—notepad.exe in this case. Then, you would need to specify the command that should be used to install the software. In this case, that command would *not* be notepad.exe. To understand this, let's look at what happens on the target computer.

When the time came for the package to be installed, your software distribution agent would connect to the network location where your package was stored and run the installation command line. In this case, if you specified the installation executable as `notepad.exe`, when the software installation was scheduled to begin the Notepad application would be launched (because you specified `notepad.exe`). The user would be confused, wondering why Notepad opened all by itself. They would close it and continue working. In this case the software distribution program did exactly what you wanted it to—it connected to the network share and ran `notepad.exe`. In fact, the software distribution program would report that there was a successful installation, because `notepad.exe` ran and it exited successfully. In this scenario, the software distribution utility did its job. However, the administrator that configured it did not.

In order to successfully deploy Notepad with a software distribution utility, you need to create an installation procedure. In this simple case, that is probably most easily done with a batch file. Let's create a batch file called `install.bat`. The batch file can be made up of the following line:

```
copy \\networkserver\share\notepad.exe
%systemroot%\system32\
```

As you can see, this "installation program" will copy notepad from the network share to the target computer's local hard drive. It's important to note here that the `%systemroot%` variable is used to specify the location on the target computer. That way, your program will work no matter how the target computer's drives are configured.

Once this installation program is complete, you need to update your software package. Your new package will contain two source files—`notepad.exe` and `install.bat`. You also need update your installation procedure. Instead of running `notepad.exe`, your package is now launched by running `install.bat`.

Now, when the software distribution agent needs to install your package, it will work whether or not a user is logged on, and it will not interrupt them while they're working. As you have seen, this improvement step had nothing to do with a bug in the software distribution utility. It had everything to do with the skill of the people creating the package.

Let's take a look at another example. Imagine that you want to deploy Microsoft Office XP to 100 computers. Ordinarily, you would go to each computer and execute `setup.exe`. That setup program would prompt you for several options, configurations, and information. When it had all the information it needed, the actual installation would begin.

When using automated software distribution utilities, this process is no different. If the software distribution utility decides that a computer needs to have an application installed, then the software distribution utility instructs the computer to run the application's installation program.

If you simply copied the contents of the Microsoft Office XP CD to a network share and then instructed the target computers to run the command setup.exe to install Office XP, each target computer would run the full GUI version of setup.exe. This GUI version requires user input along the way to enter the options, installation path, and CD key. Imagine what would happen in the real world if the executable for an Office XP distribution was setup.exe:

- Some computers would have no one logged on, which would mean that the software distribution would fail, because Office XP's setup.exe requires a user to be logged onto the computer in interactive mode.

- Other users would see the box pop up that said "Microsoft Office XP Setup." They would think to themselves, "Why is this happening? I didn't run this!" Then, they would immediately cancel the installation.

- Still other users would continue through the installation. In these cases, each user would probably choose different options, meaning that the Office XP installation is different on each computer.

In the real world, if you want to deploy Microsoft Office XP to your Meta-Frame XPe servers, you need to create a software installation package it.

In your package, you would specify the location of the source files and the command line needed to kickoff the installation. Instead of specifying "setup.exe" to launch the installation, it is possible to create a "silent" installation of Microsoft Office XP. This silent installation involves creating a configuration file that specifies all of the options that you want, and then running setup.exe with special command-line parameters that instruct it to read settings from the custom configuration file. This is done with the same methods used to specify "silent" installs of the ICA client software in Chapter 10.

To summarize, the important thing to remember when using any software distribution environment, including Citrix Installation Manager, is that you must first create the "silent" installation routine for your application before you can distribute it to any target computers (or target MetaFrame XPe servers in this case).

# Automated Software Distribution Considerations

If you're thinking that using automated software distribution is too much work, consider this: Would you rather spend some upfront time building packages for and testing your applications, or would you rather install your application over and over and over until it was on all your servers.

The decision of whether to use automated software distribution can be a difficult one to make. Fundamentally, everyone wants to use automated software distribution because on the surface, it simplifies the management of software and software updates. However, in the real world, it's not always that easy. To help you decide whether or not you can use automated software distribution for your applications, ask yourself the following questions:

- How difficult is it to package your applications?
- How often are your applications updated?
- How long do these updates take to deploy?

### How difficult is it to package your applications?

For each application, consider whether it comes to you ready to go in Windows Installer package or whether you need to manually create the application package. If you have an MSI file, then your application package is ready to go without much effort on your part. However, if you must manually create an application package, you need to do some testing to figure out how long it will take you to create that package.

All too often in the real world people spend four days trying to create a software installation package that they could have manually deployed to all their servers in two days.

You can download a document called "Application Compatibility Guide: Citrix Installation Manager" from www.citrix.com/support. This document contains detailed instructions on how to package dozens of popular applications for deployment with Installation Manager to MetaFrame XP servers. It provides a great starting point when determining how difficult an application will be to deploy. If your application is not listed in that document, you can always post a question on the http://thethin.net forum.

### How often are your applications updated?

If you have an application that will need to be updated frequently, then it may be worth your time to create an application package because once you figure out the tricks you should be able to package new versions of the application quickly. On the other hand, if your application is only updated every 18 months, then it might not be worth it.

## How long do these updates take to deploy?

If the application updates only take ten minutes each and you have ten servers, then you can manually deploy all of your updates to all of the servers in less than two hours. Most likely, it will take you longer than that to create an application package. However, if you have 100 servers, it could take two full days to deploy all of the updates. If you can make an application package in one afternoon, then it's worth it.

### Factors that May Lead to Automated Software Deployment

- Many MetaFrame XP servers.
- Frequent application updates.
- Applications that are easy to package, such as MSI applications.
- Good test lab environment.

### Factors that May Prevent Automated Software Deployment

- Small number of MetaFrame XP servers.
- Infrequent application updates.
- Complex applications that require significant effort to package.
- No test lab environment.

## What method of software deployment should you use?

If you decide that automated software deployment is right for your environment, there is no reason to use Citrix's Installation Manager. There are many other third-party software distribution tools to consider using instead of Citrix's tools, such as Microsoft Systems Management Server, Novell ZENworks, CA Unicenter, or Tivoli.

If you don't have these tools in your environment, then you should not introduce them for the sole purpose of deploying software applications to Meta-Frame XP servers. However, if you have them already and they are being used on a daily basis, you can extend them to the MetaFrame XP environment without much additional effort and without the need to learn Citrix's Installation Manager or purchase MetaFrame XPe.

### Advantages to Using Third Party Software Distribution Tools

- They work with any version of MetaFrame XP, not just MetaFrame XPe.
- You can use them for other, non-MetaFrame XP environments.

- You don't have to learn any new packager tools or software distribution tools.

- Their single purpose is to distribute software, so they are much more robust than Citrix Installation Manager.

### Disadvantages to Using Third Party Software Distribution Tools

- They do not integrate as tightly with MetaFrame XP.

- They require that you have the expertise and support structures in place.

- They cost more than Installation Manager, which is built into MetaFrame XPe.

## Citrix Installation Manager Overview

One of the advanced components of MetaFrame XPe that's not available with XPs or XPa is the Citrix Installation Manager (IM). IM is Citrix's automated software distribution tool that is fully integrated into the CMC and the MetaFrame XP environment. Installation Manager fundamentally works in the same fashion as any software deployment application, such as Novell's ZENWorks or Microsoft's Systems Management Server.

Before we take an in-depth look at how you can begin using Installation Manager, let's provide a real-world overview. We'll cover the components that comprise an Installation Manager environment and some of the actions that must be taken to use it.

### Installation Manager Components

Installation Manager for MetaFrame XPe is made up of several core components:

- Application Packages.
- The Citrix Packager.
- Packager Machine.
- Network Share.
- Citrix Installer Service.
- Installation Manager plug-in for the Citrix Management Console.

### Component 1. Application Package

An Installation Manager application package is a collection of source files and the scripted installation procedure needed to install a software application onto a MetaFrame XPe server. Every application or software update needs to be "packaged" in order to be installed to a MetaFrame XPe server with Installation Manager. In the real world, you will end up having dozens of application packages in your MetaFrame XPe environment.

### Component 2. The Citrix Packager
The Citrix Packager is the stand-alone utility that you use to create certain types of application packages for applications that are to be deployed to MetaFrame XPe servers. As you will see later in this chapter, the Citrix Packager is only one of the many options you have for creating application packages.

### Component 3. Packager Test Server
In order to create your application packages, you need a test server. This server is usually a non-production server that is dedicated to the use of the Citrix Packager. Ideally, the format and layout of this server will mimic your production servers.

### Component 4. Network Share
Once a package is created, it is stored on one or more network shares. From here, target MetaFrame XPe servers can download and install the package.

### Component 5. Citrix Installer Service
The Citrix Installer Service is installed on the target MetaFrame XPe servers that receive packages deployed with Installation Manager. This service is comprised of two parts: the installer subsystem and installer service. The installer subsystem manages packages and schedules installations, while the installer service runs on each server and physically installs the packages. The Citrix Installer Service must be installed on every machine that will have software applications installed via Installation Manager packages.

### Component 6. Installation Manager Snap-in for the CMC
In order to manage and configure Citrix Installation Manager, components are added to the Citrix Management Console. These components extend the functionality of the CMC by allowing you to view the status of packages and installation jobs.

## *How Citrix Installation Manager Works*
The six components of Citrix Installation Manager work together to allow applications to be deployed to MetaFrame XPe servers. That deployment process can be summarized in four steps:

1. Packages are obtained or created.

2. Packages are added to the Installation Manager database.

3. Jobs are scheduled.

4. Applications are published.

## Step 1. Packages are obtained or created.

The first step to deploying software to MetaFrame XPe servers is obtaining or creating application packages. Applications that use the Windows Installer installation method (that have .msi files) are ready for Installation Manager without any other administrative work. In these cases, the software vendor has already created the application package for you. (See Chapter 10 for more information about the Windows Installer.)

For applications whose installation routines were not built with the Windows Installer, you will need to create a package using the Citrix Packager and the Packager test server.

## Step 2. Packages are added to the Installation Manager database.

After application packages are created, they must be added to the Installation Manager database, which is part of the IMA data store. By adding packages to the database, the packages are made available to MetaFrame XPe servers. Adding packages to the database is usually as simple as copying the contents of the package to a network share or shares that are available to all the Meta-Frame XPe servers, and then using the CMC to add information about the package, such as its name, network location, and intended platform.

## Step 3. Jobs are scheduled.

After the package is added to the Installation Manager database, it needs to be installed onto the target MetaFrame XPe servers. Each software installation is known to Installation Manager as a "job." Installation jobs can be designed to run immediately or they can be scheduled to happen during off-peak hours. For each job that is executed on a target MetaFrame XP server, the package's installation script is "played back" and the needed package files are copied from the network share.

## Step 4. Applications are published.

After the application is installed on a target MetaFrame XPe server, the application must be published. This process is identical to traditional methods of deploying applications, in which after they are installed they must be published to be load-balanced across multiple servers. In most cases, publishing applications simply involves adding the new target MetaFrame XPe server to the published application's list of configured servers.

# Understanding Installation Manager Components

Now that we've reviewed the high-level Installation Manager components and the software installation process, let's take an in-depth look at each of the components.

## *Component 1. Application Packages*
An Installation Manager Application Package consists of the complete scripted installation procedure and the source files needed to perform a software installation. An application package can be created for anything, from a service pack update to a full installation of an application to a hotfix. Basically, if you can script it, it can become an application package.

Application packages exist because the MetaFrame XPe servers to which you want to deploy software must have the instructions for procedure to follow to install the new software.

MetaFrame XPe's Installation Manager recognizes two different types of packages:

- Windows Installer Packages (.msi)
- Application Deployment Files (.adf)

### Windows Installer Packages
Windows Installer packagers are regular application packages that have been created with the Windows Installer utility. The scripted installation procedures for these packages are located in files with the .msi extension. These .MSI files contain the information and instructions needed to install applications.

If the software application that you want to install with Installation Manager has an .MSI file, then the application package is already created. Every new piece of Microsoft Software and many other vendors' software products use the Windows Installer. You can import the .MSI package directly into Installation Manager. In fact, if you're using Feature Release 2, Installation Manager will even detect new .MSI files placed in designated network shares and add the packages to the installation environment automatically.

Windows Installer packages are still launched via some type of command such as setup.exe. However, that setup executable is a small stub program that launches the Windows Installer. Take a look at a Windows Installer application (such as Office 2000). You will see that there is an .MSI file in the root directory representing the instructions for the package.

Ordinarily, you wouldn't create a Windows Installer package yourself. You usually take the .MSI packages created by the software vendor and bring them directly into your Installation Manager environment so that you can begin deploying the software to your MetaFrame XP servers.

### ADF Packages

Not all software vendors choose to use the Windows Installer for their applications. (Okay, most software vendors choose not to use the Windows Installer.) As outlined previously, in order to deploy any applications to MetaFrame XPe servers with Installation Manager, they must be packaged. To package non-MSI applications, Citrix includes a utility with Installation Manager called "The Citrix Packager."

The Citrix Packager creates ADF packages. Each ADF package is composed of two components:

- The collection of files that are to be copied and installed to the target MetaFrame XP servers. This is known as the ADF package itself. Like any software package, the ADF package is the collection of the application's source files. These can be on a CD or a network share.
- The ADF software installation script. The ADF script is a file with the extension .wfs. This file is a text file created by the Citrix Packager. It is the actual script played back on the target machine that copies files and modifies registry keys.

The ADF script file is named with the application to be installed, based on the project in the Citrix Packager.

### *Component 2. The Citrix Packager*

The Citrix Packager is a stand-alone utility that watches how applications are installed on test servers and then creates ADF packages that can be used to deploy the applications to target MetaFrame XPe servers. It monitors applications as they are installed and records any registry keys or .INI files that are added, modified, or deleted. It also creates a list of any files that were added.

From this information, the Citrix Packager gathers all of the new files together into a package. It then creates an ADF installation script that can be used to play back the installation on future servers.

Using the Citrix Packager, you can create projects for each software application that you want to deploy. A Citrix Packager project stores all sorts of information about the environment, changes, setups, and additions, as well as your settings for how the scripts play back on target MetaFrame XPe servers.

By creating a different project for each software application, you can easily modify pieces of the installation without having to build a new package from scratch. Even after a project's ADF has been entered into the CMC and deployed, you can still work with the packager and modify the project. For example, you can add outside files to the package. Many people use this when a new version of a file is available, when a new hotfix is released.

When your project is configured as you want it, the Citrix Packager allows you to "build" the project. This build process creates the actual ADF script file.

Everything that a software application does as it's being installed on your test MetaFrame XPe server while the Citrix Packager is running is logged. This allows you to use the packager's "rollback" feature, which essentially removes everything that your application installation did on the test server. You can use this to quickly test new changes without having to rebuild a new MetaFrame XPe test server after each installation.

### *Component 3. Packager Test Server*

The Citrix Packager software should be installed on a dedicated MetaFrame XPe test server, informally known as the "Packager Test Server." This is the server that you will use to create ADF packages for non-MSI applications that you would like to deploy to MetaFrame XPe servers. This server should be identical to your production servers, both in terms of software and hardware.

In the real world, some people laugh when they hear that they should have a test server that is the same as their production servers. "You don't know what it's like around here!" they say. However, getting a new dedicated test server from your boss might be easier than you think. Remember that if the test server is identical to your production servers, its hardware components can be instantly swapped with a failed component in a production server. Also, because Installation Manager is only used in larger environments, you might be able to get several departments to chip in together to pay for a test server.

At a minimum, the packager test server must have the same software configuration as your production MetaFrame XPe servers. For example, if you have applications installed on your packager test server that are not installed on your MetaFrame XPe target servers, you could have problems when the packaged applications are run on the target servers. TMost software applications' installation programs will not install required shared files, like DLLs, if a current version already exists on the computer where the installation is taking place.

If you have applications already installed on your packager test server, the script for the application installation routine that you are recording may not contain information on some of the DLLs that are required since they already exist on the packager test server (causing the installation routine not to install them). If this occurs, the installation script doesn't realize that a required DLL was skipped and the required DLL is not written into the script.

Then, when the application package's script is played back on target machines, the DLL would not be copied given that it was not in the script. Even though your script was successful, the application would fail due to the missing DLL.

Because of this, your package test server should have the same software configuration as your production servers. This includes the MetaFrame XP installation and configuration as well as any published applications or other utilities.

If you have MetaFrame XPe installed on multiple platforms in your environment, you should have two test servers or (worst case) one test server with two hard drives that you can swap—one for each operating system.

### An Overview of DLL Versioning

Something that you need to be aware of when using the Citrix Packager on a test server is that the Citrix Packager is not aware of "DLL Versioning," unlike some other software packaging utilities (such as the Windows Installer).

DLL versioning is what allows an installation routine to be created on one computer for a program to be installed on another computer where the numbers and versions of DLLs could be different.

A DLL file is just a chunk of programming code. The reason developers put some code in a separate DLL file instead of the main EXE is because the code in a DLL file can be easily shared by several programs. For example, in Windows, all of the code that provides shared functionality is maintained in DLL files. This includes instructions for how to draw the menus, scroll bars and buttons, as well as code for interacting with the desktop and other programs.

All DLLs have version numbers, just like any program. Higher version numbers are used for newer versions of a DLL. Newer DLLs usually have new features while also including all of the functionality of previous versions.

The version numbers of DLLs play a big role in the software installation process. For example, if a software installation program knows that its application needs a file called `resources.dll` version 3.0, and it finds `resources.dll` version 1.0 on the computer already, it will update that DLL to version 3.0. Whichever program originally needed version 1.0 should still be able to use version 3.0. That program will just access the 1.0-level features of the DLL. If the new software application that needed `resources.dll` version 3.0 is uninstalled, its uninstallation program will leave version 3.0 of the DLL on the computer, because version 1.0 was there before it was installed.

However, this situation can become more complicated. If the new software application that needs the `resources.dll` version 3.0 sees that there is already a version 3.0 of that DLL installed on the computer, it will not copy over it. This can cause a problem if the original program that needed version 3.0 of the DLL were ever removed, because its uninstallation program would remove the DLL. Then, the new program that was installed wouldn't work, because `resources.dll` version 3.0 would not be available.

To combat this, the Windows operating system tracks the number of times a DLL file is installed. For example, if a software application needs `resources.dll` version 3.0 and it is not available on the computer, the installation program will install it. That DLL will have its installation counter set to 1. If another software application also needs `resources.dll` version 3.0, it will not be installed because it's already there. However, the DLL's installation counter will be incremented because the new program wanted to install that DLL. This would mean the `resources.dll`'s installation counter would be set to 2, indicating that 2 programs use that DLL.

If the first program is removed, when it tries to uninstall the DLL it will notice that the DLL's installation counter is greater than 1 so it will not remove the DLL. However, it will decrement the installation counter. If any program's uninstallation routine ever tries to remove a DLL whose installation counter is already set to 1, then the DLL will be deleted because no other programs need to use it.

It is important to understand DLL versioning and installation counters because the Citrix Packager is not aware of any of them. This is why it is crucial that your packager test server has the same software configuration as your production servers.

## Component 4. Network Share

To be able to use MetaFrame XPe's Installation Manager, you will need to identify at least one network share that can be used to hold all of your packages before they are deployed to the MetaFrame XPe target servers. This network share must be a Microsoft share that supports UNC naming conventions. All target servers receiving packages must be able to access a network share that you identify. This means that the account you configure for installation must have at least "Read" permissions to the shares.

Each network share must have enough free space to hold the applications package that you store on it. Each package will be the size of the installed application plus a bit of overhead for the installation script. It's important to note that the application size will be the size of the installed application, not the source files. Installation Manager does not compress application packages.

## Component 5. Citrix Installer Service

The Citrix Installer Service runs in the background on MetaFrame XPe servers that are to receive applications deployed with Installation Manager.

When application installations are scheduled, this service plays back the installation scripts for the ADF or MSI packages. When this playback occurs, no user intervention is required.

The Citrix Installer Service is always running on MetaFrame XPe servers with Installation Manager enabled. However, it requires very little memory when not in use.

## Component 6. Installation Manager Plug-in for the CMC

When Installation Manager is installed on a MetaFrame XPe server, the Citrix Management Console is extended to provide the administrative functionality of Installation Manager.

The setup routine is able to extend the functionality of the CMC by installing a Java plug-in contained in the `imsmgr.jar` Java package. This plug-in is copied to the `\Program Files\Citrix\Administration\Plugins\` folder. If you see a generic folder called `IM_FOLDER` in your CMC, that means that your IMA data store contains Installation Manager information, but that the CMC console you are using has not had the Installation Manager plug-in installed. The simplest way to install this plug-in is to use the Installation Manager setup program from the CD.

This plug-in needs to be installed on each computer that runs the CMC where you want to manage Installation Manager. Obviously, the plug-in is automatically installed on the MetaFrame XPe servers where you install Installation Manager. But, if you have the CMC installed elsewhere, such as on your workstation, you will need to manually install the plug-in.

The Installation Manager CMC plug-in allows you obtain an ADF or MSI package from the network, add it to the Installation Manager database and schedule it for installation to servers. It also allows you to view the status of pending and previous Installation Manager jobs.

## Using Installation Manager in the Real World

Remember the four steps to deploying applications with Installation Manager that we addressed previously?

1. Packages are obtained or created.
2. Packages are added to the Installation Manager database.
3. Jobs are scheduled.
4. Applications are published.

Now that we've taken a detailed look at all of the components that make up an Installation Manager environment, the four steps can be used as a high-level framework to build a detailed flowchart covering all of the steps, sub-steps, and decisions that need to be made when installing an application with Installation Manager to MetaFrame XPe servers. As you read through the steps, you can refer to the process outlined in Figure 12.1 (facing page).

### *Step 1. Creating Packages*
The first step is to create the application package. Remember, Installation Manager for MetaFrame XPe supports two types of application packages: Windows Installer packages and Citrix ADF packages. Let's take a look at the details of each type.

### Option 1. Microsoft Installer Packages
Before an application built with the Windows Installer can be used by MetaFrame XPe's Installation Manager, the package must be prepared. Microsoft calls the preparation of an MSI package an "administrative" installation. To perform an administrative installation, execute the following command:

```
msiexec /a e:\path\packagename.msi
```

*Figure 12.1 The Installation Manager application distribution process*

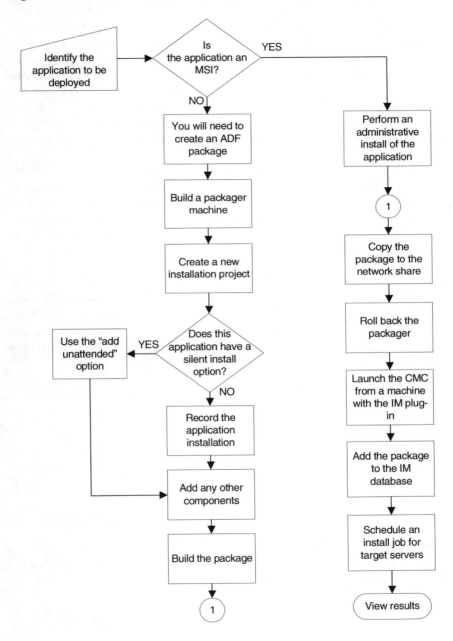

In this example, `e:\path\` is the full drive letter and path to the existing installation package and `packagename.msi` is the name of the Windows installer file. This file will always have the extension `.msi`. Its name will usually be somewhat related to the package, such as `visio.msi`, but sometimes it is not, such as `install.msi`. Also, the MSI packages are not very large. For example, Office XP's MSI file is only about 3.4MB. That is because the MSI files must only contain the instructions (or the installation playback scripts) for installing applications. Often times they do not contain the actual files themselves. MSI installation files are very similar to the Citrix ADF files generated by the Citrix Installer, which have the file extension .wfs.

When the `msiexec` command is executed, the Microsoft Installer will perform an administrative install of the application. (Hence the "`/a`" command line option.) This administrative install does not actually install the application locally. Instead, it prepares the application to be installed from a network location by decompressing any CAB files and making sure that everything is in order.

When you execute the `msiexec` command, the standard graphical application installation dialog will begin. Your only option will be to enter a location for the installation. This should be the network location where your package will sit before it is pushed out to MetaFrame XPe servers. Remember, this graphical setup program does not install the application locally.Advantages of Using Microsoft Installer Packages

- No additional configuration is needed to use them with Installation Manager.
- High success rates because the application's native installation routine is used.

### Disadvantages of Using Microsoft Installer Packages
- Not all applications are built with the Microsoft Installer.
- Okay, *most* applications are not built with the Microsoft Installer.

### Option 2. Citrix Packager
If the application that you want to deploy does not have an MSI file, you will have to package it with the Citrix Packager.

Packaging applications for automated deployment is more of an art than a science. In fact, there are entire books dedicated to this single topic. (Check out *The SMS Installer* by Rod Trent.) While it's not practical to discuss every possible scenario that you might run into when packaging an application, there are several tips and techniques that real world administrators use:

- The package server where the Citrix Packager is loaded should be identical to the target MetaFrame XPe servers, in terms of software configuration and applications that are installed.

- Application Packages should not be packaged through ICA sessions.

- You should incorporate some sort of structured naming convention for your packages. This will help you identify packages that need to be updated months after they were created.

- When you record your installation, it is important that there are no unnecessary programs running in the background. If there are, anything that they do will become part of the recording and will be played back on all of your target servers.

- If you are using Feature Release 1 or 2, you will have a "Project Wizard" option that will walk you through creating an application package with the Citrix Installer.

- If the software application that you want to package has a silent install option, you should use the "add unattended install" option of the Citrix Packager instead of recording it yourself. After all, you never can tell exactly what the programmer intended to do with the installation routine. By using the silent install, you are effectively using their installation routine instead of creating your own.

- Become familiar with InstallShield. As discussed in Chapter 10, InstallShield is a program that application developers use to create the installation routines for their software applications. InstallShield is similar to the Windows Installer. While Installation Manager cannot support InstallShield applications directly, the Citrix Packager can support their silent installs. Even if it's not mentioned in the software application's product documentation, every single application whose installation routine is built with InstallShield can be installed in a silent mode. You can learn more about InstallShield, and how to use it from www.installshield.com. One of the great things about this is that you can purchase the InstallShield product manual for about US$60. That manual gives you all the information that you need to create silent installs for any commercial applications that use InstallShield. This will put you in a very good position, because about 95% of all commercial applications have installation routines that are built with either the Windows Installer or InstallShield.

- Get to know the application packaging resources that are available. One of the best websites for information about application packaging is www.myITforum.com run by Rob Trent.

### Advantages of Citrix Installer ADF Packages

- Allows non-MSI applications to be deployed via Installation Manager.

### Disadvantages of Citrix Installer ADF Packages

- Creating the packages requires skill.
- Packages that are not created properly can break target servers.
- The Citrix Packager requires a dedicated test server.

## Step 2. Adding Packages to Installation Manager

Once you've identified, created and/or prepared your application package, you need to let Installation Manager know that it exists. In order to do this, you tell Installation Manager which user account it should use to find and install the package and where on the network the package is located.

In order for Installation Manager to be able to access your package on the network, you need to specify which user account you would like Installation Manager to use when working with the package (CMC | Citrix Installation Manager | Properties | Network Account). This user account needs to have "Read" access rights to the package source files on the network and administrative rights on each MetaFrame XPe target server where the package will be installed. In the real world, most people create a dedicated service account in the domain, called something like "IMS_Service" that they use exclusively use for Installation Manager. By creating a dedicated account, you can give it only the security rights that it needs to perform Installation Manager functions, without giving it full Domain Admin rights.

Once you specify which account is to be used, you need to add the package to the IMA data store by telling Installation Manager where your package is located on the network (CMC | Installation Manager | Add Package, or with FR-2, CMC | Installation Manager | Packages | Add Package). If this network location is not the original location of the application package that you have created, then you should copy the package to its permanent location before adding it to the IMA data store. As soon as this step is complete, the application package will be primed and ready to be installed to target MetaFrame XPe servers.

If you're using Feature Release 2, you can create "Package Groups." By using package groups, you can create a folder structure in the CMC that helps your organize your packages. Also, each package group can contain its own network account and file share location, allowing you to segment packages in large environments.

Do not confuse FR-2's Package Groups with FR-1's Package Groups. While FR-1 does allow you to create Package Groups, they are nothing more than folders for sorting your packages. For "true" package groups, including the ability to store a package on multiple network share points, you need FR-2.

### Creating Packages in WAN Environments

You should not use Installation Manager to deploy packages to MetaFrame XPe servers across slow WAN links. If you do this, you not only risk saturating the WAN, but you could also render your target server unavailable as the package is accessed across the WAN.

*Figure 12.2  Installation Manager in a WAN environment*

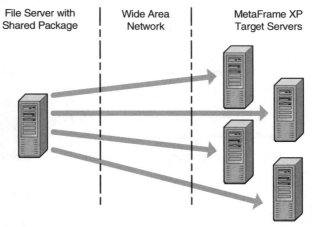

If you choose to use Installation Manager with multiple instances of one application, then you should develop a naming convention or implement package groups for your packages that indicate not only the application, but also the location where it is to be deployed. Sample package names include the following:

- IE Security Update – All
- MS Office SP-2 – North
- MS Office SP-2 – Corporate
- Sales Tracker – North

- Sales Tracker – Corporate

*Figure 12.3 Proper use of Installation Manager in a WAN environment*

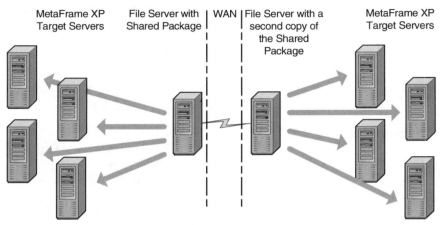

## Advantages of Creating Multiple Instances of One Package

- In large environments, the package can be deployed faster.
- Efficient use of WAN bandwidth.
- With FR-2, you can create multiple package groups. Each group can contain the same packages with different package source network shares.

### Disadvantages of Creating Multiple Instances of One Package
- More network storage space required.
- Each instance of the package must be manually added to the IMA data store.
- Prior to FR-2, each instance of the package must have its own unique name.

## Step 3. Job Scheduling and Package Installation
Once an application has been copied to the network share locations and added to the IMA data store, the package must be installed to the target MetaFrame XPe servers. This is done by creating a package installation job. There are two different ways a job can be created:

- Use the CMC to create an installation job.
- Use the CMC to publish a package to a server where it is not installed.

## Creating Installation Jobs for Servers

If you use the CMC to create an installation job (CMC I Installation Manager I Right Click on Package I Install Package), you can create a job that will install an application package to a server or a server group. This job can be set to run immediately or it can be scheduled so that the package is installed at some point in the future.

When a package installation job begins, all existing ICA connections are terminated. If necessary, you can configure the job not to begin until all of the ICA connections are closed. If you are using Feature Release 1 or 2, you can create a customized message that is sent to current users when a job is scheduled to run, notifying them of their impending session termination.

Whenever a job is finished, you should delete it to save space in the data store and keep your job list from becoming cluttered. If you create the job manually, you can specify the number of days before the job expires and is automatically removed from the job list, anywhere from "never" to 90 days.

If you are using Feature Release 2, you can filter your MetaFrame XPe servers by platform or by Installation Manager server group when you are creating a job. Without Feature Release 2, you will have to do this manually. Also, with Feature Release 2, you can specify in the job options that the target MetaFrame XPe servers should automatically reboot after the package has been installed. Without Feature Release 2, you will have to add the server reboot into your installation script.

### Advantages of Creating Installation Jobs for Servers

- Application installations can be scheduled for off-peak hours.
- You can specify granular job options.

### Disadvantages of Creating Installation Jobs for Servers

- Applications must be manually published after they are installed.

## Publishing Uninstalled Packages

Alternately, you can use the CMC to publish an uninstalled Installation Manager package to a target MetaFrame XPe server (CMC I Applications I Publish Application I Choose Installation Manager Package). When publishing an Installation Manager package with the CMC, all packages will be in the drop down list, regardless of whether or not a package has been deployed to any servers. This allows you to configure an application package for any MetaFrame XPe server, and if the application is published to a server where it has not been installed, the installation will start immediately after the application is published.

For farms containing more than 20 servers, you should not use this "single step" publish and install option to publish uninstalled application packages. This method will cause the application installation to start as soon as the application is published, and with more than 20 servers, your systems and networks will become overwhelmed.

If you need to deploy an application to more than 20 servers, then you should first deploy the application to the MetaFrame XPe servers by creating several smaller installation jobs, and then publish the application with the Citrix Management Console.

### Advantages of Publishing Uninstalled Packages

- Application installation, publication, and load management are combined into one step.

### Disadvantages of Publishing Uninstalled Packages

- The application installation job is launched immediately.

Regardless of the package installation method used, the following process shows how the various Installation Management components work together to install an application package to a target MetaFrame XP server:

*Figure 12.4  Installation Manager's Package Installation Process*

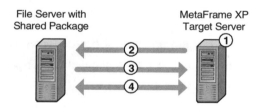

1. The installation job is initiated, either because the scheduled date and time has arrived or because the administrator has manually started it.
2. The installer service on the target MetaFrame XP server connects to the package source file share.
3. The installation package and script are copied to the MetaFrame XP server, then executed.
4. The status of the package is changed to "installed."

### Segmenting Target Servers into Server Groups

When using Installation Manager, you can choose to use MetaFrame XP server groups to deploy packages to more than one server at a time. To do this, combine multiple servers into logical groups, giving each group a name. Then, create application installation jobs that deploy packages to the entire group instead of to just one server.

The server groups that you create for Installation Manager are logical groups used only for Installation Manager application deployments. Group membership has no bearing on anything outside of Installation Manager. A MetaFrame XPe server can belong to more than one server group.

Because server groups only affect deployment, changing a server's group membership after an application has been installed will not cause application packages to be installed or removed.

Use common sense when creating your server groups. It is probably not a good idea to create a group of 50 MetaFrame XPe servers. When a package is deployed to a single server group, a network connection is still opened between the package share and each MetaFrame XPe server. A package deployed to a group of 50 servers will cause 50 servers to try to download the package from the same share at the same time. Also, because all 50 servers would probably finish the application installation at about the same time, they would all reboot at about the same time, which means that they would all be downloading their IMA data at the same time.

Most people create server groups based on WAN locations, business units, or the application sets that different servers need. A server can belong to multiple groups, but it doesn't have to belong to any group.

### Advantages of Using Server Groups

- Packages can easily be deployed to multiple servers.
- Multiple servers can maintain identical application sets.

### Disadvantages of Using Server Groups

- Server groups do not affect security.
- Each group member server must obtain its own copy of the package from the package share.
- Groups affect package deployment only.
- Moving a server to a new group does not cause that server to receive new applications.

### Viewing Package Installation Status

You can use the CMC (CMC | Installation Manager | Summary with FR-2, or CMC | Installation Manager without FR-2) to view the status of packages and installation jobs.

The applications tab shows you details about each package that has been added to the IMA data store, including its name and the executable used to launch it.

The "jobs" tab shows you details about each scheduled job, including the job name, the package it installs, its scheduled installation time, and the current status. Be careful when reading the status of a job, because it changes to "success" as soon as the job is successfully started. Installation Manager does not verify whether a job actually finishes.

## Step 4. Application Publishing

If you manually created an installation job, the last thing to do is publish the application. Once the application has been deployed to all of your target Meta-Frame XP servers, you can publish it just like any other application. If you chose to create the installation job by publishing the application directly, then the application will be ready to go and you can skip this step.

# CHAPTER 13

# MetaFrame 1.8 Migration and Integration

In this chapter

Concepts for Mixing MetaFrame 1.8 and XP     534

Native Mode Server Farms     549

Add-on Management Services from 1.8 to XP     551

MetaFrame 1.8 to XP Server Farm Migrations     557

Real World Case Study     571

Few of us have the luxury of building a MetaFrame XP environment from scratch. Many of us will need to upgrade or migrate from a current Meta-Frame 1.8 environment. While the other chapters in this book will help you design the final MetaFrame XP environment, this chapter will help you get there from your current MetaFrame 1.8 environment. Most likely, the migration plan that you create will call for a temporary coexistence period in which both MetaFrame 1.8 and MetaFrame XP servers will work together.

In this chapter, we'll look at how MetaFrame 1.8 and MetaFrame XP are fundamentally different and what it takes to get them to work together. We will study various interoperability and migration concepts and look at the various components that will be key elements in your migration strategy.

# Concepts for Mixing MetaFrame 1.8 and XP

Before we dive into the details of what it takes to integrate MetaFrame XP with MetaFrame 1.8, let's study some basic concepts relating to the interaction of MetaFrame XP and MetaFrame 1.8.

First, we'll look at the three levels of MetaFrame XP and how they compare to MetaFrame 1.8's add-on packages. Then, we'll see how MetaFrame XP servers can be configured for various levels of interaction with MetaFrame 1.8 servers. We'll also review some of the key MetaFrame 1.8 architectural components—components that you'll need to understand to successfully build an environment consisting of MetaFrame 1.8 and XP servers.

## MetaFrame 1.8 and XP Product Level Correlations

Unlike the multiple product levels available with MetaFrame XP, MetaFrame 1.8 came in one version—MetaFrame 1.8. (Technically, there were two different packages, MetaFrame 1.8 for Windows NT 4 Terminal Server Edition, and MetaFrame 1.8 for Windows 2000. However, these two packages were 100% identical from a features standpoint.) Additionally, there were several option packs that could be purchased a la cart to extend MetaFrame 1.8's basic functionality. Those options are detailed in Figure 13.1 (facing page).

*Figure 13.1  MetaFrame 1.8 add-on management services*

| Option Pack | Function |
| --- | --- |
| Load Balancing | Publish applications across servers |
| Resource Management Services | Performance management |
| Installation Management Services | Automate the installation of applications across multiple servers. |
| SecureICA | Encrypt ICA sessions. |
| Feature Release 1 | Added functionality that is now standard in MetaFrame XP. Replaced the Secure ICA add on. |

With MetaFrame XP, there are different levels with different features that roughly correspond to versions of MetaFrame 1.8. Of course, MetaFrame XP has dozens of other benefits over MetaFrame 1.8, but Figure 13.2 shows the basic equivalencies.

*Figure 13.2 Correlations between MetaFrame 1.8 and XP products*

| XP Level | Old Rough Equivalent |
| --- | --- |
| MetaFrame XPs | MetaFrame 1.8 |
| MetaFrame XPa | MetaFrame 1.8 + Load Balancing Pack |
| MetaFrame XPe | MetaFrame 1.8 + Load Balancing Pack + Resource Management Services + Installation Management Services |

# MetaFrame XP Interaction with MetaFrame 1.8

MetaFrame XP servers must be configured to enable or disable interaction with older MetaFrame 1.8 servers. This configuration, set for an entire Meta-Frame XP server farm, is known as the "mode of operation." MetaFrame XP server farms can be configured for one of two modes of operation: native mode or mixed mode. Native mode is used when no MetaFrame 1.8 servers exist and MetaFrame XP servers are operating "natively" in their own language and only with their own kind. Mixed mode is used when MetaFrame XP servers will be in "mixed" environments, communicating with other Meta-Frame XP and MetaFrame 1.8 servers. Some other aspects of each mode of operation are shown below.

### Native Mode (MetaFrame XP server farms operating in Native Mode)

- MetaFrame XP servers communicate with only other MetaFrame XP servers.

- No interoperability with MetaFrame 1.8 servers. (They don't even know that they exist.)

- Designed for the final state, for organizations after all MetaFrame 1.8 servers have been migrated to XP and no more MetaFrame 1.8 servers exist.

### Mixed Mode (MetaFrame XP server farms operating in Mixed Mode)

- Server farms may contain both MetaFrame 1.8 and XP servers.

- MetaFrame XP servers communicate with XP and 1.8 servers.

- MetaFrame 1.8 and XP servers appear to ICA clients as one unified farm. Clients do not know (or care) to which platform they actually connect.

- Designed for periods of migration, this mode allows MetaFrame 1.8 and XP servers to be integrated with each other while the migration is taking place.

- MetaFrame XP Feature Releases cannot be used.

The "mode of operation" for a MetaFrame XP server is a farm-wide setting. Changing the mode of the server farm changes the operating mode of all the MetaFrame XP servers in the farm. There is no way to set the mode on a server-by-server basis (unless each server is its own farm). The mode of a MetaFrame XP server farm can be changed at any time, and changed in any direction (native-to-mixed and mixed-to-native). There is no limit to the number of times that a farm can change modes. The server farm's mode is configured via the Citrix Management Console (CMC | Farm Properties).

You can only set the mode of operation for MetaFrame XP server farms. MetaFrame 1.8 server farms do not have a mode of operation—they are always operating with other MetaFrame 1.8 servers only or mixed-mode MetaFrame XP servers.

## MetaFrame 1.8 Technical Components

Before we progress too far into looking at the details of integrating MetaFrame XP server farms with MetaFrame 1.8 server farms, let's review the technical components of a MetaFrame 1.8 environment to ensure we have a full, fresh understanding of how they work. For this review, we will only focus on the MetaFrame 1.8 components relevant to integration with MetaFrame XP servers: the ICA Browser and the Program Neighborhood services.

## *ICA Browser*

Last century, MetaFrame 1.8 servers ran a service known as the "ICA Browser Service." This service performed many of the tasks that the IMA service and data store handle for MetaFrame XP servers today.

When multiple MetaFrame 1.8 servers exist on the same subnet, they collectively appoint one of them to become the "ICA Master Browser" through an election process similar to the zone data collector elections that take place in MetaFrame XP. The ICA master browser is responsible for maintaining information about user connections, published applications, ICA licenses, and server load. An ICA client can request information about the MetaFrame environment by sending out a broadcast on UDP Port 1604 requesting the information. The elected ICA master browser responds to the ICA client with the appropriate information. If something happens to the ICA master browser causing it to become unavailable, a new election is held to appoint a new ICA master browser.

One ICA Master Browser must exist on each subnet on which MetaFrame 1.8 runs. If MetaFrame 1.8 server farms span multiple subnets, then "ICA Gateways" must be defined to relay ICA browser information from one subnet to the other.

The ICA browser architecture of MetaFrame 1.8 is inefficient, a far cry from the IMA architecture of MetaFrame XP. But, when it comes to the integration of MetaFrame 1.8 servers with MetaFrame XP servers, the ICA browser service is the lowest common denominator. It is the only method of information sharing that MetaFrame 1.8 servers understand, and so we have no choice but to work with it.

## *Program Neighborhood Service*

In addition to the ICA browser service, the Program Neighborhood service plays a big role in MetaFrame 1.8 server farms. It too has been replaced by the IMA service in MetaFrame XP.

The Program Neighborhood service is responsible for building application lists and keeping track of those applications which are available on Meta-Frame 1.8 servers. A web of persistent server connections is created, as every MetaFrame 1.8 server creates a connection with every other MetaFrame 1.8 server in the farm. For example, ten MetaFrame 1.8 servers will have 45 connections between them, as shown in the following formula:

$$\text{servers} \; \times \; \left( \frac{\text{servers} - 1}{2} \right)$$

Be careful not to confuse the Program Neighborhood service with the Program Neighborhood client. The two are not the same. The latter is an ICA client executable that displays the results of the former.

## Mixed Mode Server Farms

Setting a MetaFrame XP server farm to mixed mode will enable the XP servers to communicate and integrate with 1.8 servers. You can then publish and load-balance applications across both platforms. Users will see one unified server farm that consists of MetaFrame 1.8 and XP servers.

Mixed mode is designed to be a temporary solution—to only be used for integration between MetaFrame 1.8 and XP servers. Citrix is very adamant about this. Of course, they have a vested interest (from the revenue standpoint) in moving everyone to XP. Rather than making a recommendation, let's look at all the aspects of mixed mode operation. You can be the judge as to whether this is something you want to support in your environment for an extended period of time.

For mixed mode farm operation, we will look at the following technical components:

- IMA Service
- Server Farm Design
- Administration Tools
- ICA Browser Service
- ICA Client to MetaFrame Server Communication
- Network Ports and Protocols
- Published Applications
- Load Balancing
- Licenses

## IMA Service

In order for a MetaFrame XP server farm to interoperate and communicate with MetaFrame 1.8 servers, it is necessary for the MetaFrame XP servers to fully emulate the MetaFrame 1.8 environment. Remember that MetaFrame XP completely replaced the Program Neighborhood service and ICA browser service with the new IMA service and architecture. This is great for pure (native) MetaFrame XP environments, but MetaFrame 1.8 servers are not able to communicate with or understand the IMA service. As a result, MetaFrame XP servers operating in mixed mode must run the legacy ICA browser and Program Neighborhood services in addition to the IMA service and all of its components (zones, IMA data store, etc.). Running these services might seem like a high price to pay for simple interoperability, but it is absolutely necessary since the architecture changed so drastically from MetaFrame 1.8 to MetaFrame XP.

The following chart details the differences in the IMA service between MetaFrame XP servers running in native mode and mixed mode.

When a MetaFrame XP server farm is set for mixed mode operation, a flag is set in the IMA data store. All MetaFrame XP servers check that flag to see which mode of operation they should be set to, and their IMA services are configured accordingly. MetaFrame XP servers check for the mode setting flag when the IMA service is started and periodically after that. Because of this, MetaFrame XP servers do not need to be rebooted in order to switch from native to mixed mode or vice versa. When the MetaFrame XP servers notice that the flag has been modified, they modify their configuration of the IMA service as outlined in Figure 13.3 (next page).

## Server Farm Design

Contrary to everything discussed so far, it is not *technically* possible to create one server farm that includes both MetaFrame 1.8 and MetaFrame XP servers. However, you can create two separate server farms (one for each platform) that have identical names.

Once both farms have the same name, the ICA browsers from each platform will share information—enabling the mixed mode, multi-platform integration.

From the management perspective, the MetaFrame 1.8 and MetaFrame XP mixed mode farms are two different farms. They must each be managed with their own versions of the management tools. Naming them identically does not allow them to be managed as one farm.

*Figure 13.3  IMA mixed and native mode differences*

| XP Servers in Native Mode | XP Servers in Mixed Mode |
| --- | --- |
| XP Servers use IMA-based Program Neighborhood and ICA Browser subsystems, which interact with the IMA data store. | XP Servers do NOT use IMA-based Program Neighborhood and ICA Browser subsystems. Instead, they use the Program Neighborhood service and the ICA browser services (which are stand-alone, backwards-compatible services). These two services interact with the local registry and the elected ICA master browser. |
| IMA service does not interact with local server registry. All configuration is stored in the IMA data store. | IMA service interacts with local server registry, in addition to the IMA data store. |
| Program Neighborhood and ICA Browser services are not used | Program Neighborhood and ICA Browser subsystems of the IMA service are disabled (because full ICA browser and PN services are used) |
| XML Service connects to IMA Service via Remote Procedure Calls | XML Service connects to Program Neighborhood Service via Named Pipes |
| ICA client connects to the Program Neighborhood Subsystem of IMA service | ICA client connects to Program Neighborhood Service |
| ICA client connects to the ICA browser subsystem of the IMA service | ICA client connects to ICA Browser service (via ICA Browser protocol, UDP 1604) |
| Citrix Server Administrator makes RPC connections to only MetaFrame 1.8 servers | Citrix Server Administrator makes RPC connections to all farm servers (1.8 and XP) |

## Administration Tools

MetaFrame XP and MetaFrame 1.8 farms must each be managed by its native administration tools. In addition to the Citrix Management Console for managing MetaFrame XP servers, the MetaFrame XP CD contains updated versions of the MetaFrame 1.8 administration tools that should be used to manage MetaFrame 1.8 servers that are participating in mixed mode XP server farms.

Let's look at some specific features of the updated administration tools for MetaFrame 1.8, included on the MetaFrame XP CD:

- **Citrix Server Administration Utility**. The version of Citrix Server Administration that is included with MetaFrame XP has been modified to allow configuration of MetaFrame 1.8 and MetaFrame XP servers, as long as the MetaFrame XP servers are operating in mixed mode.

- **Published Application Manager**. Published Application Manager should not be used to manage applications that have been migrated to MetaFrame XP servers. It can be used to manage published applications on MetaFrame 1.8 servers in mixed mode farms. See the published applications section of this chapter for more details.

- **Shadow Taskbar**. In native mode, the shadow taskbar only displays MetaFrame XP servers. Mixed mode farms allow the Shadow Taskbar to be used for MetaFrame 1.8 and MetaFrame XP servers.

- **License Manager**. The Citrix License Manager will continue to manage licenses for MetaFrame 1.8 servers, even in mixed mode farms. MetaFrame XP licenses, regardless of the server farm mode, are managed through the Citrix Management Console. See Chapter 14 for more information.

- **Citrix Connection Configuration**. Citrix server connections are basically the same on MetaFrame 1.8 and MetaFrame XP servers. Because this information is server specific, connection configurations are stored in the local server's registry. Use this tool to configure connections on MetaFrame 1.8 or XP servers, operating in farms that are native or mixed mode.

## ICA Browser Service

The real reason ICA clients can view MetaFrame 1.8 and MetaFrame XP servers as a unified farm in mixed mode environments is that both server platforms join information to form one unified ICA browser service. The unified ICA browser maintains information about applications and servers across both platforms.

Any MetaFrame XP server that is part of a server farm operating in mixed mode will automatically participate in ICA master browser elections. Thinking back to Citrix classes from a few years ago, you undoubtedly remember that the number one ICA master browser election criterion is the version of the ICA browser software. Since MetaFrame XP is newer than MetaFrame 1.8, if there is a MetaFrame XP server on the same subnet as a MetaFrame 1.8 server, the XP server will always win the ICA master browser election, regardless of its configured election preference.

If a single MetaFrame 1.8 server farm spans multiple subnets, ICA gateways are used to pass ICA browser information between the subnets. Because mixed mode MetaFrame XP farms fully emulate the ICA browser service of MetaFrame 1.8 farms, ICA gateways can exist in XP mixed farms.

Two servers are needed to form an ICA gateway, one to initiate the gateway and one to receive. These gateway servers can be configured with Citrix Server Administration (All Servers | ICA Gateways). Any MetaFrame 1.8 servers that are migrated to MetaFrame XP will retain their ICA gateway role.

## ICA Client to MetaFrame Server Communication

Let's look at how ICA clients interact with MetaFrame servers in mixed mode farms. An ICA client will contact a MetaFrame server for the following reasons:

- **Application Launch.** The client needs to get the address of the server to run the application.
- **Find New Application Set.** The client needs to get the list of applications that are available in the server farm.

An ICA client always uses one of the two high-level methods described below to contact MetaFrame servers. Refer to Chapter 10 for more.

- **Default Server Location.** The ICA client is preconfigured with known addresses of MetaFrame servers. The client systematically steps through the list, trying individual addresses, until a server responds.
- **Auto-Locate.** The ICA client has no idea where the server is. It sends out a generic broadcast request or tries to connect to a generic address. If this fails, the client request fails.

If a MetaFrame XP server farm is operating in mixed mode, XP servers will respond to ICA client "auto-locate" broadcasts. In a mixed mode environment, it really doesn't matter whether a 1.8 or an XP server responds because it doesn't matter which platform the ICA client successfully contacts. Because the servers of both platforms share information via the communal ICA browser service, the ICA client can receive information about applications on both platforms by contacting a server from either platform.

In reality, the ICA clients don't ever know (or care) to which platform they connect. The Default Server Location configuration on ICA clients can point to MetaFrame 1.8, XP, or a mixture of both.

## Network Ports and Protocols

MetaFrame XP servers operating in mixed mode will require the ports and protocols of MetaFrame XP servers and MetaFrame 1.8 servers.

For interaction with MetaFrame 1.8 servers, ICA browser communication will take place via UDP Port 1604. The standard IMA communication for MetaFrame XP will also take place over TCP port 2512.

Full port communication and usage information for both modes of operation can be found in the Appendix.

## Published Applications

When a MetaFrame 1.8 server is migrated to MetaFrame XP, any published applications on that server are automatically upgraded, regardless of whether the target server farm is running in mixed mode or native mode. These applications are immediately accessible to end users, and you can begin administering the applications via the Citrix Management Console. A log file created in the `%systemroot%\system32\` directory contains details regarding published applications that were migrated.

Complications arise in environments in which applications are published in a load-balanced fashion across multiple servers. If all of the servers to which an application is published are upgraded to MetaFrame XP at the same time, then there are no problems. The challenges occur when you need to make changes to a published application that is published to multiple servers after some of those servers have been upgraded to MetaFrame XP and some of them are still MetaFrame 1.8.

In order to understand the complications that could arise, let's take a look at the differences in how MetaFrame 1.8 and MetaFrame XP servers store configuration information for published applications.

First, consider the many components required of applications published to multiple MetaFrame platforms, including:

- MetaFrame 1.8 Servers
- MetaFrame XP Servers
- Citrix Management Console (for managing published applications on MetaFrame XP)

- Published Application Manager (for managing published applications on MetaFrame 1.8)

Each of the components plays specific roles, as outlined below.

### Citrix Management Console (CMC)

- Connects to the IMA data store.
- Reads / writes published application configuration to the IMA data store.
- Capable of configuring XP servers only.

### Published Application Manager (PAM)

- When launched, it systematically connects to the registry of every server in the farm, including XP and 1.8 servers. (It gets the server list from the ICA master browser via UDP port 1604.)
- Reads / writes published application configuration to the registries of each server.

### MetaFrame XP Servers Operating in Mixed Mode

- Maintain published application configuration in the IMA data store.
- Because they are in mixed mode, they also maintain published application configuration in their local registries, for the purposes of backward compatibility with MetaFrame 1.8 servers and PAM.

### MetaFrame 1.8 Servers

- Maintain published application configuration in their local registries.

Now that we've outlined how the components relate to each other when working with applications published across MetaFrame 1.8 and MetaFrame XP servers, let's take a look at the troubles that could arise. There are actually five different scenarios that could cause problems in this situation:

## Potential Trouble Scenario 1

If you publish an application to the MetaFrame XP servers by using the CMC, you will not be able to publish that application to the MetaFrame 1.8 servers.

### Why does this Happen?

When you use the CMC to publish an application to the MetaFrame XP servers, the servers write the published application information to the IMA data store. But, because the servers are operating in mixed mode, they also write the published application information to their local registries. Then, when you open Published Application Manager (PAM) to publish the application to the MetaFrame 1.8 servers, PAM connects to the registries of all the servers in the server farm, including the MetaFrame XP servers operating in mixed mode. When you try to add your application to the MetaFrame 1.8 servers, you will receive an error indicating that the application name is already in use, because PAM knows that the application is published on the MetaFrame XP servers from when it connected to their registries. If, as a work-around, you decide to publish the application under a different name on the Meta-Frame 1.8 servers, it will not be load-balanced with the MetaFrame XP version of the application.

### Solution

If you want to publish a new application to both platforms, you must publish it with Published Application Manager to the MetaFrame 1.8 servers first, and then publish it with the CMC to the MetaFrame XP servers.

## Potential Trouble Scenario 2

If there is an application that is published across MetaFrame 1.8 and XP servers, the application's icon disappears when the Published Application Manager that ships with MetaFrame 1.8 is refreshed. It will reappear after PAM is closed and opened again.

### Why does this Happen?

When you launch the version of Published Application Manager that ships with MetaFrame 1.8, it reads the registry of every single MetaFrame server in the server farm (in this case, both MetaFrame 1.8 servers and MetaFrame XP servers in mixed mode). From these servers, it builds a list of all the published applications in the farm. When you refresh the application list from within PAM, it only reads the registry of the MetaFrame XP servers. (Call it a "bug.") The registries of the MetaFrame XP servers (operating in mixed mode) list only the applications that are published locally. They do not list all of the servers that have the applications published, which is unlike the registries of MetaFrame 1.8 servers. With MetaFrame XP, the list of all servers that have an application published is stored in the IMA data store, not the local server's registry.

### Solution

The MetaFrame XP CD includes an updated version of Published Application Manager. The above problem will only occur if you are using the version of PAM that ships with MetaFrame 1.8.

## Potential Trouble Scenario 3

If a published application is modified with the version of Published Application Manager that ships with MetaFrame XP, that same application cannot be later modified with the version of PAM that ships with MetaFrame 1.8.

### Why does this Happen?

The version of Published Application Manager included with MetaFrame XP has been modified and recognizes applications differently than previous versions.

### Solution

Ideally, you should not modify any published application properties while your server farm is operating in mixed mode. (Remember that mixed mode is a "temporary" solution.) If this is absolutely necessary, the best method is to use the new version of Published Application Manager included on the MetaFrame XP CD.

## Potential Trouble Scenario 4

When mixed mode farms are being created, many administrators choose to automatically migrate the published applications on the MetaFrame 1.8 servers that they are migrating to XP. However, if circumstances force you to add or modify a published application on both platforms before all of your 1.8 servers have been migrated to XP, then you should not migrate any published applications on the remaining 1.8 servers when you migrate them to XP.

### Why does this Happen?

When the first server in a MetaFrame 1.8 server farm is migrated to a MetaFrame XP server in a mixed mode farm, a snapshot is taken of all published applications that are automatically migrated during the upgrade process. Any applications that are modified or added during the migration (i.e. after the first but before the last server has been migrated) cause inconsistencies, because these modifications or additions are not reflected in the snapshot that was taken. If you attempt to migrate any of these published applications that have been modified or added, it will have a random eight character suffix appended to the end of its name in the new environment to ensure that it is not integrated with a previously migrated version.

### Solution

Migrate the MetaFrame 1.8 server to XP without migrating any published applications. Then, use the Citrix Management Console to manually add the recently migrated server to the configured server list for the published application.

Alternately, you could choose not to modify the properties of any published applications until after your migration from MetaFrame 1.8 to XP is complete.

### Potential Trouble Scenario 5

After a published application has been automatically migrated from Meta-Frame 1.8 to XP, the new XP server will still show up in the configured server list from within Published Application Manager. However, if you use PAM to remove the XP server from the configured server list, you will not be able to use PAM to add the XP server back.

#### Why does this Happen?

Published applications on MetaFrame XP servers can only be managed with the Citrix Management Console, not Published Application Manager.

#### Solution

Manage the application with the Citrix Management Console.

### Published Application Migration Summary

In summary, given all the goofy things that can happen with published applications in mixed environments, there are two golden rules for working with published applications in mixed mode:

1. Do not make changes to or add published applications after they have been migrated to MetaFrame XP on some servers and not migrated on others.

2. When administering mixed mode farms, always use the updated versions of the MetaFrame 1.8 tools that shipped on the MetaFrame XP CD.

Now, let's continue progressing through our list of topics that you need to understand for mixed mode environments. Load balancing next.

## Load Balancing

Most real world environments have published applications load balanced across multiple servers. In a mixed mode server farm, it is possible to load balance published applications across MetaFrame 1.8 and MetaFrame XP servers.

As previously discussed, when publishing applications that are to be load balanced across both MetaFrame 1.8 and XP platforms, there are a few quirks that must be considered. Because you can only use the native tools to work with each platform, you must publish an application to MetaFrame 1.8 servers in the farm using Published Application Manager and publish the same application to MetaFrame XP servers using the Citrix Management Console. The published application must have the same name (case sensitive) on both platforms or MetaFrame won't realize that it's the same application.

After the application is published to both platforms, you can use each platform's native tools to configure load balancing. Let's look at what happens when an ICA client launches a published application that is load balanced across Meta-Frame 1.8 and mixed mode MetaFrame XP servers:

1. The user clicks an icon to launch the published application.

2. The ICA client requests the address for the least loaded server from the ICA master browser. In this case, the ICA master browser will be a MetaFrame XP server.

3. The ICA master browser looks at the load of all the MetaFrame XP servers and chooses the least loaded.

4. The ICA master browser then looks at the load of all the MetaFrame 1.8 servers and chooses the least loaded.

5. The ICA master browser compares the two semifinalist servers (one XP and one 1.8) by looking at number of active sessions. The address of the server with the least number of active sessions wins and is sent to the ICA client. If there is a tie, XP wins.

This approach is needed because the load balancing algorithms used in Meta-Frame 1.8 and MetaFrame XP are totally different. You should not be surprised if the server load is not "perfectly" balanced across platforms.

In mixed farm environments, any Load Evaluators attached to applications on MetaFrame XP servers (see Chapter 4) are ignored, because those evaluators could not apply to the instances of the applications on the MetaFrame 1.8 servers. When configuring Load Evaluators for XP servers that have published applications shared across platforms, you should only use the default load evaluators.

In mixed mode environments, you can use two different command-line tools to get information about load balanced applications—qfarm and qserver. The qserver tool has been around since before MetaFrame XP. Using qserver will display information obtained from the ICA master browser. Qfarm is the new tool for use with MetaFrame XP. It queries the zone data collector. If you want accurate information about applications load balanced across MetaFrame 1.8 and XP platforms, you should always use qserver.

## Licenses

MetaFrame 1.8 ICA licenses can be pooled between XP and 1.8 servers. However, because the licensing models for MetaFrame 1.8 and MetaFrame XP are so different, there are several requirements that must be met:

- The MetaFrame servers must reside on same subnet for license pooling to work.
- The MetaFrame XP ICA master browsers convert MetaFrame 1.8 license gateways to regular ICA gateways.
- MetaFrame XP ICA connection licenses are statically assigned to subnets that contain other XP farm servers. This means that XP connection licenses cannot be pooled across subnets (just like 1.8 licenses).

Basically, in mixed mode farms, MetaFrame XP will break the license gateway and you will only be able to pool licenses on local subnets, though you will be able to combine 1.8 and XP licenses for that local subnet pool. More MetaFrame licensing details are discussed in Chapter 14.

# Native Mode Server Farms

This section, which explores the inner workings of a MetaFrame XP server farm operating in native mode, is considerably shorter than the previous section covering mixed mode. This is because native mode acts as MetaFrame XP was designed. Basically the remainder of this book deals with native mode. However, there are some technical aspects to be aware of when native mode MetaFrame XP servers are operating in environments that also contain MetaFrame 1.8 servers.

Native mode is the default configuration for MetaFrame XP server farms. In native mode, MetaFrame XP server farms do not run any of the MetaFrame 1.8 legacy services, such as the ICA browser. In native mode:

- No communication is conducted between the MetaFrame XP and the MetaFrame 1.8 servers.
- The ICA browser and Program Neighborhood services are not used in the MetaFrame XP server farm.
- MetaFrame XP licenses are not pooled with MetaFrame 1.8 licenses.

- Published applications cannot be load balanced across MetaFrame 1.8 and MetaFrame XP servers.

## Client Communication with Native XP and 1.8 Farms

For the most part, MetaFrame XP servers operating in native mode will work in the exact same manner regardless of whether or not any MetaFrame 1.8 servers are present. There is only one small difference that you should be aware of.

MetaFrame XP servers operating in native mode will detect if there are any MetaFrame 1.8 servers on the same subnet as any XP servers in the farm. If there are, then the MetaFrame XP servers will not respond to ICA client broadcasts (when clients are trying to "auto-locate" MetaFrame servers). If the MetaFrame XP servers do not detect any MetaFrame 1.8 servers, then the XP servers will respond to ICA client broadcast requests. This behavior is so that native mode MetaFrame XP servers do not intercept client "auto-locate" broadcasts that are meant for MetaFrame 1.8 servers. (After all, new ICA clients that are looking for MetaFrame XP servers do not use the "auto-locate" broadcast behavior anymore.)

This default behavior of MetaFrame XP can be changed. In the MetaFrame settings of the farm (CMC I Farm Properties I MetaFrame Settings Tab I Broadcast Response), you can configure the zone data collectors or the RAS servers to respond to ICA client broadcasts. If you had a mixed mode farm that you have since migrated to a native XP farm after eliminating all of your MetaFrame 1.8 servers, you will need to manually configure your XP farm servers to respond to ICA client broadcasts.

On subnets with MetaFrame XP servers in native mode and unrelated MetaFrame 1.8 servers:

- ICA clients that find MetaFrame servers via the "auto-locate" method will get a server list of only MetaFrame 1.8 servers. This occurs because the XP servers will not respond to the client's "auto-locate" UDP broadcast, and the 1.8 servers do not know anything about the XP servers since the XP servers are in native mode and not running the ICA browser.

- If an ICA client is configured to "auto-locate" a server via the TCP/IP+HTTP protocol, whichever MetaFrame server is configured for the "ica" DNS hostname will determine the platform of the servers that are returned to the client.

- To view MetaFrame XP servers, ICA clients must specify the address of an XP server in the "Default Server Location" field. When this occurs, only MetaFrame XP servers are listed.

- If the ICA client's "Default Server Location" list is made up of both MetaFrame 1.8 and XP servers, whichever platform responds first will determine the resources that are shown to the client.

As you can see, in native mode there is no communication between the MetaFrame XP and the MetaFrame 1.8 servers. If you have both of these servers on the same subnet with your MetaFrame XP servers operating in native mode, you can avoid this potential confusion by doing one of the following:

- Set your MetaFrame XP server farm to mixed mode.

- Put the MetaFrame XP and MetaFrame 1.8 servers on separate subnets.

- Ensure that ICA clients are explicitly pointed towards the correct servers.

On subnets with only MetaFrame XP servers that are part of a farm running in native mode:

- By default, ICA clients using the "auto-locate" discovery method will not find anything, because the XP servers do not respond to the clients' auto locate UDP broadcast, and that broadcast will not travel across subnets to find other MetaFrame 1.8 servers.

- You can configure the XP servers to respond to ICA clients' UDP broadcast requests through the CMC (as outlined previously).

- If the servers are not configured to respond to UDP requests, the "default server location" must be configured to connect to MetaFrame XP servers.

- The DNS hostname "ica" can be used to point to a MetaFrame XP server that will be discovered via "auto-locate" if the ICA client uses the TCP/IP+HTTP protocol.

# Add-on Management Services from 1.8 to XP

Each of the MetaFrame add-on services (NFuse, Resource Management, and Installation Management) interacts with MetaFrame XP in a unique way. For the purpose of these services' interactions, we are concerned only with the interaction that occurs when MetaFrame XP server farms operate in mixed mode. Native mode XP server farms do not interact in any way with Meta-Frame 1.8 server farms. The add-on management features of XP and 1.8 do not have anything to do with each other.

Let's take a look at each of the following add-on services:

- NFuse Classic
- Installation Manager
- Resource Manager

We are not looking at the Network Manager add-on for MetaFrame XPe because there is no equivalent service in the MetaFrame 1.8 product line.

## NFuse Classic

NFuse provides a means of accessing MetaFrame environments through exposed Java objects. NFuse itself is not actually part of MetaFrame 1.8 or XP. It does not need to run on a MetaFrame server. The current version of NFuse can communicate with both MetaFrame 1.8 and MetaFrame XP platforms.

### Using NFuse in Mixed Environments

Not only does NFuse work well in mixed environments, it is the highly recommended method of simultaneously accessing multiple environments. NFuse web pages can be configured to build single lists of applications from multiple server farms, including servers that are MetaFrame 1.8 and MetaFrame XP. In fact, NFuse can be used to build application lists that contain published applications from native mode XP farms and 1.8 farms. Refer to Chapter 11 for more details.

### Migrating NFuse from 1.8 to XP

NFuse will seamlessly plug into both platforms. In migration scenarios, NFuse is a preferred method of access. When end users access MetaFrame servers through NFuse, the NFuse server holds the configuration information for the ICA client. The end user only needs to know one configuration parameter—the NFuse web server's URL. Everything else is maintained on the NFuse server. This makes "cutovers" from 1.8 to XP simple. For example, you can configure an NFuse server to point to an old MetaFrame 1.8 server farm one day and a new MetaFrame XP server farm the next. Even with thousands of end users accessing the environment, everything is changed by the one NFuse parameter. This is not possible with traditional ICA clients.

# Installation Manager

Installation Management Services (IMS) for MetaFrame 1.8 was released as an add-on management option. All IMS versions were variations of IMS 1.0x, with the most recent being 1.0b. Installation Manager is included with MetaFrame XP in the XPe product. This Installation Manager is essentially an upgraded version of IMS 1.0, and is known internally as IM 2.0. (IM 2.0 comes with MetaFrame XPe. Feature Release 1 updates MetaFrame XPe's IM to 2.1, and Feature Release 2 updates it to 2.2.)

Throughout this chapter, we will use three acronyms to differentiate the multiple versions of Installation Manager:

- IMS 1.0x – Installation Management Services 1.0x for MetaFrame 1.8.

- IM 2.0 – The Installation Manager component of MetaFrame XPe that is used without any XPe Feature Releases. This version of IM can be used in mixed mode farms.

- IM 2.x – This refers generically to all versions of IM for MetaFrame XPe, regardless of the Feature Release level. Since MetaFrame XPe with any Feature Release cannot operate in mixed mode server farms, IM 2.x in this chapter is used to describe the upgrade path from IMS 1.0x to IM 2.x.

For the purposes of working with Installation Manager, it's important to remember that there is a difference between "packages" and "applications published via Installation Manager."

- A package is the compiled scripted installation procedure that is created by the application packager portion of the Installation Manager software. These packages are then deployed to MetaFrame servers.

- An application published via Installation Manager is the actual published application that is maintained on the MetaFrame servers. Users launching these published applications invoke the "packages" that were previously created with the application packager and deployed to multiple MetaFrame servers.

### Installation Manager Technical Background

Installation Manager 2.x for MetaFrame XPe is covered in detail in Chapter 12. Even so, we'll take a brief look here at its technical components and the technical components of IMS 1.0x for MetaFrame 1.8. Though IM 2.x is essentially an upgraded version of IMS 1.0x, there are several changes that you must understand to be able to design an Installation Manager environment that works in both MetaFrame 1.8 and XP environments.

Installation Manager (across both platforms) consists of two components— the application packager and application installer.

IMS 1.0x and IM 2.x each have different versions of the application packager. IM 2.x can read IMS 1.0x packages, but IMS 1.0x cannot read IM 2.x packages.

The application installer and the associated IM service that runs on the MetaFrame servers has also changed from IMS 1.0x to IM 2.x. IM 2.x cannot read published applications that were created with IMS 1.0x.

This incompatibility occurs because IMS 1.0x packages use a "player" to run the published applications on MetaFrame 1.8 servers. In these environments, the published application path is not the executable of the application. The published application path is actually the IMS 1.0x package player (player.exe) and the package script (with the ".wfs" file extension). As long as the IMS 1.0x service is running on that server, the WFS script launches the IMS 1.0x player that reads the script, ultimately launching the published application. For example, if Microsoft Word is published with IMS 1.0x, the path for the published application in the MetaFrame 1.8 server's registry would be:

```
C:\Program Files\Citrix\Citrix Installer\player.exe word.wfs
```

In IM 2.x, this player no longer exists. The published application path for IM 2.x applications is the actual path, such as:

```
C:\Program Files\Microsoft Office\Office\winword.exe
```

### *Using Installation Manager in Mixed Environments*

There are some cases, particularly in large environments, where a mix of MetaFrame 1.8 and MetaFrame XP servers will exist together. If Installation Manager is to exist in these environments, then it too must be a mixed environment, containing IMS 1.0x services for MetaFrame 1.8 and IM 2.0 services for MetaFrame XP. The two Installation Manager environments are able to partially interoperate with each other.

### Application Packages

IMS 1.0x packages can be used by IM 2.0. To do this, you must manually add the package to the IM 2.0 system through the CMC. At this point, you don't technically have to make any changes to the package itself, although the packager that ships with IM 2.0 has many advanced packaging features that were not part of IMS 1.0x's packager.

If you would like to create new packages that are to be deployed to both IMS 1.0x and IM 2.0 servers, you may do so using the IMS 1.0x version of the application packager. Any packages created with the IM 2.0 packager will work without issues in mixed environments, but they will not be available to the IMS 1.0x environment.

### Installation Manager Published Applications

When you introduce MetaFrame XP servers with IM 2.0 into your environment, there is no need to make any changes to your MetaFrame 1.8 servers running IMS 1.0x. The two platforms will not affect each other in any way. In fact, each platform's Installation Manager configuration components will continue to work independently of each other in mixed IMS 1.0x and IM 2.0 environments. To manage the IMS 1.0x environment, you must use the Published Application Manager that shipped with IMS 1.0x. To manage the IM 2.0 environment, use the Citrix Management Console. There is no way to use one tool for Installation Manager on both platforms (just as with regular published applications that must be managed separately in mixed environments).

In most organizations, this mixed mode scenario is a temporary solution, as old MetaFrame 1.8 servers are being upgraded to MetaFrame XP.

### *Migrating Installation Manager from 1.8 to XP*

As servers are migrated from MetaFrame 1.8 to MetaFrame XP, you will most likely encounter servers using IMS 1.0x that will need to be migrated to IM 2.x. Fortunately, the migration process is automatic, with the installation of IM 2.x cleanly removing IMS 1.0x.

One migration task must be completed outside of the automatic setup of IM 2.x. Because IM 2.x does not use the "player" to launch IM published applications, the launch path of those published applications must be changed (from the player and WFS script to the actual executable location) before IM 2.x is installed. Citrix provides a utility that does this automatically. The utility, called IM_App_Upgrd.exe is located in the \support\debug\i386\ directory of the "Application Packaging & Delivery" CD included with MetaFrame XPe. This utility needs to be run on each MetaFrame 1.8 server with IMS 1.0x before it is migrated to MetaFrame XP.

After the `IM_App_Upgrd.exe` utility is used, published applications will still work on MetaFrame 1.8 servers. It's just that IMS 1.0x will no longer recognize them as an IMS 1.0x applications.

In an Installation Manager environment, the following steps must be taken to upgrade a server from MetaFrame 1.8 to MetaFrame XP:

1. Run the `IM_App_Upgrd.exe` application migration utility.
2. Migrate the MetaFrame 1.8 server to MetaFrame XPe.
3. Install MetaFrame XPe's Installation Manager. The IM 2.x setup utility will detect the legacy version of IMS 1.0x, remove it, and install IM 2.x. Any published application settings associated with IMS 1.0x will be retained.

If a MetaFrame 1.8 server with IMS 1.0x is upgraded to MetaFrame XP and IM 2.x without first running the Im_App_Upgrd.exe utility, it is possible to manually migrate the applications. From the CMC, change the properties of each published application from the WFS script to the actual executable.

Regardless of how an IMS 1.0x application was migrated (with the utility or manually), you will not be able to use IM 2.x to automatically remove the application.

## Resource Manager

Resource Management Services (RMS) for MetaFrame 1.8 was released as an add-on management option. All RMS versions were variations of RMS 1.0x, with the final version being RMS 1.0b. At the XPe level, MetaFrame XPe Resource Management is installed as the functional component of the System Monitoring & Analysis add-on.

Throughout this chapter, we will use two acronyms to differentiate between the two versions of Resource Management:

- RMS 1.0x – Resource Management Services 1.0x for MetaFrame 1.8.
- RM 2.x – The Resource Manager component of MetaFrame XPe. (RM 2.0 comes with MetaFrame XP. Feature Release 1 updates it to RM 2.1 and Feature Release 2 updates it to RM 2.2.)

### Using Resource Manager in Mixed Environments

The Resource Manager 2.x software that ships with MetaFrame XPe is tightly integrated with MetaFrame XP. It requires MetaFrame XPe, both from a licensing and a technical standpoint. However, RMS 1.0x is not tightly integrated with MetaFrame. (In fact, it can be used on non-MetaFrame servers, or even workstations.) If you need to use a common resource management interface across both MetaFrame 1.8 and MetaFrame XP servers, use RMS 1.0x.

RMS 1.0x can be installed on MetaFrame XP servers. However, it must be installed after MetaFrame XP is installed. If you install RMS 1.0x before you install or upgrade to MetaFrame XP, you must manually reinstall the old Citrix licensing service (`%systemroot%\system32\ctxlic\setup.exe`). The MetaFrame XP installation will destroy the licensing engine used by RMS 1.0x. As an interesting side note, RMS 1.0x can be used with any version of MetaFrame XP, not just XPe.

### Migrating Resource Management from 1.8 to XP

Because RMS 1.0x is very different from RM 2.x, there is no automatic upgrade path from RMS to RM 2.x. With the vastly increased functionality of RM 2.x, most organizations choose to redesign their Resource Management environments when migrating to MetaFrame XP.

# MetaFrame 1.8 to XP Server Farm Migrations

This section outlines concepts related to the migration of the actual MetaFrame servers. After you design your migration plan and strategy, at some point you will physically need to transform old MetaFrame 1.8 servers into new MetaFrame XP servers.

## Prerequisites

Migrating a MetaFrame 1.8 server to MetaFrame XP is fairly straightforward. When you run the MetaFrame XP installation program, it will automatically recognize the existing installation of MetaFrame 1.8. The installation program proceeds just like a new installation, with user input for the server farm, farm mode, and data store. There is only one real step (the last step) that needs to be considered carefully—when you are asked:

*Do you want to migrate published applications?*

Throughout this chapter we have reviewed the benefits and challenges to automatically migrating published applications. It is important to remember that it is possible to automatically migrate a server from MetaFrame 1.8 to MetaFrame XP without migrating any of the published applications. If no published applications are migrated, the applications do remain installed on the MetaFrame server. You must then manually republish the applications with the CMC after the migration is complete. It's also possible to not migrate applications, manually republish them in XP, and still have them load-balance with identically named applications on MetaFrame 1.8 servers.

Other than the application migration question, all of the standard server migration best practices apply, including:

- Making sure you have a good backup of the server before you start anything.
- Ensuring that you have plenty of room in the Windows event logs.
- Verifying that you have recent service packs and any necessary hotfixes installed.
- Disabling logons.

You need to ensure that your source environment is a supported migration path. You can only migrate from MetaFrame 1.8 to MetaFrame XP. If you still have MetaFrame 1.0 in your environment, you will need to do a clean install of MetaFrame XP. Even so, you should not have to reinstall all of your applications. You will simply need to republish them and reconfigure security.

You also need to ensure that your target environment is a supported migration path. Remember that Feature Release 1 and 2 for MetaFrame XP cannot operate in a mixed mode farm with MetaFrame 1.8.

When performing the actual MetaFrame server migration, if server drive letters were remapped during the initial installation of MetaFrame 1.8, you should not allow MetaFrame XP to remap the drive letters (unless you want to break things).

If you're migrating the underlying operating system in addition to MetaFrame, you should upgrade the operating system first. After the operating system upgrade, perform the MetaFrame XP migration. Of course, during this migration, all users should be logged off and all Citrix management tools should be closed.

Ideally, in a mixed mode migration, you will migrate the ICA master browser first. Once that server migration is complete, it will become the ICA master browser and the zone data collector. If the zone data collector will not be the server that was the old ICA master browser, then migrate the server you want to be the zone data collector first. Basically, the first MetaFrame XP server will create whatever it needs to support a MetaFrame XP server farm. This all can be changed at a later time, but you can save configuration down the road by migrating your servers in the proper order.

If a MetaFrame 1.8 server that is set to "always attempt to become master browser" is on same subnet as a MetaFrame XP server that has a zone data collector "Most Preferred" setting, elections will occur continuously (because they will both fight each other). This is a "feature" that has been corrected in Service Pack 1 for MetaFrame XP.

## Farm Migration Strategies

There are dozens of MetaFrame migration methodologies and strategies. Some are better than others and none are absolutely right or wrong.

There are many books and white papers that go through different MetaFrame migration case studies and scenarios, but these case studies always seem to be "a little too perfect" to be found in the real world. Usually they just "happen" to be an exact fit to the illustrated migration methodology.

Another problem with many of the published recommended methodologies is that most of the readers work for companies that have their own internal methodologies that must be used. There are so many different methodologies floating around. Microsoft recommends their Microsoft Solution Framework. Citrix Consulting Services has written multiple white papers touting their field-proven MetaFrame migration strategies. Online virtual support groups such as The THIN List are full of postings from people in the real world advocating different migration strategies.

In this book, rather than focusing on specific migration methodologies, we will study the elements that need to be considered for successful MetaFrame XP migrations. Remember, we are looking at this from a technical standpoint. If you are not familiar with methodologies, check into some of the resources previously mentioned.

Some people try to break down MetaFrame migrations into broad types or categories and then present the details of each migration type. For the most part, these broad migration types aren't significant. What is important is that you have a solid understanding of the technology, both from where you are in your MetaFrame 1.8 environment and where you are going in your Meta-

Frame XP environment. You must also understand how these two environments can work together. You need a good technical understanding of your options as well as the advantages and disadvantages of each. From there, you can develop your migration strategy based on sound technical expertise.

That being said, when looking at MetaFrame XP migrations from a technical standpoint, there are really just a few issues that need to be considered when migrating from MetaFrame 1.8 to MetaFrame XP. These issues are:

- **Target XP Farm Operating Mode**. Are you going to build a temporary mixed mode farm or are you going to create a new MetaFrame XP native farm, managed separately, until all 1.8 servers have been migrated?

- **Users Access**. What are you going to do with the users during the migration? How will they connect to the new environment?

- **Farm Consolidation**. Do you have multiple MetaFrame 1.8 server farms that you will consolidate into fewer XP server farms, now that XP farms have much better scalability than 1.8?

- **Other Upgrades**. Are you going to upgrade the operating systems of your MetaFrame servers along with the MetaFrame migration? How about Active Directory?

- **Server Migration**. Are you getting all new servers for XP? If not, are you going to upgrade the existing servers or wipe them clean and install XP from scratch?

- **Published Application Migration**. Based on the technical details and challenges presented in this chapter, are you going to migrate published applications or republish them from scratch in the new environment?

Let's examine each of these issues separately, beginning with the new MetaFrame XP server farm operating mode.

## Target XP Farm Operating Mode

By now you are fully aware of the two operating modes of MetaFrame XP server farms and the advantages and disadvantages of each.

### *What are the Target XP Farm Operating Mode Options?*

There are two main options to consider when selecting the operating mode of the new farm:

1. Create a new native mode MetaFrame XP farm. Bring new XP servers into that farm as they are brought online.

2. Integrate new MetaFrame XP servers into the existing MetaFrame 1.8 farm by configuring the new MetaFrame XP servers to operate in mixed mode.

## Option 1. Create a new native mode MetaFrame XP farm.

Building a new MetaFrame XP environment involves creating a new MetaFrame XP server farm operating in native mode built right alongside the old farm.

### Advantages of Creating a New Native MetaFrame XP Farm

- Mixed mode is not used.
- No published application migrations.
- NFuse can provide seamless client access.
- Great opportunity to overhaul your environment (spring cleaning).

### Disadvantages of Creating a New Native MetaFrame XP Farm

- User access must be addressed if users are to simultaneously access both farms.
- The entire environment must be reconfigured.
- If Citrix licenses are to be upgraded, users cannot simultaneously access both farms.

## Option 2. Integrate new XP servers into the existing 1.8 farm.

Other than the technology benefits discussed previously in this chapter, the following advantages and disadvantages apply to the migration method itself.

### Advantages of Integrating New XP Servers into the Existing 1.8 Farm

- Licenses are pooled.
- Published applications can be load balanced across both platforms.
- The XP migration can be phased over time.

### Disadvantages of Integrating New XP Servers into the Existing Farm

- Published applications cannot be modified until all servers are MetaFrame XP.
- The MetaFrame XP farm must operate in mixed mode.
- Published applications can be easily broken, due to the quirks associated with their migration.

### What Factors Affect This Decision?

- *Load Balanced Applications.* If you have published applications that will need to be load balanced across both MetaFrame 1.8 and MetaFrame XP servers during the migration process, you must integrate new servers into the existing farm by configuring the XP servers to operate in mixed mode. If you can arrange to migrate servers in groups so that you do not need to have the same application load balanced to both platforms, then you can build a separate, new XP farm operating in native mode.

- *Size of the Source Server Farm.* If the source MetaFrame 1.8 server farm is large, it may not be possible to migrate all of one published application's servers at the same time. If this is the case, you must allow the new XP servers to interoperate with the existing 1.8 server farm.

- *Migration Timeframe.* If the migration can be done all at once, then the MetaFrame XP servers can operate in native mode because there will not be any legacy MetaFrame 1.8 servers.

- *Frequency of Changes to Published Applications.* Published applications cannot be added, altered, or modified if some of the servers they are published to have been migrated to XP while others have not, even if the new XP farm is operating in mixed mode. If you will need to modify or add published applications during the migration process, then you must create a new, unrelated MetaFrame XP farm and manually modify the applications in each separate environment.

- *Licensing.* If you intend to create a new native XP farm that does not integrate into the existing farm, users accessing published applications from both platforms will require two Citrix licenses – one for the 1.8 environment and one for the XP environment. This can be avoided by building a mixed mode XP farm or by signing a volume licensing agreement with Citrix.

## User Access during the Migration

When adopting a new MetaFrame XP environment, it's important that the people using the system are not forgotten. Are the users going to need to access two different server farms during the migration? How will the users' ICA clients be configured to access the new MetaFrame XP environment?

### What are the User Access Options during the Migration?

1. Use NFuse.

2.  Use the Traditional ICA Client.

## Option 1. Use NFuse

NFuse can be used to provide simultaneous access to both the source farms and the new target farms for MetaFrame migrations. Because NFuse runs on servers, NFuse web pages can be easily changed to provide access to different or multiple server farms. This can have the effect of migrating thousands of clients just by changing the farm configuration parameter of one NFuse server. NFuse web pages can be customized to fit any environment, even providing quick and easy user access to multiple, totally unrelated server farms.

### *Advantages of Using NFuse During the Migration*

- Single point of configuration for all users.
- Provides seamless access to multiple server farms.
- Allows for quick transition to a new farm environment.

### *Disadvantages of Using NFuse During the Migration*

- Learning curve (for users and administrators) if it is not currently in use.
- Requires MetaFrame 1.8 Feature Release 1 in order to use it for source 1.8 farms.

## Option 2. Use the Traditional ICA Client

Many companies today use the traditional ICA client to access MetaFrame servers. While the ICA client is popular, the fact that a local copy of it exists on each and every client device can make it a nightmare to reconfigure on an enterprise basis. Many companies resort to sending out email attachments with scripts that change local .INI files. It is also difficult to use when connecting to more than one server farm. Through Program Neighborhood, a user is forced to back out of one application set and to enter another when looking for an application that resides on a different server farm.

### *Advantages of Using the Traditional ICA Client During the Migration*

- Most users are familiar with it.

### *Disadvantages of Using the Traditional ICA Client During the Migration*

- Users must access different farms via multiple Application Sets.
- Complex or manual configuration.

### What Factors Affect this Decision?

- *User Access during the Migration.* If users will not need to simultaneously access both the new and the old farms, there are no additional design concerns. However, if users will need to access both the new and the old environments, considerations must be made.

- *XP Target Farm Mode of Operation.* If the XP target farm will operate in mixed mode along with the old farm during the migration, users will only need to access one application set. However, if the new XP server farm is configured for native mode, then users will need to be able to access the old farm and the new farm at the same time.

- *Current User Access to the MetaFrame 1.8 Servers.* Are users currently using NFuse or traditional clients? If everyone currently uses traditional clients and you want them to use NFuse, then NFuse must be built and configured. The end users also must be trained to use it.

- *Planned User Access to the MetaFrame XP Servers.* Will users be using NFuse or will they access the servers via the traditional ICA client? The method used during the migration should match what they're used to in the current environment, or what is planned for the new environment.

## Farm Consolidation

Many current environments in which MetaFrame is in use consist of several small, non-connected MetaFrame 1.8 server farms. Often these farms are owned and controlled by different groups within the company. Time and money is wasted administering multiple, unnecessary server farms. When migrating to MetaFrame XP, companies often decide to consolidate MetaFrame server farms. This does not mean that they eliminate MetaFrame servers, nor does it mean that they physically consolidate the servers into fewer locations. It simply means that companies understand that MetaFrame XP server farms can scale much larger than MetaFrame 1.8 server farms. Certain economies of scale can be attained by creating larger server farms that include all of the servers.

### What are the Server Farm Consolidation Options?

1. Consolidate server farms.
2. Create multiple XP server farms, one for each 1.8 farm.

## Option 1. Consolidate Server Farms

Consolidating server farms might save money by not requiring that users have multiple licenses to access multiple farms, but fewer farms can mean less flexibility as well. Because farms are essentially managed together as one unit, individual MetaFrame options are not as freely applied to specific servers. MetaFrame XP server farms can scale to support hundreds of servers worldwide, but rarely in the real world would such an environment be managed by one group. More likely, companies will create multiple farms that can be individually managed by local administrators.

### *Advantages of Consolidating Server Farms During the Migration*

- Fewer farms to administer.
- Fewer ICA connection licenses required.
- Since you are touching all of the servers anyway, it's a good time to change their farm configuration.

### *Disadvantages of Consolidating Server Farms During the Migration*

- Administration cannot be granular.
- Less flexible.

## Option 2. Create Multiple XP Farms

Creating multiple XP server farms allows for a flexible, supportable environment—but one that could get expensive to keep legal. The politics of many organizations force them to adopt a server farm model that allows for local administration of servers, and in the MetaFrame XP world, that means creating multiple server farms. While this allows local administrators to have the autonomy that they desire, it also increases the chances that work efforts are being duplicated within the organization. This model also does not allow the enforcement of corporate standards in MetaFrame implementation.

### *Advantages of Creating Multiple XP Farms in the New Environment*

- Administration can be distributed.
- The old MetaFrame XP farm boundaries will remain the same.

### *Disadvantages of Creating Multiple XP Farms in the New Environment*

- More administrative overhead.
- Individual licenses must be used for each farm.
- Access methods must allow for the seamless access to multiple farms.
- Difficult to enforce corporate standards.

### Real World Hidden Option 3. Hybrid Approach

In the real world, many organizations adopt a hybrid approach to the migration of server farms. They choose to consolidate many similar farms into one "corporate wide applications" farm, while allowing local farms to exist with custom applications. An NFuse interface can provide seamless access to all farms for all users.

## What Factors Affect this Decision?

- *MetaFrame Server Management.* How are the current server farms managed? If they're all managed by one group, server farm consolidation is extremely attractive. On the other hand, if different departments or different business units each manage their own server farms, consolidation is probably not the answer, especially considering that MetaFrame XP server farm administration is "all or nothing" for the entire farm.

- *Application Scopes.* Will end users need to access applications from many different server farms or do end users only access their own local server farms?

- *Licensing.* Citrix ICA connection licenses used in MetaFrame XP are not valid for servers in multiple server farms. That is, one user connecting to two servers from separate farms requires two licenses. If users will need to access many applications from multiple farms, consolidation may save licensing costs. Of course, many companies are signing Enterprise Agreements with Citrix, eliminating the licensing issue.

# Other Product Upgrades / Migrations

Often, when performing a major migration, such as MetaFrame 1.8 to MetaFrame XP, organizations decide to upgrade other components at the same time. These components are sometimes required by or related to the core product migration and are sometimes totally unrelated. A good example of this is that many companies' source environments in MetaFrame migrations are built on Windows NT 4.0; they decide to upgrade to Windows 2000 as part of the MetaFrame XP migration.

## What are the Options for Upgrading Other Products?

1. Migrate, update, repair, patch, fix, or otherwise change additional, non-Citrix, non-MetaFrame XP-related components.

2. Perform the MetaFrame XP migration without updating anything else.

## Option 1. Migrate Other Components with MetaFrame.

This refers to other, non-MetaFrame components. For example, many companies choose to upgrade the underlying MetaFrame server operating system from Windows NT 4 to Windows 2000 when they adopt MetaFrame XP. Some companies choose to begin using Active Directory at this time, and others will begin using a new network segment or switch.

Migrating other server components along with MetaFrame can efficiently use the server downtime that is already planned. It also can allow the MetaFrame XP environment to significantly impact end users, by having other components upgraded that further enhance the user experience.

The main downside to many of these tertiary migrations is that they are outside the scope of the core MetaFrame environment. Can the MetaFrame XP migration afford to be slowed down by upgrading other server components? What happens if there is a failure involving the other, non-MetaFrame components? Will the MetaFrame XP migration be perceived as a failure because the Active Directory team didn't prepare well enough, and just the Active Directory failed?

### *Advantages of Migrating Other Components with MetaFrame*

- Efficient use of server downtime that is already planned.
- Allows the addition of other components that may positively impact end users' experience.

### *Disadvantages of Migrating Other Components with MetaFrame*

- May increase time needed to perform the MetaFrame migration.
- Increased risk of a failed component of the update.

## Option 2. Migrate MetaFrame Only.

Pure and simple, you can choose to migrate the MetaFrame components of the servers only. This is a good option for large organizations in which different people or groups own different parts of the environment. For example, the person doing the MetaFrame migration is probably responsible only for Meta-Frame—someone else maintains the server operating system, a different group maintains the applications, etc.

### *Advantages of Migrating MetaFrame Only*

- Fastest migration times.
- Least risk.

### Disadvantages of Migrating MetaFrame Only

- Missed opportunities for other product updates.

## What Factors Affect Other Product Upgrade Decisions?

- *Political Impact.* Are there any political advantages or disadvantages to upgrading non-Citrix components? Is one group going to be offended if you don't follow its recommendations for some components of the MetaFrame XP servers?

- *Risk.* What happens if one of the non-MetaFrame components breaks the server or causes extended migration times? Will people look to the MetaFrame XP server as the culprit? Or a failure?

- *Is it broken now?* The old adage "if it ain't broke, don't fix it" applies here. Should you take on new or updated components if there were no problems with the old environment?

# Server Migration

When considering strategies to migrate to MetaFrame XP, at some point you must convert the actual servers from MetaFrame 1.8 to MetaFrame XP.

## What are the Server Migration Options?

There are two different methods that can be used to migrate MetaFrame 1.8 servers to MetaFrame XP.

1. Upgrade the current software to MetaFrame XP.

2. Reformat the hard drive and start over, installing the operating system and MetaFrame XP from scratch.

### Option 1. Upgrade to MetaFrame XP.

Performing an upgrade from MetaFrame 1.8 to MetaFrame XP takes the least amount of effort. Your upgraded MetaFrame XP server will maintain all of the applications, settings, and configurations of the old environment. Of course, it will also maintain all of the quirks, misconfigurations, and history of the old environment.

### Advantages of Performing a MetaFrame Upgrade

- Maintains previous environment.

### Disadvantages of Performing a MetaFrame Upgrade

- Maintains previous environment.

## Option 2. Install MetaFrame XP from Scratch.

Installing MetaFrame XP from scratch on new servers will yield the most pristine environment. This does not mean that you need to physically procure new servers. Many companies pull existing servers out of the rotation, wipe them clean, and install everything anew. Your environment will be configured perfectly the way you want it, but you will pay for that with the time and effort it takes to perform the reinstallation.

### *Advantages of Installing MetaFrame XP from Scratch*

- Fresh install.

### *Disadvantages of Installing MetaFrame XP from Scratch*

- Everything must be reconfigured.
- Time consuming.

### *What Factors Affect this Decision?*

- *Current Server Standards*. Do server standards exist for the server environment? These standards might include partition sizes, drive letters, and naming conventions.

- *Server / Standards Alignment*. Assuming that you have server standards, how closely does the server in question line up with those standards?

- *Server Stability*. Is the current server stable or are there quirks? It may not be worth taking the time to reinstall everything if the current server works well.

# Published Application Migration

When you upgrade servers from MetaFrame 1.8 to MetaFrame XP, you have the choice as to whether you will migrate the existing published applications or republish them manually in the new environment.

## *What are the Published Application Migration Options?*

1. Migrate published applications to XP.
2. Manually republish applications in XP.

### Option 1. Migrate Applications.

Migrating published applications is a way to save time when migrating a server to MetaFrame XP. Problems can arise; however, if your entire farm migration is scheduled to take some time and you need to modify or add any published applications after the first server has been migrated but before the last. In this case, it's better to not migrate any published applications and just manage them separately on each platform. Remember, just because you don't migrate an application doesn't mean that you can't load balance it across new and old servers. You can always republish an application manually in the new server farm with the same name as the application in the old farm, which will cause it to load balance between the two.

### *Advantages of Migrating Applications*

* Applications do not need to be reconfigured in the new farm.

### *Disadvantages of Migrating Applications*

* Migrated applications cannot be modified until all servers have been migrated.

### Option 2. Do Not Migrate Applications.

Choosing not to automatically migrate any published applications is the conservative, safest approach. Migrating applications does not really save too much time unless you have a long, complex user access list.

### *Advantages of not Migrating Applications*

* Low risk of breaking applications.

### *Disadvantages of not Migrating Applications*

* Applications must be manually republished in the new farm.

## *What Factors Affect this Decision?*

* *Target Farm Operability Mode.* If the target farm is operating in native mode, you won't have to worry about your published applications because they won't interact with the old MetaFrame 1.8 anyway.

* *Migration Timeframe.* If the timeframe of your migration is short, you don't have to worry about trying to manage your applications during the migration; you can choose to automatically migrate the applications. If your migration is planned to take awhile, then you need to consider whether or not you'll need to modify or add any published applications.

# Real World Case Study

## Zem Zem Publishing

## Current Business Environment

Zem Zem Publishing is an Italian company that produces high quality books to markets throughout Europe. They currently have three large offices in Italy and fifteen smaller offices throughout Europe. Zem Zem is in the middle of a buying spree, as twelve of their current eighteen offices were not part of Zem Zem 18 months ago.

Each of the eighteen offices is fairly autonomous. Because each has its own "speciality," each office also has its own unique applications that must be supported. This means that each office has its own local IT support staff for the local applications. However, there are several corporate-wide applications that the central IT department is responsible for.

## Current Technology Environment

The three large offices are connected to each other via 1.5Mbps point-to-point communication lines, dedicated to data traffic. All of the fifteen smaller offices are connected to the large offices via frame relay, with connections ranging from 56k to 240k.

Historically, Zem Zem Publishing's network was run entirely on NetWare. They had a single NDS tree for all their employees before they started buying up small companies. Now, of the eighteen offices, eleven of them are part of the corporate NDS tree. Of the remaining seven offices, four have their own NDS trees. The other three have only an NT domain. Overall, Zem Zem Publishing is planning to move towards Active Directory, bringing the entire corporation into a single tree. However, that project is not going to get started until next year.

As far as applications are concerned, there are many pockets of MetaFrame 1.8 servers throughout the environment. At the corporate level, there is a good sized server farm that provides corporate applications to users from all eighteen offices.

At the local office level, most offices provide at least some applications via MetaFrame 1.8. Some offices use MetaFrame 1.8 for everything, while others use it strictly for remote access. (In all cases, only the local "speciality" applications are loaded on local MetaFrame 1.8 servers.) Some of the Zem Zem offices have as many as six MetaFrame 1.8 servers, while others only have one or two. In most cases, the offices with more than one MetaFrame 1.8 server are using Load Balancing Services to publish applications across multiple servers. In these cases, all of the servers are configured in an identical fashion.

## Future MetaFrame XP Environment

The Zem Zem Publishing project team has already created the design of their future MetaFrame XP environment. They've decided to create one large Meta-Frame XP server farm that spans servers in all eighteen offices. All of the local MetaFrame XP servers will continue to be located throughout the environment at the local offices. They decided that this would be the most convenient arrangement, because each office has its own unique applications and those applications are administered locally. The centralized corporate-wide applications will still be located on MetaFrame XP servers in the central office.

Zem Zem Publishing's large vision is to be able to provide access to applications for end users, no matter what type of device they use, and no matter where they are. For that reason, they have decided that they would make NFuse the corporate standard for accessing MetaFrame applications.

Finally, due to the amount of NetWare in their environment, the project team felt that it was necessary to build their MetaFrame XP environment with Feature Release 1, so that they could maintain NDS accounts for all of their users. This was especially necessary for users that access applications at the corporate level, with different NDS contexts. By using Feature Release 1, those users would always be able to log on to the MetaFrame XP servers with their proper NDS context.

## The Project Team's Thoughts about the Migration

Before creating the actual migration plan, the Zem Zem Publishing project team decided to outline all of the issues they would need to consider. From there, it would be a simple matter to assemble the issues into a logical order and to create the plan. Following are the items that they outlined.

### Ease of Access

Currently, users access the MetaFrame 1.8 servers via the 32-bit ICA client. The project team knew that if they continued to use this, the users would need to manually find the new application set to connect to the new farm (after the migration to MetaFrame XP took place). They felt that the users would not be capable of doing this, and that it would cause excessive confusion. An easier way to perform the user "cutover" had to be found.

**Mixed Mode Farm**

Obviously, the final MetaFrame XP server farm would operate in native mode. What the project team didn't know was how they should build that farm. Some team members wanted to create the central farm in mixed mode, and then add the outlying servers to the farm. After everything was upgraded to MetaFrame XP, they could switch the farm over to native mode. There were a few problems with this.

First of all, Feature Release 1 for MetaFrame XP cannot be used in mixed mode farms. That meant that they would not be able to log on with their proper NDS contexts until all servers had been migrated. It also meant that they would have more work to do after all the servers were running Meta-Frame XP.

Also, the project team did not feel comfortable that a mixed mode farm could support their distributed, WAN-based environment. (After all, that's why they built separate MetaFrame 1.8 farms in the first place.) They knew that there was no efficient way to build an ICA browser-based farm in their environment.

# Migration Plan

Based on what their current environment looks like, where they want to go, and the issues that they outlined, the project team was able to build the following migration plan. This plan is split into three phases:

- **Prerequisites**. Things that must be done in all offices before any migrations can take place.
- **Central Office Migration**. The steps that must be taken once at the central office to move to MetaFrame XP.
- **Local Office Migrations**. The steps that must be taken at each local office, after the first two phases are complete.

## *Prerequisites (All Offices)*

1. **Install Feature Release 1 for MetaFrame 1.8**. This will allow NFuse to be used during the migration process. Most of Zem Zem's servers already had Feature Release 1, but there were two offices

that were not using it. Amazingly, Zem Zem successfully negotiated with Citrix directly to acquire the FR-1 licenses for MetaFrame 1.8, because they were buying so many MetaFrame XP licenses and they needed the old FR-1 licenses for the sole purpose of their migration.

2. **Implement NFuse.** By moving to NFuse now, the users could accustom themselves to the new way of accessing their MetaFrame applications. More importantly, this allowed the project team to seamlessly switch users from one server farm to another. (In this case, from the old local farm to the new corporate farm.)

### Central Office Migration

These three steps must be performed at the central office before any migrations can take place at the local offices:

1. **Migrate the Servers.** Each MetaFrame 1.8 server would be migrated to MetaFrame XP, to a farm of the same name operating in mixed mode. This will allow users from all eighteen offices to be able to continually access the applications.

2. **Switch to Native Mode**. After the last corporate server has been migrated, switch the farm from mixed mode to native mode.

3. **Implement Feature Release 1**. This can only be done once the farm is in native mode.

### Local Offices

Each local office will do their own migration, based on the plan below.

1. **Migrate the Servers**. Upgrade servers one by one, to a farm operating in mixed mode, so that users can continue to access local applications.

2. **Switch to Native Mode**. After the last local server has been migrated, switch the local server farm to native mode.

3. **Implement Feature Release 1**. This should be done on all local servers so that the servers are at the same level as the corporate servers.

4. **Move Servers into the Permanent Farm**. Add the local servers to the corporate MetaFrame XP server farm. Ensure that the zone memberships and zone data collector properties are configured according to the final server farm design.

5. **Republish Applications**. The existing applications will be lost when the farm membership is changed.

6. **Reconfigure Security**. Set the security as needed on the newly-published applications.

7. **Reconfigure NFuse as Needed**. The old URL that the local users accessed pointed to an old NFuse environment. To point the users to the new server farm, the project team simply needed to update the NFuse web page.

By following this implementation plan, Zem Zem Publishing was able to successfully implement MetaFrame XP. The users had little disruption to their work, and the IT department was able to fully implement their planned MetaFrame XP environment.

# CHAPTER 14

# Licensing

**In this chapter**

| | |
|---|---|
| Microsoft Licensing | 578 |
| Citrix Licensing | 601 |
| Application Licensing | 615 |
| Real World Case Study | 618 |

Licensing is probably the most dreaded component that administrators ever deal with. In MetaFrame XP environments, you need to work with both Citrix and Microsoft licenses, in addition to the licenses for your applications. Both MetaFrame XP and Windows 2000 Terminal Services have significant licensing provisions to ensure that licenses are paid for. Gone are the days when you could carelessly install applications and assume that the accounting department paid for them.

The only thing that changes faster than technology is the licensing of technology. For that reason, it is important to note that this licensing chapter was up-to-date when this book was printed. However, it's possible that the details of Microsoft or Citrix licensing have changed since then. You can find the latest details on the web at `www.microsoft.com/licensing` or `www.citrix.com/licensing`.

Because Microsoft Windows licensing and the MetaFrame XP licensing are so different, we will address each one separately in this chapter. We'll also look at how third-party applications are licensed in MetaFrame XP environments before closing this chapter with a real world case study.

# Microsoft Licensing

It's necessary to license the underlying Microsoft operating system components in a MetaFrame XP environments. Before we study the technical details of Microsoft's licensing and how it works, let's review their policy and which licenses are required in different scenarios.

## Microsoft Licensing Requirements

The Microsoft licenses required for your MetaFrame XP environment are conceptually identical whether your servers are running on Terminal Server 4.0 or Windows 2000 platforms. Because of this, we can look at the two platforms together. Also, it is important to keep in mind that all Microsoft licenses are automatically backwards compatible, so when a Windows NT 4.0 Workstation license is required, a Windows 2000 Professional license will be sufficient.

Microsoft licenses can be divided into three groups:

- Licenses required for each server.
- Licenses required for each unique client device.

- Internet Connector licenses.

The actual Microsoft licenses required for your environment will be a combination of server and client licenses.

## Licenses Required for Each Terminal Server

Microsoft requires one license for each server in a terminal services environment. That license is known as a "Server License."

### License 1. Windows Server License

Each server that runs Terminal Services requires its own server license. This is the license that allows you to run the actual server itself. Windows 2000 servers require a Windows 2000 Server license. Windows NT 4.0 Terminal Server Edition servers require a Windows NT 4.0 Terminal Server Edition server license.

## Licenses Required for Each Client Device

All Microsoft client device licensing is done "per seat." Microsoft defines one "seat" as a unique hardware device used to access a server. This means that if you have two computers and you access the same server from each of them, you have two different seats and need a separate "per seat" license for each device. This applies even if you never use both devices at the same time. In Terminal Services or Citrix MetaFrame environments, each seat requires *both* of the following licenses:

- Server Client Access License.
- Terminal Server Client Access License.

### License 1. Windows Server Client Access License (Server CAL)

The server client access license (CAL) is the license that allows a client device to access a Microsoft Windows server over the network. As with other Microsoft licenses, accessing Windows 2000 servers requires a Windows 2000 Server or Core CAL, and accessing Windows NT 4.0 Servers requires a Windows NT 4.0 or a BackOffice 4.5 CAL.

### License 2. Terminal Services Client Access License (TS CAL)

In addition to the server CAL, each client device that connects via a remote Windows session to a Windows Terminal Services-enabled server needs to have a Terminal Services Client Access License (TS CAL). This license is more expensive then the regular server CAL. Microsoft created this TS CAL because they felt that if you were experiencing the full Windows environment (as through a Terminal Services or MetaFrame ICA session) then you should be paying for the full Windows environment.

Since Windows NT, 2000, and XP Professional already give you the right to run the Windows professional desktop environment, client devices running these operating systems have the ability to obtain a "free" TS CAL. You only need to purchase a TS CAL for every client device that runs an operating system that is a lower or older version than the operating system of your Terminal Server.

For example, if your client device is running Windows 2000 Professional, Server, or Advanced Server, then you do not need to purchase a TS CAL to connect to a Windows 2000 Terminal Server because your Windows 2000 client device has the right to obtain a free Windows 2000 TS CAL. Also, since these licenses are backwards compatible, the Windows 2000 TS CAL would also apply if you were using a Windows XP Professional client to connect to a Windows 2000 Terminal Server.

If your client device is running Windows NT 4.0 Workstation, you would not need to purchase a Windows NT 4.0 TS CAL to connect to Windows NT 4.0 Terminal Servers, but you would need a Windows NT 4.0 to Windows 2000 TS CAL upgrade to connect to Windows 2000 Terminal Servers. This is because each TS CAL is version-specific. The free TS CAL that is included with Windows NT 4.0 is a version 4.0 of the TS CAL, and it is only valid for connecting to other NT 4.0 Terminal Servers.

Essentially, if you have the license to run the operating system locally on your client device then you also automatically have the right to run that same operating system via remote sessions due to the free TS CAL.

In the event that you do not have a full Windows NT or 2000 license for your client device (such as if your client device is running Windows CE, 95, 98, ME, UNIX, Macintosh, etc.), you need to purchase the appropriate TS CAL for that client device in order to access MetaFrame XP servers.

For Windows 2000 servers, client devices only need TS CALs if Terminal Services is configured to operate in application mode. For administration mode, only two concurrent connections are allowed; you do not need TS CALs for those clients, regardless of the client device platform.

### (Optional) Work-at-Home TS CAL

By Microsoft's definition, you need a separate TS CAL for each client device. If you access MetaFrame XP sessions from a computer on your desk at the office and from a computer at home, you need to have two separate TS CAL licenses (one for each device). Some of the Microsoft licensing agreements provide work at home licenses, which are basically additional, cheap

TS CALs for these scenarios. The terms for use of these work at home TS CALs change regularly, but it is worth checking into whether your agreement has a provision for these before you spend a lot of money to provide home access to business applications.

### Internet Connector Licenses

There is one additional type of Microsoft license that is required in some situations where Terminal Servers provide applications via the Internet. This license is known as a "Terminal Services Internet Connector License." We'll this license later in this chapter.

## How Microsoft Licenses Work

Windows NT 4.0 Terminal Server Edition uses the "honor system" for tracking licenses. This system works in the same way that licensing has worked for the past twenty years. While you are legally supposed to purchase the correct licenses, there is nothing technically stopping you from connecting more users than you paid for. While the honor system has traditionally worked well for system administrators and thieves, it has not worked well for Microsoft shareholders.

In Terminal Services for Windows 2000, Microsoft introduced the "Terminal Services Licensing Service"—a service that runs on one or more servers on your network. This TS licensing service is responsible for monitoring, distributing, and enforcing TS CAL usage. Microsoft implemented this licensing architecture as a "service to their customers" who were "deeply concerned that they might accidentally forget to pay for a license or two, every once in awhile." In MetaFrame XP environments running on Windows 2000 platforms, there will be no "accidentally forgetting" to buy all the needed licenses with this new licensing service structure.

If you decide that you would rather not build this TS licensing infrastructure and that you want to continue using the honor system, you will change your mind 91 days after you start using Windows 2000 Terminal Services. At that point everything will stop working until you install and activate a TS licensing server.

### Windows 2000 License Components

There are four main technical components that make up the Terminal Services licensing service infrastructure in Windows 2000:

- Client devices.

- Windows 2000 Terminal Servers.
- Terminal Services licensing servers.
- Microsoft license clearinghouse.

*Figure 14.1 Microsoft licensing components*

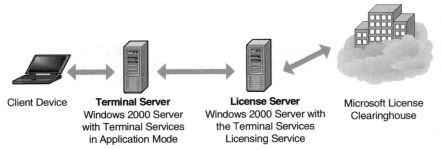

| Client Device | **Terminal Server**<br>Windows 2000 Server<br>with Terminal Services<br>in Application Mode | **License Server**<br>Windows 2000 Server with<br>the Terminal Services<br>Licensing Service | Microsoft License<br>Clearinghouse |

Let's take a look at the licensing–related roles of each of the four components.

### Client Devices

Each client device that connects to a Windows 2000 server via Terminal Services must have a valid Terminal Services Client Access License (TS CAL). The TS CAL is stored locally on the client device in the form of a secure token, similar to a digital certificate.

All client devices must obtain their TS CALs from a TS Licensing Server.

### Windows 2000 Terminal Server

Windows 2000 Terminal Services plays a large role in the licensing process. A Windows 2000 Terminal Server operating in Application Mode will check to make sure that every client device that connects to it to run a session has a valid TS CAL. If not, the Terminal Server will contact a Terminal Services Licensing Server to assign a TS CAL to the client device.

### Terminal Services License Server

A Terminal Services License Server is a Windows 2000 server that is running the Terminal Services Licensing (TSL) service. The TS licensing service can be installed on any Windows 2000 server. It does not need to be installed on a Windows 2000 server that has Terminal Services enabled. Many companies choose a standard file server or domain controller to be their TS Licensing server.

TS license servers maintain the inventory of TS CALs. These license servers then distribute these licenses to client devices the first time they log on to a

Terminal Server. If you purchase additional TS CALs for your growing environment, you add them to the license database on the TS Licensing server. That way, the licenses are ready to be distributed to end-user client devices.

Every Windows 2000 TS Licensing Server has a built-in unlimited supply of TS CALs that can only be granted to Windows 2000 or Windows XP Professional client devices. For any other client platform, including Mac, UNIX, Linux, Windows 9x, and Windows XP Home Edition, a TS CAL needs to be purchased for each device.

### Microsoft License Clearinghouse and Certificate Authority

The Microsoft License Clearinghouse is a big server in the sky maintained by Microsoft. This clearinghouse is used to activate TS License Servers and TS CALs. TS license servers and the licenses they maintain must be activated via this clearinghouse so that Microsoft can make sure that no licenses are stolen or pirated. Before a TS license server is activated, it will still function; however, the TS CAL digital certificates that it distributes will be temporary, expiring after 90 days. These temporary CALs cannot be renewed until the license server has been activated by the clearinghouse. This clearinghouse is accessed using the Terminal Services Licensing Wizard utility via the Internet, a web page, fax, or telephone.

## *The Windows 2000 Licensing Process*

Now that we've looked at the components that make up the Windows 2000 Terminal Services licensing environment, let's take a look at how the entire licensing process works. Figure 14.2 diagrams the high-level process described in the following steps. This example starts from the beginning, when you first purchase the licenses.

*Figure 14.2  Microsoft licensing process*

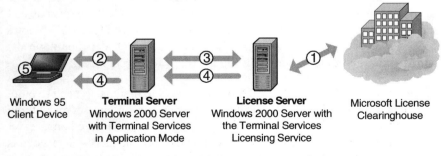

| Windows 95 Client Device | Terminal Server Windows 2000 Server with Terminal Services in Application Mode | License Server Windows 2000 Server with the Terminal Services Licensing Service | Microsoft License Clearinghouse |

1. Terminal Server CALs are purchased and installed into the license database on the TS Licensing Server. The TS CALs are then activated via the Microsoft License clearinghouse. The activated

licenses remain on the license server, waiting for assignment to client devices.

2. A new Windows 95 client successfully authenticates and establishes an ICA session with the Terminal Server running MetaFrame XP.

3. The Terminal Server contacts the licensing server to obtain a TS CAL for the client device.

4. If the licensing server has enough licenses, it grants one to the client. The license server's available license count is decremented by one, and the TS CAL is sent down to the client device itself. The TS CAL is physically maintained on the client device in the form of a digital certificate.

5. For future sessions, the Windows 95 client device will already have the TS CAL certificate which it will present to the Terminal Server when the session is started. When that happens, the Terminal Server does not contact the license server.

### *The Windows 2000 Terminal Services Licensing Service*

The TS Licensing Service forms the core of Microsoft's Windows 2000 TS license tracking and enforcement program. This service is responsible for managing the distribution of the digital certificates representing TS CALs and TS Internet Connector Licenses. Interestingly, this service is not responsible for determining whether or not a particular computer needs a license; that determination is made by the Terminal Server itself. The TS Licensing Service is invoked only after a Terminal Server requests a license.

#### TS Licensing Service Server Location

The Terminal Services licensing service is 100% separate from the actual Terminal Services components that allow users to run remote sessions. The TS licensing service must be installed on a Windows 2000 server, but that server does not need to be running Terminal Services. The type of Windows 2000 server that the TS licensing service is installed on depends upon the domain configuration, as shown in Figure 14.3 (facing page).

Regardless of the location of the TS licensing server, there is no need to build a dedicated server. The TS licensing service can run on any server without adversely affecting performance, and does not need to be installed on a server that has access to the Internet. The only time that Internet access is needed is for the activation of the server or the licenses, although that Internet access is required by the computer that you are activating the licenses from, not the TS license server itself. The TS licensing service does not need to access the Internet every time it assigns a TS CAL to a client device.

*Figure 14.3  Valid license server locations*

| Domain | TS Licensing Server Location |
| --- | --- |
| Active Directory | W2K domain controller for automatic discovery, Any W2K server for manual discovery |
| NT 4 Domain w/ Windows 2000 servers | W2K member server |
| Workgroup (non-domain) environment | Any W2K server |

## TS Licensing Service Impact to Existing Servers

The TS licensing service does not require many resources from the server on which it is installed. It uses no CPU time except for when a license is requested or a Terminal Server pings it. Memory utilization is always under 10 MB, even for large organizations. The license database, which is stored on the server running the TS licensing service, requires less than 1k of hard drive space per client license. All this means that the TS licensing service can be installed on a busy domain controller or Terminal Server without adversely affecting the performance of that server.

## TS Licensing Scope for Active Directory Environments

In Windows 2000 Active Directory environments, the TS licensing service will register itself with a domain controller. This will provide a method for Terminal Servers to use the directory to find license servers. When you perform the actual license service installation in such an environment, you must decide in what "scope" you want the licensing server to operate. There are two options.

- Domain scope.
- Enterprise scope.

### Domain Scope

In domain scope, TS licensing servers only respond to license requests from the Terminal Servers that are in the same Active Directory domain. If an Active Directory domain crosses multiple Active Directory sites, then the TS licensing server will respond to requests from multiple sites.

This is useful if there are multiple business units on the same network that are partitioned into different domains. With a domain scope, you can prevent your license server from providing licenses to other domains. This is also the mode that you should use if your license servers are member servers in a Windows NT 4.0 domain.

When the TS licensing service is installed on a Windows 2000 server that is a member server in a Windows 2000 domain, the license server will register itself with a domain controller, allowing for Terminal Services to find licensing services via that domain controller.

### Enterprise Scope

Enterprise scope TS licensing servers respond to license requests from Terminal Servers that are in the same Active Directory site as they are. If that Active Directory site is comprised of several domains, then the license servers will provide licenses to clients from several domains.

Upon service start, an enterprise scope TS licensing server will register itself with the Active Directory via a domain controller for its domain. This will allow Terminal Servers from any domain to be able to locate it. The TS licensing server will create an Active Directory object called "TS-Licensing." The FQDN of this object is `CN=TS-Enterprise-License-Server`, `CN=YourSite`, `CN=Configuration`, `DC=YourDomain`, where *YourSite* is the Active Directory site and *YourDomain* is the Active Directory domain.

### Terminal Server Discovery of TS Licensing Servers

Merely installing TS license servers in your network does not necessarily mean that they will work properly. You also need to ensure that there is a way for the Terminal Servers to find the TS license servers when they need a license for a client.

License server "discovery" is the process by which Windows 2000 Terminal Servers locate and connect to TS licensing servers. As soon as Terminal Services is enabled in Application Mode on a Windows 2000 server, the server will immediately begin the discovery process. License server discovery can happen in one of three ways, depending on which of the following environments the Terminal Server finds itself in:

- Windows NT 4 domain or workgroup.
- Windows 2000 domain, with the TS license servers operating in domain mode.
- Windows 2000 domain, with the TS license servers operating in enterprise mode.

### Discovery in Windows NT 4 Domains or Workgroup Environments

If the Windows 2000 Terminal Server is in a Windows NT 4 domain or a workgroup, it will send out a NetBIOS broadcast on the local subnet to the "\TermServLicensing" named pipe. All TS license servers on the same subnet will reply. The Terminal Server will record the names of the servers that replied and randomly pick one to use as its licensing server by opening a "\HydraLs" named pipe to that server.

Once a TS license server is found, the Terminal Server will periodically verify that it exists. (See Figure 14.4.) If the Terminal Server "loses" the TS license server because that license server did not reply to a verification by the Terminal Server, the Terminal Server will attempt to connect to one of the other TS licensing servers that responded during the initial discovery. If no connection can be made to a license server, the Terminal Server will attempt to find a license server by starting the discovery process over again.

### Discovery in Windows 2000 domain Environments

If the Windows 2000 Terminal Server is a member of a Windows 2000 Active Directory domain, the Terminal Server will use two methods to try to find the TS licensing server.

Via the first method, a Terminal Server will query a domain controller for the "TS-Licensing" object. If that object exists, that means that a TS license server has been configured and is operating with a domain scope.

Next, the Terminal Server will query the domain controller for a list of servers whose names are listed in that domain object. It will then randomly pick a server from the list and try to open the "\TermServLicensing" named pipe connection. If that is successful, the Terminal Server tries to open a "\HydraLs" named pipe through which licenses can be requested from the TS licensing server.

If that connection fails, the Terminal Server will pick another server from the list and try again. If all servers fail, then the Terminal Server will connect to another domain controller and start the whole process over again.

Meanwhile, a Terminal Server in a Windows 2000 domain attempts to find an enterprise license server by reading the value of the "TS-Enterprise-License Server" Active Directory object. If that object exists, the Terminal Server will try to connect to the TS license server specified by that AD object.

If the Terminal Server establishes a connection with two different TS licensing servers—one at the domain level and one at the enterprise level, the domain level license server will take precedence. However, if that server runs out of licenses and cannot find any more among other domain–level license servers, the Terminal Server will try to obtain licenses from the enterprise–level license server.

In all cases, after a Terminal Server finds a TS licensing server, the Terminal Server will use that specific TS licensing server exclusively until that server fails to respond to a request, forcing the Terminal Server to connect to another license server.

When a Terminal Server successfully establishes a connection with a TS license server, the Terminal Server will perform a connection test to verify that the TS license server is still there. The timing of that test varies with the type of license server found, as shown in Figure 14.4. If that test fails and the Terminal Server cannot connect to any of the TS license servers it discovered the first time around, the discovery process is restarted.

*Figure 14.4  Microsoft License Discovery*

|  | License server verified to exist if no activity every | If no license server is found, discovery process occurs every |
| --- | --- | --- |
| NT 4 domain or workgroup | 120 min | 15 min |
| Windows 2000 – Domain | 120 min | 15 min |
| Windows 2000 – Enterprise | 60 min | 60 min |

## Manually Specifying Default License Servers

If a TS licensing server is located or configured in such a way that a Terminal Server is not able to automatically discover it with the aforementioned methods, it is possible to manually configure the Terminal Server to connect to a specific TS licensing server. By doing this, license servers can be located in different subnets, domains, or sites than the Terminal Servers.

To manually specify the location of a TS licensing sever, you must add the NetBIOS name of the licensing server to the registry of each Terminal Server.

Key:`HKLM\SYSTEM\CurrentControlSet\Services\TermService` `\Parameters`

Value: `DefaultLicenseServer`

Type: `REG_SZ`

Data: `servername`

Note that this entry must be a NetBIOS server name. IP addresses will not work. (If NetBIOS name resolution is not working in your environment, you can always add an `lmhosts` file to the Terminal Server with an entry for the TS licensing server.)

*Figure 14.5 Microsoft License Server Discovery Process*

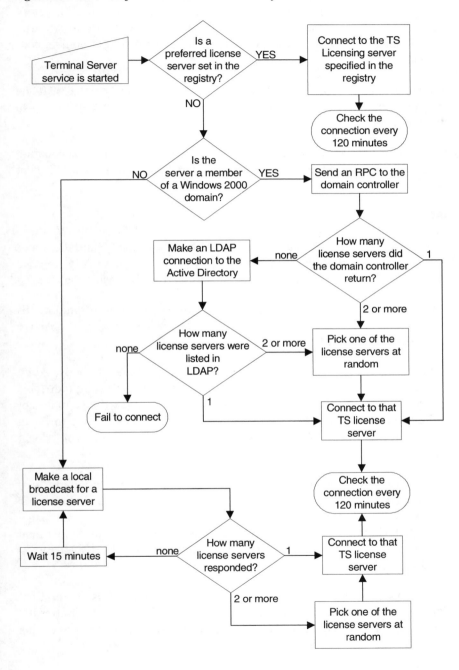

You can even use this manual method of specifying a license server as a way to run your license server on a non-domain controller in Active Directory environments. This is useful in many situations because the people who run the Terminal Servers are not always allowed to add services to domain controllers.

Adding this registry key will override the natural discovery process. If the specified license server is not available, the Terminal Server will not try to discover another license server on its own.

Many organizations make use of this manual configuration for accounting purposes, allowing different departments to purchase and maintain different pools of TS CALs.

### Installing the TS Licensing Service

The Terminal Services Licensing Service can be installed on any Windows 2000 server. This installation can be done at the time of the OS installation or at any time after that via the Control Panel (Control Panel | Add Remove Programs | Windows Components | Terminal Services Licensing Service).

When the installation routine begins, it will ask if you want to setup the license server in "Enterprise" or "Domain" scope for license servers in Active Directory environments.

After the TS licensing service is installed on a server, it must be activated by the Microsoft clearinghouse via the Terminal Services Licensing tool. This activation gives the license server the digital certificate it will use to accept and activate TS CALs. Activation also enables the license server to begin issuing the "free" TS CALs to Windows 2000 and Windows XP Professional clients.

The license server activation is fairly straightforward (Start | Programs | Administrative Tools | Terminal Services Licensing Tool | Right click on server | Activate). Activation can be done directly via the Internet or via a web page, fax, or telephone call. If you run the licensing tool on a computer other than the license server, the computer that you are using needs access to the Internet—not the license server.

Install and activate a TS licensing server within 90 days of using Terminal Services. If a Terminal Server can't find an activated license server after it's been used for 90 days, the Terminal Server will refuse connections to clients that do not have valid TS CALs.

If an activated license server ever depletes its inventory of TS CALs, it will issue 90 day temporary CALs. These temporary licenses are only valid for 90 days. They can only be replaced by a permanent license. They cannot be replaced by another 90-day temporary license. Temporary TS CALs are only issued to clients that require TS CALs to be purchased. An activated TS license server can never run out of the "free" TS CALs for qualifying clients such as Windows 2000 and Windows XP Professional.

## Managing TS Licensing Servers

Managing Windows 2000 Terminal Services license servers should not take much of your time. There are only two tasks you need to know about:

- Adding new licenses to the license pool.
- Administering the license server.

### Adding Licenses to a TS License Server

All newly–purchased Terminal Services Client Access Licensing must be installed onto a TS license server. These licenses are purchased in the same manner they have always been. Traditionally, if you bought a Client Access License pack, that pack only contained a license agreement—a useless piece of paper. Now, when you buy a Windows 2000 TS CAL license pack, it comes with a 25 character license code. This code must be entered into the TS Licensing Wizard for the TS licensing servers. If you buy licenses through a volume license agreement such as Select or an Enterprise Agreement, you will need to enter that agreement number into the Licensing Wizard when you add the licenses.

After the licenses have been installed, you need to activate them. You can activate the licenses via the same four methods you use to activate the license server (Internet, phone, fax, or email). Once activated, the licenses are ready to be distributed to client devices. Any clients that previously received the 90-day temporary licenses will be upgraded to full licenses the next time they connect.

### Administering License Servers

The TS licensing service is a "set it and forget it" kind of service. Theoretically, it only needs to be administered when new licenses are purchased or old licenses are removed.

However, there are times when it would be convenient to administer TS licensing servers remotely. For technical reasons, the TS Licensing Tool cannot be run via a remote Terminal Services session. However, this tool can be executed locally on any Windows 2000 computer and used to connect back to one or more TS license servers. In order to do this, copy the `licmgr.exe` and the `lrwizdll.dll` files from the `\system32\` directory of the TS licensing server to the `\system32\` directory of the computer you would like to use. Run `licmgr.exe` to use the tool.

As was mentioned previously, running the tool in this manner can be helpful when activating TS licensing servers or TS CAL packs. This is because during the activation, the machine that is running the TS Licensing Tool needs access to the Internet—not the actual license server itself. This works well in scenarios in which the Terminal Servers are not connected to the Internet but there are certain administrator workstations connected to the Internet and the internal network.

Maintaining the TS license servers is simple. One TS licensing console can connect to all of the license servers in your environment, facilitating centralized administration.

If you ever lose your TS license server, you will need to contact Microsoft to have your licenses re-issued. (This can be prevented if your license server is backed up properly. See Chapter 17 for details.)

You can generate a report that shows all of the licenses that have been issued, including temporary ones, with the "`lsreport`" tool available in the Windows 2000 Server Resource Kit.

### Client Device License Acquisition Process

The process by which a client device is granted a Terminal Services Client Access License is fairly complex, but interesting nonetheless. It is important that you have a good understanding of how the client device, Terminal Server, and license server all work together.

Before we sdelve into the details of the client device license acquisition process, there is an important technical note to cover.

In order for the licensing to work as described here, you must have hotfix Q287687 or Windows 2000 Service Pack 3 installed on all of your Terminal Servers and your TS licensing servers. Ideally, this hotfix or Service Pack 3 will be installed before any users ever connect to the server.

We'll talk about how horrible things would be without this hotfix or Service Pack later in this chapter since the changes that this hotfix applies are more relevant once we study how the process works. For now, know that hotfix Q287687 or Service Pack 3 is a good thing. Always.

## License Distribution to New, Unlicensed Client Devices

When a client device connects to a Windows 2000 Terminal Server, the server checks to make sure that the client device has a TS CAL (in the form of a digital certificate). If the client has a valid TS CAL, it is allowed to connect to the Terminal Server. In this case, there is no need for the Terminal Server to contact the license server because the client already has a TS CAL.

If the client device does not present a valid TS CAL, the Terminal Server will connect to the license server to obtain one. The license server will send a digital certificate for a temporary 90-day TS CAL to the Terminal Server, which passes it down to the client.

In the event that the license server does not respond to the Terminal Server, the Terminal Server will try to connect to one of the other license servers from its internal list of servers that was built as a result of the license server discovery process. If it can't connect to a license server, it will start the license server discovery process again. If this happens, because the client device does not have a TS CAL, the Terminal Server will be forced to deny the connection. The only exception to this is if the Terminal Server has been in use for less than 90 days. If so, the server will ignore the fact that it cannot find a license server. All of this action takes place a soon as the connection is made—before the user even authenticates!

After the user successfully authenticates, the Terminal Server will again contact the license server. This time the Terminal Server will tell the license server that the TS CAL that was sent to the user should be marked as "valid." If the user did not successfully authenticate, (i.e. the connection was from an inappropriate user), the Terminal Server will not contact the license server, and the license that was sent out will not be marked as "valid."

The next time that client device connects, its 90-day temporary TS CAL is upgraded to a full TS CAL. The Terminal Server notices that the client device has presented a temporary TS CAL certificate upon connection. The Terminal Server contacts the license server and requests a digital certificate for a full TS CAL which it then passes on to the client device. If, for some reason, all of the license servers have depleted their inventories of TS CALs, the client device will keep its temporary 90-day TS CAL certificate. As long as the 90-day certificate has not expired, the client device can still connect, even with no licenses available on any license servers.

The key to remember with the TS CAL certificate assignment process is that an unlicensed client device will always be granted a temporary 90-day TS CAL at the time of its first connection. Only after successful authentication and a second logon is the temporary TS CAL upgraded to a full TS CAL. This two–stage licensing process is used to ensure that TS CALs are only assigned to authenticated users. Previously (before hotfix 287687 or Windows 2000 Service Pack 3) any user that connected was assigned a full TS CAL, even if they did not belong on the system. This was because the full TS CAL certificate was granted at connection time, before the logon screen even popped up. If a user thought, "Oops, I don't belong on this system!" it was too late. Their client device had already received a full TS CAL certificate, even if the administrator never meant for them to access the system. This often lead to license servers running out of TS CALs.

### TS CAL License Certificate Storage on Client Devices

When a client device receives a TS CAL from a Terminal Server, it receives it in the form of a digital certificate from a license server. This is why you have to activate the license server with the Microsoft clearinghouse (a certificate authority). This digital certificate is an actual certificate copied to the client device (even with Windows CE). Microsoft has chosen to do this because Terminal Services client devices are licensed separately for each physical client device. The idea is that once a client device connects to a Terminal Server, a TS CAL digital certificate is transferred from the license server to the client device. The license server loses one of its licenses from inventory, and the client device has the digital certificate that it can present to any Windows 2000 Terminal Server for future logons.

This digital certificate is stored in different places in different operating systems. For example, on 32-bit Windows platforms, the TS CAL digital certificate is stored in the registry, at `HKLM\Software\Microsoft\MSLicensing\Store\License00x`. In the event that the client device has no local storage, its TS CAL certificate is stored on the Terminal Server.

When this license transfer plan was created, the security gurus and bankers at Microsoft thought it was a fantastic idea, because each client device that connected (even once) would be forced to take a permanent TS CAL license (just like the license agreement mandated). While this has always been the way that licensing was *supposed* to work, there was previously no way for Microsoft to enforce it, and practically every organization that used Terminal Server was under licensed.

Anyone who has been in the computer industry for more than five minutes knows that this license transfer scheme is a horrible idea, mainly because client devices tend to break. Windows-based terminals constantly have their ROMs reflashed. Operating systems are reinstalled on client PCs. Whenever this happens, the TS CAL digital certificate stored on the client device is lost forever because the TS CAL doesn't exist on the license server after it's transferred to a client device. When that client connects back to a Terminal Server, it has no digital certificate to present. The server thinks that it has no license, and so it instructs the license server to use a new TS CAL in the form of a new digital certificate to send down to the client device. In effect, that one client device ends up consuming two TS CALs—the old one that was lost and the new one that was just assigned. If the client device is reset again then a third TS CAL would be used. The only way to fix this is to call the Microsoft licensing clearinghouse (telephone only in this case) and have them release the duplicate TS CAL licenses. (It's kind of funny. When you call them, Microsoft always seems surprised, like they had never heard of this before, and that they would do it "just this once.")

Clearly, this gets very old. The fix to this is the other major component of hotfix Q287687 or Windows 2000 Service Pack 3. With the hotfix installed on your Terminal Servers and license servers, the full TS CAL certificates are no longer permanent (non-expiring). With the hotfix applied, when a Terminal Server requests a TS CAL from the license server for a client device, a full TS CAL certificate is granted that has an expiration date randomly selected between 52 and 89 days from the current date. The license server keeps track of this expiration date and it is also imbedded into the digital certificate that represents the actual license that is passed down to the client device.

Then, every time the client device connects to a Terminal Server, the client device presents its TS CAL certificate to the server. The server checks not only whether the client device has a valid certificate, but also the expiration date of that certificate. If the expiration date of the certificate is within 7 days of the current date, the Terminal Server connects to the license server to renew the license for another random period of 52 to 89 days. Because the license server also tracks the expiration date of TS CALs, if for some reason the CAL is never renewed and it expires, the license server returns that TS CAL to the inventory of available unused licenses. If a client device with a TS CAL were to blow up or be rebuilt, the license server automatically adds the TS CAL back into its available license pool after it expires (a maximum of 89 days).

If the Terminal Server is not able to obtain a TS CAL renewal when the client device's TS CAL certificate expires after the 52 – 89 days, the client is denied access. A temporary 90-day certificate cannot replace a full certificate that has expired. If you don't properly manage your CALs, it is possible that you could end up with users that cannot connect.

This system is actually very cool. Someone at Microsoft deserves an award for designing the temporary TS CALs to be valid for 90 days and the full TS CALs to be valid for a maximum of 89 days, conveniently one day less than the temporary licenses. Consider the following scenario:

Assume that a client device successfully authenticates to a Terminal Server and is granted a full TS CAL certificate that was (worst case) randomly selected to expire at the 89 day maximum. When it passes down the certificate, the license server decrements its total TS CAL license count by one, also noting that particular certificate's expiration date. Now, assume that a catastrophic event occurs at the client, causing its local operating system to be reinstalled and its local TS CAL certificate to be lost. When that client authenticates to a Terminal Server, the Terminal Server will request a new TS CAL certificate from the license server and the license server (again) decrements its TS CAL inventory by one. At this point there have been two TS CAL licenses given out to that one client, but the first one will never be renewed because the certificate was lost when the client was rebuilt. After 89 days (the randomly selected duration of the first certificate), the first TS CAL is returned to the pool by the license server.

As most people would, an administrator in this situation probably bought just enough TS CALs to cover the exact number of client devices. They did not buy extras to cover the 52 – 89 day period that the two licenses were used by one client. By purchasing the exact amount of TS CALs, the license server would not have any more TS CALs to give out when the client device asked for the new TS CAL certificate after the first was lost. In this case, the license server would grant a temporary 90-day TS CAL certificate to the client device because the client device appears to the server as a brand new machine.

Because the temporary TS CAL certificate is always valid at least one day longer then the full CAL certificate (90 days verses a maximum of 89 days), the old, lost full TS CAL will always be returned to the inventory on the license server at least one day before the temporary TS CAL certificate would expire. For example, after day 88, the client device's temporary TS CAL certificate will expire in 2 days, but the license server is tracking the expiration of the full TS CAL that was originally granted for 89 days. That full TS CAL only has 1 day left before it expires. The following day, when the client device's temporary TS CAL certificate has only 1 day remaining, the license server will add the original TS CAL back in its inventory pool, making it available to grant to the client as a permanent license for another random period of 52 – 89 days.

There is one last thing that should be mentioned about the TS CAL expiration period and the Q287687 hotfix or Service Pack 3 change. Any TS CALs distributed to client devices before the hotfix or Service Pack was applied will never expire, unlike the 52 – 89 day expiration of TS CALs distributed after the hotfix is applied. Applying the hotfix does not change the expiration date of the licenses that were previously applied. In this case, if you lose a client device with a TS CAL that was granted before the hotfix was applied, you will have to call the Microsoft clearinghouse to get them to release the license. After this, the next time the license is distributed, it will have the 52 – 89 day expiration date.

If you are a true geek, then you will enjoy tracing the entire licensing flow in Windows 2000 Terminal Server environments in Figure 14.6 on the next page. (Non-geeks may skip this.)

Either way, geek or non-geek, it's worth reiterating that you must install the Microsoft hotfix Q287687 or Windows 2000 Service Pack 3 on your Terminal Servers and license servers before you begin using your environment.

## Multiple 90-day Thresholds Explained

Throughout this license distribution and acquisition process, we have mentioned two different 90-day thresholds. While both are related to Windows 2000 Terminal Services licensing, they are actually two completely different things.

- Terminal Server will work without a license server for 90 days.
- If an activated license server runs out of TS CALs (licenses), it will issue 90-day temporary ones.

The first item relates to the presence of a license server. If a Terminal Server cannot locate a license server, it will still allow unlicensed client devices to log on. The Terminal Server itself does *not* grant 90-day temporary licenses if it cannot find a license server. Instead, if a license server cannot be located, the Terminal Server simply "looks the other way" for 90 days. After the 90-day period ends, unlicensed client device connections are refused. This 90-day countdown begins the first time a user connects to the Terminal Server via a terminal session, regardless of whether or not that user has a valid TS CAL.

The second 90-day item relates to the license server itself. If, over the course of business, an activated TS licensing server runs out of licenses, it will begin to grant 90-day temporary license certificates to client devices. Only an activated license server can grant temporary licenses.

*Figure 14.6  Client Device Licensing Process*

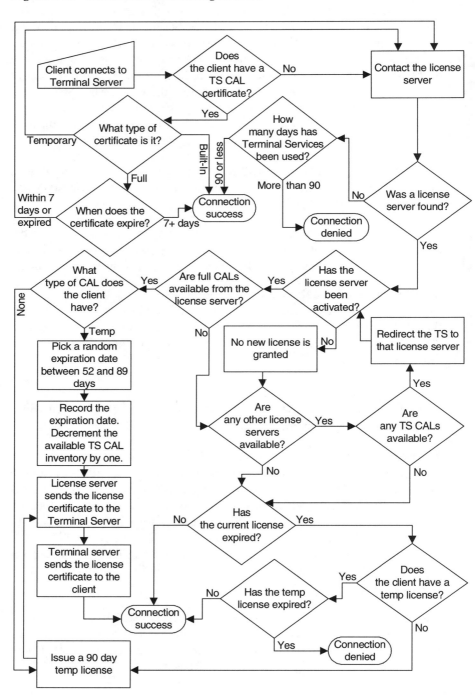

These temporary licenses can only be replaced by full TS CAL licenses— they cannot be replaced by additional temporary licenses. There is no limit to the number of temporary licenses that a license server can grant. Also, the 90-day timer for the expiration of the TS CALs is client specific, meaning that different temporary licenses can expire on different days—even if they were all granted by the same license server.

These two different thresholds inevitably lead to one question:

*Can I somehow combine these two thresholds to go 180 days without adding any Microsoft licenses?*

The answer to this is "yes." In the event that the licenses you've purchased are taking an extremely long time to come in, you can go 180 days without applying any Microsoft licenses. To do this, set up your Terminal Server without a license server. After 90 days, set up and activate a license server. If you activate the license server but do not add any licenses, the server will grant temporary licenses that are valid for 90 days.

### Terminal Services Internet Connector License (TS ICL)

There is one additional Microsoft license that is needed in special situations. This license is known as the "Terminal Services Internet Connector License" and it is required if you want to use your Terminal Server to provide access to anonymous users that will by connecting via the Internet.

This license stemmed from the clause in the Microsoft licensing agreement that mandated that every client device that could connect to a particular server needed to have a separate TS CAL. Wisecracking administrators wondered what would happen if they had applications for the public to use via the Internet. Would they need to buy 200 million licenses, one for every client device on the Internet? Of course Microsoft could not jeopardize their "one license per each unique device" scheme, so they created this Terminal Services Internet Connector License (TS ICL). This license, one of which is required for each Terminal Server that is used this way (next paragraph), costs a cool US$10,000 and is valid for up to 200 users per server. Users using this license do not require any of the TS CALs or server CALs outlined previously. However, there are very strict usage guidelines.

Users of the TS ICL license cannot be employees of the organization that bought the license and they are forced to log on anonymously to the server. The TS ICL license is an "all or nothing" license, meaning that you cannot have one server that hosts some users that connect via the TS ICL anonymously while others are employees that connect via TS CALs. From a practical sense, it's hard to imagine any scenario where this license is useful, except for Citrix's web-based demo room (www.citrix.com/demoroom).

Incidentally, do not confuse this Terminal Services Internet Connector License (US$10,000) with the Internet Connector License (US$2,000). The latter of the two is used for connecting server applications to the Internet (like web servers), and is not valid for Terminal Services sessions.

### How the Terminal Services Internet Connector License Works

One TS ICL is required for each Terminal Server (NT4 or W2K) that provides anonymous non-employees access to Terminal Services sessions. Each TS ICL may be used for up to 200 concurrent connections. This license replaces TS CALs and server CALs for these servers.

The TS ICL is installed and activated on a TS licensing server just like any other Terminal Services license. When a Terminal Server is configured to operate in Internet Connector mode, it contacts the TS licensing server and a digital certificate for the ICL is transmitted to the Terminal Server. Then the TS license server's inventory of available TS ICL's is decremented by one.

You can switch a Terminal Server into "Internet Connector" mode at any time via the Terminal Services Configuration Utility. When the switch to Internet Connector mode is made, if the Terminal Server cannot contact the license server, or the license server does not have any available TS ICLs, then the server will not go into Internet Connector mode. There is no grace period and there are no temporary TS ICLs.

Once a Terminal Server is in Internet Connector mode, all Terminal Services connections (even those via MetaFrame) are automatically logged on as the local account "TSInternetUser." This cannot be overridden and was done by design to force users to log on anonymously. Whenever a user logs onto a Terminal Services or ICA session on a server that is operating in Internet Connector mode, the user will always use one of the 200 ICL users, even if the user has his own local TS CAL certificate. However, that one user can still log on to multiple Terminal Servers, even if some are operating in Internet Connector mode while others are not.

If you disable Internet Connector mode, then the TS ICL is automatically returned to the available pool on the TS license server. Immediately after disabling this mode, users may log on with any account. TS CALs and server CALs will be required for each client device.

# Citrix Licensing

All of the Microsoft licensing described in this chapter is required as the foundation for your MetaFrame XP environment. The Citrix licensing discussed in this section is *in addition to* the required Microsoft licensing. The Citrix licenses do *not* replace the Microsoft licenses.

## Citrix MetaFrame XP Licensing Requirements

There are two types of Citrix licenses required for MetaFrame XP: product licenses and connection licenses. Product licenses *roughly* represent "server" licenses, and connection licenses *roughly* represent "user" licenses.

### Product Licenses

MetaFrame XP product licenses are required for MetaFrame XP server products. Each type of MetaFrame XP server in an environment requires its own product license. There are different versions of this product license for each version of MetaFrame XP (i.e. XPs, XPa, XPe, FR-1, etc.).

Only one product license is needed for a particular MetaFrame XP version per server farm. They are *not* based on concurrency. From the server standpoint, that means that if you have one MetaFrame XPe product licenses, you can have as many servers running XPe as you want.

Product licenses are version–specific. For example, you must have a MetaFrame XPe product license to run a MetaFrame XPe server. Higher level product licenses cannot be used for lower level servers. This means that an XPs server cannot use an XPe product license.

Each product license includes one "free" connection license so that administrators can connect if a product license pack was installed without a connection (user) license pack (described below).

### Connection Licenses

One connection license is required for each user ICA connection to a MetaFrame XP server farm. Connection licenses are based on concurrent connections. If you have 500 users but only 100 connect simultaneously, you only need 100 MetaFrame XP connection licenses.

MetaFrame XP connection licenses are based on user connections into the server farm. One user may connect to and run applications from multiple

MetaFrame XP servers, even at the same time, and only use one connection license.

Just like product licenses, MetaFrame XP connection licenses are also version–specific. A user cannot use a MetaFrame XPs connection license to run an ICA session on a MetaFrame XPe server, even if that server had a MetaFrame XPe product license. However, unlike product licenses, the reverse is not true. A user with a MetaFrame XPe connection license may use that license to connect to lower–level MetaFrame XP servers in the farm, such as MetaFrame XPs or XPa.

# How MetaFrame XP Licensing Works

All MetaFrame XP licensing is done at the server farm level. All licenses are installed into the server farm can be shared between users and servers in the farm. The actual license keys are stored in the farm's IMA data store. Each server's local host cache database contains a copy of the farm licensing information.

The zone data collectors work to police the license usage within the server farm. They are constantly kept up to date as to the total number of licenses that are available and in use.

Because license keys are stored in the IMA data store, each farm member MetaFrame XP server must not lose connectivity to the data store. If a MetaFrame XP server loses contact with the IMA data store for more than 48 hours (96 hours with Feature Release 2), the licensing component of the IMA service stops and no users are able to log on.

## License Storage and Usage

All Citrix license numbers are stored in the IMA data store. This includes both the user connection licenses and the server product licenses.

Each MetaFrame XP server knows what type of product license it requires. When the IMA service is started (usually when the server is booted), it connects to the IMA data store to ensure that it contains the proper type of product license.

The version of the product license in the IMA data store must match the version of the MetaFrame XP server requesting the license. For example, when a MetaFrame XPe server boots, it checks the IMA data store to see if it contains a MetaFrame XPe product license. If it does not, then the MetaFrame XPe server will not allow any users to connect. Similarly, a MetaFrame XPa server will check the IMA data store for an XPa product license.

Client connection licenses are also stored in the IMA data store. When a user starts an ICA session with a MetaFrame XP server, a license is granted from the available pool in the server farm's IMA data store. These client connection licenses are valid for multiple concurrent server connections. If an ICA client connects to a server in the farm where that ICA client already has another ICA session open, the client will not consume another license.

When the ICA client logs off, the connection license is automatically returned to the pool of available licenses in the data store.

## Components that make up a MetaFrame XP License

With the two different types of MetaFrame XP licenses available and Citrix's strict anti-piracy measures, there are actually several technical components that make up a MetaFrame XP license. Let's take a look at each of the components:

- Serial Number.
- Machine Code.
- Activation Code.
- License Number.
- Product Code.
- Feature Release Level.

### Serial Number

Every MetaFrame XP license starts out as a 25-character serial number. This serial number is entered into the licensing component of the CMC when you add the license to your farm. The serial number is a unique number that represents the licenses purchased. No two serial numbers in the world are the same.

Based on the serial number entered, MetaFrame XP knows how many connection and product licenses you've purchased. A single 25-character serial number can represent multiple connection licenses or a product license. In fact, some 25-character serial numbers represent a product license and multiple connection licenses—all with the same serial number. These are usually seen in the MetaFrame XP starter kits, where a single serial number represents 20 user connection licenses and one MetaFrame XP product license.

## Machine Code

The machine code is a random 8 digit character string that is added to a license serial number as soon as you enter it into the CMC. This machine code is automatically created when the license is entered and there is no way to change it. If you remove a license and then re-add it, that license will receive a new machine code. The reason for having the machine code will become evident in the next section.

## Activation Code

All MetaFrame XP licenses (product and connection) must be "activated" before they can be permanently used. Activating a license involves registering the license number with Citrix and then entering an activation confirmation code into the CMC.

Citrix created the activation process to prevent licenses from being stolen or pirated. By activating MetaFrame XP licenses, Citrix can ensure that license numbers are not shared via the Internet or that one company isn't using a single connection license for 20,000 users.

When a license is installed (by entering its 25-character serial number into the CMC), the server will specify a certain "grace period." This grace period represents the number of days the license will be valid before it must be activated. If the license is not activated before the grace period runs out, it will cease to function until it is activated. Once a license has ceased to function, only one user will be able to log on. (So you see, there is no way around the license activation procedure.) For most standard licenses, the grace period is 35 days, although some demonstration and evaluation licenses have shorter grace periods.

When you activate a license, you must provide Citrix with the 25-character license serial number and the 8-digit machine code. Citrix uses these two numbers to generate a 10-digit activation code. The activation code will only work with that specific combination of the license serial number and machine code.

If you remove and re-add a license or transfer a license to a different server farm, the license will need to be reactivated because a new machine code will have been generated when the 25-character license serial number was entered into the new farm. Now you can see why the machine code exists. Because the activation code is based on the serial number and the machine code, it is not possible to use an old activation code to activate a single license serial number over and over. Every time the license is installed into a farm, a new machine code is generated. The old activation code will only work with the license number and the original machine code.

You can activate licenses via the Citrix Management Console (CMC | Licensing | Right-click on license | Activate). Activation codes are most easily attainable via Citrix's NFuse Elite-based user portal at www.citrix.com/mycitrix.

It is recommended that you do not activate a license until a server is proven production ready. After all, there is no impact to a system that has unactivated licenses as long as the grace period doesn't run out. If you activate a license too soon and you end up rebuilding the server, you will need to reactivate the license. Citrix gets suspicious if you activate the same license number and you'll have to explain to them that you are not pirating licenses. The only exception to this rule is Feature Release 1 licenses, which for some unexplained reason, must be activated before they work. (Feature Release 2 does not have this "feature.")

## License Number

The "license number" is the generic term given to the combined serial number, machine code, and activation code for a specific license. Within the Citrix Management Console, activated licenses are referred to by their "license number."

## Product Code

Every MetaFrame XP server has a product code. The product code is an 8-digit number that tells the server what version of MetaFrame XP it is. Product codes differentiate between MetaFrame XPs, XPa, and XPe. They also tell the server if the product license is a retail, not-for-resale, evaluation, demonstration or beta version, or if it is an upgrade or migration version. As you can see, there are many different packages and distributions of MetaFrame XP, and each specific combination of these options has a different 8-digit product code so that the MetaFrame XP server knows exactly what it is.

You're probably wondering why product codes exist, especially given that all the above mentioned information can be found in the license number itself? Product codes exist for one reason. They tell the MetaFrame XP server what type of product license it should request from the server farm's license pool in the IMA data store when the server is started. Remember that all farm licenses are stored in the IMA data store. Before a server can request a license, it must know what type of license to request. This is because the IMA data store might have multiple XPs, XPa, and XPe licenses available. The product code is how the MetaFrame XP server knows what type it is. It also tells the server what type of connection licenses are required for user connections to it.

Based on this, there are four licensing steps that a MetaFrame XP server takes when it is started:

1. Server is booted.

2. Server checks its own product code to see what type of licenses it needs.

3. Server checks the IMA data store for the appropriate license type.

4. Server waits for users to connect. When they do, it makes sure that they have the right level of connection license, based on its product code. (i.e. XPe connection licenses for an XPe server, etc.)

For example, a large server farm might have many different product licenses available in the license pool in the IMA data store. If the pool contains XPs, XPa, and XPe licenses, then each server that comes online cannot blindly ask for a license—it must know which type of license it needs. This is where the product code comes in.

As an administrator, you can modify a server's MetaFrame XP product code at any time without reinstalling a thing (CMC | Server Name | Set MetaFrame Product Code). You can update an evaluation server to a permanent server or you can upgrade an XPs server to XPe without running a single line of executable code. All you have to do is add the new license or licenses to the server farm and change the server's product code (which will tell the server to look for the new license). After this, stop and start the IMA service. You're all set!

For those crafty readers, be aware that you cannot trick the licensing component of MetaFrame by entering an XPe product code with an XPs license. If you do this, the server with the XPe product code will request an XPe level license from the server farm's license pool in the IMA data store. If there is no XPe license available, the server won't accept any user connections. To remedy this, set the server's product code back to the proper XPs product code and restart the IMA service.

If you choose to install a license during the MetaFrame XP setup, the setup program will suggest that you set the server's product code to the one that matches the licenses you are adding.

## Feature Release Level

The Feature Release Level is a property of a MetaFrame XP server that is similar in concept to the product code. As with any licenses, Feature Release licenses are added to the license pool in the IMA data store. In order for a MetaFrame XP server to use the Feature Release functions, you need to tell it to acquire a Feature Release license from the license pool in addition to its standard product license when it is booted. You can set the Feature Release level of a MetaFrame XP server via the CMC (CMC | Right-click server | Set Feature Release Level). In order to set this, use a version of the Citrix Management Console that has had Service Pack 1 or newer applied.

As with product codes, you must have a Feature Release license available if you set a server's Feature Release level to anything other than "Not Installed." If you don't have the correct Feature Release product license available, the server will not be able to accept any user connections.

## License Component Summary

After reading through the license components that are available, you should be glad to know that most of this will not affect you on a day-to-day basis. You will not need to worry about which product licenses are allocated to which servers. From a licensing standpoint, all you need to do is make sure that:

1. The right product codes are configured on each MetaFrame XP server.

2. You have the proper, activated licenses added to the license pool.

## *Other Types of MetaFrame XP Licenses*

In addition to the standard license types discussed so far, there are situations alternate licensing schemes exist. Often these can save an organization time and money over buying standard licenses. Four types of nonstandard licenses are most often used:

- Migration licenses.
- Upgrade licenses.
- Enterprise licensing agreements.
- ASP licensing agreements.

### Migration Licenses from Older Citrix Products

If you have older versions of Citrix products, you can usually purchase migration licenses for the migration to MetaFrame XP. These migration licenses are less expensive than full version MetaFrame XP licenses.

Using migration licenses can save your organization thousands of dollars. You can migrate from old Citrix products, including MetaFrame and some versions of WinFrame. You can also migrate to MetaFrame XP from some OEM versions of Citrix products such as NCD WinCenter Pro, Tektronix WinDD, and Insignia NTrigure. Most of these OEM products have user connection licenses that Citrix recognizes as equivalent to MetaFrame 1.8 connection licenses—which means that there might be some real value in those old boxes in your IT closet. Even if you have old products that cannot be directly migrated to MetaFrame XP, some of them can be migrated to Meta-Frame 1.8 which in turn can be migrated to MetaFrame XP for less than it costs to purchase MetaFrame XP from scratch.

There is one little quirk that you will find when using migration licenses. To use them, you must enter and activate the old product licenses into the server farm's license pool first and then enter and activate the new MetaFrame XP migration licenses. Citrix has been using the license serial number / machine code / activation code scheme for a while, and MetaFrame XP will recognize the old licenses (and know what they're from!)

When you use a MetaFrame XP migration license, you will get a different product code and license serial number for MetaFrame XP than if you purchased a regular off-the-shelf copy of MetaFrame XP. The product code will let the server know that a migration license was used. Then, when the server is started, it requests the old license and the new MetaFrame XP migration license from the license pool.

For example, if you own a copy of MetaFrame 1.8 and you would like to use MetaFrame XPs, you can purchase a MetaFrame 1.8 to MetaFrame XPs migration license for far less than purchasing a full MetaFrame XPs license. When you install MetaFrame XPs, it will ask you to enter your license number. The XPs license number that is included with your copy of MetaFrame XPs will reflect that the version of XPs you bought was a migration from MetaFrame 1.8. If you are installing the server from scratch, you will be required to enter and activate both your old MetaFrame 1.8 license and your new MetaFrame XPs migration licenses. (If you are just performing an upgrade, then you will not have to reenter your MetaFrame 1.8 licensing information.) The product code provided to you will also reflect that your version of MetaFrame XP is a MetaFrame 1.8 to MetaFrame XPs migration license. This product code will be different from the regular MetaFrame XPs product code.

In this case, when your new MetaFrame XPs server is booted, the local IMA service will read the product code. Based on that product code (and the fact that it is a MetaFrame 1.8 to XP migration license), it will verify that both the old MetaFrame 1.8 product license and the 1.8 to XPs migration license are present in the data store. By doing so, the server ensures that the MetaFrame 1.8 license you entered will not be illegally used for more than one migration to MetaFrame XP.

It's important to note that it is not necessary to actually physically install MetaFrame 1.8 before installing MetaFrame XP. It is just necessary that you have the MetaFrame 1.8 server license available and that you add it to your MetaFrame XP license pool.

## Upgrade Licenses

MetaFrame XP upgrade licenses are similar to migration licenses, except that upgrade licenses are for use exclusively within the MetaFrame XP family. You can upgrade from XPs to XPa, XPa or XPe, or from XPa to XPe. To do this, purchase an upgrade license, change the product code on the server, and add and activate the upgrade license to the data store.

In a similar fashion to the migration licenses, the new product code and license will represent that an upgrade took place. When a server is booted with an upgrade license, the product code will require that the server uses the old full version license and the new upgrade license.

Both server product licenses and connection licenses can be upgraded. Any server can use either full versions or upgraded versions of connection licenses. Consider the following scenario. Imagine that your four-server MetaFrame XP environment has the licenses outlined in Figure 14.7.

*Figure 14.7  Current licenses*

| Product Licenses | | Connection Licenses | |
| --- | --- | --- | --- |
| XPa | qty. 1 | XPa | qty. 50 |
| XPe | qty. 1 | XPe | qty. 50 |

Currently, you have two servers at the XPe level and two servers at the XPa level. You also have 50 users at each level. You must have one XPe product license and one XPa product license in your data store, because each server type needs to have its own version of the product license available.

In this environment it would be legal for you to change the product codes on your two XPa servers to match the codes of your XPe servers. The only problem is that if you did this, your two XPa servers would essentially become

XPe servers and your 50 XPa connection licenses would be useless (leaving you with only 50 XPe connection licenses).

However, if you decide that you like the advanced features of MetaFrame XPe and you would like to have all 100 users and all four servers at the Meta-Frame XPe level, all you need to do is purchase the licenses outlined in Figure 14.8.

*Figure 14.8  Upgrade licenses needed*

| Product Licenses | | Connection Licenses | |
| --- | --- | --- | --- |
| none | | XPa to XPe | qty. 50 |

By purchasing these licenses, your environment would be equivalent to that in Figure 14.9.

*Figure 14.9  New environment license equivalence*

| Product Licenses | | Connection Licenses | |
| --- | --- | --- | --- |
| XPe | qty. 1 | XPe | qty. 100 |

However, if you looked at the actual licenses that were maintained in the IMA data store, you would see the licenses outlined in Figure 14.10.

*Figure 14.10  New environment – actual licenses in the data store*

| Product Licenses | | Connection Licenses | |
| --- | --- | --- | --- |
| XPa (no longer used) | qty. 1 | XPa | qty. 50 |
| XPe | qty. 1 | XPe | qty. 50 |
| | | XPa to XPe | qty. 50 |

The server farm (via the IMA data store) tracks all of the licenses that you have purchased. For the environment outlined on the previous page, you would simply add the 50 XPa to XPe upgrade connections licenses to the data store and then change the product code on your XPa servers to match the code on the XPe servers.

The user connection licenses would be used interchangeably. For each user that connected to an XPe server, that XPe server would request an XPe connection license from the server farm's license pool. It doesn't matter if that server gets a full XPe connection license or a full XPa connection license coupled with an XPa to XPe upgrade connection license. The licenses can be used either way on any of the four servers.

## Volume License Agreements

If MetaFrame XP is going to large a large part of your organization, Citrix now offers several different licensing programs with various discounts and degrees of flexibility. The terms of these programs change as fast as Microsoft's do, so it's not worth detailing them here since they'll be different by the time you read this.

In addition to price breaks, many of Citrix's volume license programs have special licensing hotfixes that you install on your Citrix servers to prevent you from having to manually type in license numbers and activate licenses. There are also licensing programs for service providers that allow you to pay for licenses based on actual per-month usage of your customers.

Full details about Citrix's licensing programs are available at www.citrix.com/licensing.

# Configuring MetaFrame XP Server License Usage

By default, any licenses that are added to the server farm's IMA data store are automatically added to the license pool. This license pool combines identical types of connection licenses, making them available use by any server in the farm. This license pooling simplifies administration sincelicenses are not tied to specific servers. The servers take licenses from the pool as they are needed.

This generally works well, but there are times when it is necessary to reserve a certain number of user connection licenses for specific servers. To do this, you can "assign" connection licenses to specific servers via the Citrix Management Console (CMC | Licenses | Right-click license set | New assignment). When licenses are assigned to servers, the licenses are removed from the shared license pool and made available only for the server to which they have been assigned. Only activated, permanent (non-demonstration, non-evaluation) licenses can be assigned to servers.

When you assign connection licenses with the license assignment wizard in the Citrix Management Console, be sure that you assign the proper type of licenses. The wizard does not enforce this, so be careful! If you assign MetaFrame XPa licenses to an XPe server, the licenses won't work.

A server that has licenses assigned to it will still be able to accept connections above and beyond the number of assigned licenses so long as pooled licenses are still available. The assigned licenses merely represent the minimum number of licenses that must be reserved.

If a server is offline, its assigned licenses are not pooled and are still reserved for it, which is necessary so that the licenses don't get used while the server is offline. Consequently, if a server is lost, its assigned licenses are not automatically returned to the pool. Of course you can add them back to the pool with the click of the mouse in the CMC.

Because licensing is done by concurrent connection, ordinarily one user can connect to multiple MetaFrame XP servers and use one only connection license. If a user connects to a server that uses pooled licenses and then connects to a server that has licenses assigned to it, the user will only use one license because the pooled license will "travel" with the user to the second server. However, the opposite is not true. Consider the user in Figure 14.11. If a user first connects to "Server A" that has licenses assigned to it and then that user connects to "Server B," the "Server B" connection will use a second license. This is because the first license is "assigned" to the "Server A" and cannot be used for other servers. Some people wonder why that assigned license can't be used for both. If it could, the user could use the assigned license for the two connections and then terminate the connection with the first server. In this case, the user would be using the assigned license on the wrong server.

*Figure 14.11 Users with assigned licenses*

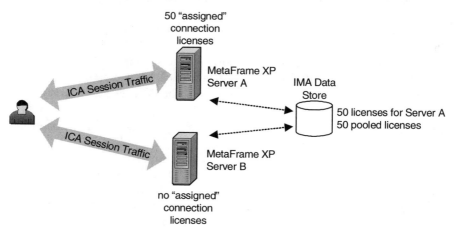

Best practices dictate that you do not pool all of the licenses on all of the servers. By assigning one or two licenses per server, you will always ensure that at least one user can connect. This is useful for administration purposes. By assigning one or two licenses, you are not wasting them. In fact, they may be used by regular users throughout the day.

## Managing Licenses with the Citrix Management Console

The Licensing Area of the Citrix Management Console has three tabs: Connection, Product, and License Numbers. It can be confusing to understand what information is displayed on each tab because some of the license numbers are the same from tab to tab. The following section should help decipher exactly what the CMC licensing tabs are displaying.

### Connection

All of the same type of connection licenses are combined together on the connection tab. These combined licenses are called "license sets." There is only one line per type of connection license even though more than one license number may contribute to the total number of licenses. For example, MetaFrame XPa connection licenses are different than MetaFrame XPe connection licenses and each would be displayed on a separate line. The MetaFrame XPa license set may show that there are 35 connection licenses available. This one line could contain combined license information from a 20 pack, a 10 pack, and a 5 pack. You can double click to see more details, including which license numbers make up the license set.

When you view licenses with the Citrix Management Console, the display does not automatically refresh even if you have "auto-refresh" enabled for the CMC. You can easily perform a manual refresh by pressing the F5 key.

### Product

The product tab works in the same manner as the connection tab except that it shows server product licenses. Again, all similar product licenses are combined to form one line entry for each type. This combination can include dedicated product license packs and the single product license that comes with starter pack combination licenses.

By viewing the product licenses, you will notice that a MetaFrame XPe license is a single license, unlike MetaFrame 1.8 that had separate licenses for Load Balancing, Installation Management, and Resource Management. In MetaFrame XPe, it is not possible to separate these advanced components from each other. You cannot use part of an XPe license for Resource Management on one server with the same license number's Installation Management on another. In this case, each server (and user connection) would require a full XPe license.

### License Numbers

The license numbers tab displays the actual license numbers that have been entered and activated.

### Viewing Licenses in Use

By selecting a server in the CMC, you can use the licensing tab to view the licenses that are in use by that server, including connection licenses and product licenses.

### SNMP License Notification

For environments in which SNMP management and monitoring tools are used, MetaFrame XP servers can be configured to send traps relating to license usage. This component is similar to a functionality of the Network Management component of MetaFrame XPe described in Chapter 16 except that this SNMP license notification will work with any version of MetaFrame XP.

Options for SNMP license notification can be configured on a farm-wide (CMC I server farm I properties) or individual server (CMC I server I properties) basis.

You can configure alerts to be sent when the percentage of pooled licenses drops below the entered threshold and reset when that percentage rises above another entered threshold.

## When Multiple Licenses are Applied to One User

Under some circumstances, one user may consume more than one connection license. This usually happens when a user connects to multiple servers or applications that have conflicting parameters.

For example, if one server is configured not to use compression and another server requires compression, it is not possible for a user to connect to both with one session. The user will still be able to simultaneously connect to both, but two sessions will be started and two licenses will be consumed. This occurs when one of the following does not match between sessions:

- Protocol.
- Encryption Level.
- Color Depth.

- Disk Cache.
- Compression.
- Queue mouse and keystrokes values.
- Audio Settings.

Additionally, as previously mentioned, if a user connects to a MetaFrame XP server where a connection license has been assigned and then that user connects to another server, a new license will be used since the assigned license cannot travel with the user.

## License Differences Between MetaFrame XP and 1.8

Citrix licensing varies with the version of MetaFrame being used. In both MetaFrame 1.8 and MetaFrame XP, user licenses are connection–based. However, the definition of "connection–based" changes depending on the version of MetaFrame.

In MetaFrame 1.8, one "connection" is defined as a single user with a single user ID on a single subnet, regardless of the number of ICA sessions actually opened or servers actually connected to by that user.

In MetaFrame XP, one "connection" is defined as a single user with a single user ID connecting to a single server farm, regardless of the number of ICA sessions actually opened or servers actually connected to by that user.

The key difference is the designation between "subnet" and "server farm." In actuality, the products were licensed this way due to the internal differences of the ICA browser and IMA data store and their respective ability to track licenses.

Regardless of MetaFrame version, Citrix licenses are based on concurrent connections as opposed to Microsoft's "per device" approach.

# Application Licensing

When you think about the licenses you will need for your MetaFrame XP environment, you can't forget about the licensing of the actual applications that your users will access. While the purpose of this book is to focus on MetaFrame XP, there are some common threads worth pointing out regarding application licensing.

Because there are so many different ways that applications can be licensed, it's impossible go into specifics here. However, in almost all cases, the application usage license is tied in some way to the number of users or client devices. Most application licenses are not linked to the number of times the application is installed because the application vendors don't want you to buy one copy of the application for each MetaFrame XP server that you have and then publish that application to hundreds of users per server.

Most of the applications out there today have licensing agreements that fall into one of two categories:

- *Per Named User*. One license for each user that *could* execute the application. (Microsoft applications)
- *Per Concurrent User*. One license for each concurrent copy of the application that is executed. (Everybody else)

### Enforcing Named User Application Licenses

Applications that are licensed "per named user" require that you have a license for each user that could access the application. That means that if you have 100 users that have access to an application but no more than 10 ever connect at the same time, you still need to purchase 100 application licenses. Most Microsoft applications are licensed this way, in addition to many expensive line-of-business applications.

The key to properly enforcing per named user application licenses is permitting or preventing users from being able to access the applications. One easy way to do this is to create a domain group with all the user accounts of the users that will need to access the application. Then, set the permissions on the published application so that only members of that domain group can use it. Or, if your users are connecting to a published desktop instead of a published application, set the NTFS permissions on the application executable.

By restricting access to the application itself, you are guaranteeing that only appropriate users will ever use the application. When it comes time to pay for your application licenses, all you have to do is count the number of users that are in your application group and buy that number of licenses.

### Enforcing Concurrent User Application Licenses

Applications whose licenses are based on the number of concurrent users only require that an application license is purchased for each concurrent connection. If you have 100 users that have access to an application but no more than 10 ever connect at the same time, you only need to purchase 10 licenses. Your company's accountants will appreciate applications that are based on concurrency because they are a lot cheaper. You will probably not appreciate applications that are based on concurrency because they are harder to enforce from a technical standpoint.

Within MetaFrame XP, there are really three ways to enforce concurrent users. We'll look at them in order, from the easiest to the most difficult:

- The easiest way to limit the number of concurrent applications is to install Feature Release 1 or 2. Feature Release 1 and newer includes a "connection control" feature that lets you specify the maximum number of concurrent published application instances in a server farm. It also lets you limit each user to only running one instance of the application. It's based on all instances of the application on all servers, so you can easily limit application access while still getting the benefits of a load balanced application. The disadvantages of this connection control is that it requires Feature Release 1 and MetaFrame XPa or XPe. See Chapter 4 for details on connection control.

- Another way to limit the number of concurrent connections to an application is to use the Load Evaluators available in MetaFrame XPa or XPe. You can create load evaluators that are based on ICA connection thresholds or published application thresholds. They can be configured so as not to allow any more connections once their threshold is reached. See Chapter 4 for more details on configuring load evaluators.

- The last way to limit the number of concurrent connections to an application is known as "really fancy scripting." It is possible to create a batch file that writes to a flag file before an application is launched. That batch file can be configured to check the flag file to see how many other instances of the application are running. For environments in which applications are published across more than one server, the flag file can be stored on a network drive. When users quit the application, the flag file is updated to reflect the user change. The only problem with this (other than the complexity of writing the scripts in the first place) is that the flag file is not updated if users do not exit the application properly. These days this method is not really used anymore, especially since Feature Release 1 simplifies limiting users.

The only other item worth mentioning about application licensing relates to applications that require a hardware key. If you have an application that requires a hardware key, or "dongle," it probably won't work on a Terminal Server. Microsoft has disabled this functionality because the sole purpose of a hardware key is to prevent multiple users from using an application, and Terminal Services' sole purpose is to allow multiple users to use an application.

If your hardware key vendor did not use the standard Microsoft APIs when writing the application, the hardware key may work on a Terminal Server. If this is the case for your application you need to ensure that its use in a MetaFrame environment is acceptable from a licensing standpoint.

### IMA Data Store Database Licensing

If you use SQL, Oracle, or DB-2 for your IMA data store, you will need have the proper licenses for it as well. Fortunately, the licensing of these databases allows for licenses based on the number of connections to the database.

If your MetaFrame XP servers are configured to access the IMA data store via direct mode, you will need a database license for each of your servers. If your servers will access the data store via indirect mode, you will only need a single connection license for the MetaFrame XP server directly connected to the database.

Either way, your Citrix ICA clients will never directly access the IMA data store, so at worst you will have to buy a database client license for each MetaFrame XP server, not for each Citrix ICA client.

# Real World Case Study

## Tyler Treats Gourmet Pet Foods

Tyler Treats Gourmet Pet Foods chose to use MetaFrame XP to provide a new warehousing application to about 120 users scattered throughout Brazil. They had never really used MetaFrame before, although they did have a copy of WinFrame 1.6 sitting in the closet. Let's take a look at the licenses that they ordered for their environment.

### Current Environment

The first table shows the breakdown of users and what operating system they were using.

| Number of Users | Platform |
| --- | --- |
| 20 | Windows 2000 |
| 40 | Windows NT 4.0 Workstation |
| 60 | Windows 95 or 98 |

Every one of the 120 users had a Windows NT 4.0 Server Client Access License which they used to log onto the existing Windows NT 4.0 domain for file and print sharing.

Additionally, while cleaning out an old desk, they found a 20-user copy of WinFrame 1.7. They decided to save it to see if they could upgrade the licenses to MetaFrame XP. The following table summarizes the additional licenses that they had.

| Number of Licenses | License Description |
|---|---|
| 1 | WinFrame 1.7 Server License |
| 15 | WinFrame 1.7 User Licenses |
| 120 | Windows NT 4.0 Server CALs |

### New MetaFrame XP Environment

In their new MetaFrame XP environment, Tyler Treats figured that they would have about 100 concurrent users accessing their MetaFrame XP environment. They built three MetaFrame XPa Servers, and planed on using Feature Release 2.

Based on this, the project team figured that they needed the following licenses.

| Number of Licenses | License Description |
|---|---|
| 1 | MetaFrame XPa Product License |
| 1 | MetaFrame Feature Release 2 Product License |
| 100 | XPa Connection Licenses |
| 100 | XP Feature Release 2 connection licenses |
| 3 | Windows 2000 Server Licenses |
| 120 | Windows 2000 Server CALs |
| 120 | Windows 2000 Terminal Services CALs |

### Actual Licenses Purchased

Based on their current environment and the licenses that they figured they needed, the Tyler Treats project team purchased several different types of licenses as shown in the following chart. Notice that they only needed to purchase full version TS CALs for their Windows 95 and 98 users. The 60 users running Windows 2000 professional could use the free Windows 2000

TS CALs, and the 40 users running Windows NT 4.0 Workstation only needed TS CAL upgrades.

| Number of Licenses | License Description |
|---|---|
| 120 | NT 4 Server to Windows 2000 Server CAL Upgrades |
| 40 | NT 4 TS CAL to Windows 2000 TS CAL Upgrades |
| 60 | Full Version Windows 2000 TS CALs |
| 3 | Windows 2000 Server Licenses |
| 1 | MetaFrame 1.7 to MetaFrame XPa Migration Kit (Server and 15 users) |
| 1 | MetaFrame XPa Starter kit (with one MetaFrame XPa product license and 20 XPa connection licenses) |
| 3 | 20-user MetaFrame XPa connection license packs |
| 1 | 5-user MetaFrame XPa connection license pack |
| 2 | 50-user Feature Release 2 connection license packs |

## How Tyler Treats Installed Their Licensing Components

After all the licenses were acquired, the project team decided to implement the various licensing components in the following order:

1. *Install Windows 2000 Terminal Servers and MetaFrame XP with FR-2.* The project team installed Windows 2000 with Service Pack 3. They then downloaded FR-2 from the Citrix website and used it to install MetaFrame XP (which was then automatically at the SP-2/FR-2 level). Even though Tyler Treats had the old copy of WinFrame 1.7, they used the same full version XPa product code for all three of their MetaFrame XPa servers.

2. *Activate all Citrix licenses.* The project team already performed extensive lab tests, so they knew that they would not have to worry about rebuilding these servers anytime soon.

3. *Install the Terminal Services License Service.* Because the three MetaFrame XP servers were the only three servers in Tyler Treat's environment that are running Windows 2000, one of them had to be the TS licensing server. The project team picked one and added the TS licensing service.

4. *Activate the TS License Service.* The TS license server had to be activated before it could accept any Terminal Services Client Access Licenses. Tyler Treats activated the TS licensing server automatically through the Internet.

5. *Install TS CALs*. Next, the project team installed the TS CALs onto the license server by typing the numbers into the TS Licensing Wizard.

6. *Activate TS CALs*. The TS CALs were then activated through the Internet.

With that, the Tyler Treats Gourmet Pet Foods' MetaFrame XP environment was all set and ready to go. Clients could start connecting and would automatically be issued a TS CAL if they did not have one.

# PART V

## Running your MetaFrame XP System

In this section

15. Security                                          625

16. Server Management and Maintenance          719

17. Ensuring Availability and Server Redundancy 751

CHAPTER **15**

# Security

In this chapter

Server Security                              629

Application Security                         636

Connection Security                          643

Network Security                             652

Client Device Security                       693

User Account Security                        703

Secure Systems Administration Environments   712

A major part of any computing environment is security. As you have probably noticed, we have not dwelled much on security in the preceeding chapters. That's due to the fact that when you focus on the security of your MetaFrame XP environment, you need to do it from end-to-end. You can't just "do a little security here, and a little there." For example, it would have done no good to talk about security of NFuse in the NFuse chapter because even if you did everything NFuse–related to tighten security you might have overlooked a major security hole somewhere else.

To prevent this, we will analyze the security elements of a complete Meta-Frame XP system in this chapter. We will systematically analyze every Meta-Frame XP component, taking note of what the potential security risks are and what to do to minimize each of them.

Let's begin by reviewing all of the components that make up a MetaFrame XP system. This will help us design the components of our security plan. We can represent the individual components as layers in the complete MetaFrame XP system, as shown in Figure 15.1. (These layers are kind of like the OSI model applied to MetaFrame.)

*Figure 15.1  MetaFrame XP layers*

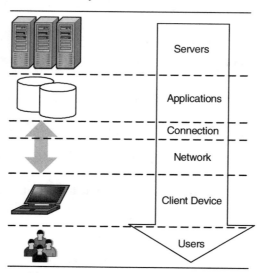

Using the MetaFrame XP components outlined in the Figure 15.1 as our guide, we can methodically step through each one, analyzing the security as we go along. We'll start from the server layer and move our way down to the user layer, touching on the security aspects of each component.

After we study the security requirements and techniques related to each of these technical components, we'll look at what it takes to build a secure administrative environment.

One thing that you must remember as you read this chapter is that it focuses primarily on the security of the MetaFrame XP components. This chapter is not meant to be an end-to-end security manual. Your MetaFrame XP environment is only as secure as its weakest link, and often human elements are involved that no technical manual can prepare you for.

## Security Configuration Layers

Before diving into the technical details of the security options, we need to take another look at the different layers in which many of the security-related settings can be made. For example, the encryption level of an ICA session can be configured as a property of the server connection, the ICA client, a Citrix user policy (with Feature Release 2), or the published application. Beyond that, applications launched via an ICA file can also have the level of encryption configured within the ICA file itself.

*Figure 15.2  Example security parameter configured at multiple layers*

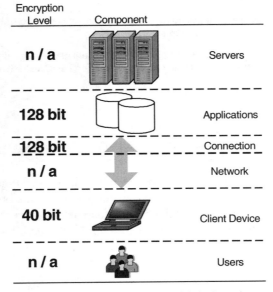

When a single parameter is configured in multiple locations with conflicting settings, the most restrictive configuration will always take precedence. Referring to Figure 15.2, if the client device and the published application were configured for a minimum of 40-bit encryption, but the server connection was set to a minimum of 128-bit, no session connecting via that connection would be able to connect at anything less than 128-bit. Even though the client and application are set lower, they must still traverse the connection configured for the 128-bit minimum.In this example, we can say that the "client layer" was set to 40-bit encryption, and the "connection layer" and "published application layer" were encryption was set to 128-bit.

Figure 15.3 shows all of the possible layers where one security parameter can be configured. Of course, not every security parameter can be configured at every layer. It's important to look at the MetaFrame XP settings and determine the proper layer that the security parameter should be applied. Do all users require 128-bit encryption or only users connecting to certain applications? Maybe only users coming from specific IP addresses need encryption?

*Figure 15.3 Various configuration scope layers*

| Level | Scope |
| --- | --- |
| Farm | Every MetaFrame XP server in the entire server farm. |
| Server | All users connecting to one server. |
| Application | All users connecting to one particular published application, even across multiple servers. |
| Connection | All users attaching via one defined server connection. Multiple connections can exist on one server. |
| Client | All users connecting from one ICA client device, regardless of the user rights or the server or farm hosting the ICA session. |
| Citrix User Policy | All users to which the policy is applied. |
| Users | User profile settings. These settings follow the user, regardless of the farm, server, or connection used. |
| ICA File | Settings affect anyone using the ICA file, regardless of settings in other locations. |

Throughout this chapter we'll look at dozens more security settings configurable at all layers. Beyond that, the appendix of this book contains a "MetaFrame XP Component Configuration" chart detailing every setting within the MetaFrame XP environment and listing the layer where it can be configured.

# Server Security

In order to adequately analyze server security in MetaFrame XP environments, we need to break up the servers into their multiple roles and then look at the security of each server role separately. We'll examine each of the following three MetaFrame XP server roles:

- MetaFrame XP application servers.
- IMA data store servers.
- NFuse Classic web servers.

## MetaFrame XP Application Server Security

Since the MetaFrame XP servers are where the actual user sessions are executed, it makes sense that there are several things to look at when it comes to security. To begin with, let's outline the basic points that you must consider when you are securing your MetaFrame XP servers. These security points are as follows:

- Use the NTFS file system.
- Configure NTFS file permissions.
- Do not install MetaFrame XP on a domain controller.
- Disable the "RunAs" Service.
- Do not use Windows RAS or VPNs for ICA–only sessions.
- Delete the MetaFrame XP installation log file.
- Apply hotfixes and service packs.

### Use the NTFS File System

Remember, each user that runs a session on a MetaFrame XP server is essentially running a remote control console session. Without an NTFS file system, you will not be able to set any file–level security permissions. This will allow any user that is logged in to be able to access files in use by other users. Even worse, there would be no mechanism to prevent users from deleting key system files, potentially crashing the server!

There is no reason not to use NTFS on your servers. Every user will be able to access NTFS files via an ICA session, even if his ICA client is running on an operating system that cannot support NTFS, like Windows 95.

## Configure NTFS File Permissions

Just using the NTFS file system might not provide enough security with its default permissions in your environment. Even if you do not intend to fully lock-down your MetaFrame XP servers or if you plan to only run published applications, you should secure the basic file system.

If you're using Windows 2000, as you install Terminal Services in application mode you are asked whether you want to use permissions that are compatible with Terminal Services 4.0 or Windows 2000. This "permissions compatibility" has nothing to do with your domain configuration or your Active Directory environment. It only affects the level of security that users are given when they access your server via a Terminal Services or Citrix ICA session. There are a few differences between the two settings:

- *Permissions compatible with Windows 2000.* This setting results in Terminal Services users having the same permissions as regular members of the local users group. This is very secure, because regular users are not able to write to inappropriate registry keys or tamper with sensitive system files. Of course, with this security comes additional risk. In this case, users will sometimes not be able to run legacy applications. If you choose this W2K permissions compatibility, you should thoroughly test your applications before enabling them for any users.

- *Permissions compatible with Terminal Server 4.0 Users.* This setting results in Terminal Services users having more access on the server than regular users because Terminal Service and Citrix ICA users will have full access to the registry and system files. This is not very secure, but it lets some older applications run.

To understand the difference between the two permissions modes, you need to understand the "Terminal Server Users" group. Whenever you install Terminal Services in applications mode on a Windows 2000 server, a local group called "Terminal Server Users" is created. Members of this group have the ability to access the critical registry keys and system files. Regardless of the permissions compatibility mode that you choose, this group always exists with its advanced permissions.

The only technical difference between the two permissions compatibility settings is whether the "Terminal Server Users" local group is used. If you set permissions compatibility to "TSE 4.0," users are added to the "Terminal Server Users" local group while they are logged on and are removed from the group when they log off. On the other hand, if you set your permissions compatible to "Windows 2000," users are *not* added to the "Terminal Server Users" group when they log on. The use of this group is how the two modes can provide different levels of access.

There are some situations in which it would be nice to give users "special" permissions while they were logged onto a MetaFrame XP Server. It seems that the "Terminal Server Users" group is perfect for this, except that by default, it has all sorts of advanced permissions already set throughout the server. In order to effectively use this group for your own purposes, you need a way to strip the "Terminal Server Users" group permissions from the server. Fortunately, Microsoft thought of this and there is an easy way to do it. In the `%systemroot%\Security\Templates\` folder, there is a security template, `notssid.inf`, that you can apply to a Terminal Server to remove the permissions of the "Terminal Server Users" local group. You can apply this security template with the `secedit.exe` security command line tool, with the command "`secedit.exe /configure /db notssid.sdb / cfg notssid.inf`." For more details about using this tool, see Microsoft article Q216735.

After you use the security template to remove the default permissions of the "Terminal Server Users" local group, there will effectively be no difference on the server between the W2K permission compatibility and the TSE 4.0 permission compatibility because the "Terminal Server Users" group will not have any special rights or permissions assigned to it. From there, you can manually set any permissions for the "Terminal Server Users" group that you want. If you later decide that you would like to reinstate the default "Terminal Server User" permissions, you can use the included `defltsv.inf` security template.

Even after you select the "permissions compatibility" mode during the installation of Terminal Services, you can change it at any time via the Terminal Services Configuration MMC snap-in (Administrative Tools | Terminal Services Configuration | Server Settings | Permissions Compatibility). Setting this compatibility affects the following registry key:

Key: `HKLM\System\CurrentControlSet\Control\ Terminal Server\`

Value: `TSUserEnabled`

Type: `REG_DWORD`

Data: 1 = Unsecured TSE 4.0 permissions (use the Terminal Server User group). 0 = Secured W2K permissions (do not use the Terminal Server Users group).

### Do Not Install MetaFrame XP on a Domain Controller

Individual domain controllers cannot be managed separately from each other. For example, in order for a user to be able to log on to MetaFrame XP sessions they must have "log on interactively" (called "log on locally" in Windows 2000) rights. If the MetaFrame XP server is a domain controller, granting a user "log on interactively" rights on the server will allow that user to log on to any domain controller, even ones that are not MetaFrame XP servers.

Also, domain controllers in Active Directory environments must be located in the "Domain Controllers" OU. This means that you can't use OU-based Group Policy Objects if your MetaFrame XP servers are installed on domain controllers.

Lastly, there are several security holes associated with the operation of the Local System Account on domain controllers. In order to have a secure environment, you should never have users log onto a domain controller. Installing MetaFrame XP on a domain controller makes it difficult to follow this recommendation.

### Disable the "RunAs" Service

Windows 2000 introduced a secondary logon ability which allows users to run programs with different user rights. Within Windows Explorer, a user can shift-right-click on a file and select "Run as..." from the context menu. Alternately a user can use the "runas" command from the command line. With this service, a user could connect to an anonymous application and then launch additional processes with his native user account, bypassing the anonymous user security that you configured on the server. This secondary logon ability can be disabled at the server by stopping and disabling the "RunAs" service." It is important to disable the service after you stop it, or the system will start it again when it is needed.

### Do not use RAS or VPNs for ICA-only access

Often times, users will connect into a company's computer system with a Windows RAS or VPN connection and launch MetaFrame XP applications on internal company servers. If you choose this setup for your environment, remember that the users of those RAS or VPN sessions are usually not limited to running only MetaFrame XP sessions. Once a user establishes a connection, they are able to access any network resource, even outside of the MetaFrame XP environment.

If you have users that need dial-in access to MetaFrame XP servers and nothing else, you should consider establishing ICA dial-in sessions or using MetaFrame XP via the Internet and having users connect via their own local ISP.

That way, you can ensure that users do not connect to inappropriate servers or services in your environment.

### Delete the MetaFrame XP Installation Log File

During the installation of MetaFrame XP, everything is captured in a setup log file. If your data store is on a SQL Server with SQL authentication, and if you're not using the newest version of the Windows Installer (part of Windows 2000 Service Pack 3), the database login credentials will be contained in the installation log file. The easiest way to fix this is to delete the log file once MetaFrame XP is installed. It is located at the following path: `%systemroot%\Imainxxxxxx.log` ("xxxxxx" is a time stamp). You should delete this file from every one of your MetaFrame XP servers.

### Apply Hotfixes

As in any computer environment, maintaining security means that you must frequently check for new hotfixes that address security issues, even if you keep your servers up to date with the latest service packs.

For example, just two weeks after Service Pack 1 was released for MetaFrame XP, Citrix released a Security Bulletin (ID# CTX654124) and hotfix that addressed a denial-of-service attack. In this case, an attacker could send malformed ICA packets to a MetaFrame XP server, spiking the server at 100% CPU utilization. The only remedy after this happened was a reboot.

You should check for new hotfixes from Microsoft and Citrix at least once a week. However, because history has shown that neither Microsoft nor Citrix has had a perfect track record for creating bug-free hotfixes, you should also check with an online discussion group (such as The THIN List at `http://thethin.net`) to see if there are any issues surrounding new hotfixes that are released.

To help maintain your hotfix environment, Microsoft has released at security hotifx checker utility (detailed in article Q303215). This utility will allow you to quickly and easily check the status of hotfixes on multiple Windows NT 4.0 or Windows 2000 servers.

## IMA Data Store Server Security

The IMA Data Store contains most of the critical configuration information for your MetaFrame XP server farm. The risk of compromising sensitive data from the data store is low. Opening the database natively does not reveal much useful information and even with the Citrix SDK it is not possible to directly access the database.

However, it is possible that someone with database administration rights could delete key portions of the database. While your environment should be designed so that the database is backed up and could be restored in case of a loss (see Chapter 17), this is an inconvenience that you probably want to avoid.

To address this security risk, ensure that the database account used by your MetaFrame XP servers is secure. By default, all MetaFrame XP servers access MS Access-based IMA Data Stores with the username "citrix" and the password "citrix." (SQL, Oracle, and DB-2 data stores ask for the credentials when MetaFrame XP is installed.) This can be changed with the "dsmaint" command line utility (dsmaint config /user:username / pwd:password). Using the dsmaint utility on a MetaFrame XP server does not change the permissions of the database itself. Dsmaint merely changes the account that the local MetaFrame XP server uses to access the data store. To create a new account or change the account permissions of the database itself, use your native database tools.

For extra security, you can restrict the database rights that you grant to the account that the MetaFrame XP servers will use to access the IMA data store. For example, if your IMA data store is on a Microsoft SQL server, the account that your MetaFrame XP servers use to access the database must have "db_owner" rights to the IMA data store database. Some people choose to not give the MetaFrame XP database account "db_owner" rights, instead simply granting read and write access to the database. If you set the security like this, MetaFrame XP will still function. However, you will not be able to install any service packs or feature releases because the database account that MetaFrame XP is configured for would not have the permissions to change the layouts of any tables.

## NFuse Server Security

Fortunately, NFuse behaves like a standard web application. This is good when it comes to applying security because you don't have to do anything out of the ordinary with NFuse. You can treat it like a regular application and apply all the standard security. Let's examine some standard security practices that can be done on your NFuse web server.

### Using the Microsoft IIS Lockdown Tool

If your NFuse web server is running IIS on a Microsoft platform, the Microsoft IIS security lockdown tool provides an automated, easy to use way to lock down your web servers. You can download the IIS lockdown tool for no charge from Microsoft's website. (www.microsoft.com/technet/security/ tools/locktool.asp)

When you run this tool on your web server, you are given a list of "server templates." Each server template corresponds to a different role that an IIS web server could play. For NFuse web servers, highlight the "Dynamic Web server (ASP enabled)" template.

Before you click "Next," be sure to check the "View template settings" box. This will allow you to customize the settings that the IIS lockdown tool applies from the template. If you don't check this box and you accept the default settings of the Dynamic Web server template, NFuse will stop working.

After you click next, you are given the option to disable certain Internet services on your web server. NFuse only requires that the Web service be present. You can disable the FTP, SMTP, and NNTP services.

The next screen allows you to enable and disable certain scripts. You can leave the default settings as they are.

The third configuration screen is where you need to make the change in order for NFuse to work. In the section that removes selected virtual directions, uncheck the "Scripts" box, since NFuse stores some scripts in the "\Scripts\" web folder. Other than that, the rest of the IIS lockdown tool options can be left at the default settings.

### Configuring NFuse Web Pages to Time Out

One potential downside to using NFuse is that after a user logs in and receives his list of applications, the web page remains open after his MetaFrame XP session is started on the server. This could be a problem because he could walk away from his computer and leave that web page open, allowing anyone who passes by to be able to access his applications. To mitigate this, you can change the amount of time that the session information is retained for a user's session. The default is 20 minutes. If, after 20 minutes, a user tries to click on a link to launch an application, he will be sent back to the login page because the web server would have deleted his session information, including his user credentials. You can set the session timeout to be longer or shorter, depending on the security you need in your environment. To change this timeout in IIS 5.0, navigate to the following location: Internet Services Manager | Right-click website | Properties | Home Directory tab | Application Settings | Configuration Button | App Options Tab | Session Timeout. If you change this timeout, you will need to stop and start the web server service for the settings to take affect.

# Application Security

The next layer that we will look at in our approach to MetaFrame XP security is the application layer. Here, we'll consider the applications that users run, how they access them, and what they can do with them. To begin with, let's review how applications are launched by users. There are two ways that users can launch applications on a MetaFrame XP server:

- By connecting to a published application.
- By running the Windows desktop and launching applications from within their established session.

When looking at application security, we first need to examine the security of these two different ways of launching applications. Before we do that, though, we should note that complete details of the ways users launch applications and when different methods should be used, are covered back in Chapter 4. In this current chapter, we'll focus on application access strictly in terms of security.

Now, let's look at the security aspects of these two methods of accessing applications, starting with published applications.

## Published Application Security

The ability to publish applications to users is one of the main benefits that MetaFrame XP offers over pure Terminal Services environments. After all, this is what allows users to connect to an application by its name alone without needing to know which servers it uses. Also, published applications provide an easy way for us, as administrators, to set permissions as to which users can access specific applications. From a security standpoint, there are two things to look at with respect to MetaFrame XP published applications:

- Published application permissions.
- How to limit users to only running published applications.

### *Published Application Permissions*
As outlined in Chapter 4, individual applications (or the entire desktop) can be published "Explicitly" or "Anonymously" in MetaFrame XP. Remember that an explicitly published application requires that a user authenticate with valid credentials before the application session is started and an anonymous application requires no credentials allowing any user that discovers the Meta-Frame XP server to run the application. These two methods of securing pub-

lished applications have an effect on the security of the MetaFrame XP environment.

## Explicit Applications

Explicitly published applications are the most common in the real world. You can set the permissions on explicit applications to make them available to local or domain groups, or local or domain user accounts. Most likely, you'll choose to set the permissions for domain groups because then you can easily grant a user access to a published application simply by adding him to the appropriate domain group instead of having to use the Citrix Management Console to change the permissions of the published application. By setting published application security at the group level, you can also publish multiple applications (such as entire application suites), to the same domain group. Then, by adding a user account to that domain group, you can instantly give him access to the entire application suite. By using domain groups instead of local MetaFrame XP server groups, the user's group membership will apply on any MetaFrame XP server to which he connects, which works well in environments where applications are published across multiple MetaFrame XP servers.

There are no restrictions to the number of groups to which a user can belong. Many companies that have dozens of applications published set the permissions of each application so that each is available to a different domain group. Users that need access to multiple applications are simply added to multiple domain groups.

Another advantage to giving users access to published applications by adding them to domain groups is that the domain groups can be used as a basis for additional security configuration outside of the published application. For example, a domain group could be used to assign NTFS rights to files or network shares that the published application needs.

By configuring multiple security items for the same domain group, adding a user to a single domain group gives access to the application, the files, and the settings he needs to use the application.

## Anonymous Applications

Applications published anonymously work well in two scenarios:

- *The application provides its own security.* This means that any user can connect to the application because the user will need to log into the application itself before it can be used. Many line-of-business applications are configured in this way since they contain their own internal user databases.

- *The application is accessed by a wide variety of users*, without formal user accounts. This is usually seen in public or kiosk applications as well as demonstration and sample applications.

When a user establishes an ICA session with an anonymous application, he is automatically logged on with one of the local anonymous user accounts that was created when MetaFrame XP was installed. All of the local anonymous user accounts (named anon000, anon001...) belong to a local group called "Anonymous Users." This group membership is important to remember when you create the security model for your environment because you can assign or deny permissions elsewhere on the MetaFrame XP server based on this group. Just because anonymous users don't officially log on doesn't mean that they can't be granted rights.

On a side note, applications cannot be published anonymously if the Meta-Frame XP server is also a domain controller because domain controllers don't have local groups, and so the anonymous accounts cannot be created.

### Forcing Users to Run Only Published Applications

One mistake that many administrators make is to assume that once the security is set properly on published applications, there is nothing more to worry about. They forget that even with only published applications available, any user can create a custom ICA connection within his ICA client software. In the custom connection properties, he could choose to connect to a specific MetaFrame XP server instead of a published application. Using that new custom connection, he would be able to logon to a full Windows desktop. Even if you use NFuse to connect to MetaFrame XP applications, anyone can download and install the full ICA client from Citrix's website and create a custom connection to one of your MetaFrame XP server's desktop.

If this happens, it is usually the case that the administrator did not anticipate that the users would ever connect to the desktop. The administrator probably did not make any effort to lock down or secure the desktop and the user would have free access to inappropriate applications, data, or configuration settings.

To prevent this from happening, you can configure your MetaFrame XP server ICA connections so that they only allow users to connect to published applications, preventing them from connecting directly to the server desktop.

This setting is configured via the Citrix Connection Configuration utility (Citrix Connection Configuration | Right-click the connection | Properties | Advanced Button I Only run published applications checkbox). If you check this box, it will apply to all users that access the MetaFrame XP server via the connection where it is applied, including administrators. There is no way to limit some users to published applications while giving others access to the full Windows desktop over a single connection. However, this can be easily remedied by publishing the desktop as an application. By doing so, you can configure the needed security for the desktop application. For example, you might choose to allow administrators to use the "desktop" published application while denying everyone else.

### Advantages of Forcing Users to Published Applications Only

- Useful for preventing users from connecting to the desktop of a server.

- There is no way around this setting over a specific connection. The connection would be very secure.

### Disadvantages of Forcing Users to Published Applications Only

- All users are restricted to running published applications— including administrators.

## Windows Desktop Application Security

The other way that users access applications is by connecting to a Windows desktop and then launching applications through icons on the Start menu just as in any regular environment.

If you plan to use this method to provide users access to applications on Meta-Frame XP servers, you need to ensure that the user environment is protected and secured so that users cannot do things that they are not supposed to do. There are four strategies that you can use to secure your Windows desktops:

- Apply appropriate policies or profiles.
- Use the AppSec utility.
- Configure NTFS security.
- Prevent users from installing applications.

### Applying Policies and Profiles

The Windows desktop shell can be "locked down" so that users are limited by the rights that they have and the actions that they are able to perform. In MetaFrame XP environments, locked down desktops are often used when users connect to the actual server desktop instead of the individual published applications.

In the simplest sense, a locked down desktop could be a Windows desktop that has the "Shutdown" or "Run" commands removed from the Start menu. On the other end of the spectrum, a locked down desktop can be created that gives users almost no access to the system—no "My Computer," no "Network Neighborhood," and no access to local system drives.

There are several methods that can be used to lock down Windows desktops on MetaFrame XP servers. The most popular methods involve using policies to restrict user shell access and applications that can be executed. Policies are discussed in detail in Chapter 5.

Locking down a Windows desktop is a function of the underlying Windows operating system. MetaFrame XP does not provide any additional mechanisms to help lock down a Windows desktop. What MetaFrame XP does provide is the published application alternative to users accessing the Windows desktop at all. With MetaFrame XP, many people avoid the hassle of locked down desktops by only allowing users to run published applications and not allowing general users to access the desktop.

### Advantages of Enforcing Application Security with System Policies

- Can be easily applied across multiple servers.

### Disadvantages of Enforcing Application Security with System Policies

- Policies only watch over the Windows shell. If you restrict certain areas or applications, users can get around that restriction by launching applications via the command prompt.

## Limiting Application Execution with the AppSec Utility

The Application Security (`appsec.exe`) utility can be used to enforce application execution security by allowing you to specify exactly which executables users are able run. This is similar to applying a policy restriction, although this AppSec utility works without policies. Any users that connect to your servers with administrative rights will not be affected by the AppSec security policy.

The AppSec utility is part of the Server Resource Kit. It is available for both NT 4.0 and Windows 2000. However, the version that shipped with the Windows 2000 resource kit was missing three critical files, so if you want to use AppSec for Windows 2000, you should download it from the Microsoft FTP site. (`ftp.microsoft.com/reskit/win2000/appsec.zip`)

When this tool is used, the server is set to a restricted state, and you can add application executables that you want users to be able to run. This makes the AppSec tool extremely granular. However, because you must specify every single executable that is permitted, the configuration can become very complex for large numbers of applications. This happens because you must find all of the exact executables that an application needs, which can be a dozen or more. For example, if you use the tool to provide access to the Windows desktop, you must allow access to both explorer.exe and systray.exe. For many applications, you can only find all of the executables that are needed through trial and error.

Whenever you run the AppSec utility, you have the option to enable or disable AppSec security. If you disable it, any of the settings that you made do not apply. This is good, especially if you make a change that adversely affects users. By running the tool and disabling security, you can "fix" whatever problems you caused by enabling security.

AppSec is an execution-layer security tool, so it cannot technically prevent users from connecting to the system. However, if you enable AppSec security without giving any executable rights to users, you can effectively prevent them from connecting. In this case, your users will get this error when they try to connect:

```
An error (193) occurred while creating user logon.
Failing component: explorer.exe.
```

When the user clicks "OK," his session is terminated.

If, through the course of his session, a user tries to run an application that is not on the AppSec authorized list, he will get the following error:

```
yourapp.exe in not a valid Windows NT application
```

AppSec can also be used to allow users to run 16-bit applications. To do this, you should use the 16-bit version of AppSec. This will automatically allow the users to use the necessary 16-bit support files, like ntvdm.exe (the virtual DOS machine) and the WOW subsystem (Windows on Windows).

### Advantages of Limiting Application Execution with AppSec

- Very granular control.
- Users cannot get around this by going to a command prompt.
- Does not affect administrators.
- Can be easily turned off.

### Disadvantages of Limiting Application Execution with AppSec

- Every application executable must be listed.
- Must be configured on every server.

## Setting NTFS Security

Another way to restrict the applications that a user can access is to configure the NTFS security on the application executables themselves. The nice thing about setting NTFS-level security is that once set, there is no way around it. No matter how the user accesses the server, the application won't run if the user doesn't have NTFS rights to the application.

### Advantages of Limiting Application Execution with NTFS Security

- NTFS permissions that prevent users from accessing certain files or applications are absolute—there is no way for a user to get around them.
- Very granular control of who can and cannot access applications.

### Disadvantages of Limiting Application Execution with NTFS Security

- Must be set on every MetaFrame XP server.
- NTFS permissions do not prevent users from running applications from other, non-local locations. Even if you restrict access to a local copy of Word, a user might find `winword.exe` on a network share and be able to execute it from there.

## Preventing Users from Installing Applications

Undoubtedly, if users run remote Windows desktops on your MetaFrame XP servers, you do not want them to be able to install any software applications. The easiest way to do this is to remove the users' "write" permissions from the software installation registry key. Use `regedt32.exe` to browse to the following registry location:

```
HKLM\Software\Microsoft\WindowsNT\CurrentVersion\Terminal
Server\Install\Software
```

From the Security menu, choose "Permissions." From there you can configure your users with read-only permissions. Be sure that you propagate these permissions to the subkeys below the key where they are applied. In order to configure registry security, you must use `regedt32.exe` instead of `regedit.exe`. `Regedit.exe` does not allow you to set permissions on registry keys.

# Connection Security

Remember from Chapter 2 that "connections" in the MetaFrame XP environment refer to the groups of settings that apply to a specific Session Protocol / Network Protocol / Network Interface combination. There are multiple options configured at this "connection layer." Many of them directly impact the overall security of the system. Additionally, there are many neat tricks that you can do to provide different levels of security to different interfaces.

## Connection Properties

When configuring the properties of a connection (Citrix Connection Configuration Utility | Right-click on connection | Edit | Advanced Button), it is important to remember that those properties will affect all users that connect to the MetaFrame XP server via that connection unless you check the box for each item that allows the server to use the settings in each user's profile. (Checking this box will actually allow the setting to be configured from the user's profile or by a Citrix user policy.)

Let's examine each of the following connection layer security settings:

- Session timeouts.
- Working with broken connections.
- Auto session logon.
- Limiting the number of sessions per connection.
- Disabling logons.
- Encryption.
- Using default NT authentication.
- Initial programs to be executed.
- Forcing Users to Run Only Published Applications
- Session shadowing.
- ICA TCP port.

### Session Timeouts

You can configure three different timeout periods for each connection: connection timeout, disconnection timeout, and idle timeout. Each of these choices allows you to specify the timeout in minutes. The checkbox allows the timeout settings of the connection to default to those specified in the user profile as opposed to by the connection itself. This allows for different settings on a user-by-user basis. Selecting "no timeout" disables that specific session timer for that connection.

The "Connection" timeout allows you to specify the maximum time that an ICA session can stay connected. After this time passes, the server either disconnects or terminates the session. (The decision to terminate or disconnect the session is determined by the connection property setting outlined later.)

The "Disconnection" timeout causes the server to reset a disconnected session after the specified time has passed. This will cause the current user to lose any work that was in progress. The disconnection timer is a good way clean up any disconnected sessions that users have forgotten about. Many companies set this to something like 2880 minutes (48 hours). If they have some situations that require less time, they configure those in the user profile. If you configure disconnection timeouts for users in addition to the connection properties, the more restrictive setting will always take precedence.

The "Idle" timeout specifies the amount of time that a live connection can stay in an idle state (no activity) before the server automatically disconnects or resets the session. From a security standpoint, the idle timeout works well as an "automatic lock-down." Many companies set their idle timeouts relatively low so that if a user leaves his desk with an active ICA session open, the server will disconnect the session after a few minutes. Then, when the user returns to his desk, he can conveniently reconnect to his disconnected session, without losing any work.

Extreme care must be taken when working with these connection timeouts. Almost all environments that utilize connection timeouts configure them as a property of the user account (at the "user layer"), instead of configuring them here as a property of a connection. The one exception is the disconnection timeout, which are used to clean up any old sessions.

### Working with Broken Connections

The term "Broken Connection" is used to specify what happens when an ICA client stops responding to the MetaFrame XP server during an ICA session. There are many things that can cause broken sessions, including network failures, power failures, and crashed client devices.

At the connection layer, you can specify what action should be taken when a connection is broken. Choosing to have the server disconnect the session will allow the session to maintain its state on the server, enabling the user to reconnect and pick up right where they left off. This often happens when client computers crash. After the crash, the user reboots, mutters a curse word or two, and reconnects to his existing session that is still running on the server. The server will maintain the disconnected session as long as the timeout period allows, with the "timeout period" being the shorter of the connection-layer disconnection timeout or user-layer disconnection timeout.

From a security standpoint, the broken connection action does not pose much of a security risk because users must successfully authenticate before they are given the option to reconnect to a broken session.

Reconnecting to broken sessions generally works best with explicit connections because anonymous users are not guaranteed that they will authenticate with the same anonymous account each time. If this happens, the server has no way of knowing which disconnected session belongs to that user.

You might be wondering about the "Auto Client Reconnection" that is available with Feature Release 1 and 2 and how it relates to the broken connection detection of a MetaFrame XP server. Auto client reconnect allows ICA clients to automatically reconnect to a MetaFrame XP server if their ICA session is interrupted. Auto client reconnection is a property of the client devices themselves and cannot be configured at the connection layer. For details on configuring auto client reconnection, see Chapter 10.

## Reconnecting From Any Client

You can also decide whether you want to allow users to reconnect to disconnected sessions from any client device or whether users should be restricted to reconnecting only from the client device on which their ICA session was originally established. Some people perceive the ability to reconnect from any client as a security problem. In actuality, the security consequences are not that great because the user must authenticate on the new client before being able to reconnect to a session. Also, the user can only reconnect if the disconnected session was started with the same credentials as the new user. This means that one user cannot reconnect to another user's disconnected session.

Potential security problems arise when multiple users logon with the same user account to access MetaFrame XP servers. This is common in many environments for kiosks, common applications, or task-based workers. If a user authenticates with credentials that were used to start multiple sessions (which have since been disconnected) on one server, the user will be presented with an option to choose the disconnected session to connect to. It is possible that the user might pick a session that does not belong to him and be able to view privileged information or data.

## Auto Session Logon

The AutoLogon parameters of a connection's advanced configuration will use one set of credentials to automatically log on any user that attempts to start an ICA session via that connection. This can pose a tremendous security risk, as any person could access to the system without being officially set up or authorized. It is relatively simple for a user/attacker to download and install the Citrix ICA client software and then to "discover" the Citrix server, connect to it, and be automatically logged on.

The AutoLogon settings are intended for point-to-point connections, such as the asynchronous RAS. AutoLogon in these cases is nice because users usually need to authenticate at other levels, as when the RAS connection is established. In these cases, AutoLogon prevents users from having to log on twice.

## Limiting the Number of Sessions per Connection

The maximum number of concurrent sessions can be limited per connection on the connection's main property page. In general, this is not used to limit user connections because this limit applies to all users, including administrators. More often, administrators will create a dedicated connection for their own use (over a specific network interface), and limit the number of sessions to one or two as an additional security precaution,

## Disabling Logons

Disabling logons is useful if a custom connection is needed from time to time, but you do not want to have the connection open all the time or have to recreate the connection each time it is needed.

Remember that disabling the logons of a connection does not cause existing sessions to be broken—it merely prevents additional users from being able to log on.

## Encryption

The required level of encryption can be set at the connection level, affecting all sessions on the connection. The encryption levels are self-explanatory, except for "Basic." Basic encryption is not really secure and should not be used if you care about protecting your environment. Encryption is detailed fully in the "Network Security" section of this chapter.

## Use Default NT Authentication

Checking this box forces user authentication to occur through the standard Windows authentication DLL, `msgina.dll`.

For example, if you install the Novell NDS Client on your MetaFrame server, the Novell client authentication and logon DLL (nwgina.dll) will replace the Microsoft DLL. This is why the "Press CTRL+ALT+DEL" logon screen is a Novell screen instead of the standard Microsoft screen after you install Novell's NDS Client. Checking the "Use default NT Authentication" checkbox will force ICA sessions to be logged on via the Microsoft client when that connection is used.

This is useful if you have two groups of users that connect to the same Meta-Frame XP server. You can create two separate connections—one for each group of users. One connection ("ICA-IPX") for users that use the IPX proto-col, can have the "Use Default NT Authentication" box unchecked, allowing them to logon with the Novell authentication. The other connection ("ICA-TCP") will be for users connecting via the TCP/IP protocol. This connection should have the box checked, forcing users to authenticate via the Microsoft logon DLL.

It should be noted that the end user experience is the same, regardless of whether the "User default NT authentication" box is checked or unchecked. The ICA client only passes the basic authentication parameters to the Meta-Frame XP, and this checkbox merely specifies which DLL handles those pa-rameters after they are received by the server. See Chapter 8 for more infor-mation about the GINA DLL.

## *Specifying an Initial Program to be Executed*

A MetaFrame XP server connection can be configured to set the initial pro-gram for every user that connects via the connection. Setting the initial pro-gram at the connection layer functions in the exact same way as setting it for one specific user, except that the connection layer setting applies to all users on that connection, without exception. As soon as the user logs on, the speci-fied program is run. As soon as the user closes that program, he is automati-cally logged off. At no time will the user ever see a desktop unless the desktop is specified as the initial program to run.

Specifying an initial program that is executed is a good way to lock down your server if all users will only need to use one program. The nice thing about it is that users still need to authenticate before the program is run (un-less the AutoLogon is configured).

The downside to it is that since this is set at the connection layer, the initial program will affect everyone who connects, including administrators.

In the real world, setting the initial program at the connection level is most useful for MetaFrame XP servers that serve as public terminals or kiosk devices. In these cases, administrators often connect via a different protocol (such as RDP), ensuring that it is not possible to run any other application from the kiosk client devices.

As an interesting side note, even if a user connects to a published application over a connection that has the initial program specified, the initial program will run, not the published application. When the user closes that initial program, the connection is terminated. As you can see, when an initial program is specified, it doesn't matter how the user connects (full desktop or published application), the user will always run the program specified in the initial program setting.

### Only Run Published Applications

Instead of forcing all users on one connection to run one specific program, you can require that all users only run published applications. Checking this box will prevent users from connecting to the server's desktop directly, unless the desktop is a published application.

Checking this box does not set any file or system-level security. For example, if this box is checked, but `explorer.exe` is a published application, a user could use explorer to run additional, non-published applications.

Full details of the security of applications on MetaFrame XP servers can be found in the preceding section of this chapter, "Application Security."

### Session Shadowing

Basic session shadowing parameters can be set at the connection layer, such as whether shadowing is enabled and what type of notification or input the shadowed sessions have. Many organizations choose to set different shadowing parameters for different connections. Refer to the "Administrative Environment" segment of this chapter for more information on session shadowing.

### TCP Port Used for ICA Sessions

By default, MetaFrame XP servers accept inbound ICA sessions via TCP port 1494. For added security, some administrators like to change this port number. This port can be changed in the registry in the following path:

Key: HKLM\System\CurrentControlSet\Control\
    Terminal Server\WinStations\*ICAConnectionName*\
Value: PortNumber

Type: REG_DWORD

Data: Port number in hex (default 1494 = 5D6)

The "*ICAConnectionName*" in the above registry path is the name of the ICA connection you would like to change, for example "ICA-TCP." Because the ICA port configuration is a connection layer setting, you can configure different ports for different connections. After changing this port number, you need to stop and start the IMA service.

Remember that if you change the ICA port on the server, you must also change the port that the ICA client looks for.

In the real world, very few people change the ICA port, mainly because there are plenty of other security measures that can provide excellent security without the need to change the ICA port and they don't want to deal with configuring all of their ICA clients to use a nonstandard port. "Security through obscurity" has never worked well for anything.

## Connection Permissions

In addition to the parameters of server connections that we reviewed previously, you can set user permissions separately for each connection. (Citrix Connection Configuration Utility | Right-click on connection | Permissions)

This allows you to specify user and group permissions at the connection layer, with the permissions affecting the configured users for each connection. You can select any user or group and then give them Guest, User, or Full Control for a given connection. You can also give a user or group "No Access" by unchecking every box.

In the event of a conflict (one user belonging to multiple groups with different permission levels), the most restrictive permissions apply.

It is important to understand that these permissions only affect the one connection where they are applied. It is possible for one user to have "Full Control" rights on one connection and "No access" rights to another.

Clicking on the "Advanced" button allows you to create granular permissions as needed. This does not allow you to give any more permissions than you could with the regular guest, user, or full access checkboxes. The "Advanced" button simply allows you to select only the specific options you need. For example, you could give one group "shadowing" permissions without having to give them full access rights. This would be accomplished by clicking the "advanced" button, selecting the group, clicking the "view/edit" button, and selecting the rights needed for that group.

*Figure 15.4  Basic connection permission levels*

|  | Guest | User | Full Control |
|---|---|---|---|
| Logon Rights (basic session use) | X | X | X |
| Query information about the session |  | X | X |
| Send Messages |  | X | X |
| Connect to a disconnected session |  | X | X |
| Modify connection properties |  |  | X |
| Delete the connection |  |  | X |
| Reset ICA sessions |  | X |  |
| Log off ICA session |  |  | X |
| Disconnect ICA session |  |  | X |
| Shadow ICA sessions |  |  | X |

For each line-item property, there are two boxes: allow and deny. If you select the deny box, the option is explicitly denied for that user or group, and this "deny" takes precedence over any other allow permissions configured in any other group, similar to the "no access" NTFS permission.

*Figure 15.5  Advanced connection permission properties*

| Advanced Permission | Allows the User or Group to... |
|---|---|
| Query Information | Obtain information about the current session |
| Set Information | Configure connection parameters |
| Reset | Reset other peoples' sessions |
| Shadow | Shadow other users(1) |
| Logon | Connect via selected connection |
| Logoff | Log off other users |
| Message | Send popup messages to other sessions |
| Connect | Reconnect to disconnected sessions |
| Disconnect | Disconnect other peoples' sessions |
| Virtual Channels | Use ICA virtual channel in a session |

(1) Note: If shadowing permissions are configured that do not give users shadow rights, the users can still shadow themselves. There have been instances where helpdesk personnel

without shadowing rights would ask an end user for their name and password. With that, the helpdesk people could log on as that user and then shadow them, even though the user was not given shadow rights.

In the past, some people have recommended that you disable the RDP connection. While doing this would minimize your security risk, it actually increases your overall risk, because if there is a problem with your MetaFrame XP server that prevents an ICA session from connecting, you have no recourse unless you are physically located near the server. In the real world, most people choose to leave the default RDP connection active, but to configure the permissions so that only administrators are able to connect. That way you protect the connection while giving your own group a back door connection in case of trouble. (Of course if your administrator account is called "administrator" and its password is "password," keeping RDP active is a valid risk. If this is the case in your environment, you should put this book down and pick up a copy of *Security for Dummies*.)

## Strategies for Using Multiple Server Connections

MetaFrame XP server connections can be used in creative ways to provide different types of security. All security configuration settings that are applied at the connection layer apply to all users that connect via the same protocol pair. However, there is nothing to say that you can't have more than one connection for each protocol.

If you put multiple network cards in a MetaFrame XP server, you can create multiple ICA-TCP connections, one for each card. To do this, change the LAN adapter for the connection's properties (Citrix Connection Configuration | Right-click the connection | Edit). Change the LAN adapter from "All network adapters configured with this protocol" to just the network adapter that you want to use. Then create a new connection for the other LAN adapter. Because each network card will have a different IP address, each connection will be accessible via a unique IP address and therefore a unique DNS name.

This will allow you to have a completely different set of properties for the same server, each accessible via its own unique address. This is useful if you want to provide different groups of users access to the same server, but you want different connection–layer settings to apply to each group. One group could access server1.yourcompany.com and the other group could access server2.yourcompany.com. In reality each would be using a different connection of the same server.

### Advantages of Configuring Multiple Connections

- If you need different connection layer settings on one server, this is the only way to do it.

### Disadvantages of Configuring Multiple Connections

- You need one physical network card for each unique connection.

- Applications can only be published to the server. You cannot specify the connection over which an application is available.

## Connection Configuration in the Registry

Because the connection parameters are properties of the MetaFrame XP servers, these parameters are not stored in the IMA data store. Instead, all of the connection configuration information is stored in the registry in the following location:

```
HKLM\System\CurrentControlSet\Control\TerminalServer
\WinStations\ICAConnectionName
```

Because this configuration information is stored in the registry, you can allow or deny specific users access to the appropriate registry keys. If a user has the ability to write to this registry key, then he will have the ability to change the parameters of MetaFrame XP connections, regardless of the permissions that are configured in the connection configuration.

# Network Security

Any traffic that crosses a computer network is susceptible to being captured and viewed by unauthorized people. Because of this, the networks must be secured. There are two ways that this can be done:

- Protect the physical network connections so that no one can access the network to compromise the data.

- Protect the logical data on the network so that if the data is compromised it is meaningless to the person who found it.

Protecting physical connections is not really practical in today's world, especially over the Internet. When addressing network security, most people focus on protecting the data that crosses the network. The common approach is "I don't care if you actually capture my data, because if you do, it will be totally meaningless to you." The networks over which MetaFrame XP traffic flows are no different than any other computer networks in the world. To secure your MetaFrame XP network, you need to look at two components:

- Network data security. (Encryption)
- Network perimeter security. (Firewalls)

Let's begin by examining your MetaFrame XP network's data security.

## MetaFrame XP Network Data Security / Encryption

In MetaFrame XP environments, there are multiple types of network communications that need to be secured. Figure 15.6 shows all of the various network communications that take place in a standard MetaFrame XP environment. Each of the five arrows in that diagram represents a network segment that has data that must be protected. As we analyze the security of these links, we'll break them down into "front-end" and "back-end" network communications.

*Figure 15.6  MetaFrame XP Network Segments*

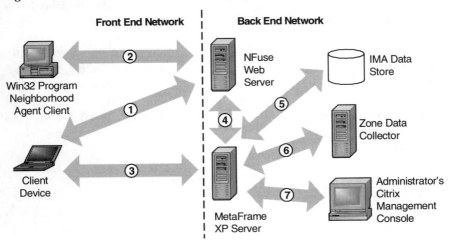

As you can see in Figure 15.6, the front-end communication includes all of the traffic that travels between client devices and the servers; the back-end communication includes all of the network traffic that travels between the various server components. Let's analyze the security needs of each of these network communication links, starting with the front-end. As we analyze these, we will refer to each network segment by its number in Figure 15.6.

### Segment 1. Client Device Web Browser to NFuse Web Server

The network connection between the end user's web browser and the web server is usually a very susceptible connection because it often travels the public Internet. When we look at security on this connection, we're only concerned with the actual NFuse web traffic. We are not concerned about ICA traffic because after an ICA session is launched via NFuse the network connection moves from the web server (Segment #1 in Figure 15.6) to the MetaFrame XP server (Segment #2 in Figure 15.6). We'll study Segment 2 later.

Even though the client device web browser to the NFuse web server network communication takes place before the ICA session is started, there are several security risks at this point. The main risk stems from the fact that standard web server to web browser HTTP traffic is not secure. When a user logs in to an NFuse web server, his credentials are passed over the standard web connection. If that connection is not secure, the credentials are not secure. When a user clicks a hyperlink on an NFuse web page to launch a published application, the information for that published application is sent down to the client's web browser. Again, the standard web connection is used and it must be secure to protect the data. Anything else that traverses this connection, including application set lists, HTML forms data, clear text credentials for launching ICA sessions, and cookies are not secure.

Fortunately, the World Wide Web and web security have been around a lot longer than NFuse and MetaFrame XP. This means that there are standard ways to address this problem. The easiest and most effective way to secure this network segment is to use Secure Socket Layers, or SSL. SSL is a form of encryption used to secure TCP/IP-based communications in everything from online banking to book selling. The encryption process is transparent to the end user.

### An Overview of Secure Socket Layers (SSL)

Using SSL is pretty straightforward. As an administrator, you must first purchase an X.509 digital certificate for your web server which contains the web server's DNS name. This digital certificate is nothing more than a bit of information that positively binds the details of your web server (such as its name) to a public key. As long as the client's web browser trusts the holder of your public key, then it will trust your web server. This will allow the client to send and receive encrypted information.

In order for client web browsers to trust that your X.509 digital certificate is real, you need to obtain it from a Certificate Authority (CA) that the client web browsers already trust. Examples of widely-trusted CAs include Baltimore, Equifax, GTE, Thawte, and VeriSign. By default, most client web browsers are configured to trust all of the big-name CAs. You can check this out yourself. For example, in Internet Explorer 6 there are dozens of "pre-trusted" CAs (IE6 | Tools | Internet Options | Content Tab | Certificates Button | Trusted Root Certification Authorities).

In order to purchase the X.509 digital certificate from a "pre-trusted" CA, specify the DNS name of your web server, choose the encryption strength (such as 40- or 128-bit), and select the expiration date. After you purchase the X.509 digital certificate, install it on your web server. The exact process varies depending on your web platform, but it usually involves cutting and pasting a really long certificate number into your web server's administrative console. Once you have installed the certificate, you can enable secure communications on specific (or all) directories for your website. This will allow your web server to securely communicate with your web users, causing the little padlock icon to appear in the corner their IE web browsers.

Because your website will now be secure, your users will need to access it using an address that begins with an https: prefix instead of http:. This is something that you'll need to think about because in the real world, most users will access your website by typing www.yourcompany.com without any prefix. Today's web browsers will automatically add the http:// prefix when the user presses enter. However, if the user is trying to access your secure website, they will get an error if they enter the address without the https: prefix. This error occurs because the web browser automatically adds the http:// prefix, creating http://www.yourcompany.com. But, because your web server is now secure, it needs the address in the secure format, https://www.yourcompany.com.

To alleviate this problem, you can create a non-secure web page that automatically forwards users to the secure web page. In our example, we could create a non-secure page called default.asp that contained the one line of code that would forward users to the secure page, complete with the prefix, to https://www.yourcompany.com/secure/login.asp. By doing this, your users can simply type www.yourcompany.com into their browsers and be connected to the secure page. For the non-programmers out there, the default.asp page on an IIS web server would only need a single line of code:

```
<%response.redirect("https://www.yourcompany.com/
secure/login.asp")%>
```

Using SSL encryption will not require you to change your NFuse web site in any way. NFuse does not know (or care) whether or not the connection is secure. You should also keep in mind that once the ICA session is started on the MetaFrame XP server, NFuse, the web server, and the client's web browser all drop out of the picture—the ICA session is a direct connection between the MetaFrame XP server and the ICA client.

By using SSL encryption on your NFuse web server, anyone, even attackers, will be able to establish a secure connection with your web server. In this case, the SSL encryption is designed to prevent attackers from reading user credentials as they pass by on the network. It is not designed to only allow certain users to connect to your web server.

However, even if an attacker established a secure session with your web server, they would still not be able to get anywhere because the only web page that they would be able to see is the secure NFuse login page that asks them to enter their user credentials. The attacker won't have any valid user credentials, and so they will not be able to continue. Furthermore, the attacker won't be able to read anyone else's credentials because the other users' credentials are encrypted with SSL as they are passed over the network to the web server. This SSL encryption is the same method that every commercial site uses, including online banks, brokers, and the Social Security Administration.

### Advantages of Protecting Web Traffic with an X.509 Certificate

- SSL is the industry standard for TCP/IP web site encryption.
- Users can use any standard web browser. No specialized VPN client software is needed.
- X.509 Certificates are available from several vendors.
- The complete process is transparent to the end user.

### Disadvantages of Protecting Web Traffic with an X.509 Certificate

- X.509 certificates can be expensive, anywhere from US$100 to US$1000 per year.
- Requires extra configuration of the web server.
- Multiple web servers with their own addresses each require their own X.509 digital certificates.

### Segment 2. PN Agent Client to NFuse Web Server

32-bit Windows clients that use the Program Neighborhood Agent ICA client get all of their configuration information from the config.xml file located on an NFuse web server. By default, this communication is an unencrypted HTTP transfer. If the PN Agent clients must cross public networks to receive their configuration information, it is possible to configure them to use SSL encryption. Configuring SSL encryption for the PN Agent clients can be done in two simple steps:

1. Secure the NFuse Web Server. Because the PN Agent uses NFuse, you must configure your NFuse web server to be able to use SSL encryption. This means that you must have an X.509 certificate for your web server, as outlined in the previous section. Once you have this, you can configure the "PNAgent" web directory to only be accessed via secure sessions. This directory contains all of the PN Agent files.

2. Change the PN Agent configuration URL prefixes to "https." The easiest way to do this is to edit the `config.xml` file. Full details of that file are covered in Chapter 11, but for the purposes of security, all you need to do is find all of the URL links and change the prefixes from `http` to `https`. You can use your text editor's "find and replace" function to do this. All in all, there should be a total of four URLs that you need to update. Each of the following sections of `config.xml` has a "Location" tag that contains the URL:

   - FolderDisplay | DesktopDisplay | Icon
   - ConfigurationFile
   - Request | Enumeration
   - Request | Resource

Once you make these updates, the Program Neighborhood Agent client devices will begin using SSL to download their configurations. As with the SSL used in other areas, each client device must have a root certificate installed for the certificate authority that generated the X.509 certificate for you NFuse web server.

## Segment 3. ICA Client Device to MetaFrame XP Server

The ICA session communication usually travels across public networks. In order to secure this network link, there are two aspects of ICA session traffic that we need to look at: ICA session creation and ICA session use.

- *Session creation*. When an ICA session is created, the user credentials are passed from the client device to the MetaFrame XP server. This poses a security risk because stolen user credentials could be used to invoke pirated ICA sessions. Even worse, because many companies are consolidating their user directories, stolen user credentials from an ICA session could most likely be used to access email or other network resources.

- *Session use.* While an ICA session is in use, a packet sniffer could be used to capture the ICA session packets. Because these packets contain all the keystrokes that a user types, anything that the user types could be compromised, including passwords.

Incidentally, you'll notice that during an ICA session, we're only really worried about the keystrokes, not the screen display data. It is highly unlikely that an attacker could capture the screen shot information from ICA session packets. Screen shot captures would require that the attacker crack the binary ICA protocol, which is highly unlikely. Of course, there are many hacker websites and the Citrix SDK that could change this in the future.

Either way, ICA session traffic must be protected. As with HTTP web traffic, the most effective way to do this is with encryption. Encrypting ICA traffic does not make it any harder for an attacker to obtain, but it does render the data unreadable to an attacker. There are four methods that can be used to encrypt ICA session traffic:

- Create an encrypted tunnel (VPN) between the end user and the server, through which ICA session data flows.
- Encrypt only the ICA traffic with the SecureICA protocol extensions.
- Use the Citrix SSL Relay service to encrypt the ICA traffic with SSL or TLS encryption.
- Use Citrix Secure Gateway to encrypt the ICA traffic with SSL or TLS encryption.

### Segment 3 Method 1. Encrypt ICA Traffic with a VPN Tunnel
Third party Virtual Private Networking (VPN) software can be used to create a secure, encrypted "tunnel" from the client device to the MetaFrame XP servers. In these scenarios, each user has VPN client software installed locally on his client machine. This software utilizes the user's local ISP and the Internet to connect to the corporate office. Once this secure connection is established, a private tunnel is created that connects the local user to the corporate network. The local user can access the corporate network as if he was attached to the network locally. In actuality, the VPN software on the user's client device connects to the VPN software at the corporate office via the Internet. All traffic that flows back and forth is encrypted by the VPN software. Through this VPN tunnel, the user can launch MetaFrame XP ICA sessions. The ICA protocol itself is not encrypted directly; rather, it is encrypted by the VPN software automatically.

*Figure 15.7  An ICA session encrypted via a VPN tunnel*

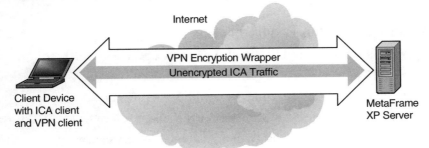

Many companies choose to use VPNs like this for their users to access Meta-Frame XP applications from remote locations. In most instances, VPN access to MetaFrame XP applications is chosen because the company already has an existing VPN solution in place for remote access to other applications. They can easily extend their existing VPN environment to support MetaFrame XP ICA session traffic from remote users.

The major downfall to these types of VPNs is that the VPN client software must be installed on every single client device. Often the configuration of this client software is complex and users are not able to do it on their own. Also, the platforms on which VPN software runs is usually limited. Many times users with Macintosh computers are not able to use the VPN software. Lastly, because the VPN software must be physically installed before it can be used, it is often difficult to use it on a guest computer.

For example, imagine you were at a friend's house when your pager went off, notifying you that there was an urgent work–related matter that needed to be addressed immediately. Fortunately for you, your company built MetaFrame XP servers that will allow you to connect from home. You can go to your friend's PC, log onto the Internet, and begin accessing your MetaFrame XP applications. But, because your company chose to secure their MetaFrame XP servers with a VPN, before you can connect you must first go to your company's intranet site to download and install the VPN software. Only after this is configured are you able to access your MetaFrame XP applications. When you are done, you uninstall the VPN software from your friend's computer.

### Advantages of Using VPN Tunnels

- All traffic is encrypted.
- Users are not limited to accessing only MetaFrame XP applications.

- If the VPN is already in place, it can be easily extended to support MetaFrame XP.

### Disadvantages of Using VPN Tunnels

- VPN software must be installed on every client device.
- VPN software must be configured before it can be used.
- Some clients are not compatible with VPN software.
- Many corporate firewalls block VPN traffic.
- The VPN software costs money, and may be very expensive.
- Some bandwidth is wasted by the VPN tunnel overhead.

Ultimately, VPNs are good solutions if you have users that will use the same computer over and over to remotely connect to your MetaFrame XP servers. VPNs are not good solutions if remote users will need to connect from many different random computers.

In case you are wondering, Citrix used to sell their own VPN software solution called "Citrix Extranet." While the name of this product suggests that it was a fully integrated solution that combines the benefits of ICA clients and VPN software, Citrix Extranet is little more than a third-party VPN software tool that Citrix OEM'ed from a VPN vendor (V-ONE). Citrix Extranet has been discontinued now that there are better ways of securely accessing remote MetaFrame XP servers. (Keep reading for details.)

### Segment 3 Method 2. Encrypt ICA Traffic with SecureICA

Instead of encrypting the entire ICA client to MetaFrame XP server network connection with a VPN solution, it is possible to encrypt just the ICA session traffic itself, as shown in Figure 15.8.

*Figure 15.8 Encrypting the ICA session*

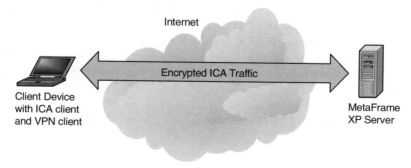

One method that can be used to encrypt ICA traffic is Citrix's SecureICA protocol extensions. All Citrix ICA clients version 6.01 and above have the native capability to encrypt ICA sessions with SecureICA. For those of you who remember, this used to be a separate purchase option, but it is now a built-in feature in all versions of MetaFrame XP.

The built-in ICA session encryption uses the RSA RC5 encryption model to encrypt ICA session traffic. This encryption scheme uses a 1024-bit key to generate a pair of RC5 keys. From there, 128-bit encryption is used for authentication, with the rest of the ICA session encrypted in both directions at the 40-, 56-, or 128- bit levels (depending on your requirements).

This ICA session encryption can be configured at the server, connection, application, or client device layer. When you configure it, you can choose to enforce minimum encryption levels. For example, you might have a Meta-Frame XP server configured to allow users to connect with any level of encryption, but you may publish one sensitive application for which you choose to enforce 128-bit encryption. If a user attempts to connect to that application without an ICA client that can support 128-bit encryption, they will be refused a connection.

This encryption is completely transparent to the user. It does not add any overhead to the ICA network traffic, although it does add a touch of overhead to the server and client processors as they encrypt and decrypt all ICA session data.

If you configure ICA encryption, you will not be able to configure your ICA clients for automatic logon. This is by design, because when automatic logon is used the user credentials are stored locally on the client device and passed to the MetaFrame XP when the session is initiated. This session initiation occurs before the server and client negotiate the secure session so that the credentials are passed in clear text. Citrix figures that if you have configured encryption, there must be a reason, so they don't let you pass credentials in clear text, which means they don't let you configure automatic logon when ICA encryption is used.

### *Advantages of Citrix SecureICA Session Encryption*

- Works on any ICA client platform.
- Transparent to the user.
- Easy to configure.
- Can be configured at multiple layers.
- Does not require an X.509 certificate.

The only real disadvantage to using Citrix's SecureICA encryption is that you need to open a nonstandard port (TCP port 1494, for the ICA session) on your firewall to receive the ICA traffic from the outside clients. This topic will be covered in greater detail in the "Perimeter Security" section of this chapter.

### Disadvantages of Citrix SecureICA Session Encryption

- Requires nonstandard ports to be opened on the firewall when ICA clients connect across the Internet.
- Does not verify the identity of the MetaFrame XP server.

### Segment 3 Method 3. Encrypt ICA Traffic with the Citrix SSL Service

If you're using Feature Release 1 for MetaFrame XP and your ICA clients are at least version 6.20, you can use Citrix SSL Relay Service to enable the industry standard SSL encryption to secure your ICA session traffic. With Feature Release 2, this service can also be used to encrypt your ICA sessions with TLS.

This encryption has the same effect as the proprietary Citrix SecureICA encryption except that everything conforms to industry standards when SSL or TLS is used. You'll probably have more success implementing SSL or TLS ICA encryption than the native ICA encryption because it can communicate via TCP port 443, which is open on most firewalls.

However, with SSL and TLS encryption, the client device must support the level of encryption that you want to use. For example, Windows 2000 clients will need to download and install the Windows 2000 High Encryption Pack in order to use 128 bit encryption.

### Advantages of SSL/TLS Encryption with the Citrix SSL Relay

- Industry standard encryption algorithm.
- Does not require any nonstandard ports to be opened on the firewall.
- Supports verification of the identity of MetaFrame XP servers.
- Each MetaFrame XP server can run its own Citrix SSL Service
- Transparent to the end user.

### Disadvantages of SSL/TLS Encryption with the Citrix SSL Relay

- Requires Feature Release 1 for SSL and Feature Release 2 for TLS.
- Requires that the client device supports encryption.
- All traffic must flow through a Citrix SSL Relay server which acts like a SOCKS proxy,

- You must add every SSL Relay Server to each client's server list.
- Requires a dedicated port which cannot be shared with any other SSL services on a MetaFrame XP server.
- Requires an X.509 certificate for each MetaFrame XP server.
- Requires that the client device supports encryption.
- Requires ICA clients version 6.20 or newer for SSL and 6.30 or newer for TLS.

### Segment 3 Method 4. Encrypt ICA Traffic with Citrix Secure Gateway

If you're using Feature Release 2 and NFuse, you can use Citrix Secure Gateway 1.1 to encrypt the ICA sessions with SSL or TLS encryption.

Citrix Secure Gateway is a stand-alone gateway server that acts as the liaison between your ICA clients and your MetaFrame XP servers. ICA clients securely communicate with the Citrix Secure Gateway server (which usually sits behind a firewall) and the Citrix Secure Gateway server communicates with the MetaFrame XP servers.

### *Advantages of Citrix Secure Gateway*

- One X.509 digital certificate can be used for multiple MetaFrame XP servers.
- MetaFrame XP server addresses are hidden from the outside world.
- Industry standard SSL or TLS encryption.
- Does not require any nonstandard ports to be opened on the firewall.
- Supports verification of the identity of the MetaFrame XP servers.
- Transparent to the end user.

### *Disadvantages of Citrix Secure Gateway*

- Requires Feature Release 2.
- Requires that the client device supports encryption.
- Requires ICA clients version 6.30 or newer.
- The ICA session path between the Citrix Secure Gateway server and MetaFrame XP server is unencrypted.
- All ICA session traffic must flow through a gateway server.

### How to Use the Citrix SSL Relay Service to Encrypt ICA Traffic

The Citrix SSL Relay Service is a Citrix service that acts as a SOCKS proxy. It receives SSL- or TLS-encrypted data from the ICA clients, decrypts it, and forwards it on to the MetaFrame XP ICA session components of the server. When the MetaFrame XP server needs to send ICA session traffic back to the ICA client, the traffic is routed back through the SSL Relay Service to be encrypted. The SSL Relay Service then sends it on to the ICA client.

*Figure 15.9 The Citrix SSL Relay Service in action*

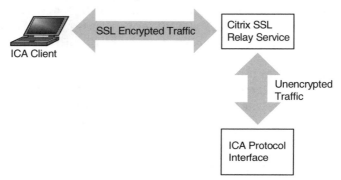

Let's look at the steps needed to configure the Citrix SSL Relay Service. Once this is configured, your clients can begin to use SSL- or TLS-encrypted ICA sessions. There are seven steps that you need to perform to make this happen:

### Step 1. Obtain an X.509 digital certificate.

First obtain an X.509 digital certificate for each MetaFrame XP server that will use SSL or TLS–encrypted ICA sessions.

If the MetaFrame XP server that you are using for the Citrix SSL Relay Service is also running an SSL–secured web server, you can use the same X.509 digital certificate that your web server uses. However, if you already purchased an X.509 digital certificate for your web server but your web server is not the same physical server that you are using for the Citrix SSL Relay, then you will need to purchase an additional X.509 digital certificate for the SSL Relay server, because each digital certificate is server–specific.

You have two options for obtaining the X.509 digital certificates needed for the SSL Relay service on your MetaFrame XP servers. You can either purchase a certificate from a professional certificate authority or you can build your own certificate authority and issue you own certificates.

## Option 1. Buy a Digital Certificate

Your first option is to buy an X.509 digital certificate from a real certificate authority. Send the details of each of your SSL Relay servers to the certificate authority and give them some money. They will send you back a digital certificate which will be nothing more than a computer file that contains some information about your server and a very long string of numbers. Because you bought this certificate from a real certificate authority, most client devices or web browsers worldwide will trust that your certificate is valid. Windows clients automatically trust almost every big-name certificate authority. For non-Windows clients, Citrix includes the root certificates (trust) for VeriSign and Baltimore Technologies in the ICA client software.

### *Advantages of Buying a Certificate from a Real Certificate Authority*

- If you buy your certificate from a big name certificate authority, all of your clients will trust it without any additional configuration on your part.
- Clients can connect from guest computers and begin using secure applications immediately.

### *Disadvantages of Buying a Certificate from a Real Certificate Authority*

- You must pay for each certificate.
- There may be a delay in receiving new certificates.

## Option 2. Create your own Certificate Authority

Instead of buying certificates from someone else, you can create your own root certificate authority and issue your own X.509 digital certificates. Pick a server in your environments and install a certificate authority service. For example, in a Windows 2000 server, you install a certificate authority just like any other Windows component (Control Panel | Add/Remove Programs | Add/Remove Windows Components | Certificate Services). When you install this component, it will ask you for the details of your certificate authority, including your name, its name, and the desired expiration period for the certificates that you will issue. (See Microsoft article Q231881 for a Certificate Services "How-To" guide.) It doesn't really matter what you enter into these fields. They don't affect anything except the data contained in the certificates that your server issues.

The certificates that you issue with your certificate authority are technically no different than the certificates that a real certificate authority would issue. The only difference is the source. Instead of being issued by "VeriSign," your certificate would be issued by "Brian's Citrix Certificates," or whatever name you choose when installing your certificate authority service.

This is important because every client device in the world trusts "VeriSign," but no client device in the world trusts "Brian's Citrix Certificates." In order to get a client device to trust you, you must install your root certificate (or your new certificate authority's root certificate, in this case). Windows 32-bit ICA clients automatically use the root certificates that are installed into Internet Explorer. Other platforms require that you install the root certificates into the ICA client software itself. Once your root certificate is installed on a client, the client device will trust you, which means that it will trust any certificates that you create. Therefore you can use your certificate authority to mass-produce the X.509 certificates that you need for each MetaFrame XP server that will run the Citrix SSL Relay Service.

### Advantages of Creating your own Certificate Authority

- No cost for your certificates.

- You can configure the expiration date and encryption strength of each certificate.

- Fast turnaround time when new certificates are needed.

- You can push your certificate authority's root certificate out with an Active Directory policy or the Internet Explorer Administration Kit.

### Disadvantages of Creating your own Certificate Authority

- Your certificates will not be automatically trusted.

- If you lose your certificate server, no new clients will be able to trust the old certificates.

- If a user connects from a new machine, they will have to first install your root certificate before they can securely communicate with you.

Now that you've decided how you will obtain your X.509 digital certificates, let's continue stepping through the process needed to use SSL to encrypt ICA sessions.

### Step 2. Configure the SSL Relay TCP listener port.

Configure the TCP port that the Citrix SSL Relay Service will listen on (Start | Programs | Citrix | MetaFrame XP | Citrix SSL Relay Configuration Tool | Connection Tab | Relay Listening Port). By default, this port is 443, which is the industry standard SSL port. In most situations, 443 should work fine. However, the Citrix SSL Relay Service cannot share its port with any other service. This means that if the SSL Relay is installed on the same server that hosts secure web pages via port 443, you will have to change one of them. If you choose to change the Citrix SSL Relay port, you will need to configure your client devices to use the nonstandard port. If you change the web servers SSL port, then your users or hyperlinks will have to refer to the new port in the web address when they request secure pages. For example, if you change the SSL web server port from 443 to 4443, you users will need to request the port number when opening a web page, such as `https://www.yourcompany.com:4443`.

### Step 3. Copy the digital certificate to the SSL Relay server.

Once you configure the SSL Relay port, copy your X.509 digital certificate onto the MetaFrame XP server that is running the SSL Relay Service. Remember that each digital certificate is server–specific and tied to that server's DNS name, so you can't use the same certificate twice and you can't mix them up.

Copy the certificate to the SSL Relay certificate directory on your MetaFrame XP server. By default, this directory is `%systemroot%\sslrelay\keystore\certs`. You can change this path with the SSL Relay Configuration Tool (Citrix SSL Relay Configuration Tool I Relay Credentials Tab I Key Store Location). When you specify the path in the configuration tool, you must specify a directory that has two subdirectories under it: `\cacerts` and `\certs`. You need to copy your certificate into the `\certs` directory.

The Citrix SSL Relay Service needs to have a certificate that is in the Personal Electronic Mail (PEM) format. A PEM certificate will have the file extension `.pem`.

Often , you will receive certificates that are not in the PEM format. They may be in other formats that have different file extensions, such as .CER or .PFX. In order to use these types of certificates, you will need to convert them into the PEM format. You can convert certificates to the PEM format with the `keytopem.exe` utility, located in the `%systemroot%\sslrelay` directory of your MetaFrame XP server. To use the conversion utility, open a command prompt and type:

```
keytopem sourcecertificate.cer newcertificatename.pem
```

`Sourcecertificate.cer` is the name of your existing certificate and `newcertificate.pem` is the name you want for the newly-converted PEM certificate. When you convert your certificate to PEM format, you should always specify the file extension PEM.

If your MetaFrame XP server running the SSL relay is also running an IIS web server that already has an X.509 digital certificate, you can export IIS's certificate for use by the SSL Relay Service (MMC I Add Snap-In I Certificates (for the local computer) I Double click certificate I Details tab I Copy to File button). You must remember to convert the certificate to PEM format after you copy it. Also, remember to configure either the SSL Relay or IIS so that they are both not trying to use port 443.

## Step 4. Configure the SSL Relay to use the digital certificate.

Once the digital certificate is copied to the MetaFrame XP server, configure the Citrix SSL Relay Service to use your new certificate (Citrix SSL Relay Configuration I Relay Credentials). Choose your certificate from the drop-down list and enter the password if needed. Once you click "OK," the Citrix SSL Relay Service will be installed and started on that server. This service works just like any other service. It will show up in the list of Windows services.

## Step 5. Verify the SSL Relay Cipher Suites.

After the certificate is installed, you should verify that you have the correct cipher suites enabled (Citrix SSL Relay Configuration Tool I Ciphersuites tab). A cipher suite is a specific encryption/decryption algorithm. When using SSL, the client and server look at all the available cipher suites and mutually agree on one. Different cipher suites have different properties, such as encryption strength or speed. Any client that connects to the Citrix SSL Relay Service must support at least one of the cipher suites that you have enabled. There is no way to add additional cipher suites. By default, the Citrix SSL Relay Configuration enables all of the available cipher suites, which should be fine for most environments.

## Step 6. Configure SSL Relay target addresses.

Once the certificate is installed and the service is running, you need to edit the target addresses for the SSL Relay Service (Citrix SSL Relay Configuration Tool I Connection Tab). The SSL Relay only sends decrypted packets to IP addresses and ports listed here. By default, the local server's primary IP address and the Citrix XML service port are listed.

Since you want to use the SSL Relay Service to send decrypted ICA packets to the local MetaFrame XP server, you need to add the TCP port that ICA uses, which is 1494 unless you changed it (Highlight the IP Address I Click "Edit" I Type in new destination port 1494 I Click "Add" I Click "OK"). When done, you should see both the XML service port (default 80) and the ICA service port listed next to your server's IP address.

Configure the SSL Relay service to forward packets to any host or any port by clicking the corresponding "Any" button when you are adding an address or port. However, by doing this you increase the risk that unencrypted data will be sent to the wrong location.

### Step 7. Configure your ICA client devices to use SSL for ICA encryption.

After you'ave performed the previous six steps, your MetaFrame XP server will be ready to support SSL– or TLS-encrypted ICA sessions. The only thing left to do is configure your ICA clients to connect via SSL. For information regarding specific client configurations, refer to Chapter 10. If you're using NFuse Classic or the Program Neighborhood Agent to provide access to your MetaFrame XP servers, you are in luck because you can change the ICA client settings centrally. Once you make the change, all client devices automatically receive the new settings the next time they connect. Let's take a look at what it takes to configure NFuse Classic and the Program Neighborhood Agent to communicate via SSL-encrypted ICA sessions. We'll start with NFuse.

### Configuring NFuse to use SSL Encrypted ICA Sessions

Remember that NFuse Classic's main role is getting ICA sessions started. You can enable SSL encryption of your ICA sessions by setting just one configuration item. Edit the NFuse.conf file on your NFuse web server. Refer to Chapter 11 for details on this file. Locate the "AddressResolution Type" setting. Ensure that its value is set to DNS (or DNS-port if your ICA protocol is configured for a port other than 1494). The new line should look like this:

```
AddressResolutionType=DNS
```

As with all NFuse settings, you will need to stop and start the web server service for this change to take effect. This change will ensure that the MetaFrame XP server addresses passed to clients are the full DNS names instead of the IP addresses.

### Configuring the PN Agent to use Encrypted ICA Sessions

Configuring the Program Neighborhood Agent to use SSL encryption for ICA sessions is easy. If the published application is configured to use SSL (CMC | Right-click Published Application | Properties | ICA Client Settings Tab | Enable SSL), the PN Agent will automatically use SSL.

## How to use Citrix Secure Gateway to Encrypt ICA Traffic

A Citrix Secure Gateway (CSG) server can support thousands of users simultaneously accessing multiple MetaFrame XP servers as seen in Figure 15.10.

*Figure 15.10 How CSG is used*

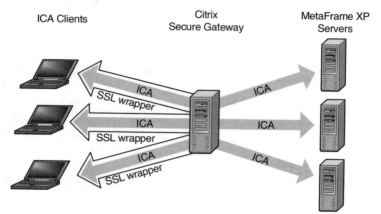

Using CSG is completely transparent to your users. In fact, because it's so easy to use, CSG is widely thought of as the "VPN" killer. In order to understand CSG, let's take a look at how it works.

### How Citrix Secure Gateway Works

Citrix Secure Gateway is made up of two components: the Citrix Secure Gateway server and the optional Secure Ticket Authority:

- Citrix Secure Gateway server. This is a dedicated server that acts as the proxy between users and MetaFrame XP servers. Since a single CSG server can interface to multiple MetaFrame XP servers, you can have a fully SSL/TLS-encrypted environment without needing certificates for all of your individual MetaFrame XP servers.

- Secure Ticket Authority. The Secure Ticket Authority (STA) is an optional component of CSG that runs on a separate server. The STA can be used to generate tickets that are sent to the user instead of credentials and server information. Using a STA renders an intercepted packet useless, since it would only contain a temporary ticket number instead of real data. To see how this works, let's take a detailed look at how CSG functions.

In most environments, CSG is used in combination with NFuse Classic. For this reason, you'll notice that the first several steps that take place to start an application in a CSG environment are identical to when they are started in NFuse Classic environments.

*Figure 15.11 Citrix Secure Gateway in action*

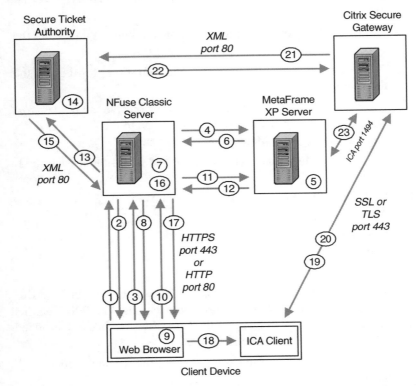

1. A user with a web browser and an ICA client requests the NFuse Classic portal web page by typing in a URL.

2. The web server sends down the HTML login page via the HTTP protocol. In secure environments, this can be via the HTTPS protocol.

3. The web user types in their credentials and clicks the "Submit" button which sends them to the web server.

4. The web server forwards the user's information to a MetaFrame XP server running the Citrix XML service.

5. The MetaFrame XP server validates the credentials and retrieves the user's list of applications for the server farm.

6. The MetaFrame XP server sends the application list to the NFuse web server.

7. The NFuse web server builds a web page that contains all of the user's application icons. Each icon is hyperlinked with its application properties.

8. The web page is sent to the user's browser via the HTTP or HTTPS protocol.

9. The user selects an application to run by clicking on an icon in the web browser.

10. The web browser sends a request to the web server for the link that the user selected.

11. The NFuse Java Objects on the web server receive the request for the application. They forward the request on to the Citrix XML service running on a MetaFrame XP server.

12. The Citrix XML service returns the IP address of the least-loaded server.

13. The NFuse Java Objects send the IP address to the Secure Ticket Authority (STA).

14. The STA saves the IP address into memory and generates a random ticket number.

15. The STA sends the ticket number to NFuse.

16. NFuse retrieves the ICA file template. The ticket number is added to the ICA file in place of the user's credentials. The fully qualified domain name or DNS name of the Citrix Secure Gateway is added in place of the MetaFrame XP server.

17. The custom-built ICA file is sent to web browser on the client device.

18. The web browser receives the ICA file and passes it to ICA client software that is also loaded on the ICA client device.

19. The user's local ICA client starts the MetaFrame XP session with the information contained in the custom ICA file. Since the server specified is the Citrix Secure Gateway, the client contacts the CSG.

20. The SSL/TLS handshaking process takes place. The ICA client verifies that the CSG is valid based on its installed root certificate.

21. The CSG passes the ticket number to the STA.

22. The STA examines ticket and (if it's valid), sends the IP address of the MetaFrame XP server to the CSG.

23. The CSG establishes an ICA session with the MetaFrame XP server. The CSG then encrypts and decrypts the ICA session traffic,

passing decrypted traffic to the MetaFrame XP server and encrypted traffic to the ICA client.

As you can see, the way that the Citrix Secure Gateway works is pretty simple. Let's now take a look at how you can get it installed in your environment.

### Step 1. Install the (Optional) Secure Ticket Authority

We mentioned previously that using the STA with CSG is optional. While this is true, the advantages of using the STA far outweigh the disadvantages. Before we look at how the STA is installed, let's take another look at how CSG works with a focus on how the STA helps to secure the environment.

Think back to how NFuse works. After a user logs in, they click a hyperlink to launch an ICA session. The NFuse web server builds a custom, dynamic, behind-the-scenes ICA file and sends it down to the client. That ICA file has the user's credentials imbedded into it since the NFuse server remembered the user's credentials because an NFuse Session Object was set when the user logged into the NFuse web page. The user's local ICA client software then launches the ICA session with the information (and credentials) from that ICA file.

This leaves a gaping security hole. Instead of clicking an NFuse application hyperlink to launch an application, a savvy end user could right-click the link, choose "Save target as..." from the context menu, and save a local copy of the ICA file. That ICA file could then be used to access the application at any time. Even worse, because that ICA file contains that user's credentials, it could be passed around and used by any user.

To combat this shortcoming, Citrix Secure Gateway uses the Secure Ticket Authority to create tickets. Ticketing was first introduced with NFuse 1.5 several years ago, and CSG ticketing is still based on that technology. Remember from Figure 15.11 that when CSG and STA are used, the user clicks on a hyperlink to launch an ICA session from the NFuse web page and the NFuse server builds a custom ICA file for the user, as usual.

However, instead of placing the user's credentials and the target MetaFrame XP server in the ICA file, NFuse sends the information to the STA. The STA then creates a totally random 30-character string called a "ticket" that it associates with those specific credentials. The STA maintains a list in memory that maps authenticated users, their servers, and their ticket numbers. It then returns the ticket to the NFuse web server.

When the ICA file is created and sent down to the user's client device, it contains the 30-character ticket instead of the actual user credentials. It also contains the name of the CSG as the server instead of the actual MetaFrame XP server. When the client device receives the ICA file, an ICA session is launched as usual. The ticket number is sent to the CSG server, and that server communicates with the STA to retrieve the actual user credentials based on the user's ticket number.

By using ticketing, a user's real credentials are not sent across the network multiple times and they are not placed in the ICA file. But wait! It gets even cooler for the following two reasons:

- Tickets are configured with a timeout period.
- Tickets are only valid for one time use.

Every ticket is configured with a timeout period (based on settings of the STA server). Once a certain amount of time passes after the ticket has been created, the STA destroys the ticket along with the associated user credentials. For example, if the timeout is set for 100 seconds, a user that "right-click" captures the dynamic ICA file from the NFuse web page will not be able to use that file after 100 seconds have passed because the STA server would not have the user credentials associated with the ticket number contained in the ICA file.

One of the great things about this timeout feature is that the ticket timeout period begins when the ticket is created. The ticket is created when a user clicks a hyperlink to launch an ICA session, *not* when the user first accesses the application list webpage. Because of this, there is no risk that a user will log in to the web page and then wait too long, causing the ticket to expire.

The other major advantage to using the STA for ticketing is that each ticket can only be used once. After a user logs on with a ticket, the STA destroys the 30-character ticket and the associated user credentials. Therefore, even if the timeout for tickets has not expired, a single NFuse-generated ICA file cannot be used by multiple users.

### Advantages of STA Ticketing

- Very cool.
- Protects ICA files from users' friends.
- Tickets are only valid once.
- Tickets expire after a configurable amount of time.
- Clear text user credentials are not placed in the ICA files.

- Clear text user credentials are not passed across the network when ICA sessions are launched.

### Disadvantages of STA Ticketing

- Unencrypted data is still sent over the network once.
- NFuse is required.

In reality, the Secure Ticket Authority is nothing more than a DLL installed into the \scripts\ directory of an IIS web server running on Windows 2000 with Service Pack 2 or newer. When you install it (from the "Components" section of the main MetaFrame XP SP-2/FR-2 splashscreen), you will need to know the path to your IIS scripts folder (%systemroot%\inetpub\scripts by default).

As soon as the STA is installed, the STA configuration tool is launched. You will need to specify an STA ID that is a unique character string made up of a maximum of 16 uppercase and numeric characters. This ID is used to differentiate multiple STA servers in your environment. This name doesn't really matter, and the default of "STA01" should be fine.

If you click the "advanced options" of the STA configuration screen, you are also given the option to specify the timeout period of the tickets that this STA generates and the maximum number of concurrent tickets that can be generated.

By default, the ticket timeout is 10000 milliseconds, or 100 seconds. This should be acceptable for most environments, although you can change it at any time if you need to (Start | Programs | Citrix | Citrix Secure Gateway | Secure Ticket Authority Configuration).

The STA is configured by default for a maximum of 100,000 tickets. You can drop this number considerably. Since this number only affects concurrent tickets (not total), it should roughly correspond to the number of users you have. Even with a few users, you can safely drop this number to about 1,000. An entry of 1,000 will be enough tickets that you will never run out but not enough that a brute-force attacker could find a way into your server.

If you use the IIS Lockdown Tool on to secure IIS on your STA server, you should use the same settings that you did for NFuse as outlined earlier in this chapter.

### Step 2. Build your Citrix Secure Gateway Server

Once your STA is up and running you can build your CSG server. This server can just be a standard Windows 2000 server with Service Pack 2, although it must be a physically different server from the STA.

The exact hardware requirements vary depending on your exact environment and how bust your users are. However, you'll be pleasantly surprised to know that CSG scales fairly well. In the real world, you can fit 700-1000 users on a dual 1.0GHz processor CSG server.

### Step 3. Obtain and Apply a Digital Certificate

The CSG server is the one that needs a digital certificate. (The STA does not need one, since it doesn't communicate directly with clients.) Follow Step #1 from the previous section ("How to Use the Citrix SSL Relay Service to Encrypt ICA Traffic") for detailed instructions about obtaining and installing this certificate.

### Step 4. Install the Citrix Secure Gateway Service

You can install CSG from the SP-2/FR-2 splashscreen or by running "csg_gwy.msi." If you've decided to use CSG without using a STA, the CSG will operate in "Relay Mode." To configure your CSG for Relay Mode, install it using the following command:

```
Msiexec.exe /i csg_gwy.msi RELAYMODE=1
```

### Step 5. Configure the Citrix Secure Gateway

Similar to the STA installation, the CSG configuration wizard launches as soon as the CSG installation is complete. The main option that you need to configure is the address or addresses of the STA servers that you will use. From a sizing standpoint, even the largest environments only need a single STA server. However, for purposes of redundancy, you can have multiple STA servers. (See Chapter 17 for more information.)

Keep the following points in mind as you configure CSG:

- You need to specify the IP addresses and ports that the CSG will watch. Ordinarily this would be the external interface of the server over port 443.

- The "Worker Threads" option allows you to specify how many threads the CSG service will use. The default value of 8 should work for up to two processors. You should double this to 16 on quad-processor servers.

- The connection timeout that you specify in milliseconds only affects the timeout of the security handshaking process. It does not affect overall session times. The default value of 10,000 (100 seconds) should be sufficient for most environments.

- You should also specify a connection limit to ensure that you do not get too many users on your CSG server. You can specify a connection limit and a resume limit. When the number of concurrent users hits the connection limit, all new connections will be refused until the number of connections falls to the resume limit.

- When you configure CSG, a single server can only support one secure protocol. If you want to support both TLS and SSL, you'll have to add another CSG server.

- Like the SSL Relay Service, CSG has the ability to use multiple cipher suites. Unless you have direction from your internal security team, you should keep the cipher suite settings configured for "all."

- When asked to exclude certain IP addresses from the CSG activity log file, think about anything in your environment that might access the server that you do not want to log. You don't want your CSG logs filling up because someone's copy of "What's Up Gold" keeps pinging your CSG server every three minutes.

- When you configure error logging, keep in mind that CSG errors are written to the Windows event log, not to standard log files. If you select one of the more robust logging options, be sure that your Windows event logs can handle the amount of information.

- After you finish configuring CSG, you should reboot it for the changes to take affect.

## Step 6. Configure NFuse Classic for use with CSG

If you're using CSG as it was fully intended (complete with the STA), you'll need to configure NFuse so that it knows that it should use CSG. As with the other NFuse Classic 1.7 options, you can configure NFuse CSG options via the administrative web pages (NFuse Admin Web Pages I Server-Side Firewall I Secure Gateway Server) or by editing the NFuse.conf file directly. See Chapter 11 for more information about configuring NFuse.

First put the NFuse web server into CSG operating mode. This is done with the following line in the NFuse.conf file:

```
SessionField.NFuse_CSG_Enable=On
```

Then, to complete the configuration of NFuse, you need to know the addresses of both the STA and the CSG. You can point a single NFuse web server to up to 256 different Secure Ticket Authorities (in case you want a really redundant environment). This is done via the NFuse session field called "NFuse_CSG_STA_URLx." (The "x" is a number from 1 to 256.)

For example, to configure two STAs, add or modify the following two lines in the NFuse.conf file:

```
SessionField.NFuse_CSG_STA_URL1=http://
staserver1.yourcompany.com/scripts/CtxSta.dll
SessionField.NFuse_CSG_STA_URL2=http://
staserver2.yourcompany.com/scripts/CtxSta.dll
```

Then, use these two lines in the NFuse.conf file to specify the name and port of the CSG server:

```
SessionField.NFuse_CSG_Server=yourcsgserver.yourcompany.com
SessionField.NFuse_CSG_ServerPort=443
```

After you enter these settings, you're all set. Stop and start the web server service and you can begin using CSG. As you use CSG, you'll notice that your NFuse web pages (and the entire experience) is the same as when CSG was not used. While this is convenient for your users, you may wonder if CSG is actually doing anything. The easiest way to check this is to go into the ICA connection manager on your client device while you have an ICA session opened. You should see that your session is encrypted via 128-bit encryption.

### *Securing Back End Network Communications*

Thinking back to Figure 15.6, we can now start to look at what needs to be done to secure the back-end network communications. In MetaFrame XP server farms, IMA and XML traffic is passed between various servers. By default, all of this communication is in clear text, unencrypted and unsecured.

Most administrators ignore the back-end network segments when evaluating security. This is usually because they don't think that there is a need to secure those segments since all of the servers are located in the same data center or within the same corporate network and so are generally considered secure.

However, there are many environments in which a single MetaFrame XP server farm will span multiple locations, causing back-end server communication security to be an issue. Within MetaFrame XP environments, there are four types of backend network communications that can be secured:

- Segment 4. NFuse web server to the MetaFrame XP XML server.
- Segment 5. MetaFrame XP farm servers to the IMA data store.

- Segment 6. MetaFrame XP farm servers to the zone data collector.
- Segment 7. The Citrix Management Console to the MetaFrame XP host server.

## Segment 4. NFuse Web Server to MetaFrame XP Server

NFuse web servers must communicate with the MetaFrame XP IMA service in order to build lists of published applications and content for users that log in. The NFuse servers access this data from the MetaFrame XP servers via the Citrix XML service. Much of this data is sensitive in nature, including user credentials and application set information. By default, this information is not encrypted (with the exception of passwords, which are encrypted at a basic level). Because this is standard XML information, it can be very easy to read if intercepted.

If you determine that the network segment between your NFuse web server and your MetaFrame XP server is not secure, there are two things that you can do:

- Encrypt the Citrix XML traffic on the network segment with SSL or TLS.
- Remove the network segment by running the NFuse web server on a MetaFrame XP server.

### Method 1. NFuse Web Server to MetaFrame XP Server SSL Encryption

In scenarios in which a public, unsecured network separates the NFuse web server and the MetaFrame XP server, you can configure NFuse so that all traffic traveling between the two servers is encrypted. Remember that NFuse 1.7 can be configured to communicate with multiple MetaFrame XP servers for load balancing. In this case, X.509 digital certificates service must be installed and configured on each MetaFrame XP server that communicates with the NFuse web server.

To allow NFuse to use SSL encryption for its communication with the Citrix XML service, all you have to do is edit the NFuse.conf file on your NFuse web server. See Chapter 11 for detailed information about NFuse and the use of this file.

With NFuse 1.7, you have two choices for encrypting this traffic. If you're running the Citrix SSL Relay service, locate the following line in the NFuse.conf file:

```
SessionField.NFuse_Transport=HTTP
```

Change the "HTTP" to "SSL," so that the line looks like this:

```
SessionField.NFuse_Transport=SSL
```

Then, in order to specify your Citrix XML servers running the Citrix SSL Relay service, add the following two lines:

```
SessionField.NFuse_RelayServer=yourserver
SessionField.NFuse_RelayServerPort=443
```

Alternately, if you are not using the Citrix SSL Relay service, you can change the transport setting to "HTTPS," so that the line looks like this:

```
SessionField.NFuse_Transport=HTTPS
```

With the "HTTPS" setting, NFuse will use the regular Citrix XML servers and ports that you specified in the `SessionField.NFuse_CitrixServer` and `SessionField.NFuse_CitrixServerPort` lines.

Just as with any other changes that you make to the `NFuse.conf` file, you must stop and start the web server service for these changes to take affect.

### Advantages of Encrypting the NFuse to MetaFrame XP Link

- Ultimate security.
- Works well when NFuse and MetaFrame XP servers are on opposite sides of an unsecured network.

### Disadvantages of Encrypting the NFuse to MetaFrame XP Link

- Extra configuration is needed.
- One X.509 certificate is needed for each MetaFrame XP server that communicates with NFuse.
- Security is usually not needed at this level because most communication is intra-site, or site-to-site with private, secure lines.

### Method 2. Use the Same Server for NFuse and MetaFrame XP

A simple way to eliminate the risk of a network segment attack between the NFuse web server and the MetaFrame XP server is to eliminate that network segment altogether. You can do that by running the NFuse web server on the same physical machine as the MetaFrame XP server. When you do this, the Citrix XML service is still used, but there is no need for its data travel to across the network.

### Advantages of Running NFuse on a MetaFrame XP server.

- Inexpensive.
- Secure.

### Disadvantages of Running NFuse on a MetaFrame XP server.

- Does not scale very well.
- Single point of failure.
- Does not allow the web pages and the SSL encrypted ICA sessions to both use the default TCP port 443.

## Segment 5. MetaFrame XP Server to the IMA Data Store

All communication between MetaFrame XP servers and the IMA Data Store is done via standard database communication traffic. There is nothing of particular value in this communication, but it can be encrypted if needed. If you decide to encrypt, you must do it with the native ODBC database tools and software. The database communication encryption is not a feature of MetaFrame XP.

## Segment 6. MetaFrame XP Server to Zone Data Collector

All zone update information is transferred between zone data collectors and MetaFrame XP servers via TCP port 2512. This communication is also done in clear text. However, this information does not contain any potentially dangerous information; it is not valuable to attackers. If you must encrypt it, then do it with non-MetaFrame products, such as a VPN or IPSec.

## Segment 7. CMC to MetaFrame XP Host Server

The CMC communicates over TCP port 2513. This communication is done in clear text, and it contains logon information including the CMC user's name and password as well as any configuration done through the CMC, such as group rights and published applications.

This security risk can be avoided by running the Citrix Management Console locally on MetaFrame XP servers. It can be made available to remote administrators by publishing the CMC itself as an explicit ICA application. In doing so, the standard ICA session security procedures will be used. See Chapter 16 for details about publishing the CMC.

# Network Perimeter Security / Firewall Configuration

In this section, we won't spend time talking about the importance of firewalls and why you need them. The truth is that most environments have them. We only care about using them with MetaFrame XP. There are really three questions that get asked when using firewalls in MetaFrame XP environments:

- Where should I put the MetaFrame XP servers in relation to the firewall?
- What ports do I need to open on the firewall?
- How do I make the MetaFrame XP servers work if the firewall is using Network Address Translation (NAT)?

Let's examine each of these questions.

## MetaFrame Server Placement in Relation to the Firewall

When deciding where to put MetaFrame XP application servers that will provide ICA access to applications across the Internet, there are three basic options:

- MetaFrame XP servers outside the firewall.
- MetaFrame XP servers inside the firewall.
- MetaFrame XP servers in a DMZ.

### Option 1. MetaFrame XP Servers outside the Firewall

Placing your MetaFrame XP servers outside of the firewall exposes them to all the attackers on the Internet. However, if a server is breached, it remains on the outside of the firewall, severely limiting any potential damage to sensitive resources on the inside of the firewall.

*Figure 15.12  A MetaFrame XP server outside the firewall*

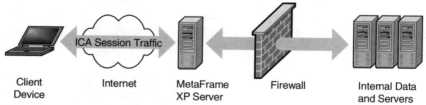

| Client Device | Internet | MetaFrame XP Server | Firewall | Internal Data and Servers |

This configuration is primarily used when MetaFrame XP applications are stand-alone (do not need to access any data from the inside of the firewall).

A major downside to putting MetaFrame servers on the outside of the firewall is that any MetaFrame XP application that accesses resources from servers on the inside of the firewall will need to have a port opened on the firewall. The more ports that are opened increase the likelihood that a breach of the firewall could occur.

Another thing that people worry about is that Microsoft software is not exactly known for being bulletproof. Very few organizations feel comfortable having unprotected Windows servers sitting on the Internet.

Putting MetaFrame XP servers on the outside of the firewall raises complexities if you have users on the inside that need to access the MetaFrame XP servers. Should they go through the firewall in the opposite direction? Should you have a MetaFrame XP server farm that has some servers on the inside and others on the outside? When users from both inside and outside need to access MetaFrame XP application servers, the servers are usually not put on the outside of the firewall.

### Advantages of Placing MetaFrame XP Servers Outside the Firewall

- Works well if no internal users will need to access the servers.
- If the MetaFrame XP server is compromised, the inside network is not affected.

### Disadvantages of Placing MetaFrame XP Servers Outside the Firewall

- Application holes need to be opened in the firewall.
- It can be difficult for some applications on the MetaFrame XP server to get through the firewall to the resources they need on the inside.
- If users connect to the MetaFrame XP servers with the same user accounts that they use on the inside, they must authenticate to the MetaFrame XP server through the firewall.

### Option 2. MetaFrame XP Servers inside the Firewall

Most companies choose to place their MetaFrame XP servers inside the firewall. By doing this, they are leveraging the true definition of the "firewall," as it will take the brunt of all Internet traffic and attacks.

*Figure 15.13 A MetaFrame XP Server behind the firewall*

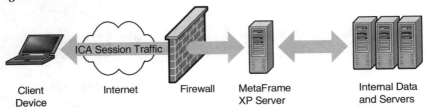

| Client Device | Internet | Firewall | MetaFrame XP Server | Internal Data and Servers |

This tends to be the most secure of all possible configurations because the only holes that need to be opened on the firewall are for ICA traffic to MetaFrame XP servers.

## Advantages of Placing MetaFrame XP Servers Inside the Firewall

- Only the MetaFrame server addresses and ports need to be opened on the firewall.
- Very Secure.

## Disadvantages of Placing MetaFrame XP Servers Inside the Firewall

- If the MetaFrame server is compromised, other servers behind the firewall could be compromised.
- The firewall must be configured to allow ICA traffic to flow to the MetaFrame XP servers.

### Option 3. MetaFrame XP server in a DMZ

Some firewalls allow for the configuration of a DMZ (Demilitarized Zone). A DMX can also be created with a pair of firewalls. This DMZ is like a combination of the two above methods. The MetaFrame XP servers aren't totally exposed on the outside of the firewall, but they also do not have free access to devices on the inside of the firewall. In this configuration, no outside traffic has direct access to devices on the inside of the firewall. Instead, the firewall is configured so that outside clients can access only the MetaFrame XP servers in the DMZ. Those MetaFrame XP servers, in turn, can access (through the firewall) network resources on the inside.

*Figure 15.14 A MetaFrame XP server in the DMZ*

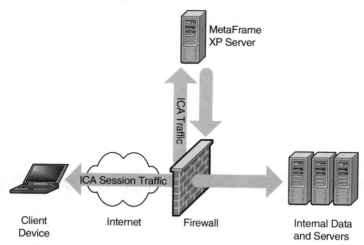

## Advantages of Placing MetaFrame XP Servers in the DMZ

- Balance between no access and all access.

## Disadvantages of Placing MetaFrame XP Servers in the DMZ

• Most complex firewall configuration.

## Firewall Ports Configuration for MetaFrame XP Environments

If you decide to put your MetaFrame XP server behind a firewall or in a DMZ, there are several TCP ports that must be configured on the firewall (if you're not using Citrix Secure Gateway).

*Figure 15.5 Firewall port usage*

| Port | Direction | Destination | Description |
|------|-----------|-------------|-------------|
| 1494 | Inbound | All MetaFrame Servers | ICA port needed for ICA sessions |
| 1023 and above | Outbound | ICA Client | MetaFrame XP will dynamically select a unique port for each ICA session. This port configuration is standard practice on firewalls. |
| 80 | Inbound | NFuse Web Server | If you are using NFuse, and your NFuse server is behind the firewall, you will need this port to allow users to access the website. |
| 80 | Inbound | Citrix XML Service on at least one MetaFrame XP Server | This port is needed on one or more MetaFrame XP servers that will be providing the application lists to external clients. If all external clients will use NFuse, this port will not be needed. |
| 443 | Inbound | NFuse Web Server or MetaFrame XP Server | If you are using an SSL connection to an internal NFuse server, or you are encrypting ICA traffic via SSL, then this port is needed. SSL session encryption uses this port in place of 1494. |

## Network Address Translation at the Firewall

Most companies that use firewalls configure them to do Network Address Translation (NAT). This allows internal servers to be configured with private IP addresses that are not valid to the outside world. Because all network traffic between the inside servers and the outside world is channeled through the firewall, the firewall maintains two addresses for each server. One address is valid to the outside world; the other address is valid to the inside network. When a request for the server hits the firewall from the outside, the firewall translates the address to the internal address of the server before passing it on to that server. Just the same, when the internal server sends network data to an external address, the firewall changes the existing sender's address (the server's internal address) to the server's valid external address. The server has no idea that its address is not valid to the outside world. Using NAT allows servers on the inside to be protected from the outside world by forcing all communication to travel through the firewall.

*Figure 15.16  Network address translation at the firewall*

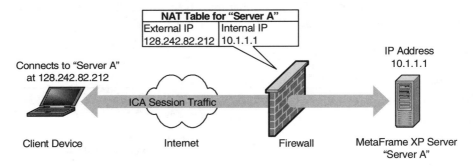

The advantage to using NAT is that because the internal IP addresses of the servers are not valid on the outside, it is technically impossible for an attacker to find a "back door" into the network. All traffic must flow through the firewall because the internal addresses are not valid to the rest of the world. Also, by using NAT, companies do not have to register the IP addresses for all of their internal devices.

In non-MetaFrame XP environments there are usually no issues with NAT because the internal server has no need to know that its IP address is being changed by the firewall. This is not the always the case in MetaFrame XP environments. To understand why, let's consider the following scenario.

A Citrix ICA client device connects to a MetaFrame XP server via the Internet. The MetaFrame XP server is accessible to the Internet via the IP address 128.242.82.212. A firewall running NAT sits between the Internet and the MetaFrame XP server. The MetaFrame XP server's IP address is configured to be 10.1.1.1. The firewall automatically translates between the two IP addresses for traffic going between the Internet and the MetaFrame XP server. This scenario is outlined in Figure 15.17 (facing page).

If an ICA client on the outside of the firewall connects directly to the MetaFrame XP server, there will be no issues. The firewall will use NAT to translate between the internal and external addresses of the MetaFrame XP server. In this case, the ICA client and the MetaFrame XP server do not know that the address is being translated. All translation occurs transparently at the firewall, and all is well.

*Figure 15.17 The firewall translates the ICA client's request*

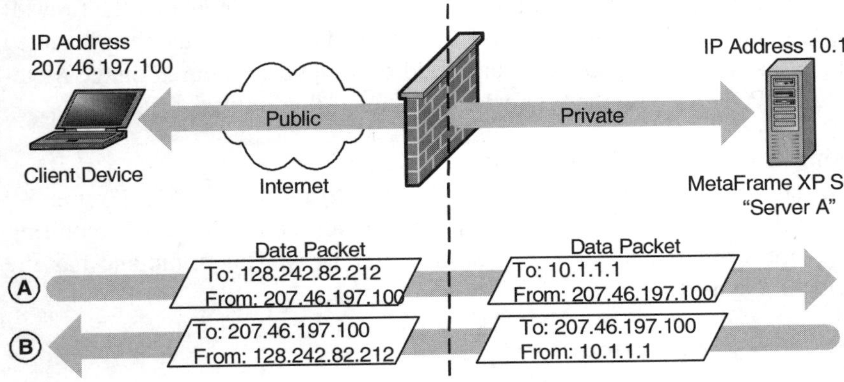


| NAT Table for "Server A" | |
|---|---|
| External IP | Internal IP |
| 128.242.82.212 | 10.1.1.1 |

However, if the external ICA client queries the MetaFrame XP server farm (via the Citrix XML service) to connect to a load-balanced published application, the user's request is sent in the form of data from his client's IP address to the server, at 128.242.82.212. The firewall gracefully intercepts that data and sends it on to the MetaFrame XP server's actual address, 10.1.1.1.

The MetaFrame XP server receives the data at its address of 10.1.1.1. It looks at which published application the user wants to connect to, queries the zone data collector, and finds the IP address of the MetaFrame XP server with the least load. In this case, the server with the least load is 10.1.1.1. The MetaFrame XP server sends this information back to the client, letting the client know that he can connect to 10.1.1.1.

The firewall will also intercept this data on its way to the client before it is sent back across the Internet. The firewall will change the sender server's address (the return address) from 10.1.1.1 to 128.242.82.212. However, the firewall will not change the actual content of the data itself. Think of it like this: A firewall running NAT will always translate the "to" and "from" addresses of the data. It will not scan the data to see if there is anything else that needs to be changed.

In this case, the ICA client will receive the data from the MetaFrame XP server without incident. That data will show a return address of 128.242.82.212. However, the content of the data will contain instructions for the client to connect to the server via 10.1.1.1. This IP address is not valid to the outside world. The ICA client will not be able to connect.

In order for the ICA client to connect to a MetaFrame XP server behind a firewall using NAT, the MetaFrame XP server needs to know that the firewall is translating its IP address via NAT. It also needs to know what the translated address is. This "alternate" translated address can be configured on the MetaFrame XP server with the `altaddr` command-line utility.

## Using the ALTADDR command

The `altaddr` command-line utility is used to inform the MetaFrame XP server that some clients may request information about the server requiring an address other than the server's real IP address. This command has the following syntax:

```
altaddr /set ipaddress
```

You can use "`altaddr /?`" to view the full options and syntax of the command. You can specify different alternate addresses for different NICs for servers that have multiple NICs.

In our example from the previous page, we would execute the following command from the command prompt of the MetaFrame XP server:

```
altaddr /server:ourservername /set 128.242.82.212
```

After this command has been executed (and after the server has been rebooted or the IMA service stopped and started), the MetaFrame XP server will determine which address ICA clients are looking for and return either the "real" IP address (in this case 10.1.1.1) or the "alternate" IP address (in this case 128.242.82.212).

The `altaddr` command line utility stores the alternate address in the registry in the following location.

Key: `HKLM\system\CurrentControlSet\Services\ICABrowser\`
   `Parameters\AlternateAddress\TCP`

Value: `DefaultAddress`

Type: `REG_SZ`

Data: IP address of the alternate address.

It is important to note that the `altaddr` command is used to configure IP addresses that are *not* local on the MetaFrame XP server. There is no need to open the network properties dialog box of the MetaFrame XP server to add another IP address to the network card. Remember that the firewall running NAT will make sure that the traffic gets to the proper server. All the `altaddr` command does is enable the MetaFrame XP server to provide an additional alias address to ICA clients. Configuring alternate addresses will not break any internal clients that already connect via the real IP address.

You may be wondering how the server knows when to provide the alternate address or the standard address. In actuality, it's the ICA client configuration that dictates whether the client will request the server to return to the standard address or the alternate address. For example, in the Windows ICA client, the "server location" section of a connection's properties has a "Firewalls..." button. This button leads to a screen that has a checkbox labeled "Use alternate address for firewall connection."

It is easy to be confused as to exactly which situations require the configuration of an alternate address. For example, if you have users that connect directly to one server via an IP address, the alternate address is not needed. An easy way to remember it is that the alternate address is only needed if the MetaFrame XP server will be providing its own IP address to the ICA client through a NAT firewall. The alternate address is not needed if the ICA client already knows the IP address of the MetaFrame XP server.

## Port Translation

Some firewalls can also be configured for port translation in addition to address translation. This can be used if you have multiple MetaFrame XP servers that you would like to make available via the Internet on a single IP address. Look at the environment in Figure 15.18.

*Figure 15.18  Port translation at the firewall*

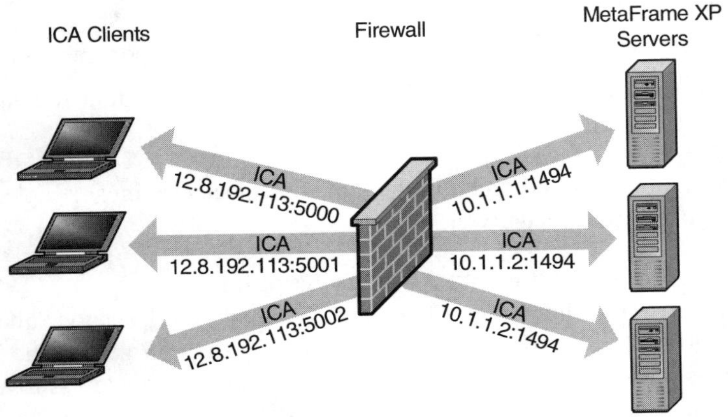

This company has three MetaFrame XP servers. All of them have private IP addresses and host ICA sessions via port 1494. When this company extended their environment to the Internet, they only had a single external IP address available: 12.8.192.113. Since they would like external users to be able to access all of their servers, they configured different ports on the firewall to map to different servers. For example, port 5000 on the firewall maps to port 1494 on Server 1 at 10.1.1.1 on. Port 5001 maps to 10.1.1.2 port 1494 and port 5002 maps to 10.1.1.3 port 1494.

In this situation, the `altaddr` command is also used. If you're using it to map a port, simply append the port number to the end of the IP address. For example:

```
altaddr /server:server1 /set 12.8.192.113:5000
```

In this situation, you wouldn't have to configure the server for port 1494 since that's the port that the ICA sessions are already using. (You would, of course, still need to manually configure the 12.8.192.113:5000 to 10.1.1.1:1494 mapping on the firewall.)

While this solution may not be pretty, it does allow users from outside the network to access any MetaFrame XP server via that single 12.8.192.113 IP address. Of course all of the users inside the network continue to access the servers as usual.

### Advantages of Port Translation

- Multiple MetaFrame XP servers can share the same external IP address.
- The servers' real IP addresses are not exposed to the outside world.

### Disadvantages of Port Translation

- It requires a firewall that can support address and port mapping.
- Client devices must be configured to connect to the non-standard port.

Port translation is not common in the real world, because most people in this situation use Citrix Secure Gateway.

### Using NFuse with Alternate Address Mapping

Since it's up to the client device to determine whether it needs the "alternate" address or the "standard" address from a MetaFrame XP server, the NFuse web pages must be configured to tell the ICA client which address to ask for. In the past, you had to manually modify the default NFuse web pages to use different ICA template files depending on the IP addresses of the clients. With NFuse 1.7, this functionality is built in.

## Configuring Default Address Behavior

On the "Server-Side Firewall" configuration page (NFuse Admin Web Pages I Server-Side Firewall), the first section titled "Default address translation setting" allows you to specify what type of address is provided to NFuse clients for the MetaFrame XP servers. There are four options:

- Normal Address.
- Alternate Address.
- Citrix Secure Gateway.
- Translated Address.

The Normal Address setting causes the NFuse server to send the client the actual address of the MetaFrame XP server. As detailed in Chapter 11, the exact format of that address (IP address or fully qualified domain name) and whether a TCP port is supplied is dictated by the "AddressResolution Type" entry in the NFuse.conf file.

The Alternate Address setting causes the NFuse server to send the client the alternate address of the MetaFrame XP server as configured on each server via the altaddr command.

The Citrix Secure Gateway setting causes the NFuse server to send the client the address of the Citrix Secure Gateway server instead of the MetaFrame XP server's address. In order for this option to work, NFuse must be configured for use with CSG as previously detailed in this chapter.

The Translated Address option uses a network address mapping table to map specific external IP addresses or server names to specific internal IP addresses or server names. This table is maintained by NFuse. Conceptually, this mapping is identical to the "alternate" address mapping, except that translated addresses are managed centrally on the NFuse web server whereas alternate addresses are manually configured at each server. If you plan on using NFuse for outside clients exclusively, you will not need to use the altaddr command. (If you plan to use CSG and NAT together you'll still have to use the altaddr command.)

In order for the translated address option to function, Enter at least one pair of translated addresses. (This is done further down the "Server-Side Firewall" NFuse admin web page via the "MetaFrame server address translation map" section.) To use this map, simply specify the actual MetaFrame XP server address and port and the associated translated (or external) address and port. These addresses must be fully qualified domain names or IP addresses, again depending on the "AddressResolutionType" entry in the NFuse.conf file.

For example, if you flip back to the altaddr diagram in Figure 15.17, you would add a translation entry of 10.1.1.1:1494 for the server address and port and 128.242.82.212:1494 for the translated address and port. You can add as many entries as you want, which is a good thing since you'll need one for each MetaFrame XP server that is accessible from the outside if your firewall is using NAT.

### Applying Conditional Address Translation based on Client Address

Now that you've configured your default address types and your translation maps, you can set specific rules that will override these default settings based on the actual IP address of each client.

Take one last look at Figure 15.17. If NFuse Classic was used in that environment, you would have specified a "translated address mapping" that mapped 10.1.1.1 to 128.242.82.212. Then, you would also have configured NFuse's default address setting to use the "translated" address. However, internal users would need the server's actual IP address, not the translated address. Therefore, you would configure the "Specific address translation settings" section of NFuse so that the client address prefix of your users ("10." in this case) would use the normal address.

When you configure "specific address translation settings," the NFuse server searches through its list of IP address prefixes every time a client user connects. If that user's IP address prefix is on the list, NFuse sends the client the address of the MetaFrame XP server in the format that is configured for that prefix. Otherwise, it sends the address to the MetaFrame XP server in the format specified by the default address translation setting.

You can configure client address prefixes for the level of detail you require. For example, you could specify "10." or "10.1.2." for whatever you need in your situation. The important thing is that client IP addresses are matched to this list based on identical patterns in the client address and the address on the list. Therefore, you cannot specify addresses based on subnet masks or wildcards.

### *Advantages of NFuse Classic's Specific Address Translation*

- Very easy to apply
- Works well
- Can also translate ports

*Disadvantages of NFuse Classic's Specific Address Translation*
- Wildcards cannot be used in addresses.
- Client address searching is only based on pattern matches, not IP subnets.

# Client Device Security

Client devices often pose one of the biggest security risks because they are inherently the least secure. This stems from the fact that clients are scattered throughout the world and are generally unprotected. Poorly configured client devices are much more susceptible to a security breach then a network connection any day.

The main thing that people worry about concerning client devices are the "leave behinds." These are the remnants of a MetaFrame XP ICA session that can be left on a client device after a user is done using it, potentially allowing other users to access the same MetaFrame XP ICA sessions with the permissions of the first user.

Another security risk associated with client devices is that often users are able to change the settings of their clients. While this doesn't usually allow them to access things that they normally wouldn't be able to, it does increase the risk that they could change a setting and lessen the security of their client device.

## Saving User Credentials on ICA Client Devices

It is possible for ICA clients to be configured to save the user's credentials so that a user does not have to type in his username and password each time his ICA client is launched. When a user saves his user credentials, the credentials are encrypted and written to an INI file (`appsrv.ini` for custom connections and `pn.ini` for application sets) on the client computer.

While it is generally not possible to decrypt the credentials stored in these files, it is possible that the files could be used by another user to gain the access rights of the first user. These INI files are stored in each user's profile. If a non-secure operating system is used, like Windows 98, any user could copy the files from one user's profile into his own. They could then connect to MetaFrame XP servers as the original user. Even worse, an advanced attacker could use the credentials saved in the INI configuration files to create ICA sessions to other MetaFrame XP servers.

### Saving User Credential Security Risks

- User credentials could be compromised.

If security is a top priority in your environment, you should not allow your users to save the credentials for their ICA client applications.

# Using Local ICA Files to Connect to ICA Applications

ICA files are a convenient way to allow users to access MetaFrame XP servers and published applications—especially when those users are connecting from different computer networks in many locations. Often it is easy for an administrator to send a remote user an ICA file, encouraging them to "just double-click the file" to launch their ICA session.

Because many of these remote users are often in different domains than the MetaFrame XP servers, it is tempting to embed the logon credentials into the ICA file to prevent the user from having to enter a second set of credentials to launch the ICA application.

As with all aspects of computing, ease-of-use is inversely proportional to security. In this case, you need to carefully evaluate the security risk of passing out ICA files with embedded logon credentials. Remember that once ICA file is given to an end user, it could end up anywhere. Because the file will automatically launch an ICA session, end users tend to pass these files to each other. This can enable other users to get access to inappropriate applications.

Since ICA files are easy to edit and understand, it is easy to modify an ICA file to point to another server or application and to use the embedded user credentials to log onto that server or application.

### Local ICA File Security Risks

- Not secure.
- End users can pass the files to friends.
- Files can be modified to use the embedded credentials to connect to other applications or servers.

If you want to create the most secure environment possible, you should not pass out preconfigured ICA files to anyone. Ever.

## Pass-Through Authentication

Pass-through authentication allows users with Windows clients to start Program Neighborhood without having to retype their usernames or passwords. When pass-through authentication is enabled, the Citrix ICA client software is able to extract their user credentials from the local workstation.

While pass-through authentication seems convenient, there are several issues that must be considered. The main security risk is derived from the manner in which pass through authentication works. At logon time, a process called ssonsrv.exe is started with three command-line parameters: username, domain, and password. These parameters are not encrypted, and any shareware debugger program can be used to view them.

The second issue with pass-through authentication has to do with the method by which it determines the current logged on user. The pass-through authentication engine looks at the last logged on user when Program Neighborhood is started. The problem with this is that some interactive services confuse the pass-through authentication service. For example, if SMS is installed, the SMS client service can sometimes start (and log on) after the user logs on. When this happens, the Citrix pass-through authentication engine will use the SMS account instead of the user account to log in to Program Neighborhood. In some cases the SMS account has more rights than the user, allowing users to launch inappropriate ICA sessions as that account.

### Pass Through Authentication Security Risks

- User credentials can be exposed.
- Doesn't always work.

Even if you disable pass-through authentication on a client, there is a chance that the user could re-enable it. To prevent this, you should either install the "gray version" of Program Neighborhood (described next), or delete the files that pass-through authentication uses. These files are ssoncom.exe, ssonstub.dll, and ssonsvr.exe. They are located in the ICA client installation directory.

## Preventing Users from Changing Their Client Settings

One of the big security problems with ICA clients is that users can change the settings of their client software. For example, even if it is your policy not to save passwords, users can access the options menu and change that option. In fact, just about everything in your ICA client can be changed or modified by the end user. Fortunately, there are a few tricks that MetaFrame administrators have learned over the years that will prevent users from breaking their ICA clients. These can be broken into two options/

## Option 1. Do Not Use a Full Program Neighborhood ICA Client

The easiest way to prevent users from changing client settings is to use an ICA client that does not have a local Program Neighborhood interface. This would include the web clients that are used with NFuse or the Program Neighborhood Agent. With both of these clients, the configuration information is maintained and controlled on the NFuse web server, where local users cannot access it or change it. See Chapter 11 for the full details of these two clients.

### Advantages of Not Using the Full Program Neighborhood

- You can enforce client settings with no loopholes.

- NFuse is becoming the de facto standard for accessing MetaFrame environments.

### Disadvantages of Not Using the Full Program Neighborhood

- An NFuse server is required.

- Program Neighborhood Agent requires Feature Release 1 and Windows 32-bit clients.

## Option 2. Use the "Gray Version" of Program Neighborhood

Another easy way to prevent users from being able to change ICA client settings is to remove their ability to set anything via the menus of Program Neighborhood. If configuration menu items are "grayed out," the users will not be able to change anything. In order to do this, you can download a "gray version" of Program Neighborhood. This gray version has all of the configuration menu items disabled.

The gray version of Program Neighborhood is available from Jim Kenzig who edits the regular pn.exe file and disables certain menu items. He posts the gray version http://thethin.net. With the download, you simply get one file: pn.exe. To use it, replace the client's original pn.exe with the newly-downloaded version. There is a different gray version pn.exe for each ICA client version.

Of course, once you copy over the original pn.exe with the gray version, you will not be able to make any configuration changes on that client via Program Neighborhood. If you need to make changes after you install the gray version, you can either edit the INI files directly or temporarily use the original pn.exe. (You should probably name the original executable something like goodpn.exe so it's there if you ever need to make a change.) See Chapter 10 for the details of ICA client configuration.

The gray version of Program Neighborhood is not *technically* supported by Citrix, but they don't seem to mind it. It's kind of a "don't ask, don't tell" thing. In the real world, probably 75% of companies that use the full Program Neighborhood client replace the default pn.exe with the gray version.

One thing that's important to keep in mind when using the gray version of Program Neighborhood is that users can still change their settings if they edit the INI files directly. The gray version of Program Neighborhood simply removes the GUI interface (and the easy way) for changing client settings.

### Advantages of Using the Gray Version of Program Neighborhood

- Easy to use.
- No additional cost.
- Works with any version of MetaFrame.

### Disadvantages of Using the Gray Version of Program Neighborhood

- Users can get around it by editing INI files.
- Users can get around it by downloading a new ICA client.
- Not "technically" supported by Citrix.

## Client Web Browser Security

Today, most MetaFrame XP environments are accessed through NFuse web portals which means that the client devices connect via a web browser. In order to secure the client devices in these situations, you need to look at ways to secure the local client web browser. There are means by which this can be accomplished:

- Understand browser cookies.
- Use NFuse ticketing.
- Remove credentials from ICA files.
- Prevent browsers from caching ICA files.
- Permit users to only connect from certain IP addresses.
- Control the amount of access that remote MetaFrame XP applications have to local client drives through web browsers.

## Understanding Browser Cookies

Client-side browser cookies might seem like an easy way to remember a user's credentials from page to page within NFuse-based websites that you create, but be aware that cookies are generally not secure. There are two areas of concern with browser cookies.

The first concern is a factor if an NFuse website stores permanent cookies on the client device. Many websites use these types of cookies to automatically log users in when they connect to a site. If these cookies are used in an NFuse environment, it's possible that anyone who accesses the website will be automatically logged in with the stored cookie information. By default, NFuse does not do this. If you change the NFuse web pages to allow this, you need to be aware of the security risks that it introduces.

The other concern with cookies is the data (user credentials) stored within the cookies. Because it's possible that someone could read the values of the stored cookies, usernames and passwords could be compromised. Again, this is not a risk with the default NFuse pages, but if you create your own NFuse web pages it's best to maintain user information from page to page without using client-side cookies, such as using web server session variables.

The default web pages that come with NFuse 1.7 do use client cookies to hold user credentials during their visit to the web site. Fortunately, those default pages use a 512-bit session key to encrypt the visitor's password. That password encryption process is very interesting and worth studying. Here's how it works:

*Figure 15.19  NFuse encrypted cookie creation*

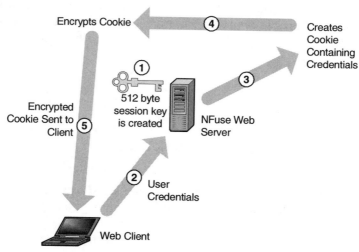

1. When the web browser session is started with the web server, the web server creates a random 512-character session key which is stored as a session object on the web server.

2. The client sends user credentials to the web server.

3. The web server creates a cookie with the user credentials.

4. The web server encrypts the cookie with session key.

5. The web server sends the encrypted cookie to the client.

After the encrypted cookie is stored on the client, the following process takes place when the client retrieves an application list or launches an application.

*Figure 15.20  Web clients use of the encrypted cookie*

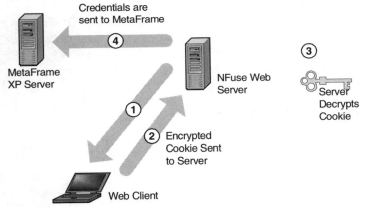

1. The web server requests user credentials.

2. The client browser sends the encrypted cookie to the web server.

3. The web server executes code to decrypt the cookie, retrieving the user credentials.

4. The web server sends the credentials to the MetaFrame XP server.

It's important to note that the default NFuse web site that uses cookie data encryption does *not* replace the need for SSL encryption between the web server and the client web browser. As you can clearly see, the user credentials are sent across the network in clear text before the encrypted cookie is created. This cookie encryption is designed to prevent people on the client device from reading the credentials. It does not offer network protection.

## Using NFuse Ticketing

NFuse ticketing was covered in depth earlier in this chapter as it related to Citrix Secure Gateway. Standalone NFuse 1.7 Classic websites also make use of NFuse ticketing. By default, ticketing is enabled in NFuse environments. NFuse ticketing is configured at the NFuse server in the same way that most NFuse system components are configured—the NFuse.conf INI file. The following line dictates the expiration time of the NFuse ticket, in seconds:

```
SessionField.NFuse_TicketTimeToLive=200
```

Also, the template.ica file must contain the following two lines:

```
AutologonAllowed=ON
[NFuse_Ticket]
```

The AutologonAllowed line allows the MetaFrame XP server to receive user credentials from the ICA file. The NFuse_Ticket substitution tag is the segment of the template ICA file that the NFuse server replaces with the actual 30-character ticket when the template.ica file is parsed for an end user.

### Advantages of NFuse Ticketing

- Very cool.
- Protects ICA files from users' friends.
- Tickets are only valid once.
- Tickets expire after a configurable amount of time.
- Clear text user credentials are not placed in the ICA files.
- Clear text user credentials are not passed across the network when ICA sessions are launched.

### Disadvantages of NFuse Ticketing

- Unencrypted data is still sent over the network once.
- Ticketing does *not* replace the need for SSL encryption from browser to web server.

## Removing User Credentials from ICA Files

If you cannot use ticketing (perhaps with MetaFrame for UNIX) or if you need extra security, you can remove user credentials from NFuse-generated ICA files altogether by deleting the AutologonAllowed=ON and [NFuse_Ticket] entries in the template.ica file. Of course, if you choose to do so, your users will need to manually log into each ICA session in addition to logging into the NFuse web page. This loss of convenience is the price you pay for higher security.

## Preventing Browsers from Caching ICA Files

As an additional security precaution, you can write your web pages so that they do not allow web clients to cache the ICA files. Again, this is a feature of the web scripting languages, not NFuse itself. In order to do this, add the code to the web page that actually creates the ICA file (`launch.asp` or `launch.jsp`).

For example, if you are using active server pages, you should add the following two lines of code after the `Response.ContentType="application-x/ica"` line.

```
Response.CacheControl="no-cache"
Response.AddHeader "Pragma","no-cache"
```

Adding these lines will create dynamic ICA files containing instructions for the local browser not to cache the file.

There is one other cache–related security item that you should be aware of. Whenever a user connects to an ICA session through an NFuse web page, a temporary file will be written to that user's hard drive. This file will be named `ica*.tmp`. Whenever your session is closed, that file will be deleted. However, if the ICA session is not terminated properly, that file night not be deleted. If this happens, the file could be read, exposing the logged on user's username and the IP address of the MetaFrame XP server. In actuality this security risk is not that significant, but it is a risk nonetheless.

## Permitting Users to Only Connect from Certain Client Devices

As an added security measure, you can configure your MetaFrame XP servers or your NFuse web servers so that they only accept incoming connections from certain IP addresses.

For MetaFrame XP servers, this is accomplished by configuring a Load Evaluator to be available with MetaFrame XPa or XPe. Specific load evaluators can be configured that only allow users to connect to published applications if the client's IP address falls within a specified range. From a security standpoint, this can be useful in mandating that users connect to applications from certain machines or certain sites. For example, this load evaluator can be useful if you want to allow users to log on from their homes, but you also have some sensitive applications that you want them to only be able to run from the office. By using the IP address–based Load Evaluator, you can still publish all the applications to the users and have the Load Evaluator check to make sure that they are connecting from a valid IP address. More detail on this configuration is available in Chapter 4.

Additionally, you can configure your web server to only allow connections from certain IP address or to deny connections from certain IP addresses. Because this security is configured at your web server-level, you can stop unauthorized users before they ever see an NFuse login page.

### Controlling Local Drive Access through Web Browsers

Since the ICA protocol allows MetaFrame XP remote applications to access local hard drives through the web, many of people became concerned that this was a security hole, because users were taught that the websites could not directly access, change, or delete their local files. While this is technically not true (because the web browser actually launches the local ICA client software, as discussed in Chapters 10 and 11), Citrix decided to modify the behavior of the ICA client when it is used to access MetaFrame XP applications through web sites.

With the current version of the ICA client, each user can specify the amount of access he wants a remote MetaFrame XP application to have to his local hard drive. This is done through a pop-up box that appears the first time the user accesses an ICA session launched via their web browser. This box allows him to choose "No Access," "Read Access," or "Full Access" to the local hard drives for the application. Additionally, the user can select to "Always ask me once per connection," "Never ask me again for this application," or "Never ask me again for any application."

The choices that the user enters into this security dialog box are saved locally on his client device in a file called "webica.ini." This file is stored in the Windows directory. Let's take a look at a sample webica.ini file now.

*Figure 15.21 A Sample webica.ini file*
```
[Access]
CurrentConnection=MS WORD10.1.1.2
GlobalSecurityAccess=-1
MS WORD10.1.1.2=405
128.242.82.212=-1
```

The CurrentConnection= line always lists the last server connection that was made. This list includes the published application name (MS WORD in this case) and the IP address of the MetaFrame XP server where the application was executed (10.1.1.2 in this case).

For the remaining lines in the `webica.ini` file, there are four different values that can be configured.

*Figure 15.22 Security values for webica.ini files*

| Value | Meaning |
|---|---|
| -1 | The security setting has not been configured. |
| 403 | No access. |
| 404 | Read access. |
| 405 | Full access. |

The `GlobalSecurityAccess` line controls the behavior of the popup security window for all web sites. By default, this value is not set (-1) and the popup windows always appears. However, if the user selects the "Never ask me again for any application" button, then the `GlobalSecurityAccess` line changes to the value that corresponds to the user's selection. For example, if the user chooses to give the remote ICA applications read only access to local drives, the line would read `GlobalSecurityAccess=404`. When this value is set, the rest of the `webica.ini` file is ignored and the `GlobalSecurityAccess` setting is used for all applications and all servers.

Further down in the file, the line MS `WORD10.1.1.2=405` contains the user's preference for the MS WORD published application on the MetaFrame XP server with the IP address of 10.1.1.2. If MS WORD is load balanced between multiple servers, load balancing will randomly pick a server for a user, causing the user to sometimes get the popup window (when they are routed to 10.1.1.2) and sometimes not get the popup window (when they are routed to a server other than 10.1.1.2). To get around this, you could manually add lines for the other MetaFrame XP servers that are running the MS WORD published application, which might be something like MS `WORD10.1.1.3=405` and MS `WORD10.1.1.4=405`. Otherwise, the user will need to specify the connection security preferences manually.

## Navigating Client-Side Proxy Servers

32-bit Windows ICA clients can automatically configure their proxy settings based on the settings in Internet Explorer 4.0 or Netscape Navigator 4.76 or newer. This prevents you from having to manually configure the proxy server on your client devices.

If you're using NFuse 1.7, you can use NFuse to send proxy server settings to the client that will override the automatic configuration (NFuse Admin Web Pages I Client-Side Firewall). These settings work in the same way as the network address translation maps. You can apply default settings that will apply to all clients or specific settings that will only apply to clients whose IP addresses match a defined prefix.

Any client-side proxy settings that you configure via NFuse are added into the ICA file that NFuse dynamically creates and passed down to the client device at application launch.

# User Account Security

The last layer of security that we need to look at is the security and configuration of the user accounts themselves. When addressing security from a user perspective, there are three different items that must be addressed:

- The user account configuration.
- Secure user authentication
- The domain configuration and trust relationships.

## User Account Configuration

You can configure several security options at the user layer. The advantage to configuring security at this layer is that the settings follow the user no matter where he logs on. In both Windows NT 4.0 and Windows 2000, there are several user properties that affect the security of your MetaFrame XP environment. These user-layer security configuration options can be broken down into three broad categories:

- Options that are configured as part of the user's domain account.
- Options that are configured per user or group as part of a server's local security rights.
- Options that are configured as part of a policy.

### User Domain Account Configuration

The security options that are configured as part of a user's account properties are literally properties of the user account itself. In Windows NT 4.0, these properties are configured via user manager for domains and the configured options become part of a user's account in the SAM. In Windows 2000, they are configured as part of a user's Active Directory account properties and the options become part of that user's Active Directory user object.

There are only a few user account properties specific to MetaFrame XP (or any Terminal Services) environments. First, each domain user that will use any MetaFrame XP server must have the "Allow logon to Terminal Services" box checked in their account properties. If you have particular users that you do not want to use any MetaFrame XP servers, you can uncheck this box. Unchecking this box affects the user for both RDP and ICA connections.

Each user's account also has properties similar to those that you can config-ure at the connection layer. These properties include the timeouts for ending disconnected sessions, active and idle session limits, and whether the user can reconnect to disconnected sessions from any client or only the original client. These settings apply to the user whether they connect via RDP or ICA.

Not immediately obvious is how the "run program on startup" options work within a user's account properties. This option is similar to the initial program option that you can specify at the connection layer because when the user exits from the program, their Terminal Services session is ended. However, be aware that any initial program that you specify in a user's domain account property only affects him when he logs onto Terminal Services with the RDP protocol. MetaFrame XP ICA connections are unaffected.

### *Server Local Security Rights*

Each server can have a local policy in place that affects users' local security rights. The way you configure these local user rights depends on the platform on which your MetaFrame XP servers are running. In Windows NT 4.0, user rights are configured via user manager on the target server (user manager | policies menu | user rights). In Windows 2000, local user rights are set via the local security policy of a server (administrative tools | local security settings | security settings | user rights assignments). On both platforms, you can con-figure local or domain users or groups with various user rights. While many of these user rights are not relevant to the security of MetaFrame XP environ-ments, there are several that are. Some of the security-related rights include a user's ability to shut down the computer, change the system time, manage the auditing and security log, and take ownership of files.

One of these security rights that is particularly useful in MetaFrame XP envi-ronments is the "log on locally" right (log on interactively in Windows NT 4.0). In order for a user to be able to use a MetaFrame XP server, he must have the rights to log on locally to the server. In the real world, you might have 10 or 12 servers for 2 or 3 different departments. You can create a global group for each department, called "Dept A Citrix Users." Then, on the Meta-Frame XP servers that serve applications to Department A, you can remove the "log on locally" right from "Domain Users" and grant it to "Dept A Citrix Users." Configuring the local security rights of the server gives you an extra level of protection beyond your published application and NTFS security. If you do this, remember also to grant "log on locally rights" to the group that contains the MetaFrame XP administrators.

In addition to the "log on locally" security right, you'll notice there is a "deny log on locally" security right. You might be confused as to why there are two of these and how they should be used. Normally, if you have users that you do not want to use Terminal Services, you can just choose not to give them the "log on locally" security right. That way, if the user is a member of multiple groups, they can get the "log on locally" security rights from any one of their group memberships. However, if you have specific users or groups that you definitely do not want to use the MetaFrame XP server no matter what, then you can add them to the "deny log on locally list." This security right will always take precedence if a user is on the list for both "log on locally" and "deny log on locally." You need to use the "deny log on locally" carefully because it is possible that one user might be a member of multiple groups and each group could have conflicting rights.

### User Policies

All of the local security rights from the previous section can be deployed across multiple servers as part of a domain policy (NT 4) or group policy (Windows 2000). They are tied to specific user accounts only when those user accounts are added to the system policy or to an organizational unit where the group policy is applied. For detailed information regarding the use of policies in a MetaFrame XP environment, refer to Chapter 7. In all cases, domain policy or group policy settings will take precedence over the config-ured local security rights.

## Secure User Authentication

One way that many organizations are securing their user environments is by implementing secure user authentication mechanisms. There are two meth-ods that work well in MetaFrame XP environments:

- Smart cards.
- RSA SecurID hardware tokens.

## Smart Cards

In environments in which positive user identification is important, smart card technology if often used to authenticate users.

In MetaFrame XP environments, smart card readers can be attached directly to ICA client devices. In order for a user to logon to run their ICA applications, they insert their smart card into the card reader. Their smart card contains a digital certificate which is transmitted to the MetaFrame XP server. The server (which has its own X.509 digital certificate) checks the user's certificate from the smart card to verify that it matches the certificate on file. If so, the user is authenticated and their MetaFrame session is launched.

For added security, policy options are usually configured on the MetaFrame XP servers that dictate the action taken when the smart card is removed from the reader. Many companies configure their environments so that a user's session is immediately disconnected if their smart card is removed from the card reader attached to the client device.

Using smart cards in MetaFrame XP environments is no more difficult than using them in standard Windows 2000 environments. Getting your existing Windows servers, clients, and Active Directory configured for smart cards represents the bulk of your work. Extending MetaFrame XP to work with smart cards is the easy part.

This section is not intended to teach you everything there is to know about using smart cards in Windows. That would require an additional 800 pages. The purpose of rather is to provide information about how existing smart card implementations can be extended with MetaFrame XP. For more information about smart card usage in Windows 2000 environments, check out Microsoft article Q313274. This article describes the process to configure a Windows 2000 certificate authority to issue smart card certificates. It also contains links to other Microsoft articles that step through the process of getting a background smart card environment set up.

To secure your MetaFrame XP environments with smart cards, you need to use Feature Release 2. Also, your client devices must use the 32-bit Windows or Java ICA client, version 6.30 or newer.

Windows 2000 and Windows XP are the only Microsoft operating systems that directly support smart cards. However, so long as your MetaFrame XP server is running Windows 2000, you can use smart cards from any 32-bit Windows client, including Windows 9x.

This is possible because the ICA protocol has been extended with Feature Release 2 and version 6.30 clients. A smart card channel has been added that passes smart card information from client devices to the MetaFrame XP server.

Therefore, if your clients are using Windows 9x, a locally attached smart card reader cannot prevent a user from logging on locally to the client desktop. However, they can be prevented from logging on to MetaFrame XP without proper smart card authentication.

If your ICA clients are running Windows 2000 or Windows XP, the smart card software and drivers can be installed locally on them to enforce local logons. In this situation, the smart card reader would be used for local logon and remote MetaFrame XP logon.

### Advantages of using Smart Cards

- Ultimate security.
- Easy for users to use and understand.

### Disadvantages of using Smart Cards

- Requires Feature Release 2.
- Requires the Citrix ICA Win32 or Java client.
- Requires substantial smart card infrastructure (cards, readers, certificates, etc.).

Before you begin using smartcards in your MetaFrame XP environment, you should have them working in your existing environment. This means that you should have individual cards with user's certificates and PINs on them. Your backend directory (such as AD) should be ready to go. Your certificate authorities and digital certificates should be all set up. Once all this is in place, smart card usage with MetaFrame XP is very straightforward.

## RSA SecurID Hardware Tokens

If you use RSA SecurID hardware tokens in your environment for two-factor authentication, you can easily extend their use to NFuse 1.7 Classic environments. Out of the box, your users must access a web page to authenticate with their token (against an RSA "ACE" server). Then, users must access a second web page where they enter their credentials to authenticate to NFuse.

However, you can use "Project Willamette" to consolidate these authentication pages so that your users' standard NFuse login page asks for their username, password, and SecurID token passcode. Project William is written by some very smart people from a company called ISC (www.iscnet.

co.uk). You can download Project Willamette for free from www.tweakcitrix.com/sections/wilakenz.htm. In order to use Project Willamette with NFuse 1.7, download Project Willamette version 2.0 or newer.

Project Willamette only has a few requirements:

- Your NFuse web server must be running on a Microsoft Windows 2000 Server with Service Pack 2 or newer.
- You must be using IIS as your web server.
- You must have an X.509 digital certificate for your NFuse web server.
- The RSA ACE Agent for Windows v5.0x or newer must be installed on your NFuse web server.
- You need to use Citrix Secure Gateway with a Secure Ticket Authority.
- Your users' SecurID usernames (their "ACE" accounts) need to match the usernames of their domain accounts.

Using Project Willamette is simple. It basically includes modified NFuse web pages, and all you have to do to use it is to copy a few files from Project Willamette over the original files on your NFuse web server.

### Advantages of Project Willamette
- Easy to install and configure.
- Simplifies and clarifies the user login process.
- It's free (thanks to Chris Walsh and Martin Hodgson).

### Disadvantages of Project Willamette
- It's not "officially" supported by anyone (although plenty of help is available at www.tweakcitrix.com and http://thethin.net.)

## Domain Configuration

MetaFrame XP server farms are extremely flexible. This flexibility allows one server farm to span multiple domains or forests. However, just because a server farm can technically span multiple domains or forests, extreme caution must be exercised with this option. There can be conflicts with user credentials and permissions. Consider the following scenario.

The Burning Troll Lumber Company has two Windows 2000 domains, EAST and WEST. Each domain has a domain local group (DLG) for users: EAST-USERS and WEST-USERS. By definition, a DLG cannot contain members of other domains. (Hence the "L" in "DLG.")

*Figure 15.23  Burning Troll Lumber's Windows 2000 domains*

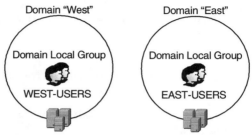

The Burning Troll Lumber Company has one MetaFrame XP server farm for their entire enterprise with servers in both the EAST and the WEST domains. They have one published application, "LumberTracker," which they load-balanced on all MetaFrame XP servers. They want to publish the application explicitly to both the EAST-USERS and WEST-USERS groups.

As you may have figured out, this configuration will cause a problem. Consider how load-balanced published applications work. A user requests the application—LumberTracker in this case. The MetaFrame XP back-end determines which server is least busy and returns that server address to the user. For the Burning Troll Lumber Company, this could cause a technical short-circuit. What if a user from the west is given the address for a server in the east? Because the WEST-USERS group is a domain local group, the east servers do not recognize it. The server would not allow the user to start a session.

The Burning Troll Lumber Scenario could never happen in the real world. There are two ways that MetaFrame XP automatically addresses this situation to prevent it from occurring:

- *Trust Intersections*. MetaFrame XP does not allow the permissions of the published applications to be set unless all target users and groups can access the application on all servers where it is published.
- *Trust–Based Routing*. MetaFrame XP will dynamically route authentication to a server on which the user has permissions.

## Trust Intersections

When setting the permissions of an explicit application via the CMC, Meta-Frame XP only shows users and groups that have permission to access the application on all the servers where the published application is configured. If you try to be crafty by setting the permissions first and then going back and adding servers where those permissions would not be valid, MetaFrame XP produces an error message and automatically removes the users or groups that cannot access the application on every server where it is published.

## Trust-Based Routing

Even though you cannot configure applications to be published to users that don't have rights on all the servers where the application is published, it's still possible that a user could do something that would require him to be authenticated by a server where he doesn't have rights. If this happens, the user's authentication is transparently passed on to another farm server where the user does have access. This is known as "trust-based routing." It's possible because MetaFrame XP keeps track of Windows domain trust relationships via the IMA data store. The domains and associated trust relationships of all farm servers are updated during a trust query cycle. A trust query cycle occurs when the IMA service starts and every six hours thereafter.

Trust based routing can occur in the following situations:

- A user refreshes the application list or launches a published application.
- An administrator launches the CMC.
- Anytime accounts are listed in the CMC, including adding users or groups to applications, printer auto-creation, and adding farm administrators.

Looking back to the lumber example, if a farm administrator from the WEST domain tried to use the CMC to connect to a server in the EAST domain, the server from the east would route the authentication to a server in the WEST. This routing would be necessary because the server in the east would recognize that the administrator has farm administrator rights, but would not be able to authenticate the user because the user account is in a different domain.

## How to Mitigate Domain Trust Issues

If you decide that trust intersections and trust based routing is too risky or confusing, you can follow these guidelines to avoid having MetaFrame XP invoke its trust voodoo. Think of these as the three golden rules of server farm design if you don't want to troubleshoot weird trust problems:

- Do not publish applications across servers in different domains to domain local groups.

- Do not publish applications across servers in different forests to domain local groups.

- Do not publish applications across servers in different non-trusted domains in Windows NT 4.

To summarize, you should really make sure that all of your farm administrators have administrative rights on all your MetaFrame XP servers and that all of your users have rights on any servers that they would ever access. Remember that MetaFrame XP server farms operate totally independently of domain boundaries, so using some sense when you design your farms will save you from headaches down the road. The simplest way to avoid all this is to not create server farms that include servers from multiple non-trusted domains.

# Secure System Administration Environments

The last thing that we need to look at when considering MetaFrame XP security is how your MetaFrame XP servers will be administered. This is often overlooked, but very important. Even the world's most technically secure environments won't actually be secure if too many people have administrative rights.

Another big part of the administration of your MetaFrame XP servers relates to how the servers are actually used. This includes how administrators or help desk personnel shadow end users and how everyone's actions are logged, recorded, and audited.

As we look at the security of the MetaFrame XP administrative environment, we'll focus on three areas:

- MetaFrame XP administrators.
- Shadowing end users.
- Auditing and usage logs.

## MetaFrame XP Administrators

You can configure your server farm administrators using the Citrix Management Console (CMC | Farm | Citrix Administrators). Farm administrators can be added by group or by user. In environments with Feature Release 1 and lower, there are two levels of farm administrator: "Read-Only" and "Read-Write." In Feature Release 2 environments, you can also configure custom levels of farm administration.

When granting accounts different levels of administrative access, there are two things to consider:

1. Administrative rights apply to the IMA Data Store only.
2. Administrative rights can only be assigned on a farm-wide basis.

When you assign MetaFrame XP administrator rights to the server farm, you are actually assigning rights to the IMA data store itself. Assigning administrator rights in the CMC does *not* change any NTFS file rights anywhere and it does *not* add the user to any Windows domain groups. It is not necessary for a user to have domain administrator or server administrator rights for him to be granted farm administrator rights—although these rights are usually granted for convenience.

Assigning Read-Only farm administrator rights allows the assigned user to read any information about any server from the IMA data store, and the Read-Write privilege allows users to add, delete, change, and reconfigure the information on MetaFrame XP farm servers that is contained in the IMA data store.

You can use the custom rights in Feature Release 2 environments to customize the specific administrative rights that a user has. When you configure custom rights, you have extremely granular control over the *type* of rights that an administrator has. You do not have control over the *where* those rights are applied.

For example, you can use custom administrator rights to grant a user the ability to edit load evaluators without giving him the ability do anything else in the farm. However, since all farm administrative settings apply on a farm-wide basis, that administrator would be able to edit load evaluators on any server in the farm. There is no way to allow users to administer certain servers while preventing them from administering others. Think of these rights as "options-based," not "server-based."

In fact, all administrative rights assigned through the CMC always apply on a farm-wide basis. If you have some administrators that you only want to administer certain farm servers, you need to break the server farm into multiple farms, or trust the administrators not to touch the wrong servers.

Some crafty people have thought that they could find a way around this "all or nothing" limitation, by creating one single server farm with granular administration by setting local rights on MetaFrame XP servers. They created three servers in one farm. Each server had its own administrator, and each administrator only had administrative level access on his own server—with no rights on the other servers. All three administrators were configured with server farm Read-Write administrator privileges.

The problem with this scenario is that all of the administrators have full read-write administrative access to the IMA data store. Administrator "A" cannot access Administrator "B's" server directly through the network, but Administrator "A" can launch the CMC and delete users, applications, and configuration information for Administrator "B's" server. This is because this server farm information does not reside on the local server, but rather in the IMA data store, where Administrator "A" is a full Read-Write administrator.

### Help Desk Security Rights

One of the nice things about the ability to set custom administrative rights in your server farm with Feature Release 2 is that it allows you to give your help desk analysts the power to do their jobs without giving them full farm administration rights.

Most people create a Windows domain group called "Helpdesk" and give them the following custom rights in the server farm:

- Log on to Citrix Management Console
- View Printers and Printer Drivers
- View Published Applications and Content
- View Resource Management Configuration
- View Server Information
- Disconnect Users
- Log Off Users
- Reset Sessions
- Send Messages
- View Session Management
- View User Policies

## *MetaFrame Administration in Active Directory Environments*

Just as publishing applications to users in AD environments is no different than in non-AD environments, MetaFrame XP administration is the same in both environments. MetaFrame XP does not extend the Active Directory schema. The "limitation" of only having farm–wide administrators still holds true in the AD environment. The only change from an administration stand-point with in AD environment is that MetaFrame XP administrators can be assigned based on the AD–only groups. (Universal, etc.)

# Session Shadowing

MetaFrame XP shadowing allows administrators to remotely view a selected end user's ICA session. There are several security and privacy concerns raised when deciding how to use shadowing. These stem from the fact that a malicious user could shadow another user's session without them knowing it. They would be able to view potential sensitive or personal information.

To mitigate this security risk, you have the option of choosing not to enable any of the shadowing features or choosing to manage the shadowing environment so that only authorized users are able to shadow other users. Additionally, if you do enable shadowing, you can log all shadow requests for security purposes. Let's look at how these two options can be applied in the real world.

### *Choosing not to Enable Shadowing*

When you install MetaFrame XP, you have the option of choosing not to install the shadowing capabilities. If the security principles of your environment prevent you from using shadowing, this allows you to easily turn off shadowing for your environment.

### *Shadowing Rights*

You also have the ability to configure which users are able to shadow other users. These rights are configured at the connection layer via the Citrix Connection Configuration utility (CCC | Right-click connection | Permissions). The "Full Control" default rights give users shadowing rights over a connection. Alternately, you can select "Advanced..." ("Special Access" in NT 4) for access to granular rights, where you can assign shadowing permissions without assigning the "Full Control" rights.

If you are using Feature Release 2, you can also configure shadowing permissions as part of a Citrix user policy. (See Chapter 5 for more information.)

### Shadowee / Shadower Interaction

Even with permissions to shadow users, there are two shadowing parameters that can be configured, "Input" and "Notification." Each of these can be set to "ON" or "OFF." These can be configured as a property of a connection via the Citrix Connection Configuration (CCC | Edit Connection | Advanced Button) or as a property of the user's account via the user management tool for your platform. If you're using Feature Release 2, you can also specify the minimum settings for shadowing users with a Citrix user policy.

As always, if the user layer settings do not match the connection layer settings, the most restrictive setting applies ("ON" for "Notify" and "OFF" for "Input"). "Input" specifies whether a shadowed user's keyboard and mouse are enabled while being shadowed (ON), or if the user has no interaction and cannot control the session (OFF). "Notify" specifies whether a user is notified before they are shadowed (ON) or if the shadower is able to covertly begin a shadow session (OFF). This notification setting is the most sensitive, as a setting of "OFF" will essentially allow administrators to "spy" on end-users. Before setting this to "OFF" be sure to check your company's privacy policy and local laws.

### Shadow Session Logging

The MetaFrame XP shadow taskbar can be configured to log all shadow events (Right click on Shadow taskbar | Logging Options... | Enable logging). The logs that are produced are by default not secure—making them not very useful. Most people want to log shadowing so that they can watch potentially mischievous employees who might want to spy on other users.

Fortunately, in MetaFrame XP, there is a special DLL (shdwhook.dll) that is responsible for logging shadowed sessions. This DLL watches all applications that could be used for shadowing (cshadow.exe, mfadmin.exe, shadow.exe, and tsadmin.exe) and logs the sessions to the event viewer.

# MetaFrame XP User Auditing

Often times MetaFrame XP administrators want to be able to create log files that they can use to audit specific MetaFrame XP user events, such as user session logons and logoffs. There are three ways that audit logs can be created:

- MetaFrame XPa or XPe load manager.
- Windows user account auditing.
- Third party auditing and logging tools.

## Logging Users with MetaFrame XPa or XPe Load Manager

When thinking of ways that user actions can be logged, most people immediately think of the logging that is available with MetaFrame XP load manager in MetaFrame XPa and XPe. This logging, which is enabled via the Citrix Management Console (CMC | Load Evaluators | Log Tab | Enable Logging Button), will show ICA user requests and resolutions of those requests.

The MetaFrame XP load manager log is secure (except for farm administrators with Read-Write privileges) and it works well for what it was intended for. The problem is that this log was intended for load balancing troubleshooting purposes. It has a small size limitation. After it reaches 16k it stops logging events until it is manually cleared and reset.

The load manager log should not be used for security purposes.

## Logging Users with Windows Auditing

For more industrial–strength user logging, it's best to think back to your Windows NT administration 101 class:

- In NT 4 environments, you can enable user auditing via user manager for domains (Security Menu | Auditing).

- In Windows 2000 environments, auditing can be configured via a group policy in Active Directory environments (Group Policy Object | Computer Configuration | Windows Settings | Security Settings | Local Policies | Audit Policy), or via the local computer policy when group policies are not used (Administrative Tools | Local Security Settings | Local Policies | Audit Policy). When Active Directory is used, most people configure the audit policies for the Group Policy Object that has the OU that contains their MetaFrame XP servers.

Once your servers are set to allow auditing, you can configure auditing for any item via the audit dialog box (Item Properties | Security Tab | Advanced Button | Audit Tab). There are many books dedicated to Windows 2000 security that can take you step by step through the various security and audit log elements of Windows 2000.

All of the user and computer auditing information is written to the security event log. There is a utility included on the MetaFrame XP CD, auditlog.exe, that can be used to dump the contents of the security event log to a CSV file. From there, you can import that file into a spreadsheet to generate audit reports.

## Logging Users with Third Party Tools

If you need heavy duty security auditing and logging in your MetaFrame XP environment, you will probably be disappointed with the native components that are available from Microsoft of Citrix. Most likely, you will want to use a third party security tool, such as Techtonik's ONEAPP utility. Details are available from www.oneapp.co.uk. New information about other third party tools is constantly available at http://thethin.net.

CHAPTER **16**

# MetaFrame XP Server Management and Maintenance

In this chapter

Managing Servers with the CMC     720

Server Farm Maintenance     724

Periodic Farm Maintenance Tasks     729

Citrix Resource Manager     731

Citrix Network Manager     744

Real World Case Study     748

Once your MetaFrame XP environment is designed and implemented, you will need to manage it on a day-to-day basis. In this chapter, we will focus on the tasks that you will have to perform in the management of your servers and the tools that you can leverage.

This chapter is laid out in the following order:

- Managing Servers with the Citrix Management Console.
- Procedures for routine server farm maintenance tasks.
- Important periodic farm maintenance tasks that should be proactively performed.
- Using Citrix Resource Manager to monitor your servers.
- Using Citrix Network Manager to monitor and administer your servers.

# Managing Servers with the CMC

By now, you have probably realized that the Citrix Management Console is the primary tool by which you will administer your MetaFrame XP servers. Because you will spend so much time managing with this tool, it is appropriate to consider best practices regarding its use.

## Choosing a CMC Connection Server

When launching the Citrix Management Console, you are asked to choose the MetaFrame XP server you would like to connect to. From a functionality standpoint, all servers within your server farm will provide access to the exact same data and configuration options. From a performance standpoint, you need to consider how the CMC works.

As you can see in Figure 16.1 (facing page), the Citrix Management Console gets its information from the Zone Data Collector for the zone of the server to which you connected your CMC. To save network bandwidth and increase CMC responsiveness, always connect your CMC to a Zone Data Collector, effectively eliminating one complete hop for your configuration information.

*Figure 16.1 How the CMC receives its data*

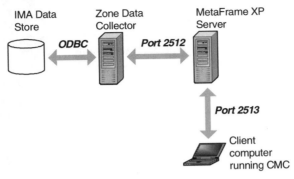

## Run the CMC Locally on a MetaFrame XP Server

For even greater performance gains, you should run the CMC locally on a MetaFrame XP server that is a zone data collector. You can then connect to the CMC via a standard ICA session. By doing this, all three CMC components outlined in Figure 16.1 (CMC, MetaFrame XP server, and Zone Data Collector) are located on one physical server.

Many companies that do this then choose to publish the CMC as an ICA application, allowing their administrators to access it no matter where they are. You can publish the CMC by publishing the command line "`java -jar tool.jar`" from the CMC directory, which is usually `\Program Files\Citrix\Administration\`.

## Configuring Data Refresh in the CMC

Every time you refresh the information presented in the CMC, the zone data collector is queried to resend the data that is on the screen of the CMC requesting the refresh. Such a refresh takes computing power and cycles away from the zone data collector.

While it is tempting to configure the CMC to automatically refresh its screen, this is not recommended. Usually you do not want to add the burden to your zone data collectors when you can very easily press the "F5" key while using the CMC for an on-the-spot refresh. If you configure auto-refresh and then walk away from your workstation, the zone data collector will continue to waste cycles refreshing your screen.

## Number of Concurrent CMC Consoles

Every open Citrix Management Console adds load to the zone data collector of the server to which the CMC is connected. For this reason, it's important to that you keep the number of open CMCs to a minimum.

If some people only need to gather basic information, you should show them how to use command-line tools. Of course the command-line tools are going to utilize the zone data collector just as much as the CMC, but they are generally used only as needed.

## Configuring Server and Application Folders

From within the Citrix Management Console, you can create server and application folders. These folders can be used to organize and sort the large numbers of applications and servers that you might have in your server farm. It's usually easier to find specific applications or servers if they are logically grouped together. This is especially true in large, multi-location environments that have some corporate-wide applications and some local applications.

It's important to note that grouping applications into CMC folders is *not* the same as configuring Program Neighborhood folders. CMC folders only affect the display of applications to administrators connecting via the CMC.

Also, when you refresh the CMC view, only the currently displayed information is re-queried. If there are 100 applications with no folders, information for all 100 applications needs to be collected and sent to the CMC. If these same 100 applications were spit into 10 folders with 10 applications each, a screen refresh will only request information from the zone data collector on those 10 applications. Multiply this savings by the number of administrators in your farm and you can see how creating CMC folders can save some real processing power on your zone data collectors.

Many organizations choose to create both application and server folders based on their zone boundaries.

### *Advantages of Creating Application and Server Folders in the CMC*

- Ease of use.
- Increased performance.

### Disadvantages of Creating Application and Server Folders in the CMC

- Sometimes it can be difficult to find the particular server or application that you are looking for.
- Everyone must agree on a common naming convention.

## Using the Citrix Web Console

If you are using Feature Release 1 or 2, you can monitor and manage your MetaFrame XP servers with the Citrix Web Console (CWC). The CWC is a web interface version of the Citrix Management Console, although the CWC does not have as much functionality.

With the CWC, you can view active sessions and applications as well as information about servers and users. You can also perform basic administrative tasks, such as logging off and disconnecting sessions, sending messages to users, and shadowing sessions.

In order to use the CWC, you must use IIS 5.0 or newer as your web server. This means that the CWC cannot be used with Terminal Server 4.0 servers. Also, the CWC only supports Internet Explorer 4.0 or newer. You cannot access it with Netscape.

You can install the CWC from the Feature Release 1 CD. The CWC URL is then set to http://servername/Citrix/WebConsole. When you access that URL, you will be presented with a logon box. That logon box only has two fields—username and password. If you need to log into the CWC with an account from a domain other than that where the CWC is running, you will need to use the "domain\username" syntax in the username field to specify your domain.

### Advantages of the Citrix Web Console

- Does not require NFuse.
- Does not require the ICA client software be installed on the client computer.

### Disadvantages of the Citrix Web Console

- Requires Feature Release 1 or 2.
- Requires IIS 5.0 or newer, so it does not work with Terminal Server 4.0.
- Only supports IE web browsers.
- It is not secure. (Although SSL can be used to secure it. See

Chapter 15 for details.)

- Limited functionality.
- Why not just publish the real CMC and access it via a web link?

# Server Farm Maintenance

Throughout the life of your MetaFrame XP implementation, you will most likely need to change some of the configuration parameters of your server farm. Let's look at the following fairly common maintenance tasks:

- Changing zones.
- Changing farm membership.
- Changing the IMA data store.
- Replacing servers.
- Renaming servers.

## Changing Zones

Moving a server between zones is very common in the real world. This is especially true for new MetaFrame XP environments that are growing and changing rapidly. Fortunately, changing a MetaFrame XP server's zone is easy to do via the Citrix Management Console (CMC | Server | Properties | Zones Tab). From here, zones can be created, deleted, and renamed.

At installation time, all MetaFrame XP servers on the same subnet are automatically configured to be members of the same zone.

## Changing Farm Membership

As your MetaFrame XP environment grows, it may become necessary to move servers from one MetaFrame XP server farm to another. Fortunately, this is a simple process, automated by the "chfarm" utility which is included on the MetaFrame XP CD. CHFARM is located in the W2K\MF or TSE\MF directory. With FR-2/SP-2, it's is located in the MF\Program Files\Citrix \System32\Citrix\IMA directory.

Remember that each MetaFrame XP server farm has its own IMA data store. If you change the farm membership of a server, you are really removing it from one data store and adding it to another.

CHFARM is a GUI application that leads you through the process of changing a server's farm membership. The CHFARM utility requires the MetaFrame XP installation files in order to work properly because it essentially reruns the MetaFrame XP setup program beginning with the farm membership questions.

The CHFARM utility performs several tasks:

1. CHFARM removes the server from the current farm. To do this, it:
   a. Stops the local IMA service.
   b. Uninstalls the IMA service.
   c. Removes all local IMA settings.
2. CHFARM installs the server into the new farm. To do this, it:
   a. Launches the MetaFrame setup program, starting with the farm setup screen. From here, you can choose to create a new farm or to add the server to an existing farm.
   b. Installs the IMA service.
   c. Starts the IMA service.
   d. Reinitializes the licensing database.

If you decide to use the CHFARM utility, there are some factors that you should be aware of:

- If you cancel part way through the CHFARM process, you run the risk of breaking everything without the ability to recover.
- CHFARM deletes the old local IMA Data Store. If the server you are changing is a host to other MetaFrame XP servers, those servers will no longer work. If you would like to migrate many servers that use an Access IMA data store, migrate the server that hosts the data store last.
- Close any CMC connections before you use the CHFARM utility. If you do not close them, they will be dropped when the CHFARM utility stops the IMA service.
- You cannot use CHFARM if a server was removed from a farm through the CMC. Removing a server from a farm through the CMC deletes all of the server's information from the IMA data store. The CHFARM utility will not be able to locate that server's information.
- CHFARM does not migrate any published applications or

configuration settings. If these settings are different in the new farm, you will need to manually reconfigure them on the server.

## Migrating to a New IMA Data Store

Often it's necessary to migrate the IMA data store from one database platform to another. This is usually the case when MetaFrame XP environments start out small with an Access IMA data store. After some growth, administrators choose to migrate the data store to a more robust platform, such as SQL Server, Oracle, or DB-2.

The DSMAINT utility is used to configure parameters and data relating to the IMA data store. The DSMAINT utility serves two purposes:

- To migrate data from an old data store to a new data store during IMA data store platform migrations.
- To reconfigure MetaFrame XP servers to point to new data stores (without changing their farm membership).

### Migrating IMA Data

The DSMAINT command-line utility can be used to migrate from Access to SQL, Oracle, or DB-2. It can also be used to migrate from between SQL, Oracle, and DB-2. DSMAINT cannot be used to migrate data from Oracle, SQL, or DB-2 to Access.

In order to use DSMAINT, you must have the necessary parameters for your old data store (source) and your new data store (destination). Those parameters include the DSN, the username, and the password. Once you have these parameters, use the following syntax at the command-line to use DSMAINT. The DSMAINT utility is located in the `%systemroot%\system32\Citrix\IMA\` directory, but MetaFrame XP adds this folder to your PATH statement when it's installed so you should be able to execute this command from any location.

```
dsmaint migrate /srcdsn:dsnfilename /srcuser:username
/srcpwd:password /dstdsn:dsnfilename /dstuser:username
/dstpwd:password
```

The "migrate" option of the DSMAINT command does not reconfigure the local server to use the new database. It simply copies all of the information from the old database into the new database. It is possible to run the DSMAINT migration command with users logged into the MetaFrame XP server.

## Reconfiguring a Server's IMA Data Store Connection

The DSMAINT utility can also reconfigure MetaFrame XP servers to point to new data stores. This is most often used to point all farm servers to the new database just after a database migration. Using DSMAINT to reconfigure the IMA data store connection requires three parameters for the new connection: the DSN to be used, the username, and the password. Use the following syntax to connect to a new data store:

```
dsmaint config /user:username /pwd:password /
dsn:dsnfilename
```

After the server is reconfigured for the new data store, you should stop and start the IMA service so that it connects to the proper data store. You can perform this IMA data store reconfiguration with users logged in because stopping and starting the IMA service does not kick off current users—it only prevents new users from logging in (while the IMA service is stopped).

# Replacing MetaFrame XP Servers

Every so often, it will become necessary for you to replace MetaFrame XP servers. This may be because a server had a hardware failure or because a server is being upgraded to a more powerful server.

In traditional environments, it was necessary to remove the old server and all of its related configuration information and to install a new server and manually reconfigure it as needed.

Fortunately, there is a shortcut when replacing MetaFrame XP servers. All of the information stored in the IMA data store is based on each server's computer name. There is no unique serial number or SID. One MetaFrame XP server can be removed and another server with the same computer name can be installed and the new server will get all of the settings and configurations of the old server. The IMA data store will not realize that the server ever changed.

To replace a MetaFrame XP server:

1. Turn off the old server. Do not use any tools to remove this server from the farm. If you do, all of the server's information will be removed from the IMA data store and the entire automatic replacement will be pointless.

2. Turn on the new server. Make sure that the computer name of the

new server is identical to the computer name of the old server that it is replacing.

3. Run "dsmaint config" to point the new server to the proper IMA data store.

4. Stop and start the IMA service. This will ensure that the new server points to the proper data store and that it is initialized with the current information in the new data store.

5. Run "qfarm" to ensure that everything looks good.

6. Verify the licensing information.

The only caveat to this is that only the information stored in the IMA data store is retained for the new server. This includes farm roles and published application information. Configuration elements that are local to the server are not retained, such as Citrix connections. Refer to the Appendix for a full list of all configuration information and where it is stored.

If you choose to replace a server in this manner, make sure that the applications that were published on the old server are located in the same paths on the new server. The IMA data store keeps a record of the applications that are published on each server, but it does not check to see whether the application paths are valid. If your old server had a published application called "Word" with the command line c:\Program Files\Office\Office10 \winword.exe and the new server has Word in the path c:\office\winword.exe, you would need to change the properties of the published application for the new server. If you do not change the properties, users will not be able to access the published application on the new server.

## Renaming a MetaFrame XP Server

It is possible to rename a MetaFrame XP server that is a member of a server farm. However, in doing so, you will lose any published application configuration information for that server. If your published applications are load balanced across multiple servers, this should not be a problem. You can just add the applications back to the server after it has been renamed. To rename a MetaFrame XP server:

1. Remove the server from any lists of published applications. This does not mean that you have to physically uninstall any applications. It just means that you should use the CMC to remove the server from the application lists.

2. Stop the IMA service.

3. Delete the file `wfcname.ini` from the root directory of the system drive (if the file exists).

4. Change the server name.

5. Reboot the server.

6. Once the IMA service starts after the server has been rebooted, the server's zone membership will be reset to the default zone. If this is not appropriate, change the zone membership via the CMC.

7. Use the CMC to reconfigure any published applications that were removed in Step 1.

# Periodic Farm Maintenance Tasks

Even after your MetaFrame XP server farm is "perfect," there are preventative maintenance tasks that you should perform in order to keep the farm running smoothly and to ensure that you do not find any surprises. Performing the following basic tasks will keep your system running in order:

- Compact the MS Access database.
- Cycle boot the MetaFrame XP servers.
- Stop and start the IMA service.
- Keep the operating system warm and clean.
- Check Resource Manager or Load Manager logs.
- Check for new hotfixes or service packs.

## Compact the Access Database

If your IMA data store is Microsoft Access-based, you can use the "`dsmaint compactdb`" command to compact it. This should be done nightly in MS Access-based farms with more than a few servers. You can actually create a batch file and use the Windows task scheduler (or the "AT" command scheduler in NT 4) to automate this process.

In addition to the IMA data store, each MetaFrame XP server contains a local host cache copy of the data store. By default, the local host cache copy is located at the `\Program Files\Citrix\Independent Management Architecture\imalhc.mdb`. It is not a bad idea to compact this database as well, although it doesn't have to be done every night.

## Cycle Boot MetaFrame XP Servers

Cycle booting refers to shutting down and restarting MetaFrame XP servers on some sort of predefined schedule. People usually cycle boot servers to fix any memory leaks or other random issues associated with keeping [Microsoft] servers on for long periods of time. Interestingly, Citrix feels that there is no need to cycle boot MetaFrame XP servers, but they do admit that "it might not be a bad idea" and include functionality in the CMC to manage automated server reboots.

Each time you reboot a server, the IMA service must recreate that server's local host cache which requires downloading the needed information from the IMA data store. In large environments this can take several minutes. For this reason, it is critical that you do not reboot too many servers at once. If you do, a bottleneck can occur and the IMA service might timeout on some servers.

## Stop and Start the IMA Service

There are many administrators that regularly stop and start the IMA service on MetaFrame XP servers. This sometimes helps servers clear any strange problems related to IMA communication. While it is possible to stop and start this service with users connected, it's usually better done at night.

Again, you can automate the stopping and starting of the IMA service at night. Be sure that you don't have all your servers set to do it at the same time.

Stopping and staring the IMA service automatically compacts the local Resource Management database.

## Keep the Operating System Warm and Clean

Because the scope of this book is MetaFrame XP, we will not address the details of tasks that should be performed at the operating system level. There are many great books on this topic. Just keep in mind that MetaFrame XP runs on top of Windows and if Windows is not cared for, MetaFrame XP will be vulnerable.

## Check Resource Manager or Load Manager Logs

Checking the logs often serves two purposes. First, you can analyze the content of the logs to look for any problems that might be developing. Second, you can make sure the log files are not too large. If you find them to be extensive you can save or clear the contents.

## Check for New Hotfixes or Service Packs

It is important to check Microsoft's and Citrix's website periodically for new hotfixes or service packs. For example, the IMA service that ships with MetaFrame XP experiences some trouble right out of the box. The current problems have been addressed with hotfixes and service packs and it is a good idea to keep an eye out for more.

# Citrix Resource Manager

In your day-to-day management of your MetaFrame XPe environment, Citrix Resource Manager will be one of your most valuable tools. Resource Manager (RM) serves three purposes:

- Real time monitoring of MetaFrame XPe servers.
- Historic reports containing information about MetaFrame XPe servers.
- A central repository of usage information and statistics across all servers in your farm.

Real time monitoring allows you to view the status of different components of the MetaFrame XP server. Each component (known to Resource Manager as a "metric") is viewed via the CMC, and has a green icon next to it if everything is okay. If there are problems, the icon will turn a different color, depending on what the problem is. You can configure the system to send alerts to SNMP traps, email addresses, or short message service pagers if problems occur. You can completely customize the types, behaviors and thresholds of each metric in your environment.

In addition to displaying the live status of MetaFrame XPe servers, Resource Manager can also be used to collect and store detailed data about individual servers. A system snapshot is taken every 15 seconds, and a report can be generated on any timeframe in the past 96 hours, allowing you to see exactly what the condition of the server was at a specific time.

Finally, if you are using Feature Release 2, MetaFrame XPe servers running Resource Manager can periodically send statistics and data to a centralized database. From there you can generate reports about overall farm usage. You can even set up pricing information and generate invoices based on which users accessed the systems.

The newest version of Citrix Resource Manager has evolved quite a bit in the past few years, even since MetaFrame XP was first released. For that reason, this section addresses the Resource Manager component of MetaFrame XPe with Service Pack 2 applied. Since Service Pack 2 is free, you can use it even if you don't plan on using Feature Release 2.

## Technical Overview

Even though Citrix Resource Manager is fairly straightforward, there are several components required to make it work. These components include:

- Citrix Resource Manager software.
- Metrics.
- Farm metric server.
- IMA data store.
- Local resource manager database.
- Summary database.
- Database connection server.

*Resource Manager Software.* In order to use Resource Manager, you need to ensure that the Resource Manager components are enabled when you install MetaFrame XPe. If not, you can install them at any time by running the SP-2/ FR-2 installation program. The Resource Manager software must be locally installed on each MetaFrame XPe server that you want to monitor. This software extends the functionality of the IMA service, allowing it to collect metrics on various server components.

*Metrics.* A metric is a component (and its associated parameters) that is monitored, including the thresholds for changing the status of the metric and sending alerts. Each metric has an icon that changes colors to indicate its current status. Metrics are configured in the server farm and applied to specific servers or published applications. Examples of the hundreds of metrics available include current user load, CPU utilization, and number of published applications in use.

*Farm Metric Server.* The Farm Metric Server (FMS) is responsible for monitoring the status of the metrics of all servers and published applications in the entire server farm. This server actually controls the metric icons, changing their status as conditions warrant. The FMS gets its information from the zone data collector, which is updated every 15 seconds by each MetaFrame XPe server.

*IMA Data Store*. All Resource Manager configuration information is stored in the IMA data store. This includes the metrics and their associated configurations and thresholds, as well as alert parameters and which metrics are applied to which servers and published applications. Just like the other information in the IMA data store, each MetaFrame XPe server's local host cache contains its local subset of the Resource Manager information from the IMA data store.

*Local Resource Manager Database*. While the Resource Manager configuration information is stored in the IMA data store, each MetaFrame XPe server is responsible for locally maintaining its own Resource Manager data. This data, stored in `\Program Files\Citrix\Citrix Resource Manager\LocalDB\RMLocalDatabase.mdb` on each server, is maintained for the previous 96 hours, with new data overwriting the oldest data.

*Summary Database*. In Feature Release 2 environments, the summary database is a SQL or Oracle database that stores long term information about server usage. You can configure this data to be whatever you want, but most people store only a small subset of the local resource manager data in the summary database. The difference is that the summary database is used to store the data for weeks or months.

*Database Connection Server*. This server is responsible for receiving summary data from all MetaFrame XPe servers and writing it to the summary database. This is the only server that directly connects to the summary database.

Figure 16.2 (next page) shows how the various Resource Manager components work together in the MetaFrame XPe environment.

*Figure 16.2 The components of Citrix Resource Manager*

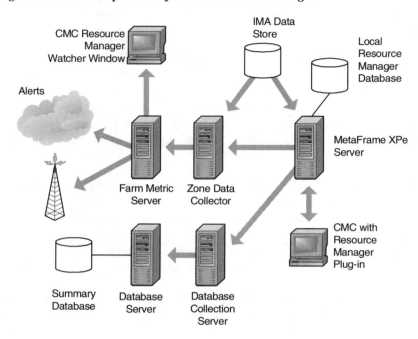

## Monitoring Servers and Applications

Everything in Resource Manager is monitored via the metrics that you configure. After installation, default server metrics are in place so you can begin monitoring a server immediately without any additional configuration.

How you view the current status of the metrics depends on which type of metric you are interested in viewing. There are essentially two types of metrics: published application metrics and server metrics. Obviously, the published application metrics show information relating to each specific published application. They can be viewed in the published application's area in the CMC (CMC I Published Applications I Your Application I Resource Manager Tab). The server metrics, which contain server-specific status and information, can also be viewed via the CMC (CMC I Servers I Your Server I Resource Manager Tab).

### Metric Status

When viewing metrics, each specific metric has an icon whose color corresponds to the state of the metric. Each metric type, both for published applications and servers, has six possible states, as outlined below:

- *Green*. The metric is operating within its acceptable limits as configured in its properties.

- *Yellow*. The metric has exceeded the limits of the green state and switched to yellow, having exceeded the time and value limit threshold you configured.

- *Red*. The metric has exceeded the time and limit thresholds of the yellow state and switched to red. Any configured SNMP, SMS or email alerts have been sent.

- *Blue*. The metric has been added, but it has not yet been configured, so it can't change color. This blue status will not change until you edit the properties of the metric and configure it for use.

- *Gray (Paused)*. The metric has entered a "snooze" state, manually invoked by an administrator. During this snooze period the metric will not activate any red alarms, and yellow and red conditions will not cause the metric to appear in the watcher window. However, during this snooze state, the metric is still active and it is still collecting data. The metric will exit the snooze state and become green, yellow, or red, after a preconfigured amount of snooze time has passed, as configured in the metric's properties.

- *Black (Stopped)*. The metric has entered a "sleep" state, manually invoked by an administrator. During this sleep period, the metric will not activate any red alarms. Also, yellow or red conditions will not cause the metric to appear in the watcher window. However, during this sleep state, the metric is still active, and it is still collecting data. The metric will not exit the sleep state until it is manually "woken up" by an administrator.

## *Metric Options*

In addition to the colored status indicators of a metric, you can configure the metric options by right-clicking on the metric's name. These options include:

- *Snooze*. This is where you set the metric to the "snooze" state, silencing any red or yellow conditions. The snooze state is temporary, and the snooze time is configurable in the metric properties. This is thought of as "pausing" a metric.

- *Sleep*. This is where you set the metric to the "sleep" state. Like the snooze state, the sleep state will silence red or yellow conditions. However, unlike the snooze metric which is temporary, the metric will remain in the sleep state indefinitely until you manually wake it up. This is thought of as "stopping" a metric.

- *Real time graph*. This option displays a real time graph of the metric's values, updated every 15 seconds. This graph is similar to the graphs available in Performance Monitor. You can also view this graph by double-clicking on a metric in the CMC.

- *Properties*. This is where you configure the specific behavior of a metric (such as the parameters for going red, yellow, or green). See the "Metric Properties" section of this chapter for more information.

- *Add/Remove Metric*. This option allows you to add additional metrics to the server to be monitored. There is no limit to the total number of metrics that can be added.

### Watching for Critical Metrics

One of the downsides to watching the colored status of metrics for each server in the CMC is that you can only view the status of one server at a time. To address this, MetaFrame XPe includes a "metrics watcher." The metrics watcher is a window that will show all of the yellow or red metrics for the entire farm. If a metric's status becomes yellow or red while the watcher window is open, that metric and its status will appear in the watcher window. If any metric in the watcher windows turns green, or if it is set to snooze or sleep, the metric disappears out of the watch window.

You can access the watcher window in two ways:

- CMC I Resource Manager I Watcher Tab
- CMC I Resource Manager I Click on the "Watcher Window" icon in the toolbar

The watcher window is a small Java window that pops up independently of the CMC (although the CMC must be open in order to use it). Through this window, you can keep an eye on MetaFrame XP servers and published applications while performing other server tasks.

In addition to the watcher window, you can also get an overview of the colors of metrics for all the servers in the farm through the Resource Manager tab (CMC I Servers I Resource Manager Tab). This screen will show the six status icon colors and the number of metrics for each server of each color.

## Working with Metrics

After Resource Manager is installed, you need to tell it what you would like to monitor. This is done by configuring the metrics. Each metric is a set of parameters that Resource Manager will watch. Metrics exist at the server farm level. After defining the parameters for a metric, you need to apply the metric to published applications or to servers. There are two types of metrics.

- Server Metrics.
- Application Metrics.

*Server Metrics.* Server metrics can be created for any object available within Performance Monitor, including any performance monitor object, counter, or instance combination. This is very cool.

*Application Metrics.* Published applications have only one metric available to them. This metric is the "count," metric—the current number of users connected to a published application.

### Metric Properties

Each metric has properties and parameters that can be configured for it. By default, these parameters are configured individually per metric, but you can copy configuration parameters from one metric to another.

All of the following parameters apply to both types of metrics. (The "count" metric for published applications and any performance monitor object, counter, and instance for the server metrics.)

The metric's configurable parameters are as follows:

- *Yellow Limit.* The level that the metric must hit to turn from "green" state to "yellow" state.
- *Yellow Time.* The time (HH:MM:SS) that the metric must exceed the yellow limit before the metric changes to a "yellow" state.
- *Red Limit.* The level that the metric must hit to turn from "yellow" state to "red" state.
- *Red Time.* The time (HH:MM:SS) that the metric must exceed the red limit before the metric changes to a "red" state.
- *Incremental.* This is a Yes / No option. Checking this box (yes) means that the metric is incremental and that lower is better (i.e. Processor Utilization). Leaving this box unchecked (no) means that the metric is decremental and that higher is better (i.e. Free Disk Space).
- *Snooze Time.* You can temporarily silence a red alarm by hitting a "snooze" button. This snooze time property configures the time

(HH:MM:SS) that the metric remains in the snooze state before returning to an active color and state.

- *Summary Data.* When this box is checked, this metric will be included in the server farm's permanent summary database.

- *Email, SNMP, or SMS on Red.* This checkbox will cause the metric to send an alert when it enters the "red" state. The recipients of the alerts must be configured in the farm or on the server in order for these alerts work.

- *Email, SNMP, or SMS on Green.* This checkbox will cause the metric to send an alert when it enters the "green" state, from a yellow or red state. The recipients of the alerts must be configured in the farm or on the server in order for these alerts work.

- *Script on Red.* You can specify a script or program that is executed when the metric enters the "red" state. This script runs with the local system account privileges, and it runs every time the status changes to red. This script must be located on the local server. If this metric is copied and applied to multiple servers, the script must be in the same location on all of the servers.

### Configuring Metrics

After a metric has been added to the server you can enter metric values by viewing a real–time graph that displays the counter of the value of the metric that you are setting (CMC | Metric Properties | Advanced Threshold Configuration button).

Once you configure a metric the way you want it, you can copy it to other servers or applications. Remember that if you copy a metric that is configured to execute a script when its status changes to red, you must also manually copy the script to the same location on every server where that metric is applied.

### Configuring Alerts

Resource Manager "alerts" is the generic term applied to the external notification process that can occur when a metric's status changes to red or to green. These alerts can be in the form of an email, and SNMP trap, or a Short Message Service alert (such as an alphanumeric pager). The alerts are configured as part of the metric's properties as described previously.

An important aspect of alerts relates to how you configure the recipients of an alert. When you are configuring the metric, the only alert options you have are checkboxes that allow you to turn the different types of alerts on or off. So how do you specify the recipients of an alert if you turn it on?

There are two ways, depending on the scope of the alerts. You can configure alert recipients per farm or per server. Both types of recipients are configured via the CMC. If you configure alerts for the server farm (CMC | Resource Manager | SMS, SNMP, or E-mail tab), any time a metric needs to send an alert, the alert will be sent to the list of recipients configured for that type of alert for the server farm.

In addition to the farm-wide alert recipients, you can configure alerts that replace or are an addition to farm-wide alert recipients (CMC | Right click on server | Server Properties | Resource Manager Alerts Recipients tab). If you uncheck one of the alert recipient methods (either the SNMP, SMS, or Email) and leave the boxes blank, no alerts of that type will be sent for that server.

Any manual customization of the alert recipients that you configure for one server must be manually reproduced on other servers if you want them to have the same configuration. There is no way to copy the recipient properties from one server to the next.

### Adding Metrics to be Monitored

Adding new metrics is fairly sinple (CMC | Server | Resource Manager tab). As you add a metric, its status light will remain blue until you configure it.

When you add a metric (which is based on Performance Monitor counters), you have the option of adding all instances of a particular counter. If you do this, Resource Manager will add each and every instance of that counter, not an aggregate. If you need an aggregate, most performance counter objects have specific instances that represent the total of all instances.

For example, the "% Processor Utilization" counter of the Processor performance monitor object has one instance for each processor, named 0, 1, 2, or 3. Additionally, there is an instance named "_Total" that is the aggregate of all the instances. If you want to create a Resource Manager metric for the aggregate, create a single metric that tracks the "_Total" instance, rather than separate metrics for each instance.

### Real World Settings for Server Metrics

After Resource Manager installation, default server metrics are automatically created and configured. Before you configure the red alerts to be sent to your pager, it's probably a good idea to take a look at the default parameters and to see how accurately they fit your server. If you don't do this, you will probably have a conversation that goes something like this:

**Your Pager:** <beep beep beep>

**You:** I see that Server A has gone red.

**Other Citrix Administrator:** Really?

**You:** Yeah, the context switches have hit 14,000 per second.

**Other Citrix Administrator:** Really?

**You:** Yeah, they've been that way for over two minutes now.

**Other Citrix Administrator:** Really?

**You:** Yeah, really.

**Other Citrix Administrator:** Is that bad?

**You:** ?

**Other Citrix Administrator:** ?

**You:** It's red.

**Other Citrix Administrator:** So that's bad?

**You:** ?

The point of this dialog is that the default metric configurations are rather generic, so it's important that you configure them in a meaningful way for your servers and your situation before you set the system to start bothering people at home via their pagers.

Monitor some of the metrics in real time with various loads on the servers to establish baseline settings. These settings will to evolve over time. As you become more aware of your servers, you'll get a feel for what "looks right" and what you need to set your metrics for.

When configuring your metrics, remember that the only metric available for individual applications is the count of the current users. All of the other performance monitor metrics must be applied to a server, not an application.

You should also keep in mind that you can use Resource Manager to monitor folders of applications or servers together as a single unit, in case you have any parameters that you need to monitor across groups.

### Metrics' Impact to Servers

The local IMA service processes and records data for the Resource Manager metrics. If you decide to create a lot of metrics on one single server, keep an eye on the IMAServe.exe in the task manager to make sure that it is not using too much memory or CPU time. Don't go overboard with the number of metrics you configure on one server because the IMA service must record the data for every single one.

### Viewing Historic Metric States and Values

You can use Resource Manager to view the states and values of metrics from any time in the last 96 hours. This is useful if a server starts performing poorly because you can step backwards in time to see exactly what happened when the performance became poor.

You can use the CMC to view a log that indicates the date and time that the status of any metric changed (CMC | Right click on server | Resource Manager Server Log). You can also view a historic graph for each metric that shows the real time value and the recent history.

You can use the CMC to generate a system snapshot that will indicate the values of any of the metrics for a specific time in the last 96 hours (CMC | Resource Manager | Reports Tab). System snapshots are automatically generated every 15 seconds, so that at any given time you will be able to look at server status in 15 second intervals for the past 96 hours.

Lastly, you can run a process report that will show all the details of all processes, except for system related processes, the system account, and the Resource Manager tools themselves. If you like, you can configure additional processes to be ignored (CMC | right click on server | properties | ignored processes tab). You can even use the "Apply to other Servers..." button to copy the list to other servers in your farm.

## How Resource Manager Works

Now that you understand the components of Resource Manager and how it is used, we should look at some of the behind-the-scenes technical components that make it all come together. These components include:

- The farm metric server.
- The local Resource Manager database.
- The summary database.
- The database connection server.

## The Farm Metric Server

Every server farm that has at least one server that uses Resource Manager has a farm metric server. The farm metric server is responsible for interpreting the metrics, monitoring them, and sending the alerts. It provides the backend data that shows each metric's status in the CMC or the watcher windows.

By default, the farm metric server will be the first server that you installed Resource Manager on. However, as an administrator, you can specify which server is your Farm Metric Server. (CMC | Resource Manager | Farm Metric Server Tab) When you are choosing this server, you will be able to get a bit of a performance gain if you choose a zone data collector.

In addition to the farm metric server, each farm also has a backup farm metric server. If the farm metric server does not respond to a request, the backup server becomes the farm metric server. If the main farm metric server comes back online, it becomes the backup farm metric server.

## Local Resource Manager Database

After you install Resource Manager, a Jet (MS Access) database is created on the local MetaFrame XP server in the following location: `Program Files\Citrix\Citrix Resource Manager\LocalDB\RMLocalDatabase.mdb`. An ODBC DSN called `RMLocalDatabase` is also created that points to this local database.

As the server is used, Resource Manager writes performance information to the local database every 15 seconds. After 96 hours, the old information is continuously overwritten by the new information, meaning that at any given time, you will always have a record of the last 96 hours.

When you use the CMC to produce a Resource Manager report for a Meta-Frame XPe server, the IMA service on that server reads the information needed for the report from its local Resource Manager database. It then sends that information to the server running the CMC. The only time any performance data is read or sent across the network is when a report or a graph is generated.

Resource Manager only saves information in the local database for the metrics that are configured for a server. Each entry only requires a few hundred bytes, which means that the 96 hour history of 15-second intervals requires about 7MB for each metric.

In addition to the server-based metrics, an entry is written to the local database whenever a published application is launched. This entry is updated every 20 seconds so long as the application is in use. This happens for all published applications, not just ones that have the "count" application metric applied. However, for applications that do have the "count" application metric applied, the farm metric server is also updated every 20 seconds so that it constantly knows how many instances of the application are running in the farm.

## Summary Database

If you're using Feature Release 2, you can create a "summary database" that aggregates and stores (long-term) certain Resource Manager data from multiple servers in your farm. You can configure different types of data to be retained for different amounts of time (or even indefinitely) via the CMC (CMC | Resource Manager | Summary Database tab | Configure | Purge Settings).

Once the data is in the database, you can run reports against it via the CMC (CMC | Resource Manager | Reports tab). or with any tool that you choose (such as Crystal Reports). If you choose to use Crystal Reports, there are free Citrix-specific templates that you can download from www.citrix.com/ download. (Click the "MetaFrame XPe" link.)

## Database Connection Server

The database connection server (DCN) is the single MetaFrame XP server in your farm responsible for receiving summary data from farm servers and writing it to the database.

Each MetaFrame XP server stores its data for the summary database locally in a summary file. This file is updated whenever any user session ends, a process ends, or an event occurs. It is also updated once an hour with new metric data. After 24 hours, this data is sent to the DCN which adds it to the database.

You can configure the time of day that the summary data is sent (CMC | Resource Manager | Summary Database tab | Configure button). Unfortunately, the update time is not time-zone specific. For example, if you set your update time for "23:00" (11:00 PM), each server will send its updated information when its own clock reaches 11:00 PM.

In order to setup your DCN, you need to create a system DSN called "rmsummarydatabase." You can point this DSN to an Oracle or SQL database. Then, use the CMC to configure the farm to use this DSN (CMC | Resource Manager | Summary Database tab | Configure button).

It's important to note that the farm metric server and the database connection server are not the same thing, although you could run them both on the same server if you wanted to.

## Using Resource Manager in the Real World

Citrix Resource Manager is useful in many situations. However, you should keep the following tips in mind when you decide how it will be used in your environment:

- Remember that Resource Manager is a "farm-wide" resource. For example, there is only one database connection server and one farm metric server per server farm. If you have a server farm that spans multiple WAN locations, you must consider the bandwidth that will be consumed by Resource Manager.

- The act of collecting metrics consumes server resources. In the real world, you should only choose to collect server metrics that are actually useful to you.

- Resource Manager works best when it monitors high-level usage information. It's not really designed to be used as an in-depth troubleshooting or server sizing tool.

# Citrix Network Manager

MetaFrame XPe's Network Manager allows you to view various statistics of your MetaFrame XPe servers with third party SNMP management applications, including Tivoli NetView, HP OpenView, and if you have Feature Release 1, CA Unicenter. Citrix Network Manager also allows you to perform some limited management tasks from those management applications.

When considering the Citrix Network Manager, a lot of people ask one question: Is it worth the trouble?

Some feel that network manager is more trouble than its worth. Realistically, if you currently use NetView, OpenView, or Unicenter, the network manager may not be a bad idea. However, if you don't already use one of these products, Citrix Network Manager is not worth your time.

# Network Manager Installation

To begin using MetaFrame XPe's Network Manager, install and configure the Microsoft SNMP service. Once you do that, you can set your SNMP options for network manager from within the CMC.

The Network Manager CD that ships with MetaFrame XPe only has plug-ins for the SNMP management tool consoles, and the related MIBs. The CD contains nothing that needs to be installed on your MetaFrame XPe servers.

## Installing the CMC on the Management Console Computers

Some people choose to install the Citrix Management Console on the same workstation as their SNMP management console software. This allows the two management products to be integrated—the CMC can be launched right from the SNMP tool. Also, it is convenient because you can do more with the CMC than you can through your SNMP management tool and SNMP. The CMC is also more secure than SNMP tools.

However, remember that best practices dictate that you should install the CMC onto the zone data collectors, and use it remotely via ICA sessions. In the end, it's really up to you to determine whether the convenience of having the CMC installed locally on your SNMP management console computer is worth the performance lag of not having it installed on a zone data collector.

MetaFrame XPe's Network Manager only has a few requirements:

- You must have MetaFrame XPe.
- You must have the Microsoft SNMP service installed on the MetaFrame XPs server.
- If you are not using Feature Release 1, the SNMP management console must be Tivoli NetView 5.1.2 or HP OpenView 6.1 or newer.
- If you have Feature Release 1, you can also use CA Unicenter TNG 2.4 or later.

# Network Manager Configuration

Once the Microsoft SNMP service is installed, all you need to do is to configure the traps that you want to send to the SNMP console. For those of you not familiar with the SNMP world, a "trap" is a condition or event that generates an alert. This alert is then sent to an SNMP management console that displays it, logs it, or performs some other action.

MetaFrame XPe's Network Manager can send traps for eleven different events, as outlined in Figure 16.3.

*Figure 16.3 Network Manager's available event traps*

| Number | Name | Description |
|---|---|---|
| 1 | trapSessionLogoff | Any logoff. |
| 2 | trapSessionLogon | Any logon. |
| 3 | trapSessionDisc | Any disconnect. |
| 4 | trapSessionThreshold | Each time the number of sessions exceeds the limit as configured. |
| 5 | trapLicLowThreshold | Number of available licenses has reached the warning threshold, as configured. |
| 6 | trapLicOut | All pooled connection licenses have been used. |
| 7 | trapLicDenied | Not used. |
| 8 | trapMFAgentUp | The SNMP agent has successfully started. |
| 9 | trapSessionThresholdNormal | Back to normal from event number 4. |
| 10 | trapLicLowThresholdNormal | Back to normal from event number 5. |
| 11 | trapLicOutNormal | Back to normal from event number 6. |

Using the CMC, you can configure which traps are sent to the SNMP console. Some of the traps are configured with thresholds that cause an alert to be sent. These include the session limit per server (default 100) and the license thresholds. For the license and session limit thresholds, if the value falls below a set percentage, then a notification is sent. When it climbs back above the reset percentage, notification is sent. The reset value must be higher or equal to the set value.

These settings are different from the Resource Manager settings and thresholds.

All of the license traps are farm wide settings (CMC | Farm | Properties | SNMP Tab). The rest can either be set farm-wide (CMC | Farm | Properties | SNMP Tab) or per-server (CMC | Server | Properties | SNMP Tab).

## SNMP Security

There are several potential security issues exposed if you choose to use the remote SNMP management tools.

## SNMP Rights

First, if you decide to use the SNMP management consoles for monitoring only (and use the CMC for any actual management), then you want to ensure that the SNMP service on the MetaFrame XPe server is set to "Read Only."

On Windows NT 4.0 Terminal Edition servers, the SNMP service will need to be manually set to Read Only.

On Windows 2000 servers, all remote users of the SNMP service are limited to the "read_only" SNMP right by default. This is fine if you only want to view the status and traps of MetaFrame XP servers. If you want to actively manage them, then grant the "read_create" or "read_write" rights.

## SNMP Consoles

If you do decide to actively manage MetaFrame XPe servers with SNMP management consoles, configure the SNMP service on your servers to only accept packets from the specific IP addresses of the management consoles. Do this because the SNMP protocol is inherently not secure. You do need want anyone on the network to be able to send management commands to a MetaFrame XP server.

## SNMP Clear text

If you have the CMC installed locally on the SNMP management console workstation, then your farm logins will be sent to the server in clear text. Alternately, you can connect to the CMC via a published application on one of the MetaFrame XP servers, and use MetaFrame's native security and encryption.

## *SNMP Uses in MetaFrame XPe Environments*

Via the SNMP management console, the following administrative activities can be performed on MetaFrame XP servers:

- Restart.
- Shutdown.
- Logoff sessions.
- Disconnect sessions.
- Send messages.
- Terminate processes.

# Real World Case Study

### eHolli.com

eHolli.com is an Internet clearing house portal for the mergers of dot-com start-ups. They currently have a MetaFrame XP server farm consisting of fifteen servers. They started with three servers last year, but strong growth and success with MetaFrame XP has enabled them to grow quickly.

Because they spent so much money on Mission District rent last year, they didn't have enough cash to purchase a real database server for their Meta-Frame XP server farm. Fortunately, their fifth-round VC funding came through, and they can now migrate their MS Access data store to Microsoft SQL server. This will give them the increased speed and reliability that they desire.

Here is the migration plan that they put in place:

1. Create the new database. This will be done with the SQL server tools on the SQL server.

2. Create a DSN. The default DSN is called `mf20.dsn` and is located in the `\Program Files\Citrix\Independent Management Architecture\` directory on each MetaFrame XP server. The new DSN file should contain all of the configuration parameters for the new SQL database. The DSN file will be created with the ODBC utility (located in the control panel in Terminal Server 4.0 and the administrative tools in Windows 2000).

3. Make a backup copy of the current IMA data store. On the MetaFrame XP server that hosts the MS Access version of the data store, they will make a backup copy of the database. The database is located at `\Program Files\Citrix\Independent Management Architecture\mf20.mdb`.

4. Verify that they have the correct version of MDAC installed to support the desired target migration platform. In this case, they will be migrating to SQL Server 2000, which requires MDAC 2.5. Check the SQL or Oracle documentation to see which version is needed in the environment.

5. Run "`dsmaint`" on the MetaFrame XP server that hosts the existing MS Access data store to migrate the data to the new SQL database. This is done with the "`dsmaint migrate`" command.

6. Run "`dsmaint config`" on the MetaFrame XP server that hosts

the existing Access data store to configure it to use the new SQL data store.

7. Stop and start the IMA service. This will allow the MetaFrame XP server to begin using the new data store.

At this point, the other MetaFrame XP servers will begin using the new SQL-based data store. They will access the data store via "indirect" mode, which means that all of their access will be channeled through one designated MetaFrame XP server. This happens automatically, because all of the servers are configured to use the data store of the MetaFrame XP server that used to be running the data store locally as an MS Access file. The other servers don't even know that the server has been converted from Access to SQL. All they know is that their requests are all sent to one server; it is up to that server to see that they are handled.

At this point, eHolli.com will configure all of the remaining MetaFrame XP servers to access the IMA data store in a direct mode, so that they will each contact the SQL server, rather than funneling their requests through the one server that used to house the MS Access version of the data store. In order to configure the other MetaFrame XP servers for direct access mode, there are several steps that must be taken at each server:

1. Copy the DSN file from the initial server to the MetaFrame XP server that is to be converted to direct mode.

2. Run the "dsmaint config" command on that server to instruct it to use the new DSN, thus giving it the information it needs to access the new SQL server.

3. Stop and start the IMA service, allowing the MetaFrame XP server to begin using the new IMA data store.

Once these steps are complete, all fifteen of eHolli.com's MetaFrame XP servers will be configured to work with the new SQL Server 2000 IMA Data Store.

# CHAPTER 17

# Ensuring Availability and System Redundancy

In this chapter

MetaFrame XP High Availability Strategies        752

MetaFrame XP Backup Strategies        762

The final component of your MetaFrame XP environment that you need to consider is how to ensure that it is sufficiently available and reliable. By thinking about how MetaFrame XP works and how your users will use it, you can create a strategy to guarantee that the system has the redundancy to absorb small "hiccups" and that it is properly backed up to survive major disasters.

The redundancy of many MetaFrame XP components is discussed throughout this book. This chapter pulls them together to create a holistic strategy that you can apply to your entire MetaFrame XP server farm.

# MetaFrame XP High Availability Strategies

Your users have one objective—to access their applications. They don't care about uptime percentages or system backups or server hot-swap components. They just know that when they click the button, their application had better start loading.

It's up to you to determine how available your system needs to be. (This actually means that it's up to you to determine how much money to spend on making your system redundant.) For example, it's possible to create a system that is online and available 24 hours a day, 7 days a week, 365 days per year. There are many real world manufacturing companies who use MetaFrame XP to serve applications to their assembly line workers. These plants operate 24 hours a day; a single hour of downtime costs them millions of dollars.

On the other hand, there are quite a few companies that only have a few MetaFrame XP servers for a few dozen users. In these environments, system downtime might only cost a few thousand dollars per hour in lost business.

In order to determine what is required for your environment, we need to look at the various components of a MetaFrame XP system from the perspective of redundancy. Figure 17.1 shows a generic view of the technical components required for a user to access a MetaFrame XP application. If any one of these components is not available, the user will not be able to do so.

Throughout the remainder of this section, we'll analyze how each component in Figure 17.1 affects overall redundancy and what can be done to that component to strengthen the redundancy of the overall system. It's important to remember that all of these components work together as a system. Therefore, it does no good to think about the redundancy of one component without considering the redundancy of others. Your MetaFrame XP environment is only as strong as its weakest link.

*Figure 17.1 The MetaFrame XP components that must be functional*

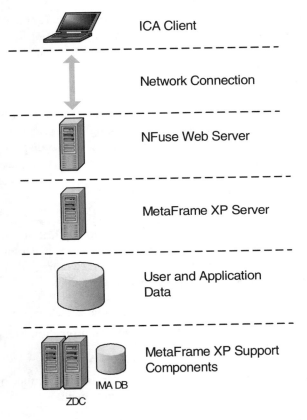

ICA Client

Network Connection

NFuse Web Server

MetaFrame XP Server

User and Application
Data

MetaFrame XP Support
Components

IMA DB

ZDC

## ICA Client Devices

Of course by this point you are well aware that one of the major architectural advantages of thin client environments is that any user can connect from any client device. If a client device ever fails, a user can begin using a different device and pick up right where he left off.

Chapter 9 presented the issues to consider when designing your client device strategy. It can be summarized as follows: With ICA clients, apply "high availability" not by changing anything on the client itself, but rather by having a spare client device available to quickly replace a failed unit.

## Network Connection

In a MetaFrame XP environment (or any thin client environment), your users instantly become unproductive if their network connection is lost. Short of running dual network cables to every user's ICA client device, you can configure clients to point to multiple MetaFrame XP servers on multiple network segments (as covered in Chapter 10).

You can also put dual network cards in your MetaFrame XP servers, configuring them for failover in case one stops working. Best practices suggest that each network card be connected to a different switch so that the servers can still function if a switch is lost.

## NFuse Web Server

Since most people use NFuse to provide access to applications, take the necessary steps to ensure that a working NFuse web page appears whenever users enter the URL into their browser. There are two areas that need to be addressed to ensure that an NFuse web site is available:

- Users must be able to find a functional NFuse web server.
- The NFuse web server must be able to find a function MetaFrame XP server.

Let's examine the steps that can be taken to ensure that neither one of these becomes the Achilles' heal in your NFuse environment.

### Ensuring Users can find an NFuse Server

The first item to consider when designing highly available NFuse environments is to ensure that your users will always be able to connect to a functioning NFuse web server, even if your primary server is down. Fortunately, people have been focusing on creating redundant websites for years, and there is nothing proprietary to prevent NFuse from working like a regular website. Three of the most common ways of ensuring website availability are:

- Connect to the server via a DNS name.
- Cluster the web servers.
- Create a manual backup address.

### Option 1. Use a DNS Name to Connect to the NFuse Web Server

By connecting to an NFuse website via a DNS name rather than to an IP address, the DNS name can be configured to point to any IP address. If something happens to the main server, the DNS table can be modified to point to a backup server. The disadvantage here is that the failover must be done manually.

### Advantages of Using a DNS Name for Redundancy

- Quick to implement.
- Transparent to end users.
- Inexpensive.

### Disadvantages of Using a DNS Name for Redundancy

- Manual failover.

### Option 2. Create a Web Server Cluster

Many web servers can be configured in a cluster format, allowing one web server to take over if the other fails. Cluster failover is automatic, although the hardware and software needed to run them can get expensive.

### Advantages of Building a Web Cluster for Redundancy

- Fast, automatic failover.

### Disadvantages of Building a Web Cluster for Redundancy

- Specialized cluster hardware and software can be pricey.

### Option 3. Manual Backup Address

Some people configure two identical web servers and instruct their users to try the alternate address if the first is not available. This is cheap and easy to implement, although it requires that your users remember a second address.

### Advantages of Using a Manual Address for Redundancy

- Inexpensive.

### Disadvantages of Using a Manual Address for Redundancy

- Requires user competence.

## Ensuring NFuse can find a MetaFrame XP Server

When using NFuse, in addition to making sure that an NFuse web server actually responds to user requests, make sure that the NFuse server is able to find a MetaFrame XP server running the Citrix XML service. There are two ways that this can be done:

- Configure multiple Citrix XML Service server addresses.

> • Use Enterprise Services for NFuse to connect to multiple server farms.

This section describes how to configure these two options so that your overall environment is as highly available as possible. Full details about the advantages and disadvantages of these options, as well as how they are configured, are included in Chapter 11.

### Option 1. Specifying Multiple Citrix XML Service Addresses

Remember that you can configure the Java Objects on an NFuse Classic web server to cycle through a list of MetaFrame XP servers when contacting the Citrix XML Service. While this list is primarily designed for load-balancing purposes, it can also alleviate the risk of a server being lost. If you specify multiple servers for the NFuse web server to contact, the loss of a single server will not affect the availability of the NFuse web site.

### Option 2. Using Enterprise Services for NFuse

Since you can use Enterprise Services for NFuse to connect load-balance users across server farms, your users can still access their MetaFrame XP applications even if an entire server farm is lost (or more likely if communication to an entire server farm is lost).

## MetaFrame Server Redundancy

The actual MetaFrame XP servers that host users' sessions are usually the first target when people begin to think about how to increase the availability of their MetaFrame XP environments. Similar to making NFuse available, there are two aspects that must be considered with MetaFrame servers:

> • A functioning MetaFrame XP server must be available for users.
>
> • The users must be able to seamlessly find that functioning server.

### *Ensuring a Functioning MetaFrame XP Server is Available*

Make sure that there will always be a MetaFrame XP server available when users need to connect to one. There are two different strategies that can be used for this:

> • Try to make each individual server's hardware as redundant as possible.
>
> • View each MetaFrame XP server as "expendable." Build redundancy by having extra servers.

Chapter 4 outlined strategies for the "farm / silo" model of deploying Meta-Frame XP servers and Chapter 6 detailed the advantages and disadvantages of building large or small servers. This section builds upon those two chapters by addressing the design options of whether you should approach server redundancy with "quality" or "quantity."

The exact approach that you take depends on your environment. What does "high availability" mean for you? Does this mean users' sessions can never go down, or does it mean that they can go down as long as they are restored quickly?

## Option 1. Build Redundancy with High Quality Servers

One approach to making MetaFrame XP servers highly available is to increase the redundancy of the systems themselves. This usually involves servers with redundant hardware, including disks, power supplies, network cards, fans, and memory. (Yes, today's newest servers have RAID-like configurations for redundant memory banks.)

### *Advantages of Building Servers with Redundant Hardware*

- By using redundant server hardware, you are assured that a simple hardware failure will not kick users off the system.

### *Disadvantages of Building Servers with Redundant Hardware*

- No economies of scale. Every server must contain it's own redundant equipment.
- This strategy still doesn't mean that your servers are bullet-proof.
- What happens if you lose a server even after your planning? Will you have the capacity to handle the load?

## Option 2. Build Redundancy with a High Quantity of Servers

As outlined in Chapters 4 and 6, you'll most likely need to build multiple identical servers to support all of your users and their applications regardless of your availability strategy. In most cases it's more efficient to purchase an extra server (for N+1 redundancy) than it is to worry about many different redundant components on each individual server.

### *Advantages of Building Extra Servers*

- Better economies of scale.
- You will have the capacity to handle user load shifts after a server failure.

### • Disadvantages of Building Extra Servers

- If a simple failure takes down a server, all users on that server will need to reconnect to establish their ICA sessions on another server.

- An extra server might cost more than simply adding a few redundant components as needed.

If you have applications that cannot go down (because users would lose work), you'll have to spend money buying redundant components for individual servers. However, if it's okay to lose a server as long as the user can instantly connect back to another server, you can use the "high quantity" approach. Of course it is never okay to "lose a server." However, even without redundant components, losing a server is a rare event. Users are always safer on a server than on their workstations since the configuration and security rights are always configured on the server. Traditional environments don't have redundant components on every single desktop and they're still widely accepted, so not having redundant components on servers should also be acceptable as long as users can connect back in

### Ensuring Users are Routed to a Functioning Server

Chapter 4 included details about how Citrix Load Manager functions in MetaFrame XPa and XPe environments. In addition to the obvious ways that Load Manager can be used to load balance multiple MetaFrame XP servers (and therefore enable users to always find a functioning server), it can be used to route users to "backup" sets of MetaFrame XP servers.

### A Note about Server "Clustering"

Many people think of clustering when they think of high availability and redundant environments. Some people use the terms "load balancing" and "clustering" interchangeably. In MetaFrame XP environments, Citrix Load Manager performs load balancing. Load-balanced groups of MetaFrame servers should *not* be thought of as clusters.

The term "load balancing" is used to describe a mechanism that distributes load across multiple resources. "Clustering" is used to describe multiple resources that support a single load that is dynamically transferred from one resource to another in the event of a failure. Clustering is possible because the members of the cluster share certain common components, such as storage.

While it's true that Microsoft Terminal Services can be used in Microsoft Clusters, a user's remote session cannot be "clustered." What this means is that if a user's session is running on a server that goes down, it is not possible for that session to be dynamically switched over to another server. (Of course the user could instantly reconnect to the server environment, but they would lose whatever changes they made after they last hit "save."

Clustering in a Terminal Services environment presents several significant technical challenges and it will most likely be several years before we see a true clustered environment. To understand why, think about what happens when a user logs on to a MetaFrame XP server. To function as a cluster, the users' applications and memory spaces would have to be loaded onto multiple servers so that one server could pick up when another failed.

## User and Application Data

When determining the actions that you will take to ensure that your data is highly available, you need to first classify your data. All data can be divided into two categories:

- *Unique data* is the important data that is unique to your environment that you don't want to lose. This includes user profiles, home drives, databases, the IMA data store, and application data.
- *Non-unique data* is anything that you can load off of a CD from a vendor, such as Windows 2000 server, MetaFrame XP, SQL Server, and your applications.

In the real world, it's unrealistic to build a server that "can't fail." Therefore, when designing redundant environments, assume that certain failures will occur and make the necessary provisions to deal with them. This is where the "redundant array of inexpensive servers" comes into play.

When thinking about your data, you need to ensure that your MetaFrame XP servers only contain non-unique data. Your environments unique data should be stored elsewhere, such as on a SAN or NAS device, as shown in Figure 17.2.

*Figure 17.2  Redundant servers with data on a SAN*

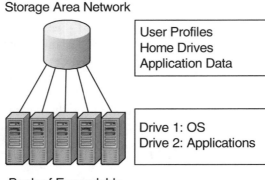

Storage Area Network

User Profiles
Home Drives
Application Data

Drive 1: OS
Drive 2: Applications

Bank of Expendable
MetaFrame XP Servers

In this environment, your data is protected if you lose one or more Meta-Frame XP servers. Your SAN should have the necessary redundancy built into it, such as RAID, multiple power supplies, multiple controller cards, and multiple interfaces to the servers. Instead of using a SAN, you can use a standard Windows 2000 Server file share driven by a Microsoft Cluster.

### Advantages of using RAIS for Data Redundancy

• Quick recovery in the event of a failure

### Disadvantages of using RAIS for Data Redundancy

• Doesn't work in smaller environments.

• Requires an "extra" server (for N+1 redundancy).

• Since all your non-unique data is on a SAN or NAS, you'd better make sure that's backed up.

## MetaFrame XP Support Components

The final aspect to consider when designing a highly available MetaFrame XP environment is the back-end support components that MetaFrame XP requires.

### Zone Data Collectors

As outlined in Chapter 3, zone data collectors are dynamically elected. If one is ever lost, an election will take place and another server will assume that role. Because the zone data collector plays such an important role in Meta-Frame XP server farms, Citrix has designed it to be highly-available. As long as your server farm is designed following the practices from Chapter 3, your zone data collectors will be able to perform their jobs.

## Ensuring IMA Data Store Availability

Since the IMA data store contains all of the information about the configuration of a server farm, you need to protect it and to ensure that your MetaFrame XP servers will always be able to access it. Remember from Chapter 3 that each MetaFrame XP server creates a local host cache from the IMA data store. This allows that server to function even if it loses communication with the data store. A MetaFrame XP server running Service Pack 2 will continue to function for up to 96 hours without any communication with the IMA data store. This is an increase from the 48 hour limit in environments prior to Service Pack 2.

Because of this, a loss of the IMA data store is not necessarily catastrophic. While it's true that you will not be able to make any administrative changes to your server farm without a data store, your servers will continue to function for a few days. Losing a data store does not affect in any way the operation of zone data collectors and the election process. It just means that you cannot manage or view your environment with the CMC (although you will be able to use the command-line tools since they query the ZDC).

If you lose the data store, you can take a few hours or days to get the database server rebuilt and the IMA data store restored from tape.

Your only real concern during the temporary timeframe while you're operating without a data store is what would happen if you had to reboot one of your MetaFrame XP servers. You can control whether the IMA Service needs to connect to the data store in order to start via the following registry key:

Key: `HKLM\Software\Citrix\IMA\Runtime`

Value: `PSRequired`

Type: `REG_DWORD`

Data: 0 = No connection required, 1 = connection required

If you ensure that your MetaFrame XP servers have this registry value set to "0," they will be able to be rebooted even though the IMA Service will not be able to access the IMA data store after the reboot. In this case, the server will simply use its existing local host cache. If you plan to use this strategy, remember that it will only work for 96 (or 48 hours), even if you never reboot a server.

# MetaFrame XP Backup Strategies

By focusing on high availability, your environment will be able to survive the small day-to-day events that occur. Your backup strategy will kick in when there is a major disaster or component failure.

Focus your backups on the unique data. Since there should be no user data stored on a MetaFrame XP server, you shouldn't need to back up a Meta-Frame XP server. You do need to backup:

- IMA data store.
- Resource Manager database.
- User profiles.
- User home drives.
- Application data.
- Terminal Services Licensing Service Database.
- One MetaFrame XP server from each silo (if you do not use server imaging to deploy new servers).

If you do not use server imaging, you should backup a single server that you can use as a master to restore a failed server. Since MetaFrame XP servers should not contain any unique data, you should be able to restore any server image to any target server within the same silo. (See Chapter 4 for more information about silos.)

This allows you to have a quick recovery in the event of a MetaFrame XP server failure. Store the server images on the SAN or the network. Then, if one should fail, you can kick off an automated process to restore it.

You can make a bootable DOS floppy disk with an `autoexec.bat` file that connects to the SAN and kicks off the server imaging process. You can even configure it so that a server is imaged with a generic name and IP address and then a lookup file is accessed based on the server's MAC address and the proper server name and IP address are automatically set after the imaging process is complete.

Many companies print step-by-step restore instructions and put them and the bootable floppy disk in a safe location. That way, they are always available in the event of an emergency. You might use a red-colored floppy disk and place it behind glass, for an "in case of emergency, break glass" effect.

Alternately, many of the new blade servers have auto-provisioning software available that can automatically detect a failed server and automatically initiate the rebuilding process. Some environments that use this have less than a one-hour turn around time from the instant a server fails until it is rebuilt and ready to go.

## Backing Up the License Database

Fortunately, it's easy to backup most of the components of MetaFrame XP environments that require it. However, backing up the license database is not that intuitive.

If you ever lose your server that is hosting the Terminal Services Licensing Service, you're officially supposed to contact the Microsoft license clearinghouse to get your licenses restored.

This is generally acceptable, because if you have a disaster you can easily build and activate new a TS Licensing Server. As soon as you do this it will immediately start handing out 90-day temporary TS CALs, meaning that you essentially have 90 days to get everything straightened out before your environment would stop working.

However, it is possible to back up the TS licensing database by backing up the LServer directory on the license server. This directory is in the location that you specified during the installation of the TS Licensing setup, %systemroot%\System32\LServer by default. The TS licensing database is similar to a Microsoft Exchange database. The LServer directory contains a couple of .edb files, a few .log files, and a .chk file.

If you ever need to restore a TS licensing server, rebuild the server with the same name as the old server; install the TS licensing service; stop the service; copy the contents of your backed-up LServer directory into the new LServer directory; and start the service.

APPENDIXES

# Appendixes & Index

In this section

A. The Future of Citrix in a .NET World     766

B. Acronyms Used in this Book     772

C. MetaFrame XP Component Configuration     774

D. MetaFrame XP TCP Ports     775

E. MetaFrame XP Scheduled Events     775

F. Websites Referenced in this Book     776

Index     778

# A. The Future of Citrix in a Microsoft .NET World

Many people wonder about the future of Citrix and the future of MetaFrame XP. The future is always uncertain, but this uncertainty is heightened by Microsoft's .NET strategy. How will Citrix and MetaFrame XP fit into the .NET world? To think about the future requires an understanding of the future as defined by today's players. In order to understand how the .NET strategy will affect Citrix, let's consider what Microsoft's .NET strategy really is.

## Microsoft's .NET Strategy

As the name implies, .NET is a strategy, not a product. It is the strategy that describes how Microsoft components will exist and work together using the Internet, web services, and many different types of client devices. This strategy will be implemented through the release and sale of several Microsoft products. Some of them are out there today. Others are just around the corner.

Let's take a look at some of the main components that make up Microsoft's .NET strategy.

### Application Development

From an application developer's standpoint, Microsoft's .NET strategy will change the way that traditional applications are developed, compiled, and deployed. These changes are possible with the release of Microsoft's new application development environment—Visual Studio .NET. There are two significant new features in Visual Studio .NET.

- Applications that are developed with Visual Studio .NET can be executed on any Microsoft platform, from a Pocket PC to a Windows PC to a smart phone. This allows developers to focus on the content of their applications without needing to worry about how to program for many different client devices.

- Visual Studio .NET applications can be written in any programming language. Historically, developers had to choose their language and develop applications based on that choice. Visual Studio .NET supports four different languages out of the box— Visual Basic, C++, C# (Microsoft's new version of C++), and J# (kind of like Java, although different enough to not get sued).

## Application Strategies

With Visual Studio .NET, developers can create applications that have rich user interfaces without worrying about what type of client devices users have. Historically, developers were forced to write web applications because they didn't know what types of client devices were being utilized. Unfortunately, due to the static nature of the web, most web applications were more difficult to use than their "full client" counterparts (think of Outlook 2000 compared to Outlook Web Access). However, developers had no choice but to write web applications because they didn't know about or couldn't control the client devices. Also, web applications had the advantage of not needing to be "deployed." In order for a user to use a web application, all they had to do was access a web site.

With .NET, full Windows applications are back. Users can run full, rich Windows applications merely by accessing a website. They can access applications without running an "install" program, and without the application touching the client's registry. These applications are full, rich applications that run locally on client devices.

## .NET Client Devices

As with almost everything in the computer world, these new .NET applications require that client devices have new client software in order to access them. For .NET client devices, there are three requirements.

- Operating System. The client operating system must be Windows 98 or newer or Windows NT 4.0 or newer. Additionally, PocketPC will be supported for mobile devices.

- Web Browser. The client device must have Internet Explorer 5.5 or newer.

- .NET Framework. The bulk of the client software is called the ".NET Redistributable Framework." This can be thought of as the ".NET client." Just as you need Citrix ICA client software to access MetaFrame XP applications, you need .NET client software to access .NET applications.

Microsoft's vision is that the operating system and client device will be removed from the application access equation, so that everything is abstracted up a level to the .NET redistributable framework. This framework is available as a free download for users (~20MB) and built-in to future versions of Microsoft operating systems. There is also be a "compact" version of the .NET framework that installs onto things like PDAs, smart phones, set top boxes, and the X-Box.

## Application Deployment

Historically, application development has only been half the battle. The other half was trying to figure out how to get a newly developed application deployed to your users. For web applications, deployment was simple. All you had to do was copy your files to your web server and send out an email that gave everyone the URL for your application. However, for developers that chose to create applications with full, rich user interfaces, the application (and its related DLLs and supporting files) had to be physically installed on every client device.

In .NET environments, the traditional application deployment challenge is completely removed from the picture. .NET applications can be accessed directly from web servers via Internet Explorer. From a user's standpoint, a .NET application looks and feels the same as any traditional application. This is essentially a "no touch" application deployment. Users can still access the full, rich application, but there are no install or uninstall routines. The registry and system folders are not be touched. Users can access the application via a simple URL.

When a user accesses a .NET web server, the .NET application is dynamically downloaded from the server and executed on the user's client device, similar to a Java application. However, unlike Java applications, the application execution begins on the client device without waiting for the entire application to be downloaded. Any necessary DLLs are trickled down from the server as they are needed (in the background) after application execution begins.

There are no install or uninstall routines for .NET applications. When a user closes his browser, the application is gone. As an administrator, you can configure applications to remain cached on the local client devices so that they do not need to be downloaded every time they are used. You can even configure applications so that they can be executed from the local cache, allowing users to access the applications when they are offline.

## The Concept of Web Services

Another advantage of .NET applications is the ability to integrate and interact with other applications and services via XML and the Internet. .NET applications' ability to interact with each other addresses two fundamental problems with traditional applications.

- Integration. It has been difficult for applications to effectively integrate with one another, especially if each application's developers do not know too much about the other application. In reality, most applications only integrate via a user "cutting and pasting" from one application to another. Even in these cases, application integration only occurs at the local level.

- Basic Services. Traditionally, developers have had to custom build many rudimentary components of their applications. For example, people who developed web–based shopping applications would have to develop components that contacted shippers and calculated shipping costs. Even though there are probably 10,000 applications that need to calculate shipping, each developer wrote their own shipping routine.

A large part of Microsoft's .NET strategy is XML–based web services. These web services act as the building blocks for .NET applications, allowing them to be distributed and interact with other applications via XML and the Internet. This common service interaction allows any program written in any language running on any computer, to be able to interact with any other. For example, in the web shopping application discussed previously, one company might create a XML shipping service that all of the other 10,000 applications use, with each application sending and receiving data to the shipping module via XML files sent over the Internet.

## The Future of .NET

Microsoft executives have said again and again that they are "betting the company" on their .NET strategy. They understand that the key to .NET's success will be getting the application developers to accept and embrace it. However, it will probably take a year or two before the critical mass of new applications are developed on the .NET platform.

Based on this overview, it's easy to see the advantages and disadvantages of .NET applications.

### Advantages of .NET Applications

- They can be executed from the device's cache, without connectivity to the server.
- They can interact with other web services and applications.
- Developers have a lot of control over the screen. The applications are smart enough to display a different user interface when running on a PDA or a full computer.

### Disadvantages of .NET Applications

- Unproven.

- A critical mass of developers and applications is needed.
- Only Microsoft client devices are supported.

# How does .NET Relate to MetaFrame?

Before we look at how Citrix and MetaFrame fit into Microsoft's .NET strategy, let's look at the advantages and disadvantages of the current MetaFrame architecture as it relates to Microsoft's .NET strategy.

### *Advantages of MetaFrame Applications*

- The client software is smaller.
- Many client devices and platforms are supported, including non-Microsoft solutions.

### *Disadvantages of MetaFrame Applications*

- MetaFrame applications execute in their own silos. The only integration that multiple applications have with each other is "cut" and "paste."
- 100% of application execution occurs on the server, and applications cannot be used if connectivity to the server is lost.

Based on this high–level overview of Microsoft's .NET strategy and your understanding of MetaFrame XP, you can easily see that there are a lot of similarities between the two.

### *Similarities Between .NET and MetaFrame Architectures*

- Client devices must have client software installed in order to access applications. (The .NET Framework for .NET and the ICA client for MetaFrame.)
- Users can run new applications simply by accessing a URL.
- The client software works on many different types of devices.
- Both strategies focus on "anytime, any where" (ubiquitous) access to applications.

However, these similarities are more coincidental than planned. This comes from the fact that both architectures are trying to solve the same business problem (access to applications). Citrix created an ingenious "retrofit" solution that provides ubiquitous access to legacy Windows applications, and Microsoft is designing a new solution from scratch that provides ubiquitous access to future Windows applications.

### *Primary Difference Between .NET and MetaFrame Applications*

- MetaFrame is a solution that provides ubiquitous access to legacy applications, whereas .NET is a solution that provides ubiquitous access to future applications.

When you look out a few years, you can see that the whole world is moving towards "smart" XML–enabled applications, and that MetaFrame is doomed because it focuses on legacy Windows applications.

## The Evolution of Citrix

Even though Citrix began life as a company that provides remote access to Windows applications, they are looking forward to a bright future.

- Citrix has a least a few good years left with their current MetaFrame architecture. Most of the .NET development components were not released by Microsoft until 2002, and Windows .NET server is slated for 2003. It will take a while for the development community to begin producing true .NET applications. Also, .NET applications require a lot of XML web services infrastructure, which will take some time to put in place.

- Citrix purchased an XML web portal company called Sequoia. Citrix is now beginning to integrate true XML services into their existing technology. This will first be seen in their "South Beach" product portals—portals that will drive the future of NFuse.

- Citrix has perfected the technology that allows applications to execute in one location while providing a user interface in another location. There will always be a need for this technology, even in the .NET world.

- Citrix applications will continue to evolve, and the Citrix middleware software will become smart enough to know what type of data is contained in the applications that are executing. For example, in today's environment MetaFrame XP is very good at allowing users to connect to applications via the ICA protocol. The ICA protocol allows users to see the content of their applications, but it doesn't allow them to be able to do anything with that content (other than cutting and pasting it). In the future, the ICA protocol will be able to work with and understand the data from ICA applications, interfacing it with other portals, users, systems, and XML web services.

# B. Acronyms Used in this Book

| | |
|---|---|
| AD | Active Directory (W2K) |
| ADF | Application Deployment File |
| ADM | Policy Template File |
| ASP(1) | Active Server Pages |
| ASP(2) | Application Service Provider |
| CA | Certificate Authority |
| CAB | Cabinet File Archive |
| CAL | Client Access License |
| CCC | Citrix Connection Configuration Utility |
| CDN | Citrix Developer's Network |
| CMC | Citrix Management Console (XP) |
| COM | Component Object Model |
| CSA | Citrix Server Administration Utility |
| CSG | Citrix Secure Gateway |
| CSNW | Client Services for NetWare |
| CSV | Comma Delimited Text File |
| CUP | Citrix User Profile |
| CWC | Citrix Web Console |
| DCS | Database Connection Server |
| DLG | Domain Local Group (W2K) |
| DLU | Dynamic Local User (NDS) |
| DMZ | Demilitarized Zone (Firewalls) |
| DSL | Default Server Location |
| EMF | Enhanced Metafile |
| EULA | End User License Agreement |
| FMS | Farm Metric Server (XP) |
| FQDN | Fully Qualified Domain Name |
| FR1 | Feature Release 1 |
| GDI | Graphics Device Interface |
| GINA | Graphical Identification and Authentication |
| GPO | Group Policy Object (W2K) |
| GSNW | Gateway Services for NetWare |
| GUI | Graphical User Interface |
| HKCU | HKEY_CURRENT_USER (registry hive) |
| HKLM | HKEY_LOCAL_MACHINE (registry hive) |
| IASP | Internal Application Service Provider |
| ICA | Independent Computing Architecture (Protocol or File Type) |
| IDS | IMA Data Store (XP) |
| IIS | Internet Information Server (NT4) or Services (W2K+) |
| IM | Installation Management (XP) |
| IMA | Independent Management Architecture (XP) |
| IMS | Installation Management Services (1.8) |
| INI | Configuration File with .ini file extension |
| ISS | InstallShield Script |
| JAR | Java Archive |
| JDK | Java Development Kit |
| JRE | Java Runtime Environment |
| JSP | Java Server Pages |
| JVM | Java Virtual Machine |
| LBS | Load Balancing Services (1.8) |
| LE | Load Evaluator (XP) |

| | |
|---|---|
| LHC | Local Host Cache (XP) |
| LM | Load Management (XP) |
| MB | ICA Master Browser |
| MDAC | Microsoft Data Access Components |
| MMC | Microsoft Management Console (W2K) |
| MSI | Microsoft Installer File |
| NAL | NetWare Application Launcher |
| NAT | Network Address Translation |
| NDPS | Novell Directory Printing Service |
| NDS | Novell Directory Services |
| NIC | Network Interface Card |
| ODBC | Open Database Connectivity |
| OEM | Original Equipment Manufacturer |
| OS | Operating System |
| OU | Organizational Unit (W2K or NDS) |
| PAM | Published Application Manager (1.8) |
| PEM | Personal Electronic Mail |
| PN | Program Neighborhood |
| PNA | Program Neighborhood Agent |
| POL | Policy File (NT4) |
| RC5 | Rivest version 5 Encryption Algorithm |
| RDP | Remote Display Protocol |
| REG | Registry Entries |
| RM | Resource Management (XP) |
| RMS | Resource Management Services (1.8) |
| RPC | Remote Procedure Call |
| RSA | Rivest Shamir Adleman |
| SAM | Security Account Manager (NT4) |
| SDB | Summary Database |
| SID | Security Identifier |
| SMS(1) | Microsoft Systems Management Server |
| SMS(2) | Short Message Service |
| SNMP | Simple Network Management Protocol |
| SP1 | Service Pack 1 |
| SPL | Print Spooler File |
| SQL | Microsoft SQL Server |
| SRC | Source INI Configuration File |
| SSL | Secure Socket Layer |
| STA | Secure Ticket Authority |
| TSCAL | Terminal Services Client Access License |
| TSICL | Terminal Services Internet Connector License |
| TSE | Windows NT Server 4.0, Terminal Server Edition |
| TSL | Terminal Services Licensing (Service) |
| TTA | The TTA Acronym |
| UNC | Universal Naming Convention |
| VBS | Visual Basic Script |
| VPN | Virtual Private Network |
| W2K | Windows 2000 |
| WAN | Wide Area Network |
| WFS | File extension for IMS script |
| XML | Extensible Markup Language |
| XP | eXtended Platform (not eXtra Pricey) |
| ZDC | Zone Data Collector (XP) |

## C. MetaFrame Component Configuration

| Feature | Server | Connection | User | ICA Client | Farm | ICA File | Application | Ctx User Profile |
|---|---|---|---|---|---|---|---|---|
| Maximum Connections | FR1 | X | | | | | FR1 | FR2 |
| Logons Enabled / Disabled | X | X | X | | | | | |
| Connection Timeout | | X | X | | | | | |
| Disconnection Timeout | | X | X | | | | | |
| Idle Timeout | | X | X | | | | | |
| Encryption Level | | X | | X | | X | X | FR2 |
| Auto Logon w/ Password | | X | | X | | | X | |
| Auto Logon prompt for Password | | X | | X | | | X | |
| Initial Program to be Run | | X | X | X | | | X | |
| Only run published Apps | | X | | | | | | |
| Disable Wallpaper | | X | | | | | | |
| Action on broken connection | | X | X | | | | | |
| Reconnect location | | X | X | | | | | |
| Shadowing Configuration | X | X | X | | | | | FR2 |
| Audio Quality Settings | | X | | X | | X | X | |
| Connect Client Drives at Logon | | X | X | | | | | FR2 |
| Connect Client Printers at Logon | | X | X | | | | | FR2 |
| Default to Main Client Printer | | X | X | | | | | FR2 |
| Connect only client's main printer | | X | | | | | | FR2 |
| Disable Client Drive Mapping | | X | | | | | | FR2 |
| Disable Client Printer Mapping | | X | | | | | | FR2 |
| Disable Client LPT Port Mapping | | X | | | | | | FR2 |
| Disable Client COM Port Mapping | | X | | | | | | FR2 |
| Disable Client Clipboard Mapping | | X | | | | | | FR2 |
| Disable Client Audio Mapping | | X | | | | | | FR2 |
| Permissions | X | X | | | | | X | |
| Speed Screen Options | X | | | X | | | | |
| Resolution | | | | X | | X | X | |
| Color Depth | | | | X | | X | X | |
| Data Compression | | | | X | | X | | |
| Disk Cache for Bitmaps | | | | X | | | | |
| Queue mouse and keystrokes | | | | X | | | | |
| Discard redundant graphics ops | X | | | | X | | | |
| Alternate caching method | X | | | | X | | | |
| Max Memory for session graphics | X | | | | X | | | |
| Session degradation method | X | | | | X | | | |
| Notify user of session degredation | X | | | | X | | | |
| SNMP Trap Settings | X | | | | X | | | |
| SNMP License Notification | | | | | X | | | |
| ZDCs repond to ICA broadcasts | | | | | X | | | |
| RAS servers respond ICA brdcst | | | | | X | | | |
| Client time zone configuration | | | | | X | | | FR2 |
| Mixed mode farm | | | | | X | | | |

# (continued)   C. MetaFrame Component Configuration

| Feature | Server | Connection | User | ICA Client | Farm | ICA File | Application | Ctx User Profile |
|---|---|---|---|---|---|---|---|---|
| Zones | | | | | X | | | |
| Shadow Logging | X | | | | | | | |
| Respond to ICA broadcasts | X | | | | | | | |
| Do not listen on UDP | X | | | | | | | |
| Do not listen on IPX | X | | | | | | | |
| Do not listen on NetBIOS | X | | | | | | | |
| Printer bandwidth limit | X | | | | | | | FR2 |
| Admin Rights | | | | | X | | | |
| Load Evaluators | X | | | | | | X | |
| Terminal Services Profile | | | X | | | | | |
| TS Home Directory | | | X | | | | | |
| Auto reconnect | | | | FR1 | | | | |
| Auto Client Update | X | | | | | X | | FR2 |
| Server Content Redirection | X | | | FR1 | X | | | FR2 |

# D. MetaFrame XP TCP Ports

| Port | Component | How to change the port |
|---|---|---|
| 80 | XML Service | CTXXMLSS |
| 139 | Server to Oracle | Oracle Tools |
| 443 | SSL | SSL Relay Config Tool |
| 1433 | Server to SQL | SQL Tools |
| 1494 | ICA Sessions | ICAPORT |
| 1604 | ICA UDP Broadcast | n/a |
| 2512 | Server to ZDC | Registry |
| 2513 | CMC to Server | Registry |
| 3389 | RDP Sessions | Registry |

# E. MetaFrame XP Scheduled Events

| Interval | Comm. Path | What Happens? |
|---|---|---|
| 15 sec | Internal | RM Metric Update |
| 30 sec | Server to ZDC | Load info, if no change |
| 60 sec | ZDC to server | IMA ping, if no info |
| 5 min | ZDC to ZDC | Failed update retry |
| 10 min | Server to IMA DS | Query for changes |
| 15 min | TS to subnet | Looks for Lic. Server |
| 60 min | TS to Lic. Serv. | Verifies it's there (Ent / AD) |
| 120 min | TS to Lic. Serv. | Verifies it's there (domain) |
| 6 hours | Server to IMA | Domain trust refresh |

# F. Websites Referenced in this Book

**Active Server Page (ASP) References and Tutorials**
www.4guysfromrolla.com

**AppSec (Application Security Utility)**
ftp.microsoft.com/reskit/win2000/appsec.zip

**Brian Madden (Author/Publisher of this book)**
www.brianmadden.com

**Citrix Demoroom (Live Demos of MetaFrame XP)**
www.citrix.com/demoroom

**Citrix Developer Network**
www.citrix.com/cdn

**Citrix Licensing Information**
www.citrix.com/licensing

**Citrix Product Activation**
www.citrix.com/activate

**Emergent Online (Citrix Management & Printing Utilties)**
www.go-eol.com

**FutureLink Canada (Printing Utilities)**
www.uniprint.net

**Hiddensoft (AutoIT scripting utility)**
www.hiddensoft.com/autoit

**InstallShield**
www.installshield.com

**Kixtart (Batch Scripting Language)**
www.kixtart.org

**LearnCitrix.com (Citrix Certification Practice Exams)**
www.learncitrix.com

**Mercury Interactive (Loadrunner Sizing Utilities)**
www.mercuryinteractive.com

**Microsoft Developer Network**
msdn.microsoft.com

**Microsoft Licensing Information**
www.microsoft.com/licensing

**Microsoft .NET Home**
www.microsoft.com/net

**Microsoft Universal Data Access Website (MDAC, Jet, etc.)**
www.microsoft.com/data

**Norton Ghost (Server Imaging Software)**
www.symmantec.com

**Novell NDS Client Download**
download.novell.com

**Packeteer Packetshaper (Bandwidth Management Hardware)**
www.packeteer.com

**Project-in-a-Box (Doug Brown's Website)**
www.dabcc.com

**Scapa Technologies (StressTest Server Sizing Utility)**
www.scapatech.com

**Sitara QoSWorks (Bandwidth Management Hardware)**
www.sitaranetworks.com

**StorageSoft ImageCast (Server Imaging Software)**
www.storagesoft.com

**Sun (Java Runtime Environment)**
www.sun.com/java

**T-scale (Server Optimization Software)**
www.kevsoft.com

**Techtonik ONEAPP (Audit Logging)**
www.oneapp.co.uk

**The THIN List (Portal for Thin Client Solutions)**
thethin.net

**Thin Print (Printing Utilities)**
www.thinprint.com

**triCerat (Printing Utilities)**
www.tricerat.com

**TweakCitrix (Rick Dehlinger's Tips Site)**
www.tweakcitrix.com

**VeriSign Internet Software Distribution Certificates**
www.verisign.com/installshield

**WinBatch (Scripting Utility)**
www.winbatch.com

**Willamette (SecurID with NFuse Project)**
www.tweakcitrix.com/sections/wilakenz.htm

**XML File Editors**
www.download.com

# Index

Based on reader feedback, I spent more time on this index than I did in the first edition of this book. If you have trouble finding something in this index, please let me know by emailing me at brian@brianmadden.com. I am always looking for ways to improve it.

## Numbers

1.8 to XP Migration  533-576

90-day License Limit  593, 597

## A

Access-based Data Stores  89, 92
    Compacting  729

Access Methods  338–342

Account Mapping (ESN)  478

Active Directory
    Support by MetaFrame XP  29

Active Server Pages  456

Add/Remove Programs  113

ADF Packages  517

ADM Policy Templates  180

Administration  34, 106, 712

Alerts  738

Altaddr Command  692688

Anonymous Applications  637

Answer File for Unattended Installs  506

Applet Tag (Java Clients)  412

Applet Mode (Java Clients)  404

Application Mode  405

Applications
    Compatibility  115–116
    Config Files  111
    Deploying  507
    Enumeration  82
    Folders  722
    Installation Groups  147–149
    Installing  110
    Load Rule  138
    Packages  513, 516–517
    Publishing  118–122
        Overview of  27
    Security  636

Simulation and Test Scripts 241, 247
Strategies 118-122

AppSec Utility 640

Appsrv.ini Client Configuration File 381, 387, 411, 417, 429

Architecture
Network 55-105
Server 37-54

Associations of File Types 126

Assigning Licenses 612

Async Connections 356

ASP Pages 456

Audio 361

Auditing 716

Auto Client Update 369

Auto Session Reconnect 372

Auto-created Printers
Enabling 269
Naming 269

Automatic Logon 324

AutoAdminQueryNDS Registry Key 326

AutoIt Scripting Utility 241

Automated Software Distribution 508

Automobile Story 254

**B**

Backing up MetaFrame 762

Bandwidth 254
ICA 61

Bitmap Caching 365

Boolean Rules 139

Broken Connections 644

Browser Cookies 698

Browser Service 57, 79, 537, 541

Broomhall, Shane 186

Business Recovery 371

**C**

CA 392, 654

CAB Packages 386

Caching
Bitmap 365

CAL 579

Capacity Planning  239

Centralized Servers  63

Certificate Authority  392,  654

Certificate Services  665

"Change User" Command  49

"Chfarm" Utility  725

Cipher Suites  668

Citrix Connection Configuration  45,  268

Citrix Installer
    Service  514,  521
    Packages  517

Citrix Licensing  601–615

Citrix Management Console  521,  720
    Application Folders  722
    Choosing a Connection Server  720
    Data Refresh  721
    Details Mode  184
    Mixed Mode  544
    Overview  31
    Publishing  721

Citrix Packager  514,  517,  524

Citrix Secure Gateway  663
    Building the Server  676
    Configuration  676
    How it Works  670

Citrix Server Test Kit  246–247
    Client  246
    Client Launcher Utility  247
    Console  246

Citrix SSL Relay Service  662
    How to use it  664

Citrix User Policies  181–185,  268
    Applying  182
    Creating  182
    Disabling  185
    Managing  184
    Priority  183
    Resultant Policy  184

Citrix Web Console  723
    Overview of  33

Citrix XML Service  439,  447,  478,756
    Overview of  43
    Interaction with NFuse  445

.Class Files  406

Class ID  393,  400

Client Audio  361

Client Auto Update  369

Client Access License  579

Client Devices
    Drive Mapping  51, 359
    Hotkey Mapping  362
    Logging  369
    Network  359
    Planning Considerations  343
    Port Mapping  360
    Printers  263, 264–282
        Configuring  267
        Configuring the Server for  268
        Mapping 360
        Performance  279
    Security  693
    Types of  348–352

Client Launcher Utility  247

Client Software
    Download Mode  423

Client Services for NetWare  319–321

Clientdb Folder  420

Clipboard Integration  363

CMC  521, 720
    Application Folders  722
    Choosing a Connection Server  720
    Data Refresh  721
    Details Mode  184
    Mixed Mode  544
    Overview  31
    Publishing  721

CMD scripts  210

Codebase  Tag 400

Cold Fusion Pages  456

Color Depths  363

Columbia, Project  497

COM Components  393

Compacting the Access Database  729

Computer-Based Policies  189

Config.xml File  402, 485
    Explanation of Tags  487

Configuring Files  375, 381

Connection Configuration  44
    Async  356
    Listeners  44
    Permissions  649
    Registry Location  652
    Security  643
    Utility  45, 268

Connection Control  617
    Overview  33

Connection Server (Summary DB)  733, 743

Consolidation  564

Content Redirection  125–131

Content Publishing  32,  123-125

Context Switches Rules  137

Control Panel
    Add/Remove Programs  113

Cookies  698

CPU Prioritization  253
    Overview of  33

CPU Utilization Rule  137

Csrss.exe  40

CSTK  246–247
    Client  246
    Client Launcher Utility  247
    Console  246

Ctxgina.dll  323

CWC  723

Cycle Booting Servers  730


# D


Data Collector  720
    Dedicated Servers  81
    in Load-Managed Environments  132
    Overview of  77
    Role in Load Management  140
    Update Interval  80

Data Store  87–96
    Access Mode  89
    Default Update Interval  88
    DSN  87
    In Load-Managed Environments  132
    Local Host Cache  88,  185
    Overview  of87
    Replication  89–91
    Size  91

Database Connection Server  733, 743

Database Licensing  618

Database Types  89

DB2  35,  89, 90, 93–96

Dedicated Data Collectors  81

Deep Shares  196

Default User Profile  164

DefaultLocationProfile  Key 325

Dehlinger, Rick  252

Delegated Administration  106
    Overview of MetaFrame's  34

Depth of Color  363

Deployment
    Applications  507
    MetaFrame XP  502–507

Desktop
    Integration  372
    Profile Folder  168
    Publishing the Server Desktop  121
    Security  639

Devices
    Drive Mapping  51, 359
    Hotkey Mapping  362
    Logging  369
    Network  359
    Planning Considerations  343
    Port Mapping  360
    Printers  263, 264–282
        Configuring  267
        Configuring the Server for  268
        Mapping 360
        Performance  279
    Security  693
    Types of  348–352

Dialing Prefixes  372

Digital Certificates  393, 676

Direct Mode  89, 95

Disabling Logons  646

Discovery of TS Licensing Servers  586

Disk Administrator  50

Disk
        Data I/O Rules  138
        Operation Rule  138
        Quotas  200
        Time Counter  244

Distributed Servers  62

DLL Versioning  519

DLU  330, 331

DMZ  684

Domain Configuration  709

Domain Controllers  632

Domain Policies  188

Dongle  617

Drive Imaging  502

Drive Letter Remapping  50

Drive Mapping  51, 359

Drive RPMs  234

DSMAINT Command  634, 726, 748

DSN 87

Dynamic Local User 330, 331

# E

.EDB Files 763

EMF Files 261,301

Encryption 646, 653, 679

Enterprise Scope 586

Enterprise Services for NFuse 472–481
    Components 475
    Configuring 481
    Database 477
    How it Works 473
    Server Location 480
    User Account Mapping 478

Enumeration of Published Applications 82

Equifax 654

EXE Client Packages 386

Execute Mode 113

Explicit Applications 637

Extracting Client Files 385

Extranet 660

# F

Farm
    Design 69
    Consolidation 564
    Membership Changing 724
    Migration Strategies 559
    Overview 27
    Role with NFuse 436

Farm Metric Server 732, 742

Farmlet 148

Feature Releases
    Overview 31
    Feature Release 1
        Installation 52
        List of Features 31
    Feature Release 2
        Installation 52
        List of Features 34

Features of MetaFrame 27

File Access Speed 199

File Associations 126, 372

Firewalls 681–693
    Placing MetaFrame Servers 682

Ports  685

Folder Redirection  206

Full Program Neighborhood Client  376

# G

Gateway Services for NetWare  318–319

Ghost  502

GINA  321, 323, 327, 647

Graphics Device Interface  261

Gray Version of PN  696

Group Policy  170, 191,172, 206
     Logon Scripts  212

GTE  654

Guest_template.ica  File  463

# H

Hard Drive Usage  233

Hardware Key  617

Hardware Redundancy  234

Help Desk Security Rights  714

High Availibility  752-763

HIPAA  217

HKCU  112, 113, 169, 179
     use with Profiles  179

HKLM  111–112, 113, 114, 179
     use with Profiles  179

HKU  111

Home Drives  195–208
     Design Options  199
     How they Work  195
     Location of  201
     Mapping Process  197
     Number of  203
     Size Limits  200
     Specifying  201, 204
          via a Logon Script  206
          via a User Account  205
          via Group Policy  206
     Replication  204
     TS Home Drive Location  196
     Usage  198

%homedrive% Variable  196

%homepath% Variable  196

Host ID  78

Hotfixes  633

Hotkey Mapping 362

# I

IBM DB2 35, 89, 90, 93–96

ICA Browser Service 57, 79, 537, 541

ICA Client Auto Update 418
    Configuring 420
    How it Works 419
    Version Checking 424

ICA Clients
    Automatically Uninstalling 428
    Connection Process 355
    Desktop Integration 372
    Download Mode 423
    Features 357–374
    Functional Overview 354–357
    Extracting Installation Files 385
    Java Launch Parameters

ICA Files 26

ICA Overview 26

ICA Master Browser 79

ICA Protocol 57
    Bandwidth 61
    Overview of 26

ICA Template Files 462

ica32.exe Package 376

ica32a. msi Package 377

ica32a.exe Package 377

ica32t.exe Package 377

Idle Sessions 40

Ignored Processes 741

IIS Lockdown Tool 634

IM_App_Upgrd.exe Utility 555

IMA 56
    Data Store *see* Data Store
    Ping 80

IMA Service 57
    Mixed Mode Changes 538
    Overview 43
    Startup Speed 92

Imaging Servers 502

ImageCast 502

Importing Print Servers 294, 311

Incremental Rules 138

Indirect Mode 89, 93, 94

INI Configuration Files
    Application  111
    ICA Client  375, 381

Initial Program  647

InprocServer32  393

Install Mode  49, 112, 156

Install.ini  File402

Installation
    of MetaFrame XP  49
    Registry Keys  113

Installation Groups  147-149

Installation Jobs  515, 529

Installation Manager  508
    Components  516
    How it Works  514
    Jobs  515
    Mixed Mode  553
    Overview  513
    Using  522

Installing Applications
    Best Practices  114

InstallShield  388, 391

IntelliMirror  508

Interactive Log Ons  110

Internet Connector Licenses  581, 599

IP Range Rule  140

IPX/SPX  43, 356

**J**

JAR  Files  407

Java .Class Files  406

Java ICA Client  403–418
    Applet Mode  404, 412
    Graphical Command Line  415

Java Virtual Machine  405

JavaServer Pages  456

JDK  404

JET  48

Jicasession.bat  File  406

Jobs (IM)  515, 529

**K**

Kevsoft  252

Keytopem Utility  667

Kixtart Scripts 211, 296

# L

Latency 254

Launch.asp file 440

License
    Components 581

License Clearinghouse 583

License Database
    Backing Up 763

License Server 584
    Adding Licenses 591
    Installation 590
    Discovery 586
    License Storage 602
    Managing 591
    Scope of Operation 585

License Threshold Rule 139

License Verification Process 40

Licenses
    Applications 615
    Assigning 612
    Citrix 601-615
    Data Store Requirements 618
    Microsoft 578
    Mixed Mode 549
    Requirements 579
    Serial Numbers 605
    Usage in Server Farms 74

Load Balancing  *see* Load Management

Load Evaluators 135–136, 701
    Applying to Published Applications 146
    Fine Tuning 144
    Overview 132

Load Evalutors
    Using Multiple Rules 145

Load Index 135, 140, 146
    Changing the Update Interval 141
    List of Possible Values 145
    Overview 132

Load Management 131-146
    Components 132
    How it Works 131
    Logging 147
    Mixed Mode 547
    Performance 147
    Strategies 142

LoadRunner Software 251

Local Computer Policies 187, 191

Local Drive Access  702

Local File Type Support  372

Local Host Cache  88, 185

Local ICA Files  694

Local Log Ons  110

Local Profiles  157

Local Resource Manager Database  733, 742

Local Text Echo  367

Local Time Zone Support  364

Lockdown Tool for IIS  634

Locked Down Desktops  640

Log on Locally Security Rights  706

Logons, Disabling  646

Logging
    Client Device  369

Logoff Scripts  208–217
    How They Work  209

Logon Automatically  324

Logon Interactively  110

Logon Scripts  208–217
    Design Considerations  216
    How They Work  209
    Language  210

Logon Speed  199

LPT Mapping  268

LServer Directory  763

# M

Maintenance  724-731

Managing Servers  720-748

Mandatory Roaming Profile  161

Mapping
    Client Drives  51, 359
    Client Hotkeys  362
    Client LPT Ports  268
    Client Ports  360
    Client Printers  360

MDAC  48

Membership  724

Memory Usage  231

Memory Usage Rule  137

Mercury Interactive  251

MetaFrame 1.8 Migration and Integration  533-576

MetaFrame XP
  Components  42
  Deployment  502-507
  Features  27
  Installation  49

Metrics  734
  Configuration  738
  Farm Metric Server  732, 742
  History  741
  Options  735
  Properties  737
  Status  734

MF:PCL4 Driver  282

mf20.dsn  87, 504

Microsoft Installer Packages  522

Microsoft Licensing  578–600

Microsoft Office (Installing)  114

Migration
  from MetaFrame 1.8 to XP  533-576
  IMA Data  726
  Licenses  607
  Strategies  559

Mixed Mode Farm Operation  538

Mobile Wireless Devices  352

Modifying Client Source Files  401

Module.ini File382, 387, 411, 418

Mouse Click Feedback  366

Moving Average Rules  138

MSI Packages  386, 507

msiexec.exe  429, 507, 524

Multi-Button Mouse Support  365

Multiple Monitor Support  364

Multiple Sessions  372

**N**

Native Mode  549–551

NDS Integration  372, 493, 572
  Using FR 1 or 2  328

NetBIOS  43, 356

NetWare Location Profiles  325

Network Address Translation  685

Network Architecture  55

Network Counters  244

Network Data Security  653

Network Manager  744–747

Configuration  745
Installation  745

Network Security  652–693

Network Tuning  254

NFuse Classic
Alternate Address Mapping  690
Components  435
Configuration  441
Configuring for CSG  677
Configuring for SSL  669
How it Works  437
Mixed Mode  552
Using for Farm Migration  563
Versions  433
Web Page Flowchart  458

NFuse Java Objects  435, 457
Configuring  445

NFuse Server Security  634

NFuse Web Server

NFuse.conf File  439
Overview  441
Sample  442

NICs  44

Norton  502

Nnotssid.inf File  631

Novell NDS Client  321–328

Novell NetWare
Integration with MetaFrame  316–324

NT Authentication  646

NTFS  629, 642

Ntuser.dat File  155, 156

Nwgina.dll File  323, 647

**O**

ONEAPP Utility  718

Operating System Versions  47

Oracle  89, 90, 93–96
Versions  93

Oorca.exe  507

**P**

Package Groups  527

PackageForTheWeb  Tool391

Packager (Installation Manager)  514, 517, 524

Packager Test Server  514, 518

Packeteer 257

PacketShaper 257

Page Fault Rule 138

Page Faults 243

Page Swap Rule 138

Page Table Entry 237

Pages/sec Performance Counter 243

Panning 30

Param Java Client Tag 413

Parameter Passing 126

Pass-Through Authentication 371, 695

PEM Certificate 667

Performance Counters 243

Performance Monitor 242, 737

Performance Tuning 252–256

Periodic Farm Maintenance Tasks 729

Ping Command 256

Placement of Servers 58

PN Agent *see* Program Neighborhood Agent

Pn.ini 382, 387, 429

Policies
    Citrix User Policies 181–185, 268
        Applying 182
        Creating 182
        Disabling 185
        Managing 184
        Priority 183
        Resultant Policy 184
    Windows Policies
        Computer-Based 189
        Creating 180
        Design Options 186
        Domain-based 188
        Editing 180
        Group Policies 170, 172, 191, 202, 212
        Templates 180

Political Issues 344

Port Mapping on ICA Clients 360

Port Translation 690

Ports Required by Citrix 685, 775

Preconfigure ICA Client Options 385-387

Print Migrator 2000 291

Print Servers, Importing 294

Print Spooler 261–262, 287

Printer Auto-creation 278

Printer Driver Names, Finding  271

Printer Drivers
    Combatibility  273
    How They Work  285
    Installing  267, 286
    Issues with Client Printers  269
    Managing  285–293, 300
    Mapping with MetaFrame XP  270 - 273
    Removing  286
    Replication  288
    Replication Performance  292
    Updating with the CMC  288

Printers
    Auto-Created  269
    Configuring for Users  293
    Configuring via Logon Scripts  295
    Client Printers  263, 264–282
        Configuring  267
        Configuring the Server for  268
        Mapping  360
        Performance  279
    Mapping  360

Printers Folder
    Publishing  297

Printing
    How it Works  260–262
    In WAN Environments  303
    Installing Local Print Queues  310
    Performance Issues  265, 279
    Permissions  268
    Questions to Ask Users  308
    Third Party Tools  299
    Types of MetaFrame Printers  263

Processor Queue Length Counter  244

Processor Time Counter  244

Processor Usage  233

Product Code  605

Profile Path  161

Program Neighborhood  341, 370, 377
    Overview  27

Program Neighborhood Agent  342, 370, 401, 484–497, 656
    Client  377
    Configuring  485
    Files  485
    Overview  32

Program Neighborhood Service  537

Project Columbia  497

Project Willamette  709

Proxy Servers  703

Published Applications

Anonymous Applications  637
Explicit Applications  637
Migration  569
Mixed Mode  543
Permissions  636
Security  638

Published Application Manager  544

Published Content  32,123–125

Publishing Uninstalled Packages  529

# Q

Qfarm Utility  145

QoSWorks  257

Querydc Command  79

Queue Key Strokes  368

Queue Mouse Movements  368

Quotas  200

# R

RAS  646

RDP Protocol  40

ReadMe Files  114

Real Time Graph  736

Rebooting Servers  730

Reconnecting Sessions  645
Automatically  372

Redirection of Content  125-131

Reducing Web Client Size  395

Redundancy  234

Registry  111–112, 113

Relocation
Impact to Design  97

Remapping Server Drives  50

Renaming a MetaFrame XP Server  728

Replacing MetaFrame XP Servers  727

Replication of the Data Store  89-91

Requirements for MetaFrame XP  47

Resource Manager  242, 504, 731–744
Alerts  738
How it Works  741
Monitoring Servers and Applications  734
Technical Overview  732

Response Times  240

Resultant Policy  184

RMLocalDatabase.mdb  733, 742

RPMs of Server Drives  234

Roaming Profiles  159–161
    Cached Copies  174
    Slow Network Detection  226

ROOTDRIVE System Variable  116

Rules (for Load Management)  136-140
    Overiew of  132

"Run program on startup" Account Setting  705

RunAs Service  632

Runonce Registry Key  114

## S

Saving User Credentials  693

Scaling  30

Scapa Technologies  251

Scheduling Rule  140

Screen Resolution  364

Scripts
    Launching  211

Seamless Windows  122
    Overview  28
    Use in Load Managed Environments  142

Secedit.exe Utility  631

Secure Gateway  663
    Building the Server  676
    Configuration  676
    How it Works  670

Secure Ticket Authority  673

SecureICA  660

SecurID  708

Security
    Application  636
    Auditing  716
    Client Device  693
    Configuration Layers  626
    Connection  643
    Desktop  639
    Firewalls  681-693
    Network  652
    Policies  186
    Security  629
    User Account  704
    User Policies  195

Serial Connections  356

Server
   Browsing 355
   Deployment 502-507
   Folders 722
   Maintenance 724
   Migration 572
   Printers 283
   Security 629
   Sizing 230–239

Server User Load Rule 139

Server-Based Computing Components 25

Services for NetWare 319-321

Sessions
   Compression 366
   Limiting 646
   Manager 40
   Monitoring Overview 33
   Shadowing 648, 715
   Timeouts 643

Set Command 198

Setup.class File 406

Setup.iss File 389, 427

Shadowing 28, 715

SID 112, 504

Signed Package 391

Silent Install 388

Silo 148,757

Simulation Scripts 241, 247

Sitara Networks 257

Size of the Data Store 91

Sinzing Servers 230-250

Slow Logons 167

Smart Cards35, 707

Smss.exe 40

SNMP 745, 746

SNMP License Notification 614

Software Distribution 508

Source Server for Imaging 503

SpeedScreen Latency Reduction
   Configuration 366
   Overview 30

Spooler Directory 268

SQL Server 89, 90, 93–96
   Versions 93

SRC Files 387

Ss3config Folder  368

SSL  355
    Overview  654

SSL Relay Service  662
    How to use it  664

Start Time of Sessions  163

StorageSoft  502

StressTest Software  251

Subst Command  51

Substitution Tags  461

Summary Database  733, 743

SyncedDomainName Registry Key  332

System Administration  712

System Information Utility  120

System Policies
    Editor  170, 172, 188
    Updates  190

Systems Management Server  508

**T**

Task Manager  253

TCP Port  648

TCP/IP  43

TCP/IP Printing  294

Techtonik  718

Template.ica File  463

Terminal Server Interaction with MetaFrame  41

Terminal Services Client Access License  579

Test Kit  *see* Citrix Server Test Kit

Test Scripts  247

Text Echo  367

Thawte  654

thethin.net  253, 277, 300, 511, 633, 696, 718

Thin Client Devices  349

Ticketing  700

Time Zone Support  29, 364

Tivoli  508

TLS Encryption Overview  34

Tomcat Jakarta  476

Traditional Computer Workstations  348

Transform Files  507

Trust Intersections  711

Trust-Based Routing 711

Trusted Printer Drivers 275

TS CALs
  Backing Up 763

TS License Server 584
    Adding Licenses 591
    Installation 590
    Discovery 586
    License Storage 602
    Managing 591
    Scope of Operation 585

TScale Utility 252

TSClientAutoAdminLogon Key 325

Tuning Applications 253

Tuning Servers 252

TweakCitrix.com 252

# U

Uistate.ini File 383

Unattended Installations 505
    Answer File 506

Unicenter 508
    Support by MetaFrame XP 34

UninstallString Registry Key 428

Universal Print Driver 279, 303,310
    How it Works 280

Universal Win32 Clients 374

Update.ini File 422

Updating ICA Clients 369

Upgrade Licenses 609

User Access Methods 338–342

User Account
    Configuration 704
    Security 704
    Settings 268

User Data 198

User Location 65, 74

User Policies 178–195, 706
    Design Considerations 194
    Overview of MetaFrame's 34

User Profiles 154–178
    Default User Profile 164
    Differences from Policies 179
    Directory Exclusion 170
    Folder Redirection 168
    Local Profiles 157

Mandatory Profiles  161
Master Roaming Copies  173
Overview of  155
Preconfiguring  164
with Published Applications  156
Registry Location  155
Size Limit  172

User Simulation Scripts  246

%username%  Variable  169, 202, 206, 220

Usrlogon.cmd Script  116

# V

V-ONE  660

VeriSign  392, 654

Volume License Agreements  611

VPN  658

# W

WAN  69, 82, 92, 96

Watcher Window  736

Web Browser Launching  371

Web Browser Security  697

Web Client  376, 392, 466
    Installation and Deployment  394

Web Page Scripting  460

Web Server for NFuse  435

Web Site Wizard  454

Webica.ini  384, 702

Wfclient.ini  383, 411, 418

Wfcname.ini  384

Wfcwin32.log  384

wfica32.exe  375

wficat.cab  377

Wheel Mouse Support  365

Willamette, Project  709

WinBatch  241

Windows 2000 Versions  48

Windows 32-bit ICA Clients  374–403

Windows Batch Scripts  210

Windows Installer  387
    Versions  53

Windows Installer Packages  516

WinTask  241

Wireless Client Devices  352

Worker Threads  676

wtsuprn.txt File  270

# X

X.509 Digital Certificate  654,  664-665

XML  486

XML Service  439,  447,  478,756
    Overview of  43
    Interaction with NFuse  445

# Z

ZENWorks  330-331,  508

Zone Data Collector  720
    Dedicated Servers  81
    in Load-Managed Environments  132
    Overview of  77
    Role in Load Management  140
    Update Interval  80

Zones  74–87
    Changing a Server  724
    Communication  79
    Design Options  83
    Overview  74